Early Childhood
Curriculum for All Learners

To Greg, who taught me all about building "major construction sites."

—AMS

To Karen and Sean, thank you for your love, support, and inspiration.

—RJG

To my family, who always puts a smile on my face when I am knee-deep in work. Thank you for making it all worthwhile. I do it all for you!

—ERMF

Early Childhood Curriculum for All Learners

Integrating Play and Literacy Activities

Ann M. Selmi

California State University, Dominguez Hills

Raymond J. Gallagher

University of Southern California

Eugenia R. Mora-Flores

University of Southern California

Los Angeles | London | New Delhi
Singapore | Washington DC

Los Angeles | London | New Delhi
Singapore | Washington DC

FOR INFORMATION:

SAGE Publications, Inc.
2455 Teller Road
Thousand Oaks, California 91320
E-mail: order@sagepub.com

SAGE Publications Ltd.
1 Oliver's Yard
55 City Road
London EC1Y 1SP
United Kingdom

SAGE Publications India Pvt. Ltd.
B 1/I 1 Mohan Cooperative Industrial Area
Mathura Road, New Delhi 110 044
India

SAGE Publications Asia-Pacific Pte. Ltd.
3 Church Street
#10-04 Samsung Hub
Singapore 049483

Copyright © 2015 by SAGE Publications, Inc.

Printed in the United States of America.

A catalog record of this book is available from the Library of Congress.

ISBN 978-1-4522-4029-9 (pbk)

This book is printed on acid-press paper.

SFI label applies to text stock

Acquisitions Editor: Theresa Accomazzo
Editorial Assistant: Georgia McLaughlin
Associate Digital Content Editor: Rachael
    Leblond
Production Editor: David C. Felts
Copy Editor: Kristin Bergstad
Typesetter: C&M Digitals (P) Ltd.
Proofreader: Bonnie Moore
Indexer: Mary Mortensen
Cover Designer: Gail Buschman
Marketing Manager: Terra Schultz

14 15 16 17 18 10 9 8 7 6 5 4 3 2 1

Brief Contents

Preface   xv

PART I. WORKING WITH YOUNG LEARNERS   1

Chapter 1. The Need for Developmentally Appropriate Practices   3

Chapter 2. Learning Through Play   29

Chapter 3. Play and Pretending   57

Chapter 4. Language and Literacy Development   85

Chapter 5. Collaborating With Families and Professionals   113

PART II. PLANNING AND DESIGNING A CLASSROOM
FOR LEARNING THROUGH PLAY   135

Chapter 6. Planning for Effective Learning   137

Chapter 7. Designing High-Quality Centers for Learning   169

Chapter 8. Strategies for Guiding Play and Producing High-Quality Learning Activities   201

Chapter 9. Observing and Assessing to Promote Learning   225

PART III. INTEGRATING PLAY ACTIVITIES ACROSS THE CURRICULUM   267

Chapter 10. Integrating Literacy Skills Into the Play Centers   269

Chapter 11. Integrating Play Activities in the Science Centers   301

Chapter 12. Integrating Play Activities in the Mathematics Centers   329

Chapter 13. Integrating Play Activities in the Social Studies and Book Centers   369

Chapter 14. Integrating Play Activities in the Creative Arts Centers   401

References   443

Glossary   459

Index   467

About the Authors   483

Detailed Contents

Preface   xv

PART I. WORKING WITH YOUNG LEARNERS   1

Chapter 1. The Need for Developmentally Appropriate Practices   3

    Scenario/Introduction: The Poison Syrup   3
    Developmentally Appropriate Practices   4
        Early Action and Intervention   6
        Academic Precursors   6
        Letter and Sound Knowledge   7
        Ability to Self-Regulate   7
    Common Core State Standards   8
    Current Demographic: Benefits and Challenges   9
        Economic Diversity   12
        Ethnic Diversity   13
        Developmental Diversity   14
    Current Curriculum Challenges   17
        Decreased Play Opportunities   17
        Increased Adult-Directed Activities 18
        Addressing Current Changes   20
        Engaging in "Guided Play" Activities 20
    Implementing NAEYC's Principles   22
    Chapter Summary   25
    First-Person Interview #1   25
    First-Person Interview #2   26
    Key Terms   27
    Useful Websites   28
    Reflective Questions   28

Chapter 2. Learning Through Play   29

    Scenario/Introduction: To the Fire   29
    Early Learning   30
        Jean Piaget (1886–1980)   32
        Lev Vygotsky (1896–1934)   34
    Play and Learning Theories   36
    Influence of Play and Learning Theories on Early Childhood Programs 43
        Montessori Programs and Learning Theory 43
        Reggio Emilia Programs and Learning Theory 45
        HighScope Programs and Learning Theory 46
        Multiple Intelligences Programs and Learning Theory 50
    Chapter Summary   53

Home and Community Connections · 53
First-Person Interview · 54
Key Terms · 55
Useful Websites · 55
Reflective Questions · 55

Chapter 3. Play and Pretending · 57

Scenario/Introduction: The Castle House · 57
The Development of Love, Work, and Play · 58
Types of Play · 60
   Solitary Play · 61
   Parallel Play · 61
   Social Play · 62
   Team Play · 63
Sequential Development of Symbolic Play Representations · 64
   Level 1: Functional Unitary Activity · 65
   Level 2: Inappropriate Combinational Activity · 65
   Level 3: Appropriate Combinational Activity · 66
   Level 4: Transitional Activities · 66
   Level 5: Self-Directed Pretense · 67
   Level 6: Other-Directed Pretense · 67
   Level 7: Sequential Pretense · 68
   Level 8: Substitution Pretense · 69
The Importance of Socio-Dramatic Play · 71
   Socio-Dramatic Play Representations · 72
   Socio-Dramatic Play Language · 74
   Socio-Dramatic Play and Self-Regulation · 76
   Socio-Dramatic Play and Autism · 77
Play and Friendships · 80
Chapter Summary · 82
Home and Community Connections · 82
First-Person Interview · 83
Key Terms · 84
Useful Websites · 84
Reflective Activity · 84

Chapter 4. Language and Literacy Development · 85

Scenario/Introduction: It's Not a Knock-Knock Joke · 85
Language Development · 86
Bilingual Development in Young Children · 89
Speech and Language Developmental Delays · 91
Language Development and Socio-Dramatic Play · 95
Communicating During Socio-Dramatic Play · 97
   Play Communications · 98
   Metacommunications · 99
Narrative Development · 101
   Emergent Literacy Development · 103
   Outside-In and Inside-Out Processes · 104
   Home Literacy Programs · 107
Chapter Summary · 109
Home and Community Connections · 109
First-Person Interview · 109
Key Terms · 110

Useful Websites   111
Reflective Questions   111

Chapter 5. Collaborating With Families and Professionals   113

Scenario/Introduction: Enhancing Collaborative Classrooms   113
Justification for Collaboration   114
Collaboration With All Families   116
   Importance of Family Collaboration   118
Collaboration With Professionals   121
Collaboration and Language-Rich Classrooms   124
   Creating a Team   125
   Developing a Philosophy Statement   125
Co-Teaching/Co-Partnering   125
   One Teaching, One Observing   127
   Center Teaching   127
   Parallel Teaching   128
   Alternating Teaching   128
   Teaming   128
   One Teaching, One Assisting   128
Reciprocal Relationships   129
Chapter Summary   132
Home and Community Connections   132
First-Person Interview   132
Key Terms   133
Useful Websites   134
Reflective Question   134

PART II. PLANNING AND DESIGNING A CLASSROOM FOR LEARNING THROUGH PLAY   135

Chapter 6. Planning for Effective Learning   137

Scenario/Introduction: Preparing for Morning "Circle Time"   137
Effective Early Learning   138
Creating Effective Learning Contexts   139
   Getting Started   140
   Indoor and Outdoor Learning   141
   Rough-and-Tumble Play With Young Children   144
   Outdoor Learning and Disabilities   147
Creating Effective Schedules   148
   A Sample Day   149
   Posting a Schedule   149
   Using Visual Schedules   150
   Teaching Transitions   153
Effective Flexible Groupings   155
   Large Group Learning   155
   Small Group Learning   156
   Center Learning   157
Effective Classroom Management   159
   Creating a Responsive Classroom   159
   Addressing Unacceptable Behaviors   161
   Addressing Challenging Unacceptable Behaviors   162
Chapter Summary   164
Home and Community Connections   165

First-Person Interview   165
Key Terms   166
Useful Websites   166
Reflective Questions   167

Chapter 7. Designing High-Quality Centers for Learning   169

Scenario/Introduction: Outdoor Activities Reflecting Indoor Activities   169
Creating High-Quality Classrooms   170
Developing High-Quality Teaching Strategies   172
    Intentional Teaching   172
    Integrating Child-Centered and Adult-Guided Activities   173
    Using Open-Ended Prompts   175
    Designing Differentiated Learning Opportunities   177
    Creating High-Quality Lesson Plans   181
Designing High-Quality Learning Centers   181
    Encouraging Pretend Narrative Activities   184
    Utilizing Familiar and Unfamiliar Activities   186
Developing High-Quality Learning Centers   191
    Center Management   191
    Center Time   192
    Center Space   193
    Center Materials   193
Integrating Early Learning and Common Core Standards Into Play Centers   197
Chapter Summary   198
First-Person Interview   199
Key Terms   200
Useful Websites   200
Reflective Questions   200

Chapter 8. Strategies for Guiding Play and Producing High-Quality Learning Activities   201

Scenario/Introduction: Teacher Rosie's Phone Call   201
Guided Learning   202
    Scaffolding   203
    Guided Play   204
    Guided Play Challenges   207
Guiding From Outside the Play Setting   209
    Guiding With Space and Time   209
    Guiding With Players   209
    Guiding With Themes and Props   210
    Guiding With Play Objects   210
    Guiding With Literacy-Enriched Objects   212
    Guiding With Adult Suggestions   213
Guiding From Inside the Play Setting   214
    Welcoming Adults Who Do Not Take Control   214
    Providing New Information, Redirecting Activities, and Having Fun   215
    Modeling Unfamiliar Roles   216
Chapter Summary   221
Home and Community Connections   221
First-Person Interview   221
Key Terms   222
Useful Websites   223
Reflective Questions   223

Chapter 9. Observing and Assessing to Promote Learning   225

   Scenario/Introduction: A New Year and a New Classroom   225
   Assessing Young Children   227
   Authentic Assessments   231
     Observational Notes   233
     Portfolios   234
     Journals   235
     Checklists   235
   Assessment of the Learning-Teaching Process   237
     Involving Families in the Assessment of Learning   238
     Integrating Cameras Into the Assessment Process   238
   Assessment of Challenging Abilities   239
     Response to Intervention   239
     Determining Special Education Eligibility   242
     Implementing a Transactive Analysis Model for Authentic Assessment   243
     Transactive Observations   243
   Observing Young Children   246
     Observing Children Planning Activities   246
     Observing Children's Participation in Activities   260
     Observing Social Skills   261
     Observing Communication Skills   261
     Observing Play Activities   262
   Chapter Summary   263
   Home and Community Connections   263
   First-Person Interview #1   263
   First-Person Interview #2   264
   Key Terms   265
   Useful Websites   265
   Reflective Questions   266

PART III. INTEGRATING PLAY ACTIVITIES ACROSS THE CURRICULUM   267

Chapter 10. Integrating Literacy Skills Into the Play Centers   269

   Scenario/Introduction: Playing "Beach Trip"   269
   The Head Start Child Development and Early Learning Framework   271
   K–12 Common Core State Standards   272
   Play and Literacy   275
     Common Characteristics of Play and Literacy   276
     Early Writing Skills   278
     Spoken Language   279
     Spoken Language Activities and English Language Learners   280
   Creating Play Centers to Expand Literacy Skills   280
     Creating Multifaceted Learning Opportunities   280
     Selecting Appropriate Socio-Dramatic Play Themes   281
     Organizing Socio-Dramatic Play Materials   282
   Integrating Literacy Activities Into Play Center Activities   283
     Guided Activity #1: Play Plans   284
     Guided Activity #2: Searching for Words   286
     Guided Activity #3: Dissecting Words   289
     Guided Activity #4: Reporting Shared Writings   292
   Chapter Summary   297
   Home and Community Connections   297
   First-Person Interview   297

Sample Learning Activities 298
Key Terms 300
Some Children's Books About Home and Literacy 300
Useful Websites 300
Reflective Questions 300

Chapter 11. Integrating Play Activities in the Science Centers 301

Scenario/Introduction: How Have You Changed? 301
Expanding Early Science Skills 302
    Planned Inquiry Activities 303
    Creating an Environment for Inquiry 305
Science and Play 309
    Functional Play 309
    Symbolic Play 310
    Games With Rules 311
Science Learning Elements and Core Standards 311
    Head Start Science Knowledge and Skills Elements 311
    Kindergarten Common Core State Standards 313
Developing Science Centers 316
    Science as an Integrative Curriculum 316
    Implementing the Inquiry Process 317
    Big Ideas That Guide Science Centers 321
Chapter Summary 324
Home and Community Connections 324
First-Person Interview 325
Sample Learning Activities 326
Key Terms 327
Useful Websites 327
Reflective Questions 328

Chapter 12. Integrating Play Activities in the Mathematics Centers 329

Scenario/Introduction: "Remember to Use the Data Sheets" 329
Developing Early Mathematics Skills 330
    Mathematics Challenge: Amount of Time Spent on Mathematics 332
    Mathematics Challenge: Gender-Biased Issues 335
Mathematics and Play 337
Guiding Mathematics Skills With Learning Standards 339
    Head Start Mathematics Elements 339
    Kindergarten Common Core State Mathematics Standards 342
Block Centers 343
    Developmental Stages of Block Play 344
    Guided Block Play 346
    Kindergarten and Blocks 353
Manipulatives Centers 355
    Commercial Manipulatives 355
    Common Manipulatives 356
    Performing Statistics With Manipulatives: A Four-Step Process 357
    Creating a Mathematics Learning Environment With Manipulatives 358
    Kindergarteners and Manipulatives 359
Woodcraft Centers 361
    Creating a Mathematics Learning Environment With Woodcraft 361
    Woodcraft and Materials 363
Chapter Summary 365
Home and Community Connections 365

First-Person Interview 365
Sample Learning Activities 366
Key Term 367
Some Children's Books About Mathematics and Blocks 367
Useful Websites 368
Reflective Question 368

Chapter 13. Integrating Play Activities in the Social Studies and Book Centers ... 369

Scenario/Introduction: The Bus Trip 369
Early Social Studies Skills 371
Social Studies and Play 373
   Neighborhood and Community Outings 376
Social Studies Standards 377
   Head Start Early Learning Social Studies Elements 377
   National Council for the Social Studies (NCSS) Standards 378
Social Studies Centers 378
   Social Studies Centers: Concept of Time 379
   Social Studies Centers: Anti-Bias Activities 381
Technology Use and Young Children 383
Book Centers 384
   Interacting With Books 387
   Designing Book Centers 388
Book Center Activities 392
   Game: Count the letter: _____. 393
   Guided Questions 393
   Dialogic Reading 394
Chapter Summary 396
Home and Community Connections 396
First-Person Interview 396
Sample Learning Activities 398
Key Terms 398
Some Children's Books About Social Studies 399
Useful Websites 399
Reflective Question 399

Chapter 14. Integrating Play Activities in the Creative Arts Centers ... 401

Scenario/Introduction: Busy Expressing Their Ideas 401
Early Creative Arts Skills and Development 403
   Current Status of Creative Arts in the Schools 405
Creative Arts, Play, and Literacy 406
Creative Arts and Motor Standards 408
   Early Creative Arts Standards 408
   Head Start Motor Skills Elements 409
   Kindergarten Standards 411
Art Centers 413
   Stages of Drawing 416
   Guiding With Open-Ended Art Materials 416
Music and Movement Centers 420
   Motor Skills Development 423
   Social and Emotional Development 423
   Cognitive Development 424
   Language and Literacy Development 425
   Pretense Development 426
   Classroom Transitions 428

Outdoor Activities 429
Guiding Music and Movement Activities 430
Drama Centers 432
Guiding Children's Drama Productions 432
Puppet Centers 434
Designing Puppet Centers 436
Guiding Children's Puppet Productions 436
Chapter Summary 437
Home and Community Connections 438
First-Person Interview 438
Sample Learning Activities 440
Key Terms 440
Some Children's Books About Creative Arts 441
Useful Websites 441
Reflective Questions 441

References 443
Glossary 459
Index 467
About the Authors 483

Preface

Over the past two decades, a growing number of parents, principals, primary teachers, and politicians have identified traditional, developmentally appropriate early education practices—particularly play—as non-essential academic activities for children from 2 to 8 years of age. They have demanded that formal academic accountability start in the early learning settings, arguing that this strategy will minimize the academic gap that has occurred between children of different socioeconomic groups, racial and ethnic groups, special education populations, and English language learner groups. In response to this criticism, early education curricula have changed to emphasize daily activities that focus on direct instruction led by adults rather than on child-centered activities. However, results to date indicate that, even with the increase in formal educational time, significant academic gaps still exist when children enter the formal education system.

In response to the existing significant academic gap, a growing number of today's teachers, caregivers, and researchers have asserted that children's classrooms must become more natural and playful learning environments. Findings now demonstrate that young children can expand their academic skills through the practice of guided play activities. Guided play is a form of child-centered play where adults structure the environment around general curricular goals designed to stimulate children's natural curiosity, exploration, and play through interactions with objects and peers.

This book demonstrates how to integrate guided play activities across the curriculum so that learning will occur for all children who are enrolled in early education programs today.

Specifically, the book promotes strategies to be used during playful activities that are carefully guided by an adult so that children can reach their highest level of learning and expand their knowledge across the curriculum, and especially in the areas of language and literacy. Research on current theories of learning, language development, and play activities are presented in Part I of the book, along with an entire chapter dedicated to developing the collaborative relationships with family members and other professionals. Part II describes strategies for designing classrooms, schedules, and learning activities so that children will engage in high-level, child-centered learning activities. Also included in Part II is a chapter on observation and assessment, along with an observation tool for assessing young children's general play, academic, communication, and social abilities. Part III provides comprehensive strategies for integrating guided play activities into the learning centers typically found in early education classrooms, such as literacy, science, mathematics, social studies, and creative arts.

Each of the book's 14 chapters begins with a factual learning *scenario* that demonstrates some of the key concepts that will be discussed in that chapter. Following each scenario are a number of *open-ended prompts* that are designed to have the instructor and students focus on the upcoming information. A large assortment of *figures* that summarize information presented in the text, and pictures demonstrating specific strategies are incorporated into each chapter. Each chapter also contains 3 or 4 *Apply and Reflect* activity boxes, which students and teachers can use to apply a specific concept to a real-life activity and to analyze the impact of this application. Toward the end of each chapter are *Key Terms*, *reflective questions*, *useful websites*, and suggested *home and community activities*. Each chapter also presents a *first-person interview* with a practitioner who is working in the early childhood field and who has exemplary skills in a specific area. Finally, the last five chapters in the book include sample developmentally appropriate *learning activities* for teachers and caregivers to use with young children.

Throughout the book evidence-based findings reinforce the premise that guided play activities must be used to integrate the early learning standards for young children and Common Core State Standards for children in early primary grade classrooms. The findings demonstrate that young children who use free and guided play activities, especially the most diverse and challenging preschoolers, have results superior to those that they would produce through activities solely directed by adults. Additionally, today's transitional kindergarten classrooms need to implement play-based curricula instead of removing it from their programs. If anything, the philosophy and pedagogical principles underlying the Common Core State Standards have more in common with the play-based learning presented in this book than past adult-directed educational practices.

The authors would like to thank the following reviewers of the draft manuscript:

Cari Lee Buckner, Dixie State College

Basanti D. Chakraborty, New Jersey City University

Cathy Coulthard, Sheridan College

Debra M. Eastman, Sierra College

Elizabeth M. Elliott, Florida Gulf Coast University

Sonya Gaches, University of Arizona

Sarah Esther Huisman, Fontbonne University

Kerri D. Mahlum, Casper College

Leslie Marlow, Berry College

Gayle Mindes, DePaul University

Sheria Slone Mitchell, Bishop State Community College

Joan Moreita, Texas State University

Kay Renken, Northern Arizona University

Jana M. Sanders, Texas A&M University–Corpus Christi

Tisha Shipley, Northwestern Oklahoma State University

Paulette Shreck, University of Central Oklahoma

Tunde Szecsi, Florida Gulf Coast University

Debra A. Troxclair, Lamar University

Nancy Winternight, SUNY New Paltz

Clover Simms Wright, California University of Pennsylvania

Chun Zhang, Fordham University

Norma Danelle Zunker, Texas A&M University–Corpus Christi

Ancillaries

Instructor Teaching Site

A password-protected site, available at www.sagepub.com/selmi, features resources that have been designed to help instructors plan and teach their courses. These resources include an extensive test bank, chapter-specific PowerPoint presentations, and links to video and web resources.

Student Study Site

A web-based study site is available at www.sagepub.com/selmi. This site provides access to several study tools including mobile-friendly eFlashcards and links to video and web resources.

PART I

Working With Young Learners

Research has shown that early language skills allow children to learn from others and provide the foundation for successful reading experiences. Young children learn language by actively participating in events. Typically, children expand their skills to a higher level when they engage in play activities with their peers. This book examines how play activities can guide children to enhance their high-quality language and literacy skills.

Part I of the book presents information on using developmentally appropriate play activities with young children to enhance early learning. Language and literacy skills can develop when children explore their environment and collaboratively produce pretend peer-play narratives. These narratives enhance language and literacy skills and influence children's future social and academic success.

Adults must have a comprehensive understanding of the similarities between play, language, and literacy development. They must know how to create contexts in which all children are self-motivated to enhance their literacy abilities and that create a strong foundation for further successful academic learning throughout their school years. Chapter 1 explains the need to modify classroom practices so that children are engaged in developmentally appropriate practices that motivate them to expand their learning. Chapter 2 addresses how play activities enhance children's learning, while Chapter 3 discusses the impact that symbolic representations have on the development of early language and literacy learning. Chapter 4 then focuses on how the development of play supports language and literacy enhancement. Finally, Chapter 5 centers on the idea that all adults, professionals, and family members must work together so children can maximize their learning of skills during the early education years. By understanding the relationships between play, language, and literacy, adults can create activities that motivate all children to achieve their highest level of learning.

1 The Need for Developmentally Appropriate Practices

THE POISON SYRUP

©iStockphoto.com/mzoroyan

Two boys walk over to the kitchen play area in a preschool classroom and start looking into the cupboards. One boy pulls out an empty paper towel roll from a cupboard and then quickly turns to the other boy saying, "Look! We found the poison syrup! Now we have to get it out of here."

The second boy, who is standing still and staring at the roll, responds, "We're right! It was here!" As he is talking, he quickly picks up a plastic shopping basket with items in it, shakes them out on to the floor, and says, "Here's the steel container to hold it. It says it here." He points to the print on the outside of the basket. Then he steadily holds out the basket with both hands towards the boy with the roll and says, "Put the poison in here so we can take it downstairs to our truck. We don't want it to spill."

The boy with the roll gently places it in the basket and then says, "Wait! We need to mark it 'dangerous.'" He picks up a pen that is in the kitchen play area and prints letter-like figures on the roll while the other boy steadily holds the basket. Then, each boy takes hold of the sides of the basket and pretends to carefully walk down some stairs, while commenting on the need to be careful and not spill.

Events similar to the ones described in this scenario appear in classrooms for young children, community centers, and homes of young children. Play events have always been considered both developmentally appropriate and a cornerstone of a young child's learning. As children engage in play they share their creativity through verbal and nonverbal language and tangible representations of their thinking. The interaction of children as they play provides a safe environment for acquiring both conversational and academic language. Through play children learn how to engage in oral discourse. They exchange their understanding and use of vocabulary, syntax, and cultural knowledge. Additionally, they also learn how to problem-solve and negotiate ideas. These rich, developmentally appropriate learning opportunities are seamless for children through play. As children develop, play allows them to escape from their present worlds and travel to fictitious worlds that are created by the intertwining of their personal knowledge, plans, and dreams. As this book will demonstrate, many of the skills that children develop during pretend play activities provide the foundation for the skills needed when they are enrolled in school and participate in common core activities. These skills include solving problems, making predictions, analyzing information, and negotiating ideas.

This chapter analyzes how adults can design developmentally appropriate practices that implement academic standards-based learning outcomes that meet the needs of all children and build both social and academic language. Additionally, it describes the diverse population that is currently enrolled in today's early childhood classrooms, and examines the benefits and challenges that they provide. Knowing how to integrate early learning standards and play activities will assist educators in responding both to current classroom challenges and when encountering concerns that can arise from administrators, parents, and politicians who are encouraging more structured learning changes.

As you read the chapter, consider the following:

> What is meant by developmentally appropriate?

> What strategies do the Common Core State Standards recommend for expanding young children's literacy skills?

> How have demographics in our classrooms changed and what does it mean for teachers and students?

Developmentally Appropriate Practices

Michael Greenberg/Photodisc/Thinkstock

Play has typically been thought to be a valuable experience for young children's learning and development.

Within the past two decades formal early learning standards have been designed and many parents, administrators, and politicians have proposed that formal academic activities replace the traditional play activities of young children (Hirsh-Pasek, Golinkoff, Berk, & Singer, 2009). Many educators are alarmed about the impact on children's overall learning with these types of curriculum changes that decrease play opportunities and **child-centered activities** where children's interactions focus on meaningful learning activities that the child is self-motivated to accomplish. Instead, those activities are being replaced with inappropriate adult-directed instruction focusing on activities where adults lead children through specific steps of a learning activity.

Educational researchers have produced a comprehensive collection of studies that clearly demonstrates a direct relationship between play activities and early academic skill development—that is, language and literacy skills, math and science skills, and social and self-regulatory skills, which are summarized below (for a complete review, see Fisher, Hirsh-Pasek, Golinkoff, Singer, & Berk, 2011).

The **National Association for the Education of Young Children (NAEYC)** is the nation's premier organization of early childhood professionals. It establishes research-based standards for programs and professionals, provides resources to improve the quality of early

Academic Skill Development	Examples From Play Activities
Language and Literacy skills	Storytelling, narrative structure, sequencing, phonemic awareness, symbolic representations, concepts about print, character development and identity, identifying, describing, questioning
Math and Science skills	Number sense, patterns, distinguishing shapes, similarities and differences, counting, making comparisons (large/small), sorting, combining
Social and Self-regulatory skills	Making decisions, turn-taking, negotiating, coordinating ideas, perspective taking, predicting, impulse control, responsible social behaviors

education programs, assists families in learning how to identify high-quality educational programs, and enhances professionals' knowledge through professional development activities such as workshops, seminars, and conferences.

In 2009 the NAEYC published a *Position Statement* that offers a framework for creating best practices for the development and learning of children birth through age 8. This report is grounded in current research findings on child development and learning and expressly identifies the following needs: (1) to reduce learning gaps in achievement, (2) to improve the connection between preschool education and elementary education, and (3) to identify teacher knowledge and decision making as vital to educational effectiveness. This statement, which addresses concerns similar to the ones addressed in this chapter, complements other NAEYC position statements (NAEYC, 2005; NAEYC & NAECS/SDE, 2002, 2003) by outlining practices for use in today's eclectic classrooms to promote optimal learning and development.

©iStockphoto.com/CEFutcher

Today's diverse classrooms promote ideal learning opportunities for all children.

For almost 20 years, the NAEYC has advocated two fundamental commitments: (1) that excellence and equality must be provided for the education of all children, and (2) that teachers must have a core understanding of how children learn and develop physically, socially, emotionally, linguistically, and cognitively. Specifically, the NAEYC endorses the concept of **Developmentally Appropriate Practices (DAP)**, which is the belief that all teaching practices should be appropriate to children's ages and developmental status, attuned to them as unique individuals, and responsive to the social and cultural contexts in which they live (Copple & Bredekamp, 2009).

Likewise, the **National Head Start Association** (NHSA) is an organization that advocates on behalf of two federally funded early education programs. One program is the **Early Start Program**, which promotes the school readiness for children birth to 2 years old from low-income families by enhancing their cognitive, social, and emotional development. Another program is the **Head Start Program**, which promotes the school readiness of children ages 3 to 5 years old from low-income families by also enhancing their cognitive, social, and emotional development. Similar to NAEYC, the mission of NHSA is to combat poverty in the United States by advocating for educational equality for all children and for early education professionals who are capable of providing high-quality, comprehensive programs in the areas of education, health, social services, and parent-community. This book fully supports the commitments of NAEYC and NHSA. However, as discussed later in this chapter, unfortunately the following trends exist (Child Trends Data Bank, 2012):

- Only 55% of 3- to 6-year-olds who were not in kindergarten attended early education programs in 2007
- Children from low-income families are less likely than children in more affluent families to attend early education programs
- Children of mothers who work are more likely than children whose mothers do not work to attend early education programs

The NAEYC (2009) proposes the following four evidence-based findings that provide the framework for efforts to increase learning levels of all children—an increase that will result in a smoother transition by children into the early elementary grades. Early childhood professionals should have a comprehensive understanding of these findings as well as the knowledge of how to integrate them into classroom practices so that all children can experience successful learning outcomes.

Early Action and Intervention

First, the research has confirmed that **early intervention** programs for families of very young children who need to develop the skills necessary for successful school participation have a more enduring impact on children's learning than does the later use of remediation techniques. All children, regardless of home and community differences are able to learn, at a very young age, many of the skills needed for successful participation in elementary school classrooms. Early Head Start has demonstrated how **high-quality programs**, programs that have low adult-child ratios, provide safe and intellectually stimulating environments, and encourage peer interactions, have a lasting, positive impact on young children's development, learning abilities, social skills, and regulation of emotions (Klein & Knitzer, 2006).

Teachers need to understand that many families of young children do not have the means to purchase books to read with their children. However, in the home environment, these children have been exposed to complex oral narratives, print in newspapers and advertisement magazines, cultural songs and chants, and peer-focused literacy activities that relate to game playing. These experiences should not be overlooked; they should be used to build a bridge between the home and school literacy activities.

Today's classrooms must engage children in playful and meaningful print-related activities.

Academic Precursors

Second, language and literacy have been identified as specific *precursors to later academic achieve*ment and thus warrant particular attention in today's early education classrooms. Language provides students access to information and a vehicle to express their thinking and learning. Vocabulary knowledge and oral language are particularly important for the development of children's reading comprehension skills and must be taught so that all children enter the formal school system ready to develop school-based literacies (Dickinson & Tabors, 2001). Home language and literacy practices are diverse and all are valuable assets for future academic success. The challenge for students from homes where the language and literacy practices are not directly reflective of those practiced or used in school is in the ability to make connections between home and school. Teachers need to be aware of the diverse forms of home literacy activities and to support families and their children in connecting these practices to the traditional literacy-based experiences of the classroom. Without a clear understanding of such connections, children find it difficult to catch up because they do not see their home practices as part of the learning process.

Letter and Sound Knowledge

Third, knowledge of the *alphabet and phonological awareness* (i.e., awareness of spoken sounds) are major predictors of later reading and writing proficiency. Preschool teachers have increasingly discovered that children's familiarity with both print and the sounds of language is a necessary part of learning in the years before kindergarten (Albert Shanker Institute, 2009; Bowman, 2005).

The foundation of phonological awareness is oral exposure and engagement with oral communication. When children hear what language sounds like, they ultimately hear patterns and norms in how sounds are connected to create meaning. This, coupled with the exposure to written language found through symbols, pictures, icons, illustrations, and text, establishes an early understanding of concepts about print. Understanding the concept that print, any print, conveys meaning prepares children to understand that letters are a form of print that can be used to create words, sentences, stories, and texts. All children need to be exposed to these precursors of successful literacy abilities through developmentally appropriate activities.

Ability to Self-Regulate

Finally, peer interactions allow children to develop **self-regulation**, or the ability to regulate their social, emotional, and cognitive abilities. Research demonstrates that these skills contribute to later classroom functioning (Raver, Farner, & Smith-Donald, 2007) and are predictors of future performance in areas of problem solving, planning, focused attention, and metacognition (Blair et al., 2007). Research has affirmed that play is the venue for all young children to enhance their peer interactions and to develop skills that will ensure success in later learning environments.

In summary, research and the NAEYC, the world's largest early childhood professional organization, emphasize the evidence-based research demonstrating that all children have a right to attend early education programs and thereby enhance their abilities through participation in developmentally appropriate practices such as interactive play activities. Unfortunately, a number of administrators, parents, and politicians disagree with this research and advocate for a more skill-based, adult-directed curriculum as a means of addressing the needs of the early education population.

Some programs offer structured academic activities in the morning and provide children opportunities to participate in more child-centered activities during the afternoon, such as exploring the sensory table, cooking recipes, singing songs, dancing to music, and creating flannel board stories. Although the schools focus on developing the same goals during the morning and afternoon activities, often the morning **adult-directed activities** can produce

At a young age, children must learn to plan and problem-solve situations with peers.

Creatas/Creatas/Thinkstock

increased negative behaviors and frustration among the children. Alternatively, when young children engage in developmentally appropriate child-centered activities such as reading, measuring, and sequencing recipe steps, their behaviors typically improve. The difference in children's behaviors can be attributed to the more developmentally appropriate practices that relate to their lives.

Common Core State Standards

A *Harvard Education Letter* article (Rothman, 2012) summarized nine ways that the then newly designed Kindergarten through Twelfth Grade Common Core State Standards change classroom practices. One substantial difference between the old and new standards that the article identified is the requirement of the new standards that literacy instruction be integrated into content areas (e.g., history, science, social science). The article cites research finding that understanding written texts for different content areas requires unique literacy skills that depend on that specific academic context. The literacy skills needed to complete a science experiment differ from those skills used to understand a historical document. Thus, kindergarten and early primary classroom literacy skills should no longer only be taught in segregated literacy lessons. Rather, some of these skills must be taught within the context in which they are used—such as science classes and social studies classes.

This same concept—that literacy learning is contextually dependent—is also true for younger children as well. The teacher for the two boys in the opening scenario had carefully planned the center where the boys were playing. There were play literacy objects in the center, such as marking pens and paper, that allowed the boys to create a sign explaining what was in the basket. These children were being provided opportunities to collaboratively create a narrative story using play items and literacy tools.

As will be explained in Chapter 4, learning to read does not simply involve learning that letters make sounds, and that those sounds can be joined together to read and write words and sentences. Instead, literacy skills emerge in children as a result of contextual clues, which is what the Common Core State Standards are promoting. Through engagement with letters in different social contexts, children actively gain knowledge of print (e.g., that it carries a message, contains letters and words, is sequentially organized) as well as knowledge of how to use it. Although books are very beneficial for the development of certain literacy skills, young children require a variety of everyday experiences to understand the multifaceted aspects of print.

Actually, the Common Core State Standards' philosophy and teaching principles have more in common with play-based learning than educational practices of the recent past. Kindergarten classrooms need to implement play-based curricula but, currently, they are having a hard time convincing many parents and administrators of this. Unfortunately, early education classrooms are being urged to implement programs that are increasingly tied to related accountability measures with more and more emphasis in print literacy early instruction.

Professionals need to be aware of what a developmentally appropriate classroom looks like and how to relate those characteristics to classroom learning activities. This information needs to be shared with families and administrators. Therefore, for all children to develop literacy skills, the following practices should be observed.

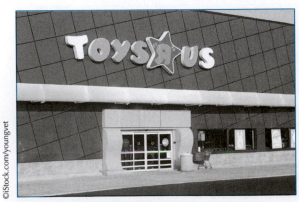

©iStock.com/youngvet

Children learn how to use print when it appears in a familiar context.

All classrooms should:

- Allow children to have ownership of the classroom and create an environment that exhibits child-made projects
- Offer choices about what children might do and respect the decisions they make
- Provide opportunities for children to participate in activities at their skill level
- Use small group activities that are interest-based for learning
- Offer hands-on experiences with real objects so that children are self-motivated to learn

Developmentally appropriate practices respect and value children as self-motivated learners.

Conversely, developmentally inappropriate practices would include the following behaviors. Classrooms should not:

- Be decorated with adult-made materials
- Expect children to complete all assigned work
- Involve children in activities that have "right" or "wrong" results
- Focus most learning activities around teacher-directed, large group interactions
- Engage children in rote-learning and memorizing activities

REFLECT AND APPLY EXERCISE 1.1

Your Early Learning Experiences

Reflect

Research confirms that the following four early education factors contribute to increased learning levels of children: early intervention, language and literacy experiences and development, familiarity with the letters of the alphabet and phonology, and positive peer interactions.

Apply

Think about your early childhood days and the ways in which you participated in activities either at home or at school and how they either encouraged or discouraged some of these four factors. What do you think was the impact of these experiences on your learning progress? If you cannot remember back to those days and have children of your own, think of their early learning years.

Current Demographic: Benefits and Challenges

Diverse populations of young children add richness to and present challenges for early educational centers. The main goals of early education programs are for children to learn how to live together, to cooperate with each other, and to share and help one another. Early education centers that are comprised of diverse students, families, and staff assist young children in learning, through their everyday experiences, how to accept differences, including differences in language, gender, ability, age, race, culture, and socioeconomics. By 5 years of age, children are capable of accurately identifying group membership on the basis on physical features. Providing opportunities for young children to interact daily with children from dissimilar family backgrounds can contribute to children's greater understanding of cultural diversity at a young age. That understanding will hopefully prevent prejudices at a later age (Sanders & Downer, 2012).

Young children tend to think in simple terms and, therefore, easily develop different stereotypes. For example, they can generalize that dresses or skirts are clothes that only women wear, and that only men have short hair. Today's early childhood professionals are responsible for continually challenging young children's simple thinking and exposing them to diverse thinking. Young children need to learn that in some cultures, men do wear skirts and that many women do choose to have very short haircuts.

Some of the ways that children can be challenged to think diversely are the following:

- **Language Diversity:** Children become aware that learning more than one language, especially at a young age, is an asset, not a deficit. In a society that uses so many languages, children should be exposed to a variety of different names for objects and actions through songs, poems, and daily interactions. Identifying the similarities and differences between words from different languages is very developmentally appropriate for children. After all, the early years are the time when children learn to enjoy and become comfortable with playing with words.
- **Cultural/Ethnic Diversity:** The early years are the time when children learn that they not only belong to a family, but they are also members of a specific culture that has certain rituals and values. As children are exposed to other children, they learn that there are many different cultures and ethnicities within their school and neighborhood communities. Along with learning self-respect and respect for others, young children must learn to respect and understand different cultural rituals and values. They need to become aware that every child, no matter what that child's ethnicity, can become whatever he or she wishes to be in life. Additionally, they must learn that people can belong to more than one ethnic group and engage in multiple cultural practices.
- **Gender Diversity:** Diverse gender experiences permeate today's world. At home, children have families that may have different sex parents, same sex parents, or a single sex parent. At a young age, children begin to classify actions and behaviors according to gender. Professionals must make certain that boys and girls realize that genders share many more similarities than they exhibit differences. Additionally, boys and girls can choose whatever profession they desire.
- **Religious Diversity:** Children need to learn that there are many ways of practicing religion, and that there is no "right" religion. Additionally, they need to understand that some families do not have a religion, and that others do not celebrate religious holidays. Talking about different religious practices, when the opportunity presents itself, helps children become comfortable with practices that may not be similar to the ones that they practice at home.
- **Economic Diversity:** Children today are exposed to families that are economically diverse. Within the past 7 years, almost all families have either personally experienced unexpected and immediate financial changes, or know of someone who has experienced such a situation. Children must learn that not having money does not mean that something is wrong with a person. They need to understand that many people have overcome poverty, neglect, and other very challenging situations.

The past two decades have seen profound changes in children attending early education programs. To design classroom activities that meet the individual needs of all children enrolled, teachers must clearly understand this population. Today, a majority of children spend 1 to 2 years in a classroom before entering the formal school system as kindergarteners. The U.S. Department of Education found that between 1970 and 2006, enrollment in preschools increased from 20% to 56% of the qualifying population (Planty et al., 2008). Milteer and Ginsburg (Milteer, Ginsburg, Council on Communication and Media, & Mulligan, 2012) report that approximately three fourths of the children in the United States between 3 and 5 years of age attend some type of a childcare program—center-based or home-based. Of this group, 56% are enrolled in formal preschool or day care centers. Table 1.1 demonstrates how the number of 4-year-olds enrolled in preschool has doubled in between 2002 and 2011.

Table 1.1   NIEER "State of Preschool 2011: State Preschool Yearbook"

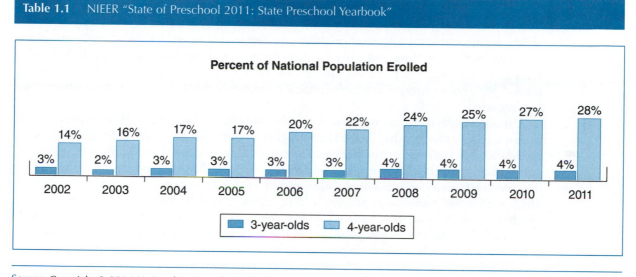

Percent of National Population Erolled

	2002	2003	2004	2005	2006	2007	2008	2009	2010	2011
3-year-olds	3%	2%	3%	3%	3%	3%	4%	4%	4%	4%
4-year-olds	14%	16%	17%	17%	20%	22%	24%	25%	27%	28%

The increased preschool population has resulted in the majority of early education classes being comprised of children from diverse economic, linguistic, ethnic, and developmental groups. Census data found that in 2000, approximately 5.5 million children were enrolled in some form of center-based preschool, and about a million of these children, or approximately one fifth, had needs that qualified them for federally supported programs. Therefore, teachers must create responsive classrooms that meet the unique needs of children who live in poverty, do not use English as their home language, and have identified special cognitive, social, or physical needs.

A long-time goal of early childhood programs has been to help children feel good about themselves, their families, and their communities. For these feelings to occur, professionals need to expose children to the ways in which families can be different, have unfamiliar customs, and might perhaps have undergone experiences that are beyond what some other children could imagine. Attention to these issues should not just be addressed on a special day or treated as an "add-on" to the curriculum. These skills cannot be efficiently taught through a planned lesson on a specific day of the year by making a headdress

©iStock.com/IPGGutenbergUKLtd

Programs need to continually support daily multicultural experiences.

or eating a particular type of food. Instead, embracing diversity involves a permanent, daily commitment to making sure that children engage in experiences similar to the following:

- Learning about and being proud of their own background
- Learning about and respecting people's different backgrounds
- Interacting with diverse families and community members in center activities
- Continually enjoying and seeking out differences
- Discovering how to respectfully problem-solve when differences occur

Economic Diversity

Family income can impact a young child's education in two fundamental ways. First, if a child's family can afford a preschool, they are better able to ensure their child's placement in a high-quality, challenging early education setting (National Institute for Early Education Research [NIEER], 2008). Second, low-income families may have a high-quality government funded preschool program available in their community that can prepare their children for kindergarten.

Although experts still do not have a specific definition of the term *high-quality* early education (see Chapter 6), they agree that a higher quality education provides a more robust foundation for later successful academic learning and for a more seamless transition into formal school programs. The government provides high-quality early education programs for low-income families and, as noted above, enrollments in these programs continue to expand. High-quality early education programs have demonstrated lifelong impacts on the lives of children raised in poverty. Geoffrey Canada's work (Tough, 2008) in the Harlem schools in New York City illustrates how funding has much more impact when it supports young children rather than children in the older grades. However, these early learning services must not focus only on the child but must be delivered through partnerships with families.

Between 1991 and 2005, the National Household Education Survey found that the preschool participation rate for children from both "poor" and "non-poor" families increased at a similar rate. However, only 59% of young poor children were participating in preschool programs, while 79% of the non-poor children were participating (Barnett & Yarosz, 2007).

An important complicating factor, as reported by the Center for American Progress in October 2011, is that a strikingly high number of children in the United States live in poverty. The 2010 Census data revealed that one out of every five American children lives with a family in poverty. According to data reported in 2006, ethnic minority children in Head Start programs demonstrate the highest rates of poverty, with approximately 40% of black children and 35% of Hispanic children falling below the poverty line. Although the majority of these children are eligible for federally sponsored programs, living in poverty creates numerous obstacles that can negatively impact the results of early education programs—such as lower levels of health, energy, transportation, and parental support. Catherine Snow (Bowman, 2005) found that, on average, 4-year-old children living in poverty had fallen about 18 months behind their typical peers. If unremediated, this gap from the preschool years will continue through elementary school and beyond.

Unfortunately, many families neither possess the means to afford high-quality preschool programs nor qualify for government-sponsored programs. Some of the children in such families are enrolled in lower-cost programs that lack staff and materials and whose staff do not understand how to address all the needs of this population. Moreover, a large number of children stay at home with family relatives and do not enter the school setting until education is free to them at 5 years of age. Although these children have had the opportunity to experience a variety of diverse language and literacy skills, some may not have paralleled the expectations for literacy in school.

Specifically, teachers must understand how to identify, access, and develop students' *funds of knowledge* (Moll, Amanti, Neff, & Gonzalez, 1992) to support ongoing language and literacy development in school. **Funds of knowledge** refers to understanding how and what children have learned as they actively participate in household and community activities. Instead of having a classroom that is isolated from what children are learning at home and in their communities, through home visits, observing students in class, and reciprocal interviews between the school staff and the families, teachers can acquire information on children's funds of knowledge. This awareness of students' funds of knowledge will assist teachers in creating classrooms that reflect activities similar to the children's personal social worlds. Moll et al. observed children in their homes and communities and learned that they were involved with family members and family friends in academic activities while they participated in skilled labors and craft activities such as carpentry, mechanics, gardening, masonry, and so on.

Teachers need to use children's familiar and real-world activities to assist them in the learning of academic content.

Teachers need to use real-world activities from the children's homes and communities to assist the children in gaining information about language, mathematics, literacy, science, and other academic areas. Using these resources as a foundation for the development of further learning will help professionals see that student diversity is an asset that we can leverage for academic success.

In sum, a growing number of children come from families who cannot afford to send their children to high-quality programs or qualify for government-funded programs. Even children who qualify for government-sponsored programs often encounter hindrances that prevent them from receiving the full value of these programs. Family income directly impacts the development of each family member physically, emotionally, socially, and cognitively, and these daily stressors severely impede healthy physical and mental development. Consequently, many families who are economically disadvantaged—both those who qualify for programs and those who do not—are not receiving the full value of early education programs. Children from these families enter preschool behind their peers and often experience higher rates of academic failure in the early years. These failures can result in an increased probability of grade retention and school dropout.

Ethnic Diversity

Most of today's early education programs are ethnically diverse. The National Household Education Survey analyzed ethnic enrollments in early education programs from 1991 through 2005. The study found that ethnicities experienced a considerable increase in enrollments during this period, with participation from Black, Hispanic, and "Other" ethnic groups exceeding those of White. Similarly, Head Start Preschool Programs reported in 2006 that Latinos made up 34% of their student population. For Head Start Programs, Latinos were the largest single ethnic minority group and were only marginally smaller than the 39% Caucasian population.

This growth in ethnic diversity in the early childhood centers has been accompanied by an increase

Ethnic diversity allows for children to develop comfortable and positive feelings about differences, newness, and unfamiliarity.

in the number of languages spoken by families and the cultural diversity of families. With such rich diversity it is almost impossible to employ a one-size-fits-all approach to learning. Understanding the complexities of diversity and the benefits and challenges it can have for classrooms is critical in meeting the needs of all children. Having the opportunity to learn from other children and families from different backgrounds and experiences enhances the learning experience for everyone. When children develop an appreciation for diversity, they learn to understand and appreciate diverse perspectives, and they develop strong language skills by interacting with different language models. The richness of the experience for children and their development is further compounded with challenges for the teachers to understand this diversity and how to cultivate a positive classroom environment where all children can learn. This challenge, unfortunately, continued to be addressed by a single approach to teaching and learning during the past decade. Many centers have implemented adult-directed, large group learning lessons in response to the sudden increase in diverse children attending early education programs. In general, this is partly due to a lack of understanding of the role of diversity in fostering high outcomes for all students. For students to fully embrace the benefits of a diverse classroom setting, all participants (i.e., adults and children) must engage in culturally responsive, interactive, child-centered, collaborative learning opportunities.

A single-minded approach to education is inadequate in providing all children with activities that will enhance their learning. Instead, programs must embrace all children's home culture and language so as to allow for the development of home language while learning English. Respecting children's home language reinforces positive feelings of self and pride in their families and communities, which results in a desire to learn and take pride in work. Chapter 5 of this book illustrates how teachers must partner with these families—many of whom are experiencing poverty, low literacy levels, and adjustment challenges in adapting to a new community—to provide opportunities for shared, school-to-family support.

Developmental Diversity

In 1986, the passage of federal law **PL 99-457** encouraged the participation of young children with disabilities in programs that had been established for children without disabilities. In 1997, the **Individuals with Disabilities Education Act (IDEA)** was amended. This federal law allows all children with disabilities to participate in a free and appropriate public education. The law also states that children with disabilities have the right to attend **natural environments**, which are learning settings that encourage inclusive practices not only in early education centers, but also in society as a whole. For over the past 25 years, a significant increase has been seen in the participation of children with disabilities of all ages in educational programs for nondisabled children. The **Council for Exceptional Children (CEC)**, a national organization, has successfully advocated for the rights for persons with disabilities. Additionally, a subgroup within CEC, the Division of Early Childhood (DEC), has focused on advocating for the rights of young children with disabilities between birth and 6 years of age and their parents.

The term **inclusion** refers to the process of combining a child or children with disabilities in a classroom or learning environment with children who do not have disabilities. Although inclusion promotes the practice of physically placing a child with a disability in a classroom of nondisabled children, it also encompasses much more, including the following, according to Odom, Buysse, and Soukakou (2011):

- Participation in activities
- Development of social relationships
- Achievement of realistic learning outcomes that are similar to those of all the children in that room

As a result of the more expansive definition of inclusion practices, professionals have ceased using earlier terms such as *mainstreaming, integrating,* and *reverse-mainstreaming.* Those terms primarily convey the idea of just a physical placement in a natural setting.

Disabilities affect all families, regardless of their culture and linguistic background or their income. Teachers need to recognize the richness in terms of diversity and interdependence that inclusion of students with varied backgrounds can bring to a classroom (Copple & Bredekamp, 2009). Young children with disabilities can either be *fully included* in a classroom, where they spend their entire day with typically developing children, or *partially included,* were a child splits the learning time between a classroom with typically developing children and a classroom with only children with disabilities. In 2000, the Office of Special Education Programs reported that 36% of preschool children with disabilities were receiving services in a classroom for typically developing children. In 2007, the same office reported that approximately half of the children with disabilities between 3 and 5 years were receiving services in a regular early education setting for more than 80% of the day. Although some believe that this increase is not exactly as high as reported because of a change in the reporting form, nonetheless inclusive educational programs for all children unquestionably have increased, including early education programs.

Enrollment in early education centers results in a number of positive impacts on both children who are typically developing and those who are atypically developing. Odom, Buysse, and Soukakou (2011) report that inclusive early childhood settings do not appear to delay the developmental gains made by the typically developing children and that, at this age, children seem to actively engage and develop friendships with each other. Nonetheless, the steady increase of the practice of inclusion means that teachers must provide activities that address the needs of all the developmentally diverse students in their classrooms. Teachers also must engage in enhancing collaborative relationships with other professionals who can assist them by working with the children in the inclusive setting.

Although limited research has examined the impact of full inclusion on children with disabilities and without disabilities, the results to date are encouraging. Families of children without disabilities tend to be concerned about three aspects of their child's education when they learn that a child with disabilities will be included in a classroom:

- Will the curriculum for the children without disabilities be "watered-down" to meet the skills of the child with disabilities?
- Will the child with disabilities require more time from the staff that, in turn, will take away from time spent by the staff with the other children?
- Will children without disabilities pick up undesirable behaviors from the child with disabilities?

So far, the research has not found that these three situations have occurred, especially when children are enrolled in high-quality, developmentally appropriate early education centers. Moreover, offering developmentally appropriate practices focuses on providing learning activities for all children at their individual skill levels. Consequently, the needs for a child with a disability can be addressed along with needs for the other children in the classroom.

For young learners, developmentally appropriate practices promote learning that occurs primarily through small group and individual activities that involve peer interactions and hands-on activities. In these activities, the role of adults is primarily to guide children, not to teach them (see Chapter 7). Adults in early childhood inclusive classrooms should spend the same amount of time guiding both children with disabilities and those without disabilities to higher levels of learning. Finally, if a classroom is truly focused on accepting and respecting differences among people, children should not find it necessary to take on the behaviors of other children.

There are a number of very positive results that can be experienced when children with disabilities are included in classrooms. Some could include:

- **Fear reduction:** Children could demonstrate an increase in the comfort and awareness of human differences. Children typically tend to fear or shy away from people who do not look or behave the same as they do. However, having daily interactions with peers who have disabilities can reduce the fear of difference.
- **Friendship development:** As children become more comfortable with differences they could begin to notice more about the similarities between themselves and their peers with disabilities. As a result, warm and caring friendships can develop between these two populations.
- **Feeling good:** When children are successful at interactions that make them feel good, they begin to enhance their self-concept. Developing a relationship with a child with a disability can make children feel good and, at the same time, bolster the child's self-image.
- **Moral and ethical principles:** During the early years, all children begin to develop moral and ethical principles. Assisting in everyday advocacy activities for a child with a disability can help children develop these important early principles.

In conclusion, today's early education classrooms are filled with children with different personalities, backgrounds, and levels of development, some with disabilities and some without. However, unlike the past, many of these children are being raised in diverse cultures with unique values, use different languages, live in challenging home environments, and have widely assorted developmental abilities. These differences affect young children's development and learning. Unfortunately, while preschool enrollments doubled and become more diverse, the average amount of funding spent per child dropped from $7,668 in 2003 to $6,780 in 2011 (see Table 1.2). As a result, programs currently must address the needs of a larger, more diverse, and challenging population with considerably fewer financial resources.

Table 1.2   NIEER "State of Preschool 2011: State Preschool Yearbook"

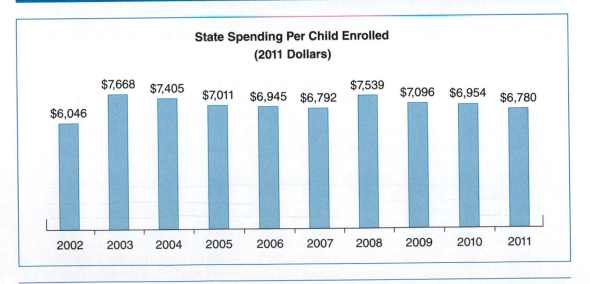

Current Curriculum Challenges

Early learning activities can have a lifelong impact on all children. The impact of early education is especially significant for young children who are at risk of developing in an atypical manner (Tough, 2008). Research demonstrates that a high-quality preschool education can enhance children's early literacy, cognitive, and social abilities, which contributes to educational and vocational success. Reflecting these findings and others from a large body of research on early childhood development, early education programs are rapidly becoming an integral component of our educational system.

During the past two decades, however, a growing number of parents, principals, primary teachers, and politicians have identified traditional, developmentally appropriate preschool practices—particularly play—as non-essential activities for young children at school. They have demanded that formal academic accountability start in the early learning settings. In response to this criticism, preschool curricula have changed to include daily activities focusing on directed instruction by adults rather than on the more traditional, child-centered activities.

Decreased Play Opportunities

For decades, early learning activities were grounded in the play activities of young children, with the goal of providing secure, harmonious, and carefree environments. Young children were offered multiple opportunities during the school day to play with their friends and to escape into various imaginative roles, such as the worlds of doctors, dragons, mothers, cowboys, and travelers. These peer play activities were commonly understood to be random and unpredictable activities that please children and promote the overall social, linguistic, and emotional development of young children. Because of the spontaneous nature of these activities, professionals have frequently labeled them **free play** activities. Adults seldom interacted with children in these activities, unless invited by them, and there were no direct connections made between these free-spirited activities and actual academic learning.

In many classrooms today, the traditional play activities, similar to the ones described in the previous paragraph and in the scenario at the beginning of this chapter, typically occur only on special occasions or when some children need to be kept busy while others complete their work. Early education professionals claim to understand the importance of active play in assisting learning and language development; however, because of the intense focus on academics, play activities have now "taken a back seat" (Milteer et al., 2012).

Howes and Wishard (2004) studied the amount of social pretend play at low-income, community childcare centers between 1982 and 2002. They found that such play decreased for 4.5 year olds from 41% to only 9% of the observed time. Miller and Almon (2009) similarly caution that, as direct instruction has gained popularity in educational settings, playtime has been all but abolished. Elkind (2007) also acknowledges that children have lost up to 8 hours a day of playtime and that 30,000 schools have substituted time at recess for time in academic activities. Finally, children's playtime has decreased so much that it has begun to impact their health and development and, as a result, the American Academy of Pediatrics now offers guidelines on ways that pediatricians can help families, schools, and communities understand the importance of play for healthy development in all areas (Ginsburg, 2007).

A decrease in play activities has begun to impact young children's health and development.

Increased Adult-Directed Activities

The pressure to increase structured instructional time for young children partly stems from the impact of the passage of the 2001 federal legislation known as the **No Child Left Behind Act (NCLB)**, which President George W. Bush proposed. This act mandates that, for states to receive federal funding for education, they must (1) annually assess elementary and secondary children's basic skills, (2) establish academic performance standards that allow for learning goals to be measured, and (3) demonstrate growth in learning through improved individual outcomes in education (see Figure 1.1).

Figure 1.1   Areas Emphasized in No Child Left Behind (NCLB)

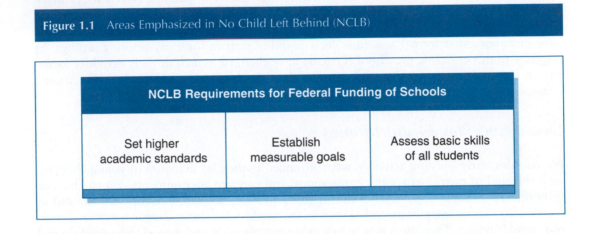

NCLB Requirements for Federal Funding of Schools		
Set higher academic standards	Establish measurable goals	Assess basic skills of all students

As a result of this insistence on operationalized learning and the demand for children's increased test scores, early childhood teachers are being pressured into turning their programs into "academic boot camps" focusing on the development of skills through academic drill, and to sharply decrease the amount of play activities offered (Hirsh-Pasek et al., 2009).

Although early learning academic environments have demonstrated some benefits from implementing the skill-and-drill learning activities proposed by NCLB, these successes have primarily occurred among children from economically advantaged homes. Interestingly, prior to entering preschool, these children typically are exposed to daily social interactions focusing on playful and meaningful activities that involve letter and number games and other academic play activities with family members—such as magnetic letters on the refrigerator, take-out menus, piggy banks with money, simple card games. These activities parallel the literacy skills and practices of school. As a result, some of these children enter preschool with a clear understanding of how to use numbers and letters in everyday life—that they are used to make lists, understand messages, pay for items, follow specific sequences. These children are then motivated to use these symbols in more abstract situations. After having such hands-on experiences, they successfully transition to more abstract activities such as reading color words, identifying geometric figures, and sequencing parts of a story.

However, the experiences of economically less advantaged students, who populate about 40% of the programs (Douglas-Hall & Chau, 2008), differ greatly from the students from middle- and upper-socioeconomic families. These children engage in and

Thinkstock/Stockbyte/Thinkstock

Some children enter educational programs having had playful home experiences using letters, words, and numbers.

experience many language- and literacy-rich activities at home, though they may not directly parallel school-like activities. There is a strong need
for professionals to understand how to connect
the home–school experiences of these children to
ensure that they all have the opportunity to succeed. Thus, as early childhood practices become
more academic and less playful, children living in
poverty can be impacted more negatively by the
trend to decrease playtime than their higher socioeconomic peers. The result is an increased disparity
between these two populations in opportunities to
develop cognitive, social, emotional, physical, creative,
and communication skills.

Many communities do not have safe areas where children can play.

At the same time, there has also been a decline in
the existence of safe outdoor play areas in most residential areas, and especially in the low-
income neighborhoods. Additionally, the impact of social, emotional, and economic stressors
on families with financial needs can cause parents to lose time and energy over these stressful situations, and this loss impacts the frequency and quality of their interactions in playful
family activities. As a result of the lack of playful activities in the home and the demand for
more academic preschool activities, less advantaged children enter the educational system
averaging a year or even two academically behind their peers from middle- and upper socioeconomic families, and never appear to catch up (Milteer et al., 2012).

The results tend to be profound for at-risk populations who enter early education settings
without experiences in meaningful and playful academic activities and face initial educational
experiences that focus on structured, teacher-instructed group activities, which are often disconnected from any of their everyday life experiences. Without the opportunity to interact with
their peers, their language development is further limited. Many of these children lose interest in
school at a young age; indeed, the number of preschoolers expelled for unmanageable behaviors

REFLECT AND APPLY EXERCISE 1.2

Your Early Play Interactions

Reflect

Think about the types of activities that you engaged in when you were 3 or 4 years old. Did
you have a park to go to where you played with your peers? Did you have neighbors that were
your age whom you had over to your house? Did you spend most of your time either in the
house with your family or out in the community with your parents doing errands or going to
work with them? Did you laugh, talk, and scream with joy with your friends and family, or were
your interactions primarily with your family members?

Apply

Evaluate how those early play experiences influenced you when it was finally time for you
to go to school. Did you feel comfortable playing with children who were not part of your
family and whom you did not know? Did you find it challenging to approach others to become
involved in play activities or did you feel comfortable with people who you did not know?
Why was that?

has greatly increased during the past two decades (Hirsh-Pasek et al., 2009). Additionally, despite the increase in children being exposed to academic skills at a younger age over the past decade, the number of student dropouts from the school system has not decreased, demonstrating that the academic challenge of better preparing students has not been accomplished (Jackson, 2011). These findings, the increase in preschoolers being expelled from school and no decrease in the school dropout rate, do not paint a successful picture for the structured preschool practices that many parents, administrators, and politicians are recommending.

Addressing Current Challenges

A growing number of today's teachers and researchers are asserting that young children's classrooms must return to being more natural and playful learning environments. In 2002 the NAEYC declared that, although play has always been considered a foundation for young children's learning and has continued to be of interest to persons working with young children, more than ever a need now exists for professionals to clearly understand the development of play and the ways to "create and support environments that enrich and extend children's play" (p. 18). NAEYC's position for *Developmentally Appropriate Practices* (2009a) focuses on five key features that early education professionals must address:

1. They must create a caring community for learners.

2. They must teach to enhance development and learning.

3. They must plan curricula to achieve important goals.

4. They must assess children's development and learning.

5. They must establish reciprocal relationships with families.

Even with the increase in formal instructional time, data continue to demonstrate the existence of significant gaps in scores between various economic groups, racial and ethnic groups, special education populations, and English language learner groups (U.S. Department of Education, 2010). The disparity that exists in educational exam scores between different groups—such as genders, ethnicities, native languages, and socioeconomic groups—is termed the **achievement gap**. During the past decade, educators, researchers, and politicians have given increased attention to strategies that might minimize these differences.

One attempt has been to close this disparity between students by providing early structured learning activities. This attempt has resulted in a wide recognition of both the value of identified preschool learning standards and the need for collaboration between preschools and early elementary teachers so that all preschool children can successfully transition into the formal educational system. However, many teachers and professional organizations object to the current practice of simply relocating elementary learning activities to within the preschool curriculum (e.g., Albert Shanker Institute, Alliance for Childhood, NAEYC). They believe that this relocation has curtailed essential early learning activities, such as ones focusing on problem solving, play, and collaborative peer interactions.

Engaging in "Guided Play" Activities

A growing body of research demonstrates that all young children can enhance their academic skills through the practice of *guided play activities* (Hirsh-Pasek et al., 2009). Guided play, which will be discussed in more detail in Chapter 8, is a form of child-centered play where adults structure the environment around general curricular goals designed to stimulate children's natural curiosity, exploration, and play through interactions with objects and peers (Hirsh-Pasek & Golinkoff, 2011). These unstructured activities integrate both core curriculum standards and playful pedagogy. Such activities are similar to the playful ones that many children from middle- and upper-socioeconomic families participate in at home with guidance from a parent before they successfully achieve formal, abstract learning lessons. Figure 1.2 illustrates the difference between free play and guided play.

Findings now demonstrate that young children who use free and guided play activities, especially the most diverse and challenging preschoolers, generate results superior to those they would have produced through adult-directed activities (Hirsh-Pasek et al., 2009).

In summary, knowledge gained in the early years of life provides a foundation for later learning. Young children from birth typically depend on social interactions with others to develop language, learn, and make sense of the world around them (Gopnik, 2009). The increase in adult-directed, structured, early learning academic activities coupled with the decrease in playtime at home or at school has led to questions about the benefits of curricula that are not rich in play activities (Hatcher & Perry, 2004). Evidence suggests that developmentally appropriate activities involving both free play and guided play can generate optimal learning outcomes that equal or surpass those of structured activities. *This book will demonstrate how to integrate play activities across the core curriculum so that learning occurs equally for all children who are enrolled in early education programs today.*

Through adult guidance, children can produce high-quality play interactions that result in the learning and development of skills.

Jupiterimages/Stockbyte/Thinkstock

Figure 1.2   Integrating Free Play and Guided Play Into Early Education Curricula

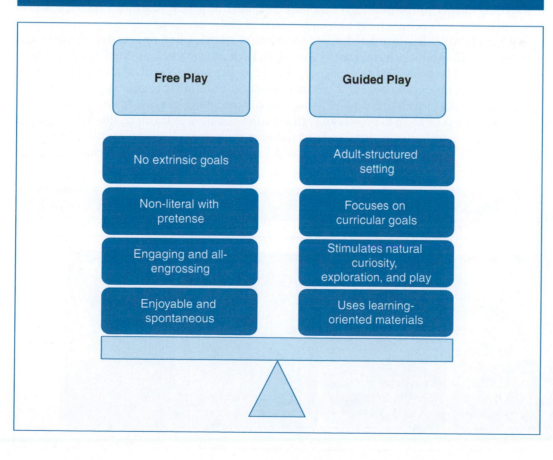

Free Play	Guided Play
No extrinsic goals	Adult-structured setting
Non-literal with pretense	Focuses on curricular goals
Engaging and all-engrossing	Stimulates natural curiosity, exploration, and play
Enjoyable and spontaneous	Uses learning-oriented materials

Implementing NAEYC's Principles

This book subscribes to the four NAEYC research principles summarized earlier in this chapter that are believed to close the achievement gap and to allow all children successful learning experiences: (1) entitlement to an early education, (2) opportunities for language and literacy development, (3) activities focusing on letter and sound recognition, and (4) enhanced learning activities embedded in social play activities. Adherence to these principles will allow professionals to promote excellence in early childhood education while, at the same time, promoting optimal learning in children.

Preschool classrooms typically include a designated play center where children are free to engage in socio-dramatic pretend play activities. These classrooms also contain other learning centers that are usually totally disconnected from the pretend play center. These learning centers are locations where children go either freely or at the request of an adult and then participate in early learning activities. Because research has demonstrated a fundamental relationship between play and learning, teachers must view all centers (including play centers) as learning centers and, therefore, coordinate all center activities so that meaningful and synthesized learning occurs. Centers must be carefully and continually designed to meet the individual and changing needs of all the classroom participants. Additionally, through skillful adult guidance in the centers, activities can reflect the learning goals for each individual. As a result, all children can expand their language abilities, enhance their literacy skills, increase their cognitive development, and develop the ability to regulate social and emotional needs (see Figure 1.3).

Today's teachers of young children need to know how to monitor play and learning activities. They also must know how to assess and readjust play when low-level activities are being implemented, interactions are limited, and language is repetitious. Allowing a low level of play to continue or stopping it does not provide children with the assistance that they need to move to a higher level of activity. By carefully guiding play enactments and encouraging children to further probe problems that they encounter in playful learning centers, teachers can move children's achievement to a higher level of understanding.

NAEYC (2009a) has translated their four areas of research findings on development and learning into 12 specific principles (see Figure 1.4). Each principle is supported by an extensive research base. The principles are designed to increase the achievement of all young students and to better connect preschool and elementary education. Similar to NAEYC's Principles of Development and Learning, this book focuses on enhancing the learning of young children by linking activities common to preschool with activities common to learning, literacy, language, mathematics, science, creative arts, and social studies skills in an elementary setting. Figure 1.4 lists NAEYC's Principles of Development and Learning and relates those principles to the

Figure 1.3 *Characteristics of Strong Early Education Learning Centers*

Learning centers should include: Activities that are playful, meaningful, and synthesized

Learning centers should include: Activities that are carefully and continually designed

Learning centers should include: Activities that reflect individual learning goals

Learning centers should include: Activities that expand language, enhance literacy, increase cognitive ability, and develop social and emotional skills

information that is presented in this book. The following three goals of this book, which are listed in Figure 1.5, address NAEYC's 12 principles.

Figure 1.4 Relating This Book's Parts to NAEYC's Principles

Book Parts I and III	• NAEYC #1: All the domains of development are important, and they are closely interrelated.
Book Parts II and III	• NAEYC #2: Many aspects of children's learning and development follow well-documented sequences.
Book Parts I and II	• NAEYC #3: Development and learning proceed at varying rates from child to child.
Book Parts I and III	• NAEYC #4: Development and learning result from a dynamic and continuous interaction of biological maturation and experience.
Book Parts I, II, and III	• NAEYC #5: Early experiences have profound effects, both cumulative and delayed, on a child's development and learning.
Book Parts I, II, and III	• NAEYC #6: Development proceeds toward greater complexity, self-regulation, and symbolic or representational capacities.
Book Parts I, II, and III	• NAEYC #7: Children develop best when they have secure, consistent relationships with responsive adults and opportunities for positive relationships with peers.
Book Parts I, II, and III	• NAEYC #8: Development and learning occur in and are influenced by multiple social and cultural contexts.
Book Parts I and III	• NAEYC #9: Always mentally active in seeking to understand the world around them, children learn in a variety of ways.
Book Parts I, II, and III	• NAEYC #10: Play is an important vehicle for developing self-regulation as well as promoting language, cognition, and social competence.
Book Parts I, II, and III	• NAEYC #11: Development and learning advance when children are challenged to achieve at a level just beyond their current mastery.
Book Parts I, II, and III	• NAEYC #12: Children's experiences shape their motivation and approaches to learning.

Source: National Association for the Education of Young Children (2009a).

Figure 1.5　Overriding Book Goals

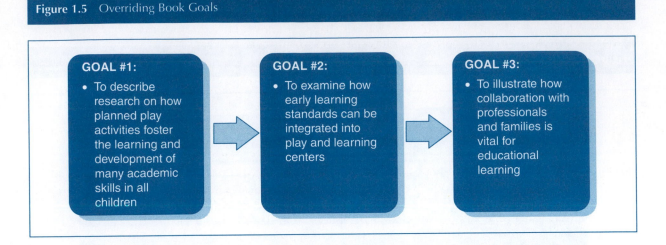

First, the book describes current research on play and how it can be used to create early intervention opportunities for children to develop and learn. Play activities can actually foster the learning and development of many academic skills in all areas. This book examines how early childhood educators who carefully attend to the play of their students can create effective child-centered play environments that allow children to acquire the skills necessary for success in the primary grades. Suggestions are presented about specific strategies that professionals can use to guide their students through developmentally appropriate preschool learning activities and then seamlessly transition them to kindergarten common core standards activities.

Second, the book explains how play and learning centers in a classroom can provide the context for integration of curricula standards. All learning activities, especially the more academically based ones such as letter and sound recognition and number and shape awareness, can be learned through playful and carefully planned and guided activities. Adults need to know how to provide children with well-designed, natural learning opportunities that are developed for children's distinct background knowledge. Through involvement in learning activities that are tightly connected to play activities, children enhance their ability to regulate their social and emotional skills as well as their cognitive skills by participating in meaningful and realistic academic activities.

Finally, this book also provides strategies for adults to use in collaborating among all concerned parties, a practice necessary for effective program implementation. Families and professionals provide necessary and vital support for the effective learning of early skills in all areas, and especially in the areas of language and literacy. Parents face many challenges during their child's early years, and these challenges affect the psychological and social-emotional stages that families experience. Teachers must understand the family system and the family's role in early education. To successfully implement an educational program, a teacher must be involved with the families of the students and must understand and respect different family values and the concerns of various cultures, as well as how a child with disabilities affects the family unit. This book explores strategies that enable teachers to more sensitively communicate with professionals and families so that development and learning can be supported to the fullest extent both at school and in the home.

When children step across the threshold of their first early education center, they are excited and motivated to learn more about the world. Adults working in these centers bear a profound responsibility to enhance that excitement and motivation so that all children—those living in poverty, learning through multiple languages, or adapting to special needs—continue to thrive and learn to their fullest potential. Research now demonstrates that successful academic learning can only occur when young children are provided with carefully planned and guided play activities that are integrated across the curriculum.

Chapter Summary

Society today expects young children to be taught skills that have traditionally been introduced in kindergarten and it expects teachers to use formal instructional methods when teaching these skills. As a result of these expectations, young children participate in fewer play activities and, when they do play, these activities are isolated from the "learning" curriculum. At the same time, national professional organizations and research recognize that young children are capable of learning more than what was expected in the past. However, they caution that early learning activities must be developmentally appropriate and grounded in child-centered play activities in which adults create an environment where they provide guidance so that learning occurs.

As a result of these findings, adults working with young, diverse, and challenging children must understand how to modify developmentally appropriate activities to produce high-level learning experiences that can be integrated into all areas of the curriculum. To successfully address this challenge, teachers must (1) understand current research on learning and play, (2) know how to design culturally responsive pedagogy for all learners, and (3) apply specific strategies that will gradually transition children during the school years from child-centered to adult-directed learning activities.

CHAPTER 1 FIRST-PERSON INTERVIEW #1

Children Need Physical Activity

Dr. Diane Craft

Professor of Physical Education, SUNY Cortland, and physical activities consultant to childcare and preschool programs, Cortland, NY

I work with childcare and preschool staffs sharing ways to engage young children in fun, inclusive, and developmentally appropriate physical activities. These activities are designed to enhance children's physical, emotional, and cognitive development. Additionally, I encourage using activities that require only inexpensive equipment and can be easily implemented in small spaces in homes or center programs. Young children need to be involved in fun, developmentally appropriate, structured physical activities that develop a wide range of motor skills. Unfortunately, many children today between 2 and 7 years of age do not have many opportunities to practice their emerging fundamental locomotor and object control skills. Young children need to participate in physical activities that encourage running, jumping, hopping, leaping, galloping, throwing, catching, and striking. Mastering these skills as young children is essential for the development of their specialized movement skills later in

(Continued)

(Continued)

life, such as the skills needed to participate in specialized sports and recreation movements like pitching a ball, striking with a badminton racket, or cross-country skiing.

Teachers can be successful in providing children opportunities to practice active physical skills by choosing activities that are fun and age appropriate, engage them with other children, and are associated with cognitive skill acquisition and the use of their imagination. I also recommend that teachers choose physical activities that can accommodate a wide variety of abilities to encourage all children's success.

Matching socks is an example of an activity that lets children practice a variety of locomotor skills while learning about sizes, colors, patterns, weaves, and textures at the same time. In addition, it allows children to practice moving in space among others as they enjoy imitating a task they see adults do at home. Many pairs of socks are separated into two groups, one sock from each pair in each group. The teacher scatters one group of socks around Point A, then scatters the second group at a distant Point B. Children choose one sock at Point A and then are told to run, hop, jump, leap, roll, skip, and so on, to get from Point A to Point B. Once they are at Point B, they have to find the matching sock. Then they run, hop, jump, leap, roll, skip, et cetera, back to Point A, where they choose another sock and repeat the activity. Teachers can talk about the different ways that socks match or do not match as they encourage the children's success. Most children enjoy the cognitive challenge of this activity and will proudly show the teacher how clever they are at matching socks. Some children, however, might find it difficult to accurately match socks. Make the task easier for them by asking them to find any other sock that has the same color, or is about the same size. Then talk about the two different socks, and why they are similar and why they are different to encourage vocabulary development. Teachers can make this activity more challenging by asking a child to find a sock that is opposite the one the child chose, such as finding a black sock while carrying a white sock. Also, the activity can be varied to keep interest levels high by substituting items other than socks just as long as you have two identical sets. Fabric swatches, letters and numbers, colors, shapes, pictures of foods, and many other everyday, inexpensive items work well in this activity.

There are some considerations that are important when choosing activities for young children. There is a lot of variation in aptitude, experience, skill level, and individual interest at this age, and activities that will accommodate the most children will have the best outcomes. Second, avoid creating an environment that might encourage behavior problems. Provide a safe play area that is adequate for the physical activity. Avoid having children wait to participate in physical activities. Choose activities that are inclusive of children of all abilities. Third, activities should be as rule-free as possible. Keep instructions to a minimum. The good activities are ones that the teacher demonstrates and then allows children to participate in, in a way that best matches their interests and abilities safely. Finally, activities that encourage children of different ages and abilities to play successfully together will help many develop physical, cognitive, emotional, and communication skills more effectively.

CHAPTER 1 FIRST-PERSON INTERVIEW #2

Listen to the Children and Be Patient—It's Going to Click

I teach for a large public school district where many of the children and their families speak very little English. With the children in my class I have found that it is very important to be interested in them by asking them what things they like to do, what foods they like to eat, and what places

Jaime Moreno

*Kindergarten Teacher,
Los Angeles, CA*

they like to visit. You really have to get a sense of who they are and what they do when they are not at school so that they begin to trust you. By making the class culturally relevant whenever possible, you make the class easier and fun. You really have to be open to the children and let them talk to you. We do a lot of talking to them, but we need to let them do more talking to us if we want them to learn.

In class I use the information that I know about them all the time. When we are working on vocabulary and if a child cannot think of a word, often I am able to assist them by suggesting something that they have told me about themselves. The children love it when I talk about something they have shared with me, and I really believe that it makes them feel closer to me and want to learn.

I also treat the families the same way that I treat the children. I let them talk to me. On Conference Days or at Open House, I don't do all the talking; I let the families tell me what they know and think. You have to reach out to the families and let them know that you are interested in them and interested in their child making progress. Most of the parents really want to help their children and want resources from the teachers. So, I am always telling them about educational materials they can buy for their children and where to get them and/or interesting places to go with their children.

I do send things home for the children to do at home, and about 90% of them bring them back done. They tell me that different people in their family help them with the work; for example, an uncle, an older sister, a dad or mom, or a grandparent will help. I also let the parents know that learning happens only if there is a partnership between them and me, and that I need them to help me with the children's learning. I make it very clear to them that I cannot do all the work, and that they need to get in there and help their children if they want to see progress. I make sure that they understand that we have to work together.

I have seen so many changes in all the children in my class. Their language, vocabulary, writing, and listening skills are all expanding so fast. But you have to be patient with each child. We know that some children get things right away. Others need more time, but they are still going to get it. You just have to be patient with them and not press them. Not all children are going to develop a skill by next Friday. They need to work on it a little bit longer at school and at home, and then it's going to click. Parents need to know that learning eventually happens for all children, if we are patient and work as a team.

Student Study Site

Visit the Student Study Site at **www.sagepub.com/selmi** to access additional study tools including mobile-friendly eFlashcards and links to video and web resources.

Key Terms

achievement gap

adult-directed learning

child-centered activities

Council for Exceptional Children (CEC)

developmentally appropriate practices (DAP)

early intervention

Early Start Program

free play

funds of knowledge

Head Start Programs

high-quality programs

inclusion

Individuals with Disabilities Education Act (IDEA)

National Association for the Education of Young Children (NAEYC)

National Head Start Association (NHSA)

natural environments

No Child Left Behind Act (NCLB)

PL 99-457

self-regulation

Useful Websites

Alliance for Childhood: http://www.allianceforchildhood.org

Council for Exceptional Children: http://www.cec.sped.org

Division for Early Childhood: http://www.dec-sped.org

National Association for the Education of Young Children (NAEYC): http://www.naeyc.org

National Head Start Association: http://www.nhsa.org

Reflective Questions

1. One of the sections in this chapter is titled "Developmentally Appropriate Practices." Reread that section and summarize what is meant by the term DAP. Additionally, in the subsection titled Increased Adult-Centered Activities the common phrase "skill and drill" is used. How does that phrase relate to DAP for preschoolers?

2. Think about the early education centers in your local area. Do you think that they are being impacted by children from poverty, diverse cultures, or with developmental and physical delays? What might be some of the benefits that these populations contribute to the centers? What might be some challenges that the centers are experiencing?

3. This chapter continually uses the following terms: child-centered activities and adult-directed activities. What are some of the differences between these two terms that you have learned about in this chapter?

2 Learning Through Play

TO THE FIRE

©iStockphoto.com/SergiyN

A caregiver and a 10-month-old child are sitting on the floor with some toys close to them. The child picks up a fire engine and starts to spin its wheels. He then places it down on its side and picks up a play gas pump. The caregiver puts the fire engine on its wheels and starts pushing it around while he is making the sound of a siren. He then says, "We need to get to the fire fast." The child first looks at the moving fire engine and next at the caregiver, and then goes back to examining the gas pump.

The caregiver moves the fire engine very close to the child and removes his hand. He looks directly at the fire engine and then at the child. The caregiver then says, "We need gas to get to the fire." The child drops the gas pump, puts his hand on the fire engine and moves it about 6 inches. He then stops.

The caregiver moves the gas pump close to the fire engine. The caregiver then says, "We need gas." The child watches as the caregiver gives the fire engine some gas. The caregiver then states, "The engine has to go to the fire now." Lastly, the caregiver quickly moves the fire engine away from the gas pump, while looking at the child.

In this scenario, a caregiver is attempting to demonstrate to the child the role of a fire engine in the community and how vehicles need gas to run. The child appears interested and seems to be learning from the caregiver. Natural learning activities such as these are common for young children. Through interactions with adults, siblings, and peers, young children learn how to "make sense" of the world around them.

This chapter examines how, at a very young age, children learn skills through playful interactions with adults. These skills form the foundation for the future learning and development that occur during the childhood and adolescent years. The chapter describes the different school programs and the methods used by them to integrate play into learning activities.

As you read the chapter, consider the following:

> How do children learn?

> How does play impact early learning?

> How has play been incorporated in early childhood curricula?

Early Learning

The seminal work of Marie Clay (1998) explains the importance of interaction between children and adults as they experience the world around them. Through interactions, children are not only learning new concepts and behaviors but are acquiring language. As children engage in an exchange of oral discourse with an adult, they learn new vocabulary and syntax through an authentic experience. For example, the young child in the opening scenario is being exposed to a specific type of vehicle, a fire engine, and the purpose of the fire engine. These rich early language experiences provide a strong foundation for future literacy development (Lawrence & Snow, 2011).

From birth, children spend their days attempting to make sense of the world around them through interactions with the people and objects that are present in the surrounding environment. Many adults have observed how an infant learns to express needs and desires over a relatively short period of time. Typically, this development occurs as the infant progresses from cries to babbling to more conventional forms of communication, such as eye gazes or gestures, and then replaces eye gazes and gestures with words and phrases (Shonkoff & Phillips, 2001). Young infants not only learn quickly, they also are capable of performing more complex tasks than researchers previously thought (Gopnik, 2009).

Xu and Garcia (2008) found that children as young as 8 months old could understand certain concepts of probabilities. For example, when several balls were removed from a box of mostly white balls and some balls of another color, the infants looked longer at the experimenter when most of the removed balls were not the white balls (see Figure 2.1). When the colors were reversed—when there were more balls of the other color than white balls and more white balls than other colored balls were removed, the infants again responded with longer looks at the experimenter. More broadly stated, very early in life children appear to interact with and learn from their environments at an amazing rate, and these interactions appear to be closely linked to their future learning behaviors.

All children can be expected to learn at complex, conceptual levels, even those who experience adversity during their early years. Young children appear to be resilient learners. They all enter school with different skills, some of which may or may not be strongly aligned with the traditional language, literacy, or social skills of a formal education. However, the differences can be used as an asset to lead children

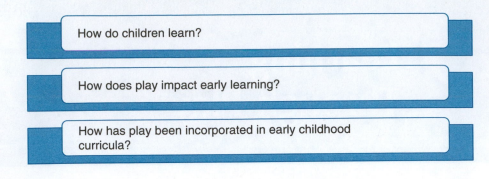

Creatas Images/Creatas/Thinkstock

Children learn through interactions with others.

Figure 2.1   Probability Experiment With Mostly White Balls and Some Balls of Another Color, Then Mostly Balls of Another Color Balls and Some White Balls

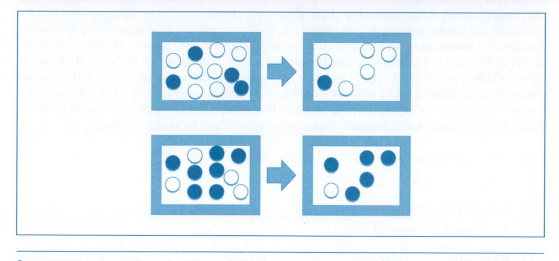

Source: Xu, F., & Garcia, V. (2008). Intuitive Statistics by 8-Month-Old Infants. *Proceedings of the National Academy of Science, 105,* 5012–5015.

towards expected school-based skills. High-quality intervention practices can substantially contribute to these children's learning processes and frequently increase their performance to a level within the norms (Reynolds & Temple, 2005).

Positive relationships and environments that support cognitive, social, emotional, and physical development provide all children with the resources and skills that they need to cope with and adapt to adversity throughout their early years and their life (Pizzolongo & Hunter, 2011). When adults provide responsive care to infants, toddlers, and preschoolers, children learn to trust others. When adults provide high expectations, children begin to believe in themselves. Specifically, Pizzolongo and Hunter recommend the following techniques that adults can use for supporting young children's resilience:

- Expressing love for children both verbally and physically
- Acknowledging children's feelings
- Keeping children safe while allowing them to explore the environment
- Modeling confidence and optimism
- Encouraging children to do things on their own

It is often difficult to imagine such young children learning at a level that may seem more reserved for older students and adults. There are indeed many complex tasks and concepts that would need further development as children mature. However, those conceptual tasks that young children are capable of are operationalized and learned differently by young children than by adults (Gopnik, 2009). For example, children seem more interested in novel activities, whereas, adults are more goal and outcome oriented. The child in the opening scenario was most likely focusing on the sound and movement of the fire engine, while the father was engaged in getting the gas and progressing to the fire. Young children tend not to focus on learning single, particular facts about a subject that is common in elementary grade classrooms. Instead, they appear to be drawn to learning through situations that are new and interesting to them.

Two prominent researchers have been at the forefront of understanding how children learn and conceptualizing the influences of the environment on the learning process. Jean Piaget and Lev Vygotsky have laid a foundation for how to understand the learning process of a young child through to adulthood.

Jean Piaget (1896–1980)

Piaget was a Swiss-born developmental psychologist who was the first to introduce the concept that children think differently than adults and, therefore, that a child was not just an immature or incomplete adult. For centuries, children's minds were mistakenly viewed as constituting blank slates waiting for adults to fill them with information (Singer, Golinkoff, & Hirsh-Pasek, 2006). As an alternative theory, Piaget proposed that children start out as egocentric beings, or self-centered thinkers, using both actions and language that focus on themselves. However, as they interact with the world around them, children are propelled by a sense of equilibrium, or the drive to balance their knowledge through learning, to progress through four stages of development that ultimately will lead to abstract thought:

1. The sensorimotor stage

2. The preoperational stage

3. The concrete operational stage

4. The formal operational stage

A child in the sensorimotor stage is interested in the sensory enjoyment that is provided when the child interacts with an object or a person—pulling a string that is attached to a wooden duck will cause the feet to move and the duck to say, "quack-quack." At the preoperational stage, children between 2 and 7 years of age begin to use language and represent objects symbolically. For example, children playing during bath time will pretend that a bar of soap is a duck by talking about it being a duck and verbalizing "quack-quack" as they push the soap along the surface of the water. During the concrete operational stage, young children develop the ability to think logically, and they learn that a big plastic blow-up duck could weigh less than a smaller wooden duck. Finally, as children approach adolescence and enter the formal operational stage, they become capable of logically thinking in abstract terms and analyzing hypothetical situations, such as a mathematics problem relating to the migration of ducks. Figure 2.2 provides a summary of Piaget's Stages of Cognitive Development.

Within each of Piaget's four stages, children incorporate new information into their already accumulated body of knowledge through assimilation. They then change their existing knowledge or assimilated information to accommodate or incorporate the new information (see Figure 2.3). For example, a young child holds a rubber duck under water in the bathtub and then lets go of it, with the duck popping up and above the water. After doing this activity several times, children learn that some items, when held under water, will be propelled upward when their grip is released.

Once children assimilate the information that holding a rubber duck under water will produce a specific phenomenon like this, they then accommodate that information into their understanding of the world and use it to produce similar responses. If the child holds a bar of soap underwater, will it do the same? What about a washcloth or a shampoo bottle? Through repetitive interactions with a variety of objects, children accommodate this information and establish new levels of knowledge and insights. In this manner, children not only learn new ways of interacting with objects, but they accommodate that information to gain knowledge about the objects themselves. For example, why do some objects pop up out of the water and others do not?

Piaget lived from 1896 to 1980 in Switzerland.

Figure 2.2 Piaget's Stages of Development

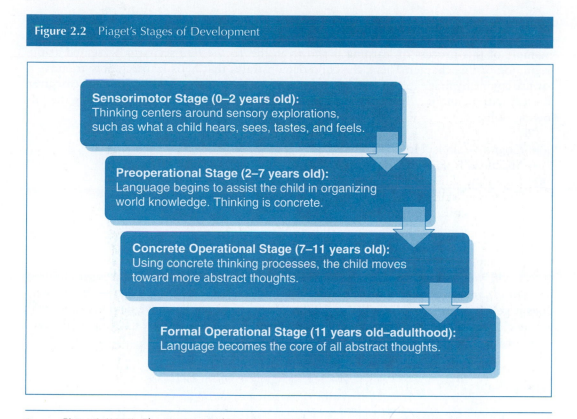

Sensorimotor Stage (0–2 years old):
Thinking centers around sensory explorations,
such as what a child hears, sees, tastes, and feels.

Preoperational Stage (2–7 years old):
Language begins to assist the child in organizing
world knowledge. Thinking is concrete.

Concrete Operational Stage (7–11 years old):
Using concrete thinking processes, the child moves
toward more abstract thoughts.

Formal Operational Stage (11 years old–adulthood):
Language becomes the core of all abstract thoughts.

Source: Piaget, J. (1962). *Play, Dreams, and Imitation in Childhood.* New York, NY: W. W. Norton.

Learning occurs when young children construct new knowledge by adapting knowledge that they already have with new information that they acquire from the external world (Piaget, 1962). By performing what Piaget termed everyday "trial and error experiments," children actively practice skills that they do not yet have by participating in step-by-step,

Figure 2.3 Piaget's Definitions of Learning Terms

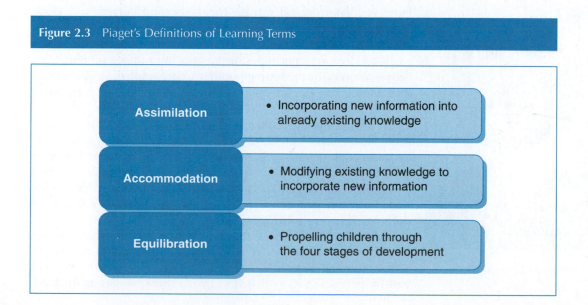

Assimilation
• Incorporating new information into already existing knowledge

Accommodation
• Modifying existing knowledge to incorporate new information

Equilibration
• Propelling children through the four stages of development

temporary rehearsals of general situations. After practicing a number of times, children eventually attain the skills that they have observed occurring in their environment. Another example of this process of learning is shown in the *To the Fire* scenario presented at the beginning of this chapter. There, the child demonstrates that he is learning how to move a toy fire engine by first exploring different parts of the vehicle, then by watching the caregiver interact with it, and finally by moving it about 6 inches. Additionally, he is learning the following skills:

- Cognitive skills: How to pretend
- Social skills: How to take turns
- Linguistic skills: How to understand and apply new vocabulary
- Emotional skills: How to wait and self-regulate himself
- Creative skills: How to develop a simple story

Although Piaget (1962) substantially advanced the understanding of learning, he viewed young children as having limited cognitive abilities (Woodward, 2003). This perception was perhaps due to the fact that the experiments performed with children focused on areas about which the children did not have much knowledge—such as, why does it get dark at night (Donaldson, 1978). More recent studies have demonstrated that young children understand much more than Piaget recognized and are capable of abstract thought.

Lev Vygotsky (1896–1934)

Although Vygotsky was born only a decade after Piaget, the two had little opportunity to interact and share ideas. Vygotsky lived in Russia, and because that country was isolated from the rest of the world for many years, much information about his theories was not disclosed to the world for some time. Additionally, Vygotsky passed away at a young age from complications due to tuberculosis. Unfortunately, he was not living when his works were made known outside of the Soviet Union and Piaget was able to review them.

Vygotsky lived from 1896 to 1934 in Russia.

Similar to Piaget's theory, **Vygotsky**'s theory (1978) proposes that learning first occurs through the *interaction* between children and the environment where the learning activity will take place. However, Vygotsky extends his theory beyond Piaget's to include two levels of learning. Children who cannot accomplish a task gradually transition into the first level of learning, which occurs when children attempt to perform a task but require support from people, objects, or the setting in order to accomplish it. The second level of learning occurs when children are capable of completing the task independently.

Children transition from learning through assistance (Level 1) to being independent learners (Level 2) by interacting with more experienced people who create a zone for learning, or what Vygotsky termed the **Zone of Proximal Development** (see Figure 2.4). Within this zone, children gradually become more capable of producing skills with less support. Eventually, they are able to acquire the skills on their own (see Figure 2.5).

For example, assume a toddler does not know that holding a rubber duck under water and then releasing it will cause it to soar above the waterline. The toddler will not acquire that skill just by practicing it, as Piaget's (1962) theory suggests. Instead,

Figure 2.4 Vygotsky's Zone of Proximal Development

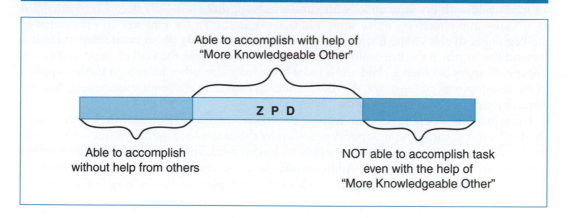

Able to accomplish with help of
"More Knowledgeable Other"

ZPD

Able to accomplish
without help from others

NOT able to accomplish task
even with the help of
"More Knowledgeable Other"

Figure 2.5 Vygotsky's Definitions of Learning Terms

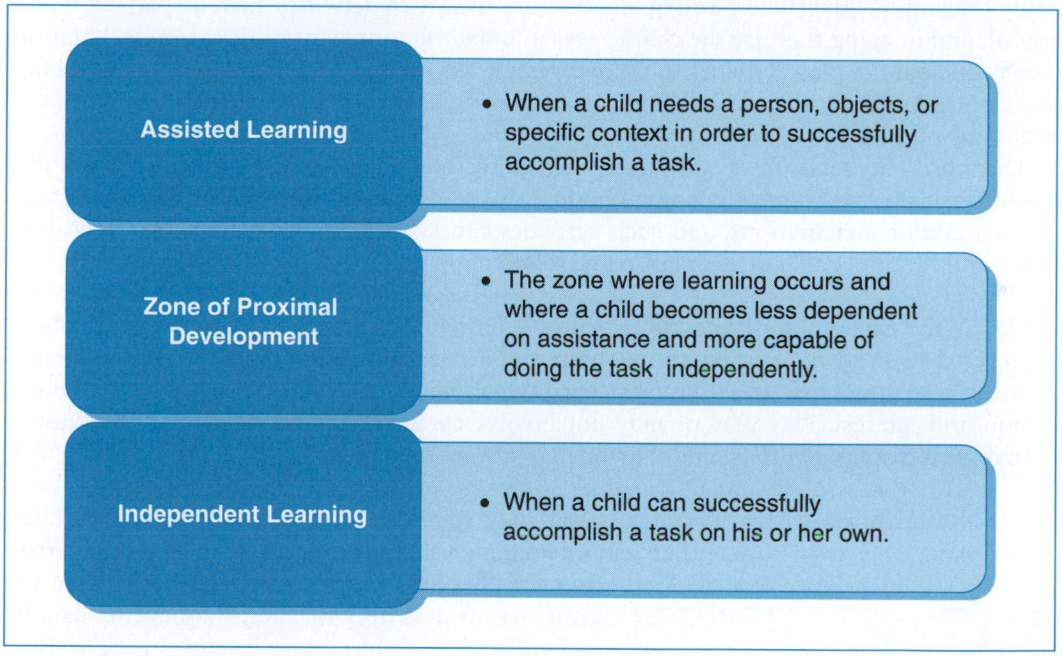

Assisted Learning
- When a child needs a person, objects, or specific context in order to successfully accomplish a task.

Zone of Proximal Development
- The zone where learning occurs and where a child becomes less dependent on assistance and more capable of doing the task independently.

Independent Learning
- When a child can successfully accomplish a task on his or her own.

Vygotsky (1978) believes that the child achieves competency with this skill through social interactions with another person who knows what will most likely happen if the duck is released. Learning occurs through activities such as modeling, pointing, or eye gazing, which assist children in becoming more knowledgeable about a task. Eventually, after being provided differing types of support from a knowledgeable person, most children become capable of independently making decisions about what will escape from the water and what will sink to the bottom. Therefore, Vygotsky's theory of learning differs from Piaget's by attributing more learning to a collaborative process and less to an independent process.

Vygotsky (1978) asserts that many observable, independent skills are eventually internalized into similar inner, cognitive skills. The situation in which the child learns what will pop up when held with pressure under water and what will sink eventually becomes internalized as a "cause and effect" cognitive skill. Additionally, in the *To the Fire* scenario presented at the beginning of this chapter, when the child can independently demonstrate that there is a pretend fire to which the fire engine must go, he has internalized the skill of cause and effect. These exchanges between a child and a more knowledgeable other have been further applied to the development of language. As young children engage in authentic experiences they are acquiring the language models of the "other."

Examining the opening scenario using a Vygotskian perspective illustrates that the young child is learning, through the support provided by the caregiver, that fire engines move from one place to another (e.g., choosing of play objects, modeling behaviors, and both verbal and nonverbal communication). Additionally, the caregiver is creating a learning context, or zone of proximal development, through the pretend play interactions with the child.

Play and Learning Theories

Play is an activity that most human beings participate in as young children and continue to enjoy throughout their lives. Young children are drawn to activities such as playing house, school, and imaging they are the characters from their favorite stories or cartoons. Later on, they participate in play activities in more diverse ways such as organized sports and hobbies and games. As adults, they will look forward to activities such as playing sports, cards games, and word puzzles.

The word *play* tends to be associated with enjoyable, free-flowing learning activities that are intrinsically motivated by young children. Play at a young age typically involves toys, objects, and/or imaginations, and such activities can last for a few minutes or a few days. Lifter and Bloom (1998) define play as the following:

> Play is the expression of intentional states—the representations in consciousness constructed from what children know about and are learning from ongoing events—and consists of spontaneous, naturally occurring activities with objects that engage attention and interest. Play may or may not involve caregivers or peers, may or may not involve a display of affect, and may or may not involve pretense. (p. 164)

For the purpose of this book, the term *play* refers to activities that young children create using objects or toys, either real or imagined. Play can occur with just one person or many people, and the participants can be the same age or a variety of ages. Play events usually conclude when children lose interest in the activity or when an adult or an uncooperative peer interrupts it.

Spontaneous, naturally occurring play activities with objects engage the attention and interest of children, and yet those activities need not involve caregivers or peers, displays of affect, and pretense (Lifter, Mason, & Barton, 2011). In other words, play is an activity that children can carry out with toys and that engages their attention and interest regardless of what is happening around them or who is present. Figure 2.6 describes play activities by using specific terms suggested by Segal (2004).

Bec Parsons/Digital Vision/Thinkstock

Children learn and develop skills while playing.

Figure 2.6 Characteristic of Play

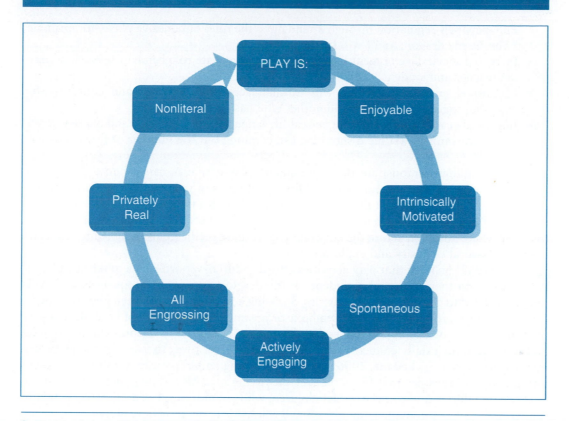

PLAY IS:

Enjoyable

Nonliteral

Intrinsically Motivated

Privately Real

Spontaneous

All Engrossing

Actively Engaging

Source: Segal, M. (2004). The Roots and Fruits of Pretending. In E. F. Zigler, D. G. Singer, & S. J. Bishop-Josef (Eds.), *Children's Play: The Roots of Reading* (pp. 33–48). Washington, DC: Zero to Three Press.

At the same time, however, play is an activity that can be enhanced by the guidance of an adult. Work by Marie Clay (1998) demonstrates that when children are exposed to and engaged in activities with adults, their language is enhanced, as opposed to when they are involved in child-child activities. Although children do acquire language and learning skills through interactions with their peers, the learning that occurs through adult-guided interactions appears to be more robust.

Recently, Burghardt (2011) identified five criteria believed to be fundamental for an activity to be identified as play. The activity must be:

- Incompletely functional in the context in which it appears
- Spontaneous, pleasurable, rewarding, or voluntary
- Different from other serious behaviors in form (e.g., exaggerated) or timing (e.g., occurring early in life)
- At times, repeated, but not in abnormal and unvarying stereotypic form (e.g., distressed, rocking, pacing)
- Initiated in the absence of acute or chronic stress. (p. 17)

To positively impact young children's learning, adults must first have a comprehensive understanding of the theories of how play impacts learning. An extensive amount of research exists promoting play as a learning tool (for a complete review of the research, see

Singer et al., 2006). However, the following are a few examples of the developmental areas that play impacts:

- Enhanced self-regulation through attending to the rules of cohesive play—for example, "You be the dragon, and I will be the queen"
- Increased social development by engaging in appropriate role behaviors—such as playing teacher and student
- Monitored emotional development through acting out feelings and concerns—for example, concerns about a grandmother who has cancer
- Improved academics by engaging in real-life language, mathematics, and literacy activities—for example, writing a shopping list, counting out the number of flowers to sell

Current findings demonstrate that high-quality play activities can enhance the specific linguistic, social, cognitive, emotional, and literacy abilities of young children. One new and particularly significant type of play is *guided play*. While this type of play will be studied in more detail in Part II of this book, Hirsh-Pasek and Golinkoff (2011) define it as a type of free play where adults structure the environment around specific goals designed to stimulate children's natural curiosity and exploration.

Piaget (1962) believes that play activities afford children opportunities to rehearse familiar activities on their own and to independently develop appropriate sequences and skills that are needed to complete these activities. Stressing a relationship between play and cognition, Piaget primarily focuses on the symbolic or pretend characteristics of play. He analyzes ways that play provides opportunities for children to learn how to decontextualize objects and roles from their daily context in life and, gradually over time, to use them as imaginary ones (Morrow & Schickedanz, 2006). As a result, young children create symbolic representation and play episodes that focus on everyday living activities: they pretend to eat food, to care for children, and to sleep. Older children, who are more experienced players and are more capable of decontextualizing objects and roles, create make-believe activities that they have never experienced: they travel into space as an astronaut, drive a train, and become a monster.

According to Piaget, play gives children the opportunity to practice and develop skills that lead to abstract learning (Soderman, Gregory, & McCarty, 2005). Piaget concluded that changes in learning occur through the interchange of a child's maturation and his or her interaction with the surrounding world. Pretend play skills occur regardless of whether there are any other human interactions and, through these pretend play activities, children develop representational thought skills that assist them with learning.

Applying a Piagetian approach to the *To the Fire* scenario at the beginning of this chapter, one might conclude:

> This child is attempting to understand the function of a fire engine.

However, within the next 6 months, the child would be expected to move the fire engine from point A to point B, and most likely the following could be assumed:

> This child has practiced moving the truck through play and has learned that fire engines move from one place to another and he would use words such as fire truck, moving, and going as he engages in the task.

After a few more months, the child might move the fire engine from one place to another, stopping it for a moment, and then moving it back to the original spot. A person with a Piagetian perspective of play might think the following:

> This child has now learned that fire engines go to a place and then return back from it. He begins to understand the meaning of words such as "go," "back," and "again."

This description of play behaviors reflects Piaget's belief (1962) that children construct their own knowledge about real-life activities by participating in them and practicing them with play materials. Over time, the child in the opening scenario would be expected to assimilate information about the function of a fire engine and to accommodate that knowledge by creating elaborate play scenarios appropriately involving fire engines going to fires. Consistent with this Piagetian concept, professionals and parents typically choose play items for children that are oriented to everyday experiences and that encourage young children to explore and experiment with those items so that learning can transpire.

Learning occurs as children experiment and explore with play items and play partners.

Similarly, Vygotsky (1978) also believes that play is a vital tool for learning. However, he suggests that when a child is playing, "it is as though he is a head taller than himself" (p. 102). Vygotsky views play as creating a context for children to stretch their abilities and perform tasks that they cannot otherwise accomplish outside of the play context. Through interactions with play objects and other people, children have opportunities to acquire skills that they cannot accomplish independently. Play partners in a play environment, with one child more experienced at play tasks, tutor or guide a less experienced child to learn so that that child can develop skills.

Vygotsky proposes that the play contexts actually create a zone of proximal development allowing for tasks to be performed at the child's highest level. Therefore, Vygotsky proposes that play interactions afford children the opportunity to interact with others and to extend their abilities to use representational thought. In contrast, Piaget suggests that play offers children opportunities to develop skills that will assist with learning.

Consistent with Vygotsky's (1978) belief, current research demonstrates that 2- and 3-year-old children are very good at discriminating between pretending and reality. If a child knows what a real object does, then the child can imagine pretend objects doing the same thing or even different things. Vygotsky suggests that knowledge about an object is what actually allows children to imagine the object differently. Once children know how something works, they can then separate the meaning of the object from the object itself. After doing so, they can imagine it operating in an altered state as something else.

As children gain knowledge about the world around them, they are then able to create new, imagined worlds through play. For example, a young child who gives a bottle to a doll and then burps it is not just imitating what a caregiver does. Rather, the child is demonstrating his or her intelligence by enacting the sequence of events related to this activity. In addition, children use language to guide their actions. They often mimic the vocabulary or syntax that was modeled by an adult. Children know what a caregiver does and, as a result, can now create that activity or a variation of that activity using pretend objects and familiar language. Research shows that, when very young children play, they reveal the ability to differentiate reality from pretending (Lillard & Witherington, 2004). They do so by providing consistent signals such as giggles, exaggerated gestures, and theatrical and melodramatic facial expressions and language, indicating that their actions are pretend actions.

A Vygotskian approach to analyzing the *To the Fire* scenario at the beginning of this chapter would focus on the context that the child is in (e.g., the caregiver's actions, language and the play objects) and how it supports the child's development. Therefore, most likely the following would occur:

> This caregiver is guiding the child's learning by modeling with the play materials and using a "think out loud" process, stating what they are doing as they are playing with the play materials.

Within the next few months, if the child moved the fire engine in a direct path, the following observation might be made:

> Through social interactions with people and objects, the child has internalized the knowledge that fire engines move from one place to another. The child begins to integrate the adult's models of language, behaviors, new content, and conceptual understanding.

After a few more months, the child might move the fire engine from one point to another, stop, and then move it back to the original spot, each time checking with the caregiver for clues. Then, the following could be assumed:

> The child has independently demonstrated that the function of a fire engine is to go from one place to another, and will soon be capable of separating the meaning from the object to use object representations, such as having a block represent the fire engine.

To summarize, Vygotsky affirms that the play partners, materials, and context collaboratively afford children the support needed to exhibit their maximum mental capabilities through actions and often language. Piaget proposes that play offers children the context to independently rehearse incomplete tasks and to learn how to do them correctly. However, both researchers propose that play is a central part of young children's social and cognitive development, and that it provides multiple opportunities for children to learn the cognitive skills that prepare them for school (Singer et al., 2006).

For several reasons, this book utilizes a Vygotskian perspective to analyze how contexts are "tools" for the development of learning, language, and literacy skills. First, research studies from the past three decades demonstrate that play activities create powerful contexts for children to transmit and acquire knowledge about the world around them. This knowledge provides the foundations for the language and literacy skills needed to

REFLECT AND APPLY EXERCISE 2.1

Differences Between Piaget and Vygotsky

Reflect

Piaget proposed that children learn through practicing skills on objects and people, exploring in their environment; whereas Vygotsky suggests that children primarily develop skills through interactions with other people in their environment.

Apply

Think about how Piaget would explain how a young child learns how to stack blocks. Now think of how Vygotsky would explain the development of that same skill. Generally, what do you think are some of the similarities between the two theories and what are some of the differences?

Figure 2.7 Summary of Early Literacy and Play Research

Background Knowledge	Oral Language	Phonological (Sound) Awareness	Print Awareness
• Play helps children intergrate experiences that appear to be unrelated and learn the natural sequence for many everyday schemas (e.g., taking the bus, washing the clothes, feeding the baby).	• The number and the variety of words that children use in pretend play positively relates to performance on kindergarten languauge measures.	• Phonological awareness has been found to be a prerequisite for learning the principle that letters represent language sounds, and it is the strongest predictor of reading learning.	• When literacy tools/props are available in a play center (e.g., doctor's office: pencils, paper, sign-in form, eye charts), a marked increase in amounts of emergent reading and writing occurs.

Source: Singer, D. G., Golinkoff, R. M., & Hirsh-Pasek, K. (2006). *Play = Learning: How Play Motivates and Enhances Children's Cognitive and Social-Emotional Growth* (pp. 62–64). New York, NY: Oxford University Press.

participate in today's world. Figure 2.7 summarizes a review of play-literacy research highlights and demonstrates that early childhood play does contain components that

A more knowledgeable person can guide children's learning through play.

Although they differ on how it happens, both Piaget and Vygotsky believed that play is a central part of young children's cognitive and social development.

are linked to later literacy achievement (for a more detailed review see Dickinson & Neuman, 2006, and Singer et al., 2006).

Second, as stated in Chapter 1 and advocated by the National Association for the Education of Young Children (NAEYC), social interactions have always been the preferred "tool" for instructing young children and have been successfully used for decades. Only recently has a movement sought to change that approach. Third, this book focuses on instructional practices for young children, an area that Vygotsky researched. Although Piaget researched how children learn, he spent little time analyzing the instructional conditions that lead to learning. Accordingly, Vygotsky has more to offer in creating instructional practices.

In alignment with the Vygotskian perspective, the book examines classroom play environments. It suggests methods for manipulating those environments to provide children with opportunities to produce activities that they normally cannot produce, rather than looking narrowly at the skills children are learning in a play context. Through cautious analysis of play and careful planning of play environments, free-play and guided play opportunities can be created that "stretch" young children's minds to the highest levels of learning. As learning is stretched, more complex language patterns are modeled, used, and internalized by children. These enjoyable play opportunities are thus used to help children to internalize cognitive behaviors and develop language.

Figure 2.8   Preschool Content Area and Play Activities

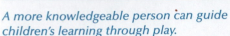

Literacy: Pretend play encourages children to use symbolic representations to create narratives and to re-create stories they read.

Math: Water, blocks, and manipulative play facilitate the development of numbers, counting, shapes, patterns, and sorting.

Science: Exploring the natural world and use of scientific instruments, children learn to problem-solve and inquire.

Social Studies: Through dramatic play children learn about cultures, communities, history, economics, and justice.

Music/Movement: Learning to move like animals or objects helps with gross motor and balance. Foreign language songs help with understanding.

Sources: (Literacy) David Woolley/Digital Vision/Thinkstock; (Math) Jupiterimages/Stockbyte/Thinkstock; (Science) Jupiterimages/ BananaStock/Thinkstock; (Social Studies) Jupiterimages/Creatas/Thinkstock; and (Music/Movement) Photodisc/Photodisc/Thinkstock.

Figure 2.8 suggests different content areas for early childhood and how play activities can be used to achieve learning development goals. These activities will be addressed in more detail in Part III of this book.

Influence of Play and Learning Theories on Early Childhood Programs

Although many early education programs implement Piaget's and Vygotsky's theories of play, four well-known programs, Montessori, Reggio Emilia, High/Scope, and Multiple Intelligences, have implemented these theories into their activities so that optimal learning occurs.

Montessori Programs and Learning Theory

Maria Montessori (1870–1952), an Italian doctor, became interested in working with economically disadvantaged children, especially those with disabilities. She designed a program that respects children as innate learners with the natural capacity to learn. Specifically, a **Montessori** environment, which respects children as innate learners with a natural capacity to learn, is well prepared with activities and materials that address the individual needs of each child. Children are afforded opportunities to choose from a variety of activities that have been specifically selected to meet their specific needs, and are provided with careful instructions on how to

©iStockphoto.com/monkeybusinessimages

Montessori classrooms offer well-planned and sequenced activities but allow children opportunities to choose their pursuits.

Figure 2.9 Montessori Four Learning Planes

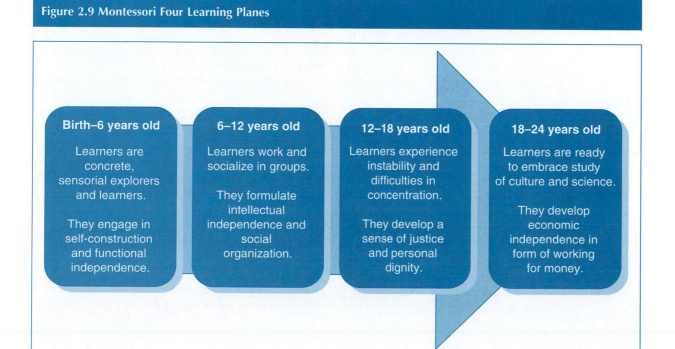

Birth–6 years old	6–12 years old	12–18 years old	18–24 years old
Learners are concrete, sensorial explorers and learners.	Learners work and socialize in groups.	Learners experience instability and difficulties in concentration.	Learners are ready to embrace study of culture and science.
They engage in self-construction and functional independence.	They formulate intellectual independence and social organization.	They develop a sense of justice and personal dignity.	They develop economic independence in form of working for money.

LEARNING FOR AL CHILDREN
Montessori and Poverty

Montessori programs can have a positive impact on young children's learning and the skills of their family members.

©iStockphoto.com/monkeybusinessimages

Some of the core values of the Montessori educational philosophy are to have children learn how to take responsibility for their own learning, to help others, and to respect individual choices (Robinson, 2006). Montessori education has primarily been associated with economically well-off private schools for children from families with financial resources to pay for the tuition.

Harger (2008) examines how children who are being raised in poverty-stricken countries that have environments of helplessness, terror, and abuse can receive the learning and language skills from a Montessori education that will allow them to develop as successful students and responsible members of a community. Situations are currently changing in a number of the poorest federal districts in Mexico. Whereas, in the past only a few Montessori schools have been in operation in Mexico and have almost exclusively been developed for children from affluent families, today some children living in poverty in that country have access to the Montessori model of education. Young, underprivileged children are being taught not to accept the status quo, but rather to think creatively and to be agents for their own change.

Because of the emphasis the Montessori philosophy places on school–family collaboration, an increasing number of programs are offering a Montessori education along with the support of social services (Bagdi & Vacca, 2005). Harger demonstrates that these programs are profoundly affecting families who were once living in poverty and now have access to jobs with insurance, holiday pay, and vacation benefits.

Collaborating professionals address parents' concerns, such as:

- Assisting them with information on everyday challenges: other childcare needs, transportation issues, scheduling concerns
- Being aware of emotional concerns: fear of entering the system, negative educational experiences by parents, concern of their child being labeled "at risk"
- Understanding philosophical beliefs: preschool is not necessary, their child is not ready for school

complete the tasks. Once the environment is prepared, successful learning should take place through independent interactions between the child and the special learning materials.

Montessori schools are known for their sturdy wooden learning materials created specifically for young children to handle. These materials are judiciously placed in the environment on child-sized shelves, allowing children to independently choose activities that are within their developmental range and sequence. When new items are introduced into the environment, the teacher models the correct approach to working with the items, and then monitors each child to make sure they are each following the appropriate procedure.

Montessori environments are controlled by teachers and designed to encourage independent exploration of adult-selected materials during uninterrupted time blocks. Teachers follow a well-defined and detailed curriculum focusing on many of Piaget's concepts. The materials, which center on using cognitive and motor skills, are arranged so children are free to access them by themselves, interact with them, and return them back to their assigned place on the shelf. Teachers oversee the children's activities and, as they learn independently and develop skills, advance them to activities that relate to, what Montessori termed as, different planes of learning (see Figure 2.9). Pretend play is not encouraged as a prominent learning activity in Montessori schools.

Reggio Emilia Programs and Learning Theory

The original Reggio Emilia program was founded after World War II by Loris Malaguzzi (1920–1994) and the parents of young children who lived in the villages around the city of Reggio Emilia in northern Italy. These parents strongly believed that the first years of life were the most valuable for learning and were anxious to swiftly rebuild their school programs that the war had destroyed. They created what has become known as the Reggio Emilia approach: supportive and enriched environments that provide child-centered, self-guided activities focusing on a sense of respect, responsibility, and community. (See Figure 2.10 Reggio Emilia's Set of Principles.)

Reggio Emilia programs, which are currently located throughout the world, recognize parents as children's primary teachers. Accordingly, these programs believe that learning should

Figure 2.10 Reggio Emilia's Set of Principles

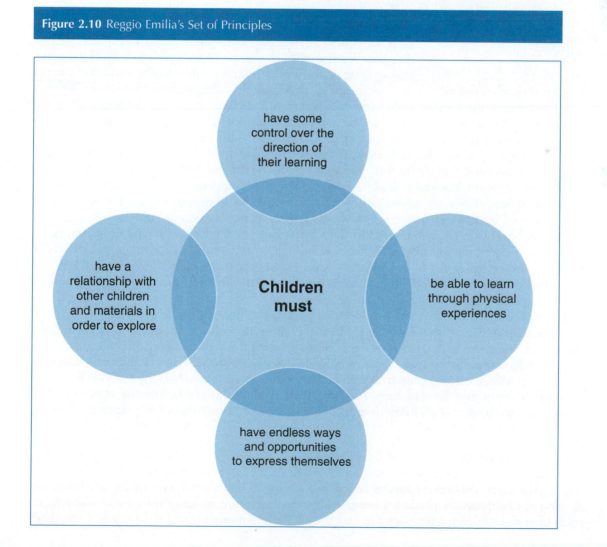

have some control over the direction of their learning

have a relationship with other children and materials in order to explore

Children must

be able to learn through physical experiences

have endless ways and opportunities to express themselves

Comstock Images/Stockbyte/Thinkstock

Reggio Emilia programs have a special room called the atelier where children can experiment with a variety of creative materials.

be extended from the school to the home and from the home to the school. Adults work as co-learners with the children by collaborating in learning activities and attempting to learn more about the children and their interests. Instead of being on the outside of the learning activity, observing children, as proposed in the Montessori method, teachers and parents are inside the activity, learning from the children what they are interested in doing and what they are thinking.

Along with children learning from themselves and adults, the Reggio Emilia approach views the environment as "the third educator." Learning environments are designed to have multiple windows and doors that open to the outside and allow for natural light to enter the room. In contrast to the Montessori method, children are free to move back and forth between the inside and outside areas, exploring their environment and engaging in problem solving with peers. All interior and exterior space is well designed for learning activities that strongly support cognitive and social goals. Particular attention is focused on cutting back clutter and overstimulation, which can be particularly helpful for some children with special needs. Children are afforded the opportunity to routinely participate in modifying the environments so that they reflect current learning experiences.

Reggio Emilia programs continually reinforce artistic activity as a tool for learning. By doing so, they integrate a variety of symbols and graphics modes into their activities. Children learn to express concepts they have learned through the use of multiple modes such as drawings, sculptures, and block structures. Additionally, teachers document learning through use of videos, photographs, and transcripts. Providing such multi-modular activities and documenting the learning contributes to a feeling of independence for all children in the classroom. Reggio Emilia programs typically include a special room or area of the room called an *atelier* or *studio*, where large and small groups engage in experimental learning activities.

In the Reggio Emilia approach, information is presented to children in terms of *projects* or *themes* that always originate from the questions posed by the children about what is happening in their environment. If a group of children find a spider and appear to be interested and curious about the spider, then a project or unit will be developed on spiders or insects. Similar to what was proposed by Vygotsky, learning in the Reggio Emilia programs occurs through peer and adult collaborative interactions. One of the cornerstones of the Reggio Emilia approach is the trust that teachers, parents, and children have in each other's ability to contribute meaningfully to what must be learned. The curriculum evolves through co-constructed, collaborated learning activities in which parents, children, and teachers trust each other to form learning communities where everyone enhances their knowledge.

Through cooperative learning and peer support at the Reggio Emilia programs, individualized goals are designed for all students. Multilevel projects evolve between the adults, children, and the environment, and these provide in-depth learning through a variety of tasks for all children with diverse abilities. These types of individualized learning activities facilitate the incorporation of specific goals and objectives for children with special needs. Making individual choices on what to learn and how to learn it both enhances all children's feelings of autonomy and contributes to children with disabilities feeling less dependent on others for successful learning.

HighScope Programs and Learning Theory

During the early 1960s in Ypsilanti, Michigan, David Weikart, a school district administrator, developed HighScope, a preschool program that focused on enhancing the educational experiences of at-risk children from poor neighborhoods. With four other teachers, he began a preschool

LEARNING FOR ALL CHILDREN
Reggio Emilia and Disabilities

The Reggio Emilia approach to learning embraces the concept of inclusion of children with disabilities. Reggio Emilia programs do not use the term "children with disabilities"; instead, they use the term "children with special rights."

With a primary goal of ensuring that every child experiences both the feeling of belonging to a community and the development of a sense of individual identity, Reggio Emilia programs welcome children with disabilities. Usually, these programs have wait lists for typically developing applicants; however, if the child has a disability, that

Reggio Emilia programs welcome the inclusion of children with different abilities.

child automatically receives acceptance into the program and is placed in a class where he or she is the only child with a disability. The teacher of that class receives an additional teacher assistant to assist with all of the students in the room.

Reggio Emilia programs promote four core learning components that facilitate successful inclusion: encouraging collaborative relationships, constructing effective environments, developing project-based curricula, and documenting learning in multiple ways (Edmiaston & Fitzgerald, 2000). Through teacher/child, child/peer, teacher/parent, and general/special educator collaborative relationships based on mutual respect and cooperation children's skills are enhanced throughout all learning activities. Collaboration is further enhanced by group meetings, which are used to discuss problems, design rules, assume responsibilities, and create a sense of concern for all the children in the class.

Strategies for encouraging adult-child collaboration:

- Talk about a joint concern
- Ask questions
- Seek help
- Encourage feedback
- Observe each other
- Combine knowledge

program that was housed at Perry Elementary School. The program, which supports an "open framework" approach to education, focuses on the interests and choices for the children. The name HighScope reflects the high level of aspiration for learning that the program has for children, along with the broad scope of things to learn.

The curriculum is organized into eight broad content areas, which are listed in Figure 2.11. Teachers organize learning experiences around 58 specific *Key Developmental Indicators* within these areas. Some concepts presented are based on Piaget's cognitive properties that apply to young children. The HighScope approach believes that children learn through interactions with both child-selected materials and adults who are continually attempting to expand the child's knowledge.

A key concept of the HighScope program is the idea of a group of activities known as *plan-do-review*. These activities involve children planning (1) what items they want to interact

Figure 2.11 HighScope Curriculum Content Areas

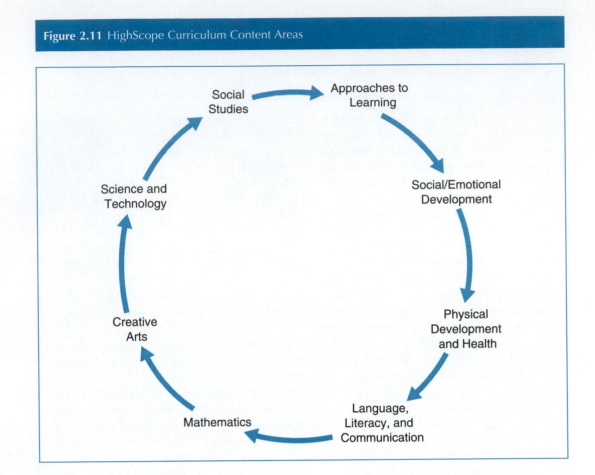

©iStockphoto.com/monkeybusinessimages

Positive research findings from the HighScope continue to impact the quest for early education programs.

with, (2) how they will interact with them, and (3) who will join them in these interactions. Once these decisions are made, the children are free to go about their activities. At the end of their experience when the children are finished, they discuss ways in which the actual activity was different from the planned activity. Therefore, discussions and plans can take place in large formal groups or in smaller informal groups, depending on which is most comfortable for children.

The HighScope Curriculum encourages the development of many of the cognitive abilities that Piaget believed were important for young children to develop during the preschool years. Additionally, the curriculum supports Vygotsky's belief that children should choose the materials and adults should support them while they interact with these materials in an effort to expand the child's knowledge and language. Similar to the Reggio Emilia program, the HighScope program views the adult as a partner or facilitator for learning instead of as a manager, a position typically assigned to the adult by the Montessori curriculum.

LEARNING FOR ALL CHILDREN
HighScope and Life Improvement

Early childhood professionals continue to reference a famous study known as the Perry Preschool Research Study. This randomized control study of 123 children consisted of 58 children who received the HighScope Curriculum and a control group of 65 students who did not receive training from the curriculum. Both groups who participated in the study were equivalent in the areas of intellectual abilities and family demographics. After the program, the educational and life experiences of the children who participated in the HighScope Curriculum were much more enhanced than those who did not receive the curriculum, particularly in the areas of school retention, legal responsibilities, and job wages. Figure 2.12 demonstrates the outcomes from research conducted 27 and 40 years after the participants enrolled in the preschool program. Current findings from this study provide the foundation for President Obama's 2013 commitment to provide prekindergarten services to all children in the United States.

Strategies for encouraging responsibility:

- Provide examples of how adults are responsible
- Create a chart that states each child's classroom responsibilities
- Have children together work with adults on classroom chores
- Share clear and consistent expectations
- Allow children to experience natural consequences of their actions

Figure 2.12 Perry Preschool Research Studies

Age	HighScope Program	Regular Program
Age 27 Follow-Up		
Years of Schooling	11.9 years	11 years
Years in Special Ed	3.9 years	5.2 years
High School Graduation Rate	66%	45%
Out-of-Wedlock Births	57%	83%
Average Teen Pregnancies	0.6%	1.2%
Age 40 Follow-Up		
Served Time in Jail/Prison	28%	52%
Arrest for Violent Crimes	32%	48%
Median Monthly Income	$1,856	$1,308
Government Assistance	59%	80%

Multiple Intelligences Programs and Learning Theory

In the early 1980s, Howard Gardner proposed a theory of **Multiple Intelligences**. The theory suggests that intelligence is not dominated by a specific continuum of single types of activities; instead, a wide range of cognitive abilities relate to the use of various modalities. The Multiple Intelligences approach somewhat conflicts with the more traditional approaches of Piaget and Vygotsky, which suggest that intelligence is related to logical and linguistic abilities. The Multiple Intelligences theory has received varied reviews, with some educational scientists referring to it as an opinion rather than a proven theory. However, educators appear to see some value in this hypothesis.

Multiple Intelligences programs respect children's capabilities. Instead of viewing a situation in which a child cannot perform a task as a child having a deficit, they propose that tasks are challenging because they are presented using inappropriate strategies for the child. If children were presented tasks through their dominant modality, or through their favored method of learning, they would most likely be successful. These various types of modalities, or what Gardner called *intelligences* and which are defined in Figure 2.13, are the following: logical-mathematical, spatial, linguistic, body-kinesthetic, musical, interpersonal, intrapersonal, naturalistic, and existential.

An example of the idea of Multiple Intelligences is a situation when children are having difficulty stringing beads using a repetitive color pattern. They might be more successful if the activity is altered to one in which the children produce a sound pattern by clapping their hands (musical) or engage in body movement patterns such as raising their arms and legs while sitting (body-kinesthetic). Multiple intelligences not only suggests that children can learn if the learning approach is altered, but also that they might be able to excel in that task through this alteration.

Figure 2.13 Howard Gardner's Multiple Intelligences Theory

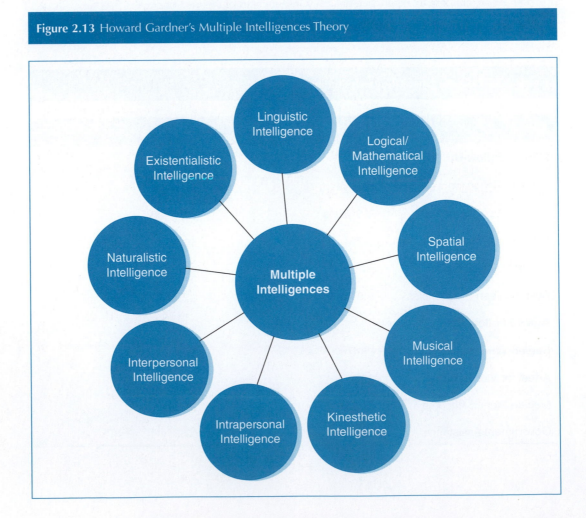

Many early childhood educators typically use some type of Multiple Intelligences approach. Many teachers, especially when confronted with struggling learners, believe that a multiple approach to intelligence makes sense and that it validates what they already know: that children learn in different ways. Most teachers already believe that one style of teaching cannot meet the needs of all young children's learning requirements. Therefore, they continually provide students with multiple approaches, activities, and experiences to enhance all children's intelligence. The goal of schools that embrace the Multiple Intelligences approach to learning is that all children are capable of learning if the activity matches their particular modality of intelligence.

Rettig (2005) suggests four ways to emphasize the use of multiple intelligences in a classroom for young children with and without disabilities. These are activities that early childhood educators should typically be involved in when designing student learning activities, and are the following: (1) selecting toys and playthings for children to interact with, (2) preparing lesson plans, (3) creating centers, and (4) planning career education activities.

Lesson Materials. Some examples of selecting toys and playthings to focus on when using a Multiple Intelligences approach to learning are the following:

Intrapersonal	• Blocks, dress-up clothes, dolls, stuffed animals
Interpersonal	• Card or board games, phones, puppets
Naturalist	• Sand, rocks, water, wood, hammer, pets
Logical	• Nesting toys, puzzles, paper, crayons, lotto

Lesson Planning. Lesson planning should incorporate a variety of types of intelligences. Rettig (2005) recommends the following when designing a lesson on the body parts:

Intrapersonal	• Identify your body parts
Naturalist	• Identify the body parts of an animal
Spatial	• Draw a picture of self and talk about the shapes and parts
Bodily	• Dance to the "Hokey Pokey" with body parts

Lesson Design. Examples of how career learning centers might be designed around different types of intelligences are as follows:

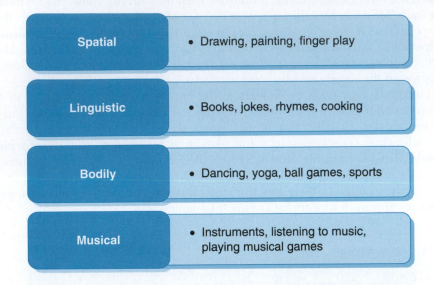

Spatial	• Drawing, painting, finger play
Linguistic	• Books, jokes, rhymes, cooking
Bodily	• Dancing, yoga, ball games, sports
Musical	• Instruments, listening to music, playing musical games

Career Awareness. Books, field trips, and guest speakers can further aid teachers in providing children with opportunities to focus on different careers. These activities can center on the integration of various intelligence preferences. The following are examples:

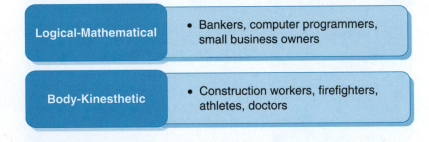

| Logical-Mathematical | • Bankers, computer programmers, small business owners |
| Body-Kinesthetic | • Construction workers, firefighters, athletes, doctors |

🦠 LEARNING FOR ALL CHILDREN
Multiple Intelligences and Disabilities

The Multiple Intelligences approach to learning can assist children with disabilities in discovering what they are good at and how to focus their abilities on such activities, instead of focusing on what they cannot do because of their disability (Rettig, 2005). Highland, McNally, and Peart (1999) found that classroom behavior improved for young children, both typically and atypically developing, who were involved in the Multiple Intelligences approach to learning. Specifically, children in prekindergarten and the first grade demonstrated a 77% improvement in not talking out, cooperating, keeping their hands to themselves, and staying on task.

Understanding and using the Multiple Intelligence approach should provide the following positive results:

- Fewer referrals to special education programs
- Focus on individuals' strengths
- Increased feeling of self-esteem in children
- Enhanced understanding of children

Integrating Play and Learning. Although the four programs just described differ somewhat in their approach to learning, all of them use play as a tool for learning. Children gain useful and adaptive skills and knowledge when they engage in playful activities. Honig (2007) describes 10 in which children learn through play:

Skill	Toddler	Preschooler	Early Elementary
1. Dexterity and grace	Reaching and stretching for toy	Stacking and balancing blocks	Throwing balls and skating
2. Social skills	Engaging with adults	Negotiating goals for play narrative	Work as a team member
3. Cognitive and language skills	Cause/effect—pull/open up	Planning and coordinating	Predicting next moves
4. Number and time concepts	Chant/song rhythm sequence	Following steps to build an object	Timed events
5. Spatial understanding	Crawling forward/backward rolling over	Fitting things together, climbing	Aiming the ball, tossing rings onto a peg
6. Reasoning of cause/effect	Putting items together	Why things sink or float	Similar characteristics and pattern design
7. Real and pretend	Pretending with self	Imaginative pretend play narratives	Reading and writing fantasy stories
8. Sensory/aesthetic appreciation	Blowing and catching bubbles	Creating art products and acting out plays	Tending to a garden or a pet
9. Attention span and persistence	Becoming absorbed in an object	Prolonged play narratives with peers	Practicing and improving skills
10. Release emotions	Delight in early pretense—feeding baby	Pretend acting of emotional concerns	Competing and winning/losing

Chapter Summary

Research demonstrates that learning can occur through play. For years, theories on learning and play have formed the foundation of early childhood education. Piaget and Vygotsky formulated theories explaining how young children actively participate in learning through the construction of play activities. Piaget suggests that play provides environments for children to rehearse skills that they already have developed. In contrast, Vygotsky proposes that play activities actually create the context for young children to engage in skills that they do not have and to develop those skills.

Today, preschool programs integrate the learning theories of Piaget and Vygotsky into their curricula and use them to guide their interactions with young children and their families. Research shows that these programs can assist children from diverse backgrounds and adverse home experiences and can

HOME AND COMMUNITY CONNECTIONS

Learning Through Play

Let your child explore the house. For example, pulling utensils, pots and pans out of the cupboard and seeing what they can do.

improve their overall life experiences and trajectories—for example, longer retention in school, less criminal activity, and higher paying work. Key to all programs outlined is this chapter is the expectation that all children are capable of learning at high levels.

CHAPTER 2 FIRST-PERSON INTERVIEW
Being a Flexible Teacher

Joanna Thrall

Preschool and PE Teacher, Dardenne Prairie, MO

I believe that the most valuable characteristics for being a successful teacher with young children is being flexible and having fun. In preschool, no two days are the same. Teachers need to feel comfortable with change and with the fact that their plans will usually have to be modified throughout the day to address unexpected situations. They also need to incorporate "active learning" into the activities, which keeps children's attention, gets them involved, and engages them in daily learning experiences.

Early education programs usually have children who attend the program two days a week, others who come three days a week, and there are those who attend five days a week. When children show up and see something that has happened on a day that they were not there, they don't understand why they cannot have the same opportunity just because they were not at school on the day that it happened. I believe that teachers need to be sensitive to this feeling that children have and to accommodate them so that they can participate in these activities. Telling them that they will not be able to do something that other children did the day before does not respect their feelings. As a teacher, I have to make sure to switch the days we work on certain activities and skills so that all children are expanding their skills. For example, I just cannot set aside Mondays to work on certain skills, because the Tuesday/Thursday children would never get a chance to work on those skills.

On top of children having varying schedules, the staff members at our center also have varying schedules. Our center is open from 6:30 AM to 6:30 PM. The hours at the beginning and the ending of the day are devoted to free choice activities chosen by the child and the hours from about 9:00 to 3:00 focus on preschool activities planned by the teacher, which include activities in the areas of math, language, science, social studies, art, and reading. Therefore, we have different shifts for the staff. Some staff members are there for the opening and others stay for the closing, and they also float around so that the other staff members can have a break. The lead teachers and co-teachers usually work between 8:00 or 8:30 AM and 4:00 or 5:00 PM. They plan the lessons, write out daily reports, send out newsletters, and so forth.

This scheduling really can get challenging when a staff member has an emergency or calls in sick. These kinds of changes usually impact everyone's schedule and require a great deal of collaboration from everyone. Somehow, though, we always make it through. I think it is because of the fact that we are so adaptable and respectful of staff and children's needs. It's a challenge because if a teacher needs time off or is sick, we end up pulling another teacher into the classroom who is not normally in that room. That teacher may not be aware of the children's routine and their behaviors, which can make the day even more stressful.

We strongly believe in co-teaching, but again, that requires a lot of flexibility to design lesson plans that incorporate the school's standards. For example, because we co-teach, I am able to pull away from my classroom and provide PE activities to all the toddler and pre-k classes. Because I can do this, the toddler staff can take breaks or attend to program issues. But, they also have to make sure that they return in time for me to leave their class on time and still stay in the student/teacher ratio. Also, teaching the PE classes takes about 2.5 hours of my time away from my preschool classroom but, when that happens, my co-teacher steps in and teaches the lessons when I am not there. At our school, what one person does almost always impacts what everyone else does!

Key Terms

accommodate

assimilation

concrete operational stage

egocentric

equilibrium

formal operational stage

HighScope

Montessori

multiple intelligences

Piaget

preoperational stage

Reggio Emilia

sensorimotor stage

Vygotsky

zone of proximal development

Useful Websites

HighScope Programs: http://www.highscope.org

Montessori Programs: http://www.montessori.edu; http://www.montessori-ami.org; http://www.amshq.org

Multiple Intelligences Programs: http://howardgardner.com/multiple-intelligences

Reggio Emilia Programs: http://www.reggiochildren.it/?lang=en; http://www.reggioalliance.org

Reflective Questions

1. Reread the opening scenario, *The Poison Syrup,* for Chapter 1. Discuss how Piaget would analyze the learning and play activities. Then discuss how Vygotsky would analyze the described activities in terms of learning and play.

2. Analyze and compare the approaches to learning, curricula, and materials for the following types of early education programs: (1) Montessori, (2) Reggio Emilia, (3) HighScope, and (4) Multiple Intelligences.

3 Play and Pretending

THE CASTLE HOUSE

©iStockphoto.com/pmphoto

Two preschool girls are walking around their school's outdoor area. One girl says to the other, "Mom, Mom, I found the castle. It's right over there." She points to the large jungle-gym/slide structure on the other side of the outside area. "Can we move into the castle? It can be our castle-house," she says. The other girl responds saying, "Sure, Honey. Remember to move the sand food with us."

The two girls fill up two buckets with sand, walk over to the jungle gym, and climb up to the open platform. There they pretend to eat the sand and talk about their pretty castle house. Other children are playing on the structure. When these others get to the platform where the two girls are playing, they appear to ignore the girls and walk around their activity.

After a short amount of time, one of the two girls says, "Mom, Mom, can I leave to go find my friend?" The second girl responds by saying, "Yes, but just bring back your special friend." The first girl climbs down the ladder and goes off. She returns with what appears to be a younger preschooler and announces, "Mom, Mom, I'm home with my friend. Can we move to another house, Mom?" The two original girls then pick up the buckets and climb over to another part of the jungle-gym structure that is enclosed and has a roof over it. The younger girl watches the two original girls move to the other spot and then walks over near them. She then picks up a bucket and independently plays with the sand.

Typically, young children participate in play activities similar to those in the scenario just described, which are created collaboratively with a caregiver, sibling, or peer. These activities are based on common actions that occur within children's worlds. They allowed them to play using pretend objects, actions, and roles, as well as to successfully create stories with familiar play partners that often took place outside of the context where the play was occurring. If a bus is needed, they simply physically and/or verbally create one, just as the children did in the scenario at the beginning of this chapter. They become proficient at scouring their play environments for objects that could be used as part of the play theme. They then transform those objects within seconds into pretend objects that sometimes have totally different meanings.

As you read the chapter, consider the following:

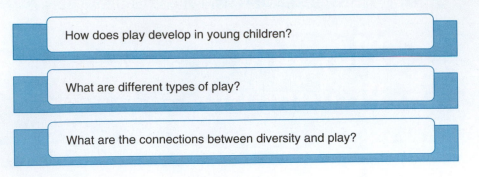

How does play develop in young children?

What are different types of play?

What are the connections between diversity and play?

The Development of Love, Work, and Play

Young children's play involves using symbolic objects, actions, and roles. Symbols can either replicate things that they represent or they can stand for something totally different—for example, a popsicle stick can become a hairbrush or a blanket can become a tent. Creating and using symbolic play items enhances a child's imagination (Vygotsky, 1978). Actually, all human beings employ imagination to do many tasks, such as to invent new things, solve problems, enjoy a book, make plans, understand another's point of view, and come up with alternative ideas.

Specifically, children use everyday objects, actions, and roles as well as hearing the natural use of language around these experiences to create simple pretend play activities with others. They gradually learn how to routinely combine these individual make-believe acts to create complex, multi-episode collaborative narratives or stories. Figure 3.1 illustrates some of the characteristics of play activities.

In his book *The Power of Play*, Elkind (2007) suggests that throughout life, human thoughts and actions are continually driven by three inborn and connected powers—love, work, and play. Infants show *love*, or the natural ability to express one's feelings, desires, and emotions, by flapping their arms and kicking their legs when they see a familiar and caring face. They demonstrate the ability to *work*, which is the skill to adapt to the physical and social demands around them, by concentrating on reaching out and grabbing an object, such as a rattle, that the person might be holding. Finally, infants *play*, or adapt the world to their own needs, by shaking an object that will create an auditory experience that they enjoy.

Early in life, love, work, and play function together as a single ability, with play being somewhat more dominant than the other two skills. As young children develop, these three traits gradually separate and become more independent. However, because of this early interconnection between love, work, and play, play is actually a critical component of social-emotional, physical, and intellectual development at all age levels; it is not just an amenity in the early childhood years.

An example of the interconnection between love, work, and play can be seen toward the end of the first year of life. Children approximately one year of age begin to develop the skill of **object permanency** (Piaget, 1962). This skill is the ability to understand that something or someone exists even if it is not visually present (see Figure 3.2). Prior to the

Children use pretend actions to create complex symbolic stories.

©iStockphoto.com/gradyreese

Figure 3.1 Characteristic of Play

Source: Segal, M. (2004). The Roots and Fruits of Pretending. In E. F. Zigler, D. G. Singer, & S. J. Bishop-Josef (Eds.). *Children's Play: The Roots of Reading*. Washington, DC: Zero to Three.

development of object permanency, children think that if they cannot see something or someone, then that person or object has ceased to exist. However, through repeated daily playful interactions (play) in which people and objects disappear and reappear to infants, children adapt (work) their understanding of *presence* and replace the feeling of surprise with that of *trust* (love).

Around 2 to 6 years of age, love, work, and play begin to separate slightly, as children spend much of their time experimenting with ways of creating **symbolic play** representations, which involves changing the meaning of objects, roles, and actions from what they typically mean to something different. Although play appears to be the dominating activity for this period of development, children actually learn through play activities how to adapt to the demands of their environment (work) by using make-believe activities (play) to create enjoyable joint enactments with friends (love).

Although children's elementary years appear filled with work, they continue to focus on enjoyable and playful activities through positive peer interactions.

As children pass through the elementary grades, their lives are typically dominated by school activities that focus on learning new content, strategies, and concepts. However, the learning of these skills (work) often occurs through creative assignments (play) requiring

Figure 3.2 Object Permanency Development

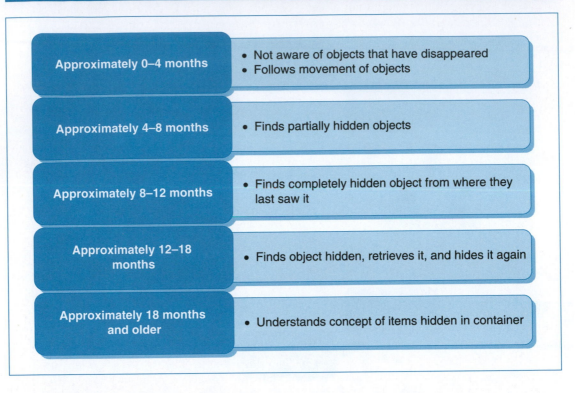

positive interactions with other students (love). Similarly, during the middle school years, learning (work) occurs through more abstract and symbolic activities (play), such as studying life science and world history, and children are taught to apply this new knowledge to enhance their own lives (love).

The adolescence years are known as a time dominated by the development of powerful friendships. Being a teenager involves exploring occupational possibilities (work), developing enhanced friendships (love), and investigating lifetime hobbies (play). As teenagers move toward adulthood, they begin to develop a more profound division between play, love, and work by balancing their career life (work) with their family life (love) and their recreational activities (play).

Elkind's (2007) theory of play and how play activities provide the groundwork for other lifelong skills provides the foundation for the development of social-emotional skills (love), intellectual or cognitive skills (play), and self-regulation skills (work). However, understanding the "power of play" requires knowledge about the different types of play and how play evolves in young children.

Types of Play

Evidence of young children's play has been documented in cultural groups all over the world. Although it is often assumed that play has general and universal characteristics, research now suggests that different ethnic-cultural groups have various forms and goals for play (Roopnarine, 2011). For example, technologically developed cultures generally regard play activities as having an impact on cognitive and social development of young children and, therefore, adults will use such activities to teach children. However, in agricultural and hunting-gathering communities where less of an emphasis might be placed on formal academic activities, adults might not always view play as a tool for development and learning. Instead, these adults view play as an intrinsic childhood behavior that children should engage in without adults.

Chapter 2 discussed how Piaget and Vygotsky viewed play as a context for learning and development with or without adult involvement. Research suggests that children appear to progress through the following three types of play during their early years:

- Solitary Play
- Parallel Play
- Social Play

Each of these types of play in turn consists of the following three cognitive levels (Shim, Herwig, & Shelley, 2001):

- Functional Level
- Constructive Level
- Dramatic Level

If children are free from serious brain disorders, social neglect, and trauma, almost all of them develop these types of play in a natural and sequential manner. Furthermore, each type of play can flourish if experienced play partners carefully assist in the planning of the activity. The role of a more knowledgeable play partner as a key participant in the overall learning process is evidence of Vygotsky's theory of the zone of proximal development (see Chapter 2).

Young children begin exploring play by interacting with objects by themselves.

Solitary Play

Very young children play independently and do not interact much with other people within the play context—that is, they engage in **solitary play**. Instead of human interaction, they typically engage in a solitary-functional interaction with objects—such as spinning the fire engine's wheels. Solitary play behaviors are typical of children within their first 24 months of life. As children develop cognitively and physically, their solitary play becomes increasingly constructive and dramatic.

Parallel Play

During the second year of life, children typically begin to observe others' play activities and replicate these play activities from afar. This type of play is known as **parallel play**. It too has three subcategories: functional, constructive, and dramatic. Again, using the scenario at the beginning of this chapter as an example, parallel functional play occurs when the younger girl follows the two other girls to the new play area and begins to play with a bucket but

At about the age of 2, children participate in parallel play activities by playing near each other but not interacting with their peers.

does not interact with the other girls. As children became more knowledgeable about the world and more comfortable playing in the vicinity of each other, they tend to play closer to each other, but do not interact or share objects. This situation would demonstrate parallel-constructive play. Finally, parallel-dramatic play would be observed when children are sitting close together engaged in pretend activities but not interacting with one another.

Social Play

With the onset of language around 2 years of age, children begin to engage in overt social play in which they directly share their play creations with their peers. Typically, children first demonstrate social play by collaboratively engaging in complementary, repetitive activities, such as two children banging teacups and saucers together while looking at and laughing with each other. Next, socio-constructive play emerges as children begin to construct single play episodes, with each child providing input into the activity. Finally, children create pretend play narratives that are collaboratively sequenced. Each child takes part in the planning, executing, negotiating, and sustaining of the activity. This form of play is called socio-dramatic play.

Definitions of the three types of play (i.e., solitary, parallel, and social) and examples of the three levels of play (i.e., functional, constructive, and dramatic) are set forth in Figure 3.3. Findings now reveal that babies as young as 18 months old, or perhaps even younger, demonstrate knowledge of the real-life function of objects and, at the same time, are able to imagine those objects in an altered pretend state (Gopnik, 2009; Howes, 1992). According to Howes, evidence of socio-dramatic play can occur prior to language when children have the support of a very familiar peer's interactions and are engaged in an activity that both understand and have experienced.

Figure 3.3   Three Types and Levels of Play

Team Play

At about 7 years of age, participation in *team play* activities becomes popular and children tend to exhibit less interest in socio-dramatic play activities. Team play activities, such as relay races, generally consist of tightly knit groups of children who do not externally discuss in detail the plans and rules of the activity as they do with socio-dramatic play. Instead, children usually regulate peer interactions by following an internal set of game rules and imagining the cause and effect of their and others' behaviors. The rules for team play activities are specific, steadfast, and penalty-based, again requiring much less external negotiating than occurs with socio-dramatic play activities.

About the age of 7, children begin to participate in team games.

Although this book discusses all different levels of play, socio-dramatic play—the most complex level of play—is the central concern. Through participation in this type of play, young children develop many of the skills necessary for the learning of language and literacy abilities such as the following:

- Use of symbolic representations
- Development of self-regulation
- Creation of stories

All of these abilities greatly contribute to a successful transition from preschool to the early primary grades.

When young children begin to produce simple social play actions, most adults tend to view these actions as spontaneous and assume that children pay little attention to the complex value of this type of play. However, these basic actions lay the foundation for the development of more complex, make-believe, goal-oriented activities shared with play partners. These partners likewise understand how to effectively create pretend play objects, roles, and actions during which language is shared and acquired. Through pretend interactions with peers, young children gradually learn how to regulate their own play behaviors (self-regulation) and those of others. As children develop a more accurate knowledge of the world around them, they demonstrate more behaviors that are thoughtful and deliberate, and fewer behaviors that are impulsive-looking in their play activities (Vygotsky, 1978).

Socio-dramatic play interactions like those in *The Castle House* occur frequently in the homes and schools of young children. Adults often marvel at how such randomly appearing enactments can be so well coordinated when children produce them swiftly and with little instruction. Socio-dramatic play affords young children opportunities to learn how to substitute one object for another object (e.g., a bucket of sand becomes a basket of food) and to feel comfortable using symbolic representations when interacting with peers. Through the changing of the context in which the object is used, *decontextualization,*

Socio-dramatic play enhances children's abilities to use their imaginations and to decontextualize information, which are the foundation for academic activities.

children transform a commonly used object into a different abstract or imagined object. By doing so, continual participation in socio-dramatic play activities enhances children's abilities to decontextualize information in their imagination (Vygotsky, 1978), similar to the way they decontextualize information through print in reading and writing. Therefore, it is important to focus closely on and guide young children's development of symbolic representations.

Sequential Development of Symbolic Play Representations

Symbolic representations of objects, actions, and roles are activities that truly define early play activities. Between the ages of 12 and 18 months, children begin to create symbolic object representations while they engage in solitary play. For example, children undertake familiar, everyday social actions, such as putting their head down to represent sleeping, turning a knob on a play faucet to represent water, and holding a purse to represent going shopping.

At this same age, children begin to develop verbal language skills. By the time children are 24 months old, they are regularly acquiring new vocabulary and develop complex oral discourse structures. As children also become better communicators, they are able to use their verbal and nonverbal communication abilities to explain their multifaceted, imagined play object representations to others. In turn, as children become more competent users of complex symbolic object representations, those representations create a context for developing more complex and sophisticated linguistic structures. They begin with labeling their world, then verbally sharing what and how they are engaged with the world around them.

Research has documented an intertwining of play and language development during the preschool years (Christie, 1991; Dickinson & Tabors, 2001; Piaget, 1962; Vygotsky, 1978). The research on language development is quite extensive (see Chapter 4), though less information has been published on how symbolic play representations develop in

Figure 3.4 Symbolic Play Levels

Play Levels	Descriptions	Examples
1. Functional unitary activity	Production of an effect unique to a single object	Push button on drill
2. Inappropriate combinational activity	Inappropriate juxtaposition of two or more objects	Put cup in vehicle
3. Appropriate combinational activity	Approximate juxtaposition of two or more objects	Nest barrels
4. Transitional activity	Approximate pretense but without confirmatory evidence	Put camera to eye (not taking picture)
5. Self-directed pretense	Clear pretense activity directed toward self	Drink from an empty cup
6. Other-directed pretense	Clear pretense activity directed toward other	Put doll to sleep
7. Sequential pretense	Link two or more pretense actions	Pour into empty cup from teapot then drink
8. Substitution pretense	Pretend activity involving one or more object substitutions	Pretend block is food to eat

Source: Bornstein, M. H., Selmi, A. M., Haynes, O. M., Painter, K. M., & Marx, E. S. (1999). Representational Abilities and the Hearing Status of Child/Mother Dyads. *Child Development, 70*, 833–852.

children. Importantly, recent work reveals a relationship between the development of symbolic play representations and the learning of language, and literacy skills. Thus, early childhood professionals must know specifically how symbolic object representations evolve in young children. Through the modification of play environments, adults can challenge children with situations in which they can stretch their skills and create well-organized, complex play narratives that incorporate abstract symbolic object representations.

At a young age children begin to pair play items together inappropriately.

Researchers have identified a sequential pattern for the development of symbolic object representations (Bornstein & O'Reilly, 1993; McCune-Nicolich, 1981). Bornstein, Selmi, Haynes, Painter, and Marx (1999) present a sequence that is illustrated in Figure 3.4. Generally, children first interact with objects in a functional, non-symbolic manner. They then pass through a transitional phase before finally progressing to a hierarchy of symbolic phases. The following paragraphs summarize eight sequential levels of symbolic play representations described by Bornstein, Selmi et al. (1999) and relate that information to common play behaviors.

Level 1: Functional Unitary Activity

This level of play occurs when children produce an activity that is unique for a single object. For example, a child sitting at the play table can demonstrate Level I activities by hitting a cup with a spoon or by pushing the buttons on the cash register. After all, spoons are meant to be used with cups and buttons are designed to be pushed. Here are a few more examples of Level 1 behaviors:

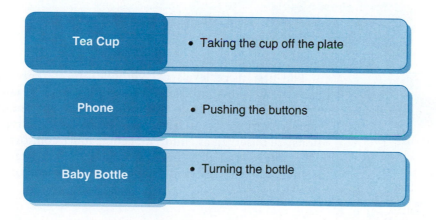

Tea Cup	• Taking the cup off the plate
Phone	• Pushing the buttons
Baby Bottle	• Turning the bottle

Level 2: Inappropriate Combinational Activity

These activities are evident when a child demonstrates an inappropriate, nonfunctional combinational activity with more than one object. An example of a Level 2 behavior could be a child placing the plastic bear in the cash register drawer. Although this behavior is not appropriate for either the bear or the cash register, the child did produce an activity that involved the use of two play objects. Other examples of Level 2 behaviors are:

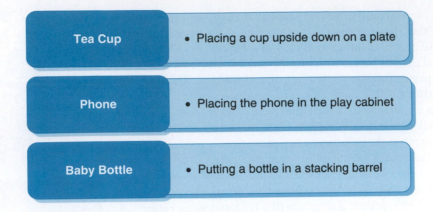

Tea Cup	• Placing a cup upside down on a plate
Phone	• Placing the phone in the play cabinet
Baby Bottle	• Putting a bottle in a stacking barrel

Level 3: Appropriate Combinational Activity

These behaviors take place with two or more objects. An example of this level of play would be when a child appropriately places the cup on a plate, for a plate is frequently used to hold things. Other examples of Level 3 behaviors are:

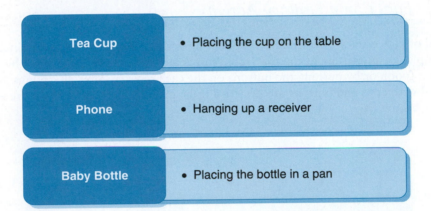

Tea Cup	• Placing the cup on the table
Phone	• Hanging up a receiver
Baby Bottle	• Placing the bottle in a pan

With time, children begin to know which items are associated with each other.

©iStock.com/dcdp

The first three levels of symbolic object representations demonstrate how children learn to play appropriately with toys, but those levels do not reflect the actual use of object representations. Faint hints of symbolic object representations are observed as children become more comfortable with play objects and play behaviors, and these representations become more complex during the development of the next five levels.

Level 4: Transitional Activities

These actions consist of making vague approximations of pretend behaviors on one's self. In the scenario at the beginning of this chapter, the younger girl played with a bucket of sand near the other girls. However, it is uncertain if the child intended this specific action or not. If it is intentional, it is a symbolic play action representing the fact that she had food or household items. However, the activity could also be coincidental. Other transitional activities similar to this one are:

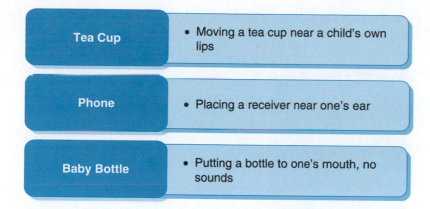

Tea Cup	• Moving a tea cup near a child's own lips
Phone	• Placing a receiver near one's ear
Baby Bottle	• Putting a bottle to one's mouth, no sounds

Play behaviors rated as Levels 5 through 8 reveal intended symbolic activities. These activities are obvious transformations that involve decontextualization of objects. The meanings of the objects and/or actions are intentionally changed to support the evolving play stories. These behaviors are initially evident when children play by themselves, but they tend to flourish when children begin to collaborate with others in creating well-coordinated play stories.

Level 5: Self-Directed Pretense

These are behaviors that demonstrate specific pretend activity toward the self. Such behaviors could have been noted in the opening scenario if the younger child had pretended to eat some of the sand from her bucket. Other common play behaviors that demonstrate this level of representation are:

Children first become familiar pretending by themselves and then they pretend with peers.

©iStockphoto.com/LP7

Tea Cup	• Drinking from a cup while making sounds
Phone	• Putting the receiver to the ear and talking
Baby Bottle	• Drinking from a bottle and sucking

Level 6: Other-Directed Pretense

This level occurs when children demonstrate a pretend activity toward another person or object. For example, in the opening scenario, the girl arrives back at the "castle house" with a "friend." Here she is specifically using pretense with the "Mom" by announcing her pretend "friend." Similar types of Level 6 behaviors are:

Tea Cup	• Giving another child a cup to drink
Phone	• Giving the phone to another person
Baby Bottle	• Giving a bottle to a doll

Brand X Pictures/Stockbyte/Thinkstock

As children become more skilled with pretending, they begin to pretend with their peers through the use of sequential interactions.

Level 7: Sequential Pretense

This level indicates that children are able to connect two or more self-directed or other-directed pretend activities and thereby create an appropriate sequence of activities. Level 7 skills are demonstrated in *The Castle House* scenario when the two girls talk about moving to the "castle house" and then actually go about doing it by packing up their "sand food" and moving to a special area. By connecting these individual pretend activities in a sequentially appropriate order, the girls develop a story: moving to the castle house. This level of symbolic representation can be demonstrated either by one child creating a sequence of linked behaviors, or by a number of children interacting to create an appropriate social sequence, as shown in the opening scenario. Other demonstrations of sequential pretense are:

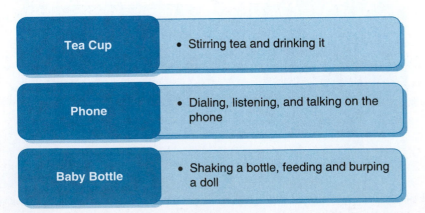

Tea Cup	• Stirring tea and drinking it
Phone	• Dialing, listening, and talking on the phone
Baby Bottle	• Shaking a bottle, feeding and burping a doll

Level 8: Substitution Pretense

This culminating level occurs when children substitute one object or action for another. An example of a pretend object substitution occurs in *The Castle House* scenario when the girls substitute buckets of sand for baskets of food or household items, a jungle gym for a house, and another girl for a friend. Additionally, pretend action substitutions occur when the girls move from place to place. Other examples of substitution pretense are:

Tea Cup	• Using a tea cup to scoop out ice cream
Phone	• Using a block as a cell phone
Baby Bottle	• Using a baby bottle as a rocket

As children become more familiar with symbolic representations and as their language expands, they begin to use object substitutions to develop complex pretend narratives.

©iStock.com/dejanristovski

As symbolic play behaviors become more abstract and complex, and language abilities are enhanced, young children begin to share information about these abstract behaviors with other players. They narrate what they are doing, demonstrating a more sophisticated language including compound sentences and detailed descriptions. Through the use of more complex thinking, children engage in more complex language demands in order to express their thinking. To successfully create and sustain play stories with another person, children must impart to peers the rules and plans that relate to the created representations. Research reveals relationships between the development of these shared play stories and successful academic achievement (Dickinson & Neuman, 2006; Dickinson & Tabors, 2001; Neuman & Dickinson, 2011; Pellegrini, 2011; Singer et al., 2006; Zigler, Gilliam, & Barnett, 2011).

REFLECT AND APPLY EXERCISE 3.1

Different Levels of Play

Reflect

Reread the scenario at the beginning of the chapter and take note of all of the different types of objects, roles, and action symbolic representations being used.

Apply

Read the opening scenario in the next chapter, Chapter 4. Identify an example of the following types of pretending: self-directed pretense, other-directed pretense, sequential pretense, and substitution pretense.

Ryan McVay/Digital Vision/Thinkstock

Interactions are dependent on different cultural beliefs and values.

LEARNING FOR ALL CHILDREN
Symbolic Play and Cultures

Symbolic play is an activity that occurs within all cultures around the world. However, cultural values and beliefs mediate play; therefore, play activities are somewhat fluid depending on the context in which they occur. Most western, highly technological societies consider play activities as a means to develop linguistic, social, and cognitive abilities. By contrast, some less developed societies value play as a means to impart cultural rituals. For example, Korean American children tend to focus their play activities on family role themes, whereas, European American children focus on fantasy themes such as superhero adventures (Farver & Shin, 1997).

Past research has found that mother-child symbolic play interactions also appear to be culture specific. They are influenced by settings, customs, and cultural belief systems, factors that might in turn impact the development of children (Farver, & Howes, 1993; Haight, & Miller, 1992). In cultures that encourage interdependency, such as the Argentine and Japanese cultures, mother-child play interactions tend to concentrate on symbolic interactions. However, in cultures that value independence, such as the United States, mother-child interactions tend to center on exploration of the environment (Bornstein & O'Reilly, 1993).

A study analyzing the behaviors of immigrants to the United States indicates that mothers rapidly and easily modify their play interactions to reflect the values of the culture of destination (Cote & Bornstein, 2005). This conclusion, however, must be taken with caution, as the researchers suggest that the modification seen in the play behaviors of immigrating parents might be somewhat influenced by the fact that so many of the mothers in this study were married to European American men. However, what can be learned from this study is how play is socioculturally constructed as children experience play in diverse contexts.

Strategies for encouraging parents to play with their children:

- Provide information to parents on the value and types of play
- Allow children to take a toy home to share with their families
- Talk to parents about their children's play habits
- Encourage parents to have confidence in their own play behaviors
- Enhance parents' understanding of the need to minimize guided and inactive activities

LEARNING FOR ALL CHILDREN
Symbolic Play and Prenatally Drug-Exposed Infants

Prenatally, drug-exposed children of chronic, substance-abusing mothers living in poverty in the inner city tend to play differently at 18 and 24 months of age than do their counterparts who were not exposed to drugs but were living in poverty (Beckwith et al., 1994). The non-drug–exposed children demonstrated natural developing skills, increasingly produced and combined socially conventional acts that were progressively more directed at others instead of themselves, and increasingly used symbols that related to an object when the object was not present in the environment. However, prenatally drug-exposed toddlers demonstrated the less mature play behaviors of mouthing, banging, and waving. They repeated one-act sequences and directed acts toward themselves rather than other players. Additionally, the more drug-exposed population demonstrated less sustained attention to play, less purposeful behaviors when choosing toys, and many more abrupt transitions from one object to another.

Strategies for encouraging sustained attention with young children with disabilities:

- Provide a sticky (underside of shelf liner) or bumpy surface that will prevent the toys from falling as much as they do on a smooth surface
- Adapt the knobs and buttons on toys so the child can use them
- Use a Velcro wristband to attach a small rattle or bell if the child cannot hold it
- Place Velcro on the corners of book pages to make them easier to turn

The Importance of Socio-Dramatic Play

Over the years, a variety of terms have been used to describe what this book labels *socio-dramatic play*. These terms include *collaborative play, interactive play, social play, pretend play, dramatic play,* and *socio-dramatic play.* This book uses the term *socio-dramatic play* because it emphasizes that younger children *interact with peers* by using play representations and language to create *jointly developed stories.*

Socio-dramatic play typically occurs when children between 3 and 5 years of age create a pretend play enactment with peers. These socio-dramatic play enactments require children to integrate their knowledge of the world, their ability to create symbolic representations, and their communication skills so that they can share pretend behaviors with other children. These children have previously demonstrated the ability to create symbolic play representations when playing by themselves. For example, a child can run a Popsicle stick over his or her hair and say to a play partner, "I'm finished brushing my hair. Let's go." The child thus indicates to the partner that they can now begin creating a pretend story about going somewhere. Similarly, a child can move a block along the floor and say "Vrrroom-vrrroom." By doing so, he or she encourages a play partner to join in with creating a car-racing story.

©iStock.com/RichVintage

Socio-dramatic play activities require children to integrate their knowledge of the world, their ability to create symbolic representations, and their communication skills.

Like adults, young children appear to know the difference between reality and make-believe. However, children engage in much more pretense than adults. They tend to find that an imaginary world is more important and appealing to them than the real world because they can have more control over it. The object in the environment is not the principal cause of creating the desire to pretend; rather, the children's desire for pretending drives them to using the objects. Participation in these pretend acts affords children the opportunity to imagine the different ways that the world could be as they are increasing their attempts to understand it.

Socio-Dramatic Play Representations

Socio-dramatic play involves the use of multiple play representations. These representations support the shared stories of young children who, at this point in their lives, have a limited knowledge of the world, limited abilities to create symbolic representations, and limited communication skills. As children's language develops, they create representations using language alone, and the need for play objects lessens.

Some representations are associated with the environment in which the play activity takes place. These *contextual representations* can be as realistic as a playhouse area, which is commonly found in preschool classrooms, or as abstract as a couple of boxes in the corner of a room. In Chapter 1's scenario, *The Poison Syrup,* the play context of the staircase was totally abstract and existed only in the minds of the players. They created pretend stairs simply by moving their legs as if they were descending a staircase and by talking about what they were doing.

Along with contextual representations, *symbolic representations* are another type of play representation used by preschool children to create socio-dramatic play stories. Typically, children use three types of symbolic representations: *objects, actions,* and *roles.* Although the actual form of these representations does not change, the function of the representations in the child's mind can quickly transform an object into something that it typically does not represent in everyday life. Young children transition from depending on the physical appearance of the representations for stimulation to becoming increasingly capable of creating pretend representations without that stimulation.

Jupiterimages/BananaStock/Thinkstock

Children can completely change their identity while involved in socio-dramatic play activities.

For example, a young child may transform a large piece of material into a tablecloth or a blanket. However, a more experienced, older child might easily change the meaning of the fabric into a villain's cape or a tent for a family's camping trip. Similarly, young children swinging an arm up and over their head could represent some type of physical hitting or swinging. In contrast, older players, with more advanced world knowledge, more experience with pretense, and greater language skills, will be able to transform that action into a person casting with a fishing rod or a fairy waving a magic wand.

The following is a summary of general pretend behaviors that occur around certain ages:

- **Around 0 to 2 years old:** Children begin to engage in symbolic activities—a doll can represent a baby, a piece of material can become a blanket.
- **Around 3 to 4 years old:** Children produce symbolic play activities that relate to real-life experiences using a lot of props and language. Peer collaboration in play begins to

occur. Imaginary friends appear in play at about 3 years old, and 4-year-olds are more focused on producing details about their symbolic play representations.

- **Around 5 to 6 years old:** Children begin to understand the differences between real and pretend and, as a result, enjoy engaging in pretend enactments. With their increased attention spans, 6-year-olds extend play themes for long periods. Pretending is social and fun at this age.

Figure 3.5 provides further examples of socio-dramatic symbolic representations.

Figure 3.5 Socio-Dramatic Play Symbolic Representations

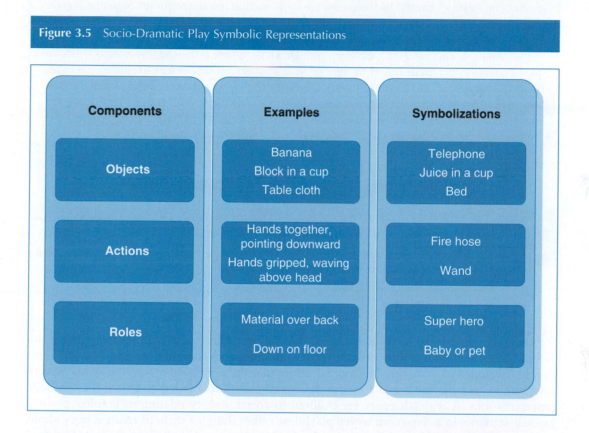

Components	Examples	Symbolizations
Objects	Banana Block in a cup Table cloth	Telephone Juice in a cup Bed
Actions	Hands together, pointing downward Hands gripped, waving above head	Fire hose Wand
Roles	Material over back Down on floor	Super hero Baby or pet

REFLECT AND APPLY EXERCISE 3.2

Contextual and Symbolic Representation

Reflect

Again, reread the scenario at the opening of this chapter.

Apply

Think of three contextual representations that the children used to sustain their play narrative and the impact that these representations had on enhancing their activities. Now do the same for three symbolic representations.

LEARNING FOR ALL CHILDREN
Symbolic Play and Disabilities

Preterm babies considered to be "high-risk" demonstrate lower play levels and less language and play growth when compared to full-term children (Hebert, Swank, Smith, & Landry, 2004). These delays could have resulted from the actual prematurity or may have been due to the impact of other complications caused by the premature birth, such as visual, motor, or cognitive impairments. Children with physical and cognitive disabilities (e.g., cerebral palsy, acquired brain injuries, congenital conditions and syndromes) tend to engage less in play activities with others (Cress, Arens, & Zajicek, 2007). Children with Down syndrome produced less-mature symbolic play behaviors that were linked to their general intellectual impairment (de Falco, Esposito, Venuti, & Bornstein, 2010). All of the children with challenges, however, tend to benefit from support by parents and are able to interact in more complex, purposeful engagements and communication behaviors when they participated in structured play activities.

Strategies for encouraging social interactions with children with disabilities:

- Use pictures, picture schedules, and symbols
- Use gestures and eye gazes
- Encourage children to "use their words"
- Provide short one-on-one reviews of materials before introducing them to the class
- Remind the children what they are going to do before it is time for a transition

Socio-Dramatic Play Language

As young children learn to create pretend play stories using contextual representations and symbolic representations, they also use verbal and nonverbal communication to expand their jointly developed play stories. The more abstract that the play context and the symbolic representations are, the more complex are the communications needed to create the symbolic representations. It is much easier for children to create a story relating to familiar pretend kitchen activities in a classroom with a playhouse center than for them to create a story about an unfamiliar pretend launching of a rocket ship in a room without supporting contextual representations.

For socio-dramatic play stories to flourish, all players must know what is happening and must abide by agreed-upon rules that are developed as the play evolves. Although these stories may appear random, explicit and implicit rules govern the roles and procedures for their creation (Curran, 1999). Some play activities, especially those of beginning players, evolve through adhering to very precise and explicit rules. These are rules that primarily focus on the roles, themes, and context. Other rules, which are typically developed by more experienced children, focus on embedded or implicit rules, such as accepting abstract symbolic representations, elaborating on a play partner's request, or inferring a more complex plot. Figure 3.6 provides information on the differences between explicit and implicit rules for socio-dramatic play activities.

In *The Castle House* scenario at the beginning of this chapter, the girls used the jungle gym to verbally create a context for their castle house. They also used symbolic object representations, such as buckets and sand, to transform themselves into people who were moving from one home to another home. Also, they used the symbolic action representations of bringing sand up toward their mouths to convey eating. Both girls were familiar with the moving

Figure 3.6   Rules of Socio-Dramatic Play

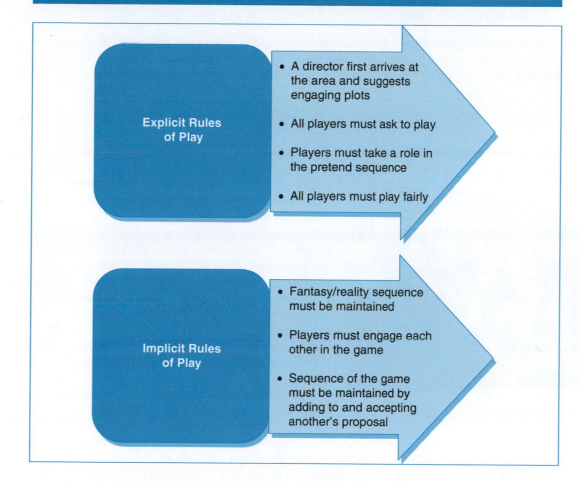

Explicit Rules of Play

- A director first arrives at the area and suggests engaging plots
- All players must ask to play
- Players must take a role in the pretend sequence
- All players must play fairly

Implicit Rules of Play

- Fantasy/reality sequence must be maintained
- Players must engage each other in the game
- Sequence of the game must be maintained by adding to and accepting another's proposal

process and demonstrated that familiarity a number of times. They were also aware of the language and syntax that a mother would use when talking to a child, and that a child would use when talking to a mother.

Children who are experienced players know which of their peers have difficulty following these explicit and implicit rules. Typically, they will attempt to avoid these children and will initiate play only with children they know will preserve and continue their play stories. When children know or suspect that another child does not understand how to play or is not a cooperative player, they will try to isolate that person from their play activity (e.g., turn their backs on the person, tell the person that he or she cannot play, or pause and move the play to another location). When these actions happen, more experienced players are often reprimanded by a teacher or parent for being unkind and not sharing the play with the other child. However, the experienced players are often simply trying to preserve or to expand and sustain their own play enactments (Corsaro, 1987).

As young children expand their abilities to collaborate with peers and to share fantasy objects and stories, they also develop a feeling of wanting to control the space in which their collaborative enactments are occurring. Professionals working with young children must recognize this theme of "control and communal sharing" as part of the preschool peer culture and should not discourage it. According to Corsaro (1987), children will attempt to maintain control over their shared activities by exhibiting the following behaviors:

- Verbally claiming ownership of objects, areas, and unfolding play events
- Saving or guarding a place or position for a peer during a temporary absence
- Resisting access attempts of other children to the play enactment

Such behaviors should not be punished but should be dealt with openly by discussing the children's concerns and how modifications could occur so that everyone's needs are met. These are wonderful situations for children to enhance their empathy and compromising skills.

Socio-Dramatic Play and Self-Regulation

Shortly after birth, infants are exposed to situations where they begin learning how to self-regulate basic activities such as sleeping and eating. The development of self-regulation is central to being a human being and is essential for both learning and social success (Baumeister & Vohs, 2004). Self-regulation involves the ability to initiate, sustain, modulate, or change the intensity or duration of feelings and motor activities in order to achieve a goal. Self-regulation is the foundation for all choice and decision-making activities and involves a number of higher cognitive processes. Children are required to anticipate when certain activities will occur and suppress their own personal desires to attain those desired goals. Self-regulation is essential for success in any structured environment, such as school.

Jupiterimages/Pixland/Thinkstock

Young children begin developing sincere friendships during their early education years.

Self-regulation is the cornerstone of early childhood development and cuts across all domains of behavior (Shonkoff & Phillips, 2001). Although rudimentary self-regulation skills are evident in children during their first year of life and continue to develop during toddlerhood, self-regulation is critical during the early education years, especially in the areas of motor control, inhibitory control, and delay of gratification. Between 3 and 5 years of age, children expand their self-regulation and cognitive skills by successfully participating in regulation tasks such as waiting for a turn, favorably entering a play activity, and delaying the need for recognition (Mezzacappa, 2003). Although these regulation and cognitive skills are predictable and somewhat universal, they can be substantially influenced by gender, temperament, parenting skills, care settings, and peer groups (McCabe, Cunnington, & Brooks-Gunn, 2004).

Research has documented a robust relationship between socio-dramatic play and the development of self-regulation (Fisher et al., 2011; McCabe et al., 2004). As children successfully create socio-dramatic play activities, they suggest and follow rules, suppress impulsive motor and emotional behaviors, and manipulate their actions so to advance the agreed-upon play theme. Specifically, while playing with peers, young children expand their self-regulatory skills by attempting the following (Berk, Mann, & Ogan, 2006):

- Understanding the mental state of their partner
- Distinguishing the symbolism of objects and actions from their reality
- Implementing appropriate social competence
- Processing divergent thinking skills

Additionally, when children are involved in challenging socio-dramatic play activities, these activities tend to produce a higher rate of self-guided speech than when the children are not involved in such challenging activities (Krafft & Berk, 1990), demonstrating Vygotsky's (1978) conclusion that children use self-guided speech to assist them with difficult situations. Not only do play activities enhance self-regulation, but the cleaning up activities that follow the play activities also improve regulation (Elias & Berk, 2002).

LEARNING FOR ALL CHILDREN
Self-Regulation and Disabilities

Preschoolers with disabilities who were premature babies and exhibited a very low birth weight tend to have early central nervous system infections, such as meningitis and neural tube defects (Isquith, Gioia, & Espy, 2004). These children usually demonstrate poor regulation abilities during the early childhood years. Early intervention programs that enhanced the development of self-regulation through respecting children's autonomy rather than through negative interactions have shown positive results in developing self-regulation skills.

Strategies to use to encourage positive self-regulation behaviors:

- Model appropriate behavior(s)
- Communicate effectively with young children
- Provide a calming activity or place where they can go
- Encourage children to discuss their feelings
- Teach conflict resolution strategies

Socio-Dramatic Play and Autism

All early education centers have witnessed enrollment increases of children with autism or autistic-like behaviors. Professionals working at early education centers must know about how autism could impact children's play behaviors.

Young children with Autism Spectrum Disorder appear to have difficulties engaging in purposeful play interactions when left on their own. Generally, their play behaviors tend to be characterized by less initiating and responding to joint attention, fewer turn-taking exchanges during play episodes, and less social communication (Williams, 2003). Young children with autism demonstrate significantly lower responses to social cue approaches made by their mothers, such as vocal prompts or facial expressions, than typically developing children (Doussard-Roosevelt et al., 2003). Preschool children with autism also produce less symbolic behaviors, use less variety in their play, exhibit less complex play behaviors, and demonstrate fewer complex play sequences (Lifter et al., 2011).

However, with systematic teaching children with autism can learn to play (Barton & Pavilanis, 2012). Implementing a system using just a few prompts can impact behaviors (National Autism Center, 2009). Specifically, the practice of using a prompt hierarchy system, which has a research body demonstrating its effectiveness, consisting of planning and delivering three to four prompts, has proven successful. The prompts include modeling, visual cues, and guiding the child's hand with an adult hand ("hand over hand"), and then transition to less intrusive prompts.

©iStock.com/Vita-lina

Although not as complex as their typically developing peers, most children with disabilities do participate in socio-dramatic play activities.

In a study by Kasari, Freeman, and Paparella (2006), young children participated in a two-tiered intervention process: first, a table-top, adult-driven training that lasted for 5 to 8 minutes. This was then followed by a floor session that was child-driven. It included following the child's lead by talking about what the child was doing and then expanding what they were saying. Interestingly, the children made significant improvements in their use of symbolic play and joint attention behaviors, and they generalized those improved skills to play activities with their mothers.

With children who have autism, positive play behavior results have been observed when teachers demonstrate how to use an object, which is of notable interest to the child, in a correct manner. After establishing "correctedness" within each activity, Sherratt and Donald (2004) suggest 10 structured activities in which the child can implement more advanced social behaviors with that object. Five of the 10 structures relate to symbolic play activities and are listed below:

- **Developing a shared understanding of symbols within play:** Adult turns an object into something else. For example a sock can become an elephant trunk, a snake, a rocket, or a hot dog.
- **Developing more complex narratives using language and symbolic play:** Adults emphasize engaging activities within and maintaining a narrative. This must be a highly flexible process where the adult sets the scene by stating something like, "Let's have a pretend birthday party." "Can this rocket ship take us to the moon?" "Did you know the dog ate all the hot dogs?" Throughout the scenario, children act out the events, sharing their ideas and feelings with the adult and peers.
- **Developing simple conversational sequences using language:** This practice involves designing an activity and then developing the language around that activity. For example, in the *Castle House* scenario, the girls wanted to move to a new house. Realizing that the jungle gym could create a context for the location of their house, one of the girls began using the term "castle house." Conversations then took place around events that occurred within the castle house.
- **Developing abstract, imaginative, and fantasy ideas as a focus of the interaction:** This type of structure occurs when adults suggest that a fantasy activity is going to happen. The opening scenario in the previous chapter, Chapter 2—*To the Fire*—demonstrates how an adult can suggest the idea that a fire truck needs to have gas in order to get to the fire.
- **Developing extended narratives using abstract mental state ideas and open-ended questions:** Having read a certain story, an adult asks children to talk about alternative outcomes. To do so, the adult uses open-ended questions such as "Can you think of another way it could end?" "I wonder what would happen if . . ." and "Why did she behave like that?" Children are asked to pretend to be a character from the story and to create an alternative ending.

Through adult support in developing a suitable pretend narrative structure, children with autism who find it difficult to develop social connectedness are provided the opportunity to elicit more sustained and coherent play, and to participate in affective engagements with adults and peers. Figure 3.7 provides further suggestions on ways that adults can work with parents to effectively support parent-child play interactions (Childress, 2011).

Ganz and Flores (2010) recommend using visual cues when children are involved in inclusive play activities with children with autism. Visual cues can be cards with drawings or short phrases written on them that provide suggestions to the child with autism. These cards give the typically developing child suggestions for getting the attention and communicating with their peer with autism. Such phrases could be "hand your friend a toy," "stand close to your friend," or "touch your friend's arm to get his attention."

Figure 3.7 Techniques for Supporting Parent-Child Play Interactions

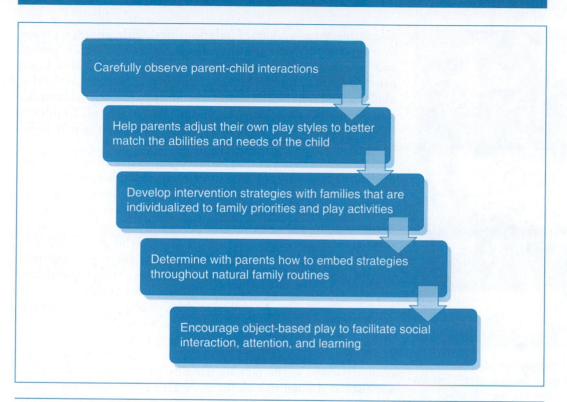

Source: Childress, D. C. (2011). Play Behaviors of Parents and Their Young Children With Disabilities. *Topics in Early Childhood Special Education, 31,* 112–120.

The following are specific reminders that Ganz and Flores suggest when using visual cues with young children:

Children with autism tend to do better in small groups of typically developing peers. They tend to be excluded in larger groups because there are so many children who have the needed social skills.

- Try to keep the same peers in the small group so that the children all become familiar with each other and comfortable with their interactions.
- Allow for time for the children with autism to adjust to the group and learn how to use the script. It may require two weeks or more for progress to be seen.
- Do not interrupt the children in an effort to have them use the cues. Let spontaneous interactions continue to occur.
- Keep using the cue cards as long as needed. Gradually discontinue the supports as the children demonstrate that they no longer need them.

As children increase their knowledge of their everyday worlds, their use of imagination, communication skills, and socio-dramatic play become more complex. When playing, children can transform a set of chairs into a city bus, a piece of string into a fishing pole, and a box into a dinosaur cave. Through explicit and implicit rules, children accept the representations of their play partners. As children become both more comfortable with the use of pretense and better communicators, simple contextual and symbolic representations develop into complex pretend narratives that are co-constructed with peers.

Play and Friendships

Christopher Robbins/Photodisc/Thinkstock

Friendships require the ability to achieve complex goals and this usually occurs for young children in play activities.

©iStock.com/Martinan

Making friends can be challenging for some children.

Friendships are voluntary relationships with another person that typically involve the sharing of companionship, intimacy, and affections (Dunn, 2006). These relationships can begin prior to attending preschool, are partially dependent on verbal abilities, and require the cognitive ability to socially understand and predict the other person's actions and emotions. Children's friendships tend to blossom through participation in collaborative pretend play activities (Dunn, 2006).

Research documents that establishing a friendship is a major developmental accomplishment of early childhood, and that the ability to establish friendships predicts later social and emotional outcomes. Typically, children who successfully develop friendships in preschool will continue to develop friendships throughout their lives. However, those who have difficulty developing friendships during their early years will continue to find it a challenge throughout their lives. Young friendships require what Dunn (2006) termed *emotional power,* which can be demonstrated by the ability to achieve complex goals usually through participation in pretend play activities.

Young friends demonstrate respect for their companions by continually negotiating, sustaining, and compromising their own activities. While playing, friends will frequently use these sophisticated cognitive skills more frequently than when they are involved in activities outside of play—for example, when they eat, draw, or read. Additionally, friendships demand that children know and predict the actions and feelings of another person. Young children somewhat effortlessly identify and predict their friends' responses when involved in pretend play enactments. Children's friendships typically involve children sharing and understanding feelings such as suffering, distress, glee, and concern when they play together. Thus, friendships affect emotional development, and emotional development affects friendships. In other words, children use play activities with friends to learn how to deal with their world, and learning how to deal with their world assists them in developing friends.

Friendly relationships can appear different depending on the personalities of the children involved. In a study reported by Dunn (2006), slightly over half of the friendships appeared to be built upon a *give and take* relationship where all the partners contributed equally to the relationship. Other children, about 20% of the population, formed *leader-follower* relationships where one partner definitely directs the activities. Children involved in these types of friendships did not complain about their roles. Finally, just fewer than 30% of the children were involved in friendships classified as *boss* relationships. Interactions occurring with this type of relationship involved a definite director of the play activity and a partner who complained about the other player being the director.

For over the past two decades, all schools have been concerned about the increase in **bullying,** or the act of using force or intimidation with others. Early childhood centers are no different. Bullying can cause extreme suffering and loss of self-confidence, and it often happens without parents or teachers noticing. To some extent, friendships can lessen the occurrence of bullying for a child.

Dunn (2006) cautions parents and teachers to be aware of the following indicators of bullying:

- Children not wanting to go to school
- Children beginning to act poorly at school
- Children becoming withdrawn
- Children crying at night, wetting the bed, or having nightmares
- Children becoming withdrawn or losing confidence

Some activities that could occur should parents or teachers suspect bullying are:

- Talk about it directly to the child—i.e., "I'm worried about you. I think you are being bullied. Can we talk?"
- Carefully keep an eye on the child and the signs that you see
- Tell the child that he/she is protected if they tell the adult
- If you are a teacher, talk about it with the parent. If you are a parent, talk about it with the teacher.
- Do not encourage the child to fight back. Both will be injured.

Friendships provide considerable information about a child's social, emotional, and cognitive abilities, and they can be predictive of future behaviors. Additionally, early friendships illuminate children's ability to successfully achieve their interpersonal goals (Guralnick, 2001). At some point in their childhood, most children experience difficulty with friendships. Friends can be a source of adverse emotions such as pain, jealousy, and hurt, and it may take a considerable period of time for a child to recover. Additionally, friendships can often involve teasing, which is also painful.

Some young children experience severe challenges when it comes to developing friendships. Among those are children who experience friendship neglect, and those who are just not interested in developing friendships and are withdrawn. These types of children typically do not participate in deviant types of behavior, and they can become more accepted by their peers as they get older or when they change schools. Additionally, there are other children who are unsuccessful at developing friendships and become frustrated and aggressive. This type of rejection is serious and could lead to outcomes such as academic failure, truancy, dropping out of school, and delinquency.

LEARNING FOR ALL CHILDREN
Friendships and Disabilities

Since friendships involve cognitive processing, social problem solving, and emotional regulation, a number of children with disabilities find it challenging to make friends. Specifically, children with certain disabilities that impact these skills are often unsuccessful at developing friendships and can become aggressive. Such disabilities could be autism, intellectual disabilities, and behavior disorders (Odom et al., 2006). In comparison, children

(Continued)

(Continued)

who experience speech impairments or physical disabilities without other disabilities tend to experience relatively less social rejection from peers. When compared with typically developing preschoolers, Odom et al., noted that children with disabilities tend to engage in fewer interactions and exhibit a more negative interaction style. As a result, they make fewer friends.

Interestingly, when children with disabilities were in childcare settings, which tend to be less structured and have high enrollments, the children with disabilities made friendships at a frequency similar to that of their nondisabled peers (Buysse, Goldman, & Skinner, 2002). However, this finding was not demonstrated in more structured inclusive preschools with smaller enrollments. This trend tends to reinforce the fact that the social context does impact friendships. It also might suggest that, when provided with the opportunity of having more children to choose from to make friends, children with disabilities actually do so. The same study found that the severity of the disability was not related to the number of friends.

The findings that the quantity of children in a class does impact friendship development, while the severity of the disability does not, should encourage the view of inclusion as an intervention that will assist in nurturing friends and enhancing cognitive, social, and emotional abilities in all young children. Additionally, having children with disabilities included in a classroom could allow opportunities for friendships to develop for those children who have challenges making friends but who are not disabled.

Strategies for encouraging friendships for young children with disabilities:

- Provide pictures to enhance the concept of friendship
- Read books about friendships with young children
- Identify children with similar interests
- Arrange for families of children who are friends to meet each other and encourage play dates

Chapter Summary

Symbolic representations typically dominate early childhood play activities. At around two years of age and concurrent with language development, children begin to utilize abstract representations while involved in play interactions. The ability to create sequential representations develops through children interacting with others in socio-dramatic play activities, resulting in more abstract and complex play and language. Socio-dramatic play activities require children to abide by implicit and explicit rules in an effort to maintain evolving play enactments and enhance friendships at a young age.

The desire to create pretend play enactments is so compelling in young children that, even if they have limited language abilities, they are self-motivated to create imagined play stories by nonverbally sharing information with their play partners. These complex activities require children to plan, predict, coordinate, and negotiate symbolic representations with others. In doing so, the activities provide the foundation for early language and literacy skills.

HOME AND COMMUNITY CONNECTIONS

Play and Pretending

Take your child to the park or other community or family events with other children to help them explore how to play in diverse ways.

CHAPTER 3 FIRST-PERSON INTERVIEW

"It's Our Big Screen TV"

Vicki Martinez

Early Childhood ESL Teacher,
Carrollton, TX

I am an Early Childhood English as a Second Language (ESL) teacher, and I co-teach in a public program with a Special Education teacher. We have a morning and afternoon session with 24 students in each session. All of our students qualify by being high-risk students. We have children who have autism, who have speech delays, who have a parent in the military, who are learning English as a second language, who are economically disadvantaged, and who are delayed but not yet diagnosed with a disability, some might be living with foster families.

Although they are all very different children with different backgrounds, the amazing thing is that they all interact with each other. You can come into our noisy classroom any time of day and you will find each child enjoying and learning from other children. They enjoy one another because they are kids, not because they have disabilities or are labeled "high risk."

We have been working hard to develop our outside area so that more focused learning can take place there. The children love going outside, and we have noticed that they talk and socialize much more with each other outside than they do inside. Therefore, we moved the large Duplo blocks outside and also set up a literacy center out there. We are also raising funds to purchase a number of large pieces of Plexiglas to hang on the chain-link fence so that the children can paint on them, using shaving cream on them, or finger painting with mud. We have a lot of different ideas for them!

An outdoor playhouse was just donated to our program. We have been busy painting roads on the cement and making traffic signs so that the children can drive bikes to and from the house. We have put a number of household play materials in the playhouse, and the children really love playing there.

The other day the most amazing thing happened. We have a sandbox that has a hard plastic cover. During the day, we take the cover off and store it under the playhouse, where it is out of the way. What happened was that I noticed a little girl trying to pull it out from under the house. I went over to her and mentioned that we like to keep it under the house so that it does not get in people's way. She looked at me and said, "But it's our big screen TV!" Intrigued, I asked her, "Where are you going to put it?" She immediately responded with, "On the wall in our house," and continued to pull it out and to take it into the playhouse. At that point, she and another little girl worked together to figure out where in the house "the big screen TV" should go.

Student Study Site

Key Terms

bullying	social play
friendships	socio-dramatic play
object permanency	solitary play
parallel play	symbolic play

Useful Websites

NAEYC's Position Statements on Play:

http://www.naeyc.org/files/naeyc/file/ecprofessional/BigIdeas_Play.pdf

http://www.naeyc.org/files/yc/file/200305/FurtherReadings.pdf

http://www.readplaylearn.com/standards/naeyc.htm

Reflective Activity

Describe the activities as they relate to the various stages using the suggested toy.

	Activities With a Toy Tow Truck	Activities With a Toy Phone
1. Functional unitary activity		
2. Inappropriate combinational activity		
3. Appropriate combinational activity		
4. Transitional play		
5. Self-directed pretense		
6. Other-directed pretense		
7. Sequential pretense		
8. Substitution pretense		

4 Language and Literacy Development

AbleStock.com/AbleStock.com/Thinkstock

Two children are in the playhouse area; Nina is a 4-year-old typically developing child, and Kara is a 4-year-old with developmental delays. Nina is standing at the stove moving her right hand in a circular motion, as if she is stirring something. Kara is lying on the ground with her head on a pillow and a doll's bottle in her mouth. Nina says, "Drink this bottle and go to sleep, Baby, so you can go to the party."

Sammy, a 4-year-old typically developing boy, is wearing a firefighter's hat and is sitting inside one of two attached boxes. The boxes are painted red and are located adjacent to the housekeeping area. The boxes have a paper ladder glued to each side. Additionally, two black Frisbees are glued on each side of the boxes and look as if they could be tires.

Sammy quickly jumps out of the "fire truck" and rushes over toward Nina, but he stays outside of the playhouse area. He then makes a knocking movement with his right hand and at the same time says, "Knock, knock." Nina responds with, "Who's there?" When Sammy says, "The fireman," Nina replies, "Fireman who?" Then Sammy frowns and says, "We're not playing the joke." Again, he says, "Knock, knock," and Nina again replies with, "Who's there?" Sammy responds with, "The fireman," and Nina says, "Come in!"

When Sammy enters the housekeeping area, he looks around and says "I am here to help you with the baby." Nina turns toward Kara and quickly rushes over to her while saying, "She ate the soap and she's going to die. I am taking her temperature because she's sick." Nina then bends down and quickly removes the bottle from Kara's mouth. Holding the bottle horizontally, she looks at it and then turns to Sammy, saying, "Oh no! She's really sick with fever. Get her to the hospital for the operation or she will die."

Kara is acting limp, and Sammy bends over and helps her sit up. He then gets behind her and puts his arms under her shoulders. He begins to drag her toward the opening in the play area's boundaries while saying, "I can get her to the hospital fast and they will operate on her and get that soap out of her so she won't die." Nina puts a hat on her head, and she then follows Sammy and Kara out of the center to the fire truck. She says, "Don't die, Kara. We will make it better. We can go in the fire engine."

85

Language is the process that we use to communicate with other people. Child development specialists, however, were traditionally uncertain about how very young children develop language. Only within the past four decades have they identified a language development sequence, one that appears to be a very robust and resilient process. In the opening scenario, young children take on adult roles and then produce sentence structures and language that are fairly close to those that an adult would produce in a similar but real situation. Additionally, two of the children in this scenario demonstrate that they know the difference between "real language" and "joking language." Finally, they use language to create a story, or narrative, that is well coordinated and is composed of beginning, middle, and end activities.

Early education professionals must clearly understand the interaction between language and literacy development, and how play impacts that development. Through carefully planned play activities, children can enhance the language and literacy abilities that are the foundation for future academic achievement.

As you read the chapter, consider the following:

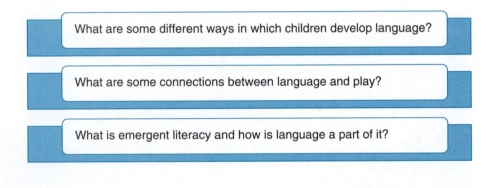

What are some different ways in which children develop language?

What are some connections between language and play?

What is emergent literacy and how is language a part of it?

Language Development

Research has found that, although adults from different cultures talk to children in various ways, children tend to develop language similarly (Ochs & Schieffelin, 1984). Only minor developmental differences occur between children raised in a culture that included children in adult conversations and children raised in a culture where adult conversations rarely included participation by the children. Additionally, when children are learning more than one language at the same time, they learn those languages at a similar rate as long as both languages are equally valued and respected by the participants in the environments where the children reside—for example, home, school, and community (Vaughn, Linan-Thompson, Pollard-Durodola, Mathes, & Hagan, 2006).

At about the age of 9 months, infants generally begin to make verbal approximations of words that are familiar to them. For example, they say "ma-ma" for "Mama" and "ba-ba" for "bye-bye." Somewhere around 10 to 15 months of age, they begin to express their first words. These expressions consist of the very shortest part of the word that contains meaning, which is called a *morpheme.*

At a very young age, children begin to communicate with each other.

Morphemes relate to affixes (prefixes and suffixes) and root words. At this age, they are experimenting with the concept that in their simplest base form, words carry meaning. The morphemes expressed by these infants are emulating base words that can stand alone as free morphemes without needing other roots or affixes to create meaning. These expressions are intended to convey much more meaning than just that single morpheme. For example, young children typically produce the morpheme "ball" when presented with a single ball. Additionally, they also use the expression "ball" when presented with a basket of balls. Here, though, they do not intend it to refer to just a single ball but to the many balls they observed. At this stage, children do not combine morphemes to convey meaning, such as "ball" + "s" to mean many balls. Additionally, they will go around a room saying, "Ball?" and meaning, "Where is my ball?" Their goal is communication and focusing on meaning.

Similarly, infants experiment with phonology. **Phonology** is the study of the sounds of English language. As infants hear how language sounds when produced, they develop **phonological awareness**: for example, when infants produce vocalizations that sound like words, such as in the example of "ma-ma," they are emulating the sounds they hear in their environment to communicate.

As children become comfortable using spoken language and receive more accurate and elaborate responses from their caregivers, they begin to produce phrases that are larger and more meaningful. The exposure to and exchange of language with caregivers furthers the development of children's vocabulary and **phonemic awareness**. During the second year of life, most children begin putting words together in an organized manner. For example, "ball" might become "my ball," and then "want my ball." Very quickly, children begin adding words and meaningful units of sounds from their environment to their vocabulary. The arrangement of words to create a correct sentence is called syntax. Around 2 years of age, it is not uncommon for children to join together subjects, verbs, and objects to express their desires, as in "I want my ball!"

Between the ages of 3 and 5 years, children become skillful at joining two separate thoughts into one complete sentence. Preschoolers typically put together the ideas of "I want to go to the park" and "I want to play ball," and produce a statement such as, "I want to go to the park and play ball."

Young children use talking and listening to learn about their world, understand the events that are taking place, and encounter diverse perspectives. Figure 4.1 presents a general overview of language development with information taken from the National Dissemination Center for Young Children with Disabilities (NICHCY) website.

Throughout the first 5 years of life, children add approximately nine new words a day to their vocabulary (Carey, 1978). Gradually, most young children learn to produce and understand longer sentences and how to use the correct word order of their culture when expressing their needs and thoughts. Again, this language acquisition process appears to be rather consistently learned. It occurs prior to children entering the primary school grades and does not require formal instruction.

Krashen and Terrell (1983) referred to this process of language learning as language acquisition. As infants interact with their environment and are exposed to meaningful language, they naturally "pick up" the language. When the process becomes intentional and requires formal instruction, the process becomes a learned process. Children then learn about the language and how to improve their language through the explicit study of language. For example, they formally learn about parts of **speech**, or the verbal production of language, and how to form proper complex sentences. However, when language acquisition occurs prior to school, children just know what does and does not sound right based on their ability to communicate effectively with others.

Early childhood professionals must be aware of three situations that may impact children's development of verbal language and alter or delay the process described above (Shonkoff & Phillips, 2001). First, children will deviate from the traditional process if they have been raised in an environment where the quantity or quality of the language input

Figure 4.1 Overview of Spoken Language

Approximate Ages	Skills	Examples
Newborn	Cries	
1–3 months	Cooing in response to speech, makes "raspberry" sounds	oo, goo
4–6 months	Plays with sounds, turns toward sounds	ba, ga
6–8 months	Babbles, imitates sounds	bababa
8–12 months	Babbles with changes, responds to own name	badaga
10–15 months	First words, waves bye-bye, imitates words	ball, shoe, mama
12–18 months	Adds morphemes, may put two words together	balls, shoes
15–20 months	Adds words, understands commands	my balls, black shoes, happy mama
24 months	Speaks several two-word phrases, uses pronouns	Get book. He bite.
36 months	Full sentences with missing articles, asks questions	My balls fall. Find black shoes.
36–48 months	Grammatical system, uses six-word sentences	These are my red balls.

©iStock.com/RyanJLane

Although most children follow a similar pattern of language development, they might accomplish it at a different rate.

is below the norm. Second, a deviation in the natural pattern of language development may occur if a child's organism of language input is affected. For example, perhaps a child suffers intermittent middle ear problems that do not allow the child to hear language correctly. Finally, children who experience severe delays in their cognitive or learning abilities might demonstrate a different sequence of language development. Otherwise, language development occurs for the majority of young children between birth and 5 years of age and without formal instruction.

Children must practice and master their native language for three important reasons (Resnick & Snow, 2009, pp. 1–2):

- Speaking and listening are the foundation skills for reading and writing
- Speaking and listening make children smarter
- Speaking and listening are academic, social, and life skills that are valued in school and the world

Interestingly, infants who learn sign language and are exposed to signs in a naturally interactive environment learn to understand and use sign language at a faster rate than they learn to understand and use verbal language. Infants who have a hearing loss and who do not learn language through signing, tend to learn verbal language at a rate slower than hearing infants.

Early education classrooms should encourage children to talk a lot so that they will enhance their vocabulary and language. Children should be encouraged to talk to their peers frequently. They should be urged to talk at great length on a specific topic, sharing their knowledge, and express what they need to know. Additionally, children should be given multiple opportunities to discuss books, stories, and play narratives. Encouraging children to express their thoughts, ideas, and interests will enhance their social and academic lives. Actually, Resnick and Snow (2009) recommend that children be provided with the following opportunities:

- To see how other people respond to what they might say
- To respond to what others ask them about what they are saying
- To hear others comment on their ideas
- To have what they say repeated or improved
- To have opportunities to practice the rules of speaking and listening

Bilingual Development in Young Children

Young children use language to communicate in and with their environment. As children interact with other speakers of language they naturally pick up language in order to receive and transmit messages to meet their needs. The **language acquisition process** is an unconscious process for young children whose focus is getting their needs met through language. This ease of learning language can help explain why learning in two or more languages can be a seamless process for very young children (Sorace & Ladd, 2005).

When children interact with their caregivers, they hear phonology, syntax, and vocabulary being used to communicate. Depending on the language being spoken, children will hear similar language constructs and sounds consistently and will create a similar language output. They may then interact with another caregiver who speaks a different language or enter a consistent setting where another language is spoken and they will acquire the second language in the same way. That is, a child may have ongoing, consistent exposure to the two languages since birth and naturally switch between languages when speaking to others in the different languages. If the caregiver is consistent with speaking and expecting a response from the child in a language, the child will know when to speak which language. For example, when talking to mom, the child may speak in Spanish, then when talking with dad, switches to English. This would be due to a consistent pattern by which the mother speaks only Spanish to the child and the father speaks only English to the child. The child then naturally comes to understand that one language is spoken with mom and another with dad. In both cases, the language development process is the same as with monolingual children. They are using language to communicate their wants and needs, and are doing so by being exposed to, mimicking, repeating, and communicating with their environment.

Bilingual children who learn a second language upon entering preschool or some other consistent new language context learn a second language with the help of their primary language experience. The second language acquisition process is similar to first language acquisition as children seek to communicate within their new context. In rich language contexts children will just pick language up. However, the process is stronger when the child has developed strong primary language skills and can then transfer what he or she has learned conceptually in one language to learning another language.

Creatas/Creatas/Thinkstock

Children have stronger language skills if they are allowed to develop their primary language skills first and then learn another language.

For example, in the opening scenario, children who do not understand English would be able to follow along with their peers as they see familiar experiences being played out and hear familiar language. As the children pretend that the baby is sick and needs to get to the hospital, children who do not speak English may recognize the motions being used as that of sick patients, and hear the word "hospital," which may sound familiar to a word known in the primary language, *hospital,* if coming from a Spanish language background. Conceptually, children learn about the world around them and the language they have learned helps them articulate those experiences. But the experiences may be the same.

Cummins (2000) referred to this as the **common underlying proficiency** (CUP) model. When people learn something, they have processed the concept and the meaning; they have registered the experience and the knowledge. The *surface level learning* is the language that is used to share that experience. As we learn a second language, we do not re-learn those experiences; we just learn the new labels or outputs to share those experiences in another language. Research has consistently shown that children learning a second language in a new context after they have developed a first language are most successful when they are allowed to use their primary language as a vehicle for learning a second language (Goldenberg, 2008).

Play provides an effective and less threatening experience for young children to learn a second language. It allows children to use and draw upon primary language experiences and "see" how English works in familiar contexts to acquire a second language. Early play experiences allow children to continue their language experiences in a bilingual world and prepare them for the ongoing English language experiences of early elementary grades. They give them the opportunity to continue to learn in and through their primary language as they build more CUP and are able to transfer their knowledge base to school across the curriculum as they continue to learn English.

All children need the caring and loving support of adults to foster communication skills. Meece and Soderman (2010) suggest the following 10 strategies for supporting safe and enriching environments that promote positive verbal exchanges:

1. Know and respect each child as an individual: Make each feel special and welcomed to the classroom

2. Show interest in children and their activities: Be actively engaged with them

3. Speak courteously: Use positive, polite language and be patient with them

4. Ask a variety of open-ended prompts: Pose questions that encourage them to think

5. Use appropriate praise to encourage them: Use sincere, constructive and appropriate praises

6. State expectations clearly: Make sure they know what to do rather than what not to do

7. Respect children's abilities: Let children seek the feelings of autonomy

8. Allow children to learn from their actions: Let them construct their own knowledge through their own actions

9. Give children choices: Provide authentic choices so that they can make decisions for themselves

10. Include and welcome families: Welcome families and communicate with them positively

Speech and Language Developmental Delays

Speech and language development are considered to be major indicators of a child's overall cognitive and academic success. In 2005–2006, the NICHCY reported that approximately one in every six children with disabilities had an identified speech and/or language disorder. This statistic did not include secondary students or students with deafness, autism, intellectual disabilities, or cerebral palsy. For children between the ages of 2 to 4.5 years old, research findings suggest that up to 19% of this population could have a language delay. Should the language delay go untreated during the early years, about 40% to 60% of these problems will persist throughout life (Nelson, Nygren, Walker, & Panoscha, 2006).

Concerns about a language delay should arise if a child does not begin to make the verbalizations typical of 1 year olds, or if the child's speech and language are different from that of their peers who use a similar language. All young children should receive a regular *screening,* or general assessment, for language delays during their early years by their primary care professionals. Nonetheless, 43% of parents of children between the ages of 10 and 35 months in a study reported that they did not receive any type of developmental assessment during their well-child visits (Halfon, Olson, Inkelas, & Lange, 2002). Additionally, 30% of these parents said that the child's physician never discussed with them how their child communicates. Obviously, a number of children with language delays are not being identified at an early age, when intervention can have a positive impact. Furthermore, findings demonstrate that young children with speech and language delays appear to be at increased risk of developing learning disabilities once they reach the school grades. Typically, this disability is manifested by poor reading skills around the age of 7 or 8 years.

Language can be identified as **receptive language**, or the ability to understanding the language that has been spoken or read, and **expressive language**, or the language that is used to share thoughts or comments through the use of voice, gestures, signs, or symbols. Young children can demonstrate a receptive and/or an expressive language delay. A receptive language delay occurs when children have difficulty understanding language being spoken to them. An expressive language delay is when children have difficulty sharing their own thoughts or comments with others.

Young child and parent participating in a friendly and playful hearing test.

Language consists of three components: form, content, and use. *Form* refers to the structure of the language, including the sounds that make up the words and that add meaning (such as "s," which makes a noun plural), and the grammatical rules of sentences. *Content* denotes the overall meaning of the language, including both the words and how they are combined. *Use* reflects the purpose of the communication. Young children learn to communicate by capturing the meaning of what they want to say (content) by using correct rules and words (form) for a number of personal purposes (use). For example, children typically will say, "Let's play" to a peer. The phrase "Let's play" conveys the meaning of a desire to create a pretend story. The contraction "let's" indicates that the child wants to do this activity collaboratively, and the use of this statement could be for enjoyment or companionship. Children who have difficulties in one or more of these areas of communication often experience communication breakdowns, which can lead to feelings of frustration and confusion for all involved.

Young children can also demonstrate difficulties with language form development when they have challenges correctly producing and understanding the language's (1) sound system *(phonology)*, (2) word structures (**morphology**). or (3) grammar (**syntax**). They demonstrate difficulties with language content when they have challenges with **semantics** or challenges developing the vocabulary. Finally, children can also face challenges using language correctly as it is influenced and governed by context (**pragmatics**). Figure 4.2 provides definitions for these different speech and language terms using information taken from the NICHCY website.

Because of the demonstrated lack of support from some professional health care providers in the identification of early speech and language disorders, early educators must carefully and regularly monitor the speech and language development of the children with whom they work. They must immediately inform parents of any concerns that they might have. Providing a child with a speech and language screening tool is a quick and uncomplicated task that can be carried out by an appropriately trained professional. If the screening device indicates a chance that a speech and language delay exists, then a more elaborate diagnostic assessment needs to occur. However, referring professionals should assist parents in seeking out services that provide child-centered assessments, as opposed to structured, formal assessments, so that an accurate appraisal occurs. Figure 4.3 provides information on different types of language delays in young children with suggested general intervention methods.

Figure 4.2   Language Terms and Definitions

Terms	Definitions
Expressive Language	The use of language to share thoughts, protests, or comments through voice, gestures, signs, or symbols
Language	The conceptual processing of communication, which may be receptive and/or expressive. Language is made up of socially shared rules such as word meanings, word order, and word combinations.
Morphology	A component of language form governing the meanings of word units (e.g., tense markers, suffices, plural markers)
Phonology	A component of language form that addresses the sound systems of language (e.g., /a/, /b/, /th/) and how they function in a language
Pragmatics	The component of language use focusing on purpose or intentions (e.g., formal, informal). Pragmatics involves three skills: use of language, changing language for different types of talk, and the rules of language (e.g., turn-taking, staying on topic).
Receptive Language	Understanding of language. The ability to listen and understand what is being communicated.
Semantics	The component of language content focusing on the words a person understands or uses (vocabulary)
Speech	Verbal production of language that is used for communicating. It consists of articulation (speech sounds), voice, and fluency (speech rhythm).
Syntax	A component of language form focusing on elements used to form phrases or sentences (grammar)

Figure 4.3 Causes for Language Delays, Impacted Areas, Language Interventions

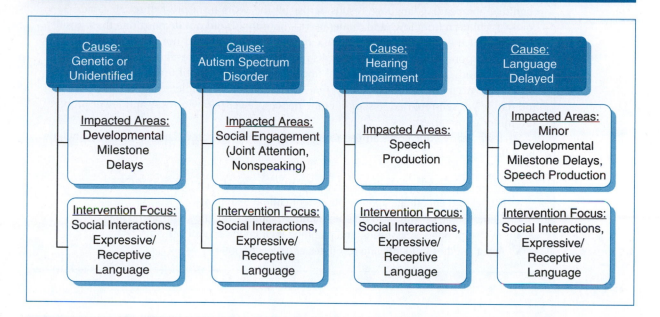

LEARNING FOR ALL CHILDREN
Language Development and Poverty

Poverty can produce an increase risk of developmental problems, which could begin as early as the time of conception and continue throughout life. Children raised in poverty are exposed to multiple risk factors that can result in developmental differences that challenge their social, behavioral, and educational outcome more severely than for children who are not living in poverty who are exposed to the same problems.

Parents of children from poverty backgrounds tend to talk less frequently to their children during their first 2-1/2 years than parents who do not come from poverty backgrounds (Hart & Risley, 1995). Using and hearing language early in a child's life affects that child's language development. For example, children living in poverty have lower vocabulary and communication skills than their peers who are not living in poverty. When these two communicatively different groups enter school, their language skills are different. The strong connection between oral language and vocabulary development and early reading success can explain why students from poverty may struggle academically. Additionally, children who are raised in poverty are exposed to other risk factors (e.g., stress, lack of nutrition, and inadequate medical care that can further affect their school performance.) No matter how many or few of these types of factors exist, findings indicate that most children being raised in poverty have lower language abilities than their non-poverty peers (Stanton-Chapman, Chapman, Kaiser, & Hancock, 2004).

Recently, however, the Head Start Research Third Grade Follow-Up Impact Study (Office of Planning, Research and Evaluation, 2012) found that children who were from high-risk households and who entered a Head Start program at 3 years of age sustained positive

(Continued)

(Continued)

cognitive and reading/language results across all the years from pre-K through Grade 3. In contrast, children from low- and moderate-risk households did not demonstrate these results. The fact that the low- and moderate-risk household children did not show positive results might correspond to the HighScope results reported in the Perry Preschool Study (see Chapter 2). In that study, a delayed or "sleeper" impact did not occur until the age of 15, when the HighScope group finally demonstrated that the students had completed more years of school and had fewer self-reported misconduct incidences, fewer felony arrests, and fewer property and minor crime arrests.

Strategies early educators can use to encourage increased parent-child interactions include the following:

- Create a positive and collaborative relationship with all families
- Model and encourage appropriate parent-child interactions
- Demonstrate sensitivity to different cultures, family structures, and social interactions
- Involve families in assessing and planning their child's school activities
- Assist families in identifying resources and their priorities

REFLECT AND APPLY EXERCISE 4.1

A Concerned Parent

Reflect

Infants and toddlers develop at different rates. As a result, parents often have concerns and questions about their child's development. They may express concerns by asking:

Why isn't my baby saying anything?
Why can't people understand what my baby is saying?
Do you think my baby has normal hearing?

Apply

It is difficult to know what to do when a parent presents such questions. They must be reminded that all children develop at their own pace. However, if the parents' concern continues, you might suggest they call a public health care provider, a community health clinic, or a public health nurse to inquire about an evaluation for their baby. Visit the following website http://www.nichcy.org and become with familiar with the information that is available to assist you in working with parents who have concerns similar to the ones mentioned above. Share two resources you learned about on this website with another student.

According to Christ and Wang (2010), there are four research-based vocabulary teaching practices that can assist all children in learning new words. Providing exposure to new words is particularly critical for children who begin school with fewer words than others. These vocabulary teaching practices are the following:

1. Provide purposeful exposure to new words through thematic activities (to be discussed in Chapter 6)

2. Teach intentionally the meaning of words (to be discussed in Chapter 7)

3. Teach word-learning strategies (to be discussed in Chapters 10 and 13)

4. Offer opportunities to use newly learned words (to be discussed in Chapter 10)

Language Development and Socio-Dramatic Play

Socio-dramatic play activities, such as those demonstrated in the scenario at the beginning of this chapter, afford children opportunities to use social dialogue to develop play scripts and activity that enhances considerable language growth. Through interactions with peers and more experienced players, and the support of play props, children produce more complex play and language activities than they do by themselves (Vygotsky, 1978). There is a meaningful exchange of language and that can lead to further development as children are exposed to new ways of labeling items (vocabulary and syntax). Children as young as 15 months of age can insightfully solve problems with play objects if they are provided the right kind of information (Gopnik, 2009; Howes, 1992). Howes found that before the age of 2, children can recruit peers to join them in engaging in similar or identical pretend play acts, such as simultaneously drinking from different teacups or moving cars. Through pretend play activities, young children gradually expand behaviors that will assist them in developing the social and cognitive skills needed later in life for (1) interacting with people and (2) planning insightful activities. These skills include coordinating and sustaining conversations, and negotiating ideas.

Socio-dramatic play is both a physical and a mental activity in which children invent roles, actions, and objects to construct and negotiate stories (Katz, 2001). These activities afford children three major opportunities. First, children participate in mental symbolic representation activities by transforming roles, objects, and actions into uncommon images. This activity was seen in the scenario at the beginning of this chapter when the baby bottle transformed into a thermometer. Here the children used labels or sounds to express their actions and thinking.

Even at a very young age, children produce playful interactions with their peers.

Hemera Technologies/AbleStock.com/Thinkstock

Second, children are motivated to share these invented representations with their playmates. Again, this activity was demonstrated in the scenario when Sammy informed Nina that they were not playing a knock-knock joke, instead, he wanted to create a pretend story so that the story would evolve. These rich exchanges expose children to sociocultural language norms and patterns. They continue to hear and learn the variations through which language can be produced.

Finally, children adhere to explicit and implicit rules in order to co-construct with their play partners well-organized play narratives or stories, most of which are structured to have beginnings, middles, and ends. The children in the scenario demonstrated the desire to construct a story, with each person taking on an authentic role and coordinating their actions and language. The level of oral discourse is strong as students learn turn-taking and engage in collaborative language experiences.

Pretend play facilitates the development of narrative productions (Ilgaz & Aksu-Koc, 2005). Creating narrative productions enhances language skills by requiring children to do the following (Champion, Katz, Muldrow, & Rochelle, 1999):

- Focus on the organizing of events
- Use storytelling form and content
- Gradually increase the use of decontextualized information

Three-year-old children do occasionally produce single episode narratives, but these do not dominate their play activities. However, by the age of 5, narratives typically dominate children's play and is primarily composed of decontextualized language that creates a well-sequenced story. Around 6 years of age, children become familiar with telling stories without the use of props or actions, and they create narratives that consist of a high point and then a related conclusion (Kaderavek & Justice, 2000).

Therefore, socio-dramatic play enactments are not the free-flowing and aimless activities that many adults think they are. Rather, they are well-planned activities that require insightful thinking. Figure 4.4 graphically illustrates how the three components of socio-dramatic play—symbolic representations, social sharing, and rule-making—interact and depend upon each other to produce well-planned play stories.

All three components of socio-dramatic play are language-based activities:

- **Symbolic representations**. Object, role, and action symbolic representations require the players to separate the label of an everyday object from the object itself. The players

Figure 4.4 Interconnected Language-Dependent Components of Socio-Dramatic Play Activities

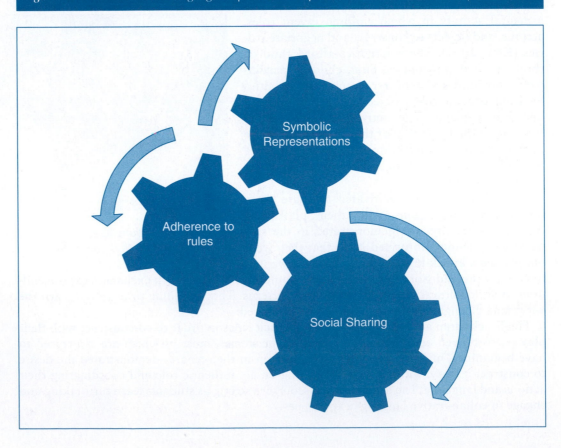

must then provide that object with another label, which in some cases might be a child-invented word (Vygotsky, 1978). For example, assume that children are playing with an empty paper towel roll and want to transform it into a telescope. To do so, they must first separate both the word from the function of the object that it typically represents. That is, they must separate "a paper towel roll" from an object that is cylinder-shaped and can be looked through. Next, they must use language to provide this new cylinder-shaped object, which in their minds is no longer a paper towel roll, with a new label, such as *a telescope* or some other label for an object that would allow them to see far distances.

- **Social sharing**. To socially share individually created symbolic representations with a play partner, children must provide their peers with explicit communications. These communications must signal that the original object has been transformed and that it now represents an imagined object with a different label and function. For example, a child might demonstrate that this paper towel roll now has a different function by using the nonverbal communication of lifting the roll to his or her eye and then verbally stating, "I see the pirate ship way over there."

- **Rule-making**. Finally, to coordinate and sustain the socially shared symbolic representations in play and to produce a co-constructed play story, play partners must use language demonstrating that they are motivated to follow explicit rules so as to expand the story. An example of this motivation would be a second child gently removing the "telescope" from the first player's eye, placing it up to his or her own eye, and stating, "It is a pirate ship, and it has a cannon with a bomb in it!" These verbal and nonverbal communications demonstrate that the second child is motivated to follow play rules and to coordinate, negotiate, and sustain a story about a threatening pirate ship that they both see through the pretend telescope. These complex and thoughtful exchanges are rich in language. As the cognitive demand of a task is increased (e.g., coordinating and negotiating), more language is required to successfully participate in the experience.

Children use language to share information about symbolic play representations.

©iStockphoto.com/ktaylorg

Communicating During Socio-Dramatic Play

Preschoolers use specific play language to clearly convey symbolic meanings, interpret shared ideas, and grasp the roles and perspectives of other peer players (Dickinson & Tabors, 2001; Goncu & Gaskins, 2011; Pellegrini, 1985; Pellegrini & Galda, 1993; Sachs, 1980). The language understood and produced by preschoolers in play contexts involves more complex structures and more interactions than the language that the players use outside of the play context (Katz, 2004). When interacting in collaborative play stories, children employ two types of communications to share symbolic information and enhance their narratives: *play communications* and *metacommunications*. These communications add to the understanding of the play story and, at the same time, coordinate, sustain, and negotiate the story's plot (see Figure 4.5). Play builds communication skills. Without play, children may miss opportunities to develop their expressive language at complex levels.

Figure 4.5   Definitions of Communications in Play

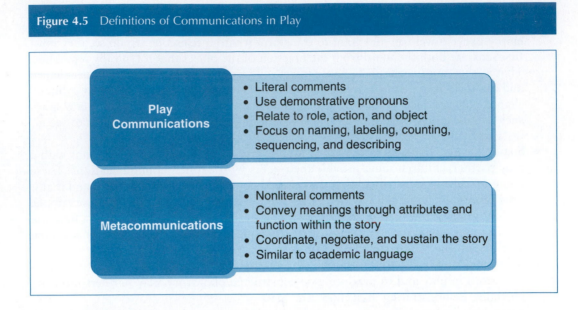

Play Communications
- Literal comments
- Use demonstrative pronouns
- Relate to role, action, and object
- Focus on naming, labeling, counting, sequencing, and describing

Metacommunications
- Nonliteral comments
- Convey meanings through attributes and function within the story
- Coordinate, negotiate, and sustain the story
- Similar to academic language

Play Communications

Play communications occur when a player creates a symbolic representation and then uses an appropriate, real-life comment in association with that representation. These **play communications** are very literal statements or behaviors and relate to the role, action, or object that is being transformed. Specifically, play communications can focus on activities such as naming, labeling, counting, sequencing, and describing. Play communications are grounded in the environment, and the players typically use a demonstrative pronoun (e.g., this, that, these, those) to refer to a tangible, visible object even though the purpose of the object might have symbolically changed.

As children develop language, they become capable of creating well-coordinated pretend stories.

For example, a play communication can be as simple as saying "That is going beep-beep" when moving a block over the carpet to represent a car, or "Meow" when the child is down on all fours limbs acting similarly to a cat. More complex examples are the following:

- When a child is pretending to be working at the car wash and says, "Do you want this super washed?"
- When a child playing a doctor says, "Open your mouth wide and swallow this" or "Take that medicine every day."

Typically, play communications do not add information to the play event; instead, they are used to confirm the symbolism by stating the appropriate sounds or words.

The following are two examples of play communications taken from the scenario at the beginning of this chapter.

Nina comments to Kara, who is lying on the floor with a bottle in her mouth, "Drink this bottle and go to sleep, Baby, so you can go to the party." The comment is typical of what an adult would say to a child who is lying in bed.

Sammy's statement "I can get her to the hospital fast and they will operate on her and get that soap out of her so she won't die." This statement is similar to what a fire fighter would say in a similar situation.

Figure 4.6 contains a list of some symbolic play contexts and examples of play communications that could occur.

Metacommunications

In contrast to play communications, **metacommunications** are verbal or nonverbal communications that contribute to the construction of the play story or context. They add specific information to the pretend creations and directly contribute to the development and organization of the play story so that the play plot is coordinated, sustained, and negotiated (Goncu & Gaskins, 2011). Metacommunications provide continual information about transformations as they are occurring. They convey meaning, such as the attributes and functions that objects, roles, and actions have within the play narrative. Through metacommunications, thoughts and feelings are shared, directions are presented, roles are assigned, and stories are coordinated, sustained, and negotiated. Most communications that occur in socio-dramatic play are metacommunications.

Language structures used for metacommunications are more complex than those that young children typically use outside the play setting, and they possess the quality of conveying meaning from beyond the immediate play context (Katz, 2001). These communications depend less on the actual sharing of the physical play environment and more on (1) the sharing of knowledge and (2) the feedback from the words and gestures that are being used. Katz notes the linguistic structures of metacommunications are similar to those used in academic settings and also contribute to the development of early literacy skills.

Metacommunications can be as simple as the planning phrases "Let's play" or "You be the doctor and I'll be the patient." Alternatively, they can be as linguistically and factually complex as "I am pouring this poisonous syrup into this lake so that the monster will die."

Figure 4.6 Communications Occurring in Play

Symbolic Representation	Play Communications	Metacommunications
• Standing on a large outdoor rock	• "Hurry before the bad pirates capture us!"	• "Now that we are at the ship (the rock) we can count the gold."
• Stuffed dog	• "Here's your bone."	• "I think the dog is barking because he is hungry."
• Wooden block used as a car	• "Vroom, vroom!"	• "The firetruck is coming to save the driver in the crashed car."

©iStockphoto.com/RichVintage

Through the use of metacommunications, children create the context for stories to develop around their favorite super heroes.

All metacommunications carry the message that the activities are pretend, in contrast to play communications that reflect real-life communications. Metacommunications are integral components of socio-dramatic play because they externally communicate complex internal images from one player to another.

In the play scenario at the beginning of this chapter, a number of metacommunications occurred. For example, the following:

Sammy, who was the fire fighter, enters the housekeeping area and announces, "I am here to help you with the baby." This message alerts Nina that the play context has changed from a peaceful setting where the baby is going to sleep to one of an emergency situation.

Nina responds to the contextual change by saying, "She ate the soap and she's going to die. I am taking her temperature because she's sick." She then takes the bottle from the baby and holds it horizontally, which is a movement that is similar to reading a thermometer.

Through her verbal metacommunications stating that the baby ate the soap and is sick, and her nonverbal metacommunication of holding the bottle sideways, Nina shared information with Sammy and the other child that the bottle had been transformed into a thermometer. Children typically use metacommunications to:

1. Announce the beginning of play (e.g., "Let's play" or "Let's pretend we went home and had our own party.")

2. Identify social positions (e.g., "I am the robber and I want all the money.")

3. Create the context or frame for the play activity (e.g., "It's dark and cold in there," or "Guys, let's go back here where the monsters live.")

4. Describe object, role, and action transformations (e.g., "This is a birthday cake for baby" or "This spaceship is crashing into a crater.").

Figure 4.6 provides more examples of metacommunications that reflect their use for specific purposes.

REFLECT AND APPLY EXERCISE 4.2

Time for You to Play

Reflect

The Socio-Dramatic Play Center in your classroom has been designed to look like a camping site. There are sleeping bags, a tent, backpacks, cookware, a plastic garbage can lid that is turned upside-down and has logs in it, fishing poles, and other outdoor equipment. Additionally, a few wood blocks are mixed in with the objects.

Apply

Think of five different ways that the wooden blocks could be transformed into a symbolic representation of another object found in a camping context. Additionally, think of the play communications and metacommunications that children would use to share with peers the information about what the wooden blocks represent.

Narrative Development

Narrative skills have been significantly related to literacy development (Lai, Lee, & Lee, 2010). Narratives require children to tell stories from outside of the context of the story. While involved in play narratives, children must continually provide information from

Figure 4.7 Suggestions for Supporting Emergent Literacy Within Classroom Contexts

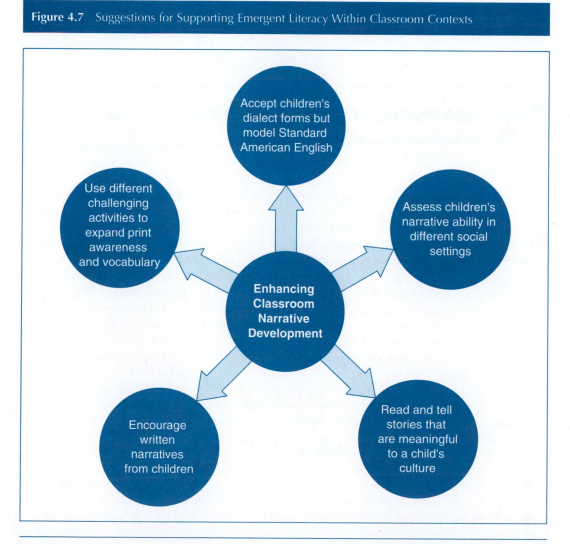

Source: Champion, T. B., Katz, L., Muldrow, R., & Rochelle, D. (1999). Storytelling and Storymaking in an Urban Preschool Classroom: Building Bridges From Home to School Culture. *Topics in Language Disorders, 19*(3), 52–67.

outside the "story" (metacommunications) so that the other participants will understand what is happening. Adults need to be aware of the variations in narrative development among different cultures and accept stories from children that might not follow the usual convention of storytelling—such as have a clear beginning, middle, and end; be topic centered; and be temporally linked. For example, African American children tend to link several events together by themes and not time. Narratives by Asian children may be brief and contain fewer details. Therefore, adults must be sensitive to the impact of culture when listening to children's narratives and encourage the children to develop their stories in a comfortable manner. Figure 4.7 provides some suggestions on ways in which this goal can be accomplished. Storytelling appears to be a strength for African American children that adults could capitalize upon in developing their language and literacy skills (Reese, Leyva, Sparks, & Grolnick, 2010).

Focusing on narrative skills is one element of a complex set of skills for developing language and literacy. With the new Common Core State Standards, classrooms will see a shift in the balance between narrative texts and nonfiction texts for academic language and literacy development. As early as kindergarten, classrooms must represent a 50/50 split of narrative and non-narrative text in the classroom. This shift supports the need to allow children more time for engaging in play. Through play, children experience the world around them and imagine it from a "real-world," "nonfiction" context and build upon that context through the application of narrative skills. Doing this exposes children to what will be demanded of students when they enter grade school—a true integration of narratives and nonfiction texts.

LEARNING FOR ALL CHILDREN
Narrative Development and Culture

Young children tend to increase their understanding of human intentions and develop an understanding of another person's intended thinking through creating shared play narratives. However, a famous study by Heath (1986) demonstrated a difference in the function, style, and expectation for storytelling across cultures. It showed that the narratives of African American children had unique functions and styles when compared to those of European American children (Price, Roberts, & Jackson, 2006). While European American cultures usually develop topic-centered narratives, African American children tend to create narratives that are exaggerated and elaborative, and those narratives are told spontaneously and with amusement. However, Price et al., found that as children got older and approached kindergarten, both cultures increasingly developed stories that were both goal-directed and more cognitively mature. Additionally, in a study that controlled for linguistic differences, Hispanic children tended to provide sparser narratives about past events than did non-Hispanic children (Leyva, Reese, Grolnick, & Price, 2008). Findings also indicated that, when comparing Korean and Taiwanese preschoolers, Taiwanese children tended to incorporate more emotions, feelings, and thoughts into their narratives than Koreans. However, 5-year-old Koreans then tended to more rapidly develop ways to organize their narratives.

These studies linked some identifiable characteristics and behaviors of students from different ethnic cultures. However, these generalizations to all children from similar cultural backgrounds cannot be made. These studies do assist in understanding that there are sociocultural variations in the narrative development of children. These differences should be seen as assets to build upon. Once we can understand the level at which children have developed their narrative skills, adults can then move them toward more academic narrative skills necessary for school success.

Ways family storytelling can impact children:

- Enhance bonding between family members
- Encourage empathy among family members
- Develop children's understanding of story components
- Enrich shared values of the family
- Enable the family to have fun

Emergent Literacy Development

Literacy is how children access information and the world around them, process its meaning, think about their world in diverse ways, and produce knowledge to be shared with others. However, today the term literacy is often narrowly understood as the ability to read and write. Teachers often think of literacy in terms of specific skills that relate to teaching standards for reading and writing. Many parents relate the term to a child's ability to interact with books and print. Lawmakers regularly refer to literacy test scores, while employers tend to connect literacy with an employee's ability to synthesize information and successfully complete a task. Today's early education teachers often view literacy abilities as a combination of all of the skills mentioned above—a child's ability to (1) achieve literacy elements or standards, (2) interact with books and print, (3) attain certain assessment scores, and (4) problem-solve situations.

In the past, teaching practices for literacy were based on the premise that oral language was necessary for literacy development to occur. Consistent with this premise, children were not usually taught to read or write until about the age of 6 or 7 years, when language was fully developed. Early education teachers and parents provided "pre-reading" or "reading readiness" activities, which were designed to introduce children to the literacy skills that they were historically taught after entrance into the formal primary education system.

During the 1980s, this pattern changed. The concept of emergent literacy, a term first coined by Marie Clay in 1966, became an accepted theoretical basis for explaining the development of early reading and writing skills. Emergent literacy theory proposes that very young children develop the skills, knowledge, and attitude to read and write by observing the use of literacy skills in their everyday environments (Clay, 1979). Whitehurst and Lonigan (1998) endorsed the conclusion that emergent literacy originates during the first years of life through the concurrent and interdependent development of reading, writing, and oral language. They posited that literacy is best conceptualized as a developmental process, rather than a learned process, and that this process is one in which skills are acquired through interactions within a stimulating and responsive environment. They found no clear demarcations between pre-reading and reading skills, as had traditionally been thought. Rather, through everyday social and linguistic interactions, children construct their own concepts about the function and structure of print. Early education professionals need then to understand what may seem to be unconventional or nontraditional forms of emergent literacy that can transfer to children building traditional literacy skills.

Lester Laminack (2013) points out that children "flirt" with literacy at a young age. Through the recognition of print in their environment, children develop a casual interest in letters and what they communicate. For example, children will identify the letters "o," "r," "e," and "o" as saying the word "Oreo" when they see it on a package of cookies. They will also have fun making letters in damp sand, and eating a piece of bread so that it looks like a "U." These types of activities demonstrate that children are always attempting to put together information that they are learning and to find logic in these new relationships. Adults need to provide an abundance of opportunities for children to "play" with literacy so they can begin to understand the logic behind it.

The National Academy of Sciences report on *Preventing Reading Difficulties in Young Children* (Snow, Burns, & Griffin, 1998) viewed literacy as more than the ability to read and write. Rather, it involves a more complex process that includes multiple cognitive, language, and social skills. The academy concluded that reading and writing development is achieved through the interaction of these multifunctional skills, which originate at the beginning of life and progress on a continuum of skill development. However, identification of the specific skills that exist on the continuum and the order in which they might occur is still debated.

Reading is a complex process that requires more than just knowing the letters of the alphabet and their sounds.

Contemporary research continues to support the conclusion that reading and writing skills do not develop in isolation from language development; instead, they start at birth and emerge through the interactions between language and other abilities (Britto, Fuligni, & Brooks-Gunn, 2006). Literacy development does not appear to be tethered to a specific chronological age or school grade; instead, it evolves throughout the childhood years. Therefore, the majority of today's preschools in some fashion now address the literacy skill development of 3- and 4-year-old children.

Outside-In and Inside-Out Processes

According to Britto, Fuligni, and Brooks-Gunn (2006), Whitehurst and Lonigan (1998) have developed the most acceptable typologies for understanding early literacy. They proposed that literacy skills emerge through two different sets of skills and processes, which they title the *outside-in* and the *inside-out processes*. Both processes are equally important to a child to succeed as a reader (Cabell, Justice, Sucker, & Kilday, 2008)

The **outside-in process** refers to a child's abilities to understand the context in which the writing is being produced. These abilities are ones that support reading comprehension skills, such as children's understanding of the world, their language skills, and their knowledge of how to use print. For example, if children know that stories typically have a beginning, middle, and end, they can anticipate the story development and climax. When children read, these are the skills that assist them in understanding the context in which the story occurs.

The **inside-out process** consists of skills that relate to the coded aspects of reading. They center on children's ability to understand rules for translating the print that they are attempting to read into meaningful sounds. Examples of these skills are alphabet letter recognition and awareness of the sounds children make.

At a young age, children begin to understand how to use print in everyday environments.

To become skilled readers, children must learn to integrate and coordinate the skills relating to their general knowledge of the world and use of language, or the *outside-in processes,* with their specific understanding of code-related skills such as letter-knowledge and phonology, or the *inside-out processes* (Lonigan, 2006). Figure 4.8 summarizes the components of these two processes.

Similarly, children learn to write by observing writing activities in their daily environments. Around the time that children are 3 years old, they begin to make marks on paper that resemble letters of the

Figure 4.8   Emergent Literacy Components Suggested by Whitehurst and Lonigan (1998)

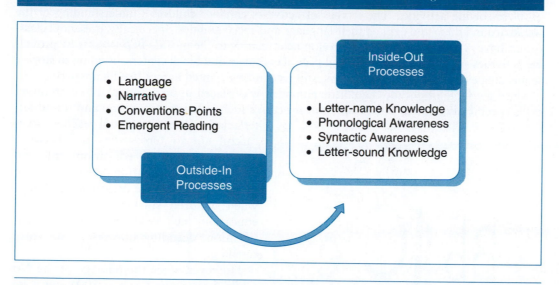

Source: Whitehurst, G. J., & Lonigan, C. J. (1998). Child Development and Emergent Literacy. *Child Development, 68*, 848–872.

alphabet. However, it takes a long time for these formations to truly reflect conventional letters and writing. Schickedanz (2009) suggest a progressive development from scribbling to writing letters of the alphabet. This progression is presented in Figure 4.9.

Figure 4.9   Making Marks: From Scribbles to Alphabet Letters

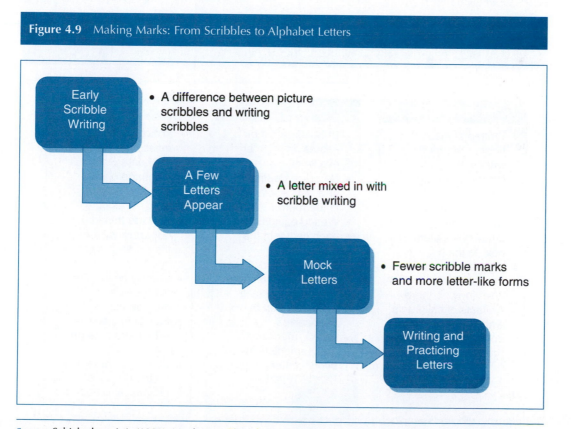

Source: Schickedanz, J. A. (1999). *Much More Than the A B Cs: The Early Stages of Reading and Writing.* Washington, DC: The National Association for the Education of Young Children.

Traditionally, preschool teachers have also encouraged the development of *outside-in processes* by providing children with opportunities to participate in child-directed peer play and problem-solving activities. These types of activities enhance children's understanding of the world around them and expand their language and social abilities. Specifically, preschool classrooms have typically fostered skill development relating to the *outside-in processes* by providing activities such as playing at pretend peer play centers and block centers, listening to stories, sequencing events, following directions, and recognizing printed names (see Figure 4.10).

Until a couple of decades ago, little emphasis was placed upon young children attaining skills specifically related to the *inside-out processes* such as letter recognition and sound-letter relationships. Preschool teachers were careful not to "cross the line" between informal preschool education and formal primary education. They did not teach skills that were typically introduced when children start their kindergarten education, such as letter and sound identification, decoding of words, and story retelling.

Jupiterimages/Photos.com/Thinkstock

Preschool classrooms today do expose children to the letters of the alphabet and the different sounds that those letters can make.

However, since the passage of the *No Child Left Behind* act in 2001, with its demand for academic accountability, an abundance of curricula for young readers has been produced. These curricula deviate from the previous child-centered focus of early literacy practices and endorse a more adult-driven, *inside-out*

Figure 4.10   Examples of Exposing and Using Print in the Classroom

In the classroom	For the children	For the families
• Written stories, poems, songs written • Displays of things that children have learned or will learn with written questions/statements next to them • Written instructions at each center on what they do there • Artifacts of children's writing on the bulletin board and around the room	• Cubbies with their names on them at eye level • Name cards (first and last) displayed in the room • Writing equipment at each center in the room • Children's work displayed around the room with their names written by themselves • Books, magazines, and pamphlets in every center	• Welcoming messages written in the home language on the classroom door (e.g., "Welcome," "We are thankful for our families," "Burr! It's starting to get cold" • Weekly newsletter that goes home to the parents • Family mailboxes with their name on them • Family news section on the door with news, recipes, and travels

process of skill development. Much attention is currently given to the visual and auditory processing components of reading and writing that typically occurred in the past in kindergarten and first grade. The new approach focuses on the concept that children must master specific reading and writing skills that enable them to interpret print and then to understand a story. Many early education centers have revamped their child-centered play and exploration environments and now organize them around a more scientific approach to literacy development that nurtures simplified visual and auditory skills as a basis for early literacy.

The initial goal of many of today's popular literacy programs is to have young children learn the letters of the alphabet and the sounds that these letters represent. Similar to elementary-grade reading programs, preschoolers are presented with stories with controlled and unnatural texts that are designed around newly learned letters and sounds. While such texts may make it easier for children to recite the words, they tend to focus on topics that children know little about. As a result, comprehension of this type of text becomes a challenging chore rather than an enjoyable, self-motivating activity grounded in children's knowledge of the world around them.

Nonetheless, many elementary teachers, parents, and lawmakers continue to pressure preschool teachers to teach the type of skills that were previously taught to children 5 years old and up (e.g., alphabet awareness, decoding, and comprehension). The preschool teachers are asked to implement teacher-directed instructional methods. Although some young preschoolers have demonstrated the ability to adjust and successfully transition into learning through teacher-directed instruction, some children have become confused and have experienced academic failure at a very young age (Albert Shanker Institute, 2009). Yet another group of children demonstrates a reasonable grasp of letter-sound correspondence at a young age but then encounters difficulties with reading during the third and fourth grades (Miller & Almon, 2009). These unsuccessful early experiences may account, at least partially, for the large increase over the past decade in the number of young children who exhibit specific social and emotional behavioral concerns.

Home Literacy Programs

Home literacy, or literacy that develops in the home through experiences that demonstrate how language and literacy are used for communication and learning, benefits children. Many families that read to their children in the home provide them with opportunities to ask questions and have those questions answered (DeTemple, 2001). This type of everyday, informal interaction typically produces young children who are interested in reading and writing (Vukelich & Christie, 2009). Through personal and meaningful interactions with books, objects, and people in their home environments, young children begin to understand how print is used in the world around them and thus enhance their *outside-in reading processes.*

The literacy skills of some children who are raised in poverty often reflect the lack of exposure to reading and other stimulating literacy experiences (Tough, 2008). Children with parents who are professionals tend to have vocabularies of about 1,100 words by the age of 3; in contrast, children whose parents receive welfare have about 525 words at that age. Some children from families living in poverty have more frequent occurrences of cognitive deficits and tend to score below average in letter-naming and phonology (Molfese et al., 2006). Research documents a relationship between early reading and academic success. Children who fail to read at a young age tend to be candidates for grade retention, which ultimately could lead to a high risk of dropping out of school (Gormley, 2005).

Dickinson and Tabors (2001) found that the home environment is one of the dominating factors that highly influence the development of early literacy abilities. Young children who read from books early are most likely to come from homes where there are many books and

©iStock.com/jarenwicklund

Children of all abilities can participate in reading activities.

the family members continually engage in book reading activities. However, many of those who struggle with reading tend to come from homes where the family members do not engage actively in literacy activities. Other emergent literacy practices can and could be valued if there was a better understanding of how nontraditional practices connect directly with school-based literacy skills. For example, children who are encouraged to share with their parents what they did each day, are building sequencing skills that are also developed as parents read stories to their children. Oral language exchanges provide rich contexts for building literacy-based skills that children can capitalize on in school, and should be encouraged.

Research does demonstrate that high-quality early education centers can and do make substantial and lifelong contributions to the development of children's literacy skills. Language activities in early education centers can affect vocabulary and early literacy development, and changes occurring in the early years endure throughout children's academic careers (for a comprehensive review of the research, see Neuman & Dickinson, 2001, 2011; and Dickinson & Neuman, 2006).

The challenge facing today's early education professionals is to ensure that all young children experience a smooth and successful transition from their early education programs to formal school settings—a transition that offers a balance of *outside-in* and *inside-out* experiences. As research in previous chapters demonstrated, young children are capable of learning and doing much more than what was thought in the past (Gopnik, 2009). To successfully meet the needs of all young children, literacy skills must be presented in a meaningful and comfortable learning context and teachers must partner with the home (see Figure 4.10). Children must be provided with developmentally appropriate practices within a context that allows them to gradually transition from child-centered activities that focus on the development of *outside-in* processes, to teacher-centered activities that focus on the development of *inside-out* processes (Lonigan, 2006). To successfully guide preschoolers through this measured transition, teachers must have a comprehensive understanding of the following:

- The components of literacy development
- The methods for systematically introducing the literacy components through child-centered activities

This information will be presented in Part III of this book.

REFLECT AND APPLY EXERCISE 4.3

Guiding Parents With Reading

Reflect

Become familiar with the International Reading Association's website at http://www.reading.org. On the left side of the home page, click "Parents" and read the brochure titled *Getting Your Child Ready to Read.*

Apply

Think of different suggestions that you could make to families to get them to realize the importance of the concepts presented in this brochure. Think of different ideas for families who have children of different ages: for example, an infant, a toddler, a preschooler, and a child in the early primary grades.

Chapter Summary

Language appears to develop similarly for most children. Children who are learning two languages at the same time from birth naturally switch between languages when speaking to others in the different languages.

The language structures used to create socio-dramatic play enactments are more complex than the language structures used outside of play activities. When children create play enactments, they produce and understand two types of languages: play communications and metacommunications. Play communications are used to add meaning to and confirm the understanding of the play enactments; in contrast, metacommunications are used to coordinate, sustain, and negotiate a play story's plot and subplots. At a young age, children learn how to use actions and language to enhance and protect their collaborative play enactments. Through the co-construction of collaborative pretend stories, children develop self-regulation skills by determining the information that their play partners need to create and enhance their play story.

HOME AND COMMUNITY CONNECTIONS

Play and Pretending

As your child explores his or her world, label things using the proper vocabulary (name of the item).

CHAPTER 4 FIRST-PERSON INTERVIEW

Teaching Life Is Good to All Children

Brian Armstrong

Play Consultant, Gales Ferry, CT

I have been working for years with children of all ages, abilities, and backgrounds, including those with social, emotional, cognitive, and physical disabilities. Through play I help them manage their challenges and increase their willingness to learn the academic and social skills they will need. Play can increase children's creativity, social connectedness with adults and peers, internal control, and feelings of joy. These are abilities that help children become more resilient and empowered to face the challenges that life can impose.

One of the keys to keeping children involved in playful activities is to encourage them to use their imaginations and participate in make-believe activities. One great activity I use with the children is to ask them to lie on their backs and move their legs as if they are pedaling a bike. I then ask the children to imagine they are riding their bikes to a place of their choice.

(Continued)

(Continued)

Each child in the group gets the opportunity to "lead" the bike trip and everyone in the group can share what they see when they arrive at the specific, real or imagined location. It's so much fun for all of us, adults also participate, and it leads us too many different imaginative places. We have gone to Italy, under water, to the flower market, to grandma's house, and other places, and have had so many exciting things happen to us by just lying on our backs, moving our legs, and using our imaginations. The children really hang together because they are all engaging with each other and get a chance to lead. The combination of movement and imagination is important and activities like this one allow children to be really honest with you.

Sometimes children will not want to participate, and that is okay. I always give them the opportunity to "Pass" and we move on to the next person. Children should not be forced to participate in activities because there are children and there are circumstances that may be interfering with their willingness to participate. Sometimes children just need some extra time to feel safe enough to participate. However, if the pattern continues a few times, I will place myself near the child and personally try to include that child in the activity.

Play is the essential tool for young children's learning and development. It is not just something for children to do when they have nothing else to do. You must maintain high goals when designing activities for every child. I will make accommodations, but not modifications to the activities. For example, if a child cannot participate in a certain activity because of a physical, cognitive, or social challenge, I will alter the way we are doing it so that each child can participate to the best of each one's ability. I will not scale-down or modify my goals and objectives. I expect greatness and allow individuality. There is always a way to do things, and an empowered child can amaze you. Along with play groups and classroom activities, a program of ours that I love is titled Success on Skateboards (SOS) for children with challenges. In this program the approach, support staff, and skateboard are very motivating and encourage the children to develop important cognitive, communication, and social skills beyond what was traditionally expected. They are truly motivated to learn.

We need to teach children that "life is good" and give them an abundance of opportunities to have "playfulness" in their lives. Play won't take away their struggles, it will help them manage those struggles through developmentally appropriate means and they will be empowered to push through the challenges they face.

Student Study Site

Visit the Student Study Site at **www.sagepub.com/selmi** to access additional study tools including mobile-friendly eFlashcards and links to video and web resources.

Key Terms

common underlying proficiency	language acquisition process
emergent literacy	literacy
expressive language	metacommunications
home literacy	morphology
inside-out process	outside-in process
language	phonemic awareness

phonological awareness	receptive language
phonology	semantics
play communications	speech
pragmatics	syntax

Useful Websites

International Reading Association: http://www.reading.org/General/AboutIRA/Position Statements/PreschoolLiteracyposition.aspx

NAEYC: http://www.naeyc.org/files/naeyc/file/positions/WWSSLearningToReadAndWrite English.pdf

NAEYC: http://www.naeyc.org/files/naeyc/file/Publications/ArticleExamples/02Neuman.pdf

Zero to Three: http://www.zerotothree.org/child-development/early-language-literacy/early literacy2pagehandout.pdf

Reflective Questions

1. Using the information presented in Figure 4.1, provide examples of what language you would expect from a child at the previous stage and at a later stage.

Previous Stage:	Current Stage: Babbling	Later Stage:
	Dadada	

Previous Stage:	Current Stage: Adds Words	Later Stage:
	Bad doggy	

Previous Stage:	Current Stage: Full Sentence	Later Stage:
	Baby go night-night	

Previous Stage:	Current Stage: Add Morphemes	Later Stage:
	Spoons	

2. Review the information presented in subsections "Play Communications" and "Metacommunications" and in Figures 4.5 and 4.6; describe examples of play communications and metacommunications that would be used with each play item.

	Play Communications	Metacommunications
Food Items		
Post Office		
Camping Tent		

5 Collaborating With Families and Professionals

ENHANCING COLLABORATIVE CLASSROOMS

©iStockphoto.com/asiseeit

There was a knock at the door of a preschool classroom. The classroom paraprofessional aide was engaged with three students in the block area next to the classroom door. Hearing the knock, the aide looked over to the teacher, and without a word left the three children and went to the door.

When the door was opened there stood the school's principal accompanied by the grandfather of one of the preschoolers in the classroom. Although this was a surprise visit, both the teacher and the aide were happy to see the two visitors, and the aide invited them into the room. Since visitors come to the room on a regular basis, there was little interruption in the general flow of the class. While children were moving from center to center, the teacher was engaged with two students discussing their plans for a play activity. At the same time, the aide was working with a small group of 4- and 5-year-old students who were building a bus with large wooden blocks to take them to the local zoo.

The other children were in other group learning areas. Some were reading individually or to one another, two children were in the play post office area, and another small group of children was at the outdoor art area with another aide. A special education teacher was working with a small group of children recording science data in their science journals.

The grandfather was visiting the room as a result of a planning meeting he had had a week ago with the teacher, the aide, and the principal. The grandfather and the principal walked slowly toward the teacher, but before reaching her they spoke to Sarah, who showed her grandfather her story journal with her illustrations. The principal was stopped by one of the children in the post office, who said that he had a package to deliver to the school. The grandfather and the principal finally got to the teacher's table and exchanged greetings. The grandfather then said, "Everything is arranged." A demonstration hive, a small three-comb beehive with two safety glass observation

(Continued)

(Continued)

walls, was ready for installation. However, the grandfather wanted to do a final check of the room and determine the best place for installing the hive. He wanted to make sure that the hive was safe for the children and at the same time was maximally available for student observations.

The teacher was happy to discuss this project with Sarah's grandfather. The project was an outgrowth of a previous child-led project. Several children had been reading a book on insects, and they began a research project on bees. Other children were included in the project, which resulted in art pieces, journal stories about bees and other insects, and a unit on the benefits of insects. Additionally, Sarah's grandfather, a professional beekeeper, had already visited the classroom to discuss beekeeping and demonstrated how honey is extracted, and the class tasted the honey. Following the tasting there was a discussion by a child and his mother that demonstrated how honey could be used.

Several of the children had asked if it would be possible to visit Sarah's grandfather's hives, so he had arranged for the class to visit one of his apiaries, an orchard, and a fruit processing plant. The children then asked if he could bring a beehive to school so that they could watch bees make honey. This request resulted in the meeting between the grandfather, the principal, and the teachers.

T he opening scenario describes a classroom that has established a culture built on trust and cooperation at several different levels. The staff is composed of two teachers, one general education and the other prepared in special education, as well as two teaching aides. Additionally, as demonstrated on the day that this scenario occurred, family members and administrators are also a vital part of the educational team. All of these primary adult stakeholders have created an environment in which the parties involved are committed to common goals, they share planning responsibilities, and their relationships are based on respect for one another. While committed to common goals and shared planning, their professional roles are preplanned and often their teaching and evaluation duties are overlapping. In short, they work well together and they respect each other as participants in a learning environment that is based on collaboration.

This chapter will discuss the following topics, which have trust and shared responsibility as their foundations:

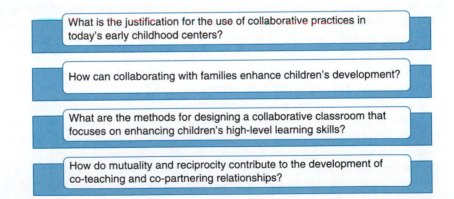

What is the justification for the use of collaborative practices in today's early childhood centers?

How can collaborating with families enhance children's development?

What are the methods for designing a collaborative classroom that focuses on enhancing children's high-level learning skills?

How do mutuality and reciprocity contribute to the development of co-teaching and co-partnering relationships?

Justification for Collaboration

For effective learning to occur in early education centers, the relationship between the staff, the children, and the children's families must build on a foundation of trust and cooperation. School professionals must skillfully collaborate with other professionals and family members to create environments that encourage children to take the lead in planning their learning activities. By fostering home–school connections, communication pathways are established with all families, including caregivers who can be parents, grandparents, uncles or aunts, foster parents, and significant others.

Additionally, in the school, collaboration among the school staff is important for planning and implementing education programs. As will be pointed out in Chapter 7, children can be guided to higher levels of learning during planning periods in which staff decide their activity, choose with whom they will interact, and later reflect on their activities.

Moreover, children engage in work that rests on cooperation and collaboration with each other. The activities in which they engage center on working together with their peers. Although adults are present, young children should take the lead in discussions, development of projects, and completion of tasks. The adults facilitate activities, orchestrate the class, and generally plan, implement, and evaluate the daily activities that comprise the sequence of events that occur throughout the school year.

In the opening scenario for this chapter, the brief conversation among the teacher, the principal, and the grandfather is an example of cooperative and collaborative teamwork between the school, a caregiver, and the community. Sarah, who is the granddaughter, prompted earlier conversations between the teacher and her grandfather about this child-developed and child-led project. The classroom visited the grandfather's apiary and his orchard. Several related classroom projects emerged from that field trip, and the students developed an idea for a class

For successful collaboration to occur, all participants must value trust and cooperation.

In collaborative classrooms, students take responsibility for developing and leading the learning projects.

beehive. The school completed negotiations with Sarah's grandfather and a community resource to establish the classroom observation center. The observation beehive will be a place for student observations, a resource leading to additional student projects, and a source of many conversations. This classroom example resulted from cooperation and collaboration among students, school staff, and families.

The opening scenario provides evidence that a culture of collaboration exists. Such a culture fosters "evolutionary relationships of openness, trust and support among teachers where they define and develop their own purposes as a community" (Pugach, Johnson, Drame, & Williamson, 2012, p. 23). Collaboration and cooperation occur at several different levels in the opening scenario. The scenario demonstrates a culture that extends beyond the teachers and aides to include the students, their caregivers, and community individuals. All the participants share a sense of joint ownership.

How did this staff establish its approach to working with children? What are the particular attributes of the staff that helped to establish this educational climate? Can such a program be replicated in other classrooms? These and other questions can be answered by understanding the qualities of collaborative professionals and how collaborative cultures can be established (Pugach et al., 2012).

Collaboration is complex and multilayered. To be successful, it requires a joint effort among staff, families, students, and community personnel. In successful collaborative efforts, all stakeholders respect the idea of collaboration and commit to working together and engaging in joint problem solving. Additionally, a culture of collaboration fosters personal and professional growth at both an individual and collective level. In such a culture all parties benefit.

Collaboration With All Families

The situation with so many diverse living arrangements today makes it challenging to define what is meant by the term *family*. While the past traditional notion of a nuclear family has been one that is usually comprised of a mother, father, and child(ren), the current definition of family has changed. In its most robust form, family is "two or more people who regard themselves as a family and who perform some of the functions that families typically perform. These people may or may not be related by blood or marriage and may or may not live together" (Turnbull, Turnbull, Erwin, & Soodak, 2006, p. 7). However, such families can be viewed as self-contained communities with their own rules, languages, rituals, and worldviews (Sameroff & Fiese, 2000; Seligman & Darling, 2007). According to Seligman and Darling (2007), a family is similar to a little society of its own, with each having its own culture, government, language, foreign policy, and traditions.

Families vary in membership and, although the membership can be relatively stable over a period of time, it also changes. Family membership can change by births, adoptions, foster children, divorces, children moving out of the home and then moving back home, changes in partnerships, grandparents needing assistance and then passing away, the death of a spouse, a parent moving to another country, remarriage, parent(s) being in the military, a parent commuting a long distance for work, relatives or friends needing a place to live, and many other reasons. These changes in family membership alter such family patterns as communication, relationships, and the general dynamics of the unit.

Therefore, today's families are defined by membership at a particular time (Seligman & Darling, 2007). That membership can be diverse and impacted by multiple contributing factors such as grandparents who provide full-day caregiving but reside elsewhere, parents living in different houses, unemployed family members, or memories of a deceased family member that influence the family's thinking and behavior.

Teachers must understand and accept the contemporary views of families, and must be open to working with all committed persons whether that person is committed but not legally married, a gay or lesbian partner, a relative or close friend, or a widow or widower. According to Burt, Gelnaw, and Lesser (2010), the NAEYC *Code of Ethical Conduct* (2005) clearly emphasizes the need for teachers to respect children within the context of their families through supporting the following guidelines:

- Appreciate and support the bond between the family and child
- Recognize that children are best understood and supported in the context of family, culture, community, and society
- Respect the dignity, worth, and uniqueness of each individual (child, family member, and colleague)
- Respect diversity in children, families, and colleagues
- Recognize that children and adults achieve their full potential in the context of relationships that are based on trust and respect (pp. 1–2)

Young children tend to understand the concept of "family" as being the people with whom you live and who take special care of you. According to this view, family members need not be related and there does not need to be a "mommy" and a "daddy." Instead, children view their family in very personal and functional terms (Derman-Sparks & Edwards, 2010). Therefore, educators should also have a broad concept of family that includes the many diverse structures that exist in society today.

Among young children, the family is of primary importance. Children are curious about their peers' families and, through experiences with other families, young children learn about different family structures and different family stories. Along with enhancing their knowledge of families, young children also develop attitudes about the differences in families that they observe. Therefore, discussions should occur at school about the variations in families and family stories, and about acceptance of all forms of families.

While all types of families today face many daily challenges, some families face unique situations. Early childhood professionals need to broaden their understanding of these situations. Specifically, as Derman-Sparks and Edwards (2010) suggest, teachers need to be thoughtful about, and understanding of, the daily challenges that some of the following **types of family structures** might be encountering:

- **Single-parent families:** This type of situation can be a result of choice or circumstance. Avoid the use of terms like "broken home" and "real home."
- **Blended and extended families:** Children have unique terms for various family members (e.g., my stepdad, "George," Papa). Whenever possible, all family members should be included in school activities.
- **Adoptive families:** Children have both adoptive and birth parents: Avoid using the terms "real parents" or "natural parents." Transracial adoptions bring questions from other children that should be addressed.
- **Foster families:** Children can be placed in foster care homes for a short period or for all of their childhood. This situation may engender a great deal of pain and confusion around issues of family. Attention should be given to the fact that these children have two equal families.
- **Conditionally separated families:** Could be for military reasons, medical reasons, transitional reasons, or incarceration. It's important to assure the child that although the family member is not around, he or she is still a member of the child's family.

Burt et al. (2010) offer 11 suggestions for including all types of families in an early education curriculum. Five of those suggestions are the following:

- Reflect on the language that is consistently used and if it includes all children. If it excludes some children, then do not use it
- Examine and use books that describe different types of families
- Make a picture display of the children, their families , and classroom staff
- Frequently discuss similarities and differences
- Have posters, puzzles, photos, and dolls around the classroom that depict different kinds of family structures

Figure 5.1 provides suggestions for welcoming children from all unique family structures at an early education center. Professionals who work

Digital Vision/Digital Vision/Thinkstock

Today's classroom diversity encourages and challenges collaboration.

Figure 5.1 Including All Families at School

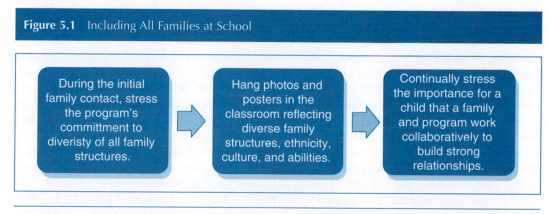

During the initial family contact, stress the program's committment to diveristy of all family structures. → Hang photos and posters in the classroom reflecting diverse family structures, ethnicity, culture, and abilities. → Continually stress the importance for a child that a family and program work collaboratively to build strong relationships.

Source: Derman-Sparks, L., & Edwards, J. O. (2010). *Anti-Bias Education for Young Children and Ourselves.* Washington, DC: National Association for the Education of Young Children.

with young children must know how to collaboratively assist families in making connections with community agencies and groups that can assist families who require social supports. Professionals need to develop partnerships with families and treat all individuals with respect and dignity, honor their values and beliefs, and provide support that will strengthen the family unit.

REFLECT AND APPLY EXERCISE 5.1

Understanding Families

Reflect

Understanding the concept of family is important to establish collaborative relationships. Conversations with a family's members can provide information about the family and the environment in which the child is being raised, along with general development information about the child. Additional information might emerge concerning the support system that surrounds the family. Ongoing communication will foster a collaborative relationship.

Apply

Engage in a conversation with another person about the person's family. Try to gain an understanding of that family and its rules, languages, rituals, and worldviews. What kinds of support systems does that family have to assist them?

Importance of Family Collaboration

An effective child-centered program must involve families as integral stakeholders in a collaborative program. In the opening scenario, families in the classroom have active roles in the program. For example, the grandfather of a child was involved in providing an observational beehive for the classroom. He helped the teachers arrange for a field trip to his orchard and apiary. In many classrooms families provide support to the teachers and engage in some student guidance. Other families are less involved in the program, but the "open door" policy of the teachers welcomes them into the classroom.

The caregivers of students who are in special education are involved in the Individualized Education Program (IEP) process. But they can also be formally engaged in the classroom and in their child's education. Thus, these families have multiple opportunities for shared decision making. For the families of children without disabilities, the active engagement of families can seem informal because it is not part of a required form of involvement; however, all forms of family engagement should be encouraged and valued by the teacher. Increasing opportunities for involvement for all families can change families' perspectives on their role as partners in the education of their children. Without a conscious effort to encourage and plan for ongoing family engagement opportunities, many families wait for the more traditional and less frequent formal events such as back-to-school nights, teacher-family conferences, and family meetings. Though these are also important events, they are limited in their potential for creating ongoing and frequent partnerships between families and teachers in the classroom that can have positive effects on student learning. In the program described in the opening scenario, family participation is fostered. The program reflects the idea, as suggested by Turnbull, Turnbull, Shank, and Leal (1995), that educational programs must increase opportunities for families to participate in their children's education to "ensure that families have an opportunity for sharing their important insights and goals" (p. 129).

REFLECT AND APPLY EXERCISE 5.2

Becoming Familiar With DEC

Reflect

The Division of Early Childhood (DEC), which supports services for families and professionals working with young children between birth and 5 years of age who have disabilities, has a website at: http://www.dec-sped.org. Visit this website.

Apply

Examine the information available on the DEC website. Think of three ways that you could use this information to collaborate with a family who has a child with a disability or with a professional working with a child in your class who has a disability.

Of course, all families do not choose to invest themselves in their child's education at the same level or to the same extent. Nonetheless, teachers need to communicate actively with all families and make the school classroom inviting to all families. The benefits of collaboration with families are transactive, that is, each individual connected with the classroom influences the others (Sameroff, 2010; Sameroff & Chandler, 1975; Sameroff & Fiese, 2000). Information is shared, and the process changes all the parties, including educators, other professionals, families, and students. More tangible benefits from a collaborative relationship with families, other professionals, and children include (1) having greater access to multiple perspectives, (2) gaining a deeper understanding of a family's support system, (3) improving a family's access to resources that can improve the educational services and outcomes of students with disabilities, and (4) increasing the families' role in decision making and responsibility of helping serve their children's needs (Friend & Cook, 2007; Turnbull & Turnbull, 2001).

Professionals must include families as equal partners in planning learning experiences.

©iStockphoto.com/asiseeit

The benefits of opening communication with the family are bi-directional. The families receive information about their child's program, open communication between teachers and families occurs, and a personal relationship between the families, teacher, and other professionals is established. The families feel more comfortable about and confident in the education that their child is receiving, and they view the educational progress of their child more positively. Beyond their understanding of the program and their confidence in the education their child is receiving, the hope is that the caregivers will become active partners in their child's education. Collaborating with families has potential positive effects on all parties.

LEARNING FOR ALL CHILDREN
Family Collaboration and Culture

Research has concluded that families play a critical role in the academic success of children (Bryk, Sebring, Allensworth, Luppescu, & Easton, 2009). Parents, guardians, and caretakers positively impact children's learning when the family, school, and community share in the educational responsibility of a child. Developing meaningful relationships with families recognizes the knowledge that families have about their children. However, some teachers have little understanding of or connection with the lives that children in their classrooms lead outside of school.

Eberly, Joshi, and Kozal (2007) suggest that teachers examine their own cultural biases about what makes a "good" parent. They emphasize that today's early education professional often works with children whose families are different from their own in composition, race, and socioeconomic status. As a result, professionals appear unsupportive of the families of children in their classrooms, as "not caring" instead of trying to understand from the parents' personal perspective why they appear to be unsupportive of their child's education program in the way that the teacher expects. Specifically, many professionals react with negative judgments about families' treatment of discipline, approach to bedtime, and attitude toward the value of education instead of trying to attribute differences to economic restraints that affect meeting basic family needs. Such negative attitudes impede the development of a trusting relationship between the school and family. Reciprocal relationships between families and professionals are important to both the school and the family. Formal and informal contacts with families can build sharing relationships that change both the school's understanding of the family and the family's understanding of their child's educational program. Familiarity reduces barriers between home and school and a collaborative relationship can eventuate. School staff should listen to families and learn about their child-rearing practices and their notions about education and the reasons for them, and gain an understanding of the family's hopes for the child. A deep understanding of the family's perspective and dialog about the differences between families and professionals can assist in building a more trusting and respectful relationship, which in turn will create a more comfortable learning environment for children.

Strategies for encouraging school-family collaborations include:

- Interact with family members during drop-off and pick-up times
- Communicate frequently with families
- Share information with families
- Encourage family-to-family networking
- Invite families to participate in school and classroom activities

As demonstrated in the opening scenario, implementing effective collaboration can involve many sources, including the students, family members, teachers, paraprofessionals, and administrators. Each stakeholder in a child's education brings to the system different skills and experiences, and the various participants can contribute to creating an effective collaborative learning community.

With commitments by individuals, an open, trusting, and collaborative relationship can be built. This relationship can create a classroom and school culture that fosters open communication and overcomes personal, professional, and organizational barriers that can obstruct such relationships. For example, from the parents' perspective, schools can be seen as unsupportive, resistant, and even malevolent. In response, the families' behaviors can range from anger to silence and withdrawal. The teacher might react to these behaviors by isolating himself and his classroom from the family. School personnel can exacerbate this negative teacher-family dynamic by interpreting the family's behaviors as indicating their general lack of interest in the child's education. The school personnel might then behave in a way that suggests that the family is one with whom it is simply too difficult to work (Harry, Klingner, & Cramer, 2007).

This division between the family and school and the teacher can inhibit a collaborative process and impacts the relationship among all parties: the family, the teachers, and the school administration. Ultimately, this situation affects the educational experiences of the students. Without changes in this dynamic, the level of collaboration that is sought will not occur (Lynch & Hanson, 2004). To transform such a culture requires the willingness and commitment of all parties. "The challenge is not whether to collaborate. Instead, it is whether, as professionals, we have the collective will to maximize our capacity to meet the needs of the students in our schools and foster their success" (Pugach et al., 2012, p. 27).

Collaboration With Professionals

Collaboration is a term often used by educators and other professionals. It is both a desired attribute for schools and organizations to incorporate into their structure, and a process in which all professionals are expected to engage. While a preferred approach in schools, collaboration is a concept that can be elusive to define, and creating an organizational culture that supports it can be difficult.

Friend and Cook (2013) define collaboration as "a style for direct interaction between at least two co-equal parties voluntarily engaged in shared decision making as they work toward a common goal" (p. 6). Embedded in this definition are several components necessary for fostering successful collaboration. The preference of each party must be equally considered when two or more parties engage in direct interactions that result in successful collaboration.

For a school or classroom to be considered an effective, collaborative learning environment, its structure must be premised on a flattened hierarchy where the interacting parties have co-equal status, engage in this voluntarily, and promote an interactive style of shared decision making. As illustrated in Figure 5.2, such an environment requires the following characteristics for collaboration to successfully occur (Friend & Cook, 2013, pp. 6–9):

- **The process is *voluntary*:** Collaboration in schools can be mandated, but unless the parties are willing participants who elect to operate in such a manner, collaboration will not occur.
- **There is *parity among participants*:** All participant interactions are valued, and there is equivalence among the collaborators when decisions are made.
- **Collaboration is *built on mutual goals*:** While participants may have different interests and/or professional backgrounds, all participants share common goals.
- **Collaboration depends on *shared responsibility* for participation and decision making:** All participants agree to actively engage in the process and be accountable for decisions made.
- **Individuals who collaborate *share resources*:** Each participant has resources to contribute in the collaborative process and in achieving common goals. Combining personal, professional, and tangible resources makes the best use of what is available and establishes unity among participants.

Figure 5.2 Collaborative Teaching Environment

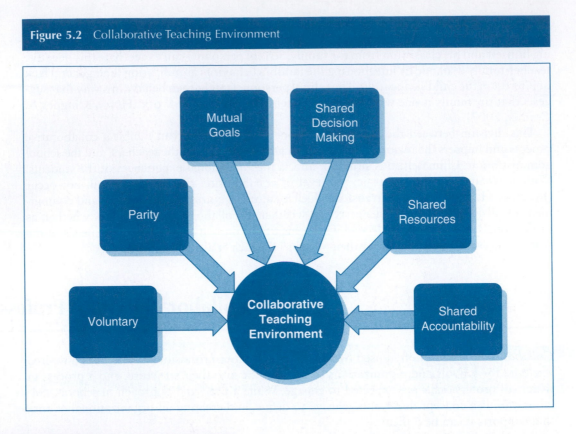

For successful collaboration to occur, team members must trust each other and share responsibilities and decision making.

©iStockphoto.com/asiseeit

Collaborative partnerships will grow when program staff value families as the primary source of information about the children with whom they work, and when families value the knowledge and personal characteristics of the program's staff members. This type of relationship will flourish only when there is reciprocal communication between the program and the families.

While collaborative environments are difficult to establish and maintain, they are rewarding for those who participate in them. The individuals establish a sense of shared trust among themselves. Moreover, the outcome for all participants is a common bond that fosters positive outcomes for children as well as a sense of community and belonging. When establishing a collaborative learning environment, the roles and responsibilities for the professional staff and their relationship with others in the classroom, such as paraprofessionals, families, support services personnel, must be considered. They participate in the classroom planning, and trust is established between and among these stakeholders. They are also personally and professionally committed to improving their skills in the classroom (Pugach et al., 2012). In the opening scenario about the beehive, four individuals were directly involved in organizing the classroom, planning for the students, and implementing the learning activity. Each of these individuals—the teacher, the grandfather, Sarah, and the principal—had a role in the success of the activity.

Turnbull et al. (1995, p. 127) detail the following three benefits from collaboration, which are also included in Figure 5.3.

- **Shared ownership of the problem definitions and solutions:** When all members of the educational team are included in decision making, they tend to take more responsibility for identifying and implementing solutions to problems.

- **Shared knowledge and expertise:** Team members with differing expertise have an opportunity to learn new skills from each other when they work together to solve problems.

- **Increased cohesiveness and willingness to work together on future projects:** Team members who work together tend to have greater persistence when tackling difficult tasks and continue to seek assistance in meeting the challenging needs of students.

The outcome for all participants in a collaborative activity is a common bond that fosters positive outcomes and a sense of community.

©iStock.com/mangostock

Figure 5.4 relates these three benefits of collaboration to the events happening in the opening scenario.

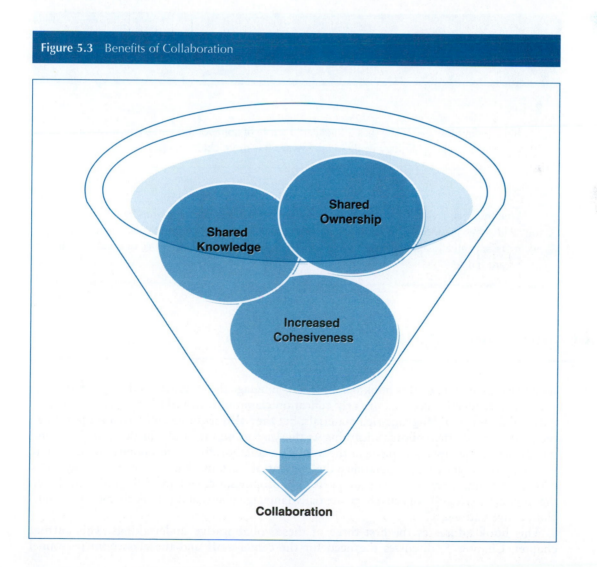

Figure 5.3 Benefits of Collaboration

Shared
Ownership

Shared
Knowledge

Increased
Cohesiveness

Collaboration

Figure 5.4 Benefits of Educational Collaboration Reflected in the Opening Scenario

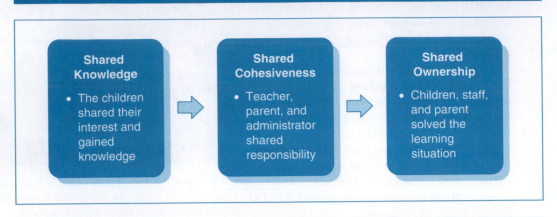

Source: Turnbull, A. P., Turnbull, H. R., Shank, M., & Leal, D. (1995). *Exceptional Lives: Special Education in Today's Schools*. Englewood Cliffs, NJ: Merrill/Prentice Hall.

REFLECT AND APPLY EXERCISE 5.3

Technology and Collaboration

Reflect

Think about how technology has influenced the role of collaboration. In some ways collaboration is easier with technology while in other ways it is more challenging.

Apply

What impacts have the Internet, e-mail, instant messaging, cellular phones, conference calling, and other technological advances generally had on collaboration? Which technological advances specifically affect educators and which ones can be used to improve our collaboration in and around schools?

Collaboration and Language-Rich Classrooms

As previous chapters of this book demonstrate, language development is the foundation for social and academic success. For early education classrooms to yield high-quality language outcomes, they need language-rich materials, but they also require team-based support from the staff to guide the children's learning as they use those materials. Justice (2004) recommends that professionals implement the following collaborative undertakings into designing their classroom activities to maximize the amount of learning that can occur: (1) develop a classroom team, (2) create a team-supported philosophy statement, (3) collaboratively design the physical space, (4) collectively create daily language plans, and (5) jointly monitor adult-child conversations.

This book addresses the first three of these collaborative undertakings. This current chapter, Chapter 5, discusses the need for the center staff and the classroom personnel to develop classroom teams that collaboratively design physical spaces for children. Additionally, Chapter 7 will present information on the need for carefully planned lessons. Finally, Chapter 8 will examine strategies that adults can use to engage children in collaborative conversations. Therefore, this chapter will discuss the remaining two collaborative characteristics needed to create a language-rich preschool environment: creating a team and developing a philosophy.

Creating a Team

A classroom should consist of a *team* of adults who support the children's activities. This team includes every adult involved with the children's education: the classroom teacher, assistants, special education personnel, and a family representative. The team's overall purpose is to monitor the curriculum activities to ensure that responsive adult-child interactions are used and that children are continually motivated to produce higher level outcomes. Just one teacher and one aide alone cannot successfully achieve this purpose when they are working with 15 to 20 children (Justice, 2004). As a result, while the teacher is usually the one who facilitates the team's activities, the entire team must commit to active involvement in providing systematic and consistent language-rich activities.

Developing a Philosophy Statement

A **philosophy statement** consists of a set of principles that defines the beliefs that the adults in the classroom put into practice every day. It typically consists of the following three components: what is important to learn, how it will be acquired, and why it is important (Justice, 2004). The principles that comprise the philosophy should be collaboratively decided upon and used to derive the classroom's operating principles.

The philosophy statement for a language- and literacy-rich classroom should provide the team's (1) definition of what the staff means by language and literacy development, (2) statement of why language and literacy experiences can develop in a playful manner, and (3) how the staff will specifically support language and literacy development through natural preschool classroom activities. Philosophy statements should be written in practical, everyday terms to ensure that all of the adults working in the classroom have a uniform understanding of the philosophy's components. Spending the time to create a philosophy statement guarantees that everyone working with the children will approach classroom activities mindful of the overall goal of enhancing linguistic and literacy skills.

Co-Teaching/Co-Partnering

The classroom in the opening scenario has a general educator, a special educator, and a paraprofessional aide. The general educator and special educator are both credentialed teachers who have several years of experience working in prekindergarten through third grade. The special educator possesses a teaching credential in high-incidence disabilities such as learning disabilities and early childhood special education that qualifies her for working with preschool students with disabilities. The paraprofessional aide has 2 years experience with young children both with and without disabilities. All three individuals have been a part of this program, and this year is their third year together.

Several factors came into play as the professional staff decided their mutual roles. For example, this particular classroom exhibits considerable diversity. Included in the student population are several students who receive special education services, and an Individualized

©iStock.com/vgajic

Collaboration with support personnel is vital when working with young children and their families.

Education Program (IEP) guides the educational program for these students. With these children with disabilities in the classroom, it is important for the team to work together on a daily basis to determine the particular roles each teacher will assume, how the children will be grouped, what co-teaching models will be incorporated in the classroom, and how educational decisions will be made.

Two additional factors need attention as well. First, what role will the paraprofessional assume in the planning and implementation of the educational program? Second, how will specific support services personnel, for example, therapists and other intervention specialists, be integrated into the program?

Each co-taught classroom requires attention to certain factors to be effective. First, it is important to recognize the skills that each professional can contribute to the planning and implementation of an effective educational program. While the instructional roles of the professional staff might differ because of training and background, the professional staff shares decision-making responsibilities. Their active engagement in instruction ensures that their specialized training can be incorporated into the learning environment, including adapting approaches to meet specific needs of particular students. By capitalizing on the professional strengths of two or more teachers, the classroom is better able to accommodate the needs of all the students. "Co-teaching allows teachers to respond effectively to the varied needs of their students, lowers the teacher-student ratio, and expands the professional expertise that can be directed to those needs" (Friend & Cook, 2013, p. 165).

Jupiterimages, Creatas Images/Creatas/Thinkstock

When working with larger groups of children with diverse abilities, co-teaching is necessary.

Second, the paraprofessional aide in this model classroom plays a central role. The traditional model for aides is one of support, with the aide often used in clerical roles. In this particular classroom, however, the role is expanded. The aide is expected to contribute to the planning of the program and, under the direction of the two credentialed teachers, to assume roles in working with individual and small groups of students. The paraprofessional aide is actively engaged in the classroom and a key stakeholder in its overall culture.

Friend and Cook (2007) offer a rationale for developing a co-teaching model. First, they see co-teaching as an effective way to provide robust and effective instruction to the diverse learning needs of students. They state that "the driving force for creating co-teaching programs between general education teachers and special educators or related services personnel is to support the students who have [an] IEP, and co-teaching should result in direct instructional and social benefits for these students" (p. 118).

A second reason for incorporating a co-teaching model is making curriculum and instruction available to all students. The collective expertise of the general and special educator, supported by intervention professionals and the paraprofessional aide, can provide all students with developmentally appropriate curricula. Specifically tailored instruction and curriculum will be constructed to meet the particular needs of all students. Third, in a co-teaching model, students with disabilities in prekindergarten through third grade are placed in the general education classroom. As a result, these students are not separated from their peers. As such, the co-teaching model eliminates the "stigma associated with students leaving their general education classrooms and going to a separate place to receive special instruction" (Friend & Cook, 2007, p. 119).

Finally, co-teaching provides teachers with collegial support. Shared decision making, planning, and implementation allows teachers to feel secure that they have support. They no longer feel the pressure of "having to know everything."

Friend and Cook (2013) present six models of co-teaching. These models are largely classroom structures for implementing direct instruction. As such, they can be implemented in classrooms where a significant portion of the instruction is completed in "teacher-as-leader" settings. Each model has its advantages and the model that best fits a program is largely determined by the match between the professional backgrounds of the teachers and the learning needs of the students. The six models are illustrated in Figure 5.5 and are described below:

Figure 5.5   Models of Co-Teaching

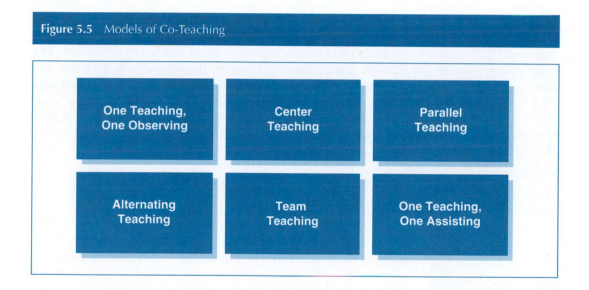

One Teaching, One Observing

In the **one teaching, one observing** model, one teacher assumes primary responsibility for delivering the lesson. The second teacher's responsibility is observing individual students or small groups of students. In this model, data can be gathered on student behaviors, the interactional patterns among students and with the teacher. One potential difficulty with this approach is that one professional could easily become relegated to assistant status, and the person's role in that situation would be diminished. An advantage to the approach is the ability to develop ongoing classroom data on students. These data could offer important information on the effectiveness of teaching over time.

Center Teaching

Center teaching occurs when both teachers are actively involved in instruction. Each assumes responsibility for planning and teaching a portion of a lesson. This approach requires planning and coordination. There is shared responsibility, and the specific roles of the participants are planned ahead of time. This arrangement requires transition time while children move from one center to another.

Parallel teaching allows for a lower child-teacher ratio during instruction.

Parallel Teaching

Teachers involved in **parallel teaching** each have a group of children that they teach. The lessons that each teacher provides are similar and are planned together, and each teacher remains with his or her group for additional lessons. The advantage of this format of collaboration is that it reduces child-teacher ratio, because each teacher instructs only half of the students. It also assumes that both teachers are equally skilled in the topic presented.

Alternating Teaching

The **alternating teaching** approach is structured around two groups of different sizes. A larger group is paced differently than a smaller group that needs additional information, slower pacing, pre-teaching, or a different curriculum. The larger group receives faster-paced, more intense instruction. In other words, over time the classroom has two different groups and the students participate in parallel lessons that take place in the same classroom. One caution is that this model can easily transform into a "class within a class" model. One class is the general education class, while the other is the special education class. The small groups should also be flexible, allowing students to move across groups as their needs change.

Teaming

In **teaming**, both teachers are involved in planning and implementing the teaching duties. They share instruction and usually teach the students in a large group. The teachers, however, may divide up tasks. For example, one may present the initial content, while the other demonstrates by modeling the concept or procedure. Alternatively, one teacher may elaborate on a point that was made during a discussion using realia or objects from real life, that could include maps, pieces of art, pictures, or other teaching materials that relate to the topic being addressed. The two teachers are located in the same room and circulate independently throughout. This approach requires careful planning to coordinate the dual roles, and on an individual level it requires considerable trust and commitment that each teacher is continually keeping track of what the other teacher is doing while also attending to the children.

Team teaching involves both teachers planning and implementing the teaching responsibilities.

One Teaching, One Assisting

In the **one teaching, one assisting** model, one teacher assumes the major responsibility for the instruction while the other teacher provides support. This particular model requires little joint planning because one teacher is charged with the responsibility of planning and implementing the lesson. The other teacher can circulate around the room and attend to students who might be having challenges. This particular model has several inherent problems. One teacher can easily become the permanent assistant if the model is used too often, as the assistant is less involved in the classroom (Friend & Cook, 2013, pp. 168–175).

REFLECT AND APPLY EXERCISE 5.4

Analyzing a Joint Position Statement

Reflect

   Visit the NAEYC website: http://www.naeyc.org. Under *Position Statements,* find the Joint Position Statement on the inclusion of children with disabilities with the Division on Early Childhood (DEC), an organization assisting families and professionals working with young children with disabilities. Review that joint NAEYC/DEC position statement.

Apply

   Choose a recommendation in the NAEYC/DEC Joint Position Statement that interests you. Share it with another student and explain the reasons why you chose it. Describe to the student how that recommendation could be demonstrated at an early education center.

In the classroom described in the opening scenario, the teacher and paraprofessional aide have implemented a center teaching model, which involves co-planning among the adults, who take preplanned roles for working with students in their particular station or center. The students also appear to be engaged and actively participating in projects that interrelate and connect to a particular theme. The adults circulate from one center to another and have a good deal of choice in what they will pursue, with whom they will work. Students are asked to share their plan with one of the adults in the room, and they then go to the particular center that addresses their needs, complete their task, and evaluate their progress with the support of an adult. In this room arrangement, collaborative planning and evaluation is a key component for all students learning.

Reciprocal Relationships

Irrespective of the model used for instruction, if a classroom or school is committed to implementing a classroom built on a culture of collaboration, a strong interpersonal foundation is needed to support reciprocal relationships between families and the staff. In such an environment, all the stakeholders must be continually aware of each other's ability to interact with children in certain content areas and their instructional skills (Friend & Cook, 2007). All families also need to be valued as teachers. Variations in a classroom can include children from various backgrounds and abilities, with families and community stakeholders who represent different cultures and varying views on childrearing and the role of education. These families and stakeholders may well have had different experiences with schools. However, a common factor that must emerge among all parties is their overarching goal of creating an effective learning environment for all children.

   Once again, effective communication is an essential component of reciprocal relationships and collaboration (Friend & Cook, 2007, 2013; Pugach & Johnson, 1995; Pugach et al., 2012). Effective communication includes the ability to listen and communicate with one another. Listening is important for establishing interpersonal rapport with others. By listening, the individual demonstrates concern for the speaker and shows his or her intent to understand what is being said.

Through the acquisition of funds of knowledge (Moll et al., 1992), as described in Chapter 1 of this text, teachers use home visits and interviews to learn from families what activities students participate in outside of the classroom. Moll et al. found that barrio families and children engaged in activities focusing on agriculture and mining, economics, household management, science, medicine, and religion. Additionally, families in rural areas knew a great deal about the cultivation of plants, animals, ranch management, mechanics, carpentry, masonry, electrical wiring, and medical remedies. By using this information, teachers were able to abandon the classroom drill and skill approach to learning that is often unsuccessful with many working-class and poor students, and instead involves their students in thoughtful learning activities that related to the familiar and socially meaningful tasks they engaged in at home.

Some strategies that contribute to teachers obtaining knowledge about the students and their families and construct activities in the classroom that are meaningful might include:

1. Making sure that students' learning activities are linked to family, home and community.

2. Engaging in ongoing parent education so parents can help their children and know more about their child's educational program.

3. Inviting family members to come into the school and share information about their home and community activities, and then relating those activities to academics.

4. Implementing ways to support students' informal home language and link it to standard English.

5. Tailoring the curriculum to the particular needs, interests, and learning styles (see Chapter 2) of individual students.

Through a reciprocal relationship based on funds of knowledge, information is transmitted with and without words. Skillful use of verbal and nonverbal behaviors is essential in successfully communicating attitudes necessary for establishing and maintaining positive collaborative relationships with families and for establishing a learning environment that becomes a tool to support student learning (Friend & Cook, 2007, p. 218).

In the classroom in the opening scenario, there are three important groups that are committed to collaboration. Each group has a role in how the classroom conducts its primary task of ensuring that the students learn, and while the membership of the groups differs, individual players can fill roles in other groups.

©iStock.com/asiseeit

Family and community collaboration builds stronger learning activities.

One group is comprised of the school's teachers, paraprofessional aides, and administrators. This group is charged with the actual planning and implementing of the instructional experiences in the classroom. The second group is comprised of the various children. While the classroom organization is established and governed by the teachers, in a child-centered classroom the children play important roles in determining the direction of the class through their child-initiated projects. A third group is composed of family and community members, such as Sarah's grandfather in the opening scenario. This group of individuals must be encouraged to provide information on particular home and community activities and also to share the expertise of their daily activities that provide the foundations for the children's learning.

Each group is part of a network of groups that are organized as part of the community or social environment. In such an environment, a structure must be established (Gallagher, LaMontagne, & Johnson, 1994). The concept of mutual and reciprocal relationships is at the heart of such an environment, and a structure must be established in which individuals feel welcome and their contributions valued. This process is dynamic, with all individuals, including family members, playing critical roles in determining the outcome of the partnerships. In such a partnership, one has to contend with dynamic change in that families, children, and community partners change, but the culture of cooperation and collaboration is stable. A program cannot mandate collaborative relationships and mutual relationships among all

iStockphoto.com/fstop123

Family-to-family collaboration can have a profound impact on all parties involved.

stakeholders, and establishing a programmatic commitment does not guarantee that groups will work together. However, barriers to collaboration and reciprocal relationships can be overcome and result in enhanced learning for all the children involved. Figure 5.6 provides NAEYC's guidelines for supporting successful family and professional collaboration.

Figure 5.6 NAEYC's Statement on Developing Collaboration Between Programs and Families

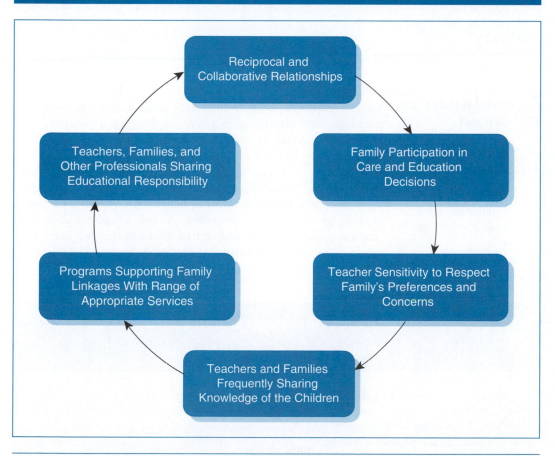

Reciprocal and Collaborative Relationships

Family Participation in Care and Education Decisions

Teachers, Families, and Other Professionals Sharing Educational Responsibility

Teacher Sensitivity to Respect Family's Preferences and Concerns

Programs Supporting Family Linkages With Range of Appropriate Services

Teachers and Families Frequently Sharing Knowledge of the Children

Source: Copple, C., & Bredekamp, S. (2009). *Developmentally Appropriate Practices in Early Childhood Programs Serving Children From Birth Through Age 8.* Washington, DC: National Association for the Education of Young Children.

Chapter Summary

HOME AND COMMUNITY CONNECTIONS

Collaborating With Families and Professionals

With your child, visit the local library and talk with the librarian about programs and resources aligned with your child's interest.

Although challenging, fostering collaboration between and among stakeholders is an important goal of co-partnering relationships and ultimately essential to creating a positive, supportive, and collaborative school culture. Such a culture creates learning opportunities for students, families, and teachers alike, and it fosters reciprocal relationships that benefit students. Friend and Cook (2013) highlight the concept of collaboration and parity among stakeholders, and the benefits of a shared decision-making process for all concerned. As this chapter has shown, authentic collaboration and shared decision making can occur when stakeholders are brought together as meaningful partners.

CHAPTER 5 FIRST-PERSON INTERVIEW
All Kids Have Very Special Needs

I may teach children with disabilities, but my children are no different than any other children. They may have some special needs, but that really does not make them different from other children. All children have special needs, and we need to recognize those needs and address them. If children are interested in something, they are going to learn about it because with young children it's all about what is relevant to them.

Katrina Jones

Early Childhood Inclusion Teacher, Los Angeles, CA

All children want to learn. I see that every day. For example, today we were just getting ready for a math lesson that I had prepared and, suddenly, it became very windy outside. Three children who were standing near the door, two typically developing children and one atypically developing, started jumping up and down and laughing and pointing. I went over to where they were and saw that they were watching all the flowers fall down from the tree on the playground. Instead of just commenting on what they were observing and calling them over to the table for my planned small group math lesson, the collaborating teacher and I agreed that I should take my small group outside for the math lesson. I gathered up some paper, glue, and crayons and we went outside.

I had the children collect flowers and glue them to the paper. We counted each child's flowers and then talked about who had more and who had less. After that, we returned to the classroom, and I wrote on each paper the following: "The wind blew the flowers off the tree. I collected _____ of them." Each child filled in the corresponding number in the blank space and read the sentences.

Although I have only been at this school for four weeks, the general education preschool staff is wonderful. I already feel as if we have all bonded. I hope it stays that way. I think it will because the beginning of the school year is always the hardest, and ours has gone smoothly so far. They treat my preschoolers with disabilities exactly the same way that they treat their own students. They don't let them get away with anything, and they seem so comfortable having them as part of the class . . . and so do their children.

It's interesting because we have begun talking about how some of the modifications for learning that I use for my students might also assist some of their students. In particular, one of my students uses a "squeeze ball" to calm himself, and yesterday my partner teacher asked if we could try and see if one of the general education students could also use the ball. I said that I thought it was a great idea, and that perhaps my student could show the student how to use it. In my mind, I was thinking how good my student would feel seeing someone else doing the same thing as he is doing. This will ensure that students with disabilities feel as if they are part of the class. Plus, general education children do not have to feel left out and say, "Why does he/she use the ball and we don't?"

I think the most important practice that my partner teacher and I have is that we share everything with each other. I let the staff know everything about the special needs that my students have, and the general education teacher makes sure that we know about the special needs that general education students have. After all, they are all kids, and every kid has some special need. We all work together like a family, both the staff and the children, and that's the way it should be.

Student Study Site

Visit the Student Study Site at **www.sagepub.com/selmi** to access additional study tools including mobile-friendly eFlashcards and links to video and web resources.

Key Terms

alternating teaching

center teaching

collaboration

one teaching, one assisting

one teaching, one observing   reciprocal relationships

parallel teaching   teaming

philosophy statement   types of family structures

Useful Websites

Division for Early Childhood: http://www.dec-sped.org

NAEYC for Families: http://families.naeyc.org

Parents Helping Parents: http://www.php.com

Reflective Question

Think back to classes that you have been in that have been collaboratively taught. Describe the procedure used and what you liked about it or did not like about it. If you have not had a collaboratively taught class, imagine what one of your classes would be like if more than one person taught it. What do you think you would like about it and what would you not like?

PART II

Planning and Designing a Classroom for Learning Through Play

Part I presented information on using developmentally appropriate play activities with young children to enhance early learning skills. Language and literacy skills can develop when children collaboratively produce pretend peer play narratives and explore their environment. Enhanced language and literacy skills influence children's future social and academic success.

Part II now examines strategies that adults can implement to design high-quality classroom settings that engage all children in self-motivated learning activities. Part II begins with Chapter 6, which explains general classroom organizational practices that create an effective learning environment, such as developing schedules, forming groups, and managing classroom activities. Strategies for designing high-quality learning centers that integrate play activities and early learning standards are examined in Chapter 7. Chapter 8 then presents techniques that adults can use when guiding children to engage in activities that reflect their highest level of learning. Finally, Chapter 9 explores the implementation of methods for continual observation and data collection that monitor children's abilities while they are involved in natural learning activities. Through organized settings that are tailored to address individual needs, all children can be guided through play activities in which learning standards are integrated to achieve their highest level of learning.

In addition to the end-of-the-chapter activities that are similar to those in Part I, each chapter in Parts II and III includes suggested activities that can occur at home or in the community.

6 Planning for Effective Learning

PREPARING FOR MORNING "CIRCLE TIME"

©iStock.com/ktaylorg

Children begin arriving at this full-day preschool program at 7:45 a.m. They play at indoor play centers (e.g., art, sorting, puzzles, and language arts) until 9:00 a.m. During that time, they are offered breakfast. At 9:00 a.m. the door to the outdoor yard opens, and children may choose to play either at indoor centers or outdoor centers until 10:00 a.m. Two adults are stationed at outdoor centers; one supervises the art center and the fine motor center, while the other supervises the gross motor activities and water/sand play. Two other adults supervise the indoor centers. All children are expected to be signed in by their parents and playing by 9:30 a.m.

At 10:00 a.m., an adult announces that it is time to clean up and have "Circle Time." The children, who have become familiar with the classroom routine, begin putting their center items away with some coaching from the adults. Four children are playing indoors with a large floor puzzle on a carpeted area. They immediately begin to break up the puzzle and put it back in the box. They then move two tables off the carpet and to the side of the room. Next, one child goes over to a bookshelf, which is on the carpeted area, takes a pillow off of the shelf, and places the pillow on the carpet. The other three children push the bookshelf off the carpet over to the side where they put the tables. They then push the bookshelf a little more so that it goes under one of the tables. This leaves only one table remaining on the carpet and off to the side.

Once the carpet area began to be cleared, little pieces of tape can be seen on the carpet. After a while, children from indoors and outdoors walk over to the carpeted area, and each one sits on a piece of tape. An adult then comes over and joins them by sitting on the pillow. The "Circle Time" activities begin.

This scenario illustrates how young children can develop the necessary skills to modify their classroom so that effective transitions occur from one learning activity to another. The children had to learn these skills, and over time they became more proficient at independently performing them. Actually, as stated above, on the day of this particular observation one table remained on the carpeted area. Of interest is that the adult who was leading the Circle Time activity did not say anything about this omission. Later during Circle Time, when children were acting out a short play, they realized that the table was in their way and moved it. Such actions convey the feeling that these children had "equal ownership" in designing a classroom where effective learning could take place.

Effective learning can occur for all young children through careful planning. Specifically, this chapter addresses the following classroom planning questions:

> How do teachers create effective settings where children are self-motivated to learn?

> What strategies can be used for organizing daily activities that enhance children's independence?

> What are some techniques that develop effective interaction and create classrooms that are responsive to children's needs?

Effective Early Learning

©iStockphoto.com/timeles

Effective learning occurs during well-planned settings where guided interactions assist children in tailored learning activities.

Organizing classrooms so that effective learning occurs is a challenging undertaking. It requires the staff to work together and carefully think through the purpose or objective for each learning activity. Today, it is not enough for professionals to create an inviting learning environment; rather, each activity must be tailored with a meaningful learning purpose for each student. In classrooms with children who are learning English as their second language, attention must be given to their unique linguistic needs. The same attention to differentiation must be addressed for children with special needs. Children who have transient home lives further require activities that will enhance their feelings of security and self-esteem.

Play generates an environment for early learning. Therefore, classrooms should not be designed to separately address play activities in one context and language, literacy, and other academic skills in another. All skills can be equally enhanced through the use of carefully planned developmental practices (Copple & Bredekamp, 2009). The following are four proven ways, some of which have already been presented in Part I of this book, in which play impacts multiple developmental areas of young children and provides a foundation for successful learning (Elkonin, 1977):

- *Play impacts children's motivation.* Play is the first context where children demonstrate the capability of delaying their gratifications through negotiating and sustaining a pretend enactment. For example, when children are pretending to shop at a market, one child will quietly wait while the "checker" is adding up the merchandise. Most children are eager to participate in playful activities and will typically seek out ways to prolong such activities on their own.

- *Play facilitates cognitive decentering.* Through play activities, children learn to take on another person's perspective and think and talk about that person's thought processes. As children's language develops, their abilities increase to negotiate, coordinate, and sustain play activities with their peers. Chapter 1's opening scenario demonstrates how two boys negotiate and coordinate their pretend activities to remove the "dangerous materials" from a home.

- *Play advances the development of mental representations.* When involved in play activities, children use their verbal abilities to develop abstract thinking and imagination. Children create complex pretend stories that have been known to last over a period of days.

- *Play fosters deliberate behaviors.* Play requires children to follow rules and consistently monitor their play activities and those of their partners. Children develop favorite play partners and tend to exclude children they believe will disrupt the smooth and cohesive development of their activities. They work hard to exclude children they know will not contribute to enhancing their play story.

Motivation, perspective taking, mental representations, monitoring, and following rules are certainly the key traits for academic success in later school years. Children who lack such skills have difficulty adapting in school. They typically have challenges when socially interacting with peers and teachers and in motivating themselves to learn about different content areas. To aid in the development of social and learning abilities, effective learning environments must focus on well-planned and guided-play activities that foster high-quality pretense and narrative development.

REFLECT AND APPLY EXERCISE 6.1

Play and Development

Reflect

Two 3-year-old children are standing at a water table splashing their hands in the green water. There is one water wheel, a number of funnels, and some plastic pipes.

Apply

Think about Elkonin's four ways that play impacts development that are listed above. How do they apply to the situation described above? How does this situation impact self-motivation? How does it impact cognitive decentering? How does it enhance mental representations? How does it foster deliberate behaviors?

The pressure to organize an early education program that will produce effective learning results is intense, to say the least. The organizational process can be divided into three areas that are vital to successful early learning: (1) the setting, (2) the activities, and (3) the interactions (Chien et al., 2010; see also Figure 6.1). This chapter primarily focuses on ways to design *effective learning settings.* Subsequently, Chapter 7 will address methods for creating *high-quality learning center activities,* and Chapter 8 will emphasize using *adult-guided interactions* that allow children to attain their highest learning level.

Creating Effective Learning Contexts

Part I affirms that classrooms should not discriminate between play activities and learning activities. Learning activities for young children should center on well-planned and playful child-centered activities that occur in both indoor and outdoor settings.

Figure 6.1   Snapshot of a Preschool Classroom

Settings	**Basics:** Napping, toileting, standing in line, cleaning up, or waiting
	Free Choice: Child selects what and where to play or learn (e.g., art, blocks, play, or reading)
	Individual Time: Class works on project independently while teacher moves around to help
	Meals: Eating breakfast, lunch, or snacks
	Whole Group: Teacher-initiated activities (e.g., stories, songs, calendar, demonstrations, book readings)
Activities	**Aesthetics:** Art, drama, music
	Fine Motor: Stringing beads, building with Legos, cutting, coloring
	Gross Motor: Running, skipping, jumping, playing games, chasing
	Mathematics: Rote counting, one-to-one correspondence, skip counting, matching numbers to pictures, making graphs
	Letters and Sounds: Identifying letters, sounding out words, making letter-sound relationships, recognizing rhyming sounds
	Oral Language: Talking about story, telling stories, answering and asking open-ended questions
	Pre-Reading: Reading stories, identifying words, recognizing meaning in symbols and pictures, practicing class poem
	Read to: Teacher reads books and stories, talks about author, talks and asks questions about book
	Science: Child explores environment, uses science equipment, reads books/talks about animals, body parts, and life cycles
	Social Studies: Talking, reading, or engaging in activities about their world (e.g., neighborhood, school, farm, community)
Interactions	**Routine:** Teacher engages in routine caregiving (e.g., wipe child's nose)
	Minimal: Teacher uses warm or helpful physical contact or verbally answers child's bids but does not elaborate
	Elaborated: Teacher engages in some physical response (e.g., thumbs up, high five, frown) or acknowledges child's statement and responds
	Scaffold: Teacher (or more capable peer) does one-on-one work with child and builds on child's initiations, using visuals, concrete objects, and gestures to help child learn; teacher elicits responses and helps child expand thoughts
	Didactic: Teacher lectures, gives instruction, models, asks close-ended questions, or demonstrates, such as counting or saying the days of the week

Source: Chien, N. C., Howes, C., Burchinal, M., Pianta, R. C., Ritchie, S., Bryant, D. M., Clifford, R. M., Early, D. M., & Barbarin, O. A. (2010). Children's Classroom Engagement and School Readiness Gains in Prekindergarten. *Child Development, 81,* 1534–1549.

Getting Started

Learning for young children is an integrative process. Children do not just learn isolated mathematics skills or social studies skills. Instead, they learn these skills by participating in interesting experiences in which they are eager to learn. Therefore, classroom learning should be organized around comprehensive units, themes, or projects instead of isolated skills from competencies or standards. The following are examples of how a teacher could present learning activities if the children were ready and interested in learning about different types of shapes:

- **Projects:** Projects are in-depth investigations that either the children or the teacher initiates, and that are geared to finding out answers to child-developed questions and interests. For example, the children in a class could find a worm outside and begin to ask questions about the worm. The teacher and the children could then research information on worms and on insects and, while doing this, the teacher could engage the children in discussions about the different shapes of insects.

- **Thematic Experiences:** Thematic activities are organized learning activities where the teacher identifies the topic, but the lessons are a combination of teacher-directed activities and child-centered activities. For example, the teacher could organize thematic experiences around the topic of "the sky" with one of the objectives being to discuss the different shapes of objects in the sky, the moon can be a circle, stars consist of triangles, and clouds can be oval shaped.

- **Units:** Units are organized learning activities in which the teacher identifies a topic, determines the content of the units over a number of unified areas of learning, and instructs the children on important facts and concepts. For example, a teacher could design a learning unit around the topic of "shapes." Each week the teacher could focus on a new shape and children could be responsible for identifying objects that are that shape.

Whenever possible, the children should be involved in selecting learning topics. However, there are times when teachers might decide that a certain topic needs to be addressed for an important reason. Once the topic is decided upon, the children and adults can brainstorm together to come up with different activities that will assist children in learning specific skills. As activities are identified, they must be modified so that they address learning content from the following areas: language/literacy, math, social science/health, science, and creative arts. Part III of this book is dedicated to explaining strategies for integrating symbolic play and content information into developmentally appropriate activities.

Indoor and Outdoor Learning

Indoor settings should incorporate multiple home-like items that allow children to feel comfortable when transitioning from home to a daycare center or school environment. Fluorescent lighting should be diminished, and lighting from natural sources and lamps should be used whenever possible. Soft pillows, household plants, and pets (e.g., fishes, birds, and gerbils) placed around the classroom also contribute to a home-like feeling. The classroom furniture should be comfortable for small children and must be child-sized. Often, children's home furniture items can be purchased at garage sales or second-hand stores for reasonable prices.

The cultural backgrounds of the children in the class should be considered by furnishing the rooms with household items that are familiar to them. Asking children's parents for suggestions of where to purchase culturally specific items often contributes to home–school collaborative relationships and can result in families contributing items to the classroom that they no longer need at home. Having items from home in the classroom provides children with a great sense of pride for their family. It makes them feel safe being with who they are and celebrating their diversity. Children gain a sense of belonging. Figure 6.2 illustrates some indoor items that can be incorporated into a classroom to create a more home-like feeling.

Planning outdoor learning activities usually allows children to use natural materials, have larger spaces where they can move their entire bodies, and have fewer noise restrictions. As a result, children can focus more on their physical and social skills when participating in outdoor activities. Reggio Emilia programs encourage that the physical connection between the indoors and outdoors should be as broad as possible; it should foster easy and natural transitions by the children between the two areas. The opportunity to move within and across contexts

Figure 6.2   Indoor Home-Like Items

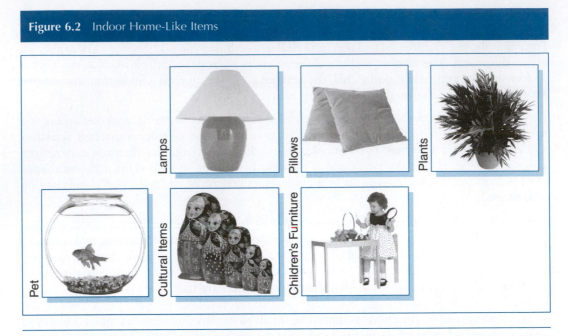

Sources: (Lamps) Hemera Technologies/PhotoObjects.net/Thinkstock; (Pillows) Hemera Technologies/PhotoObjects.net/Thinkstock; (Plants) NA/PhotoObjects.net/Thinkstock; (Pet) Comstock/Stockbyte/Thinkstock; (Cultural Items) Comstock Images/Stockbyte/Thinkstock; and (Children's Furniture) Ablestock.com/Ablestock.com/Thinkstock.

Creating an environment that has items from a home assists children in feeling comfortable at school.

further supports children's language development. Children can begin to understand that language is impacted by the context in which it is used. When they are outside they may feel a sense of freedom in raising their voices to represent their excitement for learning and use different vocabulary and language forms. When inside they may learn that they might need to lower their voices as they interact with one another and continue to learn new vocabulary to guide their play.

Teachers should strive to have their outdoor areas reflect the indoor activities and the indoor area reflect the outdoor activities. However, creating effective learning centers outdoors allows children to engage in some activities that cannot occur indoors. Many children lack outdoor experiences because of their long days away from home or because of the unsafe neighborhoods in which they live. Therefore, ample time must be set aside for children to engage in well-planned outdoor activities. Water play, mud play, sand play, and bubble play are all activities that offer opportunities for children to explore, investigate, experiment, and problem-solve. These activities contribute greatly to young children's cognitive, social, linguistic, and motor development.

Because of safety issues that exist today, young children are not as free to roam in the outdoors unsupervised by adults as children did in the past. Because outdoor activities are more limited today, Nelson (2012) has identified seven critical issues that are impacting young children's development:

- The absence of exercise that has resulted in an increase in obesity, heart disease, and diabetes
- The increased engagement with electronic toys and decrease in the amount of time spent interacting with peers in collaborative problem-solving activities

- The enhanced feeling that the outdoors is an unsafe place, and an increase in children's organized, adult-directed activities—sports, classes, and tutoring
- The decrease in interactions with nature and the feelings of peacefulness and wonder that can occur through exploring open spaces
- An unconnected feeling with neighborhoods, environments, communities, and local habitats
- Early education programs that focus more on the mental development of children's skills while overlooking the need for children to engage in independent, exploratory activities
- The increased number of young children who depend on medications so that they will not "misbehave" or can perform better and with more concentration.

Outdoor play is important because many children today do not have access to neighborhood areas or parks that they can go to and play with peers.

At all times the physical safety of the children should be at the forefront of every planned activity that will take place either inside or outside. The National Program for Playground Safety (http://playgroundsafety.org/standards/cpsc) provides suggestions, guidelines, and standards that all teachers should consider when planning activities.

Similar to the indoor learning centers, outdoor learning centers need to be tidy and well organized and have materials that are accessible and developmentally appropriate for all children. Center space should have boundaries that can be established simply by having a table with two or three chairs designating a specific interest area. The outdoor area can contain a dramatic play area, art center, block center, science center, swings and slides, bikes, trikes, and scooters, a space for children to run and chase each other, and space to be quiet, such as a book center. Some children love to take books into the playhouse or a tent to read.

Additionally, outdoor areas should have a designated area for large group meetings. Dancing, singing, reading books, problem solving, and sharing in creative productions should occur just as easily in outdoor large group meetings as they do indoors. Children can participate in fun and developmentally appropriate literacy activities outdoors (see Figure 6.3 for 10 suggestions).

Figure 6.3 Ten Simple Outdoor Literacy Activities

Painting With Water	Using rollers and large brushes, paint letters and words on a wall.
Outdoor Murals	Place butcher paper on a fence, wall, or sidewalk and have children attach objects that have a certain letter or sound.
Large Chalk Geometric Shapes	Draw large geometric shapes in a row some distance apart on sidewalk. Inside each shape is an action word. To get from one shape to the next and then to the end, read and do the activity of the word in the next shape.
Letter Hunt	Have buckets with a letter on them. Children need to go on a hunt for items that contain that letter.
Catagorize Hunt	Have children hunt for things that can be placed in a specific category—e.g., hard/soft, dry/damp, smooth/rough, smell/no smell, and firm/bends.

(Continued)

Figure 6.3   (Continued)

Sand or Mud Letters	Create mud or damp sand letters or words using alphabet cookie cutters (a set costs about $12).
Squeeze Bottle Writing	Make letters or words using squeeze bottles filled with water.
Car or Animal Wash Dramatic Play	Set up a center with instructions on how to wash a bicycle or stuffed animal.
Caterpillar Hopscotch	With chalk, draw a very hungry catepillar with names/pictures of foods in each circle. Children read the name when they jump into the square.
Treasure Hunt	Children pretend they are pirates and create a map to search for a hidden treasure.

Outdoor learning centers can provide multiple learning opportunities that indoor centers cannot provide.

Jupiterimages/BananaStock/Thinkstock

Perry (2001) suggests that benefits accrue from drawing a map of the outdoor areas and carefully planning the placement of the activities, similar to what would be done indoors. At all times, the areas should be monitored for children's use of activities, language, and imagination. For example, one preschool in California replaced a single-person slide and set of swings with a double-person slide and tire swings to encourage peer interactions and language development. Additionally, this program discovered through careful data collection that the sandbox area was not a very popular spot for children to congregate. The program was fortunate enough to secure funding to design and create a submerged sand area with a rim that was level with the ground. This modification allowed the children to more easily extend other activities into the sand area by putting wooden planks across that area and riding bikes or running over the planks. Instead of being a place just for digging, the sand area became an imagined lake, hole, cloud, freeway, and more. Figure 6.4 provides some general considerations to take into account when creating outdoor learning settings, and Figure 6.5 summarizes the benefits of using both indoor and outdoor areas for learning activities.

Rough-and-Tumble Play With Young Children

Play can become intense and vigorous, and yet still be beneficial to children's development. In the past, more aggressive types of physical play have been labeled as rough-and-tumble play, roughhousing, or horseplay. Teachers and parents often confuse this type of play with fighting and try to stop it because they believe that it will lead to an injury. Additionally, many opponents of this play state that early learning standards do not encourage such activities because they will lead to fighting. However, recent research has demonstrated many developmental benefits related to such play (Carlson, 2011a). The research has identified specific differences between this type of play and fighting, and those differences are summarized in Figure 6.6. Generally speaking, in rough-and-tumble play, children return for more play even

Figure 6.4 General Considerations for Outdoor Learning Areas

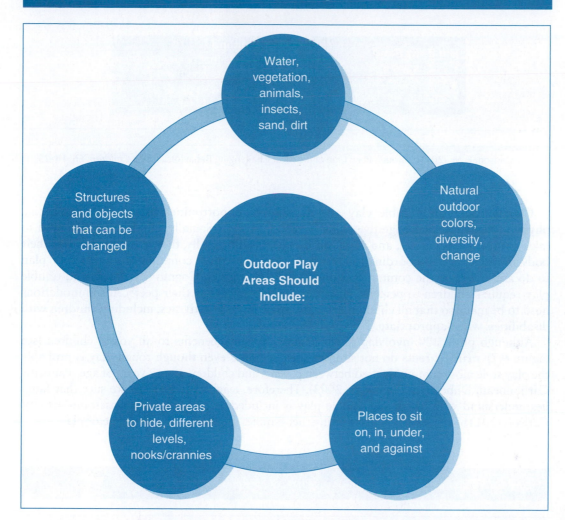

Figure 6.5 Benefits of Outdoor Learning Centers

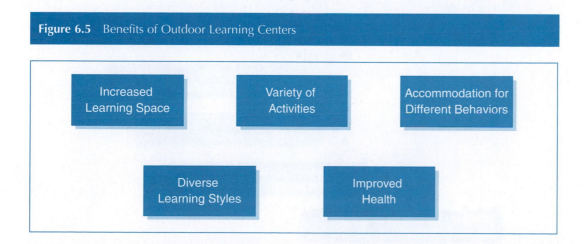

though the adult observers do not see it as play. By contrast, when children fight, they tend to get away from it, often in tears and asking for adult assistance.

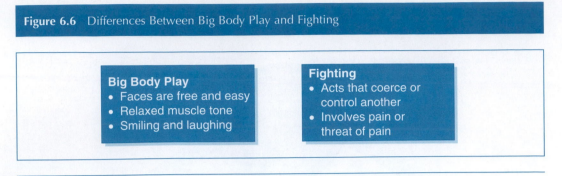

Figure 6.6 Differences Between Big Body Play and Fighting

Source: Carlson, F. M. (2011b). Rough Play: One of the Most Challenging Behaviors. *Young Children, 66,* 18–25.

Clearly, rough-and-tumble play affords children opportunities to expand their social, physical, language, and cognitive skills (Carlson, 2011a). Socially, children are required to take turns, infer, negotiate, and maintain friendships. Physically, they gain control over their body movements and coordination. Linguistically, they must communicate what they plan to do and interpret the communications of their play peers. Cognitively, rough-and-tumble play requires children to perceive and infer the movements of their peers. Accommodations need to be made so that all children can participate in these activities, including children with disabilities, when appropriate.

Although physically involving play can provide many benefits to all young children (see Figure 6.7), many parents do not support such activities even though rough play is probably the play style most commonly used between parents and children after 2 years of age (Paquette, Carbonneau, Dubeau, & Tremblay, 2003). Therefore, teachers need to make sure that families understand why rough-and-tumble play is included as an acceptable classroom activity. Carlson (2011b) suggests two ways to instruct families on the goals of this type of play:

Figure 6.7 Continuum of Young Children's Physical Development

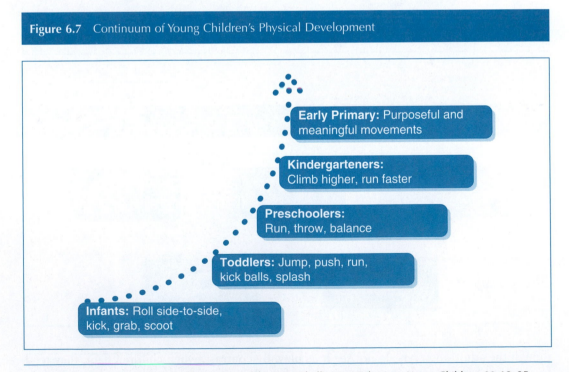

Source: Carlton, F. M. (2011). Rough Play: One of the Most Challenging Behaviors. *Young Children, 66,* 18–25.

- Provide families with a description of the activities that will take place and the justifications for those activities by creating a handbook for families. Also include how the children will be supervised.
- Show families photos of the children engaged in rough-and-tumble play activities. These pictures can go home in a class newsletter or be posted on the bulletin board near the room entrance where parents will see them.

Figure 6.8 provides suggestions for adults on strategies for designing successful rough-and-tumble activities.

Outdoor Learning and Disabilities

More and more, early education professionals are noticing the value of outdoor education. As mentioned in the *First-Person Interview* in Chapter 4 of this book, children appear to "talk much more with each other outside than they do inside." Studies are showing that hands-on, outdoor learning activities enhance children's physical skills, mental health, brainpower, and attention abilities (Gordon, 2013). These activities also assist in encouraging children's curiosity. Specifically, a growing number of teachers in Canada have found children's learning to improve when they are engaged in outdoor activities that require them to generate their own questions and explore for their own solutions. Additionally, teachers have noticed steady improvement in children's literacy and attention abilities.

Gordon describes remarkable developments made by a 4-year-old boy with autism who was included for at least an hour a day with 25 kindergarten children in **outdoor play activities**, which are well-planned learning environments that offer children opportunities to explore, investigate, experiment with, and problem-solve outdoor interests. Eventually, this child was observed gathering small sticks in a wheelbarrow, taking them to a place on the pavement, and then spelling out his name with the sticks: A-L-E-X. Additionally, other children with autism in the program, who appeared to be reluctant about getting their hands dirty at the beginning

Figure 6.8 Ways Teachers Can Support Big Body Play

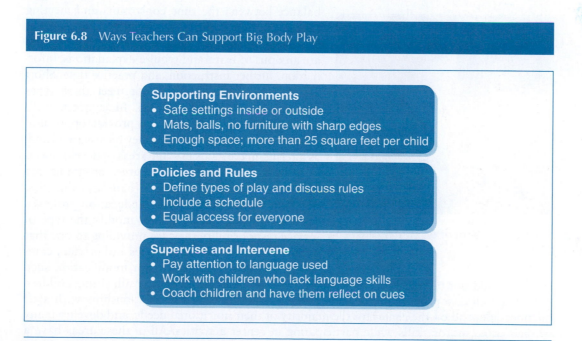

Supporting Environments
- Safe settings inside or outside
- Mats, balls, no furniture with sharp edges
- Enough space; more than 25 square feet per child

Policies and Rules
- Define types of play and discuss rules
- Include a schedule
- Equal access for everyone

Supervise and Intervene
- Pay attention to language used
- Work with children who lack language skills
- Coach children and have them reflect on cues

Source: Carlson, F. M. (2011a). *Big Body Play: Why Boisterous, Vigorous, and Very Physical Play Is Essential for Children's Development and Learning.* Washington, DC: The National Association for the Education of Young Children.

of the year, gradually became comfortable with "mucking about" in sand, paint, and water. Finally, the professionals also observed a more rapid increase in the occurrence of parallel play and a decrease in solitary play, along with an increase of muscle tone, balance, and strength. All of these skills relate to vital components of most early education curricula.

Again, outdoor centers do not require that programs invest thousands of dollars in materials and engage in special landscaping plans. Instead, local wood suppliers and hardware stores can typically provide materials for seats, benches, and activities. Teachers have been known to spend less than $1,000 to successfully create an engaging outdoor classroom for all children.

Creating Effective Schedules

Early education daily schedules for children up to 6 years of age can be designed around **half-day programs**, where children have the option of attending either a 3- or 4-hour morning or afternoon session, or **full-day programs**, where children attend for an entire day and that assume some responsibility for providing both education and childcare activities. However, with today's demands for high-quality activities, many half-day programs, are being asked to change to full-day programs. Further bolstering this trend is the fact that both parents in most families now work full-time. Additionally, many teachers in half-day programs express concern about not having adequate time to devote to all of the demands that contribute to high-quality learning activities. Young children continually make such appeals as: "Will you help me with . . . ," "I can't find the . . . ," "We want you to come over and . . . ," and "Look what I found! It reminds me of a . . ." Teachers must respond sensitively to such requests for meaningful learning to occur, but they often find it difficult to do so during a 240-minute (or 4-hour) day. In addition, taking the time to listen to children's questions and requests provides opportunities for teachers to engage in important oral discourse exchanges that can lead to ongoing language development. Finding a balance between the time constraints and meeting the needs of the children is difficult.

The number of parents dependent on all-day care continues to increase.

Effective programs seek to foster children who are anxious to learn and require explanations, information, further instruction, and practice time. Short half-day programs often cannot meet these types of demands of young children. In contrast, well-designed full-day programs can provide opportunities for children to apply what they have learned and, as a result, make gains in some areas of development.

In response to these pressures, programs are being asked to change from a half-day education program to a full-day care and education program. Such a change requires staff to modify the type of service responsibility they are providing to one that includes both education activities and primary caregiving for the children. A major modification such as this should not be treated lightly (Scales, Perry, & Tracy, 2012). After all, young children attending full-day programs will most likely develop attachment relationships with staff members, depend on the center for the majority of their nutritional needs, and develop many of their gross motor skills while participating in center activities. All of these areas have a major impact on a young child's overall social, emotional, cognitive, linguistic, and academic development.

©iStockphoto.com/MachineHeadz

A Sample Day

Generally, both half- and full-day programs should begin each day with a relaxed morning period where, as the children arrive, they are placed indoors engaging in comfortable interactions involving puzzle, book, or manipulative activities. This quiet period should include offering children either a light breakfast or a morning snack so that all children have a healthy start to their day. Once they have arrived, relaxed, and eaten, children should be encouraged to go outdoors to enjoy the fresh air, sounds, scents, and space so they can be refreshed to continue with their day. Some teachers are so committed to outdoor learning (see above) that they have the children outside during all types of weather conditions—sun, rain, wind, and snow.

As in the scenario at the beginning of this chapter, following a period of time outdoors, children should assist with tidying up the areas where they have played and then transition to the morning Circle Time activities. These activities should include large group songs, stories, sharing, plays, and classroom "business." Circle Time should be imaginative, fun, and short, not lasting more than 5 minutes for toddlers and 10 to 15 minutes for older children.

Following Circle Time, children are ready to participate in what should be considered their crucial learning time. This period, which should last for about one hour, involves activities that have been carefully prepared for children at the centers. During this time all staff members work with the children in a holistic manner by integrating play and content area skills into particular center activities. Additionally, children should be offered the opportunity to have a small snack and use the restroom. Following the play center activities, a set amount of time should be dedicated to having the children and adults clean up the areas. This is an ideal time for adults to observe and encourage peer-to-peer interactions. These peer-to-peer interactions support students' ongoing language development as they naturally exchange language in authentic learning contexts. They develop vocabulary and hear how language is produced and structured to communicate their actions, questions, and learning.

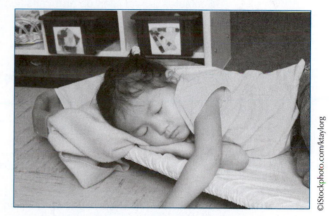

Children attending full-day programs are dependent on the program for many developmental needs.

Next, children should be brought together for a 15-minute **large group activity**, such as reading or acting out a story, learning a new song, or introducing and discussing a problem-solving situation. Following the large group activity, children attending a half-day program should be ready for dismissal. Children in a full-day program should have lunch, a nap or rest, and then follow a schedule similar to the morning for the remainder of the day, but be provided different center materials. Figure 6.9 outlines suggested schedules for 3- to 6-year-olds.

Posting a Schedule

Toddlers need predictable but flexible plans for the day. Having a regular routine for the day encourages autonomy by allowing children opportunities to independently start an activity, finish it, and transition to the next activity. Schedules should allow ample time for transitioning when children are separating from parents and participating in self-care activities (e.g., eating, toileting, sleeping). Giving young children enough time to participate in these important developmental activities for young children ensures more positive experiences and ensures effective learning of skills. A general sample of a toddler's schedule is provided in Figure 6.10.

Figure 6.9   Sample Schedules for 3- to 6-Year-Olds

	Full-Day Schedule	Half-Day Schedule
60 minutes	Arrival/Indoor activitie: Small group play, motor skills, book reading	Arrival/Indoor activities: Small group play, motor skills, book reading
30 minutes	Offer breakfast and restroom	Offer breakfast and restroom
45–50 minutes	Outdoor play	Outdoor play
10–15 minutes	Clean up and transition	Clean up and transition
15 minutes	Large group circle activities: Stories, songs, problem solving, "business"	Large group circle activities: Stories, songs, problem solving, "business"
60 minutes	Small groups/Indoor and outdoor centers/Offer snack and restroom	Small groups/Indoor and outdoor centers/Offer snack and restroom
15 minutes	Clean up and transition	Clean up and transition
30 minutes	Lunch	Departure (10 minutes)
40 minutes	Outdoor play	
15 minutes	Clean up and transition	
15 minutes	Large group share time	
60–90 minutes	Rests and naps	
60 minutes	Outdoor play/Offer snack and restroom	
15 minutes	Clean up and transition	
15 minutes	Large group circle time: Play and games	
60 minutes	Small group/Indoor and outdoor centers	
15–20 minutes	Final clean-up and transition	
10 minutes	Large group closing	
10 minutes	Restroom and prepare to go home	

Using Visual Schedules

Having a schedule posted in the room and referring to it throughout the days' activities assists children in becoming independent. These schedules can either be made commercially or by teachers, as illustrated in Figure 6.11. For a number of years, children with disabilities, such as an Autism Spectrum Disorder, and from diverse language backgrounds have benefited from visual schedules. A **visual schedule** is a line of pictures, objects, and words

Figure 6.10 Sample Schedule for 2-Year-Olds

	Full-Day Schedule
60 minutes	Arrival/Indoor activities/Wash hands/Breakfast/Diapers and toilet
15 minutes	Transition to circle time
10–15 minutes	Circle time
10–15 minutes	Clean up and transition
45 minutes	Outdoor and indoor centers/Check diapers and potty
20 minutes	Clean up/Transition
10 minutes	Story time
30 minutes	Art activity and play
10 minutes	Hand washing
30 minutes	Lunch/Check diapers and potty
90–120 minutes	Naps
30 minutes	Diapers and toilet/ Wash hands/Snack/ Transition to circle time
10 minutes	Circle time
10 minutes	Transition
45 minutes	Outdoor centers/Check diapers and potty
10–15 minutes	Clean up/Transition
10 minutes	Story time
10 minutes	Transition
45 minutes	Indoor centers
10–15 minutes	Clean up and transition
10 minutes	Check diapers and potty
10 minutes	Closing circle time

that represent each major transition during the day (see Figure 6.12). Today, the daily use of visual schedules can benefit children who have challenges with the sequential processing of events (i.e., learning the order of events) or those who have not yet been expected to follow a schedule of events.

The pictures can be displayed either from top-to-bottom or from left-to-right. For very young children, actual pictures might be used, and the printed words for the activities can be displayed for children who have begun reading words. The following is a list of the different symbolic levels that can be used on a picture schedule depending on the child's visual stage:

- **Object Stage:** Use of the actual objects can be used to communicate what the child will be doing. For example, if the child chooses to begin the day by going to the manipulatives center, an actual Lego might be placed on the schedule to represent that center.

Figure 6.11   Classroom Schedules

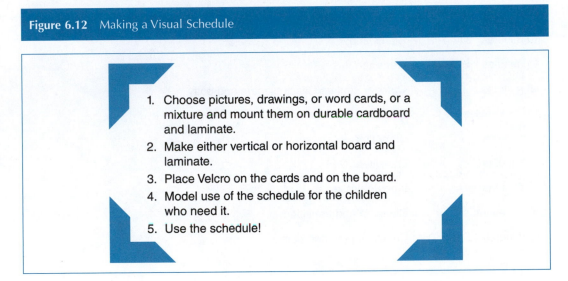

| Teacher-Made Classroom Schedule | Commercially Made Classroom Schedule |

Sources: ©iStock.com/JillianSuzanne; ©iStock.com/Kameleon007.

Figure 6.12   Making a Visual Schedule

1. Choose pictures, drawings, or word cards, or a mixture and mount them on durable cardboard and laminate.
2. Make either vertical or horizontal board and laminate.
3. Place Velcro on the cards and on the board.
4. Model use of the schedule for the children who need it.
5. Use the schedule!

- **Photograph Stage:** A real picture of the centers that the child chooses to visit can be placed on the schedule. If the child is going to an outdoor art center, then a picture of that center is placed on the schedule.
- **Symbolic Picture Stage:** Hand-drawn or commercially produced pictures can demonstrate where the child will go next. When the child is ready to go home, a drawn picture of a backpack is placed on the schedule.
- **Text Stage:** A written word for the center is used to communicate the child's schedule. For example, if the child is going to the socio-dramatic play center that is a Flower Shop, then the words "Flower Shop" are printed on the card. Children are encouraged to independently determine meaning from the text during this stage. Additionally, for second language learners, placing labeling strategically around the room can continue to support their English language development.

Figure 6.13 summarizes key elements that comprise an effective learning environment for young children.

Figure 6.13 Effective Learning Involves Careful Planning

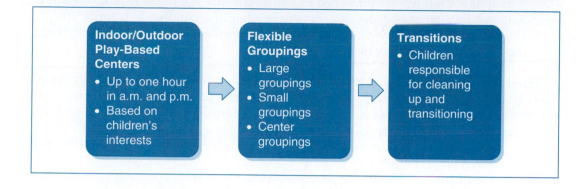

Indoor/Outdoor Play-Based Centers
- Up to one hour in a.m. and p.m.
- Based on children's interests

Flexible Groupings
- Large groupings
- Small groupings
- Center groupings

Transitions
- Children responsible for cleaning up and transitioning

Teaching Transitions

In most programs, certain times of the day are more stressful than others. These times tend to focus around major transitions when children can lose focus and become distracted. Typically, the challenging times of the day are:

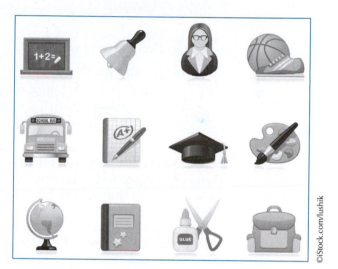

Visual schedules assist many children in understanding the sequence of their daily expectations.

- **Arrival:** Children often come to school at different times because some walk, some are driven, and others arrive on buses. Also, some children come early because they participate in a breakfast program before school. As a result, many interruptions occur during the arrival time. Having a variety of opportunities to participate in unstructured quiet activities that encourage socializing, settling down, and gradually participating at their own rate in the classroom activities helps provide a purposeful learning environment amid the interruptions.

- **Eating Time:** Prior to eating times, children are typically restless. Gathering them together to read a short story or discuss something that has happened during the morning's activities is an excellent way to settle them down. Additionally, talking about what they need to remember when transitioning to eating can assist in avoiding problems. The time before eating is a nice time to talk about the activities that the children will participate in during the remainder of the day, further providing an opportunity for teachers to model the language of the activities (i.e., vocabulary).

- **Cleaning Up:** After children are finished with an activity, they need to be responsible for cleaning up. They need to be given a warning prior to cleaning up. One successful way of having children focus on cleaning up is to have one child from each activity give a brief summary of what they have just accomplished. Having that break between the activity and cleaning up appears to focus children on the fact that the time for the activity is up.

- **Departure:** Every day should end on a happy note. To ensure it does, children should have ample time to wind down before they go home. Again, gathering the group together with enough time to talk about what they did that day, or what might happen the next day, is a good method for calming them down. Additionally, children may want to share information on what they will do after school during their afternoon or evening. Staff can also share what activities they do outside the school day. Children are interested in knowing about the home lives of the adults with whom they spend the day. Finally, reading the children a favorite story is always a good way to unwind and end the day so they are calm when their family members come to pick them up.

Transition activities should be enjoyable learning opportunities for children. They should never be tricked into transitioning; they need to be involved in the process. Therefore, teachers should seriously think about how they will alert the children that a transition time will be occurring and what they specifically want to tell them. Adults cannot expect children to transition by themselves. Instead, the adults have to be actively involved in the moment because children will get distracted.

Adults can use musical instruments to alert children that it is time to clean up and transition. Something soft and that can produce different tunes, like hand chimes, can be nice to use. Bells are a little too harsh. Also, having a simple little tune is always engaging for young children. For example, changing the words to *Frère Jacques* to the following could work nicely:

Time to clean up, time to clean up

Put things away, put things away

Everybody's working, everybody's working

Toys away, toys away.

Having a specific transition plan in place and reviewing it with the children can assist in these challenging time periods during children's long days away from home. Additionally, when beginning to transition from one activity to another, the adult who is announcing that transition might also want to briefly caution the children (1) to remain calm, (2) to beware of others' feelings, and (3) to ask questions if they have any concerns. This reminder alerts young children to the skills that they have to put in place when they are assisting adults in cleaning up the room and then moving on to another type of activity. Some of the ways to engage children in learning activities when transitioning from one place to another is choosing one of the ideas listed below and using it until they begin to lose interest in doing it:

- Transition as a story character
- Transition and only say words that start with a certain letter
- Transition saying words that rhyme with a given word
- Transition making a sound of an animal or vehicle
- Transition looking like a food
- Transition acting like the opposite of a word
- Transition if your name begins with the same sound as a word
- Transition by following the directions "I spy with my eyes someone with . . ."
- Transition by being an object—popcorn, kangaroo, a runaway rabbit
- Transition looking like a particular letter

Additionally, transitions should be made fun for children. The teacher interviewed for the *First-Person Interview* found at the end of Chapter 14 mentions how she likes to ask children to move from one activity to another in a certain way that is related to an activity that they have just completed. For example, when children are transitioning from a large group lesson after reading a book on butterflies, they are asked to flap their wings as if they were real butterflies when moving to their next activity.

Remember, correct transitions take time. However, if they are done right, actually less time will be spent transitioning during the day and more time will be spent with children involved in learning activities!

Effective Flexible Groupings

As illustrated in the daily schedule presented in the previous section, early education programs organize activities around the implementation and coordination of three different types of instructional groups: large groups, small groups, and the learning centers (DeBaryshe, Gorecki, & Mishima-Young, 2009; see Figure 6.14 and descriptions below). Effective classrooms are those that carefully plan for children to participate in each type of grouping multiple times throughout the day. Additionally, while they are in these different types of groups, the adults are responsive and sensitive to each child's abilities. The adults continually encourage the development of different skills, even though all the children in the group are working on the same activity (Howes et al., 2008).

Flexible groupings are not similar to **ability groups** where children are placed with peers with similar abilities. Instead, **flexible groupings** place children in groups of various sizes (i.e., large, small, and centers), and each group that the child is in consists of different children learning different skills. For example, in the opening scenario of this chapter, children were transitioning from working in center groups to participating in a large group learning activity. Throughout the day, children engage in activities that occur in large groups, small groups, and learning center groups. During these activities, children interact with different peers, are exposed to different language models, and develop their individualized learning skills.

Figure 6.14   Different Instructional Groups

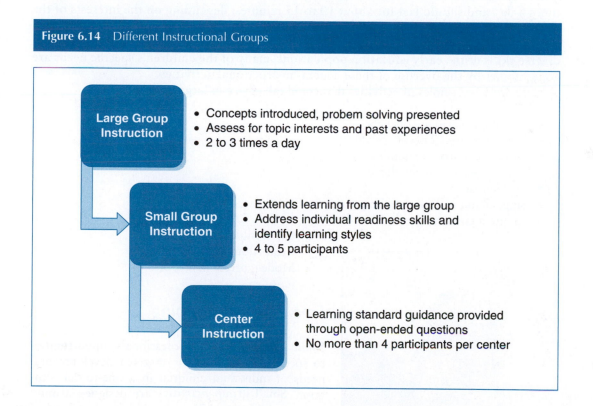

Large Group Learning

Large group lessons usually involve either the entire class or half of the class, depending on the children's ability to remain focused on an activity as a member of a large group. These lessons are generally reserved for introducing and reviewing specific concepts, problem-solving

Large group lessons are a valuable time to introduce the class to new concepts.

approaches, or developmental skills. Large group lessons tend to be adult directed, with the professional presenting general and uniform information to all the children. However, professionals should always provide opportunities for children to offer their suggestions and practice new skills that they have learned.

For example, when teachers have a book that they are going to read to the class, they can do a "Picture Walk" by showing some of the pictures from inside the book (see Chapter 10). They can ask the children, "What questions do you have about this book before we read it?" The teacher can then write the questions down on the board or a large piece of paper, and tell the children that many of the questions will be answered as they read the book over the next few days. Teachers can also remind the children that, as they read the story, they might think of more questions that will be answered in the story. Practices such as these modify the large group lesson from being totally adult directed to becoming more adult-child directed.

Information used in large group lessons is then more individually examined in small group lessons and center activities. Large group lessons should occur about two or three times a day and should last for about 10 to 15 minutes, depending on the interests of the children (Purcell & Rosemary, 2007). Unfortunately, many programs today are designed for children to spend from 20% to 25% of the day in large group activities. Given the diverse skills of the early education populations, many of the children's specific needs are going unmet by the overuse of these general instructional activities.

Here are 10 examples of activities that could take place in large groups:

- Introduce learning concepts
- Discuss a special event
- Discuss classroom routines
- Get suggestions from children
- Problem-solve
- Sing, chant, read and recite poems, do finger play, dance
- Create a class story
- Offer choices of activities
- Read Alouds
- Model correct behaviors

Small Group Learning

Small group activities afford the opportunity to address the individual skills of each child in a one-to-one context.

Small groups afford professionals opportunities to specifically address the targeted developmental needs of individual children in a one-to-one situation. **Small group activities** are designed around moving children's skills to an independent level of mastery. Effective learning occurs through the use of materials that are of interest to the children in the group and that are not based on the interest of the entire class. Small group lessons involve a staff member working with a limited number of children on activities that relate to the class unit, theme, or project. They are also specifically designed to address readiness skills within these children's zone of learning.

Small group lessons are usually structured for about 4 to 5 participants and should last for approximately 20 to 30 minutes, depending on the interests and abilities of the children. Children should participate in small group lessons at least three or four times a week. During these activities, the teacher continually provides the children with activities that are self-motivating and that are designed around their learning style.

Here are 10 examples of activities that could take place in small groups:

- Share similar interests
- Provide mini-lessons
- Write play plans
- Design a group project
- Work on specific tasks
- Provide more guidance
- Share work
- Scaffold support
- Work on similar strengths
- Introduce a task

Learning centers provide opportunities for hands-on, self-motivated learning through play activities.

Center Learning

Learning centers are distinct interest areas in a classroom that offer various materials and opportunities for hands-on learning at an individually appropriate level (Copple & Bredekamp, 2009; Epstein, 2007). Participation in learning center groups affords children opportunities to actually engage in learning. Additionally, centers provide opportunities for children to make genuine choices about working with materials selected by a knowledgeable adult with the goal of enhancing children's independence, communication competence, and academic learning. Such learning opportunities also nurture children's social, emotional, physical, creative, and cognitive development.

Learning center activities afford children opportunities to explore new skills and concepts on their own with minimal guidance from an adult. The staff carefully selects all activities presented at the play centers to meet the individual interests and developing skills of the participants. Centers are areas where children are engaged in activities. The activities are located in well-planned learning areas that are designed to meet the specific developmental needs of the children in the class.

Children must be taught how to use each center and what to do before they leave the center. The ability to choose the center at which they want to spend their time is a powerful motivator for young children. Such freedom typically results in children spending more time learning and understanding the activities at the center. As a result, the centers must

Center activities provide opportunities for children to develop independent skills as adult guidance gradually decreases.

be well stocked with materials for children with all developmental needs and interests, and with an adult to provide appropriate monitoring.

Centers should not have more than four children at them. Children need to be taught how many children can be at a center and what to do when a center they wish to visit has reached its maximum number of participants. Instructions should also be provided on how to clean up the center, how to walk from one center to another, and what to do at the new center.

The following is a list of skills that could develop while children work on activities in learning centers:

- Work as part of a small group
- Develop independent skills
- Explore ideas
- Manipulate materials
- Discover consequence
- Interact with others/exchange
- Negotiate and problem-solve using language
- Explore hands-on learning
- Develop a deeper understanding
- Demonstrate self-expressions
- Generalize concepts

Small group lessons and learning centers can be orchestrated simultaneously during the day. As mentioned earlier in this chapter, children also must be taught acceptable behaviors for transitioning from one center to another. Adults should provide a specific auditory or visual cue alerting the children that transition time is about to occur. The consistent use of a special signal creates an orderly time for groups to clean up and transition to another center.

LEARNING FOR ALL CHILDREN
Center Activities and Disabilities

Learning centers provide an excellent opportunity to address young children's individual needs. The centers can be especially helpful in supporting the learning goals for children who have disabilities or might be at risk of having disabilities and who are enrolled in inclusive educational centers. One research study found that young children with disabilities tended to gravitate to centers where the teacher was present (Odom & Diamond, 1998). The study noted that none of the nine learning centers observed in the study appeared to facilitate social interactions between children with and without disabilities. The researcher recommends that adults think carefully about how their presence and actions at learning centers for young children in inclusive classes might increase the attractiveness of centers that children typically do not choose. Additionally, adults working with inclusive groups of young children should design center activities that require two children to engage simultaneously in an activity to achieve a specific outcome. Participating in cooperative learning activities, such as two children making one clay item or collaboratively completing a puzzle, could enhance the communication and other social skills of both participants.

The following five suggestions could enhance children's participation in inclusive learning center activities:

1. Provide an in-service about different disabilities and the impact of those disabilities on children's learning and social activities, so that the staff will feel more at ease working with challenging children.

2. Have regular interactions with the children's families and discuss how they engage children in activities at home and in the community.

3. Have someone trained in special education provide modeling and supporting techniques that would encourage peer interactions between children with and without disabilities. Additionally, have the professional share ideas on ways to create, adapt, or obtain adaptive equipment—for example, creating adaptive devices for the learning of self-help skills, adapting the classroom to allow for fewer distractions or more open pathways, or finding resources for obtaining appropriate communication devices.

4. Observe the children with disabilities more frequently to obtain information on their interests and children with whom they might want to interact.

5. Work with the staff as a team to problem-solve the individual challenging situations that might occur during the day.

Effective Classroom Management

Between 3 and 6 years of age, children begin to develop *prosocial behaviors* (Copple & Bredekamp, 2009). **Prosocial behaviors** are voluntary acts that assist in showing others your concern for their well-being. These behaviors at a young age include caring, sharing, and helping peers. Typically, young children express concern to their distressed peers by hugging or using comforting words.

Creating a Responsive Classroom

Positive results have been demonstrated when professionals working with young children engage in *responsive classroom* activities (Denton & Kriete, 2000). The responsive classroom approach is an evidence-based method that increases academic achievement, decreases problem behaviors, improves social skills, and leads to more high-quality instruction. In **responsive classrooms**, through the collaborative efforts of children and adults, classroom rules are developed and enforced. Children then develop a sense of ownership for the classroom and the capacity to care about themselves, others, and the world. Teachers teach positive behavior work habits to children that focus around developing the following skills:

- How to work and play together peaceably
- How to communicate what you think and need
- How to take care of yourself, your friends, and your environment

©iStockphoto.com/ktaylor

Collaborative activities at learning centers can assist all children with learning skills.

At a young age, children begin to learn prosocial behaviors.

- How to listen to others with openness and compassion
- How to choose an effective course of action and make it happen

Through the continual use of phrases such as "Show me" and "Remind me," teachers have young children discuss how they will participate in upcoming activities that could be challenging for them. For example, before transitioning to a new activity, a teacher might say, "Remind me of how we are going to get ready to walk to a new center." Because the children provide descriptions of the acceptable behaviors for the task, they are more committed to following those behaviors. Young children, especially those between the ages of 3 and 5 years, take great interest in expressing their feelings and learn over time how to identify and express the feelings of others. Designing a responsive classroom gives them the opportunity to achieve this developmentally appropriate ability.

Returning back to the opening scenario, if it happened that two children began to argue over who would get the pillow and place it on the floor for the teacher, simply saying, "Remind me how we work together to prepare our classroom for the next activity" would likely produce a more positive response from the children than reprimanding them for arguing. Through the fostering of autonomy and the integrating of academic and social learning, children and adults build a community in which high expectations for learning and behavior exist.

LEARNING FOR ALL CHILDREN
Classroom Interactions and Culture

Early education centers are always attempting to teach children prosocial skills—that is, the ability to make friends and maintain healthy relationships. However, different cultures have different values and beliefs regarding prosocial skills. The prosocial behaviors of young children from four cultures (two Western and two Southeast Asian) were examined in a specific context when interacting with an adult (Trommsdorff, Friedlmeier, & Mayer, 2007). The results indicated that the children from the Southeast Asian cultures appeared to be more self-focused and less prosocial than the children from the Western cultures. Therefore, children may feel more comfortable when they interact with adults or peers from similar cultures because they can relate to them in diverse ways. However, a culturally responsive classroom affords children opportunities to learn about and from one another to build a strong sense of community within a diverse classroom context.

Strategies for encouraging diversity in the classroom include:

- Learn about the children's backgrounds and traditions
- Continually encourage diversity throughout the daily activities
- Help children learn more about their culture and background
- Provide activities, materials, and experiences that do not support stereotypes

Addressing Unacceptable Behaviors

Chapter 1 of this book mentions the increasing expulsion rate due to unacceptable behavior in early education centers. Research has found that this increase in aggressive behavior directly corresponds to the increase in skill-and-drill work now expected from young children. The majority of early childhood professionals believe that if young children are presented with developmentally appropriate activities that integrate learning skills, unacceptable behavior occurrences will decrease. Therefore, implementing the practices promoted in this book should directly impact the overall social climate of an early education class. Children still need to learn at a young age, however, that specific environments have specific rules of conduct that they must respect.

Although appropriate play practices contribute to children's development of their own social behaviors and the understanding of others' behaviors, all classrooms should still require children to specifically design a set of simple rules that describes what they think is acceptable behavior. A cornerstone for the HighScope program, which was mentioned in Chapter 2, is its formal, six-step conflict resolution process when someone continually refuses to follow the accepted rules. This process has proven to be very successful in addressing behavior concerns with young children before they escalate into major problems. This program encourages professionals to teach and use the following six-step process with young children:

- **Step 1: Approach the situation calmly.** Observe the situation, stop any harmful behaviors, approach the children using a calm voice, and ask the children involved to sit down on the floor.
- **Step 2: Acknowledge children's feelings.** Describe the observed activities and feelings to the children.
- **Step 3: Gather information.** Using open-ended questions, gather data from each child involved.
- **Step 4: Restate the problem.** Clarify the problem based on the information that is collected. Check each child for a clear understanding of what transpired.
- **Step 5: Ask for ideas for solutions and choose one together.** Encourage children to talk about the problem and a solution, and also be prepared to provide some suggestions. When a solution is reached, make sure that the children are in agreement.
- **Step 6: Be prepared to give follow-up support.** Sometimes the solutions must be clarified once the children resume their play activity.

Having such a plan in place and making the students aware of it, just as they learn to be aware of the daily schedule, will assist in preventing many problems.

LEARNING FOR ALL CHILDREN
Classroom Interactions and Poverty

The growing concern over the increase in unacceptable social and behavioral interactions of preschoolers who are being raised in poverty is addressed in a study by Bulotsky-Shearer, Bell, Romero, and Carter (2012). The researchers found that much of the blame for unacceptable behaviors was attributed to the use of developmentally inappropriate activities for young children.

(Continued)

(Continued)

Findings demonstrate that peer play mediates some behavior and learning challenges for young children's external activities such as aggression, inattention, and frequent disruptions, and for internal activities such as becoming withdrawn and nonsocial.

Suggestions from the American Academy of Pediatrics on encouraging family play activities for children living in poverty follow:

- Teach parents about the value of play for learning and development
- Suggest simple toys and games—balls, boxes, and buckets
- Encourage parents to use positive interactions with their children
- Help parents understand the need for children to participate in physical activities

---

REFLECT AND APPLY EXERCISE 6.2

Using Conflict Resolution

Reflect

Some preschool children find it challenging to process information about other children's feelings. Instead of using prosocial behaviors, they will frequently use hostile intentions toward other children to get what they want.

Apply

Imagine a child who is watching two children who are involved in a play enactment about a dog that escaped from the shelter and is being chased by the dogcatcher. The child watching would like to become part of the play enactment, so he trips one of the children as a way of gaining entrance to the play enactment. How would you use the six-step conflict management process described above to address this situation?

Addressing Challenging Unacceptable Behaviors

About 10% to 21% of current preschool children exhibit challenging behaviors (Powell, Fixsen, Dunlap, Smith, & Fox, 2007). Most of the inappropriate behaviors that occur are aggression, noncompliance, defiance, tantrums, and property destruction (Trommsdorff et al., 2007). As discussed earlier in this book, children who continue to have behavior problems throughout the early primary grades tend to end up failing in school and exhibiting violent behavior and mental health issues into adulthood. When children are provided with appropriate intervention, these serious behavior problems become less likely to occur.

During the past three decades, along with the use of the Response to Intervention (RtI) model (see Chapter 9), positive behavior support (PBS) has demonstrated success in addressing young children's inappropriate behavior at home and at school (Snell, Berlin, Voorhees, Stanton-Chapman, & Hadden, 2012). Using the same RtI three-tiered process for intervening, PBS addresses specific challenging behaviors that appear to recur and interfere with a child's academic and social development (see Figure 6.15).

Figure 6.15 Continuum for Academic and Behavior Supports

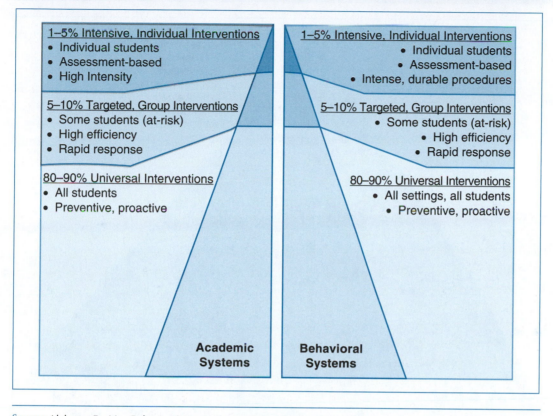

Source: Alabama Positive Behavior Support Center, Auburn University Montgomery, School of Education. Retrieved from http://www.education.aum.edu/alabama-positive-behavior-support-center.

The bottom of Figure 6.16 illustrates two dark blue levels of the pyramid: (1) how most children's inappropriate behaviors can be modified through planning natural classroom environmental activities, and (2) designing situations that enhance peer relationships. When conflicts do occur, programs such as the HighScope conflict resolution approach, which was mentioned above, can be implemented to effectively modify children's behaviors.

The Targeted Interventions level of the pyramid applies to some children in the class who do not demonstrate progress through naturally occurring situations. At this level, young children are typically able to modify their behavior if they are provided small group instructions about the specific behaviors. Using visually presented aids to assist them, such as acting out scenarios or reading stories that demonstrate how to appropriately respond, have been successful at modifying these challenging behaviors.

Finally, the top area, or Intensive Intervention, is for the few children who require a **functional behavior assessment** to determine the predictive antecedent conditions that are causing the problem (Freeman et al., 2006). The information from the functional behavior assessment assists in creating an individualized intervention plan that prevents the behavior from happening, teaches alternative behaviors, and shifts the reinforcement from the problem to the alternative behavior. At this stage, skills must be individually taught and reinforced at school as well as at home through the designing of specific behavior objects. These individual intervention plans have been shown to prevent behavior problems in preschool children and improve their social abilities (Snell et al., 2012).

Figure 6.16 The Pyramid Model: Promoting Social and Emotional Competence and Addressing Challenging Behavior

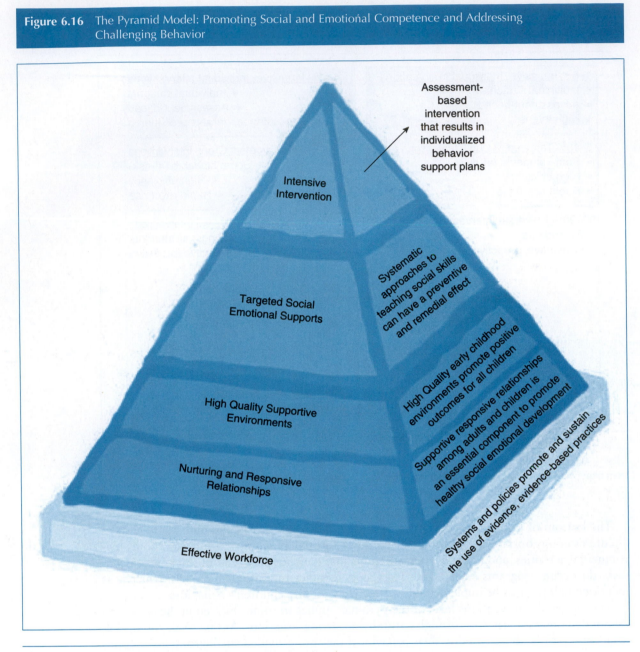

Source: © TACSEI, http://www.challengingbehavior.org/contact.htm.

Chapter Summary

Most classrooms for young children are comprised of children with diverse play skills. However, these classrooms typically have only one play center, and that center is usually designed around typical middle-class American themes of household activities—preparing meals, caring for babies, cleaning the house. To meet the diverse experiences and developmental levels found in today's classrooms, however, professionals must create play centers that have familiar items for children and that challenge them into producing high-level enactments. The "one center fits all" concept and continual exposure to the same play themes and materials will not produce high-level play activities.

When planning for effective learning to occur, classroom settings should have carefully designed learning centers both indoors and outdoors. Center activities should encourage not only the development of content-area skills but also the enhancement of pretending and narrative skills. Although children are free to participate in all center activities, adults must carefully monitor the centers. The centers must continually transform through the gradual introduction of more abstract materials and, after a period of time, the centers should be replaced with a different theme. This ongoing interaction with different content and peers supports the language acquisition process by providing continual exposure to language in context. Through the sensitive choosing of play themes, materials, and co-players, adults can interact with children by guiding their learning to higher levels of performance and language.

All members of the classroom are responsible for creating a community in which appropriate social behaviors are practiced. For children who exhibit more challenging aggressive behaviors, a more structured behavior plan might be necessary.

> ### HOME AND COMMUNITY CONNECTIONS
>
> Planning for Effective Learning
>
> Create a schedule with your child of your morning routine, take pictures of your child doing those activities to add to your schedule.

CHAPTER 6 FIRST-PERSON INTERVIEW

When Screaming Gradually Turned Into Eager Participation

Tiffany Madsen

Early Childhood Family Education and Special Education Teacher, Coleraine, MN

After teaching early childhood for 15 years now, I still love it as much as I did in the beginning. I love that every day is new and different, and you frequently witness children gaining new skills throughout the day. I am currently teaching for a school district in rural Minnesota.

All children take pride in their learning, and it is gratifying to witness as they recognize themselves accomplishing tasks that only days prior were too difficult. Early childhood is a time when the value of gaining independence in self-help skills is just as celebrated as learning academics.

When working with a child with limited social skills and language, I learned how to make and use Visual Schedules. After much success, we began to use visuals classroom-wide as a pre-teaching tool for classroom management. This practice aided individuals that had difficulty managing transitions through verbal commands as well as those that just needed a visual reminder.

At the beginning of this year, we had all our students using different types of Visual Schedules. A number of the children used a large schedule that was placed on the wall and did not require individual involvement but was introduced and referred to by the classroom teacher. Other children, however, physically interact with the schedule in order to understand the classroom's sequence of events, so teachers developed different types of visuals for them to manipulate throughout the changes of the day. They remove a picture each time that they complete an activity, and then they focus on the next picture in order to know what is going to happen next. Still other children carry their Visual Schedule with them as they move from one activity to another.

(Continued)

(Continued)

One example of our success was with a child who screamed during every transition. The improvement that we saw in him when we gave him a picture of the next activity and had him hold on to that picture as he transitioned to and joined his classmates in a large group time was amazing. The screaming gradually turned into eager participation! The other day, his classroom job was to be the ornithologist; he was to check outside for birds and count them. We were all amazed at how he went over to the Morning Circle and sat there holding his card until it was time for him to check and count the birds. He went through the entire circle activities holding on to the card with a bird on it, and he never got upset.

Student Study Site

Visit the Student Study Site at **www.sagepub.com/selmi** to access additional study tools including mobile-friendly eFlashcards and links to video and web resources.

Key Terms

ability groups

conflict resolution

flexible groupings

full-day program

functional behavior assessment

half-day program

large group activities

outdoor play activities

positive behavior support

prosocial behaviors

responsive classrooms

small group activities

visual schedules

Useful Websites

Center for Social and Emotional Foundation for Early Learning: http://csefel.vanderbilt.edu

Impact of toys on play: http://www.naeyc.org/content/what-research-says-toys-and-play

Playground safety: http://playgroundsafety.org/standards/cpsc

Responsive classrooms: http://www.responsiveclassroom.org

Visual Schedules: http://autismpdc.fpg.unc.edu/sites/autismpdc.fpg.unc.edu/files/VisualSchedules_Steps.pdf

Reflective Questions

1. Some children in your classroom who are eating their snack begin to act silly. How could you use the techniques presented under the heading "Creating a Responsive Classroom" to address this behavior? What results could you expect?

2. Go to the following website: http://csefel.vanderbilt.edu/resources/practical_%20strategies .html

   Watch the 25-minute demonstration on strategies for developing appropriate social and emotional skills with young children. The three-step process that is demonstrated in this film clip suggests the following steps for learning appropriate behaviors:

   Step 1: Introduce a behavior by using a variety of tools

   Step 2: Practice the behavior through planned and unscripted activities

   Step 3: Maintain the behavior by recognizing when children use it

   In groups of two or three people, think of a common situation where young children typically demonstrate inappropriate behaviors (e.g., not waiting to take a turn, not expressing feelings, not wanting to share). Apply the three-step process described above to the situation that you chose to improve the child's use of appropriate behavior.

7 Designing High-Quality Centers for Learning

OUTDOOR ACTIVITIES REFLECTING INDOOR ACTIVITIES

Jupiterimages/Stockbyte/Thinkstock

It is approximately 10:30 a.m. at an early childhood center. Outside, three classes, totaling about 50 children and 10 staff members, are busy participating in the morning learning activities. The majority of the children and staff are engaged in activities at different centers.

The outdoor playhouse has been designed as a travel center where tickets can be purchased and travel can take place using different types of transportation. It has a desk with a broken laptop computer, a phone, a cash register and money, a calendar, a clock, paper, small tablets, envelopes, travel brochures, magazines, a travel photo album, and different writing utensils. There are also some plastic boxes containing items such as dress-up clothes, purses and wallets, travel bags, and hats from different countries—for example, sombreros, berets, cowboy hats, a safari hat, dress hats, ski hats, beach visors and hats, and different types of travel occupation hats (e.g., hats for flight attendants, bus drivers, train conductors, and subway drivers). Travel posters are on the walls around the center along with computer-generated signs advertising travel to places and the cost of that travel. Outside the travel center there is a large refrigerator box lying on its side, and windows have been cut out of two sides. A sign on the box states, "I can become a bus, car, train, subway car, airplane, rocket, or any other type of transportation. Use your imagination!" The sign has pictures on it showing the types of transportation.

Inside the classroom is a table with an adult working with about 3 or 4 children. The children are making plans for what they will do in the travel center. At another table, a small group of children, some of whom are wearing construction hats, are watching the teacher slice large, firm pieces from a block of clay. She is instructing the children, one of whom has Down syndrome, that they need to flatten the clay and create long, thin strips that are wide enough for two traffic lanes. She then suggests that they can all connect their pieces of clay with each other's and then make a line down the middle of them with a thick pencil to make two lanes on the road. She shows them a box of small construction trucks that they can move back and forth along the road.

To prepare young children to embrace the academic challenges that they will encounter throughout their education, early learning activities must be well planned and tailored to meet each child's unique needs, especially those children who might be at risk of future academic failure. As illustrated in the opening scenario, children's early learning endeavors must provide high-quality activities that are age-appropriate, individually appropriate, and socially/culturally appropriate (Purcell & Rosemary, 2008). Well-planned and guided play activities can lead children to high-quality learning.

This chapter examines the following questions related to high-quality play activities:

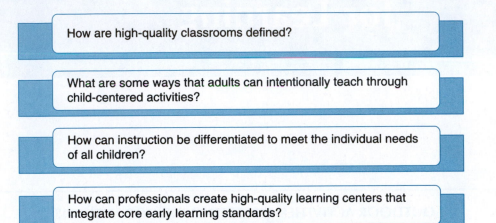

How are high-quality classrooms defined?

What are some ways that adults can intentionally teach through child-centered activities?

How can instruction be differentiated to meet the individual needs of all children?

How can professionals create high-quality learning centers that integrate core early learning standards?

Creating High-Quality Classrooms

The National Institute for Early Education Research (NIEER) has identified 10 general benchmarks to measure program quality. Although the benchmarks do not guarantee quality, they reflect the program characteristics that research has discovered for early childhood programs to be highly effective. The 10 benchmarks and recent state achievement rates for meeting these benchmarks are listed in Figure 7.1, and include general structural items such as standards, training, class size, support services, and meals provided.

Other factors that are used to determine the quality of early childhood experiences focus on features such as physical safety, high-quality teachers, adult-child interactions, and intellectually stimulating environments (Yamamoto & Li, 2012). Although all of these features are important and contribute greatly to the development of high-quality programs, adult-child ratio and class size appear to be of paramount concern, especially during an era of severe budget reductions. Understandably, programs that adhere to the state or national required adult-child class size ratio afford staff the time to continually secure a safe environment, encourage interaction with children in activities, and regularly provide intellectually stimulating exchanges with children. Additionally, programs with these high-quality features frequently attract employees who are more educated and more knowledgeable about working with children because they understand the potential that early education has for children.

Howes et al. (2008) also examined specific teachers' behaviors and found that those who engage in the following behaviors tend to have children who produced more proficient language and literacy skills:

- Participate in meaningful interactions with children
- Provide responsive and sensitive interactions

Figure 7.1 NIEER's National Quality Standards Checklist Summary

Policy	Benchmark	No. of State-Funded Pre-K Initiatives Meeting Benchmark (of 52)
Early Learning Standards	Comprehensive	51
Teacher Degree	BA	30
Teacher Specialized Training	Specializing in Pre-K	44
Assistant Teacher Degree	Child Development Associate or Equivalent	15
Teacher In-Service	At least 15 Hours/Year	42
Maximum Class Size	20 or Lower	44
Staff-Child Ratio	1:10 or Better	45
Screening/Referral/Support Services	Vision, Hearing, Health; and at Least 1 Support Service	37
Meals	At Least 1/Day	24
Monitoring	Site Visits	32

Source: NIEER. (2012). http://nieer.org/sites/nieer/files/yearbook2012_executivesummary.pdf

- Create respect, encouragement, and enthusiasm for learning
- Manage time so that children receive frequent feedback

©iStockphoto.com/shironosov

Adhering to the state or national required adult-child class size ratios affords staff the time to provide a safe environment where optimal learning can take place.

Additionally, Chien et al. (2010) identified two classroom instructional features that appear to contribute to encouraging sensitive and responsive interactions, and contribute to positive early learning outcomes. First, *free-choice play and exploration activities* afford children opportunities to construct knowledge, particularly knowledge of skills that adults cannot directly impart, such as problem solving or negotiating. Second, scaffolding, which is a process where a more knowledgeable person guides children to think through and/or complete tasks at a higher level than the children could achieve unassisted.

Therefore, high-quality early learning classrooms involve responsive and sensitive adult-child interactions that occur during play activities and that focus on language and literacy skill development (see Figure 7.2). These interactions integrate scaffolding and feedback techniques that guide children to construct knowledge by exploring materials (Piaget, 1962) and/or by interacting with a more knowledgeable person (Vygotsky, 1978). As a result, young children's learning appears to be directly affected both by the environment in which they spend their time and by the adults who tailor that environment.

High-quality classrooms involve
responsive and sensitive adults
who guide children to explore and
construct new knowledge.

Source: ©iStockphoto.com/IsaacLKoval.

For example, a toddler might try to grab a staff member's purse in an attempt to demonstrate interest in the object. A responsive and sensitive professional would later provide the child with a play purse containing a few age-appropriate objects so that the child could explore. Similarly, preschoolers are always thrilled with new materials, ideas, and activities. A responsive and sensitive preschool teacher will understand the children's excitement and will make sure to provide new ideas, materials, and activities throughout the preschool day.

Developing High-Quality Teaching Strategies

Intentional Teaching

The NAEYC position statement on developmentally appropriate practices (Copple & Bredekamp, 2009) convincingly warns about two problems: (1) the negative impact of adult-guided teaching practices that involve fragmented, discrete learning objectives, and (2) the limited exposure to child-centered play activities currently occurring in a number of preschools and K–3rd grade classrooms. The statement recommends integrating adult-guided literacy concepts into child-centered play activities, such as block activities, water activities, sand activities, and dramatic play activities. Daily participation in literacy- and content-centered, playful activities that are guided by adults can lead to successful results on traditional literacy measures (DeStefano & Rempert, 2007; DeStefano, Rempert, & O'Dell, 2008).

When children interact and use language for meaningful exchanges, they develop oral language skills and vocabulary. Oral language development has a high correlation with vocabulary development and reading comprehension. Listening to their teachers and peers use language exposes them to the phonology, prosody, and syntax of the language. This prepares students for phonemic awareness and ultimately for decoding sounds and symbols for early reading success.

By 3 years of age, children already use language for multiple purposes. Resnick and Snow (2009) claim that, early on in life, children experiment with using talking for some of the following purposes (p. 9):

- To inform, entertain, and persuade others
- To present themselves, their topic, or their point of view to others
- To negotiate or propose relationships with others
- To evaluate people, information, or events
- To think, teach, and learn

Many of these skills are ones that children use while they are talking and creating sociodramatic play enactments (e.g., informing, presenting a point of view, negotiating, evaluating events, and thinking aloud; see Chapter 2).

Although adding a robust number of positive impacts, early childhood teachers are also challenged by having classrooms full of children with diverse learning and language skills and, at the same time, by the expectation to develop high-quality programs that address each child's individual needs. Carefully crafted play environments reflecting the individual needs of the children can be created through the implementation of intentional teaching practices (Copple & Bredekamp, 2009; Epstein, 2007).

Intentional teaching is implemented in environments that are specifically designed for children, on a daily basis, to achieve new skills and knowledge that contribute to academic success and a successful life. These practices focus on creating well-planned learning opportunities that integrate information from a variety of learning content areas, instead of focusing on the development of isolated, non-meaningful skills. Therefore, children can learn language, literacy, mathematical, and motor skills while involved in carefully planned block activities, instead of learning literacy during literacy activities, mathematics during math activities, and motor skills during motor activities.

For example, a staff member might notice that a toddler has started walking around the room holding a book in one hand. This activity could arise from the fact that the child has been read to and has an interest in reading books. Therefore, the staff member should guide the child to walk over to the book area, and then join the child and perhaps a friend in reading that book. In this sensitive and responsive example of intentional teaching, the staff person would recognize the child's interest in reading and intentionally integrate that interest and those skills into other areas of development—communication, motor, social, and literacy.

Additionally, older children might demonstrate an interest in working with clay. Having noticed their curiosity, the adults might design a couple of planned activities that could guide the children into working with clay at a more sophisticated level. For example, one adult might want to work with some of the children on how to use clay tools properly. When they have become comfortable with using the tools, the adult might want to then show the children how they could create pinch clay pots or coiled clay pots. After the children have begun to use these skills somewhat independently, they could then be allowed to make choices about what they want to do with the clay and allowed to explore. While working with children in these more directed lessons, adults must always keep in mind that all the children should not be in the same place at the same time. Learning cannot be rushed. Each child needs to be given the time, support, and encouragement needed to develop skills at his or her own rate.

According to Copple and Bredekamp (2009), an intentional teacher is an excellent teacher in all areas of practice—such as developing a community of learners, teaching all children, designing self-motivating curricula, regularly assessing learning, and collaborating with families. Intentional teachers use child-centered unexpected situations as teachable moments, and they intentionally guide children during these highly motivated situations to achieve planned learning outcomes. For example, children who, on their own, have suddenly expressed an interest in dinosaurs can be guided by attentive adults to engage in activities involving this new area of interest and in the development of natural language, social, motor, cognitive, and literacy skills. Intentional teachers do not need to motivate children to learn; instead, they are motivated by the children they teach. Intentional teachers are learners because they continually learn from the children what they know and what they need and want to learn.

Integrating Child-Centered and Adult-Guided Activities

Using intentional teaching practices with play activities allows children to acquire knowledge through child-centered experiences where peers collaboratively explore and create their own learning experiences and engage in a natural flow of language. At times, however, adult-guided experiences are needed. In these situations, adults can introduce new information and vocabulary and model specific skills for children. After doing so, the adults then pull back

Comstock Images/Stockbyte/Thinkstock

Intentional teaching involves planned and integrated activities that are designed to meet the individual needs and interests of each child.

and observe the impact of their involvement. For example, older children might want to put on a production but may need assistance with planning it, creating costumes, directing each other, and assigning roles.

The opening scenario for this chapter demonstrates two specific intentional teaching situations—for example, the development of a travel agency for dramatic play and the clay project. These activities were designed by adults so that children could have opportunities to set their own goals and select the activities and materials that interested them. Additionally, the adults can encourage the children's learning by talking with them about what they are doing (e.g., "Tell me about your trip," "How does the clay feel on your hands?") and by assisting them with their problem solving activities (e.g., molding clay, what you need to take a trip). An intentional teacher uses child-centered learning and adult-guided learning throughout the day. Child-centered learning is similar to those activities that take place in learning centers where the adults have supplied the materials but the children are making the connections (or learning) on their own or through interactions with a peer. According to Epstein (2007), child-centered learning involves the child doing the following:

- **Investigating:** Children explore materials, activities, and ideas in an attempt to figure out how things work
- **Relationships:** Children make connections on their own
- **Assistance:** Children determine when they need assistance and seek it
- **Problem solving:** Children are encouraged to solve their problems on their own
- **Adult intervention:** Children focus on activities so intently that adult intervention is a disruption
- **New skills:** Children challenge themselves to master new skills
- **Existing knowledge:** Children apply their current knowledge in new ways

In contrast, adult-guided learning occurs during more structured activities in which children are more likely to be presented with information that they would not encounter on their own. This type of learning can usually occur when young children are engaged in large and small group learning activities. Adult-guided learning can occur during the following situations:

- **Unsafe actions:** Children are unaware that their actions will be hurtful
- **New experience:** Children have not encountered materials or experience
- **Lack of knowledge:** Children do not have the information
- **Not aware:** Children do not know that something will please them
- **Further learning:** Children will need information for further learning
- **Assistance when unsuccessful:** Children need assistance to complete something successfully after a number of unsuccessful attempts

Intentional teaching practices involve the careful daily and weekly planning of play activities where play contexts are cautiously chosen and designed. Children's developing skills are enhanced through exposure to deliberately selected materials that are arranged so that children will notice them and want to use them. Adults observe children's interactions and, based on these observations, design methods for challenging, scaffolding, and extending children's skills. Through the implementation of high expectations, plans, learning-oriented classrooms, and engaging activities, children learn skills (Epstein, 2007).

Using Open-Ended Prompts

Schwartz and Copeland (2010) suggest that children progress through three levels of learning, as demonstrated in Figure 7.3. Adults need to watch what children do and listen to what they say in order to identify key ideas of what information they are trying to make sense of for learning. At home, children will pick up new information and often test it and apply it to different situations at school.

For example, a family might be talking at home about having to quickly find another place to live because of an unfortunate financial situation. A child might share this information when participating in a school dramatic play activity. School staff can assist the child in dealing with the situation of quickly transitioning to another home by having books in the book center on living with other families or family members, suggesting drama or puppet enactments focusing on moving, and designing movement/music activities that encourage expressing feelings.

REFLECT AND APPLY EXERCISE 7.1

Being an Intentional Teacher

Reflect

Intentional teaching involves purposeful and thoughtful decisions on behalf of the classroom adults and program administrators. When creating a classroom environment and planning learning activities, intentional teachers and administrators have a clear idea of the outcomes that they wish to achieve. They not only know what to do, they understand why they are doing it, and they can describe their purpose to others.

Apply

Go back to the opening scenario in Chapter 6, the previous chapter. Intentional teaching must have occurred in order for the children to know exactly what to do when the adult announced that Circle Time was about to occur. Practice being an intentional teacher by (1) providing a description of the behaviors that children demonstrated when Circle Time was announced, (2) describing how the children might have learned these behaviors, and (3) justifying why those behaviors were important to learn.

Similarly, the NAEYC's work on developmentally appropriate practices (Copple & Bredekamp, 2009) suggest that through exploring, thinking, and inquiring about a variety of phenomena, high-level learning occurs. Intentional teaching that encourages self-directed and meaningful experiences assists children in attaching information to the broader themes that they already know, which in turn allows them to make connections in future learning activities. NAEYC encourages tailoring learning activities to children's interests and experiences, developmental capacities, language and culture, and abilities and disabilities.

Figure 7.3 Children as Fact Collectors

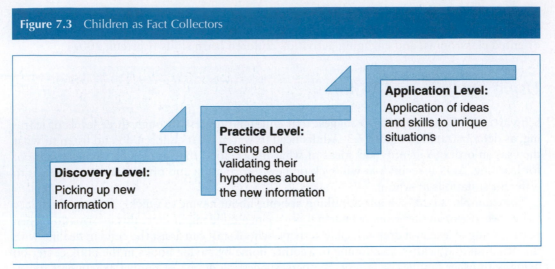

Source: Schwartz, S. L., & Copeland, S. M. (2010). *Connecting Emergent Curriculum and Standards in the Early Childhood Classroom*. New York, NY: Teachers College Press.

Intentional teachers respect children as active learners. They use open-ended prompts with children in an effort to extend conversations and invite children to share their knowledge. According to Wasik and Hindman (2013/2014) open-ended prompts are typically not just questions, but are also statements that can have more than one correct answer and require a multiple-word response. Asking a closed question typically results in ending children's learning interactions and limiting their language development. At early stages of language development children are often asked questions that require limited language output. Examples of such questions are yes/no or either/or questions where children can answer the questions using one or two word responses or simple phrases. However, when teachers use open-ended prompts that encourage children to think deeply about what they are doing, the language exchange is more sophisticated.

Open-ended prompts can be questions that begin with "why" and "how" or statements that start with phrases similar to "Tell me about" or "Describe what happened when." These prompts are valuable because they allow for children and teachers to build more language skills in the classroom than closed questions (Wasik & Hindman, 2013/2014). For example, asking a child, "Are you enjoying yourself?" would require a simple, "yes" or "no." On the other hand, asking a child, "What are you enjoying about . . ." requires the child to explain the experience. This encourages language expansion and will help children to continue to develop language fluency. The following are examples of open-ended prompts that will encourage thoughtful responses from young children:

- How does that taste to you?
- Share with us how you made that
- Tell me about the materials that you used
- I wonder what would happen if I added some sand to that
- What might be a different way to do that?
- How do you think you can make that and what will you need?
- What made you decide to put the wheels under it?

These are all thoughtful questions and statements that, when used at appropriate times by the classroom adults, will engage children in expanded exchanges and elicit longer stretches of language for continued development. Figure 7.4 provides prompts that can be used during different activities during the day.

Figure 7.4 Examples of Activities and Open-Ended Prompts

Circle Time

• Who would like to share with us something that they did over the weekend?
• What is it that you like about that poem?

Transitions

• How do you think a bird feels as it flies up into the sky?
• Tell me about how it feels to walk on the moon.

Lunch Time

• What part of your lunch tastes the best to you?
• How do you think they made that sandwich?

Designing Differentiated Learning Opportunities

Professionals must attend to the interactions that they use when engaging with young children. These interactions must address each child's individual skills and also motivate the child to attain higher levels of knowledge. The NAEYC position statement on developmentally appropriate practices (Copple & Bredekamp, 2009) strongly encourages the use of differentiated instruction to address the individual needs of all children. Differentiated instruction is a philosophy of teaching that recognizes children's individual differences in three specific, related areas of learning: readiness skills, interests, and learning styles (Figure 7.5). When planning instructional

©iStock.com/Ilona75

The use of thoughtful, open-ended prompts demonstrates an adult's respect for young children as self-motivated learners.

activities, differences in children's skills, interests, and learning styles must be recognized. Actually, providing differentiated instruction is the same as providing developmentally appropriate practices!

The term readiness skills refers to the specific skills that children cannot produce on their own but require the support of a more experienced person to successfully generate them. Readiness skills are the skills that exist in a child's zone of proximal development, or zone for learning (see Chapter 2). These skills are neither so easy for children to produce that they become bored using them, nor too difficult for them to produce so that they become frustrated attempting them. Professionals need to be aware of each child's zone of learning and must know about methods to expand those dependent skills, or those skills that can only be produced with support, to becoming independent skills, or skills that can be produced autonomously.

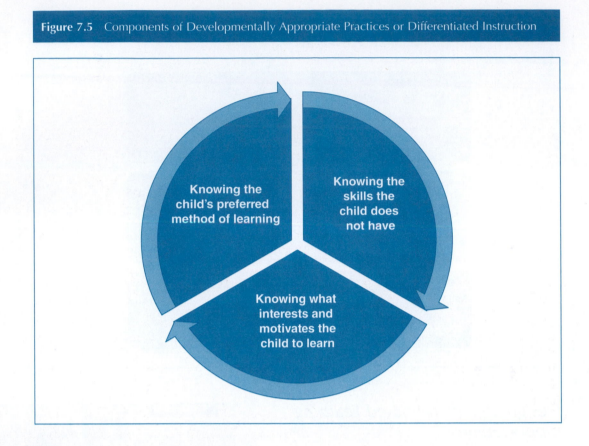

Figure 7.5 Components of Developmentally Appropriate Practices or Differentiated Instruction

Knowing the child's preferred method of learning

Knowing the skills the child does not have

Knowing what interests and motivates the child to learn

©iStockphoto.com/CEFutcher

Classrooms today are rich with diverse cultures, beliefs, and learning skills.

Almost every state in the United States has a set of early learning standards that provides sequential information on the development of readiness skills. Through careful observations and assessments (see Chapter 9), professionals can identify a child's readiness levels and create learning activities that will motivate the child's interest and curiosity to expand these skills. As professionals observe these skills maturing, they must understand how to gradually reduce the environmental supports so that the child can eventually produce these skills independently.

For example, a class may have some children who can independently engage in creating complex block structures with peers, while others might only be capable of building bridges. Adults working at the block center must be aware of these different levels of development, and they must know how to encourage the more advanced group to engage in creating patterned structures while integrating mathematics, language, and literacy skills. At the same time, these adults must nurture the younger group in building enclosures and engaging in peer interactions. Recognizing different learning interests and needs, and then addressing them is key to providing high-quality learning activities.

REFLECT AND APPLY EXERCISE 7.2

Identifying Zones of Learning

Reflect

Review the scenario at the beginning of the chapter where two learning activities are described that have been designed around addressing specific readiness skills. Identify the two activities.

Apply

Determine what skills might be appropriate for a child who just turned 4 years old and another who is almost 5 years old to learn, who is involved in each of the activities. Now, look up your state's Early Learning Standards. Determine what skills a child might need to perform independently if the child is working on learning the specific skills you have identified.

Another component of developing high-quality differentiated learning activities is recognizing *students' interest,* which is the ability of a teacher to identify individual activities that motivate children to learn. Because children's interests vary, teachers must be capable of identifying these interests and designing different lessons that focus around them.

From the time of birth, children are self-motivated to make sense of their worlds by participating in developmentally appropriate activities. However, the skill-and-drill activities adopted after the passage of *No Child Left Behind* did not attract the interest of many young children. As a result, few positive learning achievements have been witnessed since young children were required to participate in these structured learning activities. In contrast, activities that are differentiated around the interests of children allow them to develop more advanced skills and, concurrently, a more positive attitude about themselves, their ability to learn, and their feeling about their own creative potential.

Each child has an individual learning style that the child prefers to use.

Some children may enjoy activities that focus more on fine motor skills and the use of manipulative objects; in contrast, others may feel more comfortable expressing their thoughts and feelings through creative arts activities, such as painting, coloring, and playing with clay. Professionals need to recognize the interests of individual children and then integrate play and academic skills into those favored activities.

Identifying individual **learning styles,** the techniques that people choose for learning, also provides differentiation in instruction and can lead to high-quality learning. Chapter 2 in this book discussed how some children rely more heavily on visual information to make sense of the world around them, while others appear more dependent on auditory processing to obtain information. Additionally, children move through their zone of learning, or zone of proximal development, at different rates depending on their interest and motivation. Learning activities must accommodate the various learning styles and rates of learning. Professionals must frequently observe children's learning styles and rates while involved in activities, and then modify those activities or the contexts in which they occur in an effort to guide the children to a higher level of learning (Purcell & Rosemary, 2008). Some children may require a couple of days to complete an art project and need the encouragement of an adult to stay with the activity, while others may typically rush through activities and require an adult to remind them to slow down.

Although children vary in their readiness skills, interests, and style of learning, differentiated instruction is based on the concept that all children use the same curriculum and the same learning standards, no matter how diverse those differences might be. Children who might find a particular skill development challenging should not automatically be isolated and provided with alternative lessons. Instead, all children should be taught within their own zone of learning until, through the modification of materials, activities, and guidance, their learning is expanded. Six general principles for providing differentiated instruction to young children are provided in Figure 7.6 (Purcell & Rosemary, 2008).

The opening scenario for this chapter shows an adult working with a small group of children on a clay activity. It can be assumed that all these children, typical of other children their age, are developing fine motor skills. However, the children within this group might be

Figure 7.6   Principles of Differentiated Instruction

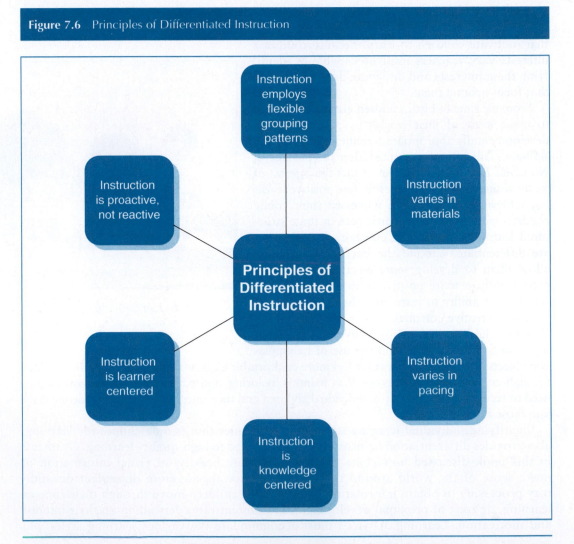

Source: Purcell, T., & Rosemary, C. (2007). Differentiating Instruction in the Preschool Classroom: Bridging Emergent Literacy Instruction and Developmentally Appropriate Practices. In L. Justice & C. Vukelich (Eds.), *Achieving Excellence in Preschool Literacy Instruction* (pp. 221–241). New York, NY: Guilford Press.

working on developing their own specific skills. The teacher might be observing one child to see how he maneuvers a pencil to draw a line in the clay. The teacher might also be assessing how other children work collaboratively with each other when joining the strips of clay to create a roadway. Finally, the teacher could be evaluating how the child with Down syndrome is using her muscle strength to flatten down the clay. All the children just mentioned are involved in the same activity; however, the guidance provided by the teacher is carefully designed to expand the differentiated skill needs of each child.

Creating High-Quality Lesson Plans

Lesson plans are "road maps" for ensuring that children are held to the highest expectations throughout the day. Although they do not always need to be written in great detail and for all activities, they must be completed for planned activities. Preschool lesson plans help teachers ensure they are meeting the needs of each child in the class. Lesson plans are crucial for staying organized and ensuring class time is used appropriately. Unstructured blocks of time lead to chaos, confusion, and behavior problems. Lesson plans also help make sure the appropriate skills are being taught in a developmentally appropriate way that benefits each child in the class.

Most early learning activity should have a plan that is prepared and agreed upon ahead of time. At a minimum, the plan must include the goals, the sequence of learning, individual language/literacy outcomes, and ways to differentiate learning for children's diverse needs. The teacher and the aides should be involved in selecting the topics that will or will not be addressed, and in how the information will be organized and presented for learning.

Each lesson should be organized around a learning standard or foundation, a topic discussed in detail in Part III. Because language and literacy goals are of primary concern at this age, each lesson plan should clearly indicate how the activity will enhance children's growth in those areas. With language goals, time should be spent considering goals for language content, form, and use (see Chapter 4). Additionally, with literacy goals, specific letter recognition, phonetic awareness, and comprehension skills must be determined (to be discussed in Chapter 10). Finally, specific material and instructional accommodations must be determined for children with disabilities who might require them.

Forty-nine of the fifty states have established early learning standards (NIEER, 2012). The following website will assist in locating information on early learning standards that your state has adopted: http://nieer.org/yearbook. Figure 7.7 contains a sample lesson plan format.

Designing High-Quality Learning Centers

Individualized learning activities should occur within well-planned and organized learning centers, both indoors and outdoors. Each center should focus on the following (Bouley-Picard, 2005):

1. Encouraging the use of pretending and narrative skills that children demonstrate in the socio-dramatic play center

2. Facilitating language and literacy development

3. Including adaptations for all children's special concerns

4. Providing adult guidance in play, language, literacy, and content area learning

The scenario in Chapter 8 focuses on a pretend telephone call that an adult and children made to Teacher Rosie, who was on vacation. On the day before that play enactment, the children had come to school and were asking why Teacher Rosie was missing. As demonstrated

Figure 7.7 *General Lesson Plan Format*

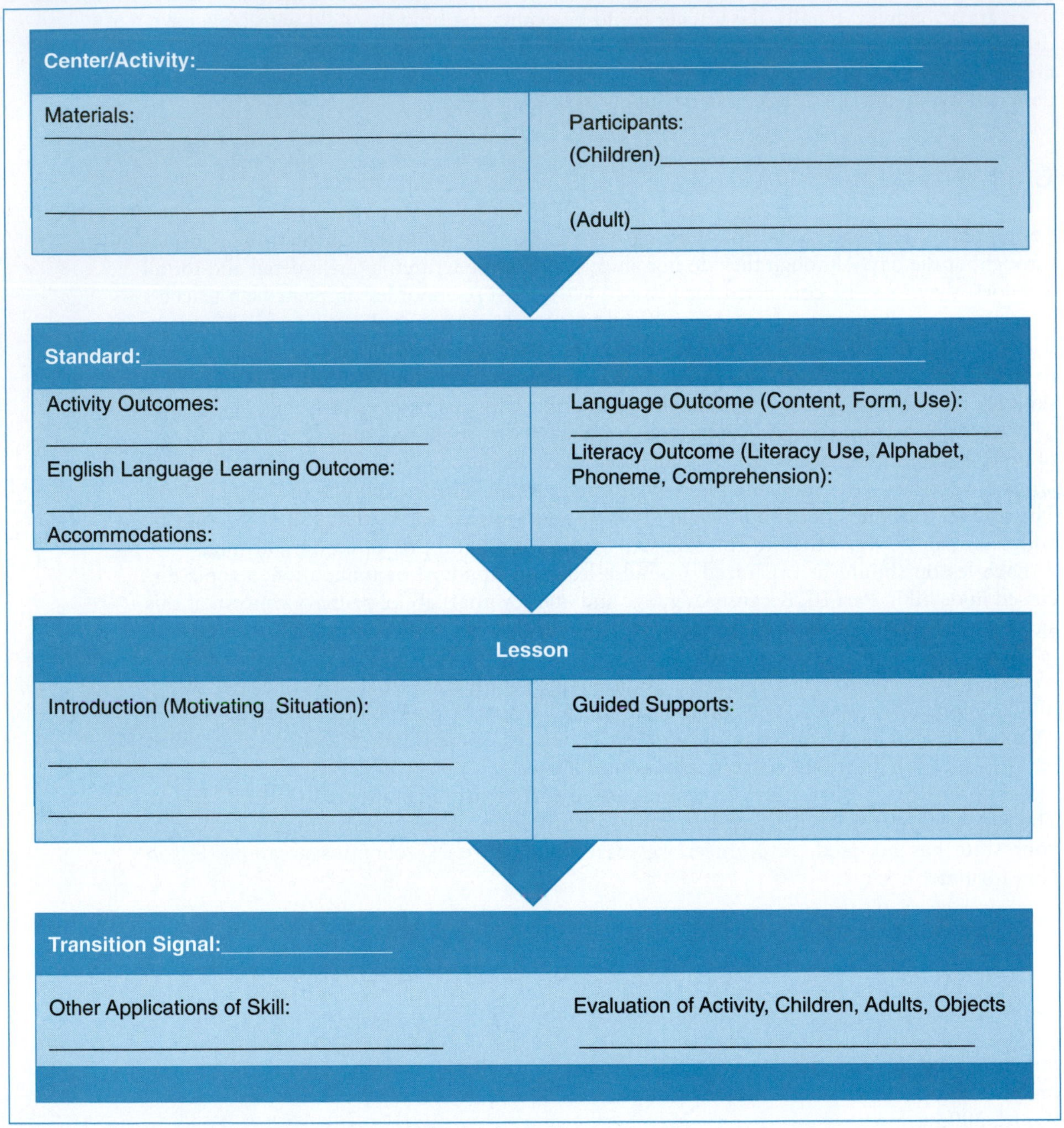

Center/Activity:_____

Materials:	Participants:
_____	(Children)_____
_____	(Adult)_____

Standard:_____

Activity Outcomes:	Language Outcome (Content, Form, Use):
_____	_____
English Language Learning Outcome:	Literacy Outcome (Literacy Use, Alphabet, Phoneme, Comprehension):
_____	_____
Accommodations:	

Lesson

Introduction (Motivating Situation):	Guided Supports:
_____	_____
_____	_____

Transition Signal:_____

Other Applications of Skill:	Evaluation of Activity, Children, Adults, Objects
_____	_____

in the next chapter, the adult, who was sensitive to the children's concerns, decided to engage them in *pretend narrative activities* that focused on Teacher Rosie being on vacation. The adult was very successful in doing so.

Learning centers also should have embedded opportunities for children to expand their *language and literacy* competencies. Socio-dramatic play activities should be at the core of all center activities for high-quality learning to occur. Figure 7.8 illustrates how learning centers can be designed around socio-dramatic play activities. Socio-dramatic play centers are not areas where children go when they have extra time; these centers are critical parts of the early learning curriculum.

Figure 7.8   Indoor and Outdoor Centers

When planning the centers, professionals must pay considerable attention to adapting the activities to *children's concerns*. One way of determining the interests or concerns of children is to watch and listen to them while, at the same time, always keeping in mind each child's sociocultural experiences. Listening to what children are talking about when they arrive at school, watching the books that they choose from the book center, and sending questionnaires home to the parents are all methods for gathering information on children's interests and concerns. Additionally, asking children at a class meeting to suggest topics and materials that they would like to have in the centers can also be useful. The last thing that teachers want is a learning center in which children do not engage in the activities. Should that happen, however, the center should be redesigned so that children are motivated to use it. Additionally, asking the children for suggestions on why they are not using a center and what they would like to have in its place is a respectful and reliable way to gather motivational data.

Learning center activities should implement strategies that allow *adults to guide children's development of language, literacy, and content area skills*. Additionally, appropriate

Preschool children engage in learning core content while participating in playful learning center activities.

early learning standards have been matched to these groups and can be integrated into the learning activities in which the children engage in the centers (see Part III). As demonstrated in the next chapter, sensitive and responsive adult interactions that occur in learning centers can motivate children to develop high-quality learning skills.

Encouraging Pretend Narrative Activities

Children who demonstrate play skills in the socio-dramatic play center should be encouraged to use these skills in other learning centers. Those children who are just learning how to participate in socio-dramatic play activities and who have limited language abilities should be provided with realistic-looking objects to use as make-believe objects. This provides a concrete example of the representation of language. Some examples are the following:

- At the sand or water tables, encouraging children to pretend they are cooks by providing them with bowls, spoons, hats/aprons, pans, and strainers.
- For more advanced play and language skills at the sand or water tables, allow children to be cooks; however, the objects should include fewer pots and pans, and more symbolic-type objects, such as pieces of wood, tongue depressors, and empty yogurt and cottage cheese containers.
- Additionally, adding play items that could add to the plot of the play narrative, such as plastic flies, ants, or other bugs could be added to guide children in the development of more complex and creative cooking narratives.

Figures 7.9 and 7.10 illustrate two classroom plans from research by Neuman and Roskos (1997). The first illustration (7.9) reflects a typical plan for an early education classroom with a housekeeping play center. Figure 7.10 illustrates a classroom with multiple play settings that focus on literacy-enriched contexts (e.g., post office, office center) and that contain literacy-related objects (e.g., pens, paper, address books, calendars). When children participate in the literacy-enriched centers, they not only engage in more literacy activities, but these activities also tend to become more complex as the children begin to master ways of integrating them into their play activities. To encourage the development of literacy and language skills, early education centers should provide multiple learning center opportunities where children can engage in literacy-enriched play activities.

When possible, children should create some of their own props and play objects by using paper plates, modeling clay, or other items (Bodrova & Leong, 2003). Although these items may not be as durable as commercially manufactured objects, making them encourages children to identify objects as having a variety of purposes. For example, a simple paper plate can represent the following objects:

Wheel

Mask

Musical instrument

Sun/moon

Pizza

Flying saucer

Figure 7.9 Classroom Environment Without Literacy-Enriched Centers

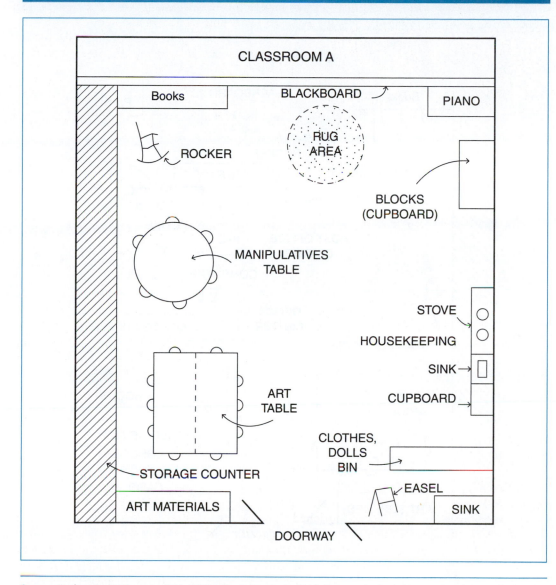

Source: Roskos, K., & Neuman, S. B. (2001). Environment and Its Influences for Early Literacy Teaching and Learning. In S. B. Neuman & D. K. Dickinson (Eds.), *Handbook of Early Literacy Research* (Vol.1, p. 285). New York, NY: Guilford Press.

Allowing children to create their own props assists with their understanding of how language and thought can change one object into another and utilizes both critical and creative thinking skills.

Make-believe play objects should gradually be introduced to the activities and should be mixed with realistic play objects. As discussed earlier in this book, children's ability to use pretense while playing depends on how familiar they are with the play theme, who is involved in the play enactment, and how comfortable the children are with the objects they are using. Adults can assist children by showing them the objects during a group lesson, naturally modeling language through labeling, and brainstorming with them on how certain objects could be integrated into the play activities. Additionally, teachers can expand children's knowledge of different roles that exist in different play themes by taking children on local field trips where the teachers not only focus on the objects at these locations, but also talk about the roles of the

Figure 7.10   Classroom Environment With Literacy-Enriched Centers

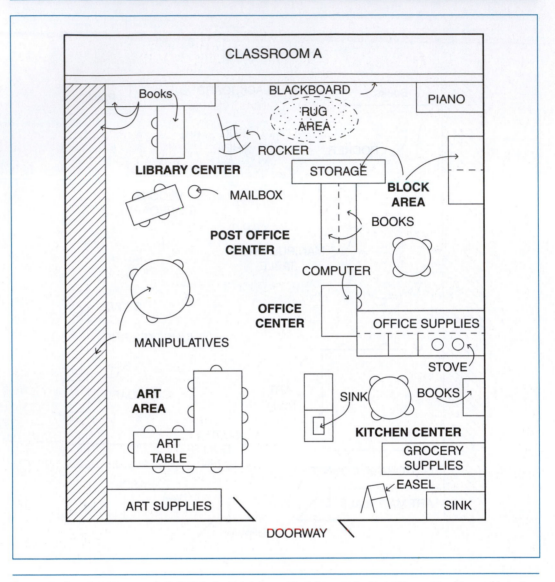

Source: Roskos, K. & Neuman, S. B. (2001). Environment and Its Influences for Early Literacy Teaching and Learning. In S. B. Neuman & D. K. Dickinson (Eds.), *Handbook of early literacy research* (Vol. 1, p. 286). New York, NY: Guilford Press.

workers and the language that is used in different contexts. Figure 7.11 describes numerous realistic and unrealistic play objects that can be used in three different types of socio-dramatic play centers.

Utilizing Familiar and Unfamiliar Activities

Play center activities must relate to experiences that the children are familiar with so that they can use more complex language and feel comfortable focusing on literacy skills. Expansion of language and literacy skills cannot occur successfully if children are attempting to connect information to make sense out of an unfamiliar event.

Figure 7.11 Integrating Realistic and Unrealistic Objects

Castle

- <u>Realistic objects:</u> Hats, dresses, shields, flags, horses
- <u>Unrealistic objects:</u> Material, pipe cleaners, poles, paper

Fix It Shop

- <u>Realistic objects:</u> Tools, appliances, cords, hammers, nails
- <u>Unrealistic objects:</u> Blocks, clamps, Styrofoam, rope, rags

Ice Cream Shop

- <u>Realistic objects:</u> Scooper, cones, cups, toppings, candies
- <u>Unrealistic objects:</u> Paper, balls, Popsicle sticks, straws

Additionally, a child might demonstrate knowledge of certain familiar play themes—like taking a bus, washing a dog, visiting the grocery store, or delivering mail. However, these situations are not similar for all children, and do require the involved participants to integrate the specific routines or customs that they have experienced with that activity and to make appropriate linguistic, emotional, and cognitive choices. As a result, taking a trip may be comprised of very different language, thoughts, and emotions, depending on the children involved. For one child, it may be a joyous time, consisting of looking at maps and travel books, purchasing tickets, and packing a suitcase. For another child, a trip may be associated with the sorrow of someone traveling far away, perhaps alone and to another country, and not being seen for a long period of time. These diverse experiences show children can have different perspectives and language around the same play theme.

Symbolic objects allow children to create decontextualized play stories.

Jupiterimages/BananaStock/Thinkstock

Chapter 8 will demonstrate that for high-quality learning to occur, adults need to guide children's learning. In order to provide appropriate guidance, adults must be cognizant of how typical play settings are influenced by individual family values and beliefs. Children are motivated by activities that they participate in with their families, communities, and cultures (Hedges, Cullen, & Jordan, 2011). Everyday roles that young children experience in their families and communities provide authentic learning opportunities for those children. Therefore, teachers must develop knowledge of the diverse experiences that occur in the home with their families and in their communities. They need to view these experiences in a positive manner and use them as the foundation for learning activities.

As discussed in Chapter 1, Moll et al., (1992) define funds of knowledge as bodies of knowledge, including information, skills, and strategies, that are related to home and community activities. Family- and community-based funds of knowledge can supply the foundation that motivates children to learn. Adults need to examine the play activities of children for the purpose of linking those activities to the child's funds of knowledge, rather than linking them to the materials being used, which is typically the pattern (Hedges et al., 2011). For example, when children engage in cooking activities at the sand and water tables, the teacher will often attribute this interest to the enjoyment of using the materials rather than linking it to the child's feeling of enjoyment in replicating a home activity that is part of the child's funds of knowledge. Additionally, if a child loves to pretend to be on a fishing trip, that child is most likely being motivated by experiences of fishing with a special family member or friend, rather than being motivated by the play materials. Observing children in these experiences helps teachers gather rich information for future activities.

Therefore, adults need to discover the children's funds of knowledge and then design learning activities around this information. For children some activities can represent extremely happy and motivating experiences from their everyday lives, while other activities might be dreaded or viewed as unpleasant. Figure 7.12 illustrates some common play themes and how they can vary in activities and emotions, depending on each child's individual experiences.

Teachers can obtain information on funds of knowledge and emotions related to the familiar, everyday activities of young children by asking caregivers to provide information on their own families' experiences to the teachers. Teachers can use this information to design play centers that will be familiar to children and assist them in utilizing more advanced social and cognitive skills. Figure 7.13 contains a sample of a survey that could

Figure 7.12   Play Activities and Diverse Behaviors and Emotions

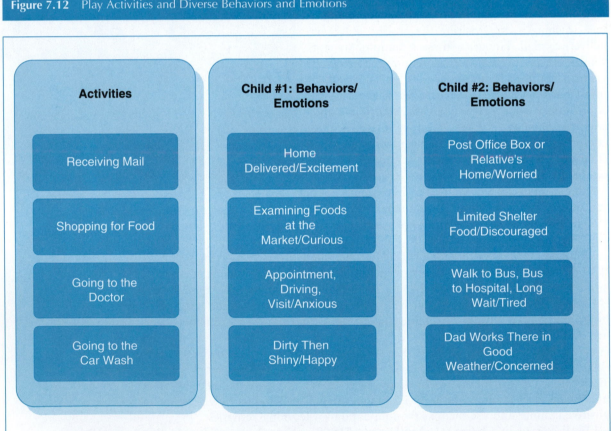

Activities	Child #1: Behaviors/Emotions	Child #2: Behaviors/Emotions
Receiving Mail	Home Delivered/Excitement	Post Office Box or Relative's Home/Worried
Shopping for Food	Examining Foods at the Market/Curious	Limited Shelter Food/Discouraged
Going to the Doctor	Appointment, Driving, Visit/Anxious	Walk to Bus, Bus to Hospital, Long Wait/Tired
Going to the Car Wash	Dirty Then Shiny/Happy	Dad Works There in Good Weather/Concerned

Figure 7.13 Survey of Familiar Everyday Activities

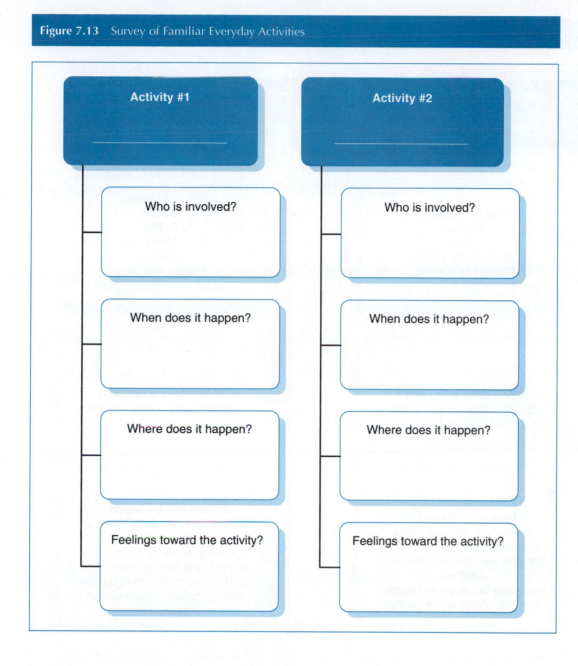

be sent home to the families during the year to gather information on the children's experiences with a certain activity and the emotional state that usually accompanies that activity. It includes a general statement explaining the need for this information. Figure 7.14 contains a survey by parents as an example of the type of information teachers are interested in obtaining.

Effective learning activities need to emphasize socio-dramatic skills along with the content area. For example, assume that children are using the outdoor climbing apparatus as a means of enhancing gross motor skills, and the socio-dramatic center represents a playhouse theme. With the addition of a few minor props, the apparatus can be modified into a store, a restaurant, or even a witch's house to encourage the development of descriptive verbal and nonverbal language and the creation of a story. The food could be

Figure 7.14 Survey of Familiar Everyday Activities

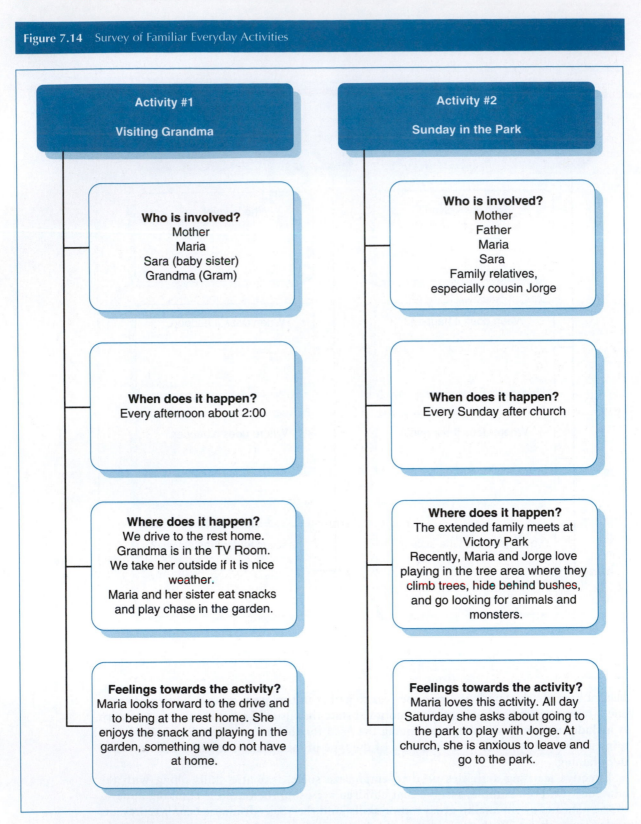

prepared at the sand table and then driven over to the house or store or restaurant. Adults must know what experiences, interests, and skills the children have, and which ones the children are working toward developing, in order to modify play and create high-quality learning. If the children rarely eat at a restaurant, then the climbing apparatus should be transformed into a fast-food eating place.

Additionally, as will be demonstrated in Chapter 8, adults can assist children in understanding new roles that might occur in settings similar to but not exactly like the one being created in a peer play episode. Through responsive observations, an adult might learn that a child is unfamiliar with ordering food at a restaurant. That adult should wait for the right moment and then suggest that the restaurant might need a cook.

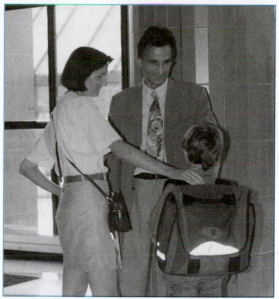

Collaboration with families should occur regularly.

Developing High-Quality Learning Centers

Work on the characteristics of high-quality classrooms by Chien et al. (2010) reflects concerns about managing children, time, space, and materials vital for positive learning outcomes. Learning centers should not just be open for children to engage in learning activities. Children need to learn how to appropriately use centers and how to participate in collaborative learning center activities. The following sections discuss how to design learning centers, and Figure 7.15 provides a 4-week guide for introducing appropriate center participation behaviors to young children.

Center Management

One of the major concerns when designing learning centers for young children is how to manage them. Not only do children need to be taught how to engage in activities that are at the center, they need to learn how to move appropriately from one center to another. Through modeling, peer role play, and group discussions, most children learn the acceptable behaviors.

Figure 7.15   Gradual Instruction on How to Use Learning Centers

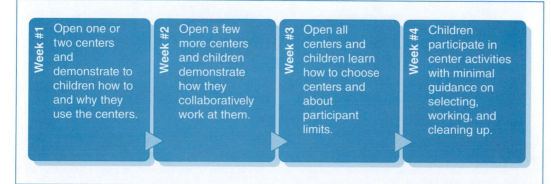

Week #1	Week #2	Week #3	Week #4
Open one or two centers and demonstrate to children how to and why they use the centers.	Open a few more centers and children demonstrate how they collaboratively work at them.	Open all centers and children learn how to choose centers and about participant limits.	Children participate in center activities with minimal guidance on selecting, working, and cleaning up.

Every learning center must be rich with print. However, professionals need to keep in mind that more print does not mean better print. Instead, having a few meaningful labels and captions around the center and in places that will get the children's attention is much more productive than cluttering the center with print. Again, using visual schedules (see Chapter 6) that combine pictures and print at each center demonstrating what the children need to do can enhance their independence and increase their literacy skills. Sometimes, having a "wash line" with clothes pins to hang pictures and/or printed cards of what needs to be done at that center allows for continual changing of the message without much trouble.

Most of the time, children should be allowed to choose the centers in which they want to participate. Setting a limited number of participants and choosing creative ways to enforce the limits, as shown in Figure 7.16, can efficiently manage the number of participants at a center. If the teacher wants to ensure that children visit specific centers at least once a week, the children can be issued a "Personal Passport" that lists required activities. Also, if cleaning up the centers is a challenge for the children, each center can be assigned a "Clean Up Captain" who attempts to organize peers into getting the center back in order.

Additionally, if too many children are interested in playing at a particular center (what a thrill!), a wait list can be created and the children can manage that wait list. Having a practice where children write their name on a list and, when one child leaves the center he or she informs the child who is waiting to play, is a natural and socially acceptable way for handling such a situation. Typically, very positive behaviors result from using such a simple procedure.

Center Time

Children require a considerable amount of time to plan and perform most activities. At the beginning of each learning center activity, children must recruit other participants,

Figure 7.16   Methods for Managing Center Participants

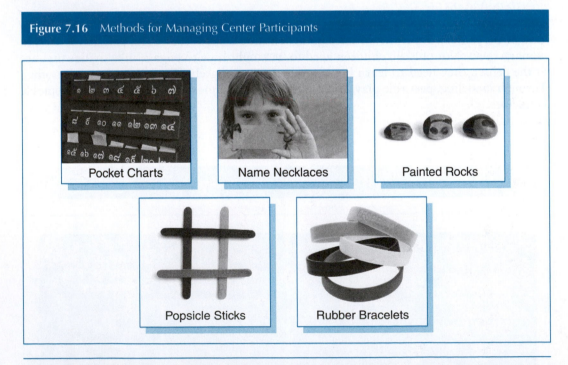

Pocket Charts

Name Necklaces

Painted Rocks

Popsicle Sticks

Rubber Bracelets

Sources: (Pocket Charts) ©iStock.com/miramalee; (Name Necklaces) ©iStock.com/lyosha_nazarenko; (Painted Rocks) Solymosi TamA!s/iStock/Thinkstock; (Popsicle Sticks) Sarah Cates/iStock/Thinkstock; and (Rubber Bracelets) Yiap See Fat/iStock/Thinkstock.

negotiate roles, and agree upon rules. All of these tasks are extremely valuable learning activities that the staff needs to monitor. The staff must also afford children as much independence and support as needed to attempt or "try out" new skills. These activities also consume a considerable amount of time due to the limited communication and social skills of young children.

When children are not provided with sufficient time, they often lack opportunities to create higher level linguistic statements, use new vocabulary, and create more abstract enactments. As a result, they construct less advanced activities than they are capable of producing. With the current trend of programs reducing the amount of time allotted for play activities (see Chapter 1), care must be taken in seeing that children are not rushed through these activities, which have been intentionally planned for them.

Children should have enough space so that they can move around and interact with the materials and peers who are in the setting.

Center Space

Children who have access to a limited amount of space might tend to quarrel and become aggressive when participating in large, small, and center group activities. Conversely, too much space might encourage them to move around and have unfocused interactions. The area designated for a center activity should be approximately 25 square feet per child involved in the activities (Roskos & Neuman, 2001). This area is necessary to ensure quality and cooperative interactions between participants. The "25 square feet per child" metric affords children enough space to comfortably move around and explore, and yet still remain focused on the learning experiences available to them and their peers.

The classroom design of locations for group and center areas should include natural boundaries that create appropriate-sized niches where children are afforded privacy to attempt the use of new interactions and language with peers and adults. These boundaries assist in regulating and guiding children's behaviors, and they can be created by portable furniture, such as the following:

Bookshelves

Cabinets

Crates

Tables

Cushions

Low-hanging shower curtains

However, centers should not be too private, as adults must be able to monitor activities from across the room to track the children's independence and to gain knowledge needed to support the children's learning.

One way to organize space in the classroom is to provide signs. Some signs should clearly instruct the students about the goals of different areas. Other signs explain what the children do in these areas.

©iStock.com/XiXinXing

The inclusion of cultural materials can assist children with transitioning from home to school.

Center Materials

During learning activities, a variety of items must be present for children to choose from, and these items should address all children's interests and abilities. Generally, very young children prefer materials that allow for pulling and stacking; in contrast, somewhat older children enjoy small manipulative items, for example vehicles, animals, people. If some children are capable of playing independently, they should be supplied with materials that encourage independence, such as puzzles and art materials (Roskos & Neuman, 2001). For children who enjoy interacting with others while playing, dolls or stuffed animals are more appropriate. Materials should be organized in child-manageable containers according to themes, functions, or skills, and not just heaped into a tub for children to tear through and dump out in search of specific items. In particular, preschool children should be developing the skills that make them more responsible, self-directed, and logical. Having centers where the children are responsible for initiating, participating in, and completing specific activities will enhance those developmental skills.

Having an abundance of materials that encourage opportunities for children to interact with and use print in the centers assists them in realizing the power of reading and writing in everyday life. All centers should contain some of the following literacy-related materials so that children can integrate them into their activities:

Blank paper	Post-its
Books	Instructions
Vocabulary boards	Stickers
Signs	Lined paper
Magazines	Stamps/pads
Word boards	Blank cards
Pencils, crayons	Keyboard
Rulers	Tape
Chalk/chalkboards	Safe scissors

Classrooms should provide continuity between all children's homes and schools. Center materials also need to reflect the diverse cultures represented in the group. A variety of objects and garments that represent different cultural groups should be available at each center. Authentic types of foods and eating utensils should also be provided in the socio-dramatic play center. Although not all staff members are proficient in children's home languages, they can learn, use, or display the words for some of the learning materials in children's home language. Doing such will convey the feelings of value, honor, and respect for the child's heritage.

Materials that children can identify as part of their cultural heritage will enhance their comfort. These materials will help offer positive play opportunities. For example, having pillows for children to sit on around one of the tables could reflect a more direct connection between the school and home for some children. Additionally, blankets or tapestries that reflect different areas of the world (e.g., Asia, Africa, India, South America) also assist in enhancing children's feelings of comfort, which should result in more effective learning.

REFLECT AND APPLY EXERCISE 7.3

Responding to Linguistic and Cultural Diversity

Reflect

Developing a classroom culture of acceptance in highly diverse ethnic and linguistic contexts can be challenging. Children are bringing to school learned behaviors, experiences, norms, and language. Think about what it would be like for children to enter a classroom where they are unable to make personal connections with the activities, routines, language, and materials all around them. Cultural and linguistic awareness on the part of the teacher can foster awareness and acceptance by children. Establishing a diverse learning experience for children encourages a sense of belonging and excitement for learning something new and unfamiliar.

Apply

Go back to the opening scenario. Knowledge of children's cultural and linguistic backgrounds can be seen in the travel center where the teacher provides transportation, clothing, and other props that represent a wide range of cultural backgrounds. Seeing themselves and their family in their classroom experiences connects children to the classroom and enhances the overall learning experience. Children can start with the familiar as a foundation for learning something new. Think of other center themes and how diversity can be integrated into those themes.

LEARNING FOR ALL CHILDREN
Activity Materials and Culture

Schools can use parents as a resource to assist children from diverse cultures in feeling comfortable in unfamiliar learning environments (Saul & Saul, 2002). Parents can be invited to share clothing, foods, items, and celebrations from their home countries. International clubs at nearby universities can be a valuable resource for arranging classroom visitors. Additionally, when a child has a birthday, classrooms can arrange a celebration using items from the child's home country—for instance, piñata, special clothing, and/or native food.

Art centers should contain shades of paper and paints that match the variety of skin colors of the children in the classroom. Music centers ought to contain music and instruments from various cultures around the world. Science centers could have activities requiring children to match

(Continued)

(Continued)

certain items with countries located in different areas around the world (e.g., seashells near coastal countries, woven baskets from grasslands, copper items from mountain areas). Children might be guided to build housing and buildings in the block center made from different materials (e.g., canvas, clay, straw). Of course, the classroom should have books, travel materials, museum advertisements, and pictures that would assist the children in creating such structures.

Exposure to these diverse cultural items assists all students in understanding and accepting cultural differences. At the same time, such exposure makes children who are unfamiliar with the mainstream culture feel more comfortable.

Sending home a survey to find out information on the families' cultures and traditions can assist in learning about similarities and differences in a positive way. Surveys can include questions on the following topics:

- Customs
- Foods
- Clothing
- Language spoken in the home and familiar phrases
- Eating and cooking utensils
- Practices for celebrating holidays and birthdays

In summary, the following are key steps that lead to the successful design of and participation in high-quality learning centers:

1. Carefully plan the lessons and how much space will be required, how the space will be used, and where the learning center space will be located.

2. Provide visual supports for each center so that the children will know what they are to do when they are at that center. Simple mini-posters with helpful reminders can assist the children (see Figure 7.17).

3. Model what is to be done at each learning center. This modeling can be done first by discussing the center in a large group activity. Later, more specific modeling can occur with small group instruction. Discussions and modeling should focus on what to do and what not to do at each center.

4. Regularly assess the group dynamics at the centers. Make sure that all the children are getting along and working together. Talk about what it means to not be a good friend. If there are conflicts, have the children talk about the problems that have occurred and how they think the problems could be solved. Remember, there is a lot more learning that goes on during learning center activities than just isolated information. Children are learning to work in groups, to interact, to be independent, to negotiate, to use different types of language, and to respect others.

5. Continually incorporate a component at each center where children can engage in sociodramatic play activities. They can dress as scientists or cooks at the water table, construction workers at the block center, artists at the art center, book characters at the book center, audience members at the puppet center, handymen at the manipulative center, and reporters at the writing center. Simple hats can be used to convey a number of these roles.

6. Create fun transition activities that relate to what the children are learning. At the beginning of the year, transitions most likely will have to be teacher directed. However, as the year progresses and students become familiar with the procedures, transitions can become more child centered. The children can flow from center to center depending where the openings are located.

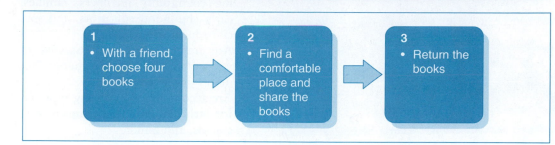

Figure 7.17 Book Learning Center Mini-Poster Instructions

1
- With a friend, choose four books

2
- Find a comfortable place and share the books

3
- Return the books

Integrating Early Learning and Common Core Standards Into Play Centers

As stated at the beginning of this chapter, high-quality programs are ones that integrate early learning standards into developmentally appropriate practices. **Early learning standards** are statements describing desired outcomes and content for young children's learning (NAEYC, 2009b). They specify the knowledge, skills, and competencies that children should master, and they provide educators with the foundation for what to teach (Stott, 2003). Standards allow teachers to focus on what has been determined as valued learning goals. They can also be used to assess progress toward attaining these goals.

In 2001, *No Child Left Behind* mandated states to develop K–12 learning standards and encouraged the development of Early Childhood standards for preschoolers in the areas of literacy and mathematics. Today, most states have early education standards in the areas of literacy, mathematics, science, social studies, health, physical development, social-emotional development, and creative arts (Early Childhood Education Assessment, 2007). Nonetheless, although standards create the foundation for the preschool education curriculum, they do not address all that must be taught (Grisham-Brown, Pretti-Frontczak, Hawkins, & Winchell, 2009). Nor do the standards provide assistance on how to teach. Additionally, one of the challenges in early childhood education is the existence of multiple sets of standards (e.g., State Standards, Head Start Standards, Early Reading First) and which set should be used.

Integrating standards into play centers can result in high-quality learning.

©iStock.com/monkeybusinessimages

The National Association for the Education of Young Children and the National Association of Early Childhood Specialists in State Departments of Education (NAECS/SDE) assert that early learning standards are a valuable component of a comprehensive, high-quality system of service for all young children. NAEYC and NAECS/SDE (2002) support standards with specific attributes. These standards:

- Emphasize significant, developmentally appropriate content and outcomes (including cognitive, language, physical, social, and emotional abilities, and accommodate for variations in culture, abilities, and disabilities)

Early standards must support the use of developmentally appropriate practices.

- Are developed and reviewed through informed, inclusive processes (including community members, families, early childhood educators, and special educators)
- Are implemented and assessed in ways that support all young children's development
- Are accompanied by strong supports for early childhood programs professionals, and families

The NIEER asserts that between 2000 and 2010, states increased the quality of pre-K standards. However, the report states that little progress had been noted in either 2009–2010 or in 2010–2011. This lack of progress with state standards for early learning has caused alarm, especially in states with large enrollments where inadequate services might be provided for low-income communities and where high concentrations of disadvantaged children could benefit from quality services.

Improper use of early standards, such as using a standard to determine the activity in which children will engage, can also lead to the designing of a sterile curriculum that is not based on the interest or experiences of children's own worlds (Kendall, 2003). Early learning standards cannot be an extension or watered-down version of K–12 standards, as has frequently been the situation. Young children have varied learning rates and interests; therefore, their learning standards should be broad and should include some learning activities different from those already established for K–12. Early education standards must guide teachers in selecting meaningful and developmentally appropriate curriculum activities in which children are motivated to learn.

Recently, common core standards have been developed for all K–12 children in the United States. These Common Core State Standards focus on core conceptual understandings and procedures that are presented to students in kindergarten. Through a high-quality education, students build each year on these foundational skills until they are able to master skills needed for college entrance. The Common Core State Standards will be discussed further, along with the early learning standards in Part III of this book.

Chapter Summary

This chapter builds upon the information presented in Part I on planning for learning. Specifically, the chapter examines how to create high-quality learning centers through the use of intentional teaching experiences that integrate differentiated instructional interactions. Learning activities must target each child's readiness level, interests, and learning preferences.

Particular attention needs to be paid to the use of time, space, and materials in order to successfully guide young children into higher levels of learning through learning center activities. The integration of core early learning standards into carefully planned learning centers will enhance high-quality learning.

CHAPTER 7 FIRST-PERSON INTERVIEW
Ever-Evolving Learning Centers

Danelle LaFoe

Associate Director and Curriculum Coordinator for the 3-, 4-, and 5-year-old program, Champaign, IL

I work at a school that is all-day and year-round. We focus on developing a whole child by enhancing their social, emotional, creative, physical, cognitive, and academic skills. At our school, teachers discover from the children what they are interested in learning, what they already know about the topic, and what they want to learn. Similarly, children learn from the teachers' new information relating to their interests through books, activities, experiments, field investigations, and free play.

Our daily schedule includes free choice play, individualized and group academics, and project-based investigations. At our school, children have choices all day long. During free choice, they choose what centers they want to play at and have continual opportunities for dramatic play activities. Free choice consists of the Dramatic Play Center, the Engineering Center, the Library Center, the Art Center, the Science Center, and other puzzles, games, and toys. Our play center, which typically starts out at the beginning of the year as a housekeeping center, changes as the children become interested in different themes. In the past, the play area has become a post office, a fire station, a pet store, and a bowling alley. The play center changes as we engage in new learning "projects." These projects last as long as the children are interested in the topic and are gaining new information related to the theme. Our teachers continually search for opportunities to expand the children's knowledge so that they are challenged to learn new skills at developmentally appropriate levels, and not just repeat familiar skills. Our projects can last one week, two weeks, one month, or two months. As long as the children are interested and motivated to learn, teachers continue to do their research on the topic and provide opportunities for the children to heighten their level of learning.

For example, one day the children showed an interest in learning more about worms. Therefore, the class sent off an order for worms to be delivered to the school. Once the worms arrived, the children had the opportunity to observe them and learn all about them, along with the worms found outside. The children then became interested in gardening and in watching how worms interact with the garden. The play center was equipped with gardening tools for the students to explore and experiment with. The students began to wonder about compost and what would assist their garden the best: their own-made compost, purchased compost, or just dirt. They conducted an experiment to see which one provided the most benefits.

Every day each child has special times when he or she can play at the play center. The project is also integrated into other activities throughout the day. For example, the teachers will read a book or create a poem about the project, and focus on developing higher language and literacy abilities. The students engage in counting and graphing activities to enhance math skills. Having children create block formations enriches motor and cognitive skills. Science skills are enhanced through child-proposed experiments while teachers help set up variables, and art skills develop by having the children create items that focus on some aspect of the project's theme.

Recently, the children have been aware of the different machines that are on the streets near the preschool. Therefore, one class started an investigation on construction. They began by having

(Continued)

(Continued)

the children answer the question, "What does the word 'construction' mean?" The teachers will send home a class letter asking parents if they can donate anything that could contribute to the project on construction, such as tools, play machines, work attire, and so on, to use in the play center, or, if they work in the field of construction, if they would like to be a guest speaker at our school. The teachers are beginning to plan some local field trips to different construction sites so that the children can make comparisons between them. Finally, the staff has been meeting collectively to share ideas on how they can incorporate the construction theme into other learning centers. At our preschool, everyone is motivated to learn, the children and the adults alike!

Student Study Site

Visit the Student Study Site at **www.sagepub.com/selmi** to access additional study tools including mobile-friendly eFlashcards and links to video and web resources.

Key Terms

differentiated instruction

early learning standards

high-quality activities

intentional teaching

learning styles

lesson plans

open-ended prompts

readiness skills

Useful Websites

NAEYC: http://www.naeyc.org

National Institute for Early Education Research: http://nieer.org

Reflective Questions

1. This chapter made reference to statistics from the National Institute for Early Education Research (NIEER). Go to their website: http://nieer.org/sites/nieer/files/2011yearbook .pdf
   Examine the data provided. Look at the current finding for your state and discuss how practices have changed during the past decade. What predictions can you make for the next decade? Compare your state with the states that have a high ranking and then with those that have a low ranking. What would your state have to do to be included as one with a high-ranking score?

2. Create a lesson plan for an activity discussed in the opening scenario for this chapter.

8 Strategies for Guiding Play and Producing High-Quality Learning Activities

TEACHER ROSIE'S PHONE CALL

Comstock/Stockbyte/Thinkstock

Some children are playing in two areas, the dramatic play area and the puzzle area. The other children are outside. A female teacher is sitting near the puzzle area, and a male university teacher candidate (TC) is sitting on the floor next to the dramatic play area. A child enters the dramatic play area. She picks up a red, "u-shaped" object, and hands it to the TC. The TC looks at the object, looks at the preschooler, and then looks back at the object while turning it around in his hands. Next, he places one end of the object near his ear and the other end near his mouth. He says, "Hello, Teacher Rosie! We miss you."

The TC then hands the object back to the preschooler and says, "It's Teacher Rosie. She's calling us from her vacation. Do you want to talk to her?" The preschooler takes the object, looks at it, and moves it near her face. However, she then immediately gives it back to the TC. The TC takes the object back and says, "It's Teacher Rosie calling us to tell us that she's having a good vacation." The child looks at the TC and then continues into the play area.

Another child then rushes over toward the TC and puts her hand on the red object that the TC is holding. The TC moves the object closer to the preschooler while saying, "It's Teacher Rosie calling from her vacation. She's having lots of fun." The child puts the object near her ear and mouth and says, "Hi Teacher Rosie. Are you on vacation?" She pauses, says, "Bye, Teacher Rosie," and then hands the object back to the TC.

The TC again puts the object to his ear and mouth, and says, "Hi Teacher Rosie. How's your vacation? Can we come visit you tomorrow and go fishing? How do we get to the beach?" The TC waits a couple of seconds, puts the phone down, and says to the child, "Could you go get a pencil and paper? Teacher Rosie is going to tell us which bus to take to the beach."

This opening scenario reveals how adults can maintain the critical aspects of socio-dramatic play (e.g., collaborative, pretend activities) while, at the same time, naturally supporting the development of academic skills (e.g., language enhancement, symbolic representation enrichment, and narrative expansion) in young children. The teacher candidate demonstrates how the use of a red, u-shaped object can symbolically represent a telephone, and he guides a preschooler in creating a narrative story around a "phone call from Teacher Rosie." This situation illustrates ways in which play and academic learning can be compatible activities.

This chapter examines how adults can guide the play activities of young children so that successful high-quality learning occurs. Specifically, this chapter addresses the following questions:

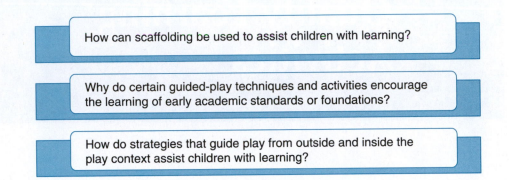

How can scaffolding be used to assist children with learning?

Why do certain guided-play techniques and activities encourage the learning of early academic standards or foundations?

How do strategies that guide play from outside and inside the play context assist children with learning?

Guided Learning

In the quest to improve student achievement scores in the elementary grades, early childhood teachers today are often pressured into replacing child-centered, learning-rich play activities with prescriptive and scripted instructional programs. Research reveals that kindergarten children commonly participate in 3 to 4 hours a day of literacy and math instruction, and spend only about 30 minutes or less in play activities (Miller & Almon, 2009). Some kindergarteners spend up to six times as much time on focused reading and math activities, and on testing and test preparation, than they spend involved in play (Wilson, 2009).

Roskos and Christie (2000), along with the National Association for the Education of Young Children, strongly advocate three principles that support learning through child-centered play activities. These principles are listed below and are related to events occurring in the opening scenario of this chapter:

- Play provides a setting that promotes *the learning of literacy activity, skills, and strategies.* (The opening scenario: Requesting a pencil and paper)
- Play serves as a language experience that *can build connections between oral and written modes of expression.* (The opening scenario: The TC writing down the number of the bus to Teacher Rosie's vacation place)
- Play provides opportunities for *teachers to teach and children to learn literacy.* (The opening scenario: Developing a narrative about Teacher Rosie's vacation)

Through the use of child-centered and teacher-guided play (not teacher-directed) activities, the learning challenges of all children can be addressed (Christie & Roskos,

2000). Part I of this book examines how children are capable of learning an enormous amount of skills. For example, children learn to use close to 300 words a year during their first 4 years of life (McAfee & Leong, 2007). Of course, some children will require more guided learning than others. However, teachers must know how to manipulate the environment so that all children successfully encounter their needed content areas while they play. Learning does not just happen independently; it is a guided process.

Scaffolding

Adults can guide children's play to enhance language, literacy, and learning abilities.

Chapter 2 of this book discussed Vygotsky's research (1978), which posits that children's potential to achieve with support is more advanced than what they can accomplish independently. Specifically, he demonstrated that in collaboration with an adult or a more capable other person, children could progress in a task through the *zone of proximal development* to the level of potential development, where the task can be performed independently. Again, the opening scenario describes one child who is hesitant about using the red object as a phone and another who definitely knew how to independently pretend.

Jerome Bruner (1986), a well-known child psychologist, determined that children actually move through the zone of proximal development by using a process he termed scaffolding. Scaffolding occurs when adults build bridges from the child's unknown and not-understood information to the child's known and understood information through the use of guided and sensitive social interactions (Henderson, Many, Wellborn, & Ward, 2002). Evidence-based research studies have found that scaffolding successfully results in learning (see Figure 8.1). Effective scaffolding occurs when those involved work toward a common goal. In this process, the less experienced person must stretch his or her understanding to obtain new information, while the more experienced person bridges unknown information with known concepts (McGee & Richgels, 2012).

REFLECT AND APPLY EXERCISE 8.1

Using Scaffolding

Reflect

Read the scenario at the beginning of Chapter 2 where a father is playing with a young child. Notice how the father is scaffolding the experience by providing support as the child attempts to organize new information to fit with what the child already knows.

Apply

Choose one of the scaffolding studies listed in Figure 8.1. Find examples of some of the scaffolding strategies that are listed in the Figure that are being used in the Chapter 2 opening scenario.

Figure 8.1   Evidence-Based Scaffolding Strategies

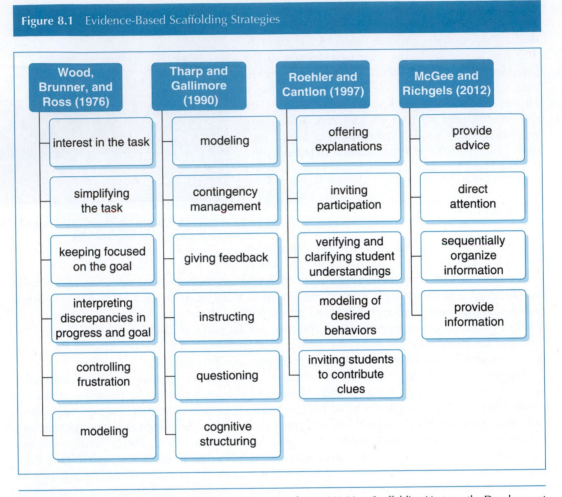

Source: Henderson, S. D., Many, J. E., Wellborn, H. P., & Ward, J. (2002). How Scaffolding Nurtures the Development of Young Children's Literacy Repertoire: Insiders' and Outsiders' Collaborative Understandings. *Reading Research and Instruction, 41,* 309–330.

Guided Play

Guided play, which is sometimes referred to as scaffolded play, is a form of child-centered play where adults structure the environment around general curricular goals designed to stimulate children's natural curiosity, exploration, and play through interactions with objects and peers. It is comprised of verbal and/or nonverbal interactions that support or scaffold the play activity, thus allowing the participants to work toward a common goal with at least one more experienced peer or adult. When more experienced persons are adults, they must be fully aware of the learner's capabilities and how to relate the desired learning task to what the child already knows. As the participants interact, the difficulty is adjusted upward or downward depending on the learner's immediate response to the challenge presented by the activity. Through joint problem-solving verbalizations and visual demonstrations or modeling, guidance is provided and the learner's skills are expanded. As the learner becomes more capable of independently performing the activity, the "guiding" or "scaffolding" is decreased, thus allowing the learner to take more of the lead in successfully completing the task. Figure 8.2 suggests steps for successful scaffolding.

Adults need to recognize that learning occurs when the child and the adult are actively involved in the activity. Learning about the interests and needs of children assists adults in

Figure 8.2 Successful Scaffolding

| Rapport has been established between the "teacher" and the "learner." | The "teacher" is sensitive to the "learner's" responses. | The task is neither too tough nor too easy. | The "teacher" knows when to let the "learner" take the next step. | The "teacher" lets the "learner" control the activity as much as possible. |

Source: Soderman, A. K., Gregory, K. M., & McCarty, L. T. (2005). *Scaffolding Emergent Literacy: A Child-Centered Approach for Preschool Through Grade 5.* New York, NY: Pearson Education.

guiding and caring for each individual child. Through the continual observation of children's play and their interactions (see Chapter 9), adults learn about each child's interests, abilities, and developmental progress.

When children are engaged in challenging puzzle activities, adults observe to learn which related skills the children might have and which ones they need. With that knowledge, the adult can then verbally encourage the children to perform specific tasks that assist in learning how to successfully complete the puzzle. Through the adult learning what the child knows, and the child learning information that the adult knows, children's skills expand.

Research now demonstrates (Hirsh-Paseket et al., 2009) that high-quality early education learning centers include places where both free play and guided play activities exist side-by-side. As mentioned in Chapter 7, high-quality early education centers do not view children as miniature elementary students. At the same time, they do not take the opposite approach by letting children run around freely. Instead, high-quality learning occurs when adults working at these centers skillfully use play as a critical component for the development of cognitive, linguistic, literacy, and social skills. Consistent with this idea, the chapters in Part III of this book provide information on designing playful learn-

Adults encourage children to use high-quality behaviors when scaffolding in playful activities.

Jupiterimages/Goodshoot/Thinkstock

ing contexts that guide young children in learning vocabulary, using print, understanding numbers, developing stories, and enhancing other skills needed for academic success.

Guided play requires teachers to be skilled at nudging children to transition from a familiar level of play activity to a higher level of unfamiliar play activity. That higher level will most likely necessitate the use of new language and more abstract symbolic representations in order to compose, negotiate, and implement complex play narratives. Specifically, teachers must have the skills and knowledge to carry out the following complex tasks (Snow et al., 1998):

- Create symbolic representations
- Use appropriate language play enactments
- Compose stories within someone else's story
- Negotiate the use of objects and others within the story
- Solve problems that occur during the development of the play narrative

©iStock.com/omgimages

Adults model pretense to young children.

Figure 8.3 illustrates how the teacher candidate in the scenario at the beginning of this chapter guided young children's learning by using these literacy supports. As children become more experienced players and language users, they also become capable of producing the five skills set forth above. They then can guide their peers in developing more advanced socio-dramatic play enactments.

In their comprehensive summary on the research of guided play and learning, Berk et al., (2006) examine caregivers' use of socio-dramatic play activities with their young children. They found that, during the second year of a child's life, mothers in Western societies typically introduce pretend play behaviors, demonstrate how one object can replace another, and create narratives. Later, around 2 years of age, mothers begin talking with their children about nonexistent fantasy objects in order to enhance the play narratives that they are collaboratively creating with the children. Such examples demonstrate how caregivers use guided play to expand learning.

Figure 8.3   Literacy Support and Scenario Examples

Literacy Supports During Play	Scenario Examples
Create symbolic representations	Transforming the red, u-shaped object into a phone
Use appropriate language for play enactments	Talking about Teacher Rosie being on vacation
Compose stories within someone else's story	During the phone conversation, asking about visiting her
Negotiate the use of objects and others within the story	Giving the "phone" back to the child to talk with Teacher Rosie
Solve problems that occur during the play activity	Asking a child to get a pencil and piece of paper to write down directions to the beach

Source: Soderman, A. K., Gregory, K. M., & McCarty, L. T. (2005). *Scaffolding Emergent Literacy: A Child-Centered Approach for Preschool Through Grade 5.* New York, NY: Pearson Education.

Mothers also used guided play strategies to create interesting and absorbing play activities. These activities encourage their children to participate in play activities much longer than the children could by themselves, and create a platform for the child to learn how to play. Through the use of demonstrations, suggestions, turn-taking, and collaborative involvement, young children—who are interested but not capable by themselves—jointly construct mature pretend narratives (Bornstein & O'Reilly, 1993). However, if 3-year-old children have parents who negate, correct, or overtly direct play activities, the children tend to manipulate play materials in a more immature manner. Conversely, 5-year-old children who have been encouraged to play tend to engage in more creative, expressive, and socially competent pretending than children with parents who were more instructive and controlling of their play (Berk et al., 2006).

Play guidance can be provided by a more experienced peer.

©iStockphoto.com/J-Roman

Guided Play Challenges

Gauging the correct sensitivity toward children's play activities is critical in guided play. Enough support must be offered to assist the learner in understanding the following (Christensen & Kelly, 2003):

- How to pretend to be someone or something else
- What behaviors and language to use
- How to compose a make-believe story
- How to negotiate and problem-solve with co-players

If the more experienced person's interactions are more directive than reciprocal, then the child's play may become less symbolic (Haight & Miller, 1993), and thus less advanced. Similarly, when children's language is directly corrected often they may "shut down" and become too intimidated to talk. More appropriately, adults should use recasting when a child might mispronounce or improperly produce language. **Recasting** is a practice in which an adult repeats the child's incorrect language properly (Gibbons, 2003). The adult doesn't tell the child he or she was wrong or ask the child to repeat it properly, but simply recasts, or restates it correctly. This creates a natural, authentic opportunity for the child to acquire language in a nonthreatening way.

Play episodes that are appropriately supported by a sensitive adult partner will be more frequent, longer, and conducted at a higher level of play than when a child plays alone (Bornstein & Tamis-LeMonda, 1997). The use of appropriate guided play strategies by an adult should result in children implementing more sophisticated language and social skills, varying viewpoints, and higher level problem-solving and persuasion skills (Soderman et al., 2005).

The guiding player must continually strive to anchor the suggested activities within the child's zone of proximal development. Predetermining the roles, content, or direction of the play must not occur; rather, the guide must be cognizant of what the child is specifically doing during "real time" and how the child is doing it. Only with this knowledge can the guiding player attempt to inspire a play partner to achieve more independent language, symbolic, and narrative skills (Bondioli, 2001).

Fisher et al. (2011) recommend the following aspects of how adults can guide children's play activities:

1. Enriching the play environment with toys, objects, people, and other items

2. Providing supporting comments about children's discoveries, co-playing with them, and posing open-ended questions about what a child has found

3. Proposing language to model vocabulary and syntax, and exploring play materials in a manner similar to that which the children might use

Again, such spontaneous guiding strategies must not be delivered in a teacher-directed manner; instead, they must allow the child the freedom to interact with the guided strategies in accordance with their own interest, pace, and inclination.

LEARNING FOR ALL CHILDREN
Guided Play and Disabilities

Childress (2011) presents a review of the literature that emphasizes the following information about the play interactions of parents of children with disabilities. Parents of children with disabilities initiate play interactions as frequently as parents of children who are typically developing. Also, parents of children with disabilities adjust their language to the abilities of their children with the intent of supporting successful interactions and positive developmental outcomes. Evidence demonstrates that parents of children with disabilities value play activities and view them as a vital tool for development. Therefore, most parents of children with disabilities should be welcomed as partners with the classroom staff in developing guided strategies for working with their children in enhancing play interactions.

Keilty and Galvin (2006) also found that parents of young children with disabilities adapt their interactions, language, and play to meet the developmental needs of their children. Parents use strategies that are responsive to their children's needs and provide support so that the children can successfully participate in activities. Play tends to be an important part of the home life for families with children with disabilities, with children participating in independent and collaborative activities throughout the day. Although there are many stressors in families with young children with disabilities, mothers were found to engage in warm, sensitive, and intentional play with their children, an activity that can provide a positive contribution to language, cognition, and social development.

Regardless of the type of disability, parents adjust their play behaviors to meet their children's needs, and that adjustment in turn appears to benefit the child by resulting in increased engagement, attention, persistence, and exploration of the play environment (Childress, 2011). Overall, most parents understand that play can be used to encourage positive developments that benefit their child with disabilities.

Suggestions for providing children with disabilities accessibility to play areas and equipment:

- Provide diverse, multisensory learning activities for all children
- Ensure that all mobility equipment can be used in all the areas
- Remove any barriers that would not allow children with equipment to freely move around
- Make sure all areas are level and have defined pathways that lead to them
- Provide wagons and other riding toys for children to use or be taken around in

Guiding From Outside the Play Setting

Adults can use tools such as space and time, themes and props, and play objects to assist in providing guidance from outside the play context with the goal of producing higher level play episodes. Providing guided play from outside the play setting allows for adult management without the adult having to enter the play context.

Guiding With Space and Time

Adults can guide children's play by providing them with ample time to develop complex pretend stories. The development of play stories involves children negotiating ideas and roles, constructing materials and stories, and actually carrying out the play activities. Play is not considered a "fill-in" activity that occurs between other curricular activities. Instead, care should be given to planning play activities for a time when children will not be interrupted by other scheduled events.

Play activities that take place in well-defined, somewhat small and intimate areas of the room appear to encourage steady interactions between the players. At the same time, an adequate amount of space should be provided so that children can easily stand, crawl, jump, lie down, and move around the area. Children need sufficient space to physically and verbally negotiate roles, construct needed materials, and carry out the actual episode play scenes. Children move unconsciously outside the defined play area to carry out some of their activities, as seen in the Chapter 4 scenario where the two girls were walking around "house-hunting." If this happen in a classroom, adults should be aware of children's need to expand their play boundaries and understand how this activity enhances and elongates the play episode. They should not always tell the young players to "return to their play area" when these activities occur.

Adults can guide children's play activities through the creative use of space.

The locations of **play center spaces**, the areas where the teachers choose to locate the play centers, should be off to the sides of the room so that the play activity is not interrupted by other children or by adults unintentionally entering the play area. At the same time, however, the play center spaces should be easily visible so that the adults can continually observe and determine when and how the activity can be guided from inside or outside the play setting.

Guiding With Players

Another way in which play can be guided from the outside is by suggesting the players who will be in the play area. Adults can recommend that same-skilled players interact together to assist them in collaboratively attaining a higher level of symbolic representation and more complex narrative development with rich language. Alternatively, they can encourage that an advance-skilled player interact with a novice player so that modeling can be demonstrated to the novice. At the same time, an adult might choose not to place a more disruptive child in the play center with other children, thus allowing those children who engage in play the maximum opportunity to enhance their skills. The disruptive child could engage in play center activities when there is an opportunity for adult engagement.

Guiding With Themes and Props

Play activities can be guided from outside the setting through the choice of the play theme. Adults must choose themes about which children have sufficient knowledge and experience so that they can successfully execute a story. Young children have limited language and cognitive skills, and are unfamiliar with play's social activities. As a result, a familiar play theme or topic for play enactment that makes the play a cohesive and integrated narrative interaction, can afford them the needed opportunities to engage in cohesive and integrated narrative interactions. They are familiar with the content, the experience, and the language that accompanies it. As children become experienced with sequencing and coordinating play stories with their peers, and as their skills and world knowledge expands, the play themes can then evolve into episodes that occur within a community. Themes for such episodes might include a car wash, the post office, a bank, or the library.

Staff members need to monitor the play enactments and, once they are satisfied that children are comfortable enacting familiar home and community activities, the staff can offer a more challenging play theme. The new theme can even reflect teaching content that is being implemented into the daily curriculum, a book that children have read as a group a couple of times, a field trip that they have recently taken, or a community speaker who has come to talk to the class. This can help students use prior knowledge and language to engage in the new activities.

The transition from familiar domestic and community play enactments to somewhat unfamiliar curriculum or book themes may present difficulties for some children. In such cases the teacher must support them at the beginning with the specific language that might be needed and some realistic-looking play materials. This support should allow the children to successfully expand their ability to create the more complex and symbolic collaborative play narratives. One other way to guide children in extending their skills is to pair one player who is more familiar with activities that involve imagination with one who is not, so that learning occurs through peer-to-peer modeling. This presents a strong opportunity for language acquisition as children listen to a more advanced language user. Additionally, pairing children who speak the same home language should produce more abstract play than pairing mixed-language users.

Once children become comfortable with familiar enactments, they then engage in more fantasy enactments.

©iStockphoto.com/patrickheagney

Once the appropriate theme is chosen, props must be gathered that will define the specific activities related to the theme. Play props are realistic- and unrealistic-looking play materials that assist children in designing their play enactments. For example, if the theme is a paint store, the adult must determine where and how to arrange the shelves for the paint cans, brushes, rollers, drop cloths, paint sample cards, buckets, sandpaper, cash register, and newspaper ads. If the theme is a car wash, then the adult must establish the space for an entering lane, a pumping gas lane, a washing and drying lane, sponges, rags, and window spray. Determining what is the appropriate number of definitive props and how to arrange them in the play setting contributes to the outside guiding of a play scenario.

Guiding With Play Objects

Choosing the number of play objects that is desirable for children to enhance their play is always a delicate decision. Adults must constantly attend to the play activities of individual children to determine how many objects are too few and how many are too many. Observing how materials are being used can determine if there are too few, too many, or just enough.

Be aware that the number of props is always a delicate balance to which adults must constantly attend (Snow et al., 1998). If too many play objects are set out in the context, the children will likely become more entertained by the objects and end up playing with them instead of using them as tools to create a play scenario. If too few play items are available for the children, the play activity often falters (Christensen & Kelly, 2003).

With younger children or children with disabilities who have limited language abilities, adults can guide their play activities by designing play environments that are rich with realistic play materials (e.g., dishes, pans, towels, aprons, food boxes, phone, and so forth). Using the real items instead of commercially made play products could assist young children in becoming comfortable with symbolic representations and confident in labeling those items. Think back to the opening scenario for this chapter and the difficulties that the younger child had using the red object as a phone.

Providing the correct level of props takes time and requires observation.

Comstock/Stockbyte/Thinkstock

Actual domestic items can be purchased at secondhand stores, flea markets, and garage sales, and include materials such as kitchenware, hats, clothing, shoes, work clothes, weather gear, and so forth. For those children who find the creation of play scenarios challenging in the beginning or who are at early stages of language development, having the actual items might assist (Neuman & Roskos, 1997). Children enjoy the following items: shoes, boots, slippers, community uniforms, ties, scarves, wallets, jewelry, aprons, badges, key rings, jackets, soft fabric, work clothes, and so forth (Machado, 2007; see also Figure 8.4).

Figure 8.4   Examples of Center Themes and Realistic Play Materials

Theme	Materials
The Bakery	• Aprons, bowls, pans, cookbooks, mixers, measuring spoons/cups, empty boxes for flour and sugar, timer, cash register/money, baked items, bags, spatula, pie tins
Camping	• Backpacks, tents, flashlight, map, mess kit, warm clothing, compass, first aid kit, fishing pole, sleeping bags, water bottles, rain poncho
Construction	• Drop cloth, tape measure, tools, toolbox, work gloves, work shirt, clamps, shovel, walkie-talkies, sandpaper, wood scraps, screws, nails, goggles
Gas Station	• Hose, funnel, rags/sponge, tire pump, supply catalogues, car ads, keys, paper towels, phone, cash register, tools, wallet/money, gas pump, inner tube, broom
Paint Store	• Drop cloth, color cards, paint cans, brushes, rollers, paint trays, stirrers, gloves, receipt pad, wall paper, wet paint signs, painting shirts

Children will transform one object into another in order to sustain the play story.

As children familiarize themselves with co-constructing play narratives with peers, and as their language develops, more neutral or non-descriptive types of materials can be introduced to support the player's development of symbolic thinking. Examples include paper towel rolls, blocks, Popsicle sticks, paper bags, fabric swatches, blankets, and ropes/cording. Realistic play props provide children with the content for their play activities while neutral toys allow children to assign meaning to the collaborative activities.

REFLECT AND APPLY EXERCISE 8.2

Using Guided Play

Reflect

Research illustrates two general aspects of guided play—such as the use of toys, objects, people, and other items, and the use of supporting comments. Assume that in your classroom, you have designed a construction center with hats, traffic signs, trucks, pieces of wood, nails, hammers, a wading pool with sand, and so forth.

Apply

Two children appear to enjoy the center but are only interested in the wood, nails, and hammers. Examine strategies for getting them to use other items and comments you might make to advance these children's learning experience to a higher level.

For children who have difficulty transitioning from realistic-looking objects to abstract objects, the teacher might want to provide a group orientation for the class by modeling some of the activities that could occur with these neutral types of objects. The teacher and a student could demonstrate how to create a socio-dramatic play narrative using these more abstract types of play objects. This provides an opportunity for the class to see and hear an oral discourse exchange. They observe turn-taking skills and see how to listen with their bodies. They are exposed to familiar and expanded vocabulary.

Guiding With Literacy-Enriched Objects

Literacy-enriched play objects are play items that encourage children to read or write, such as paper, pencils, and printed materials. The use of such objects in the dramatic play context significantly enhances children's literacy learning (Neuman & Roskos, 1997). Play settings can become more literacy focused by either introducing a literacy play context or by using literacy materials in other play contexts.

Literacy play contexts are play environments in which actual literacy skills are practiced. For example, a play context could be designed to be a library, bookstore, post office, stationery store, or office. In all of these contexts, people primarily interact with print. At the library and bookstore, books are reviewed and then either checked out or sold. In the post office, letters, packages, or postcards—all of which have been written, addressed, and stamped—are mailed or received and sorted into post office boxes. Likewise, in a stationery store, cards are viewed and purchased, pens are tried out by writing on tablets, markers are purchased to make signs, and stationery is purchased to write on. The creation of centers with such focus encourages children to collaboratively engage in play stories that use literacy behaviors in a natural and safe environment. At the same time, these play stories demonstrate real-life applications of literacy skills that are being taught at another time of the day.

Integrating literacy-enriched play objects into play centers can have beneficial impacts on children's reading and writing skills.

©iStock.com/NiseriN

The use of literacy-enriched play objects also results in beneficial impacts on children's reading and writing skills. Setting up a doctor's office that has a receptionist using a computer and issuing appointment cards can have children focus on letters and their sounds in a play environment. Additionally, placing a newspaper, cookbooks, or recipe cards in card boxes in a kitchen play context will enhance literacy awareness. They see that print conveys meaning and learn concepts about print that are foundational skills for later reading success (Clay, 1998). Finally, having magazines for those waiting for a haircut and issuing written receipts again focuses the players' attention on the print. By doing so, it assists them in expanding collaborative pretend play narratives.

Findings demonstrate a relationship between preschoolers' increased engagement in dramatic play literacy activities and formal literacy learning. Playing with literacy objects and participating in literacy routines are developmentally appropriate practices that can conceivably make literacy learning more interesting for young children and have a long-term impact on reading and writing development.

Guiding With Adult Suggestions

From outside the play center, an adult can provide suggestions that redirect or guide the play, or introduce new play props. For example, consider a situation where someone is entering the post office and the postmaster is busy putting mail into the post office boxes. An adult from outside the play context could suggest to the child entering that the child should pretend that a bell is on the counter that needs to be hit and makes a ringing sound so the postmaster knows to come to the window. For less experienced players, having an adult comment that some post offices have bells and suggest that they might look for a bell to use in the classroom, and that could keep the play episode developing.

Additionally, if novice players are having difficulty keeping their play roles straight, an adult could suggest that the "characters" wear props to identify their roles, for example, the mom can wear glasses and the dad can wear a hat. Similarly, an adult might want to make an announcement to keep the play on track, such as "Remember, Grandma might be coming tomorrow" or "I think that the baby may be coming home from the hospital soon." The guidance of such statements from outside the play activity could redirect the children's behaviors back to the original play plot.

Figure 8.5 summarizes methods for guiding children's play activities from outside the play setting.

Figure 8.5 Methods for Guiding Children's Play From Outside the Setting

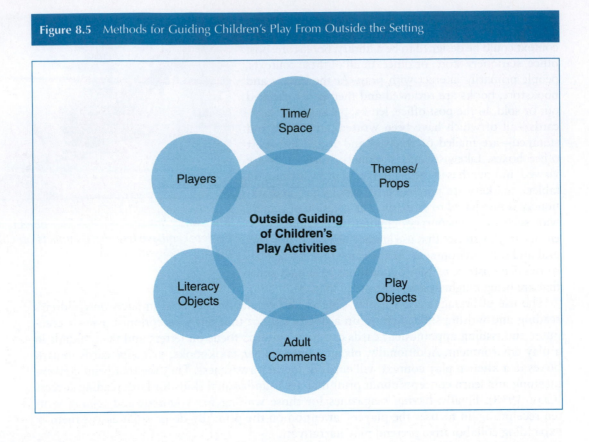

Guiding From Inside the Play Setting

Traditionally, young children's play has been viewed as an activity where only limited or no adult interactions occur from within the play setting. Research has now shown, however, that adults' regulation of children's behaviors can assist in modifying play contexts into centers for learning specific academic skills.

Dever and Falconer (2008) posit that the following premises must exist for play guidance from within the play event to be successful: (1) young children welcome adults into their play if they do not take control; (2) the purpose of entering play can be to provide new information, to redirect the activities, or just to have fun; and (3) adults can model a role that might not be familiar to a child (see Figure 8.6).

Welcoming Adults Who Do Not Take Control

In a yearlong ethnographic study of a preschool peer culture, Corsaro (1987) demonstrated the value of adult participants in children's play activities being cautiously "reactive" rather than "active." Adults typically spend their days directing and monitoring children, telling children what they can and cannot do, and assisting children who are in trouble. However, Corsaro illustrated that children would welcome adults into a play group if the adult (1) sat within the play setting's boundaries, (2) remained quiet and waited for the children to approach, and (3) followed the children's lead with respect to activities and language. Interestingly, during the yearlong ethnographic study, Corsaro himself implemented the three behaviors that encourage children to perceive an adult to be a non-authoritarian figure. At times, when he

Figure 8.6 Guiding Suggestions From Inside Children's Play Settings

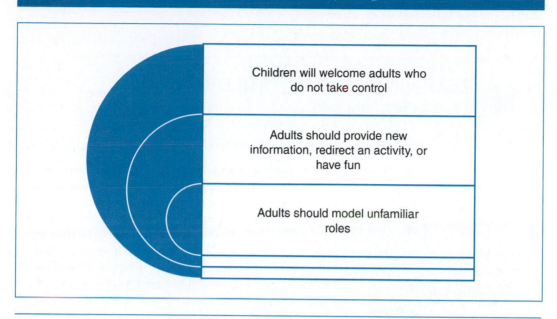

Children will welcome adults who do not take control

Adults should provide new information, redirect an activity, or have fun

Adults should model unfamiliar roles

Source: Dever, M. T., & Falconer, R. C. (2008). *Foundations and Changes in Early Childhood Education*. New York, NY: Wiley.

felt that a child was engaged in an activity that could lead to physical harm, he would say, "Be careful." However, the children would then respond to him with, "You're not the teacher!" or "You can't tell us what to do!" This demonstrates that the children may not have viewed this adult's comments as acceptable or as a natural part of their peer play.

Professionals working in early education centers need to build relationships with the children that will allow the adults to enter the play settings without altering or discouraging the natural flow of play interactions. By being non-reactive and not disrupting the natural flow of activities, adults can assess what the children need to be guided to do next and assist them with support so they can do tasks just beyond that independent performance level.

Providing New Information, Redirecting Activities, and Having Fun

In an attempt to remain reactive and not be considered as active or directing participants, adults can enter the play setting when a need exists to present new information or redirect an activity. To truly affect a play enactment from inside the context, adult-players should spend time simply sitting, observing, and waiting for the children to approach them as a participant. If a conflict should occur in another play area while an adult is attempting to become part of a play activity or is participating in it, children should be

Children need to be provided with familiar opportunities in order to have their play guided to higher levels.

Photodisc/Photodisc/Thinkstock

redirected to seek another adult for assistance. An adult should try to remain a neutral participant in the development and enhancement of the play activity in order to truly understand the behaviors of the children.

LEARNING FOR ALL CHILDREN
Guided Play and Culture

All societies appear to utilize some type of parental scaffolding techniques. These techniques reflect different forms that relate to the variety of cultural attitudes toward parenting throughout the world. Kermani and Brenner (2000) found differences in the responsiveness styles, quality of interactions, and level of control between Iranian immigrant mothers and Anglo-American mothers. The Iranian mothers used more explicit and direct forms of scaffolding; in contrast, Anglo-American mothers appeared to be more explanatory and non-direct with their scaffolding strategies. Such findings suggest that cultures have different ways of teaching and learning.

As a result of these variations, adults working with young children must recognize that children will have different abilities and ways of learning. Therefore effective instruction involves using scaffolding techniques that are appropriate for each child. These techniques are on a continuum ranging from highly directive methods to non-directive methods. No method is effective for all children when learning new material; therefore, educators and program directors must offer a variety of curricula and strategies that are sensitive to each child's home instruction. Kermani and Brenner suggest that providing such a diverse approach to the various cultural teaching and learning attitudes should not be seen as a challenge but as an opportunity to design different approaches to instruction and learning. These approaches must be sufficiently unique to correspond to and satisfy the various patterns of cultural practices but, at the same time, have overlapping practices common to all cultures. Only through sensitivity toward each child's cultural needs can teachers design programs that will allow the fine-tuning of guidance and gradual withdrawal familiar to the child. In doing such, skills will successfully transfer from social knowledge to learned knowledge.

Using culturally diverse items in the play center could also assist with the transfer of social to learned knowledge. Such items could be the following:

- Plastic play figures from different cultures
- Plastic play animals that are familiar to different cultures
- Coins from different countries
- Food boxes from different cultures
- Clothing items from different cultures

Modeling Unfamiliar Roles

Similarly, when entering a play context to model an unfamiliar role or activity, adults are moving in the direction of directing, but not all the way to the end of the continuum where overt direction is located. Therefore, the adult must select which specific activities to actively model and which will be reactively produced.

Figure 8.7 provides a graphic example of how Soderman et al. (2005) represent Vygotsky's theory of sociocultural learning. The bottom row of boxes demonstrates activities that children can do independently or without the support of a more knowledgeable other. The second row reflects activities that a child can do somewhat independently but that may require some amount of casual assistance. At the top is the skill for which a child truly requires a certain amount of fixed assistance. Modeling should be used only with the skill that occurs at the top of a child's pyramid or the one that needs structured input for a child to grasp. Similar to Vygotsky (see Chapter 2), the bottom of the image reflects skills that have been learned and can be produced unaided. The rows above the bottom row reflect those skills that are still being developed or are in the zone of proximal development. For those skills in the zone of proximal development, children need different levels of assistance to produce them.

From inside the play enactment, adults can model unfamiliar language, roles, and actions.

High-quality programs demonstrate positive results with adults respectfully moving in and out of child-centered activities and providing choices but not directing or dominating the activities. In response to thoughtful suggestions, directions, questions, and clarifications by adults, children can sustain and enhance their play behaviors with peers.

As Chapter 4 explained, language (i.e., metacommunication) is frequently used by children in socio-dramatic play to identify new situations, or changes in parts of situations, and to verbally pose a problem-solving task for those situations. According to McGee and Richgels (2012), scaffolded play talk comes in the following forms: giving advice, directing attention, alerting to a sequence of activities, and providing information for task completion. When participating in a play enactment with children, adults can provide scaffolded play talk through the use of metacommunications. West and Cox (2004) suggest the use of open-ended questions. Skibbe, Behnke, and Justice (2004) recommend responsive and directive approaches. All of these suggestions are listed in Figure 8.8.

Figure 8.7   Skill Support Needed by Children

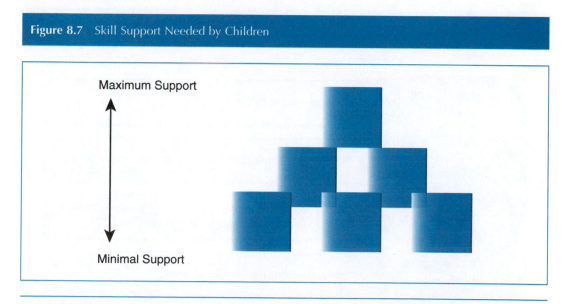

Source: Soderman, A. K., Gregory, K. M., & McCarty, L. T. (2005). *Scaffolding Emergent Literacy: A Child-Centered Approach for Preschool Through Grade 5.* New York, NY: Pearson Education.

Figure 8.8 Guided Play Language

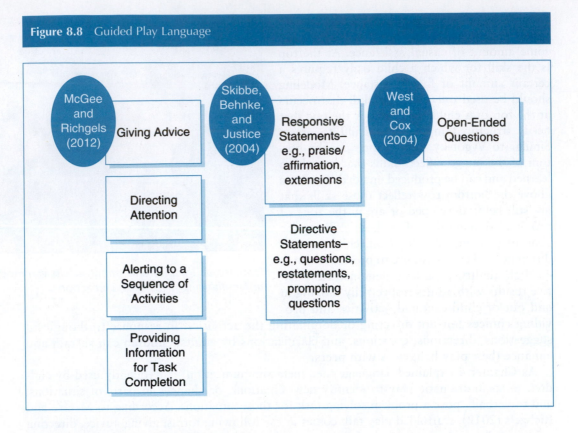

Gradually, children internalize the language that they hear and use in play. They then use it to internally direct their own attention and to plan, sustain, and negotiate their own play activities. Figure 8.9 provides suggestions on how the teacher candidate integrated suggestions from McGee and Richgels (2012) to guide the children's play behaviors.

Figure 8.9 Verbal Scaffolding Examples in Opening Scenario

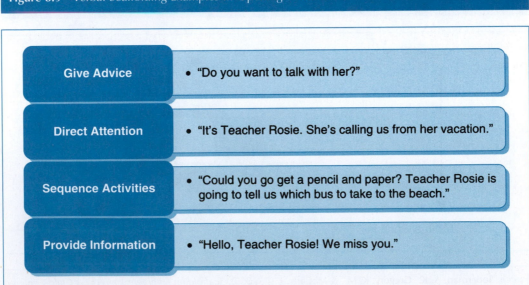

Resnick and Snow (2009) reinforce the importance of allowing children to practice and master their native language for the following three reasons (pp. 1–2):

1. Speaking and listening are the foundation skills for reading and writing.

2. Speaking and listening make children smarter.

3. Speaking and listening are academic, social, and life skills that are valued in school and the world.

Therefore, adults must spend time scaffolding children's play activities by engaging in conversations with them about their activities. Figure 8.10 provides 11 strategies that research has demonstrated are successful when used to scaffold young children's language and literacy skills.

REFLECT AND APPLY EXERCISE 8.3

Outside and Inside Guided Play

Reflect

Again, you have designed your construction site center, and you want children to integrate literacy skills into that center.

Apply

Think about different ways that you can guide the play activities from outside and inside the play setting so that literacy skills can be enhanced. How could you integrate blueprints, a city inspector, a time clock, and paychecks into the narratives to enhance literacy skills?

Adults provide guided language for literacy development by encouraging high-level socio-dramatic play activities. They can do so by implementing a number of different roles, each of which depends on each child's individual skills. For example, adults can have a more detached role in supporting the play activities and act similarly to what Enz and Christie (1997) have called a "stage manager." Being a stage manager of play activities would involve gathering materials, making props, organizing the play area, and talking with the children about their enactments. Adults can also enter the play setting and act as either "co-players" or "play leaders." The role of a co-player would primarily involve assuming minor roles in the enactment process, while acting as a play leader requires taking an active role such as selling paint at the paint store or sorting the mail at the post office.

However, no matter what role the adults take on, they must always be cognizant of the fact that play is to remain a child-centered, not teacher-directed, activity. The play ideas must originate from the child's imagination and experiences, and not from the teacher's. Through watching, but not hovering, teachers can motivate high-level play activities with the goal of having the children gradually take over these play activities without guidance.

Figure 8.10 Strategies for Enhancing Learning Interactions

Wait and Listen	• Teacher encourages children to initiate verbally and/or nonverbally by waiting expectantly for initiations, using a slow pace which allows time for children to initiate and complete their message
Follow the Children's Lead	• When children initiate verbally or nonverbally, teacher follows their lead by responding verbally to their initiations, using animation, and avoiding commands and vague acknowledgments (e.g., yeah)
Join In and Play	• Teacher actively joins in the children's play as a partner by building on their focus of interest and playing without dominating
Be Face-to-Face	• Teacher adjusts physical level by sitting on floor or small chair, leaning forward to be at face-to-face level, if above child's level, bending close when possible
Use a Variety of Questions	• Teacher uses a variety of WH questions, only using Yes/No questions to clarify message, waiting for response, and avoids test or rhetorical questions
Encourage Turn-Taking	• Teacher encourages extended verbal turn-taking by linking comments and questions to invite child to take turns. Goal is to achieve 4-4 turns on one topic
Scan	• Teacher facilitates the participation of all children in group activities by encouraging uninvolved children to participate
Imitate	• Teacher imitates the actions, gestures, sounds, or words of children who are only at a preverbal or one-word stage
Use a Variety of Labels	• Teacher uses a variety of vocabulary (nouns, verbs, adjectives, adverbs) by emphasizing, repeating, and labeling. Avoids using this, that, it, there
Expand	• Teacher expands by repeating chidren's words and correcting grammar or by adding another idea
Extend	• Teacher provides information related to children's topics or activities by using comments and questions to inform, project, pretend/imagine, explain, talk about future or feelings

Source: Roskos, K., & Neuman, S. B. (2003). Environment and Its Influences for Early Literacy Teaching and Learning. In S. B. Neuman & D. K. Dickinson (Eds.). *Handbook of Early Literacy Research: Volume 1*. New York, NY: Guilford Press.

Chapter Summary

Adults provide support to children who are involved in play activities by employing specific strategies from either outside the play context or by jointly interacting with the children and supporting them from inside the play context. Adult guidance can be provided in a number of ways both from outside and inside the play context. As young players expand their ability to perform more advanced activities, the adult "guides" decrease their assistance, allowing the learners to take more of the lead in successfully completing the task. As a result, learning occurs.

> **HOME AND COMMUNITY CONNECTIONS**
>
> Strategies for Guided Play and High-Quality Learning Activities
>
> Every few days, reintroduce a toy or activity to your child that they haven't used or played in a while.

CHAPTER 8 FIRST-PERSON INTERVIEW

Guiding as a Team

Renee Brady

Director of an employees' childcare program, Hackensack, NJ

All children have needs, and as teachers of young children we must learn how to accommodate for those needs. We must regularly ask ourselves, "What can I do to support the child?" not "How can I change the child?" It is so important that we look at how we can adjust our learning environment so that all children can learn, not so that we can teach.

Teachers need not just to teach but also to actually become part of the class. They need to learn to look at an activity in the way that a young child sees it. If the teacher is reading a book and a child appears to be uninterested, that is fine as long as the child is not disturbing the other children who are interested in the story. Being part of a class is a skill that children learn. The best way for teachers to help children learn that skill is to develop it for themselves.

Today, young children are expected to learn so much. As teachers, we have to try not to impose too much on them. We have to trust them and let things happen and evolve, while always making sure that they are safe and understand the rules. If we give them space to develop, we'll see the progress. When they are relaxed and doing something that they enjoy, they're going to grow and develop skills. Children can be allowed to do things differently, and you can still have a routine and a well-organized plan. We just have to look at what they are doing through their eyes.

For example, we had a child whom we were trying to get to comply with certain activities and he just did not want to or was not able to do things that way. So, we relaxed things a bit and let him do things his way. If he didn't want to climb on the climber, that was fine. The only thing that he could not do was aimlessly run around the outside or in the classroom. The result was amazing. He became calmer and began to participate in some of the activities more often than before. When we began to look at things through his eyes and tried to alter the environment and not the child, we began to see progress.

(Continued)

(Continued)

The staff also felt that this little boy needed more services than what we were providing at our center. Because our center is located at the parents' place of employment, parents are frequently in the classroom and interacting with the staff and children. We asked the mother of the child to come into the classroom when she had a chance to see her child and give us some suggestions on how to create a positive learning environment for her son. The mother visited the classroom a number of times and then, after meetings and discussions with the teachers and director it was mutually decided that she make an appointment for the child to be evaluated. When it came time for the evaluation's results to be shared with the mother, we asked her if she would like one of us to come along. The mother accepted our offer and we all learned a lot from being a part of that process.

The child was identified with a special need, and we all worked with the mother on determining the best placement for her son. The mother understood that her son needed special education services from a school district program but also wanted him to come to our center until she got off of work. This would involve having the child dropped off at our center by a bus at noon every day. However, we do not have children arriving and leaving the center at noon. We could have told the mother that we could not accommodate her desire, but the staff really worked hard to view this situation as the child and the mother saw it, not as we saw it. Therefore, we made arrangements for someone to be at the entrance every day when the bus was scheduled to arrive. Most of the time I do it, but we all have joined in to make this work.

We have also visited the special education classroom to observe how they are working with this child, and we keep in contact with the teacher. Similarly, the special education staff has visited our center. All of us learned so much from this situation. Through all of us collaborating we saw so many different opportunities to meet everyone's needs. I believe that the key to the success of this situation was that we all tried to see how the mother was looking at it and we were willing to try different things to accommodate the family and help the child succeed.

Student Study Site

Visit the Student Study Site at **www.sagepub.com/selmi** to access additional study tools including mobile-friendly eFlashcards and links to video and web resources.

Key Terms

guided play

literacy play contexts

literacy-enriched play objects

play center space

props

recasting

scaffolding

theme

Useful Websites

Zero to Three:

> http://main.zerotothree.org/site/PageServer?pagename=ter_par_1224_selfconfidence#
> selfconfidence—help

> http://main.zerotothree.org/site/PageServer?pagename=ter_par_2436_thinkvid

> http://main.zerotothree.org/site/PageServer?pagename=ter_par_2436_think#
> thinking—buildskills

Reflective Questions

1. Reread the opening scenario for Chapter 4, *Not a Knock-Knock Joke*. Imagine that you are the teacher. What are some ways that you could guide the play from inside the play context to move the play interactions to a higher level?

2. Review the following video clip: http://main.zerotothree.org/site/PageServer?pagename=ter_par_2436_thinkvid4

   Discuss ways in which Haley's mother has and could guide her play from outside and from inside the play context.

9 Observing and Assessing to Promote Learning

A NEW YEAR AND A NEW CLASSROOM

Comstock/Stockbyte/Thinkstock

A year ago a teacher accepted a position as a preschool/kindergarten teacher at a preschool–third grade learning center. The team at that center also consisted of a kindergarten/first grade teacher; a second grade teacher; and a third grade teacher. A special educator was the fifth member of the learning center's team.

Though the newly hired teacher was the least experienced teacher at the center, she was hired because of her knowledge of and experience with implementing child-centered preschool and kindergarten programs. During the past year, she worked hard designing various learning centers in her classroom that encouraged child-centered activities that met the learning and social needs of all her children. She knows that the best learning environments for young children are ones that foster independence, nurture social interactions, and encourage action and exploration.

Recently, the staff members were preparing their classrooms and planning for a new school year. They also were meeting individually with parents, some of whom are new to the school. These meetings provide the teachers with time to explain their classroom program to parents. Additionally, the teachers review the program portfolios for each returning student. Finally, the meetings allow parents to share their thoughts about their children and their expectations for the upcoming school year.

That day the newly hired teacher and the first grade teacher were meeting with a parent whose child was transitioning from the kindergarten classroom to the next classroom as a first grader. Then they were meeting with the parent of a child diagnosed with autism who was also transitioning from the preschool class into the kindergarten/first grade class. The special education teacher was also going to attend that meeting. The newly hired teacher was the convener for both meetings and she had reviewed the portfolios that described each student's academic and social progress since entering the school as preschoolers. Each portfolio contained samples of the

(Continued)

(Continued)

student's work from previous years and end-of-the-year summaries of the regular observations and documentations made by the previous teachers. Also included was formal assessment information that had been accumulated during the children's previous 2 years in preschool. For both children, the transition from preschool to kindergarten/first grade was considered typical, and the staff believed that the process would go smoothly for the teachers, families, and the children.

In both meetings the teachers planned to review the assessment data in each child's portfolio and discuss with parents each student's yearly goals and program plan. During the meeting the kindergarten teacher planned to provide an outline of the scope of activities that will take place during the upcoming year. A synthesis of the meeting would be added to the student portfolio and also furnished to each parent.

The only difference between the two meetings was that the special education teacher would be attending the second meeting and that the group would review and revise the Individualized Education Program (IEP) for the child with autism. In both meetings the teachers use assessment data to guide their educational decisions. Summaries would be provided of each child's progress through continuous monitoring and changes in educational programs based on data collected from natural observations and formal assessments. The teachers are proud of the school's assessment process and the data that they have gathered for children and their families, and are pleased that their school provides accessible information on the progress of all of their children.

Infants are assessed from the moment they enter the world. Immediately, the medical staff in the delivery room informally observes the infant's appearance and takes note of any obvious differences from what is expected. Next, following the first minute after birth, the infant is formally assessed using a 10-point scale called the Apgar score. Developed by Virginia Apgar, M.D. (1953), each letter of the word APGAR represents the particular area being assessed: appearance, pulse, grimace, activity, and respiration, as shown in Figure 9.1. Infants are ranked from 0 to 2 in each of the five areas. Infants receiving a total score below 7 points are given special attention in the concerned area(s). All infants are again assessed on their Apgar score when they are 5 minutes old. Once more, infants with scores under 7 points receive assistance and are reassessed every 5 minutes for up to a total of 20 minutes.

Figure 9.1   Apgar Testing at Birth

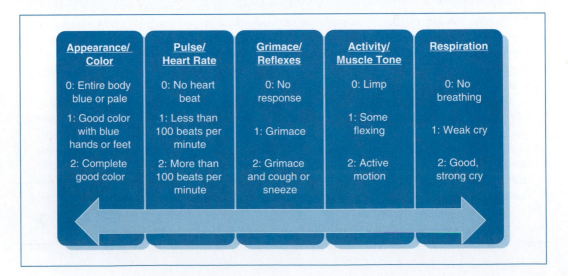

Appearance/ Color	Pulse/ Heart Rate	Grimace/ Reflexes	Activity/ Muscle Tone	Respiration
0: Entire body blue or pale	0: No heart beat	0: No response	0: Limp	0: No breathing
1: Good color with blue hands or feet	1: Less than 100 beats per minute	1: Grimace	1: Some flexing	1: Weak cry
2: Complete good color	2: More than 100 beats per minute	2: Grimace and cough or sneeze	2: Active motion	2: Good, strong cry

Informal and formal assessments that begin at birth then continue on a daily basis throughout life. Although we continually observe and assess both others and ourselves throughout each day, most people view the act of assessment as a complex and complicated mathematical process. This viewpoint is especially true for formally assessing young children's learning and developmental abilities, that people believe only trained professionals (e.g., health care specialists, educators, speech pathologists, and psychologists) are capable of administering.

Currently, for the first time in the history of education, a large proportion of children are being regularly assessed using formal measures during the years before they enter the educational system. The number of early education assessment products has grown over the past decades as a result of the expansion of private and government-sponsored early education programs. Early education centers observe and assess children to measure student progress not only in academic, social, and behavior areas as addressed in the opening scenario, but they also use assessment to plan and modify daily learning activities. Additionally, centers can also use assessments to identify children in their programs who might have educational and developmental delays, learning challenges, or be at risk for them.

This chapter will address the following questions regarding the use of assessment and observations to promote the learning for young children:

> What challenges occur when assessing young children, and how can they be addressed?

> Why is it important to observe children and collect authentic data from natural learning contexts?

> How can observations of children that include self-reflective data enrich the assessment process?

Assessing Young Children

Assessment is, simply stated, the examination of children's learning and developmental abilities, and is a planned process for systematically gathering, synthesizing, and interpreting information. The assessment of children serves many purposes and takes on different forms. It can be implemented through formal or informal procedures, and is commonly used in schools to monitor student progress, identify who needs special services, and evaluate programs. The National Association for the Education of Young Children (NAEYC) and the National Association for Early Childhood Specialists in the State Departments of Education (NAECS-SDE) (2009) advocate, and this chapter supports, the principle that valid and reliable assessment methods for young children must consist of the six characteristics listed in Figure 9.2.

More specifically, assessment is a continuous, dynamic process that provides information about six types of educational decisions: instructional planning, evaluation, diagnosis, eligibility, placement, and educational planning (Pierangelo & Guiliani, 2012; see Figure 9.3). The opening scenario for this chapter illustrates how teachers need to assess their children and then use that information to guide their instructional methods and the placement of students (Pavri, 2012; Salvia, Ysseldyke, & Bolt, 2007).

High-quality early education programs use assessment data to evaluate children's progress in development and learning, diagnose areas in which children are having difficulty, and plan large, small, and center group instruction. Informal ongoing assessment processes can provide teachers with feedback on children's understanding of specific learning concepts and the effectiveness of the instruction being implemented (see Figure 9.4). These results allow teachers to modify their instruction plans based on data. For example, some children

Figure 9.2 Valid and Reliable Characteristics of Assessments for Young Children

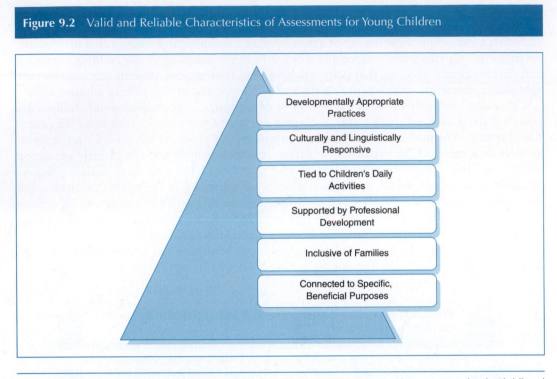

Source: National Association for the Education of Young Children (NAEYC), & National Association of Early Childhood Specialists in the State Departments of Education (NAECS/SDE). (2009). *Early Childhood Curriculum, Assessment, and Program Evaluation*. Retrieved from http://www.naeyc.org

Figure 9.3 Types of Educational Assessment

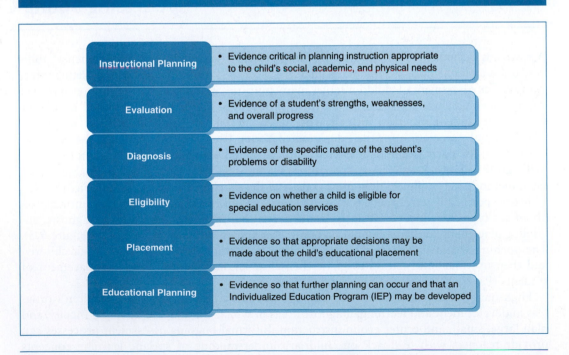

Source: Pierangelo, R., & Guiliani, G. A. (2012). *Assessment in Special Education: A Practical Approach* (4th ed.). Boston, MA: Pearson.

Figure 9.4   The Classroom Instruction and Assessment Cycle

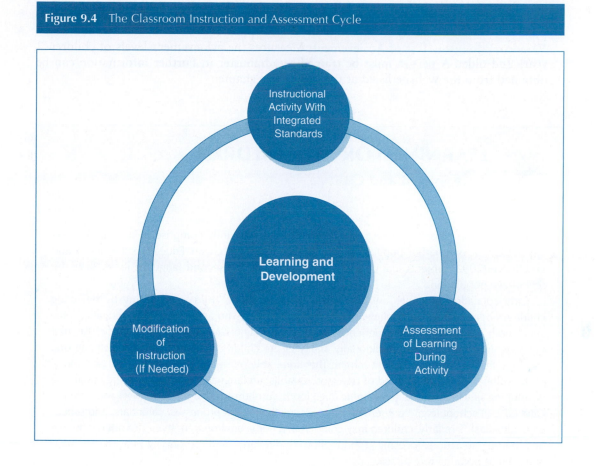

might require additional instruction to learn a specific skill before moving on to another skill, while others, who have mastered the material, can move on to more advanced materials.

Assessment data come from two sources: formal and informal assessments. A **formal assessment** is an activity that "assumes a single set of expectation for all children and comes with prescribed criteria for scoring and interpretation" (Pierangelo & Giuliani, 2012, p. 26). These published assessments tend to provide an abbreviated picture of a child—intelligence quotient (IQ), grade level equivalent, reading level, verbal skills, or specific information on measures of classroom achievement. While these data are important, they do not provide a complete picture of the child, especially when the child is young. Three examples of formal preschool language assessments are the following:

Observations of children engaged in natural learning activities provide authentic data for determining progress monitoring.

Peabody Picture Vocabulary Test: Measures the receptive and expressive vocabulary of children from two-and-a-half years and older, and has been used for over 50 years. It is easy to implement and can be used with diverse populations. For further information, use the website listed at the end of the chapter.

Preschool Language Scale: A comprehensive language assessment for children from birth through 7 years old that measures skills in the following areas: preverbal, emerging language, and early literacy in English and Spanish. The website is listed at the end of the chapter for further information.

Woodcock Johnson Test of Achievement: Measures the achievement levels of children 2 years and older. A person must be trained to administer it. Further information can be obtained from the website listed at the end of this chapter.

🌐 LEARNING FOR ALL CHILDREN
Assessment and Culture

Children from culturally and linguistically diverse backgrounds comprise a large and growing portion of our school population. The Center for Research on Education, Diversity, and Excellence (2002) projects that by 2030, English will be the second language for 40% of the school-age population.

Early education programs are intended to support young children's learning by reflecting children's home values and beliefs. However, the children who attend the early education programs do have diverse home experiences and parents may not teach them in the same way that our programs are designed. Additionally, many of the children are learning and speaking one language at home and another at school. Therefore, children many possess two less developed or transitional languages instead of one more established language. Additionally, they might be developing specific vocabulary at home (e.g., foods, furniture, and family activities) and different categories at school (e.g., components of books, mathematical processes, calendars, and scheduled activities). Similarly, children may come from a home environment that does not encourage one-to-one interactions focusing around following directions and responding in a specific manner, such as pointing to a picture.

Peña and Halle (2011) point out that all assessments, especially for young children, measure language abilities. However, children may produce inaccurate results if they are in the process of developing two languages and are not familiar with the American mainstream culture of assessment practices. Therefore, these two researchers suggest that the following recommendations be considered when reviewing assessment products for children who are dual language learners:

1. Children should continue to be assessed using both the home and school language.

2. Children may know different types of vocabulary in their home language than they do in the school language.

3. Make sure that the assessment is normed on the appropriate sample that represents the child being assessed.

4. Be cautious when using non-English assessments by making sure that the assessment being used has cultural and psychometric (reliability and validity) equivalences.

A number of professional organizations that support early learning programs believe that the assessment evidence for young children should be gathered from realistic situations that reflect children's actual performance (Barnett, Carolan, Fitzgerald, & Squires, 2012; NAEYC & NAECS/SDE, 2009). Young children's performance is highly influenced by their home experiences and emotional states. Both of these factors can impact the scores that are obtained from an inflexible and formal assessment process, resulting in unstable scores over time and an inaccurate picture of a child's abilities. To account for this potential instability, teachers must be skilled at collecting **informal assessment** data from the natural learning activities in which the children are involved. Informal assessments "are techniques that can be used at any time without interfering with instructional time. Their results are indicative of student's performance on the skill or subject of interest" (Pierangelo & Giuliani, 2012, p. 26). When informal assessments are performed in authentic learning contexts, their data provide a realistic picture of a child's everyday abilities. These informal procedures, which are incorporated in the general flow of the classroom, are used to monitor student progress and provide the teachers with ongoing information for designing high-quality learning activities to enhance children's abilities.

©iStock.com/Goldfaery

Assessing language and literacy skills in a natural environment can provide more realistic data of a young child's skills than using a formal assessment.

Authentic Assessments

Authentic assessments involve collecting evidence on young children's abilities from realistic or natural learning settings. Information obtained reflects the actual learning and instructional activities that occur in both the classroom and the world outside the classroom (Marrow, 2005). These data usually provide a more accurate picture of young children's strengths than the data collected in a formal and prescribed child-adult assessment session. However, authentic data must be systematically collected over time and grounded in research practices that are free of personal biases. Figure 9.5 provides a summary of the principles that must be a part of a valid and reliable authentic assessment procedure (Ruddell & Ruddell, 1995).

Five specific benefits accrue from observing and assessing young children while they are involved in authentic play and learning activities (Scales et al., 2012; see Figure 9.6):

1. Gathering data from children's natural learning activities is likely to guarantee that the children are engaged in developmentally appropriate activities.

2. Observing children in their daily learning settings affords professionals the opportunity to examine their own beliefs and goals about learning. It also allows professionals to assess how these beliefs and goals most likely are impacting the children's learning, either positively or negatively.

3. Authentic context observations allow professionals to refine and modify curricula based on the ease and challenges that they observe occurring during children's activities.

4. Assessing in an authentic setting allows professionals to naturally intervene and guide children to their highest level of development.

5. Finally, learning environments provide authentic assessment data on the skills that the children can and cannot actually perform independently.

Play interactions provide a context for learning and, therefore, are appropriate contexts for observing and collecting authentic assessment information relating to young children's

Figure 9.5 Principles of Authentic Assessment

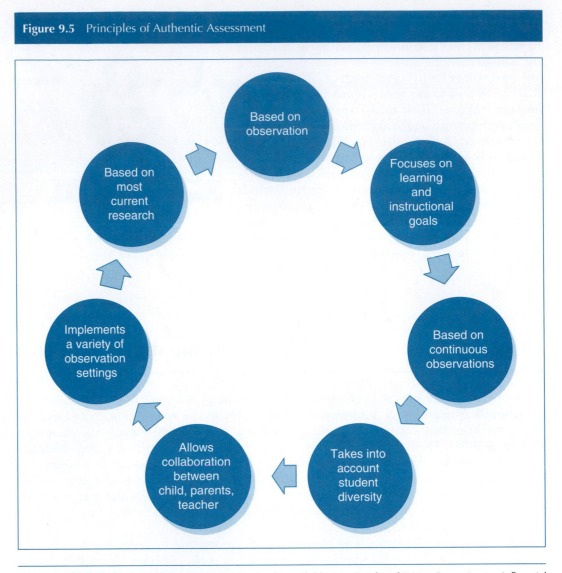

Source: Ruddell, R. B., & Ruddell, M. R. (1995). *Teaching Children to Read and Write: Becoming an Influential Teacher.* Needham Heights, MA: Allyn and Bacon.

Play activities provide opportunities for assessing how children integrate skills and use their social context for support.

development and learning of skills (Scales et al., 2012). Instead of observing and collecting information on specific, isolated behaviors, as often happens with formal assessments, play affords opportunities to examine multiple behaviors that children integrate to create meaningful experiences. It also allows examination of how the children use the social context provided to enhance their knowledge, which give children skills that will later assist with their academic learning. Authentic assessment opportunities further provide a safe context for students to demonstrate their learning. The anxiety of formal assessments can impact the ability of students to show what they are truly capable of.

Some of the informal methods for collecting authentic data during play and other learning situations

Figure 9.6 Justifications for Authentic Assessments

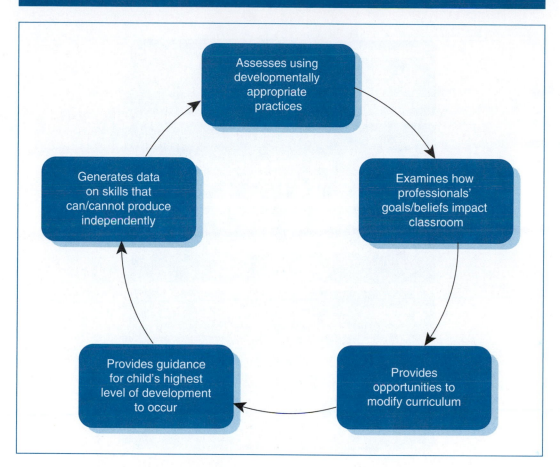

include the use of: (1) observational notes, (2) portfolio and journal documentations, (3) checklists, and (4) parents and children conferencing. Descriptions of these procedures are set forth below and are summarized in Figure 9.7.

Observational Notes

Taking **observational notes** involves watching children with a minimal amount of intrusion and in a natural learning setting, and then writing informal and brief notes about the behaviors observed. The notes can be organized in a binder and include a description of the setting, the time of day, the participants and their emotional states, their language and the behaviors observed. Following repeated observations, the organized notes can reveal patterns in behavior, document developing skills, and suggest specific behaviors on which to focus. Findings from the analysis can then be related to a developmental scale or to learning standards to determine how the children are doing and what skills need to be addressed next. Additionally, notes can be used to compare learning over different periods of time.

Reflecting on informal assessment notes and findings assists adults in determining changes that occur in a child's behavior or performance as a result of different social situations (e.g., settings, time of day, peers, materials). It also allows adults to determine the impact of instructional modifications so that high-quality learning occurs. For example, a teacher might want to determine whether a child is more engaged in learning when he or she is interacting with more skillful peers rather than with peers at a similar level. Likewise, as seen in the

Figure 9.7   Examples and Definitions of Assessment Tools

Observations and Notes

- Personal observations of natural learning activities and recording children's behaviors organized in a binder

Portfolios

- Collections of representative samples of children's work systematically arranged and analyzed

Journals

- Dated drawn and/or written entries in a notebook by children over a period of time

Checklists

- Commercially made or teacher-made lists of observable behaviors

Parent/Child Reflections

- Justifications for behaviors and insights on perception of activities

Stockbyte/Stockbyte/Thinkstock

Although formal assessments of young children provide some information, those findings need to be confirmed by informal assessments.

opening scenario for this chapter, the teacher might want to observe and take notes on how a child with a disability interacts with nondisabled peers when an adult is not present. The teacher can then compare those behaviors with the ones observed when an adult is present.

Portfolios

Portfolios involve the collection of student work data from multiple sources and using multiple methods. Using portfolios to document change in the development of skills over time can usually provide richer information on young children than using a formal assessment. In the past, teachers often kept a collection of work artifacts to create a portfolio; however, today's easy access to photos has simplified the process. If teachers wish to collect data on a child's development of skills in block building, they can take photos over time and store them on a computer file. Additionally, art projects, socio-dramatic play enactments, and peer interactions can be captured by using a photo or a recording of a child explaining an object or interaction. The teacher can later review that information to determine child growth, instruction modifications, and program effectiveness.

Journals

Journals are typically teacher-made booklets consisting of paper that is blank on the top half and lined on the bottom half. Children are encouraged to make regular entries in their journals by drawing and/or writing common letters or words. These child-produced records tell the child's "story" to an adult, and as the child narrates his or her story, the teacher writes the narration on the bottom half of the page. If the child is able to write independently, the teacher still enters text as the child reads the story. This journal provides a running record of the growth of a child's writing and language abilities over time. Journal entries can be shared with the class and used as a model for peers of ways to tell and write stories (King, 2012).

Ideally, analysis of portfolio and journal data occurs collaboratively between the professionals who are familiar with the children and their *parents*. Additionally, as addressed later in this chapter, valuable authentic information can be obtained when the analysis procedure includes the *children's own reflections* about their decisions and activities.

Checklists

Finally, either commercially made or teacher-made **checklists** offer an efficient method for observing and gathering authentic data, especially in the areas of language and cognitive abilities, and social and emotional development. For instance, and as explained later on in this chapter, the teacher can create a simple list of the developmental sequence of the symbolic representations presented in Chapter 3 of this book. Through observation and use of the checklist, adults can assess where children are with their symbolic play representations—do they make the representations by themselves, do they make object substitutions, and were there symbolic sequences? Additionally, information obtained from the use of the checklist can be related to other types of authentic assessment tools and to standardized tests as a means of validating findings.

LEARNING FOR ALL CHILDREN
Assessment and Disabilities

With the increase in the number of children with Autism Spectrum Disorder (ASD) and the need for continual progress monitoring of their academic, social and behavioral development, Charman, Howlin, Berry, and Prince (2004) pilot studied the relationship between the use of parent questionnaires and formal assessments. The results indicated it is possible to collect monitoring data on young school-age children using parent questionnaires. Using parents as informants of children's progress is much less expensive than using published formal assessments, and it also significantly contributes to enhancing home–school collaboration.

Strategies for providing an appropriate assessment session include:

- Seek input from family
- Perform in a familiar setting with familiar people
- Have short sessions
- Each session should be enjoyable and positive

When observing in natural learning settings and collecting authentic assessment data, professionals should continually ask themselves reflective questions as they organize, synthesize, and analyze observational data. This reflective analysis should be undertaken by the person collecting the data, but it should also be shared with other professionals who work with the child, the child's parents, and the child. Samples of meaningful reflective questions are presented in Figure 9.8.

Figure 9.8   Reflective Authentic Assessment Questions

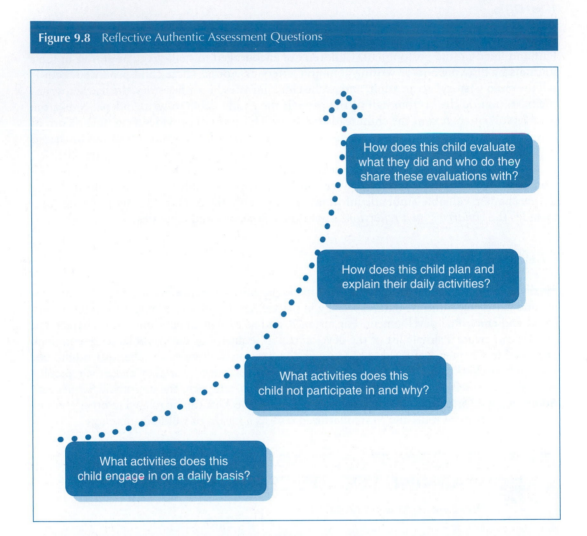

How does this child evaluate what they did and who do they share these evaluations with?

How does this child plan and explain their daily activities?

What activities does this child not participate in and why?

What activities does this child engage in on a daily basis?

REFLECT AND APPLY EXERCISE 9.1

Gathering Authentic Data

Reflect

Examine the photo on p. 232. Now examine the reflective questions for authentic data collection presented in Figure 9.8

Apply

Using the questions in Figure 9.8, try to gather authentic data about the child involved in the activities in the photo on p. 232.

There are many assessment tools out there and many ways to gather data from natural settings. Teachers need to keep some general concepts in mind when determining the type of assessment they are going to use:

- **Choose assessments that reflect what you are teaching:** Remember the point of assessment is to monitor student learning to aid instruction.
- **Assess frequently and systematically:** Remember young children are learning quickly and teachers need to know each child's skills.
- **Use several different types of assessments:** Remember that not all children are alike. The assessment procedure that you use for one child may not necessarily be the one that you should use for another child.

Assessment of the Learning-Teaching Process

Assessing and teaching go hand in hand. The assessment of learning activities can be a formal or a less structured process that informs caregivers and teachers what children can do now and what they need to learn next. For young children, direct observation during natural learning activities is often the most reliable method for the assessment of learning. Caregivers usually assess young children's motor skills by observing their mobility. Based on their findings, they determine if that child should be encouraged to take first steps, begin self-feeding with their fingers, or attempt to ride a tricycle. As children increase in age and abilities, more frequent use of formal assessments should occur. Typically, when children are in the early primary grades, they participate in multiple formal assessments across the curricula.

Early childhood professionals should be as comfortable using assessment tools as they are with using instructional strategies. Assessment practices that are integrated into daily occurring learning activities provide information on (1) what children understand now, (2) what they could understand better with more guidance, and (3) what is just too challenging for the children to understand at this time.

Children should be involved in the assessment process. For example, they benefit greatly from reviewing their work samples that have been placed in their portfolios. Examining past work allows children to observe their own growth and progress, and to talk about this growth when analyzing their ever-changing abilities. Some questions that can be used when asking children to assess their work are the following:

- What do you like best about this?
- Name two things that you would like to change.
- Tell me more about this?
- If you did this again, what would you do?
- How does this compare to what you did yesterday?
- What do you think your grandmother will think when she looks at this?

Involvement in such assessment expands children's feeling of self, use of language, cognitive abilities, and social skills.

Children in the lower primary grades should be encouraged to become adept at self-assessment, which is a skill that can assist them with future learning. As children understand the skills they have now and the ones that they will need to accomplish a certain activity, they most likely will address the achievement of a specific goal more efficiently.

Learning needs to be assessed regularly. Often, just sitting and observing a young child and writing down everything that happens over a short period of time can provide a multitude of information on that child's developmental and learning abilities. Teachers who use this "direct observation" method of assessment often observe that it takes longer than just using a checklist, but that they obtain much more valuable information. Other techniques besides using direct observation for gathering natural assessment data on children's learning activities are the following:

- Asking children to explain their drawings and work samples
- Asking children questions about what they are doing
- Asking family members about their observations of a child's learning
- Asking other professionals to observe a child's learning

To guide children's learning to a higher level of performance, adults must be able to use naturally occurring learning activities as assessment tools to enhance their curriculum.

Involving Families in the Assessment of Learning

Children's learning can be enhanced if the staff and families work together and share information. Caregivers see children in a variety of situations as they interact with diverse people. Their insights can provide robust assessment data. Therefore, family members should always be included in both the formal and informal assessment process. They should be asked to provide their information and be told that their impressions are key to assessing their child's progress.

All assessment activities and findings should be translated into everyday terms so that the parents understand them. Parents should be treated as consultants and asked for their suggestions on ways that learning can be approached with their child in the classroom. Similarly, school staff should be able to suggest resources in the community that families can access to support their child's learning.

The following are examples of everyday strategies that school staff should use to encourage assessment partnerships with families:

- Communicate regularly with families about their children's learning and development
- Explore with parents how they view the growth and development of their children
- Partner with families during all formal assessment processes
- Provide assessment tools to parents (e.g., work samples, checklists, photos) to support their understanding of their role in children's learning

Integrating Cameras Into the Assessment Process

As suggested in the *First-Person Interview* for this chapter, digital cameras can be an excellent tool for assessment. Program teachers should try to take pictures of each child at both the beginning and the end of the school year to document physical growth. Additionally, photographs afford opportunities for adults to record learning skills that cannot be displayed on paper. The following are examples of displays of learning skills that can be depicted through a photo:

- Block structures
- Large paintings
- Patterning of objects
- Puzzles that display the complexity and number of pieces
- Creations using manipulatives
- Social interactions
- Physical accomplishments
- Dramatic play enactments
- Dance and music skills

Photographs can be used to start conversations with parents about their child's accomplishments or challenges. When parents see a picture, they often can then connect the information that is being shared with other activities that they have observed outside the program setting. This information provides a much more robust assessment process. Additionally, if parents are English learners, a photo can assist with providing them with accurate information on their child's skills.

Photographs can also be used with children. They are excellent tools for initiating conversations about what children have accomplished, how they have grown, and what they would like to do differently. Additionally, taking a picture of a child involved in an activity can assist in keeping children who have challenges stay on task. Showing the child a picture of his or her current accomplishment could support the child to advance the task to a higher level of learning so that another picture could be taken.

Assessment of Challenging Abilities

Early education teachers often have concerns about the level of impact of their instruction on a specific child's academic skill, their social interactions, and their general behaviors. If a teacher is concerned about the instruction's impact on a child's progress, that teacher should always seek additional support from colleagues and from the child's family members. These resources can provide information about the child and suggestions on how to modify instructional supports so as to address the teacher's concerns. Teachers must be aware of the need to seek this assistance in a very timely manner. Putting off discussing concerns about a child's progress with the family can often have a negative impact on developmental skills.

Many programs have a **Student Assistance Team** (SAT), or a similar type of team, that supports teachers who have concerns about a particular student's progress. Such teams are often composed of general education teachers, special educators, and support services personnel—for example, speech and language therapist, psychologist, physical therapist, and an administrator. Teachers can present their formal and informal assessment information to the team by describing the student's strengths, interests, and needs, and the child's response to the instructional adaptations that have been implemented to assist the student. The SAT collaboratively evaluates the situation along with the teacher and attempts to identify intervention strategies to address the teacher's concerns. The team develops alternative plans that the teacher and family can implement to address the child's needs. Critical to this problem-solving process and the intervention that results is the use of effective observation and assessment.

©iStock.com/bowdenimages

Children who might have difficulty understanding a concept when it is presented to a large group, are provided with small group instruction through RtI.

Response to Intervention

Another classroom-based observation and assessment procedure is **Response to Intervention (RtI)**, a systematic observation and assessment process for analyzing children's learning problems. Federal law requires its use with kindergarten through twelfth-grade students who manifest learning differences.

Additionally, this process is now increasingly used to assess the learning needs of a wide variety of other students, many of whom have behavior concerns.

RtI requires teachers to use research-based interventions when children are having difficulties learning material that the other children in the classroom appear to understand through group instructional activities (Colvin, Flannery, Sugai, & Monegan, 2009; Friend & Bursuck, 2012; Lembke, McMaster, & Stecker, 2010). The RtI model, which has a similar concept as positive behavior supports (see Chapter 6), is composed of three tiers, and the intensity of the intervention increases as a student progresses through those tiers. The premise for the model is the assumption that approximately 75% to 80% of all classroom students can meet the demands of the typical classroom if they receive high-quality instruction. Of the remaining 20% to 25%, approximately 15% to 20% will require more intensive instruction in small groups to learn key concepts or skills. Finally, the remaining 5% to 10% of the students in a class will require highly intensive, more individualized instruction, or possibly be referred to a diagnostic team to be considered for placement into special education and receive services from a special educator (Friend & Bursuck, 2012).

The scenario at the beginning of this chapter gives an example of a student who might be receiving RtI services. As demonstrated in that scenario, the key to evaluating the efficacy of the RtI model is implementing a sound, pre-planned, and continuous observation and assessment process.

If observations and assessments determine that interventions for children at tiers 1 and 2 are ineffective, and those children need tier 3 interventions, assessment data are used to determine if a special education placement is appropriate. If the assessment data indicate that the intensive interventions at tier 3 are ineffective, the student is typically referred to a **multidisciplinary team (MDT)** for further observation and assessment. The MDT is comprised of educators, the child's parents, a psychologist, and support services personnel as needed—such as a speech and language specialist, nurse, occupational therapist, and social worker. The role of the MDT is to determine whether the child is eligible for special education services. That determination involves a process that relies heavily on both formal and informal classroom observational and assessment information (see Figure 9.9).

If small group instruction does not have the desired impact, children are provided with an intensive intervention through RtI.

RtI and Young Children. The underlying goal of RtI is to deliver high-quality learning opportunities to all children. High-quality early education programs use developmentally appropriate practices, that are guided by the educational team, and employ research-based instructional strategies to maximize learning (NAEYC , DEC, & NHSA,

Figure 9.9 Types of Possible Assessment Support

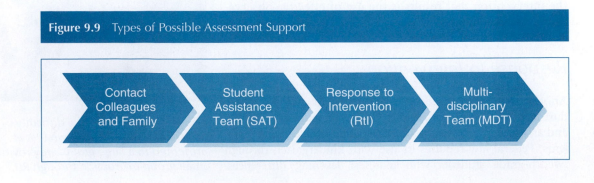

Contact Colleagues and Family → Student Assistance Team (SAT) → Response to Intervention (RtI) → Multi-disciplinary Team (MDT)

2012). The NAEYC and the Division for Early Childhood (DEC), an organization that advocates for the early education of infants, toddlers, and preschoolers with disabilities, believe that RtI is a promising approach for promoting the participation of most children in the context of inclusion (Odom et al., 2011). However, they caution that RtI activities for preschoolers must be collaboratively designed and implemented by the child's family and general and special educators. These activities must allow children to engage in types of developmentally appropriate play-based activities that research has proven effective and that build on the child's strengths, interests, and preferences. Finally, RtI with young children must involve collaborative and ongoing progress monitoring, assessment, and problem solving in natural environments—at schools, centers, homes, and community agencies.

Similar to the child in the opening scenario, the implementation of RtI in early education centers provides benefits for children who have already been diagnosed as having a special need and who are enrolled in an inclusive program with typically developing children. In that situation, RtI can provide intensive supports in needed areas within their natural learning environment. Additionally, for those children who might have a disability as yet undiagnosed, RtI replaces the traditional "wait to fail" model. Under that model, teams wait until the student demonstrates a significant discrepancy between intellectual ability and academic achievement before beginning the assessment process.

RtI is a method used for supporting children with disabilities who are included in general education classroom and who might need interventions in specific areas.

However, a number of professional organizations believe that, while early childhood education programs may benefit from an RtI framework, it is important to ensure that every child receives the developmentally appropriate practices (see Chapter 1) and intentional learning opportunities (see Chapter 6) needed for optimal growth and learning. After all, young children are beginning learners with skills that are strongly related to personal opportunities and not abilities. They caution professionals not to implement RtI in early childhood education until further research findings with older populations are available (NAEYC, DEC, & NHSA, 2012). Some of their concerns are listed in Figure 9.10.

REFLECT AND APPLY EXERCISE 9.2

Challenges and Benefits of RtI

Reflect

NAEYC, DEC, and NHSA caution about using RtI with preschoolers because research has not yet determined the impact of this model on learning.

Apply

What might be the negative impact of using the RtI model on preschool children who come from poverty backgrounds? Additionally, what might be a positive impact on that same population?

Figure 9.10   NAEYC, DEC, and NHSA Cautions Regarding Implementation of RtI Into Early Childhood Education

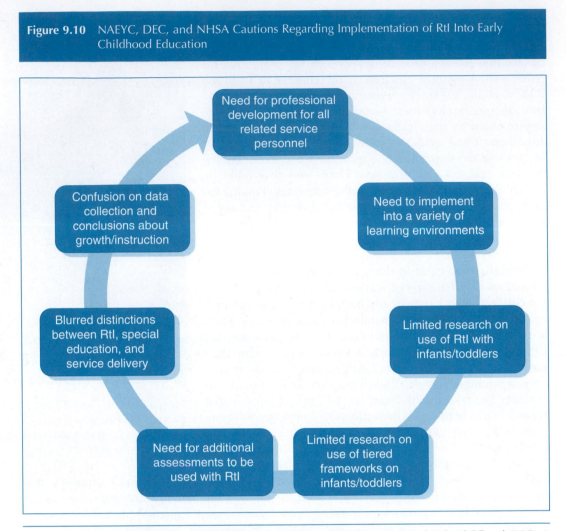

Source: National Association for the Education of Young Children (NAEYC), Division of Early Childhood (DEC), & National Head Start Association (NHSA). (2012). *Frameworks for Response to Intervention in Early Childhood Education: Description and Implications*. Retrieved from http://www.naeyc.org

Determining Special Education Eligibility

Determining the eligibility for special education services involves an assessment process that includes formal and informal data collection from several sources. For example, a school psychologist will provide data from formal assessment instruments that are typically used to determine a child's intellectual ability and academic achievement. A reading specialist might determine the student's vocabulary, decoding, or comprehension skills. Data gathered by a support services professional can provide information on the student's social/developmental background (Friend & Bursuck, 2012). When a child manifests physical and/or sensory concerns, a speech/language therapist, occupational therapist, or physical therapist might be added to the MDT to gather specific assessment data to help determine both eligibility for services and their intensity.

The combination of formal and informal assessment data helps create a detailed picture of the student's strengths and needs as well as an intervention history of the child. Based on these assessment findings, the MDT makes eligibility decisions and a placement decision for the child. The parent must agree with these decisions for the process to advance to the next step. If the parent does not agree with the team's decision, the child remains in the classroom in which he or she is currently enrolled.

If the child qualifies for special education services, the assessment findings are used to determine an appropriate education placement for the child. Additionally, an **Individual Family Service Plan (IFSP)** is developed for children from birth to 3 years of age and their families. At 3 years old, children then transition to an **Individualized Education Program (IEP)**, and they can continue with an IEP until they are 21 years old. Both the IFSP and the IEP include individually determined learning objectives for both the child and the family. The IFSP and the IEP also contain an additional assessment protocol for evaluating the student's progress.

©iStockphoto.com/azpworldwide

IEPs are Individualized Education Programs that target specific objectives that children with disabilities need to meet and that will assist them in meeting those objectives.

Implementing a Transactive Analysis Model for Authentic Assessment

For young children, obtaining valid observational and assessment information can be problematic. Early development is rapid, episodic, and highly influenced by experience. Therefore, the results of young children's assessments have to consider the emotional states of the child and the assessment conditions. The use of authentic assessments can offer the systematic gathering of information about children as they interact with different learning contexts throughout their day. This information provides a richer view of the children and a more complete understanding of their developing skills and how their daily environment is impacting the child's development (Sameroff, 2010). As discussed earlier in this chapter, instead of having an assessment provide a series of fixed data points across time, the assessment should provide teachers and families with a picture that monitors children's development as it unfolds. As one researcher recently observed, "The models we use to understand how individuals change over time have increased in complexity, from linear to interactive to transactive to multilevel dynamic systems" (Sameroff, 2010, p. 6; see Figure 9.11).

Figure 9.11 Types of Assessment Data Collection

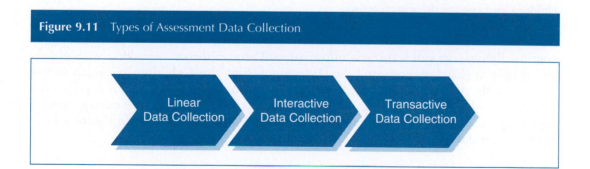

Linear Data Collection → Interactive Data Collection → Transactive Data Collection

Figure 9.14 presents a Learning Center Observation Worksheet that can be used to systematically collect data on children's play activities while they participate in learning activities. The following sections provide information on how to use that worksheet.

Transactive Observations

High-quality play center activities should have two purposes: (1) encouraging children to learn more about the world around them, and (2) encouraging adults to learn more about

Figure 9.12   Questions for Classroom Data Analysis

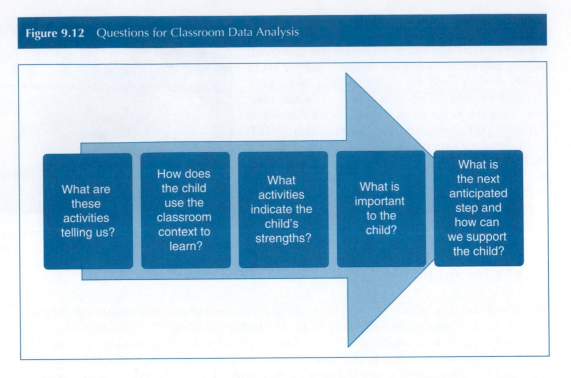

the children's knowledge of and interests in the world. Similar to the Reggio Emilia approach to learning (see Chapter 2), center time affords adults opportunities to obtain information about the children's language, knowledge, and skills, and to reflect on strategies that can be used to assist the children in enhancing their abilities. Constant and careful adult monitoring of the centers can provide valuable observational data documenting both newly acquired skills as well as skills that are still being developed at the independent level and thus currently need support. This information can be used to plan curriculum units, themes, or projects, large and small group events, and individualized center learning activities that will motivate children and engage them in learning.

The **transactive model of assessment** (see Sameroff, 2010, for a discussion of the transactional model for child development) allows both children and professionals to continually observe and learn new information. Through direct interaction with objects and people in the classroom, and the classroom setting itself, children are motivated to develop skills. Additionally, through direct interactions with observational data, professionals learn how children actually develop those specific skills. Professionals need to continually use follow-up questions such as the following and the ones in Figure 9.12 to analyze their data:

- What are the locations that the children enjoy?
- What are the general concepts at each center and how do the children engage in them?
- What are the other important features of the classroom?

The transactive model of assessment also affirms that physical space contributes to children's development. Physical space can foster the behaviors that the teacher views as important for children to develop. Furthermore, professionals must ask themselves, their coworkers, and their students' families daily questions to advance their understanding of the use of the learning spaces and the people who inhabit those spaces (Figure 9.13). For example:

Figure 9.13 Impact of Space on Learning

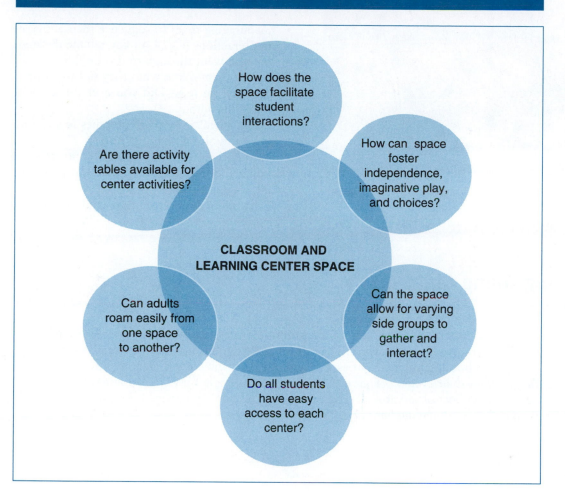

- How do children learn skills at home?
- Compare and contrast how children engage with other people at home and at school.
- Compare and contrast how children respond to sudden changes in the schedule at home and at school.

A transactive model includes children's thoughts regarding their own behaviors. Children's self-reflections can assist in portraying a clear and accurate picture of their current skills in a variety of cognitive and social areas, and the self-reflections can directly impact future instructional planning activities. Consequently, there are a number of benefits from having children participate in the assessment analysis process. First, the data that the children offer when answering questions about their own activities provide adults with information on how the children view themselves as active and contributing members of the classroom community. Additionally, their responses to reflective questions that relate to their ability provides information on children's ability to plan, negotiate, enhance, and evaluate their own activities. Finally, discussing and analyzing these questions enhances children's cognitive behaviors, and assists them in improving their self-regulation abilities.

©iStockphoto.com/Blend_Images

Adults and children collaboratively determine which centers the children will go to, with whom will they play, and in what activities they will become involved.

Questions to ask children in an effort to obtain self-reflective information from them might include:

- Encouraging them to sequence their activities or interactions (e.g., Can you tell me the steps that you went through to do this?)
- Having them relate what they did to a different situation (e.g., Did you ever think about doing this with . . . ?)
- Asking them to predict outcomes (e.g., What do you think will happen next?)
- Inviting them to compare and contrast what they are doing now to something that they did in the past
- Determining a problem that could occur and a solution to that problem

Observing Young Children

In today's diverse early childhood classrooms, professionals are compelled to regularly observe natural playful activities. They do so to determine and learn more about how each child goes about planning activities, engaging socially, and communicating information with the peers in their context. Figure 9.14 provides a sample observation worksheet that can be used to collect observational data on children's planning, participating, socializing, communicating, and playing behaviors in learning centers.

Observing Children Planning Activities

Early education professionals should not monitor only children's activities. They also should participate in conversations with the children about what those children plan to do and how they plan to go about achieving their goals. Research has examined the benefits of children and adults creating play plans together (Bodrova & Leong, 2007) and how such activities enhance the development of children's self-regulation skills (see Chapter 3). Valuable transactive information about children's ability to self-regulate their behaviors can be collected when children are observed planning the activities that they desire to accomplish before participating in an authentic learning center activity, and how successful they were in that activity.

Young children can participate regularly in short conversations where adults guide them in providing details about the activities the children want to engage in during their center activities. Children should be encouraged to describe the following:

1. The center where they will be playing

2. Who they will play with

3. The activities they want to do

Figure 9.14   Learning Center Observation Worksheet

Child's Name: _____ Emotional State: _____

Play Context: _____ Indoor or Outside Play Partners: _____

Observer: _____ Purpose: _____

GENERAL OBSERVATION NOTES

PLANNING/REFLECTING	GUIDANCE PROVIDED
Pre-Activity Dates: _____ Center(s) in which the child plans to participate: With whom they plan to participate: What does the child plan to do next: Future Activities:	
Post-Activity Dates: _____ Did the child remain at the centers as planned: Did the child participate with students as planned: Did the student complete the activity: Future Activities:	
Notes Dates: _____	

SOCIAL PARTICIPATION	GUIDANCE PROVIDED
Social Proximity Dates: _____ Individual (not interactions with others): Proximal to others with eye contact: Proximal to others with eye and body contact: Proximal to others with eye and body contact and use of same objects: Future Activities:	

(Continued)

(Continued)

SOCIAL PARTICIPATION	GUIDANCE PROVIDED
Social Interactions Dates: _____ Engages in same activity (uses same toys in same area but not actively sharing/playing): Actively shares objects, social communication, and play activity: Uses social rules (exchanging, turn-taking): Enters group: Maintains group interactions (forms friendships, assumes roles, responds to social cues): Future Activities:	
Notes Dates: _____	

COMMUNICATION PARTICIPATION	GUIDANCE PROVIDED
Receptive (spoken, nonverbal, sign, other) Dates: _____ Future Activities:	
Expressive (spoken, nonverbal, sign, other) Dates: _____ Future Activities:	
Initiator (directed to whom) Dates: _____ Future Activities:	
Responder (in response to whom) Dates: _____ Future Activities:	
Pragmatics of the communication Dates: _____ Future Activities:	

COMMUNICATION PARTICIPATION	GUIDANCE PROVIDED
Notes Dates: _____	
PLAY PARTICIPATION	**GUIDANCE PROVIDED**
Play Theme (realistic or fantasy) Dates: _____ Future Activities:	
Level of Nonrepresentational Activities (functional activity, inappropriate combinations, appropriate combinations, transitional) Dates: _____ Future Activities:	
Level of Representational Activities (self-pretense, other pretense, sequential pretense, substitution pretense) Dates: _____ Future Activities:	
Object Substitution (realistic objects or open-ended objects) Dates: _____ Future Activities:	
Role Substitution (single role or multiple roles at one time) Dates: _____ Future Activities:	
Action Substitution (props for support or language to describe actions) Dates: _____ Future Activities:	
Notes Dates: _____	

(Continued)

(Continued)

HEAD START ELEMENTS: PRESCHOOL LITERACY	GUIDANCE PROVIDED
Book Appreciation and Knowledge (interest in books/ characters; gets meaning and information from books and other texts) Dates: _____ Future Activities:	
Phonological Awareness (awareness that language can be broken down into words, syllables, and sounds) Dates: _____ Future Activities:	
Alphabet Knowledge (knows names and sounds of letters) Dates: _____ Future Activities:	
Print Concepts and Connections (understands concepts of print and early decoding—letter sound relationships) Dates: _____ Future Activities:	
Early Writing (familiar with writing implements, conventions, and emerging skills to communicate through written representations, symbols, and letters) Dates: _____ Future Activities:	
Notes Dates: _____ 	

COMMON CORE STATE STANDARDS: KINDERGARTEN READING	GUIDANCE PROVIDED
Literature Skills Dates: _____ Asks and answers questions about key details; retells familiar stories; identifies characters, settings, and events Asks and answers questions about unknown words in text; recognizes common texts; names author and illustrator of story and defines roles Describes relationship between illustration and story; compares and contrasts familiar stories Engages in reading activities with purpose and understanding Future Activities:	
Informational Text Skills Dates: _____ Asks and answers questions about key details; identifies main topic and retells key details; describes connection between two individuals, events, ideas, or pieces of information Asks and answers questions about unknown words in text; identifies front cover, back cover, and title page; names author and illustrator and defines roles Describes relationship between illustrations and text; identifies reasons author gives to identify points; identifies similarities in and differences between two texts on same topics Future Activities:	
Notes Dates: _____	

COMMON CORE STATE STANDARDS: KINDERGARTEN READING	GUIDANCE PROVIDED
Foundational Skills—Print Concepts **Dates:** _____ Follows words left-right, top-bottom, page by page; recognizes spoken words as written in sequences of letters; understands words are separated by spaces; recognizes/names upper- and lowercase letters of alphabet Future Activities:	

(Continued)

COMMON CORE STATE STANDARDS: KINDERGARTEN READING	GUIDANCE PROVIDED
Foundational Skills—Phonological Awareness Dates: _____ Recognizes/produces rhyming words; counts, pronounces, blends, and segments syllables in spoken words; blends and segments onsets and rhymes of single-syllable spoken words; isolates and pronounces initial, medial vowel, and final sounds in three phoneme words; adds or substitutes individual sounds in simple, one-syllable words to make new words Future Activities:	
Foundational Skills—Phonics and Word Recognition Dates: _____ Knowledge of one-to-one letter-sound correspondence by producing primary sounds for consonants; associates long and short sounds for spelling of five vowels; reads common high-frequency words by sight; distinguishes similarly spelled words by identifying sounds that differ Future Activities:	
Foundational Skills—Fluency Dates: _____ Reads emergent-reader texts with purpose and understanding Future Activities:	
Notes Dates: _____	
Writing—Text Types and Purpose Dates: _____ Combines drawing, dictating, and writing to (1) compose opinion and tell the topic or name of book they are writing about, (2) compose information/explanatory texts, or (3) write a narrative of a single event or several loosely linked events Future Activities:	
Writing—Production and Distribution Dates: _____ Responds to questions and suggestions from peers and adds details to strengthen writing, explores a variety of digital tools to produce and publish writings, including with peers Future Activities:	

COMMON CORE STATE STANDARDS: KINDERGARTEN READING	GUIDANCE PROVIDED
Writing—Research to Build and Present Knowledge **Dates:** _____ Participates in shared research and writing projects; recalls information from experiences or gathers information from provided sources to answer questions Future Activities:	
Notes Dates: _____	

COMMON CORE STATE STANDARDS: KINDERGARTEN READING	GUIDANCE PROVIDED
Speaking and Listening—Comprehension and Collaboration **Dates:** _____ Participates with peers and adults in conversations during small and large group activities; follows agreed-upon rules and uses multiple exchanges Understands text read aloud or information presented orally or through different media by asking and answering questions Asks and answers questions to seek help, get information, or clarify something not understood Future Activities:	
Speaking and Listening—Presentation of Knowledge **Dates:** _____ Describes familiar people, places, things, and events with details, when prompted Adds drawings or visual displays to descriptions to provide details Speaks audibly and expresses thoughts, feelings, and ideas clearly Future Activities:	
Notes Dates: _____	

(Continued)

COMMON CORE STATE STANDARDS: KINDERGARTEN READING	GUIDANCE PROVIDED
Language—Conventions of English Dates: _____ Prints many upper- and lowercase letters; uses frequently occurring nouns/verbs; forms regular plurals; understands and uses question words; uses most frequent prepositions; produces and expands complete sentences Capitalizes first word of sentence; recognizes and names ending punctuation; writes letter(s) for most consonant and short-vowel sounds; spells simple words phonetically Future Activities:	
Language—Vocabulary Acquisition and Use **Dates: _____** Sorts common objects into categories; understands frequently occurring verbs and adjectives by relating them to their opposite; identifies real-life connections between words and use; discriminates shades of meaning among verbs describing the same general action Future Activities:	
Notes Dates: _____	

HEAD START ELEMENTS: PRESCHOOL MATHEMATICS	GUIDANCE PROVIDED
Number Concepts and Quantities (understands numbers represents quantities and have ordinal properties—e.g., number words represent rank order, size, or position in a list) Dates: _____ Future Activities:	
Number Relationships and Operations (uses numbers to describe relationships and solve problems) **Dates: _____** Future Activities:	

HEAD START ELEMENTS: PRESCHOOL MATHEMATICS	GUIDANCE PROVIDED
Geometry and Spatial Sense (understands shapes, their properties, and how objects are related to one another) **Dates:** _____ Future Activities:	
Patterns (recognizes patterns, sequencing, and critical thinking skills needed to predict and classify objects in a pattern) Dates: _____ Future Activities:	
Measurement and Comparison (understands attributes and reflective properties of objects as related to size, capacity, and area) Dates: _____ Future Activities:	
Notes Dates: _____	

COMMON CORE STATE STANDARDS: KINDERGARTEN MATHEMATICS	GUIDANCE PROVIDED
Counting and Cardinality Dates: _____ Knows number names and the count sequence; counts to tell number of objects; compares numbers Future Activities:	
Operations and Algebraic Thinking Dates: _____ Understands adding as putting numbers together/adding to; understands subtracting as taking apart/taking from Future Activities:	
Number Operations in Base Ten Dates: _____ Works with numbers 11–19 to gain foundations for place value Future Activities:	

(Continued)

(Continued)

COMMON CORE STATE STANDARDS: KINDERGARTEN MATHEMATICS	GUIDANCE PROVIDED
Measurement and Data Dates: _____ Describes/compares measurable attributes; classifies objects and counts the number of objects in categories Future Activities:	
Geometry Dates: _____ Identifies/describes shapes; analyzes/compares/creates/composes shapes Future Activities:	
Notes Dates: _____	

HEAD START ELEMENTS: PRESCHOOL SOCIAL STUDIES	GUIDANCE PROVIDED
Self, Family, and Community (understands one's relationship to the family and community, roles in the family and community, and respect for diversity) **Dates:** _____ Future Activities:	
People and the Environment (understands relationship between people and the environment in which they live) **Dates:** _____ Future Activities:	
History and Events (understands that events happened in the past and how these events relate to one's self, family, and community) Dates: _____ Future Activities:	
Notes Dates: _____	

NATIONAL CURRICULUM STANDARDS FOR SOCIAL STUDIES	GUIDANCE PROVIDED
Culture (knows people create, learn, share, and adapt to culture) Dates: _____ Future Activities:	
Time, Continuity, and Change (knows about everyday life in different times and places around the world) Dates: _____ Future Activities:	
People, Places, and Environments (explores different spatial and geographic concepts and the interactions between people and places) Dates: _____ Future Activities:	
Individual Development and Identity (knows that family, friends, culture and institutions shape their personal identity) Dates: _____ Future Activities:	
Individual, Groups, and Institutions (examines families, schools, governments, and courts) Dates: _____ Future Activities:	
Power, Authority, and Governance (examine rules, fairness, and responsibilities within their families, groups, and classrooms) Dates: _____ Future Activities:	
Production, Distribution, and Consumption (relates their wants and needs to personal economic experiences) Dates: _____ Future Activities:	

(Continued)

(Continued)

NATIONAL CURRICULUM STANDARDS FOR SOCIAL STUDIES	GUIDANCE PROVIDED
Science, Technology, and Society (studies how their lives are impacted by technology) **Dates:** _____ Future Activities:	
Global Connections (discovers how things that happen around the world impact their lives) **Dates:** _____ Future Activities:	
Civic Ideals and Practices (participates in classroom communities by following rules, sharing, and collaborating) **Dates:** _____ Future Activities:	
Notes Dates: _____	

HEAD START PRESCHOOL CREATIVE ARTS FOUNDATIONS	GUIDANCE NEEDED
Music (uses voice and instruments to create sounds) **Dates:** _____	
Creative Movement and Dance (uses body to move to music/express oneself) Dates: _____	
Art (uses range of media and materials to create drawings, pictures, or projects) Dates: _____	

HEAD START PRESCHOOL CREATIVE ARTS FOUNDATIONS	GUIDANCE NEEDED
Drama (portrays events, characters, or stories by acting/ using props and language) Dates: _____	
Notes Dates: _____	

HEAD START PRESCHOOL PHYSICAL FOUNDATIONS	GUIDANCE NEEDED
Gross Motor Skills Dates: _____ Develops motor control and balance for a range of physical activities Develops motor coordination and skills using objects for a range of physical activities Understands movement concepts, such as control of body, how it moves, and that bodies can move independently or in coordination with other objects	
Fine Motor Skills Dates: _____ Develops hand strength and dexterity Develops eye-hand coordination to use everyday tools Manipulates a range of objects Manipulates writing, drawing, and art tools	
Notes Dates: _____	

For classroom management purposes, these conversations do not have to happen daily with each child and can occur with a small group of children. Additionally, the adult can suggest a couple of centers from which the children can choose. A responsive and sensitive professional will know which centers are of primary interest to each child in the classroom.

Children's planning of play activities is an important aspect of developing self-regulation skills and independence. Play plans, as defined by Bodrova and Leong (2007), require children to develop valuable cognitive skills—such as hypothesizing, negotiating, problem solving, and

Children provide valuable information when justifying the center in which they have chosen to participate.

anticipating. Children between 5 and 7 years of age do not just acquire the "absolute ability to reason." Instead, they develop the skills to reason with others and to act as if they are a reasoning member of society (White, 1996, p. 27). Therefore, long before 7 years of age, children need to participate in situations where they are not just free to play. Rather, they are responsible for planning and carrying out interactions with their peers in a cooperative and reasonable manner so that self-regulation skills can develop and language be acquired. For example, when children are required to think about the different sequences of events their play activity is going to follow and then follow those plans, they are enriching their ability to control their own actions. Children's play plans will be discussed further in Chapter 10 of this book.

Observing Children's Participation in Activities

Professionals also need to observe children's development of skills as they engage in center activities. Information should be collected on the children with whom a child engages and how long they participate in various activities. This information can assist adults in determining patterns in children's social skills and play activities.

Knowing why the child chose to go somewhere and play with someone provides insightful data to adults who are assessing children's learning.

For example, professionals will want to know which children move to different activities and interact with a variety of students, and which ones remain with the same children in the same activity. These data relate to a child's social behavior in a specific context and can assist in identifying ways to work with children so they can successfully self-select different peer groups with which to interact (Corsaro, 1987). Being comfortable and skilled at engaging with a variety of peers, instead of engaging with the same peers, can increase children's acquisition of knowledge and language and the ways in which they attain information. Additionally, guided discussions between children and adults examining what children are planning to do and with whom they want to do it can result in children expanding their interactions to include more diverse activities and people. Finally, participating in discussions about who they interacted with can also enhance children's knowledge on how to approach different learning situations.

Information should be noted on additional supports that a child might require to access a center and fully participate in the activities there. For some children, additional supports, such as the following, might be necessary for successful participation:

- An adult introducing a child to another child or group of children
- Coaching by a paraprofessional
- Adaptive equipment such as communication devices
- An interpreter

All such assistive supports should be monitored, and plans for minimizing or increasing the use of these supports should be discussed regularly with staff, family members, and the child. The goal is to maximize the number of children who are able to independently and successfully enter various playgroups.

Observing Social Skills

Gathering authentic data on children's proximity to their peers is a method for measuring their choice of social playmates (Elkind, 2007). Social proximity, or standing close enough to communicate and show interest in another person, is a gauge for determining cooperation. Elkind states that when children participate in game playing, they not only develop two conflicting skills at the same time (i.e., cooperation and competition), but they also learn how to balance and use those skills successfully at the same time. The same is true about socio-dramatic play activities. When children create socio-dramatic play enactments, they are not only developing their own play goals, but they are also simultaneously involved in self-regulation so that their play partners' goals are considered and integrated.

Adults need to observe the following social skills:

- Which children have chosen to play together
- How they get along, how they share and collaboratively engage in achieving joint goals
- How they move in and out of groups
- How they interact with members when in their groups

By maintaining these natural social data over time, a picture emerges of children's cooperation skills, competition skills, and ability to achieve goals. All of these factors contribute to the lifelong skill of being a cooperative member of a group. Attaining these social skills is typically challenging for children who have various learning or behavioral differences. For example, children with attention deficit disorders (ADD) or attention deficit hyperactive disorders (ADHD) might require guidance through discussions and modeling that can assist in modifying behaviors of concern.

Identifying skills that are challenging for children to cooperate with peers and talking about them with the children can assist in the development and understanding of appropriate social skill development.

©iStockphoto.com/RichLegg

Observing Communication Skills

While language and communication skills are traditionally identified using formal assessments, findings on these skills while children are engaged in authentic playful learning activities can provide even more comprehensive and exact information. As discussed in Chapter 2 of this book, children engaged in play activities with others tend to produce higher level skills than when they are alone. It provides a context for interacting with varied English models to acquire language. Having immediate access to information about the child's skills can assist professionals in designing high-quality learning center activities that truly meet the individual language and communication needs of all children. Additionally, through the collection and examination of young children's play narratives, adults can immediately alter classroom environments to provide earlier receptive, expressive, and pragmatic language interventions. Using observational data can provide more immediate results than waiting for formal assessment results. With the increase in the number of children with disabilities being placed in inclusive settings, teachers need to observe and document all children regularly.

Observing Play Activities

Play activities allow children to learn about objects and their properties. Additionally, they learn early that objects in themselves, while interesting, are also important tools to be used for various purposes. For example, infants explore objects to discover their shapes, how they can be held, how they taste, and how they sound when banged against a surface. Later, they learn that when an object is dropped, a sibling or adult will retrieve and return it. The objects now become important tools for learning because they are the catalyst for social interactions and evolving games.

Activities that children perform socially with their peers in play activities lead the way to working on more academically focused activities.

As children interact with play objects, they learn to differentiate among them and, based on the objects' unique properties and uses, to begin to categorize them according to their discovered properties. Through further exploration and experimentation, the properties of objects are learned. Children will learn that most round objects will roll, while something that is not round most likely will not roll. Additionally, as discussed in Chapter 3, they will learn that objects can be substituted and become something that they typically do not represent, for example a block can become a cell phone.

Children then begin to combine objects to form something novel. During this process, objects are labeled and soon associated with verbal cues. Language becomes part of children's' play. Again, as demonstrated in Chapter 3, once children begin to use language with play, a whole new type of play emerges, and children begin to participate in symbolic activities (Elkind, 2007).

Play is central to young children's development in multiple areas, and adults need a systematic method for observing and capturing the changes in children's activities as those children develop. Play remains an important part of children's development until the elementary years when play takes on new functions and gradually becomes subordinate to the dominant disposition of this age period—work as demonstrated through the development of literacy, math, and science.

In short, play is the platform upon which developmental abilities are built. Adults must carefully collect authentic data on children's use of symbolic representations and how children integrate language to describe and encourage the development of symbolic narratives.

At the end of each week adults need to analyze the authentic play data that they have collected in the classroom. Again, this process is a means for the adults to reflect upon each student's actions and developmental abilities during natural, everyday activities that motivate children. This synthesis provides the opportunity to summarize how the children interact in the classroom context, engage with other children, develop their play plans to fruition, choose play tasks in which they participate, and use language to achieve their goals. Reflecting on these data allows the adults to discuss any issues that arose during the week, including any social/behavioral concerns that might have surfaced with individual children. Through transactive observations and reflective questioning, adults both examine the learning environments and immediately implement modifications that can promote high-level learning for all young children.

Chapter Summary

There are multiple reasons for assessing young children's abilities. First, assessment assists in making sound decisions about teaching and learning. Second, assessment allows teachers to monitor the student's progress, milestones achieved, and to identify significant developmental concerns. Third, assessment assists in enhancing programs. Through the use of authentic learning settings, adults can collect information about how children are responding to their natural environments and using them to learn. Descriptive data that are gathered over time can provide an ongoing, transactive look at how children plan and engage in their activities.

Additionally, valuable information can be obtained from children when they are asked to evaluate their own activities, the peers with whom they chose to play, and the reasons for their social interactions. This observation process can be augmented with traditional linear assessment protocols to provide a more comprehensive picture of children's language, social, and cognitive skills so that high-quality learning activities can be designed.

HOME AND COMMUNITY CONNECTIONS

Observing and Assessing to Promote Learning

Encourage parents to make note of the kinds of toys your children like to play with, the topics they like to read about, the activities they like to engage in outdoors, and the materials they like to work with. Suggest that they share with the teacher what they have observed with your children's teacher.

CHAPTER 9 FIRST-PERSON INTERVIEW #1

Observing With Durable Cameras

Julie Luckenbill

Coordinator of a university infant and toddler program, Davis, CA

I constantly use a digital camera to capture images of "mindful caregiving" demonstrated by the undergraduate students who are joining us in our practicum for the first time, the intern students who are returning to gain more experience in caregiving, and our professional staff. I especially like to capture images that show our beginning undergraduates engaged in "best practice" or positive behaviors such as being tuned-in and at the level of the children at our center. I use these images to make points in the discussion component of the course. This validates each student's skill, emphasizes strengths, and invites other beginning students to imitate strong caregiving behaviors.

We also take photographs of the enrolled children. We show them along with our conference summary at parent-teacher conferences. We could just sit down with the family and tell them things like, "Jose now knows how to climb to the top of the jungle gym," but it makes a bigger impression to pair the milestone with a picture of Jose at the top of the jungle gym. Pictures are especially useful when we are communicating with family members who have limited English skills because even if they don't understand everything that is said, they can figure out a lot from the images, rather than relying solely on another person to translate. But whether they need the photos in order to follow the conference or not, all our families love seeing the pictures of their children at play in the classrooms. It helps them to trust us that we keep their children happily engaged. At the end of the year, each family takes home the file of pictures of their children participating in school activities throughout the year as well

(Continued)

(Continued)

as a printed portfolio that includes photographs, anecdotes, and artwork. This is especially nice for families who have a very limited number of photos of their children.

We use the photos of the children in the conferences, but also in classroom documentation. In our program, we use a teaching technique called "emergent curriculum," where the curriculum emerges from the children's passions and ideas. We use a technique we term "watch-ask-adapt." This technique requires the adult to "watch" what the child is doing, "ask" open-ended questions about what the adult observes, and then "adapt" the adult's behaviors to focus on the child's interest. Through this approach, the staff members at our center add challenges and expand concepts to guide children into deeper thought and play around the children's preferred ideas. For example, one of the interns working at our center observed that some of the toddlers were interested in trains. She then brought in a number of boxes and set them up as a train. By the end of the week, most of the children in the class had used the train boxes at some time or another. During the next week, we expanded her idea by making the Dramatic Play Area into a train station. Then, when we observed that the children enjoyed engaging in activities at our play train station, we planned a field trip to the Amtrak station. All of these activities—the children exploring the boxes, the activities in the play train station, and the field trip to see the real train station—were documented by taking pictures using our digital camera. At the end of the two-week period, we included many pictures of all the things that happened in our newsletter that went home to the families.

Another project that we love to do with cameras at the center is making "homemade books" about our families and the children in the classroom. This activity is designed to support home-to-school connections (reading about things that happen at home while at school) and to help children cope with separation (by looking at absent family). We also like to make social stories to teach concepts like hamster care, and to create song books that include all children in the classroom, promoting belongingness. We keep these books in our Quiet Area, and children read them when they need them. We find that they are useful in promoting social and emotional skills as well as early literacy—homemade books support early literacy by emphasizing to young children that the content in books relates to real life. We invite parents to try bookmaking at home too.

Because of the potential damage to cameras when capturing natural snapshots in the lives of infants and toddlers and their caregivers, I highly recommend that programs purchase durable cameras that are sand-proof, crush-proof, water-proof, and shock-proof. We went through a lot of cameras before figuring this out!

CHAPTER 9 FIRST-PERSON INTERVIEW #2

Enhancing and Advancing Through Assessment

I have been an early childhood teacher, an administrator, and now I am a university professor who teaches teachers. One thing I have noticed is that it is really difficult for teachers to learn how to balance academic development and developmentally appropriate practices in their teaching. They can easily create a play-based activity, but it becomes more difficult for the teacher to integrate the specific skills children need to learn and at the same time help children advance in their development while being engaged in the play activity. That's the difficult and the critical part—integration of specific skills development and advancement of learning—for the early childhood teachers to incorporate into their teaching! The key to this is assessment.

Teachers really need to know how to assess what children are doing and how to get them to do something that might be a bit more challenging. I think that most teachers know the

Dr. Elizabeth Elliott

College of Education Professor, Ft. Myers, FL

sequences of development in all the different areas. The challenge for them is to figure out how to know what children want to learn and how to go about providing children with opportunities in which that learning will occur.

In order to advance the development of children's skills, teachers have to be skilled assessors. They can see children grow, and they know when progress is being made. However, they need to know how to prove that a child has developed a specific skill. Teachers need to continually think about how they can document learning. Is the documentation going to take place through hearing certain words, or will it be the completion of a specific product? Play is fun, but when it is tied to learning, teachers really need to think beyond just designing the activity. They need to think about what they are going to do, what they want to observe, and how they will assess that learning has occurred for the child, then be able to translate that understanding that learning has occurred into something tangible.

I always tell my teachers that they need to "enhance and advance" their children's skills and development. They cannot do that unless they are continually assessing what their children are doing and what they as teachers are doing. That is why they have to be Intentional Teachers and truly know what skills they are advancing and enhancing in their students.

Student Study Site

Visit the Student Study Site at **www.sagepub.com/selmi** to access additional study tools including mobile-friendly eFlashcards and links to video and web resources.

Key Terms

Apgar score

assessment

authentic assessment

checklists

formal assessment

Individual Family Service Plan (IFSP)

Individualized Education Program (IEP)

informal assessment

journals

multidisciplinary team

observational notes

portfolios

Response to Intervention (RtI)

social proximity

Student Assistance Team

transactive model of assessment

Useful Websites

Authentic Assessment: http://jfmueller.faculty.noctrl.edu/toolbox/whatisit.htm

Center for Response to Intervention in Early Childhood: http://www.crtiec.org

Peabody Picture Vocabulary Assessment: http://psychcorp.pearsonassessments.com/HAIWEB/Cultures/en-us/Productdetail.htm?Pid=PAa30700

Woodcock Johnson Tests of Achievement: http://www.riversidepublishing.com/products/wjIIIAchievement

Reflective Questions

1. With young children, the combination of formal and informal data provides a complete picture of a child and his or her abilities. Discuss two ways that formal data can assist and two ways informal data can assist in providing data for designing instructional activities.

2. Think of a child that you have observed in a center or school. Now, read the questions in Figure 9.8 and attempt to answer them based on the data you collected during your observation.

PART III

Integrating Play Activities Across the Curriculum

Research presented in Parts I and II demonstrates that the fantasy worlds of young children, which are created through socio-dramatic play activities can positively impact their development of social, learning, language, literacy, and self-regulation abilities. Part III examines methods for integrating socio-dramatic play activities across the preschool curriculum. Because of the influence of play on learning and development, pretend activities should not be restricted to the socio-dramatic play center, nor should literacy activities be limited to the literacy and book centers. Instead, teachers must have strategies for integrating playful literacy activities into all learning center activities so that children are self-motivated to develop early academic skills.

Specifically, Part III describes strategies for integrating literacy activities into play activities, and then implementing those literacy and play activities into the science centers, mathematics centers, social studies centers, and creative arts and motor skills centers. Unlike in the past, it is no longer sufficient to provide children with an early learning curriculum based solely on their own interests. Additionally, research has shown that teacher-directed, skill-and-drill activities are unproductive for many young children who are attempting to develop academic skills.

Today's adults must understand how to modify and guide child-centered activities so that those activities address current early learning standards. Additionally, they must be knowledgeable about and skillful in using playful learning activities—similar to the ones in the opening scenario of each chapter of this book—as facilitators for transitioning children into more structured academic activities that are based on learning standards. As mentioned at the beginning of this book, many of the skills that children develop through their playful negotiations with peers provide the foundation for skills that are focused on in the Common Core State Standards.

At the end of each chapter in Part III, a new section has been added, titled *Sample Learning Activities*. This section is designed to guide teachers in integrating the chapter content into their classrooms.

10 Integrating Literacy Skills Into the Play Centers

PLAYING "BEACH TRIP"

Brand X Pictures/Stockbyte/Thinkstock

At an early education program for low-income families in the inner city, a teacher has just finished reading a story about a trip to the beach to a small group of children. The children appeared familiar with the story, and the teacher presented the information from the book using the dialogic reading technique, which allows the teacher to have conversations about the book with the students. (Information on dialogic reading will be presented later in this chapter.) Specifically, the teacher and students were discussing the use of rhyming words throughout the story, the main ideas of the story, and their own personal experiences of taking a trip to the beach or a lake.

The teacher told the children that they would be transitioning soon and that they needed to think about which center they wanted to go to next. Three of the children asked if they could play "Beach Trip," and she gave them permission to do so. Next, the teacher got all the children's attention in the room by singing "The waves at the beach go splash, splash, splash" to the tune of "The Wheels on the Bus." She then alerted them that they would need to be ready to transition to a new center in a few minutes.

She also mentioned that she was going to introduce two new activities. First, she pulled a bag out of her backpack and told the children that she and her friend had taken a trip to the beach over the weekend and that she had brought some things from the beach to their classroom. She asked the children to try to guess what could be in the bag. After about 10 appropriate guesses, the teacher said that at the beginning of center time she would be over at the Science Center with the bag. Children could come there if they were interested in seeing what she had.

Second, she announced that a group of children had asked if they could play "Beach Trip," and that this activity would be happening over by the door. She then announced again to the children that they had to clean up and be at a center in five minutes. She set a timer and began to circulate around the room with the other adults, encouraging the children to begin preparing.

(Continued)

(Continued)

The three children who were interested in playing "Beach Trip" went over by the door and opened a large plastic box. They enthusiastically took the following items out of the box: three beach towels, two pairs of sunglasses, one hat, two pails, two shovels, suntan lotion, a blue sheet (which they said was the ocean), a snorkel, a pair of goggles, a life jacket, approximately eight blocks (which they said would be the sand), and a plastic basket with plastic food. As they took the items out, they made comments about them to each other.

While the children were examining the items and commenting, one of the children, who was learning English, said that she wanted to use the "water glasses." The teacher, who was standing close by, approached the girl and said, "I'm trying to think of the special name that the glasses had in the story that we just read." Another child responded with, "They're goggles. I know—I have some." With encouragement from the teacher, the first child referred to them quietly as "goggles."

One child then announced that he was going to find rocks in the water. He began to empty the basket of its food when another child said "No, no. We need that for the food." The child with the basket responded that he needed the basket and the food because he was going into the water to get the rocks. He began to jump around on the blue sheet. Another child jumped onto the sheet with a zucchini and, holding the zucchini up high, then said, "I went down and found a fish!"

Children in today's early education classrooms come from a variety of background experiences and have varying literacy skills. Some children enter classrooms having interacted with print every day in a meaningful manner and understanding the power of print in their lives. Others—and this number appears to be rapidly growing (Resnick & Snow, 2009)—come from backgrounds that could emphasize oral stories and communications more than traditional print. These children might not feel as comfortable as other children around text-based materials. Therefore, programs cannot merely offer literacy experiences that only use print from books and on paper. Instead, all children must be afforded daily opportunities to actively and more broadly engage in familiar and meaningful print activities, so that they can be self-motivated to gradually cultivate and advance their literacy skills in a personal manner.

Play activities are developmentally appropriate activities that allow children to use self-motivation to enrich some literacy skills. Through the integration of play and literacy activities, like the ones described in this chapter's opening scenario, children can develop an early literacy foundation that will enhance successful academic skills throughout their formal educational years. Similar to the discussion in the *Harvard Education Letter* about older children's learning (Rothman, 2012), young children do not learn through isolated, domain-focused activities. Instead, learning is an interconnected process that transpires across various developmental domains (NAEYC, 2009a). Professionals need to access early learning standards or foundations when designing self-motivating learning activities for children.

This chapter answers the following questions related to integrating play and literacy development:

- Why is it important to integrate Early Learning Standards and Kindergarten Common Core Standards into play activities?

- What are some of the common skills that are enhanced in both play and early literacy activities?

- How can developmentally appropriate play activities be used to further enhance literacy skills?

The Head Start Child Development and Early Learning Framework

Most states have early learning standards or foundations. However, it is not feasible for this book to illustrate all the different ones adopted by the states. Although most of these standards or foundations are solidly grounded in research and incorporate an evidence-based sequential development of skills, each state chooses a unique method for presenting that information. Furthermore, the states use inconsistent language in describing the various standards.

To reflect the broadest approach possible, this book references the learning standard outcomes from the *Head Start Child Development and Early Learning Framework* (Head Start, 2011) to illustrate strategies for integrating standards into playful activities. The Head Start Framework consists of 11 essential learning elements that can be used for collecting data to determine developmental progress and to identify areas of focus for further learning activities. It includes what are termed "sequential elements" instead of "standards" for guiding the development of children between the ages of 3 and 5. The framework does not provide either specific benchmarks or a list of skills to be accomplished. The framework is not comprehensive and should not be used as a checklist to assess learning. Instead, supporting the NAEYC concerns about using standards with young children, the developmental and learning elements are sufficiently broad to assist with establishing readiness goals, monitoring progress, aligning curricula, and planning activities. Additionally, although the elements are organized in specific developmental and learning areas, the Head Start Framework does not imply that compartmentalized learning should occur for young children. Instead, it promotes programs that address learning in "an integrated way, using intentional instruction and scaffolded learning throughout the day" (Head Start, 2011, p. 2).

Under each of the elements is a list of examples of behaviors that support those elements. Therefore, the 2011 Head Start Framework is a tool for analyzing children's skills and for collecting data to determine developmental progress and identifying areas of focus for future learning activities. Other assessment tools and curricula should also be used when determining and designing the day-to-day activities for young children. The Head Start Framework can be found online at: http://eclkc.ohs.acf.hhs.gov/hslc/tta-system/teaching/eecd/assessment/child%20Outcomes/revised-child-outcomes.html. Head Start organized young children's competencies into the 11 domains of development illustrated in Figure 10.1.

Figure 10.1 Head Start Early Learning and Development Elements

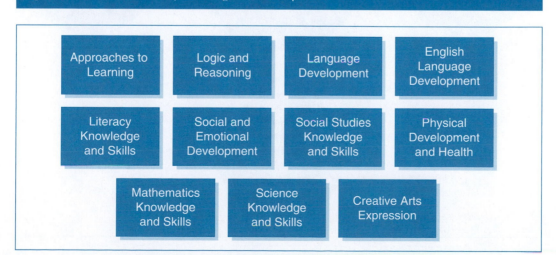

This book takes those 11 domains and associates them with a variety of learning centers that are typically found in early education classrooms: socio-dramatic play, science/health, mathematics, social studies/book, and creative arts/motor centers (see Figure 10.2). At the center of the Figure 10.2 diagram are the socio-dramatic play centers where, as discussed in Chapter 6 of this book, all other center activities should be related either to the theme and/or to the children's demonstration of socio-dramatic play skills. Note that the diagram uses double arrows, indicating and supporting NAEYC's belief that learning is not compartmentalized at this age.

K–12 Common Core State Standards

As children transition into their formal academic careers, they will be expected to build on their early learning foundation and to demonstrate enhanced reading, writing, speaking

Figure 10.2   Overview of Learning Centers and Integrated Learning Elements/Standards

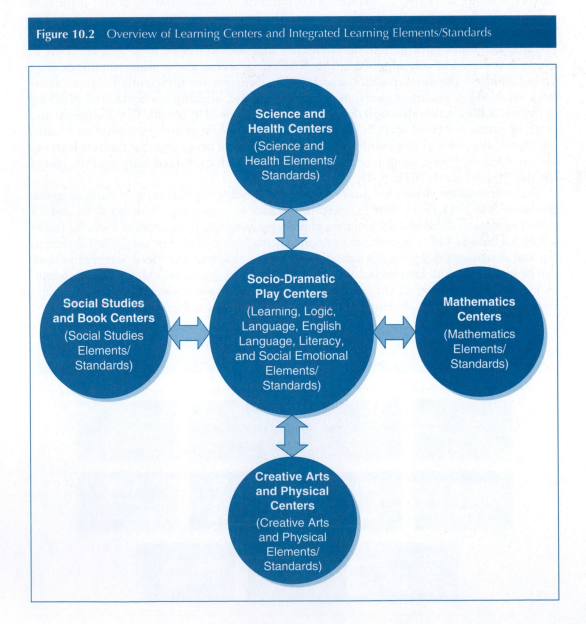

and listening, and language skills. As mentioned earlier in this chapter, **Common Core State Standards (CCSS)** are now being used by most teachers in kindergarten through high school throughout the country to integrate language arts, math, and literacy across the curriculum. The standards for kindergarten allow teachers to design formal and informal instructional opportunities in which language arts and mathematics skills are developed through small and large group activities. These standards are lists of skills that children should develop by the end of the designated grade.

Figure 10.3 demonstrates the transitions in the area of literacy development that children progress through when moving from preschool to their kindergarten year. The six Early Developmental Domains that relate to literacy development directly relate to the four CCSS English Language Arts (ELA) of speaking/listening, language, reading, and writing.

Unfortunately, the Common Core State Standards do not provide skills and competencies in the area of social and emotional development. In their joint statement on the Common Core State Standards, NAEYC and NAECS/SDE (2010) expressed concern about the developers of those standards focusing only on two content domains and strongly urged "the addition of social and emotional development . . . as the next area for high-quality, developmentally and grade appropriate common standards work" (p. 2). Because they are not currently available, social and emotional standards for kindergarten have not been included here.

Additionally, the International Reading Association (IRA) (2012) has cautioned that the Common Core State Standards establish a "one-size-fits-all" approach to learning

Figure 10.3 Transitions From Head Start Elements to Common Core State Standards

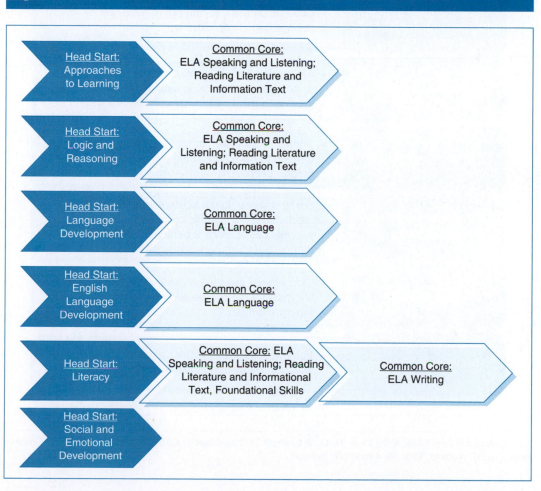

for all students. However, as presented in Part I of this book, the students attending schools today exhibit great differences, and it is impossible to believe that all students will similarly develop these learning skills, the way the CCSS suggest. The CCSS standards set a base of "what" all children must work toward but they do not dictate how to facilitate learning to meet the standards. The instructional decisions by teachers to support a diverse student body remain flexible. Differentiation continues to be an integral part of the CCSS standards in supporting all students to learn at high levels. IRA recommends more financial support that focuses on the dissemination of information addressing the wide range of needs of diverse students. Obviously, some students will require more intensive inputs than others. Figure 10.4 provides suggestions for accommodations that could assist young children who exhibit challenging learning behaviors (Cook, Klein, & Chen, 2012).

Figure 10.4   Considerations for Children Needing Extra Time or Spaced Practice

Provide concrete or multisensory tasks	• Preschool children naturally learn more easily when tasks are three-dimensional and concrete rather than abstract.
Find the child's most efficient mode of learning	• Observe carefully to determine each child's strongest mode of learning.
Monitor pacing	• Children who must work extra hard to concentrate or to process information usually tire easily. They may need more rest, quiet activities, or soft music.
Provide repetition	• Some children need to try things again and again or need to have something repeated several times before grasping it.
Plan for modeling and imitation	• Some children do not acquire information incidentally. If a specific behavior is needed, plan experiences in which a behavior can be demonstrated and provide positive feedback.
Task analysis	• Tasks might need to be broken down into simple, short steps that can be sequenced from easiest to the most difficult.
Give explicit directions	• For some children it might be necessary to give the directions slowly and in small steps.

Source: Adapted from Cook, R. E., Klein, M. D., & Chen, D. (2012). *Adapting Early Childhood Curricula for Children With Special Needs* (p. 136). New York, NY: Pearson.

REFLECT AND APPLY EXERCISE 10.1

Social and Emotional Standards

Reflect

Assume that the Common Core State Standards it agrees with the NAEYC that kindergarten children must have Social and Emotional Standards.

Apply

You have been asked to serve on the task force that will design these standards. Review the Social and Emotional Head Start Elements and Examples that are listed on this link: http://eclkc.ohs.acf.hhs.gov/hslc/tta-system/teaching/eecd/assessment/child%20Outcomes/revised-child-outcomes.html. Choose three of those examples that you believe should be continued in the kindergarten year and explain why they should be continued.

Play and Literacy

Part I of this book presented information on how learning at a young age is interrelated in a variety of developmental areas and should not be presented in fragmented and isolated activities outside children's natural, everyday learning contexts (Singer et al., 2006). For example, the opening scenario for this chapter illustrates how creating a beach trip context affords children a variety of natural learning opportunities to expand skills suggested in the Head Start Framework:

- **Logic and Reasoning Skills:** As stated in Chapter 2, play allows children to logically create more sophisticated symbolic representations. In this chapter's opening scenario, the children use a sheet for the ocean, the blocks for rocks, and a zucchini for a fish.
- **Learning Skills:** As stated in Chapter 2, children become comfortable acting out familiar schemas through play interactions. Children in the opening scenario are becoming more familiar with the schema of a "Beach Trip" as they act it out.
- **Language Skills, consistent with Second Language Learning Skills:** As stated in Chapter 4, play provides children a safe opportunity to develop language and vocabulary. The "Beach Trip" scenario allows the children to hear and use new vocabulary in a comfortable environment—for instance, goggles.
- **Literacy Skills:** Chapter 4 also describes how play enhances children's opportunities to develop well-sequenced stories. The children in this chapter's opening scenario are creating a beach trip story that has appropriately sequenced activities such as jumping into the ocean and finding rocks.

Reading and understanding informational text becomes self-motivating when children are involved in collaborative activities.

Thinkstock/Stockbyte/Thinkstock

- **Social and Emotional Skills:** Chapter 3 explains how play assists children in developing skills for negotiating and compromising. In the opening scenario for this chapter, the children are negotiating the use of the plastic food basket to catch fish or to contain lunch.

These playful opportunities contribute to an expansion of literacy skills through well-planned and carefully guided socio-dramatic play activities. For example, in the opening scenario, the teacher had specific beach items that she wanted to carefully introduce to children and, therefore, she announced that she would be opening her backpack at the science center. As previously stated, she chose to present these items in a organized situation when she could focus on new vocabulary and language structures instead of just placing the items in the Beach Box or freely giving them to the children. Most likely, once the children are familiar with the items and their purposes, the teacher will then allow them to be used to create pretend play narratives.

Chapter 4 demonstrates how children use pretending and metacommunications to develop play narratives that gradually become more *decontextualized* as children's skills improve. Decontextualized narratives are stories that are removed from the everyday, tangible, and familiar experiences within an immediate context (McKeown & Beck, 2006). They require children to make sense of the language that they hear by building on their own ideas about the words used.

Becoming comfortable with decontextualized information is vital for the development of literacy competence and academic success. Literacy activities require children to read decontextualized print to understand a story or use decontextualized printed or spoken words to develop a story. As children develop as socio-dramatic players, they design stories that are more decontextualized—that is, more dependent on shared metacommunications rather than on actions or objects. Similarly, young children's books, which gradually replace visual illustrations with printed words, are an example of the use of decontextualized print.

For example, beginning players enact stories about kitchen activities and usually use realistic-looking objects to assist with narrative creation. However, as they become more experienced players and language users, children become capable of transforming an ordinary cardboard box into a rocket ship, using language and pretending to create a complex trip to the moon story. Similarly, the young children's books, such as *The Napping House* by Audrey Wood, have pages that are mostly covered with visual illustrations, along with a small area that contains the print for the story. As children develop they become successful at reading decontextualized chapter books, such as E. B. White's *Charlotte's Web,* which have very few pictures and require children to create their own picture story based on the print they are hearing or reading. Becoming familiar with using decontextualized narratives and proficient at understanding them is a major source of learning and lies at the center of all academic achievement.

Children's thrilling and dynamic socio-dramatic play activities can significantly contribute to the expansion of decontextualized language, the enhancement of early literacy skills, and the increase of academic abilities. Consequently, adults must understand how to adapt all classroom centers into play centers that provide the following:

1. Opportunities for children to implement engaging socio-dramatic activities across the learning curriculum, and

2. Activities that foster high-quality learning by integrating early literacy learning standards into these play enactments.

Common Characteristics of Play and Literacy

As discussed in Chapter 3, young children who are involved in socio-dramatic play are *self-motivated* to use decontextualized *language* and *symbolic representations* so that they can co-construct play narratives reflecting their *knowledge of the world*. Similarly, Chapter 4 demonstrated that early literacy development depends on children being *self-motivated* to use print, which consists of the *symbolic representation* of letters and sounds, and *decontextualized language* to construct narratives that reflect *knowledge of their worlds*. Consequently, socio-dramatic play and literacy share the following common characteristics.

- **Reflect world knowledge.** Children are able to create a play narrative or understand print when they are familiar with the topic.
- **Require self-motivation.** Children must be intrinsically motivated to continue creating a play narrative or to use print meaningfully.
- **Enhance language development.** Children can safely expand their language and vocabulary when they are involved in play enactments and are exposed to print that relates to them.
- **Involve symbolic representations.** Children create symbolic action, role, and object substitutions in play, and they identify letter symbols and their sounds when interacting with print.

These similarities between play and literacy are summarized in Figure 10.5.

Figure 10.5 Common Characteristics of Play and Literacy

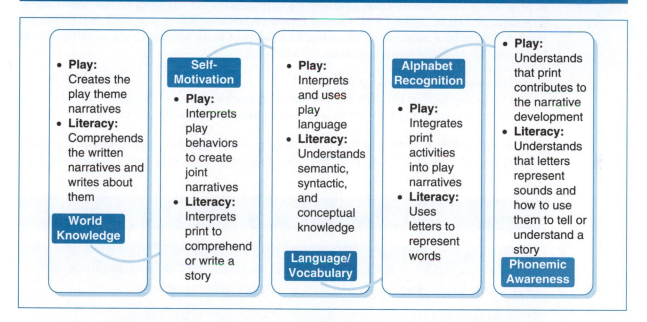

Therefore, by integrating early literacy skills into meaningful and comfortable playful activities in the classroom learning centers, children are self-motivated to expand their early literacy skills (Bowman, Donovan, & Burns, 2001; Pellegrini, 2011; Roskos & Christie, 2000; and Chapter 4 of this book). For example, the "Beach Trip" scenario at the opening of this chapter could be expanded into two other socio-dramatic play centers. One could be the "Surf and Sand Rental Stand center," which might be located outside, and the other could be the "Beach Burger Snack Stand." The following are objects that could be included at the Sand and Surf Rental Stand. Such items could be purchased at yard sales or thrift shops.

Beach chairs

Umbrellas (small)

Hats/visors

Goggles/fins

Towels

Fishing poles/nets

Life jackets

Buckets

Beach balls

Order pads/pens

Cash register

Money

Through involvement in the beach renting scenarios and decontextualized activities with the play objects, the skills listed in Figure 10.6 could be enhanced.

Early Writing Skills

In preschools today, the diversity of children's writing skills is a challenge to teachers (Cabell, Torterelli, & Gerde, 2013). Additionally, recent research indicates that very few preschool teachers know how to move children from one step of early writing to the next (Gerde & Bingham, 2012). Early writing includes the following:

- The physical act of making marks
- The meanings that children provide for their markings
- The understanding that written language represents spoken language

Although children learn at different rates, they tend to gradually progress through certain stages for writing. Figure 10.7 provides a summary of the stages as determined by

Figure 10.6   Skills That Could Develop Through Play Activities

Rental Stand	Enhanced Skills
Organizing the rental stand	Math: Classifying/ordering
Chairs and umbrellas	Motor: Opening and closing
Length of fishing poles	Math: Measuring
Size of life jackets, hats	Math: Numbers
Renting objects	Math: Numbers and money
Using beach balls	Motor: Kicking/tossing
Folding towels	Motor: Eye-hand coordination
Making sale signs	Literacy: Printing letters
Goggles/fins	Language: Vocabulary

Figure 10.7 Levels for the Development of Writing

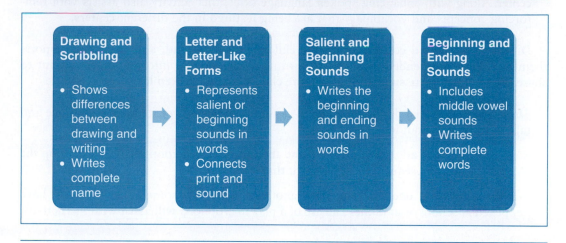

Source: Cabell, S. Q., Torterelli, L. S., & Gerde, H. K. (2013). How Do I Write. . . . ?: Scaffolding Preschoolers' Early Writing Skills. *Reading Teacher, 66,* 650–659.

Cabell et al. (2013). Teachers can use some of the guiding strategies that are presented in Chapter 8 to scaffold successful writing experiences for children.

To foster literacy skills through play, however, teachers must plan the play centers and cautiously monitor the activities there. As Chapter 7 demonstrated, early learning standards or foundations can be used to guide professionals in planning high-quality learning activities that will enhance each child's individual learning potential.

Spoken Language

All children must be provided with opportunities to participate in speaking activities during the day. These activities can be structured conversations, where adults have planned to focus the children's discussion of a specific topic. They can also be unstructured activities that are typically child-introduced, unplanned conversations.

During the structured conversations, the adult continues to direct the children's attention toward concepts, vocabulary, and grammatical structures that are appropriate for the group. Some of the more familiar activities that support structured conversations are the following:

What's in the Box/Bag? Place a specific object in a container and ask the children to guess what the object could be based on clues provided and answers to guesses.

Follow the Directions: Ask a child to do a number of tasks with items in the classroom. For example, "Take the truck and place it under the table in the art center. Next, put four large paint brushes in that truck. Finally, drive the truck back to us and tell us what you did."

Book Critics: Show the children a specific book that they are familiar with and ask them who liked the story and why. Then ask the other children why they didn't like the story and how could it be changed so that they would like it.

It Does/Does Not Belong: Tell children about two objects that are related or not related. Have them tell you why they belong or do not belong together. For example, you can say, "a bus ticket and suitcase" or "a hat and a glass of water." Although children might not give you the response that you were thinking of, if they can logically defend their choice, they are correct.

What Belongs at the Learning Center: Choose a learning center and have the children talk about the different items that they might find there and why those items are at that center. Along with enhancing spoken language skills, this activity also assists with reinforcing concepts and vocabulary that are being featured in the different centers.

During unstructured conversations, the children take the lead, and the adult supports them by asking open-ended prompts to learn more about what information they want to share. The following are suggestions for more child-centered spoken language activities:

Share Time: A special day when children can bring in some favorite item from home and talk to the class about it.

Story Starters: The adult starts a story and then the children continue it and develop the character, plot, and sequence of events for that story.

Interviewing: Have one child interview another child about something that might have happened at school or at home. The use of a play microphone will assist with this activity.

Spoken Language Activities and English Language Learners

The following are suggestions to keep in mind when working on spoken language activities with children who do not use English as a home language:

- For group activities, match English language learners with children who have strong English language skills. Also, make sure that all the children who speak the same home language are not grouped together.
- Provide opportunities for unstructured conversation activities so that English language learners can choose activities of interest that involve their language abilities.
- Provide prompts for children when they are talking. When they need to find the truck, have a picture of a truck to show them if they are not yet familiar with that word.
- Use open-ended prompts that can have multiple answers, so English language learners can expand their utterances. Use, "Which hat do you like the best?" instead of "Why do we wear this hat?"

Creating Play Centers to Expand Literacy Skills

Part I of this book and the previous section of this chapter discussed the different theoretical aspects of play and literacy development. Additionally, Chapters 6 and 7 described how to design classroom learning centers. This next section presents information on three strategies to consider when designing play centers that enhance children's literacy skills.

Creating Multifaceted Learning Opportunities

As Part I documented, socio-dramatic play behaviors do not begin in preschool. These multifaceted, highly developed skills start to develop in children at a very young age. Infants, who are busy learning about the real world around them, begin to engage in frequent play activities when provided with realistic-looking toys. Therefore, during infancy, dolls should look life-like and be accompanied by real-looking bottles, cradles, and blankets. Additionally, trucks should have an item or two placed inside them.

Toddlers typically increase their small and large muscle coordination. They also become physically capable of moving items around in their environment and arranging them in a way that is self-pleasing. They use these developing fine and gross motor skills to put on clothing, open purses and briefcases, handle small dishes/cups, hammer pegs, and coordinate the movement of rakes and brooms. The development of these motor skills directly impacts a toddler's ability to more actively participate in creating play narratives. Children at this age are able to dress up and "become" other people, and to manipulate objects into becoming other items.

As the cognitive abilities of preschool children are enriched through everyday participation in problem-solving activities, their ability to plan, negotiate, and coordinate evolves. Typically, special spaces are dedicated in the home and classroom where children participate in the planning, negotiating, and coordinating of pretend enactments. These spaces usually include props and toys that assist in the development of activities focusing on specific play themes—for example, housekeeping, workshop, medical clinic, and so forth. In these centers, teachers can guide children's development of language and literacy skills by integrating literacy objects and open-ended objects.

By using complex language structures and enhanced vocabulary, older preschoolers and kindergarteners are capable of generating complex, abstract, and engaging play stories through coordinated interactions with multiple peers. These interactions present a natural and rich opportunity for children to acquire language. These well-planned, intricate, and decontextualized stories involve the use of sophisticated symbolic representations.

Selecting Appropriate Socio-Dramatic Play Themes

Children arrive at school with some understanding of home-life and family interactions. Therefore, setting up a center with literacy items that reflect what different children would find in their homes affords opportunities for the children to re-enact those literacy activities through pretend behaviors with peers. When those familiar activities are linked with early learning standards, children receive multiple opportunities to learn, practice, and combine literacy concepts and skills.

However, once children become familiar with play activities that focus around home life, the center theme should be changed. Chapter 7 provided a number of methods for determining different play themes, and the following are four suggestions of factors to consider:

- **Not all themes are appropriate for all ages.** If a class consists of children of mixed ages, one center might be designated for the younger children and another for the older children.
- **Integrate the theme and encourage the levels of pretense and narrative development in other learning centers.** Because of the impact of socio-dramatic play on language and literacy development, pretend narratives should be encouraged in all the learning centers, not just the socio-dramatic centers.
- **Remember to change center themes throughout the year.** If behavior problems are being noted in the center, then the children are most likely bored with the activities. So change the center's theme.
- **Do not allow stereotyping based on gender.** All children should be allowed to explore any role that they choose.

Depending on the interests of the children and the topics that are being covered in the program's curriculum, Figure 10.8 suggests 20 different themes that can be used, along with suggestions for realistic objects.

Of course many more themes can be used. Furthermore, the objects listed are just a beginning of the process of creating carefully planned socio-dramatic play centers. To get ideas for

Figure 10.8   Realistic Objects That Can Be Included in Play Centers

Play Theme	Realistic Objects
Bank	Calculator, money, cash box, teller windows, checks, rubber stamp
Beach	Umbrella, pails, shovels, shells, lotion, towels, goggles, picnic basket, hats
Beauty Salon	Brushes, smocks, mirrors, spray, appointment book, hair dryer, towels
Camping	Tent, sleeping bag, back packs, flashlight, canteen, binoculars, maps
Car Wash	Rags, buckets, tricycles, hose, squeegees, specials signs, money
Fire Station	Uniform, stepladder, engine, hose, boots, phone, dog, megaphone
Gas Station	Tools, money, work clothes, tire gauge, oil/funnel, gas can, tire pump
Hardware Store	Pipes, tape, screws, tool kit, truck, rags, flash light, manual
Medical Center	Computer, eye chart, cotton, bandages, gloves, x-rays, gauze, smock
Outer Space	Flag, rocket ship, walkie-talkies, stars, food, air tank, helmet
Paint Store	Brushes, paint cans, rags, stepladder, sheets, tape, sand paper, stick
Photo Studio	Camera, tripod, film, pictures, case, photos, computer, magazines
Pizza Parlor	Oven, pans, boxes, cash register, play pizza cutter, phone, pizzas
Post Office	Boxes, tape, labels, rubber stamps, envelopes, string, computer, scale
Rock Store	Rocks, trays, cash register, order pads, rags, name tags, polish
Shoe Store	Shoes, boxes, sale receipts, floor mirror, sale signs, price tags
Theater	Tickets, projector, money, popcorn, candy, sodas, movies
Travel Agency	Tickets, tablets, maps, travel books, atlas, posters, passports
Veterinarian Office	Prescriptions, smock, stuffed animals, examining table, x-rays, carrier
Zoo	Tickets, broom, shovel, animals, blocks, peanuts, feeding schedules

more themes and objects, just look around the communities where the children live, ask the families, and listen to and watch the children!

Organizing Socio-Dramatic Play Materials

As mentioned in Chapter 7, children should be provided with play spaces that are easily organized and do not contain an excessive amount of materials at any one time. Figure 10.9 illustrates how an area can be organized by placing wooden pegs or hooks that children can reach and from which clothing can hang. Additionally, attaching a piece of pegboard with hooks to a wall of the center allows children to hang jewelry/purses, equipment, and cloth bags that are labeled for specific items that might be difficult to hang (e.g., shells and rocks, medical items, household items, beauty items). Organizing the play materials in a specific manner also assists in encouraging children to think through enactments and produce orderly sequences, instead of randomly grabbing items and pretending. Finally, having three-tiered plastic baskets, with each dedicated to certain household categories of items (e.g., beach things, table things, and rock polishing things), also contributes to well-planned play activities.

Many of these organizational materials should be labeled with pictures and/or print. For example, the hooks from which the clothing is hung can be labeled with general words such as "jackets," "dresses," "shirts," "uniforms," "aprons," and "hats." Two or three hooks may have the same label or one general label over them. Think carefully about the children's language abilities and how you will label the items. This is an excellent opportunity to introduce new and meaningful words to the children and, as the children begin to use those words

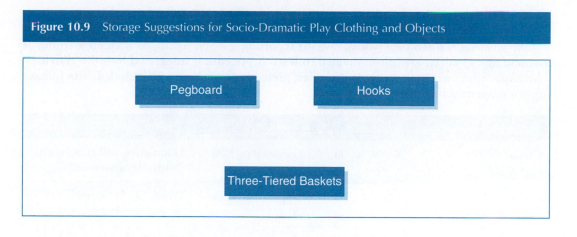

Figure 10.9 Storage Suggestions for Socio-Dramatic Play Clothing and Objects

Pegboard

Hooks

Three-Tiered Baskets

naturally, to change them so that the children are continually exposed to new words to say and read. For English learners, seeing the labels in English next to familiar items helps them use their primary language skills and language to support learning English.

Another method for organizing play activities for young children is to make sure that the play area is not overwhelmed with props. Very young children should have just a few, realistic-looking articles familiar from household environments. Then, as children enhance their world knowledge, centers can focus on community events and include items that are more abstract and that require children to use their imaginations to determine an item's function. Finally, materials associated with literacy-based activities should always be included—such as appointment books, rubber stamps, paper, pens, calendars, file folders, magazines, clipboards, maps, instructions, and measuring items.

Integrating Literacy Activities Into Play Center Activities

With careful planning and sensitive guidance, all children can develop skills that support both the Head Start Language Arts Elements and the Kindergarten Common Core State Standards when they are involved in creating socio-dramatic play narratives and when they are working with adults on small group learning activities. Small group activities provide opportunities for adults to guide children toward the independent production of target skills. As stated in Chapter 7, such activities allow an adult to work with a group of 3 or 4 children to develop their individual skills. This activity can occur while other adults in the classroom guide children at the learning centers toward achieving higher quality learning abilities.

©iStock.com/bodu9

Providing literacy objects encourages literacy activities when children play.

Chapter 7 also suggested that, every day, the teachers could schedule themselves to work with two groups of 3 or 4 children for about 20 minutes each during the approximately one hour of time scheduled for the individualized learning center. Working in a couple of small groups with a total of eight children a day on their unique literacy skills allows all the children in a class of 20 to interact with the teacher at least twice a week. During those times the teacher can guide them on the individual development of literacy skills.

The following are descriptions of four research-based, guided literacy activities that can be used in conjunction with play center activities while children are involved in small group activities with an adult. The adult integrates individualized literacy learning elements or standards into these activities. The guided strategies are: (1) planning play activities, (2) searching for words, (3) dissecting words, and (4) reporting a story. Again, as with all learning at a young age, children are self-motivated to learn if pretense is integrated into the activities. Therefore, when working on these activities, pretend props should be included. The following are suggestions:

Guided Activities	Themes	Props	Reason
Guided Activity #1: Planning Play Activities	Construction worker	Construction hats Building plans	Good plans will construct a sturdy play enactment
Guided Activity #2: Searching for Words	Detective	Magnifying glasses Hats	Words can be found all around the environment
Guided Activity #3: Dissecting Words	Scientist	Lab coats Plastic tweezers (if appropriate)	Words can be dissected into syllables, letters, and sounds
Guided Activity #4: Reporting Stories	News reporter	Microphones Cameras Notepads	Play enactments produce news-worthy events

Guided Activity #1: Play Plans

Child-created *play plans* offer a vehicle for integrating many developmental skills into play activities.

What are play plans? As mentioned in Chapter 9 on Assessment, **play plans** are proposals for what children want to do during play activities. They are created just before children participate in various play activities (Bodrova & Leong, 2007). This activity is also similar to the HighScope Curriculum concept of *Plan-Do-Review* discussed in Chapter 2. When working with children on constructing play plans, the adult might want to use the metaphor of being a construction worker who is designing a building plan. Similar to the construction worker, children will need to think through what they want to do, how they want to do it, and with whom they will engage during the activity. Having them wear construction work hats and showing them what building plans look like could encourage their motivation to design their own written plans.

How to construct play plans:

1. A group of children who want to play together in the socio-dramatic play center decide on what narrative they want to create.

2. While collaborating with play partners, each child depicts a plan of what they will do by drawing a picture on an individual piece of paper to record information about what they plan to do during the play activity.

3. Once all the children have recorded marks on their papers, they are asked to share their plans with their fellow players. After the children have done so, the adult writes the following prompt at the bottom of the paper: "I am going to _____." Then, the blank portion of the prompt is completed by the child.

4. When the play plans are completed, the children are free to implement them. Play plans should be displayed on a wall so that, when the children finish their play time in that center, they can immediately review their play plans with an adult and decide if they want to continue the same activity on the following day.

5. If the children decide to continue with their activity, they can discuss with their peers and the adult whether any further props might be needed to enhance their play. They will then modify their plans accordingly.

Figure 10.10 presents the simplified sequence for developing a play plan.

Constructing play plans with preschoolers. Preschool children are typically able to design scribble play plans or drawn play plans. In Figure 10.11, the first two descriptions are of typical preschool plans (Bodrova, Leong, Paynter, & Hensen, 2003).

Constructing play plans with kindergarteners. As children develop their literacy-related skills, they are able to work more independently with their peers and produce markings that closely reflect the letters of the alphabet. Therefore, to enhance the Common Core ELA Writing Standards, they should be encouraged to design Buddy Play Plans, as described in Figure 10.11.

Additionally, the sentences from the play plans can either be cut up into separate sentence strips or written on sentence strip cards. Then, those sentences can be cut up into words, and kindergarten children can work on a number of Common Core ELA Reading: Foundational Print Concepts, Phonological Awareness, Phonics and Word Recognition, and Fluency skills.

Using differentiated instruction when constructing play plans. The concept of designing play plans is a learning activity based on a child's play interests and literacy abilities. Therefore, because the language used reflects the child's skills, differentiated instruction is naturally embedded in this activity.

Further points about play plans. No matter what age group adults are working with, they must be aware that the main goal of play plans is not simply to adhere to the plan. Rather, the goal is to guide children into producing higher quality symbolic play representations and more complex play narratives. Additionally, the adults are focused on individual language arts skills. Finally, play plans allow adults to encourage children to develop a feeling of continuity in their day-to-day learning and language arts play activities.

Bodrova and Leong (2007) suggest that play plans not only contribute to children's understanding of the relationship between talk and print, they also assist the following

Figure 10.10 *Play Plan Sequence*

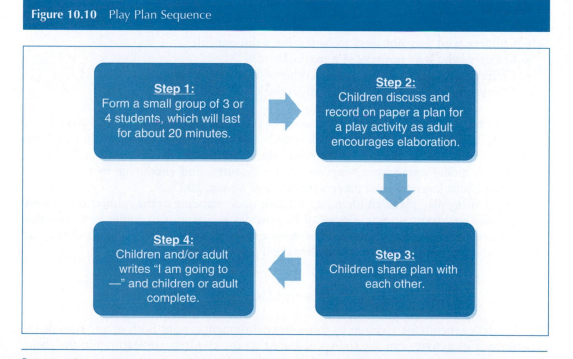

Source: Bodrova, E., & Leong, D. J. (2007). *Tools of the Mind.* Upper Saddle River, NJ: Pearson Education.

Figure 10.11   Different Types of Plans

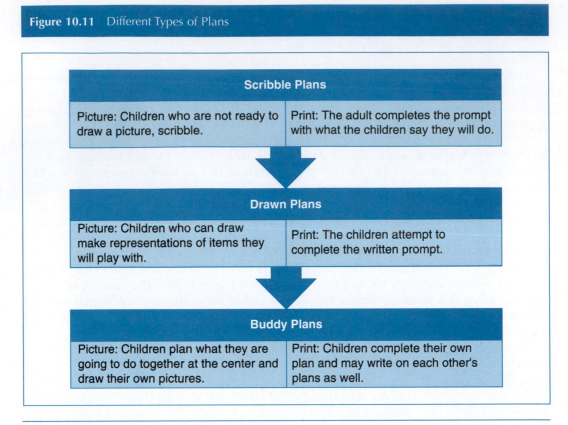

Source: Bodrova, E., Leong, D. J., Paynter, D. E., & Hensen, R. (2003). *Scaffolding Literacy Development in the Preschool Classroom*. Aurora, CO: Mid-continent Research for Education and Learning.

types of children who tend to encounter challenges when creating collaborative peer play enactments (p. 151):

- Children who may not seem to be playing a distinct role
- Children who may not stay in a particular role
- Children who may not talk to each other as they play
- Children who may be playing but might be losing the thread of the play

In addition, adults can consider using some of the suggestions presented in Chapter 8 to guide children's play behaviors from both outside and inside the play context. In particular, adults can coach individuals who might need help, suggest or model how to weave together play themes, model appropriate ways to resolve disputes, and encourage more advanced players to mentor less advanced players (Bodrova & Leong, 2007).

Through using play plans, children expand their understanding of the connection between oral language and written print. Figure 10.12 provides suggestions of games and items that can also assist in enhancing this skill. The items can be made by adults, and purchasing an extra copy of the storybook to cut up will make it easier.

Guided Activity #2: Searching for Words

Word searches encourage children to focus on environmental print both in and outside the classroom. This activity can use the vocabulary that the children are learning in the socio-dramatic play centers or use new vocabulary words.

Figure 10.12 Suggested Games for Extending Spoken and Written Language Relationship

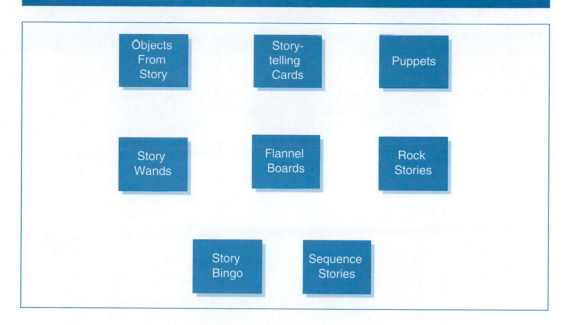

What are word searches? The adult has a card with a word written on it, and the child must match that word with the same word posted somewhere in the environment. Children become self-motivated to participate in this activity if they are told that they must act as detectives and are provided with magnifying glasses (which can even be made out of cardboard) to go around the classroom to search for these words.

How do children search for words? The words used in word searches should be of interest to the children and relate to activities in which the children have been engaged. The classroom and outdoors should have items labeled, and printed information should be posted on all the walls. The word search proceeds as follows:

1. The adult shows the children a card with a word on it and reads it to them. They then discuss the word and how it relates to what the children are learning at school. To support English learners, a picture can be added to the card to solidify comprehension of the term and help them search for the word in the room.

2. The adult then asks a child if he or she would like to search for the word in the classroom. However, before going on the search, the child can be offered the option of having a friend join in. Additionally, before leaving on the search, the child is asked to think about where this word might be posted in the room. Asking this question enhances the concept of using environmental print as a meaningful tool to provide information about a specific context.

3. The child then begins searching for the word. After finding the word, the child is allowed to take it from its place and bring it back to the table.

4. After the child(ren) return to the table, a discussion begins on topics similar to the following:
   - What letters are in the word and what sounds do the letters make?
   - Are the two words similar or different?
   - How does the word compare to other words that children have searched for in the room?
   - Do those words have letters or sounds similar to other words in the environment?

5. Use the checklist below to determine if the child can name the letter and sound.

Child's Name: _____   Date:_____

Teacher's Name:_____

Letter	Date	Comment	Letter	Date	Comment
A a			L l		
F f			Q q		
K k			M m		
P p			D d		
W w			N n		
Z z			S s		
B b			X x		
H h			I i		
O o			E e		
J j			G g		
U u			R r		
C c			V v		
Y y			T t		

Source: Adapted from University of Texas Health Science Center at Houston. (2002). *National Head Start (S.T.E.P.) Teacher's Manual.* Washington, DC: U.S. Department of Health and Human Services, Office of Human Development Services, Administration for Children, Youth and Families, Head Start Bureau.

Word searches with preschoolers. When preschoolers compare the model word card with the card that was located in the environment, their questions should focus on skills such as the following taken from the Early Learning Elements:

- Identify the beginning, middle, and end sounds of the word
- Identify the letters in the word
- Identify the word and the syllables of the word

Word searches for kindergarteners. By the end of the kindergarten year, the children should be successful at skills such as the following Common Core Standards:

- Identifying a rhyming word
- Isolating and pronouncing initial, middle, and final sounds
- Writing the words
- Identify long and short vowel sounds

Using differentiated instruction when searching for words. Some children may need to be matched with a more experienced reader if they are in earlier stages of literacy and language development. Additionally, the card could also have the word written in text, which would assist the child in focusing on the English term. Finally, continuing to discuss the word and what it means for those who might be exposed to it for the first time or for those who may be using their primary language skills to support their English language development enhances their learning of the word or phrase.

Using Word Walls. Word Walls are an organized collection of words that are printed on cards and displayed on a specific wall of the classroom. These collections of words teach children to read and spell words, see patterns and relationships in words, and apply letter-sound relationships. Through these "visual maps" children remember connections between words and characteristics that relate to the category of all the words on the wall. Word Walls can focus on different types of words, for example Theme Walls, ABC Walls, Known Words Walls, and Help Walls (for challenging words) as seen in Figure 10.13. Often words from the Word Wall can be used when playing word search games.

Figure 10.13   Different Types of Word Walls

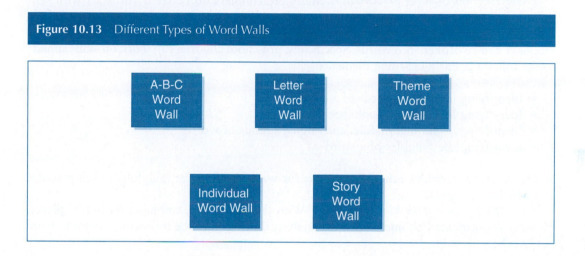

Guided Activity #3: Dissecting Words

Dissecting word activities involve having children dissect words, phrases, and sentences, and then reassemble them.

What are dissected words? Children examine a word, phrase, and/or sentence of interest that is written on a card, and then talk about the meaning, letters, sounds, and punctuation. The model card has an accompanying envelope or baggie that has in it either the sentence cut up into words or the word cut up into letters. When **dissecting words**, an activity where children take apart words, phrases, and sentences, and then reassemble them, they can pretend to be scientists by wearing laboratory coats, which can simply be old, white dress shirts.

How do children dissect words:

1. The adults select words or phrases of interest for each child. They print the word or phrase on two cards. They then take one card and cut up the individual letters (if it is a single word) or the words (if it is a phrase). The cut-up words or letters are placed in an envelope or baggie, and attached to the model card with a paperclip.

2. The child and the adult examine the model word or phrase card. They discuss what the words or letters mean, why they are important to them, and when they would use them. They then read the letters or words on the uncut card.

3. Next the children empty the contents of the envelope or baggie that has the cut-up items in it and attempt to match the individual pieces to the model.

4. This same activity can use the sentences or words from the children's own stories that are created through play plans or shared writings. Children are delighted to see some of their own work dissected and then put back together.

5. This is a very easy and inexpensive activity, so children can take the items home and show their family what they can do. Also, these cards can be kept in a box or manila envelope for each child and, when they have a few minutes, they can use them on their own.

6. Children enjoy it if you mix a few extra letters or words in with the cut-up cards. Additionally, two children can play with one model card. They can be given an equal number of cut-up cards, some of which will match and some of which will not. They can then take turns pretending that they are scientists and, one-by-one, put the dissected pieces together to make a word, phrase, or sentence.

Dissecting words with preschoolers. Many preschoolers do better if you start with sentence strips and cut-up words, instead of words and cut-up letters. Using the sentences provides more contextualized clues for younger children who are just becoming aware that language can be broken into words. Specifically, preschool children can work on skills similar to the following Early Learning Elements:

- Identifying individual words of a sentence
- Identifying letters of the alphabet
- Identifying beginning, middle, and ending sounds of words
- Identifying the syllables of a word

Figure 10.14 provides other suggestions for ways children can playfully develop sound and syllable awareness.

Dissecting words with kindergarteners. With this age group, emphasis should be placed on more sophisticated phonics and word analysis skills such as the following Common Core Standards:

- Counting, pronouncing, blending, and segmenting syllables and sounds
- Identifying one-to-one letter-sound correspondence
- Identifying high-frequency sight words
- Identifying upper- and lower-case letters and punctuation marks

Figure 10.14   Games for Developing Syllable and Sound Awareness

Clapping Syllable
Explain to the children they will clap the beats of words they speak.
Clap to the children's names.
Clap to other words that children know.
Let children provide words.
Say a sentence and then ask children to say the same sentence as adult claps.

Guess Which Object
Hold up two objects that children know and that begin with different sounds.
Identify the objects.
Tell children one beginning sound and have them guess the object.
Tell them you are thinking of a word and give them the individual sounds —/h/ /a/ /t/. Have them say the word.
Leave off beginning sound —/a/ /t/

Source: H. K. Yopp & R. H. Yopp. (2009). Phonological Awareness Is Child's Play. *Young Children, 64*(1), 1–9.

The following is a checklist for the identification of sight words.

KINDERGARTEN SIGHT WORDS								
Child's Name: _____								
Teacher's Name: _____								
Word	Date	Comment	Word	Date	Comment	Numbers	Date	Comment
1A			**2B**			two		
The			at			five		
To			him			one		
And			with			four		
He			up			three		
An			all			six		
I			look			eight		
It			is			seven		
Of			her			nine		
In			some			ten		
You			there			**Colors**		
1B			**2B**			blue		
Was			out			green		
Said			as			red		
His			be			yellow		
That			have			white		
She			go			gray		
For			we			purple		
On			am			orange		
They			then			brown		
But			little			black		
Had			down			pink		

Using differentiated instruction with dissecting words. For children who need more support while engaging in this activity, using a picture on the card with the word will assist them in feeling comfortable with the printed form. Additionally, printing the word in the home language and in English also provides support. However, remember to remove the extra clues gradually so that children can begin to feel comfortable with decontextualized print.

If children are having difficulty with this activity, dissecting a shared story into individual sentences, an activity discussed below, might assist. Using sentence strips with pictures to re-create the story provides many more clues to children who might find their initial exposure to print dissecting activities to be challenging.

Bradley and Jones (2010) suggest that teachers should point out that the most common sound that a letter represents is often the first sound of the letter name. One example is the "t" sound in the word "train." They suggest that letters can be grouped into five categories (p. 71):

- Letter sounds at the beginning of the letter name (B, D, J, K, P, Q, T, V, Z)
- Letter sounds at the end of the letter name (F, L, M, N, R, S, X,)
- Letter names that represent a sound but also represent another sound (A, E, I, O, U)
- Letter sounds at the beginning of the letter name, but the letter also represents another sound (C, G)
- Letter names that do not contain the sound that the letter represents (H, W, Y)

Examples of games that relate to dissecting words that children can play are presented in Figure 10.15.

Guided Activity #4: Reporting Shared Writings

Shared writing is a practice that implements a Vygotskian (1978) perspective of learning skills. The children first learn socially and then learn internally.

What are shared writings? Shared writings are reading texts that are composed from children's own oral language with the written support of the teacher (Vukelich & Christie, 2009). They have long been used in school programs (see Morrow, 2005). Children enjoy engaging in this activity if they are allowed to pretend that they are news reporters, and they can use a pretend microphone to be interviewed or pretend to take a picture of the story theme.

How are shared writings reported? Shared writings are about children's personal experiences. They involve talking with the children about activities that took place and then writing a story around what they said.

The child dictates to the teacher a story about a personal experience that he or she experienced in the socio-dramatic play center. The teacher concurrently takes what the child says and turns it into a written story.

The adult reads the story back to the child and asks for any edits to the story.

Figure 10.15   Examples of Dissecting Words

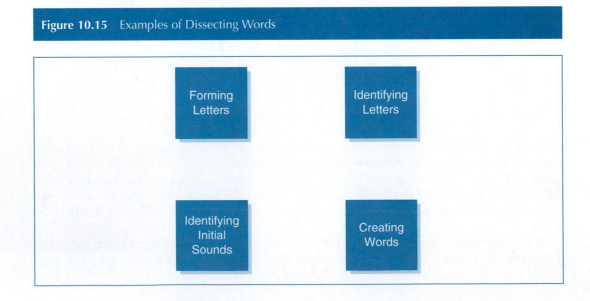

Forming Letters

Identifying Letters

Identifying Initial Sounds

Creating Words

The adult then offers the child the opportunity to read the story to the adult or to other children.

Once the story is fully composed, it should be displayed around the classroom and referred to when appropriate.

If children have the skills, they can convert the story into a book for the book center or to take home to share with their families. If a child does not yet have these skills, then an adult can write the story while the child watches and interacts with the print.

Figure 10.16 provides a summary of the steps for shared writings.

Figure 10.16   Shared Writings Sequence

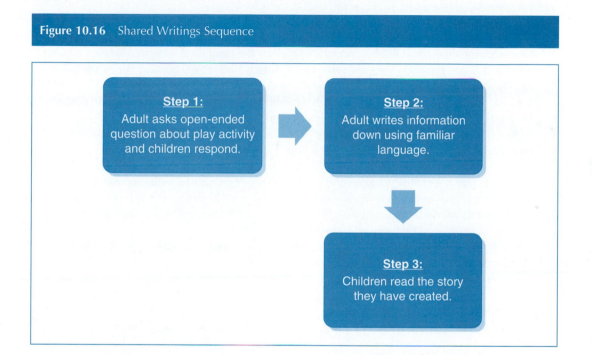

Step 1:
Adult asks open-ended question about play activity and children respond.

Step 2:
Adult writes information down using familiar language.

Step 3:
Children read the story they have created.

Shared writings with preschoolers. This strategy can be used with children as young as 2 or 3 years old and with children who are language delayed (Morrow, 2005). When working with children in these groups, the adult would write down some of the single words that the children said and then use the written format to reinforce vocabulary.

Older preschoolers can use shared stories to develop skills such as the following Early Learning Elements:

- Recognize that writing is a way of communicating for a variety of purposes
- Ask and answer questions and make comments about print materials

Shared writings with kindergarteners. For older children, skills relating to the following Common Core Standards can be encouraged:

- Retelling familiar stories using key details
- Asking and answering questions about unknown words in the text
- Engaging in group reading activities with purpose and understanding

©iStock.com/petrograd99

Children provide the language for the shared writing stories.

Using differentiated instruction with shared writings. Similar to the play plans activity, shared writings consist of stories that are differentiated according to each child's abilities and language. Depending on the child's skills, these stories can range from sequencing pictures with a minimal amount of print to composing stories with print only.

LEARNING FOR ALL CHILDREN
Print Awareness and Poverty

Neuman (2004) found that parent involvement varied dramatically among early readers from low socioeconomic communities. In this study, all of the families of early readers were living in poverty. Some provided very few resources to their children, while other families provided opportunities for and encouragement to the young children to read. However, all of the children in this study attended childcare programs that stimulated the early readers' interest and curiosity about learning to read. Although the childcare programs were frequently located in places such as church basements, storefronts, or rooms in old factories, they supported the development of literacy in many natural ways, such as the following (p. 91):

- **Print-rich environments:** Signs and symbols that communicated important messages were a central part of the daily activities.
- **A library corner:** The programs included a comfortable center where children could sit on pillows and read by themselves, to others, and to dolls.
- **Literacy-related play areas:** Literacy props such as paper, notebooks, pencils, and cook-books assisted in using print in a natural way.
- **Interactive circle times:** Instead of being read to, teachers would stop and ask questions, encourage discussions of ideas, or raise new questions for children to ponder.
- **Interactive meal times:** Teachers sat with the children and engaged in conversations with them during snack and meal times. Often the children would talk about things at home, and this conversation would allow the teacher to connect home events with school events.
- **Small group activities:** Teachers would engage in reading, writing, handwriting, or math in small groups.

In sum, the Neuman study found that high-quality early education programs could impact the development of early reading skills in much the same way that a family impacts that development. Therefore, the link between low income and poor achievement can be broken. Early education professionals can make a difference in the literacy and academic achievement of many of these young children. Professionals need to focus on each child's talents by encouraging them to develop literacy skills through natural, daily activities at school and in the homes.

Further points about shared writings. Although shared writings can be developed with large groups, small groups are the ideal format for working on this task with children who have varying abilities. Small groups allow the teacher to individually focus on enriching each child's sentence structure, vocabulary, alphabet recognition, and phonemic awareness skills, while involving the child in a self-motivating and personal activity. A chalkboard, large chart paper, or regular-sized paper can be used to record the story.

Shared writing is also used for assisting children in associating oral language with written print. The technique reinforces the concept, discussed earlier in this chapter, that print can be similar to speech. Because the writings consist of the children's own language and experiences, reading them is easier and more interesting for children who might otherwise have difficulty adjusting to the use of print (Vukelich & Christie, 2009).

According to Morrow (2005), shared writings allow children to base their stories on the following premises (p. 128):

- What I think is important.
- What I think, I can say.
- What I can say can be written down by me or by others.
- What is written down can be read by me or by others.

At a very young age, children enjoy authoring books.

A three-step process is involved in working with children on the development of a shared writing. First, shared writing typically begins with the adult asking an open-ended question of a small group of children who have been playing together at a center. For example, the adult might say something similar to "I heard some laughing coming from the block center earlier today. Could you tell me what happened?" During this step, the adult must be ready to accept all the responses by the children. The adult should not directly correct the child's grammar while he or she is talking; however, during the writing that occurs thereafter, the adult can use paraphrasing to model appropriate language.

Second, once the children have discussed their experiences in the small group, the adult begins to write the information down using grammatical structures and vocabulary that are familiar to the children. Traditional formation of letters should be followed with spacing between words and lines to enhance readability. Additionally, the adult should make a point of writing legibly and using the correct formation of letters so that children do not become confused. Illustrations should be added whenever possible to provide children with a supporting context for the print.

As the adult writes the text, he or she should discuss some of the mechanical aspects of print. Appropriate statements that the adult can use include, "I'm going to end this sentence with a dot that we call a period" or "Can someone tell me the name of the first letter in Henry's name?"

The last step of shared writings focuses on letting the group of children read the story together that they have created or allowing different children to read single phrases or sentences. As children advance toward their kindergarten year, sentences from the shared stories can be reproduced on sentence strips without picture cues, and the children can sequence the strips in the correct order. Additionally, words from the sentences can be placed on individual cards, and children can begin to learn to read those separate words. Examples of different types of shared stories are illustrated in Figure 10.17.

Figure 10.17 Examples of Shared Writings

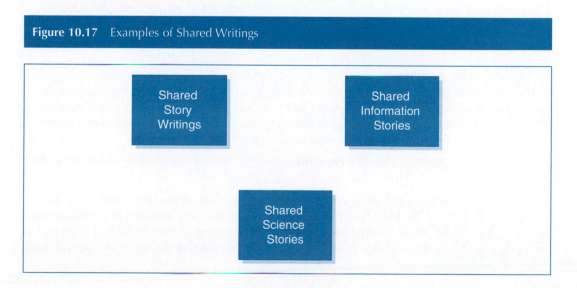

Shared Story Writings

Shared Information Stories

Shared Science Stories

The following is a checklist of 10 general literacy skills that can be identified while children are constructing play plans or reporting shared writings:

Skill	Date Not Observed	Date Observed With Guidance	Date Observed Without Guidance	Notes
Interest in print				
Print is meaningful				
Left-right and top-bottom sequence				
Shows alphabet awareness				
Shows phonemic awareness				
Sentence starts with capital letter				
Sentence ends with a mark				
Spaces between words				
Spelling conventions				
Sight vocabulary				

REFLECT AND APPLY EXERCISE 10.2

Implementing Play Plans

Reflect

Both play plans and shared writings are activities designed to enhance children's literacy skills. Think about how you could use these activities in an early education classroom.

Apply

How would you use play plans when the children in the scenario at the beginning of the chapter asked if they could play "Beach Trip"? What early literacy skills would you focus on developing? Additionally, how could you have used shared writings after the play enactment? What early literacy skills might you have focused on then?

In summary, the four activities, play plans, word searches, dissecting words, and shared writings, will increase the literacy skills of children when they are involved in socio-dramatic play activities. These activities expand children's understanding of the function of print and of how print can be used in their everyday lives for planning, sharing thoughts and information, and enjoyment. Additionally, through the integration of pretense with print, children are self-motivated to enrich their world knowledge, vocabulary, alphabet recognition, and phonemic awareness. Used daily, such an individualized enhancement of early learning skills affords children the opportunity to develop a strong platform for transitioning to more decontextualized and formal academic work during the elementary years.

One of these four activities could be used with the children each week. At the end of four weeks, the children will have completed activities involving all four strategies. This is the time when the socio-dramatic play center theme should be changed and children can then participate in these activities using another play theme.

Chapter Summary

Socio-dramatic play centers provide the core themes for the other learning centers. Socio-dramatic play centers assist children's development in a variety of situations that motivate them to physically and mentally construct narratives based on their background knowledge. These narratives use abstract symbolic representations that encourage children to develop language. Through pretend social peer interactions, children share these narratives with their play partners.

The skills used to create these play narratives are similar to those used to develop early literacy skills (e.g., motivation, background knowledge, language, and symbolic representations). Research now demonstrates that teachers can guide children in enhancing their early literacy skills by engaging them in four types of early literacy play activities: play plans, word searches, dissecting words, and shared writings.

HOME AND COMMUNITY CONNECTIONS

Integrating Literacy Skills Into the Play Centers

When reading books to your children at home, sit them on your lap while reading. Point out the pictures as you read the text and ask them to observe what they see in the pictures.

CHAPTER 10 FIRST-PERSON INTERVIEW

All Children Can Create Stories

Beverly Charsha

Director of a university toddler inclusion program, Carson, CA

One of the things that I like to do with children and that I believe truly assists them with expanding their literacy skills is to tell them that I am wondering about something. Young children are always wondering, so it feels very natural to them when we are all together in a group and I say things like, "Yesterday, I noticed that Maribel and Erika were in the play house sewing, and I began wondering if maybe they wanted to have some more fabric in that area?" Just by having me present that statement, we start talking about the play story they were enacting yesterday and expanding that story by planning new activities around the sewing and thinking of different symbolic representations that they could use. It's amazing how their language increases with a conversation like this.

One thing I have noticed is that you really need to be honest with children in conversations. They know it when you contrive

(Continued)

(Continued)

things. Therefore, you have to be up front with them and listen to what they say and respond honestly to their comments and questions. If you stay with them and respond honestly, they will continue to think about things, and this is when learning happens.

An activity that I enjoy doing is getting a tablet and pen, and sitting down and watching the children play. While they are playing, I will write down things that they say. The children love to look over at me when I am doing this, but they still continue with their play. Periodically, they will come over to look at what I have written down, and try to read it with me. They know that I am writing about them and they really want to know what those letters and words say. It is such a fun activity because they are beginning to understand that print can represent what someone does or says. Their interest really comes alive when they begin to understand they can make their own stories. I do a similar activity when I am working with toddlers. I love to take pictures of them while they are playing. Then we look at the photos, and they talk about what they were doing. Sometimes I will put a little print next to the picture and revisit their words. Again, doing this helps children see that what they are doing can be created into a story by using print and pictures. This is the core of literacy development.

Children like to use materials that they can play with when working on expanding their literacy skills. For example, they love puppets and play props, so I use a lot of puppets and props to create stories with the children. All you really need is one object, and you and the children can create an entire story around that object.

They also like making stories using the flannel board and flannel characters and shapes. It is wonderful to use flannel with children and then to let children use the flannel among themselves. I always make two sets of flannel characters—one set for me to use with the children, and one set for the children to use with each other. Children love to use real materials that they have seen the teacher using. It's real important to provide children with pieces of flannel that are different sizes and shapes so that they can make up their own story. One thing that I like to do with flannel shapes is to make stick figures that represent children in the classroom. While I am creating the character on the flannel board, I tell a story about why I think he or she decided to wear a red shirt to school that day or how their pink shoes are really magical dancing shoes. I never say the child's name while I am creating the stick figure. I always have the children try to guess who the story is about, and they love doing that. They also love playing this activity among themselves. It is wonderful to see them playing together and telling stories that use complex and new words.

Finally, I have always loved gardening with the children. I really believe that this is one of the best ways to teach them so many skills, especially literacy skills. We spend days talking about what we will plant and the sequence we need to follow for planting it. We also make lists of what we need from the market and what tools we will need. We are continually looking up photos of vegetables, fruits, and flowers and talking about what we will plant. At the same time, we talk in a very natural way about the print that we are using, the words that we are learning, and the sequence that we are following.

Children will create stories around anything. I am currently working with some young toddlers with disabilities. Although they have very little verbal language, I see them putting a block up by their ear and walking around acting as if they are talking to someone on their cell phone. I just love seeing that! It's exciting to see toddlers who may not have verbal language still expressing themselves through symbolic play.

Sample Learning Activities

Curricular Area: Language and Literacy

Core Vocabulary: Book, pages, title, author, illustrator, letters, words, sounds

Guide Questions:

What do you like to read?

What do you like to write about?

What happened in the story?

How are books put together?

How can we send a message?

Resources:

Adams, Pam. (2007). *There Was an Old Lady Who Swallowed a Fly,* Child's Play International.

Blake, Quentin. (2013). *Quentin Blake's Nursery Rhyme Book,* Trafalgar Square Publishing.

Keiko, Kasza. (2005). *My Lucky Day,* Penguin Young Readers Group.

Numeroff, Laura. (2008). *If You Give a Cat a Cupcake,* HarperCollins.

Rosen, Michael. (2003). *We're Going on a Bear Hunt,* Simon & Schuster Children's Publishing.

Core Text: I Like Myself, by Karen Beaumont

- Skills: Rhyming words, sight words (I, like, me), punctuation (periods, exclamation marks), recall details
- Levels of Questions: Who is the main character in the story? What does she like about herself? Tell me a little about you? What do you like about yourself? What things do you like to do? Why is it important to feel good about yourself?
- Product: Create a self-portrait, an "All About Me" book.

Learning Centers:

- Explore through literacy: Writing materials, abundant classroom library, listening center of songs and chants
- Create: Materials for making books: Construction paper, scraps, glue, scissors, crayons, water colors, easel and paint (for self-portrait)
- Outdoor Play: London Bridges, Ring Around the Rosie, and other singing and chanting activities
- Dramatic Play: At the library

  o Can I help you find a book?
  o What are you reading?
  o Which book are you checking out today, what is the title of it?
  o What is your book about?

Student Study Site

Visit the Student Study Site at **www.sagepub.com/selmi** to access additional study tools including mobile-friendly eFlashcards and links to video and web resources.

Key Terms

Common Core State Standards (CCSS)

decontextualized narratives

dissecting words

Head Start Framework

play plans

shared writings

word searches

Some Children's Books About Home and Literacy

Alphabet Under Construction, by Denise Fleming

Chicka Chicka Boom Boom, by Bill Martin and John Archambault

City Signs, by Zoran Milich

Goldilocks and the Three Bears, by Valeri Gorbachev

Max's ABC, by Rosemary Wells

Mother, Mother, I Feel Sick, by Remy Charlip

Pretend Soup, by Mollie Katzen

Stone Soup, by Marcia Brown

The Three Little Pigs, by Paul Galdone

Useful Websites

Books about disabilities: http://www.amazon.com/Best-Childrens-Books-on-Disability/lm/2Q14RZ7KB6IET

Information on Inclusion: http://www.naeyc.org/files/yc/file/200903/BTJWatson.pdf

Reflective Questions

The profession of Early Childhood Education is divided between having specific learning standards for young children or not. Go to the following website and read the NAEYC and NAECS-SDE response to the Common Core State Standards:

http://www.naeyc.org/files/naeyc/file/policy/NAEYC-NAECS-SDE-Core-Standards-Statement.pdf

Do you agree with NAEYC and NAECS-SDE on all of these points? Are there some that you disagree with? State your reasons why. Support your opinion with research from this chapter or from other articles that you have read.

11 Integrating Play Activities in the Science Centers

HOW HAVE YOU CHANGED?

©iStockphoto.com/bo1982

It is January and a small group of first grade children and their teacher are using various child-made instructional materials that address the current science theme of "Change in Your World." Each of the children has a personal journal that contains science notes and data that have been collected since they began kindergarten. Included in the journal are the children's baby picture and pictures of them taken throughout the school year. Other data in their journals are comparisons they made between themselves and others. For example, a small group of children compared their heights using their cutout body outlines from September. Together they gathered data and made comparisons about who was taller, shorter, or the same height. With the guidance of an adult, they also made predictions about what their height and weight would be at the end of school.

Today, the children are comparing their pictures taken at the beginning of the year and a folded colored and cutout body outline with a recently taken picture and cutout body outline. Additionally, they will compare their height and weight data from the two different times.

Before having the children gather current height and weight data and trace their updated body outlines, the teacher asked the children to describe changes they have seen at school since the beginning of the year. He also asks them to consider things that have not changed over the past portion of the school year. As the children describe their observations, the teacher writes their responses on a whiteboard. He then asks them to record two of these changes in their journals similar to the way they did at the beginning of the school year. He reminds them, "If you need help in putting your thoughts on paper, the paraprofessional or I can help you." What the teacher immediately notices is that, while most of the children needed complete transcriptions in the fall, now a few of them are independently using proper words and most of them need less assistance.

The next stage of this investigation is to gather current height and weight data and to create a body outline. Similar to the fall, the children are encouraged to make comparisons of taller, shorter, or the same height with their group partners as a result of the guided questions that are naturally posed by their teacher such as, "If we were to line up to go outside from shortest to tallest, where would you be in the line? At the beginning? Middle? End?"

Research demonstrates that children are competent thinkers who are capable of developing scientific concepts at a young age (Inan, Trundle, & Kantor, 2010). After all, science is based on asking questions, which is something that young children know how to do very well! Throughout their everyday activities they continually use questions when they encounter new experiences and organize the information that they obtain from those experiences into new information.

The scenario above is an example of a high-quality science activity that can expand children's understanding of their world and also to their cognitive, social-emotional, and language development (Conezio & French, 2002). The children are engaged in developmentally appropriate activities that enhance their inquiry techniques, self-regulation, and scientific processing skills. These learning skills contribute to these children's future academic success and to their confidence in understanding how science functions in the world around them (National Association for the Education of Young Children & National Association of Early Childhood Specialists in State Departments of Education, 2002).

In this chapter, we will learn the following:

> What are some critical science skills that children need to learn?

> What are some of the common skills that develop in science and play activities?

> How can science and language skills expand through student-led investigations, student-developed displays, and presentations?

Expanding Early Science Skills

High-quality science activities include the learning of *science content*—for example, information about living and nonliving things, the weather, air, and gravity. Additionally, high-quality science activities also include the development of *scientific* concepts, which occurs when children apply science content to different situations—such as, how do different items change over time? How and why did my friends and I change over time? Why do some items not change over time?

In the opening scenario, children are developing scientific concepts about how the world changes while they engage in science content activities related to their bodies, measurement, growth, and weight. Specifically, they are developing science concepts through the use of the scientific inquiry process, which allows children to question, explore, and problem solve as they collect and compare data. This type of learning occurs through adults carefully planning hands-on activities and guided questions that encourage the children to "put together" pieces of knowledge in order to gain an understanding about their lives and the world in which they live.

©iStockphoto.com/BartCo

Scientific inquiry encourages children to question, collaborate, predict, plan, observe, and discuss their results.

The opening scenario also demonstrates how the scientific inquiry process does not just focus on one-time activities, but rather centers on long-term investigations where, over time, children continually pose questions, use tools, work collaboratively, predict outcomes, make plans, observe, document results, and talk about their findings (Ashbrook & Chalufour, 2013). As a result, the children in the class not only learn about science, but they also learn about how science is done.

Intentional teaching is an essential component for planning inquiry-based classrooms in which individual needs of children are addressed and planned experiences that contribute to children's academic progress are provided. Such practices are important when teachers plan and create child-centered, playful environments that provide learning opportunities for the children. In this chapter's opening scenario, the teacher is using planned learning environments and implements teaching practices to develop scientific knowledge and concepts. Such an environment establishes a spirit of inquiry in which the children (1) ask questions and (2) organize their pathways to investigate phenomena related to those questions. In particular, in this class the adults are:

- **Fostering children to ask questions** by discussing things that have changed or not changed over the past half year.
- **Organizing pathways for children to investigate** by encouraging them to compare their own growth data and relate these to that of their peers.

Planned Inquiry Activities

Similar to other early education content areas, science has two primary components: what is taught and how it is taught. As demonstrated in Chapter 1, unfortunately the increasing importance that is currently being placed on academic testing scores is resulting in many early childhood teachers stressing the learning of content and, as a result, sacrificing the learning of how to use the inquiry process (Huffman, 2002). Science activities should place an equal emphasis on both the introduction of content and concepts and the guidance of children in activities that develop their scientific processing skills (Inan et al., 2010).

The teacher in the opening scenario intentionally engages the children by using **planned inquiry activities** that inspire them to investigate occurrences that are happening and allow them to use observations from these investigations to build on their current knowledge. This natural approach to science education builds on natural curiosity and allows children to become scientists when they employ systematic strategies in their natural investigations. They naturally order the data they gather from various sources and generate ideas or hypotheses that can be explored and tested. Through planned inquiries, children see how answers to initial questions can generate further questions that merit further investigation, all the while learning more and more about the topic at hand. Adults should not dispense information; instead, they should guide children through a prepared environment that motivates them to continually explore and ask questions (see Chapter 2). For example, when children are making hand shadows with a light source, instead of adults demonstrating the impact that movement to and from the light has on the size of the shadows, they should ask the children how they think they could make the shadow larger or smaller.

Adults need to observe children as they begin to generate questions and identify their areas of interest to explore. These observations allow adults to further arrange for the needed resources that

©iStockphoto.com/kali9

Through observations made during play activities, children can gather and record scientific data.

children will require in order to pursue their investigations. As children search, learn about, and explore their interests, adults clarify, prompt, and facilitate discussions related to those interests (see Figure 11.1). Specifically, the scientific inquiry process requires adults to:

- Design high-quality tasks based on children's interests
- Ask quality questions to encourage and guide students' investigations
- Listen to children as they formalize their thinking processes

And, as children's thinking is questioned and prompted, they should be encouraged to:

- Think more deeply about their learning process
- Engage in the use of higher levels of academic language

For example, with classroom pets, children can be encouraged to discuss the differences in the pets and how they feel, eat, sleep, use body parts, move around, and make sounds. Pictures can be taken and charts can be designed that demonstrate their findings. Older children can enter data regarding the pets into their journals or write stories and poems about the pets. Through continual prompting from adults, children will learn to take information from one experience and apply it to other types of learning activities.

The scientific inquiry approach to learning is similar to the Reggio Emilia approach (see Chapter 2) because they both facilitate learning through the understanding of children's interests and questions (Gadzikowski, 2013). Additionally, both approaches explore topics over time and encourage children to ask questions, make predictions, collect and analyze data, and share their findings with peers. Documentation is accomplished through drawings or charts, and children are encouraged to not only discuss what they learned but, just as important, they are supported in examining the pathways that they used to acquire this information.

Figure 11.1   Planned Inquiry Method

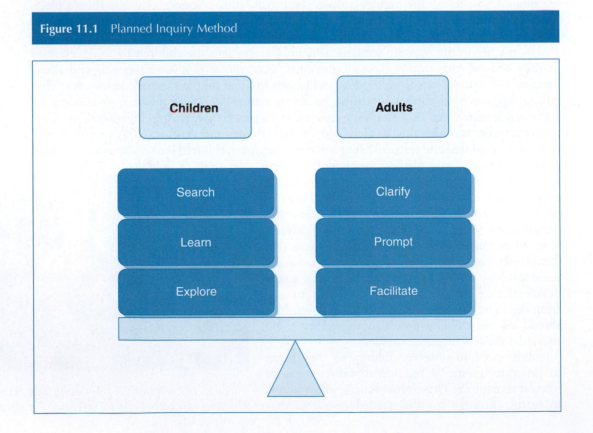

Supporting the inquiry process, Elkind (2007) states "All science begins with observation. . . . Children are natural observers and classifiers" (p. 142). As natural scientists, children learn the most when they are actively engaged in working with items found in their environment. Adults provide opportunities that challenge children as they pursue their investigations of these items. These planned inquiry activities expand children's knowledge and nurtures their spirit of inquiry (Carson, 1989).

Observing play activities provides ample evidence that children are engaged in figuring out their environments through exploring, puzzling over how something works, organizing objects based on their various features, and developing personal knowledge of their world (see Figure 11.2). "They are naturally curious and actively involved in exploring the world around them . . . young children are scientists-in-waiting" (Gelman, Brenneman, MacDonald, & Roman, 2010, p. 2).

Creating an Environment for Inquiry

Science education for children has typically been thought of from many perspectives. Some programs use an isolated approach to science in which areas of biology, physics, and geology are seen as disconnected and content specific. Another approach to science education views encouraging students to explore perplexing questions in an effort to solve problems and gain knowledge. Finally, in a number of education settings today, science education focuses on directly feeding students the content and information they need to learn, as if they are receptors of facts and information.

Figure 11.2 Techniques Promoting Inquiry Process Environments

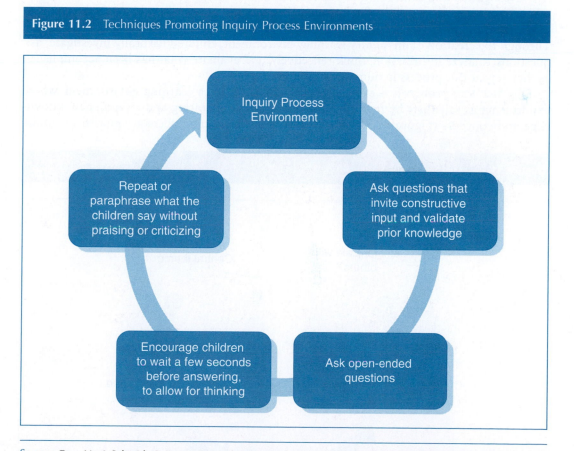

Source: Ogu, U., & Schmidt, S. R. (2013). Kindergarteners Investigate Rocks and Sand: Addressing Multiple Learning Styles Through an Inquiry-Based Approach. In A. Shillady (Ed.), *Spotlight on Young Children: Exploring Science* (pp. 61–67). Washington, DC: National Association for the Education of Young Children.

©iStockphoto.com/gbh007

Throughout their daily activities, children naturally engage in scientific activities that can be used to guide them in developing scientific concepts.

These three perspectives can create barriers that make science education unapproachable for young children and their teachers, often because each scientific domain has its own particular vocabulary, instruments, and methodologies that superficially assume content uniqueness. Typically, these specific features are presented as isolated ideas and concepts. Using such a compartmentalized approach to science learning deprives children of the demonstration of connections across areas of study and the use of generalizable language, processes, and concepts that truly relate to understanding how things work within larger systems and with one another.

Frequently, adults feel challenged by the complexities of science and inquiry-based science education. According to Hamlin and Wisneski (2012), some early educators have reservations about teaching science to young children. They believe that they have a shortage of scientific knowledge and question their ability to include more science content experiences throughout the school day.

However, in high-quality classrooms from preschool through third grade, science education should not consist of domain-specific endeavors filled with difficult vocabulary and technical knowledge. Instead, science should be an active, personal, playful, and collaborative investigation of a child's own world. Information should be presented in an environment where children understand the findings they discover and are comfortable with the methodologies they use to explore situations and apply their findings to new situations (Taba, 1962). Through the creation of an inquiry learning environment, children naturally investigate, ask questions, analyze information, think reflectively, and evaluate what has been accomplished as they repeat this process in numerous contexts.

This iterative process is a cyclical process that creates a learning environment where children act as scientists by revisiting and continually generating and refining new knowledge and concepts (Figure 11.3). Interactions with objects and peers are guided by adults

Figure 11.3   Science as an Iterative Process

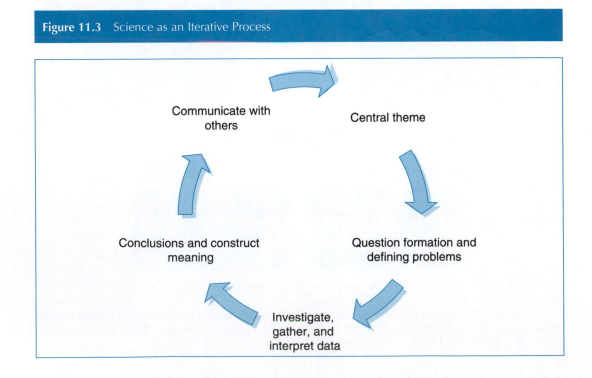

to foster a context in which children are engaged in seeking answers to their questions and engaging in a process of inquiry that builds on what they know about a topic and how prior knowledge can be used to connect with their new investigations (National Research Council [NRC], 2011; Kaplan, 2008).

In an inquiry environment, children naturally transfer knowledge from one situation to another, which leads to the emerging of new questions and new investigations. Through this continuous process, children gradually move from simple to more complex problems to investigate. As a result, the planned inquiry approach motivates children to become more refined critical thinkers who are developing the following skills:

- Asking clear questions and defining problems
- Planning and implementing investigations
- Gathering, analyzing, and interpreting data
- Drawing conclusions and constructing meaning
- Using evidence to communicate findings to others (NRC, 2012; Paul & Elder, 2009)

As this chapter's opening scenario demonstrates, a scientific inquiry environment is built on developing a foundation of inquiry in which students observe phenomena and define further problems for investigation through their own questions. "Science begins with a question about a phenomenon, such as 'Why is the sky blue?' . . . and seeks to develop theories that can provide explanatory answers to such questions" (NRC, 2012, p. 50).

REFLECT AND APPLY EXERCISE 11.1

Guiding Children's Inquiry

Reflect

Review the techniques adults can use to guide young children in developing higher level thinking skills that are presented in Chapter 7. Next, review the opening scenario for this current chapter.

Apply

Think of ways you could use the techniques presented in Chapter 7 to enhance children's use of the scientific inquiry process in this chapter's opening scenario. What skills would these techniques support—further questioning? analyzing data? drawing conclusions? using evidence to communicate findings?

An inquiry environment allows opportunities for children to connect a new problem with their established knowledge base and determine a plan for investigation (Kaplan, 2002). While they make discoveries based on their data, their questions are answered and more questions are asked. By engaging in this iterative inquiry process, children explore big ideas in their environment. With the guidance of an adult, children gather information from various sources, such as text-based planned experiments and observations, and analyze their own information. Together, children then draw conclusions and share their results. Through the drawing of conclusions and sharing them with others, children generate further questions that lead them to further investigations.

Stoll, Hamilton, Oxley, Eastman, and Brent (2012) describe a *four-step problem-solving format* that has been successful in allowing children to both (1) apply their knowledge and skills to a new situation and (2) construct new knowledge. This process centers on adults

Adults scaffold children's thinking so that they ask further questions, interpret new data, draw new conclusions, and share their new thoughts with peers.

designing problem-solving situations that are based on children's theories and questions, and it consists of the following steps:

Step 1: Define the problem

Step 2: Develop a procedure or plan

Step 3: Conduct the procedure

Step 4: Draw conclusions

Building on the learning that is occurring in the opening scenario, those children could expand their scientific knowledge by applying what they learned about their own growth and development to other objects. For example, four science centers can be created where children observe and investigate the growth and development of caterpillars, chickens, plants, and rocks. The children's knowledge will naturally grow as they ask questions, plan and carry out investigations, analyze data, formulate explanations for their findings, and communicate information on the differences they have discovered and how they discovered them. Figure 11.4 provides 11 inquiry techniques that the National Research Council recommends using with young children.

Figure 11.4   NRC's Inquiry Practices for Young Children

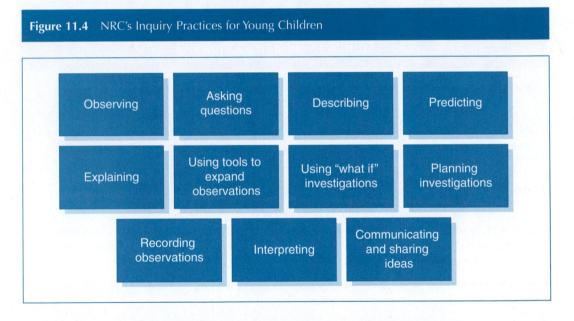

LEARNING FOR ALL CHILDREN
Science Inquiry, Reggio Emilia Approach, and Culture

The Reggio Emilia approach to learning places an intense value on the culture of each child and, therefore, does not believe that one curriculum program can address the interests and needs of all the children in a classroom (Inan et al., 2010). It requires adults to know and design learning activities around each child's individual needs, interests, questions, confusions, and inquiries. Specifically, the Reggio Emilia approach captures children's learning ambitions and develops their skills for documenting findings from their investigations using various media, and provides opportunities for them to explain what they have learned. Teachers, on the other hand, are observers, listeners, and investigative partners. They create well-planned learning environments and furnish the materials that support the children's investigations.

The characteristics of Reggio Emilia programs are similar to those of the scientific inquiry process where children are encouraged to work as members of learning communities that share ideas, collect data, discover solutions, and create further questions.

Science and Play

Play activities generate scientific environments. As the research in Part I of this book demonstrates, play affords children natural opportunities to investigate, question, construct, and problem-solve, which are engaging requisite skills for being scientists. While playing, children investigate phenomena in which they are interested. Therefore, science inquiry and play are complementary activities that are based on the same following principles:

- Learning occurs when children are personally involved in activities that relate to learning about their world through questioning, experimenting, and discussing (Bruner, 1960; Dewey, 1910, 1916/1966; Piaget, 1959).
- Early learning occurs when adults and children work in partnership by collaboratively asking questions, constructing knowledge, and providing guidance (Bruner, 1960; Piaget, 1959; Vygotsky, 1978).

Intentional planning and guided interactions in play activities (see Chapter 7) provide rich opportunities for children to learn science concepts and to become familiar with the process of scientific inquiry (Hamlin & Wisneski, 2012). In the next sections, some of the different types of play that were discussed in Chapter 3 of this book are provided to demonstrate a more comprehensive understanding of the connection between scientific inquiry and play activities.

Functional Play

Infants and toddlers learn about their own worlds primarily through play activities that require them to use their senses—for example, watching, smelling, tasting, feeling, and deliberate listening. Learning about the different senses is a scientific concept and, therefore, using sensory play activities is developmentally appropriate for science learning. For example, young children can engage in finger painting with pudding flavors to enhance their sensitivity to taste, touch, and smell. Creating structures from different types of blocks—such as cardboard, wood, sponge, plastic—encourages children to ask questions based on their experiences with vision, hearing, and touch. A light source and a background screen enables children to create

Adults create learning partnerships with children as they engage them in the inquiry process.

Jupiterimages/Goodshoot/Thinkstock

Functional play activities can engage very young children in the scientific inquiry process by using the senses to explore.

shadows and reflections. They can experiment with their shadows as the distance from the light source changes. Questions will be asked, and new problems will be solved as they actively experiment. All of these scientific play activities encourage high-quality learning. Adults enhance the children's learning if they enter into conversations with them and employ open-ended questions. Learning is also enhanced by combining their investigations with related activities like reading about the phenomena they are observing. Children can also use other media like drawings, photographs, and displays to document their investigations and findings. Finally, they can use their developing writing skills to document their findings, and record further questions they want to research. These combined data provide a source for the children to share with one another and provide a record of their investigations that documents their development as scientists.

Symbolic Play

Symbolic play activities contribute to children's learning about scientific concepts and the use of the scientific inquiry process. Preschool water tables can be filled with different materials at different times, such as sand, rice, gravel, marbles, rocks, oats, sawdust, popcorn kernels, leaves, soil, screws, pennies, and dirt. Such diverse experiences allow children to engage in a variety of symbolic representations and narratives and, at the same time, have hands-on experiences with diverse materials that encourage them to ponder, experiment, question, compare, and document differences. In so doing, children further develop important skills that benefit them academically and developmentally—including comparing and contrasting, developing causal relationships, predicting outcomes, asking questions, and developing language and vocabulary skills.

REFLECT AND APPLY EXERCISE 11.2

Designing Science Centers

Reflect

Review the opening scenario for Chapter 1 where the two boys are carrying an explosive device out of the house.

Apply

You are the teacher in the classroom and notice how interested the boys are in the explosive device. You want to create a science center that will engage the children in developmentally appropriate activities and will assist them in understanding further the concepts of explosions. What could you do? How could your suggestions enhance the understanding of science knowledge? the understanding of the scientific inquiry process? the development of symbolic play activities? the development of literacy skills?

Games With Rules

As children become older, they participate in group games with rules and scores (see Chapter 3). Through the careful arrangement of the environment and the use of guiding questions, children can engage in scientifically based games that have rules. For example, children can be arranged into teams with the quest of "finding the most different types of leaves," or "the largest shell," or "the smallest insect." All of these hands-on activities will engage children in using the scientific inquiry process for learning. Other team game suggestions are: growing the tallest bean plant, finding the most science equipment on a treasure hunt, finding the longest worm (cut up pieces of yarn), and building the tallest tower. Additionally, children are often thrilled to think of the rules or challenges for the games (Hamlin & Wisneski, 2012). Therefore, as children participate in these playful activities, adults need to continually make them more complex and abstract, based on the children's individual interests. During such naturally motivated activities, children learn more about the world they live in and ways to obtain scientific information.

Through the cautious combination of science and play activities, children learn to express their thoughts about their discoveries, describe phenomena they observe, and detail their findings. Acting as scientists, children can use an inquiry-based classroom to actively engage in playfully constructing a personal understanding of their world. As a Chinese Proverb states:

What I hear, I forget.

What I see, I remember.

What I do, I know. (Carson, 1989)

Symbolic activities and narratives can enhance children's language, literacy, and scientific concepts.

Team activities that are more organized can also engage children in developing scientific concepts.

Science Learning Elements and Core Standards

Head Start Science Knowledge and Skills Elements

Science during the younger years should engage children in discovering the world around them and refining their information about it. The Head Start Framework (Head Start, 2011) encourages early childhood professionals to focus on children's emerging ability to collect information from their natural and physical worlds and then to organize that information into knowledge and theories. Early education programs should foster a sense of curiosity and motivation that results in children learning vocabulary and ways to collaborate with peers. Placing a priority on the development of inquiry skills, the Head Start Learning Elements encourage teachers to develop children's skills to observe, collect information, ask questions, predict answers, explain their findings, and draw conclusions. The elements proposed by Head Start focus on acquiring and understanding scientific concepts and facts that relate to children's physical and natural worlds.

Most preschool curricula focus around the following domains through the use of scientific inquiry interactions (WestEd, 2011):

- Physical Sciences
- Life Sciences
- Earth Sciences

Figure 11.5 provides more specific information on some of the area that these categories can include.

Figure 11.5   Different Preschool Science Domains

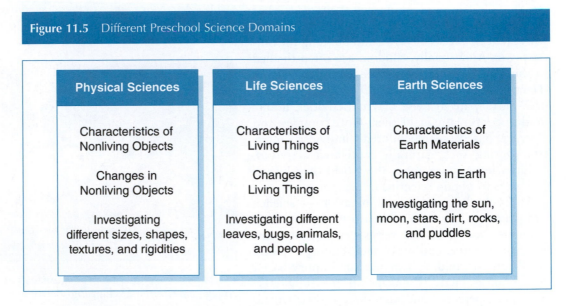

Developmentally appropriate science education activities should be integrated into the daily activities for children. Some examples of ways to integrate science learning into most young children's activities are the following:

- Cooking can provide opportunities for using specialized measuring utensils
- Magnets can allow for the exploration of physical properties
- Plants and animals can enhance the understanding of the life cycle and growth
- Balls and blocks can allow for the testing of motion and other physics properties

REFLECT AND APPLY EXERCISE 11.3

Using the Early Standards

Reflect

Find your state's early education science standards on the Internet. Go either directly to your state's Department of Education or to the U.S. Department of Education at www.usa.gov/directory/federal/department-of-education.shtm and click on Office of Elementary and Secondary Education (OESE); in the search box, enter: State Standards. Such a search will provide the K–12 standards for each state.

Kindergarten Common Core State Standards

The Next Generation Science Standards (NGSS) presents a perspective of science education that encourages inquiry-based approaches to science that are outlined by the National Academy of Sciences (NRC, 2013). These standards have been organized by integrating both science and engineering because scientists generate questions and study the world we live in and engineers generate possible solutions that lead to additional questions.

Using the inquiry-based approach, the NGSS defined eight scientific practices that are at the heart of inquiry-based science for K–12. These practices provide a structure on which to construct a science curriculum for the K–12 continuum that is not simply a compendium of facts or a domain of specific knowledge (NRC, 2011, 2012). Instead, these standards establish a "set of practices used to establish, extend, and refine knowledge," and that include central beliefs (NRC, 2012, p. 26), that sciences share at their core. Using an inquiry-based, problem-solving approach will provide children the opportunity to learn that:

- Scientifically collected data and evidence is the foundation for developing concepts
- The disagreement and analysis of data and theory are essential features of science
- Scientists examine, review, and evaluate their own knowledge and ideas and critique those of others
- Science is a collaborative endeavor and that scientists work with others as they learn about their world (NRC, 2012)

According to the National Research Council (NRC, 2012), science is fundamentally a social operation where knowledge progresses through collaboration with others. Therefore, scientific information should be obtained through *crosscutting science practices* where children are motivated to problem-solve by observing, predicting, and justifying their ideas. For example, if a class is studying plants, the teacher might want to show the children a seed and ask them questions such as the following:

- What do you think is inside of the seed?
- How do you think the inside will feel and smell?
- What will happen if we put the seed in water?

Through the use of carefully planned questions, children make predictions, observations, and communicate their knowledge to one another. Additionally, through the careful collection of data through the drawings and the recording of numbers, young children expand their literacy skills.

The NRC scientific framework for science education uses the term *practice* instead of skill to stress the need to simultaneously integrate knowledge and skill (NRC, 2013). Table 11.1 illustrates the practices that the NRC encourages young children to develop. Learning practices that focus on the inquiry-based

Formal scientific lessons should engage children in using the scientific inquiry process.

Table 11.1   Practices of Science, Their Characteristics and Examples of Each Practice

Distinguishing Practices	Characteristics	Examples in Practice
1. Asking questions and defining problems	Asking questions is essential to scientific investigations; . . . the ability to ask well-defined questions is an important component of science literacy, helping to make students critical consumers of scientific knowledge.	*Student scientists might ask:* What do we know? What changed? How do we know something changed? *Topical examples:* Why are there seasons? How do bees know where to go and get back? Why are bees attracted to flowers? Why did that bridge collapse?
2. Developing and using models	"Models make it possible to go beyond observations and imagine a world not yet seen". . . . "Models enable predictions of the language form, *if . . . then . . . therefore* to be made in order to test hypothetical explanations." (p. 50).	*Student scientists might:* Construct mental and conceptual models to think with, make predictions, make sense of experience, or demonstrate phenomena. *Topical examples:* Construct drawings of: insects with labeled features; the water cycle; a real-world object/event; represent a molecule; make a model to test a design(s) and compare designs.
3. Planning and carrying out investigations	Scientists plan and carry out "systematic investigations which requires identification of data to be recorded," those factors that are changed and those that are not. "Observations and data . . . are used to confirm existing thought or revise what is known." (p. 50)	*Student scientists will:* Ask questions to begin investigations; Pose hypotheses or make predictions; Plan data to be gathered, how to record [and] collect; Plan investigation procedures. *Topical examples:* Weather: use weather data from earlier recordings; use published weather maps from newspapers to determine factors that influence local weather; influence of geography on weather patterns; determine where weather "comes from"; Factors that affect the speed of cars going down a ramp; Growth and development changes of individuals over time.

Distinguishing Practices	Characteristics	Examples in Practice
4. Analyzing and interpreting data	"Scientists use a range of tools"—tables, graphs, visual drawings and analysis, "to identify significant relationships and patterns in data" and make the data meaningful. (p. 51)	*Student scientists will:* Organize data for analysis and communication with others: Use graphs and tables, drawings, displays to summarize data, to make meaningful presentations. *Topical examples:* Human growth/development: Height/weight tables; Human characteristics: Hair, eye color; Weather: Temperature, rainfall over time and relate to month, season, and compare with other years; Insects: Bee activity related and influencing factors.
5. Using mathematics and computational thinking	"Mathematics and computation are fundamental tools for representing variables and their relationships." "Mathematical and computational approaches enable predictions of behavior of physical systems, along with the testing of such predictions." (p. 51)	*Student scientists will:* Use of instruments: rulers, scales, thermometers, wind/rain gages, magnifiers, speedometers; understand serial order, 1:1 correspondence, more/less/same, look for patterns, use rank-ordering, range, average.
6. Constructing explanations and designing solutions	"The goal of science is the construction of theories that provide" explanations of phenomena. "The goal for students is to construct logically coherent explanations of phenomena that incorporate their current understanding of science, or a model that represents it, and are consistent with the evidence." (p. 52)	*Based on the data that student scientists gather and their analysis of data, they will:* Develop explanations for observed phenomena and predict what will happen in similar situations. *Topical examples:* Determine the relationship between the slope of a car track and the speed of the car at the end of the track—what is your hypothesis? What is the relationship between heart rate, respiration, and exercise, e.g., at rest, walking, walking fast, and running? From common paper and other classroom materials design a bridge that will support a 5-pound weight. Analyze a design, where it begins to fail, and detail the [change] needed to accomplish the goal. (p. 70)

(Continued)

Table 11.1 (Continued)

Distinguishing Practices	Characteristics	Examples in Practice
7. Engaging in argument from evidence	"Scientists must defend their explanations, formulate evidence based on a solid foundation of data, examine their own understanding in light of the evidence and comments offered by others, and collaborate with peers in searching for the best explanation for the phenomenon being investigated." (p. 52)	*Student scientists will:* Construct arguments for defending ideas or explanations of investigations. Use their gained knowledge, describe their investigations.
8. Obtaining, evaluating, and communicating information	"A major practice of science is thus the communication of ideas and the results of inquiry—orally, in writing, use of tables, diagrams, graphs, equations, and by engaging in extended discussion with peers. Science requires the student to derive meaning from texts, . . . to evaluate the scientific validity of the information acquired, and to integrate that information." (p. 53)	*Student scientists will:* Use and understand words, tables, diagrams, and graphs and mathematical expressions; Engage in critical reading of literature or media reports of science and discuss the validity and reliability of the data, hypotheses, and conclusions. *Topical examples:* Write accounts, observations, thoughts, ideas and models of their work in journals; Create diagrams, graphs, pictures, use other media to portray/ present their investigation.

Source: National Research Council. (2012). *A Framework for K–12 Science Education: Practices, Crosscutting Themes, and Core Ideas* (pp. 50–79). Washington, DC: National Academies Press.

approach allows children to explore the properties of objects, determine the relationships among these objects, ask questions, discuss their observations with others, and actively experiment to solve problems. These practices encourage the creation of an environment that presents **big ideas** or *themes* that children are interested in investigating.

As mentioned in Chapter 7 of this book, learning opportunities can be organized in many different ways. They guide children by arranging the necessary objects, asking relevant questions, and fostering and maintaining a spirit of inquiry. Adults guide and facilitate children to act as scientists by engaging in the following sequence of activities: (1) making comparisons, (2) formulating predictions based on prior experiences and current knowledge, (3) hypothesizing potential outcomes, (4) solving problems through experimentation, (5) gathering and analyzing data, and (6) drawing conclusions. Based on the children's reflections, opportunities can be presented to recycle this process with new questions based on their newly discovered knowledge (Bosse, Jacobs, & Anderson, 2009; Stoll et al., 2012).

Developing Science Centers

Science as an Integrative Curriculum

Preschoolers should learn science concepts through playful interactions with their peers in multiple places throughout the classroom and outside areas. If the dramatic play center is set up as a weather station, the following activities are simple examples of weather activities that can take place both inside and outside of the classroom:

- Caring for plants and animals depending on the weather changes
- Reading books and stories about weather in the book center
- Discussing clothing during circle time
- Creating shadow art
- Jumping over puddles of different sizes for motor skills
- Blowing bubbles to monitor the wind
- Dancing like the weather to different types of music
- Measuring the size of a shadow or puddle
- Preparing warm cocoa or making cool lemonade

Gelman et al. (2010) emphasize that a science curriculum is based on providing children readily available environments in which the tools of science are used: "redundancy and ubiquity foster organized learning" (p. 7) for children. In this manner there is a horizontal integration of a science curriculum plan. Specifically, horizontal curriculum integration involves a curriculum (science, for example) that focuses on integrating new activities with activities already learned so that children develop and use their growing knowledge base as they move through child-centered learning activities. For example, the teacher can ask children if items are living or nonliving if they have already had previously been discussing these concepts and have demonstrated an understanding of them. Through horizontal integration, children develop and use their growing knowledge base as they move through new child-centered activities. The "changing through growth" activity that was described in the opening scenario was a component of an overall unit theme examining a "change in your world." In the opening scenario, the students were comparing current data with findings that they recorded in their personal journals several months before. By comparing the two sets of personal data, children can engage in the scientific practice of reflecting on changes that occurred in themselves and their classmates over time.

"Investigative activities help to develop abilities that go far beyond the scope of what one traditionally considers as science" (Gelman et al., 2010, p. 7). Such a curriculum also manifests vertical curriculum integration. Children are counting, recording, displaying, and comparing their findings. They are using other subjects, like mathematics, reading, art, language arts, and literacy. For example, the children in the opening scenario were busy writing their observations and their predictions. Literacy skills are enhanced as children read selected stories about growth and change. When they write in their journals and construct their own stories on their personal growth they hone their developing language arts skills. As they plan and construct their visual displays and present their findings they incorporate the visual arts and use their communication skills. Children learn that the tools of scientists involve curiosity, carrying out investigations, and using their developing academic skills to record, analyze, discuss, and display their findings. Science becomes an integrated part of their learning environment, not an isolated subject.

Implementing the Inquiry Process

In the classroom described in the opening scenario for this chapter, a science unit was constructed that started during the beginning weeks of the school year. Children in this classroom will actively investigate "changes in their world" by gathering data on themselves three times over each year in the course of four school years. They will record these data

Centers should be designed so that children collaborate with their peers to engage in scientific inquiry.

in their personal science journals, where they also keep completed body tracings of themselves. These quantitative and visual data allow children to observe personal changes and determine the impact of physical growth and development across time.

Through activities similar to the ones described in the opening scenario, children actively learn about their individual and collective changes, using words, numbers, and visual representations. Classroom charts and graphs are developed and used to compare individuals with others and with the group. This long-term project allows students to gain an understanding of concepts related to change and to build an understanding of various science concepts that are associated with growth and development—for example, some things change and others do not, and weight and/or size alter as things change. Additionally, children are urged to naturally combine their science abilities with their language, literacy, and mathematics skills.

Similar to what was described in Chapter 7 of this book, the role of the adults when implementing the inquiry process is to arrange the classroom centers so they encourage the following activities:

- Asking questions
- Prompt students' curiosity
- Facilitate discussions
- Observe students' questions and interests

In other words, when using the inquiry process both the adults and students act as scientific researchers; children observing themselves and peers and adults observe the children and their interests.

In inquiry-based learning centers, children continually use language to describe, inform, and question. They also use their mathematics skills for explaining variables, determining relationships between and among those variables, and detailing similarities and differences among variables. As children attempt to record their ideas, they learn various ways to convey meaning in written form, such as the following:

- Charts
- Notes
- Lists
- Pictures
- Diagrams
- Graphs
- Text
- Photos

Table 11.1 is an adaptation of ideas that are embedded in a framework for K–12 science provided by the NRC (2012). The table provides a list of eight distinguishing practices of student scientists. Foremost among the eight characteristics presented is beginning scientific investigations by asking questions. Children are inherently inquisitive and ask "who," "what," "why," and "how" questions, and in a child-centered classroom this is a skill that should be nurtured and encouraged. Beyond framing questions, additional distinguishing science practices include planning investigations; gathering, organizing, and analyzing data; and using various methods for displaying the results of their investigations and presenting what they found. Table 11.1 also provides a brief description of the characteristics of each distinguishing practice and examples of what the student scientists might do.

These eight practices can be viewed as a framework for a science program. It is important for teachers to remember that their students are encouraged to be curious and wonder about their world. As such, the role of their teachers is to construct the learning environment in a way that encourages children to ask questions and to provide the students opportunities to plan and carry out investigations to find answers to them. Further, the students are asked to share their findings with others and provide evidence that supports those findings. Finally, it is important to note that science investigations that students complete involve topics that connect with their lives and that their findings make use of the emerging skills and knowledge gained from their curricular experiences.

While the theme might be science, activities also involve other relevant curricular domains. For example, while standards for science are primarily addressed, inquiry-based science activities also incorporate standards from other domains, such as math and English/Language Arts (ELA) and literacy. Figure 11.6 provides an example of how science (S) standards can be integrated with common core standards in mathematics (M) and English language arts (E). For example, while addressing the science standards, it is important to note that math standards are also addressed. Math skills, like reasoning abstractly, predicting, modeling and analyzing using numbers, and using appropriate tools are also addressed in science investigations. The same level of curricular integration occurs with English Language arts standards. Children are involved with text-based material when gathering background information related to their investigations. They are also synthesizing information, writing reports, reading and speaking, and using technology for gathering information and presenting their findings. This is another example of how science is complementary with other curricular domains, and that skills developed in student investigations make use of skills developed across the curriculum.

A view of how common core standards in Science (S), Math (M), and English Language Arts (E) are complementary is found in Figure 11.6. This figure is an adaptation of one developed to demonstrate the complementary nature of the Next Generation Science Standards with Common Core Standards for both Mathematics and English Language Arts and Literacy. The figure provides a teacher's view of standards that are unique to math (M1, M6, M7, M8), science (S1, S3, S4), and ELA (E1, E7). However, all three share a group of standards and include, math (M2, M3, M5) and ELA (E2, E3, E4, E5, E6). Finally, science and math share three standards (M4, S2, S5). As shown in Figure 11.7, science uses skills that span the curriculum and the developing personal skills of the student. While addressing science standards, the learning activities described in the opening scenario also address common core standards for math and ELA and literacy. The scientific inquiry process nudges students toward developing an understanding that language, literacy, and math are necessary tools in science. Children discover that asking questions, planning investigations, making predictions, and collecting and using data to answer their questions is universally important skills.

This chapter's opening scenario demonstrates how children, who are investigating the theme *Change in Your World*, examined ways that they change or do not change over time. Similarly, such a theme can also include center activities that investigate changes in the young children's observable worlds:

- Changes in substances and matter—e.g., gasses, liquids, and solids
- Changes in the seasons and the weather
- Changes in plants and animals

These themes provide opportunities for children to actively expand their scientific knowledge and scientific skills while involved in their own investigations. The children become active scientists as they complete their activities. Additionally, not only can children gather data from their observations, but adults can also make sure that they have access to other sources such as books and magazines, the Internet, guest speakers, and field trips to provide further information and encourage questioning. Hands-on experiences such as having terrariums in the science center, a classroom weather station, a light table, bug cages, bird feeders, and classroom pets can encourage children to display their findings using several different research sources, including text and dictation, photo displays, journaling, art work, and graphs and charts.

©iStock.com/robertmandel

Science centers should display symbolic reflections of children's scientific thinking and problem-solving processes.

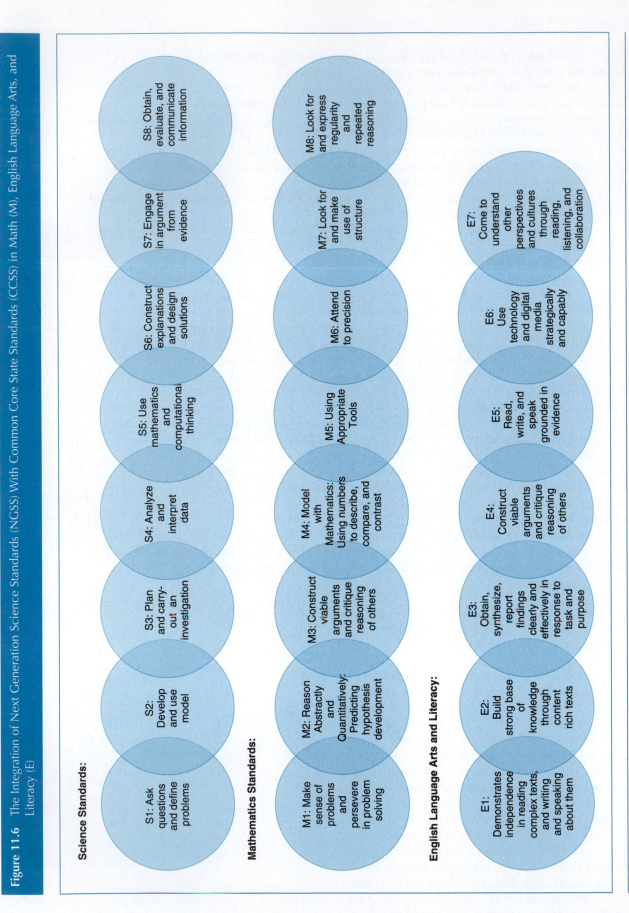

Science Standards:

S1: Ask questions and define problems

S2: Develop and use model

S3: Plan and carry-out an investigation

S4: Analyze and interpret data

S5: Use mathematics and computational thinking

S6: Construct explanations and design solutions

S7: Engage in argument from evidence

S8: Obtain, evaluate, and communicate information

Mathematics Standards:

M1: Make sense of problems and persevere in problem solving

M2: Reason Abstractly and Quantitatively: Predicting hypothesis development

M3: Construct viable arguments and critique reasoning of others

M4: Model with Mathematics: Using numbers to describe, compare, and contrast

M5: Using Appropriate Tools

M6: Attend to precision

M7: Look for and make use of structure

M8: Look for and express regularity and repeated reasoning

English Language Arts and Literacy:

E1: Demonstrates independence in reading complex texts, and writing and speaking about them

E2: Build strong base of knowledge through content rich texts

E3: Obtain, synthesize, report findings clearly and effectively in response to task and purpose

E4: Construct viable arguments and critique reasoning of others

E5: Read, write, and speak grounded in evidence

E6: Use technology and digital media strategically and capably

E7: Come to understand other perspectives and cultures through reading, listening, and collaboration

Sources: National Research Council (NRC). (2011). *Successful K–12 Education: Identifying Effective Approaches in Science, Technology, Engineering, and Mathematics.* Washington, DC: National Academies Press; National Research Council (NRC). (2013). *Next Generation Science Standards: Appendix D—All standards, All Students: Making Next Generation Science Standards Accessible to All Students.* Washington, DC: National Academies Press.

Specifically, some other possible sources for ongoing science center observations inside or outside the classroom that focus on "the way things change" are an incubator that can allow children to plot animal development and change using eggs from different birds that could include chickens, quail, pheasants, or ducks. Children can also monitor plant growth in the classroom and test how environmental differences can affect plant growth—for example, varying amount of light, water, and different soil types. School gardens afford children opportunities to grow plants, and understand the interplay between plant growth and soil, temperature, and weather. Class terrariums can be maintained throughout the school year and used as a way to understand different ecosystems and what is necessary for systems to establish balance. All these types of activities engage the students and prompt them to ask questions, make predictions, and demonstrate findings by using scientific research techniques.

Designing learning environments where projects examine the concept of "change" with different items allows core science standards to be fully integrated into other academic areas. Through a series of well-planned and related learning experiences, children naturally explore and learn (Gelman et al., 2010). Examples of different types of changes that occur in children's lives are suggested by Gelman et al. (2010, p. 26) in the following table. Each of these investigation topics in both the biological and physical sciences are embedded in big ideas that relate to a central theme of change in your world.

Brand X Pictures/Stockbyte/Thinkstock

Scientific inquiry should be integrated into many of the daily classroom activities.

Change and Transformation:	**Changing Systems/Interactions:**
Growth and Decay	Ecosystems
Seasonal/Weather	Symbiotic Relationships
Substance/Matter (Solid, Liquid, Gas)	Blood Circulation
Living/Nonliving Things	Plumbing
	Habitats and Climates
Animate/Inanimate Distinction:	**Form and Function:**
Growth and Decay	Animal and Human Movement
Living/Nonliving Things	Animal and Human Homes
Movement	Communication
	Tools and their Uses

Source: Gelman, R., Brenneman, K., MacDonald, G., & Roman, M. (2010). *Preschool Pathways to Science: Facilitating Scientific Ways of Thinking, Talking, Doing and Understanding*. Baltimore, MD: Paul H. Brookes.

Big Ideas That Guide Science Centers

Chapter 7 presented information on how early education professionals can implement many different teaching approaches such as the following: single concepts, integrated concepts, units, themes, inquiry, and projects (Helm & Katz, 2011). Figure 11.7 provides a summary progression for building a science program. Initially the teacher might introduce the big idea, for example change in your world, embedded in the topic of change and you. As in the opening scenario, the students are investigating their growth and development. While the teacher arranged this single-concept science experience, it will be the stepping stone for child-directed investigations of various topics that relate to change and you. In short, as suggested by Helm and Katz (2011), a science program may begin less child centered but as children make discoveries they ask the questions that form the basis for their next investigation and science becomes more child centered. If science is to be integrated both horizontally and vertically, the science curriculum should be designed around "central themes" or "big ideas" that guide child-centered learning. In this way children will see the relationships across science topics and make use of the tools they use in their other curricular subjects to analyze, explain, and display their science findings. Some of the big ideas for early science concept development included the following (Patrick, Mantzicoppulos, & Samarapungavan, 2013):

- Difference between living and nonliving things
- How things grow and adapt to their environments
- Interrelationships between living things—such as food chains, seeds, and plants

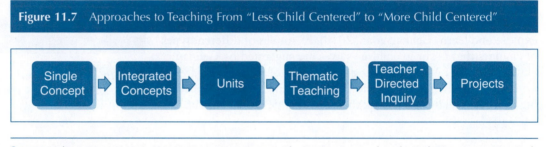

Figure 11.7   Approaches to Teaching From "Less Child Centered" to "More Child Centered"

Single Concept → Integrated Concepts → Units → Thematic Teaching → Teacher-Directed Inquiry → Projects

Source: Helm, J. H., & Katz, L. (2011). *Young Investigators: The Project Approach in the Early Years* (p. 3). New York, NY: Teachers College Press.

When children are working as scientists using science materials, and responding to guided questions or statements they discover new findings and relationships. Based on these revelations children will see additional relationships that lead to questions for further investigation from which new thoughts about their world emerge. Whether measuring body growth with rulers and scales, comparing the development of chicks in a classroom incubator, or monitoring weather changes using tools like barometers, thermometers, and computers from the classroom weather station, children need guidance on how those data relate to general unifying ideas and themes. Throughout early education programs the same themes should be addressed at more advanced levels than presented in the previous year. Doing this provides children with a framework to organize their thoughts and advance the depth of their particular investigations. In other words, the children are in control of their inquiry.

When a science curriculum is developed around general themes or big ideas, children take control of their own inquiry with the guidance of an adult. For children to have the time to investigate, explore, and reflect, the number of general themes should be limited to two or three each year (Gelman et al., 2010).

Figure 11.8 provides a sample plan for a year's science program that relates to the opening scenario. As the center square in the figure illustrates, the unifying theme in this example is change in your

Children should be provided opportunities to develop scientific concepts by comparing and contrasting a variety of activities that relate to the same concept.

Figure 11.8   Sample Pre-K–K/1 Science Curriculum

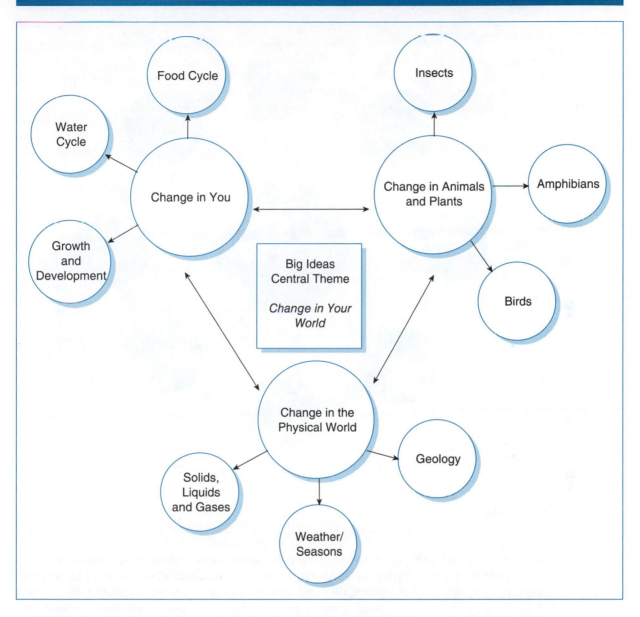

world. Under this general theme, the school staff determines topics that interest the children and that they are capable of participating in—for instance, Change in You, Change in Animals and Plants, or Change in the Physical World.

Science centers are defined as places inside or outside the classroom and are always available for students to learn. The science centers should be equipped with scientific tools (see Figure 11.9) and books that contain information relating to the themes being studied at the time. The books should be at various reading levels ranging from "big picture books" to other books that are for more advanced readers, and should consist of a mixture of informational and story books. Each child should also have a personal science journal in which to keep and update data. Classrooms should have computer access for student projects. Finally, beyond the prepared charts and figures, children's work should be displayed throughout the classroom, demonstrating their questions, predictions, and findings. In short, the classroom should have an abundance of child-created materials displayed and be an environment that suggests that science is an important area for investigation.

Figure 11.9   Materials and Displays in the Science Center

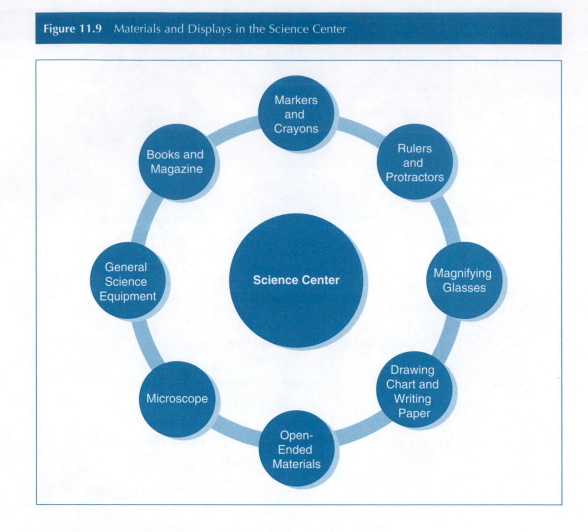

Chapter Summary

Children are naturally curious and they constantly explore their environment. As very young explorers, they gather information by using their senses and, as their physical and cognitive development continues, they collect more sophisticated information that connects their tangible physical world. Children use their accumulated information as a foundation for making decisions about new objects and spectacles, and new data are added to their growing understanding.

While children examine their environment, adults should prompt, question, and support their investigations. As children become aware of the patterns and logical order, they engage in prediction and hypothesis development. Children then develop awareness of the relationships between objects and phenomena. In other words, investigation and inquiry help student understand how objects form structures and how those structures can be interrelated to form systems.

Play and science are both grounded in observation and exploration; they both provide children opportunities to study themselves and their own world. The scientific inquiry process engages

HOME AND COMMUNITY CONNECTIONS

Implementing Play Activities in the Science Center

Nature Walk: Using an empty toilet paper roll or paper towel roll go outside and have your children observe their yard. Use the roll as a telescope to see the items more closely. Ask them, *What do you observe?*

children in activities that require them to think and speak as if they are scientists. A natural outgrowth of young children's investigations is their quest to pursue further investigations and yet more questions. Developing inquiry skills such as "What would happen if . . . ," or "If I did this, then that would happen," or "The difference between this and that is . . ." are also skills needed for academic success. Integrating science activities throughout children's daily classroom activities motivates them to seek answers to questions related to the everyday happenings that they encounter.

CHAPTER 11 FIRST-PERSON INTERVIEW

Children Leading Their Own Learning

Sandra Mora

Teacher at a parent-participation family learning center, Pasadena, CA

At our center, we work with the parents and children together. All parents are required to participate in our program. They volunteer time in the classroom with the child, participate in a parenting class, and take a language course. If their English is proficient, they take a course at the local community college. It's an amazing program because we are all learning. Naturally, the children are learning from their peers and adults in the classroom, while the adults are picking up relevant parenting skills from their peers and the center's staff. Finally, the staff is learning all the time from the children and their parents, how we can better serve our community.

Because we all understand the true value of continual learning and working together, there is no division that can sometimes develop between teachers and parents when there is a conflict between what the parent is doing and what a staff member might think the parent should be doing. Instead of just offering suggestions when I see a parent struggling with his or her child over something, I find myself saying, "Let me help you with that" and getting in and guiding the parent. We are very open and truly are a team of learners, and I just love it!

At the center, we are attempting to integrate more and more of the techniques used in the Reggio Emilia programs. We have made a lot of progress, but you can never feel as if you have done it all.

The other day, because it had just become December, a teacher brought in a lot of Christmas tree limbs and trunks that were about 8 inches tall and had been sawed off of trees. She just went by a tree lot and asked them for the pieces that were going to be thrown away. In the morning we set them out on the table and watched to see what the children did with them. Our goal was not to teach the children about trees but, instead, to provoke the children and let them lead their own learning and create their own project. We put magnifying glasses and tape measures on the table with them.

After a couple of days, some children showed an interest in examining the surface texture of the limbs. Others were using prior knowledge and counting the rings to determine the age of the tree pieces. Gradually, the children really got into it and started feeling them, smelling them, visually examining them, and experimenting with them. Eventually, some of the children began measuring them with the tape measure and talking about the different thicknesses and lengths. They began to feel excited and proud of their discoveries, and they were sharing what they were learning with each other.

This activity was interesting to use because a few months earlier, one of the teachers had to do a "measuring with your feet" activity with the children for an assignment for a class that the

(Continued)

(Continued)

teacher was taking. We thought it was a great activity, but because of the assignment deadline, we had to encourage the children to do this activity right then and couldn't wait for them to be ready for it, like we did with the Christmas tree pieces. Well, it really did not work out. The children did not appear that interested in the activity and didn't make any connections from the activity to other things that they do.

However, through the activity with the tree trunks and branches, we all learned that you have to wait and watch the children and, eventually, if you trust them, they will expand their knowledge with items that they have access to in the classroom. Often, if you push them too hard, as we did with the "measuring with the feet" activity, we find that the real learning just does not happen.

Sample Learning Activities

Curricular Area: Science

Core Vocabulary: Observe, discover, explore, question, living things, animals, plants, people, five senses: see, hear, feel, taste, smell

Guide Questions:

What questions do you have about . . . ?

What do you observe?

How do things work?

What have you discovered about . . . ?

What are you interested in learning about?

How can we learn about something new?

Resources:

Baby Animals (Kingfisher Series)

Baby Animals in the Snow

Baby Animals in the Jungle

I Wonder Why Series

I Wonder Why Penguins Can't Fly, by Pat Jacobs

I Wonder Why Snakes Shed Their Skin and Other Questions About Reptiles, by Amanda O'Neill

I Wonder Why Stars Twinkle, by Carole Stott

Jenkins, Steve. (2003). *What Do You Do With a Tail Like This?* Houghton Mifflin.

Martin, Bill. (1991). *Polar Bear, Polar Bear What Do You Hear?* Henry Holt and Co.

Rosenthal, Amy Krouse. (2011). *Plant a Kiss,* HarperCollins.

Core Text: Where's My Mom? by Julia Donaldson

- Skills: Prediction, description (animals), types of sentences and punctuation (questions and exclamations), rhyming, life cycles
- Levels of Questions: Who was looking for his mom? Who helped the monkey? Which animals and insects did he meet along the way? Describe those animals. Why didn't the butterfly know the monkey's mom looks like him? What is a "baby" butterfly? Why do you think the baby got lost? What should you do if you're lost?
- Product: Animal collage, animal matching (baby and adult animals), animal parade (students pretend to be animals)

Learning Centers:

- Explore through literacy: Provide an abundance of books and other resources such as pamphlets and magazines about animals.
- Create: Magazines, Internet sources, coloring books and other sources with pictures of animals that students can cut up to create a collage. Paper, scissors, glue, and construction paper or tag board.
- Outdoor Play: Magnifying glasses to let students explore their outside world. Ask questions as they explore—What do you see? What do you wonder about . . . ? What are you observing?
- Dramatic Play: At the zoo—Zoo Tour Guide, Exhibit presenter

Student Study Site

Visit the Student Study Site at **www.sagepub.com/selmi** to access additional study tools including mobile-friendly eFlashcards and links to video and web resources.

Key Terms

big ideas	planned inquiry activities
horizontal curriculum integration	scientific inquiry process
iterative process	vertical curriculum integration

Useful Websites

Connecting science, math, and play: http://www.naeyc.org/books/from_play_to_practice/excerpt

NAEYC/Science: http://www.naeyc.org/files/yc/file/200911/BosseWeb1109.pdf

National Research Council (NRC): http://www.nationalacademies.org/nrc/

Next Generation of Science Standards: http://www.nextgenscience.org

Reflective Questions

Young children are always asking causal questions using the word "Why?" Research appears to suggest that children ask these questions precisely when they are in the process of developing more complex knowledge structures (Chouinard, Harris, & Maratsos, 2007). Pretend that your classroom has a balance scale out for the children to use when they need information that it can produce. Read the *First-Person Interview* for this chapter. What are some questions that children might pose that could be answered by using a balance scale? How would you encourage children to observe, predict, and record information related to these questions?

12 Integrating Play Activities in the Mathematics Centers

"REMEMBER TO USE THE DATA SHEETS"

Jupiterimages/Goodshoot/Think stock

Three boys are playing with magnetic tiles in the manipulative toy center. Two of the boys are creating what appear to be spaceship-like objects. They are also discussing how to use "tall and short triangles," "large and small squares," and "constructing sides that are the same," and they are modifying their shapes so the "object can be balanced." After completing their creations, they begin walking around the area, moving their spaceships up and down while making sounds that represent those that could come from an aircraft. The third boy sits off to the side attempting to put together some of the magnetic tiles while periodically watching the other two boys.

One of the boys with a spaceship says to the other boy with the spaceship, "Let's play a game. I will look out for the monster." The other boy appears to agree and moves away from his partner, circling the area with his spaceship. The first boy, who is looking out for the monster, confines himself to a small area, moving his spaceship up and down and from side to side. When the other boy returns from traveling around the center, the boy keeping watch announces, "Everything's okay." The traveling boy takes off again, and this pattern of play continues for about a minute. The boy who is keeping watch then says, "Okay, I'm done." He puts his spaceship down on the floor and walks over to another area of the room.

Sometime later, when the learning center time was up, the teacher announced to the class, "Remember, if you created an object with the manipulatives and still have it, please take it apart and, before you put the pieces away, complete our Data Sheet that tells us what you used to make it. Also, remember to put an 'l' next to the number if the shape was large and an 's' next to the number if the shape was small. I will be over in the Manipulatives Center to assist any of you who might want help with the data sheets."

Playing with manipulative objects, known as "manipulatives," requires children to imagine, create, and explore objects and to move them through space. Many of these types of activities afford children opportunities to design objects that are either familiar to human beings or that are unique to images in the children's minds. As they build and move their objects, children are also involved in making spatial judgments that allow them to become more aware of concepts such as balance, depth, length, and width, and that familiarize them with part-to-whole relationships. These concepts also develop as children engage in other developmentally appropriate activities, such as building with blocks and designing and creating woodcraft objects. All of these activities also encourage children to classify, measure, order, and count items with which they are engaged.

Thus, when children create structures or objects with blocks, pieces of wood, or other manipulative items, they can learn how to interpret information from their senses, solve problems, and think logically. They also enhance their language and social skills, and develop foundational concepts for mathematics and early literacy learning (see Figure 12.1).

This chapter's opening scenario demonstrates how children not only enjoy designing and creating objects but also engage in meaningful social pretend interactions with peers during these processes. The chapter will address the importance of children being involved with manipulative creations that enhance concepts of mathematics. It also will suggest techniques that assist them in participating in playful social interactions while involved in these activities, so that children are self-motivated to enhance their mathematical abilities. The everyday lives of young children are filled with natural mathematical activities. Some examples are, counting steps as they go up and down them, classifying their toys, drawing a map to a hidden treasure, measuring water and sand, and moving their bodies using specific movement patterns. Specifically, this chapter will address the following questions:

> What early mathematics skills would be important for children to learn?

> How are early mathematics and play abilities common?

> How can mathematics skills be expanded through playful uses of blocks, commercial manipulatives, everyday manipulatives, and wooden creations?

Developing Early Mathematics Skills

Children tend to develop mathematical concepts at a very young age. Reflect back on Chapter 1 of this book, which presented research findings by Xu and Garcia (2008) on how children around 8 months of age are capable of determining the probability of remaining colored balls.

Although research has concluded that young children are self-motivated to learn mathematics concepts through participation in everyday, child-centered activities, the use today of manipulatives, such as those mentioned in the scenario above, and blocks are ignored in many early childhood classrooms. Instead, many classrooms now emphasize

Figure 12.1 Development and Learning Skills From Block, Manipulative, and Wood Play

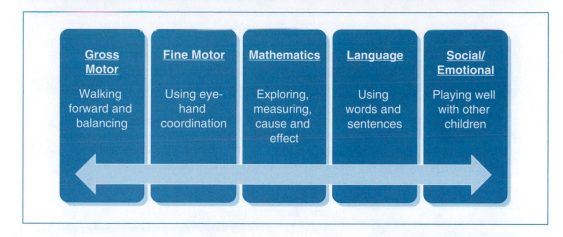

Gross Motor	Fine Motor	Mathematics	Language	Social/Emotional
Walking forward and balancing	Using eye-hand coordination	Exploring, measuring, cause and effect	Using words and sentences	Playing well with other children

having children recite rote counting, memorize mathematics facts, and drill mathematics concepts. In these early education classrooms, blocks and manipulatives are just items that children can play with once they have completed their "math work" and demonstrated their ability to be successful in teacher-directed rote activities that usually involve numbers.

Early mathematics skills, however, do not merely concern learning numbers and methods of combining them. Instead, a large portion of early mathematics focuses on a far-reaching understanding of abstractions and generalizations that assist young children in connecting ideas, developing logical thinking, and analyzing events that occur in the world around them. For example, having children measure the length of a long block bridge structure by using bananas and then by using lemons can assist with counting and also with discussions about the differences in numbers and the reasons for those differences.

According to Copley (2010), being proficient in mathematics involves children feeling comfortable with using five mathematical processes. Children must be able to implement *problem-solving* and *reasoning* skills. Next, children must be capable of *communicating* with mathematical terms when explaining what they have done or are thinking of doing. Finally, mathematical *concepts* must be understood and connected to the use of mathematical *representations*, such as numbers, patterns, and mathematical operations. Figure 12.2 provides examples of the five processes and describes how these processes can be enhanced in sociodramatic play activities.

Additionally, Copley recommends that children develop an understanding of five basic mathematical content areas: (1) numbers and operations, (2) patterns, functions, and algebra, (3) geometry and spatial sense, (4) measurement, and (5) data analysis and probability. Examples of these skills are provided in Figure 12.3 and later in this chapter.

Mathematics activities can be integrated into most daily activities. Math concepts can be expanded through very simple activities while children are lining up to go outside by talking about the different heights of the children, the number of children wearing brown socks, counting how many groups of five children the class can be divided into, discussing the time of day, and analyzing the temperatures outside and inside the classroom. Additionally, at snack time flip cards with pictures of "recipes" can be used for the snacks. If the children are to have four crackers for a snack, they can search through the recipes for the card that has the number "4" on it and a picture of four crackers. Simple everyday activities such as these make children feel comfortable with mathematic concepts and help them realize how useful these concepts can be to them.

Figure 12.2   Mathematics Processes: Everyday Examples and Socio-Dramatic Play Examples

Problem Solving	• <u>Everyday Example:</u> Children making sure there are enough materials for everyone. • <u>Play Example:</u> Standing outside the pretend bus with hand out for the fare.
Reasoning	• <u>Everyday Example:</u> Classifying objects with multiple similar attributes. • <u>Play Example:</u> Making sure each stuffed animal at the Pet Store has water.
Communicate	• <u>Everyday Example:</u> Explaining answers using graphs, diagrams, charts, and symbols • <u>Play Example:</u> Telling the patient that he or she needs to take larger spoonfuls of the medicine.
Connections	• <u>Everyday Example:</u> Understanding concepts and their impact on everyday activities. • <u>Play Example:</u> Putting two triangle blocks together to make a turret for a castle.
Representations	• <u>Everyday Example:</u> Creating a map of a proposed new learning center. • <u>Play Example:</u> Drawing a map for finding the hidden treasure.

Source: Copley, J. V. (2010). *The Young Child and Mathematics*. Washington, DC: National Association for the Education of Young Children.

Mathematics Challenge: Amount of Time Spent on Mathematics

The National Council of Teachers of Mathematics (NCTM) reported that a number of early childhood curricula that claim to be "complete" programs dedicate only about 58 seconds a day to mathematics (Kepner, 2010). Additionally, this research found that these programs do not continue to advance children's knowledge and reasoning abilities to higher levels; rather, they merely repeat concepts that children already know using varied strategies.

The NCTM is also alarmed by the findings that, generally, children from low socioeconomic backgrounds enter preschool being at risk in the area of mathematics by having abilities that are not as high as those of their peers from higher socioeconomic backgrounds. It cautions that early education professionals are responsible for designing ways in which all young children can interact with mathematics concepts in developmentally appropriate ways so that they can learn about their world and expand their thinking skills.

In play activities using blocks, manipulatives, and wood, and interacting with their peers while doing so, children naturally compare qualities of items, identify patterns, move through space, and problem solve. Additionally, by having data sheets in the opening scenario for children to complete, they are provided with opportunities to further use numbers and size in a real-life and self-motivating situation.

Figure 12.3 Activities Occurring in Mathematics Content Areas

The simple implementation of a data collection binder to the manipulatives center allowed the children to expand their knowledge by:

- Counting and understand "how many"
- Writing numerals
- Adding by counting the total number of large and small similar shapes
- Recognizing and learning the names of shapes
- Combining shapes to make other shapes
- Recognizing different shape attributes
- Recognizing relationships between size and quantity
- Noticing patterns
- Analyzing data

Additionally, to successfully develop skills in these common core areas, Van de Walle, Lovin, Karp, and Williams (2013) recommend that teachers embrace the following responsibilities (p. 13):

- Design high-quality tasks that allow children to use their own strategies to learn mathematics skills,
- Ask high-quality questions encouraging children to verify the strategies that they are using, and
- Listen to children's responses and extend and formalize their thinking processes.

Through the use of these three recommended responsibilities, which appear to be different from those that are presented in many preschool curricula, children can successfully achieve higher level mathematical knowledge and reasoning skills. Additionally, these three responsibilities are similar to the guided-play strategies presented in Chapter 8 of this book. Examples of guided prompts for specific mathematics are presented in Figure 12.4.

Figure 12.4　Examples of Teachers' Guiding Prompts

Clarifying Ideas	• "So, both of you used the same number of squares for your different looking objects?" • "Who used the most pieces, and is the one with the most pieces bigger than the other ones?"
Emphasizing Reasoning	• "What would happen if...?" • "Why does it make sense that the larger object has fewer pieces?"
Encourage Student-Student Dialogue	• "Why don't you two discuss your ideas and come back to me with one answer?" • "Could you look in the Data Book to see who made a similar object and ask them what they did?"

Source: Van de Walle, J. A., Lovin, L. A. H., Karp, K. H., & Williams, J. M. B. (2013). *Teaching Student-Centered Mathematics: Developmentally Appropriate Instruction for Grades Pre K–2* (Vol. I). New York, NY: Pearson.

In 2002, the NAEYC and the NCTM published the position paper *Early Childhood Mathematics: Promoting Good Beginnings*. This paper asserts that mathematics is as critical to early childhood experiences as are reading and writing. Young children take a natural interest in mathematical concepts as they attempt to make sense of the world around them. Throughout their day, they encounter situations that require problem-solving and reasoning abilities. These skills further transfer to students' literacy development as they apply these skills when reading and making meaning of text. Therefore, early childhood professionals should continually expose children throughout the day to activities that require them to use mathematical concepts, methods, and language. Figure 12.5 summarizes 10 recommendations from NCTM and NAEYC for a high-quality early mathematics education.

One of these recommendations—to provide ample "time, materials, and teacher support for children to engage in play, a context in which they explore and manipulate mathematical ideas with keen interest"—relates to the heart of this chapter. While children are involved in play interactions that focus on mathematical activities, teachers can guide their learning by asking questions like:

- How did you decide to do that?
- Can you tell me more about what you are doing?
- How do you know if that is the correct answer?
- Does this activity remind you of another activity that you have already done?
- Did you try some things that did not work? If so, why don't you think they worked in this situation?

Conceptually, questions such as these further support students' literacy development as well. They are often asked to explain their reading and writing processes. They justify their decisions and thinking and make comparisons across texts. These cognitively similar learning

Figure 12.5 Recommendations From NCTM and NAEYC for Early Childhood Mathematics (2010)

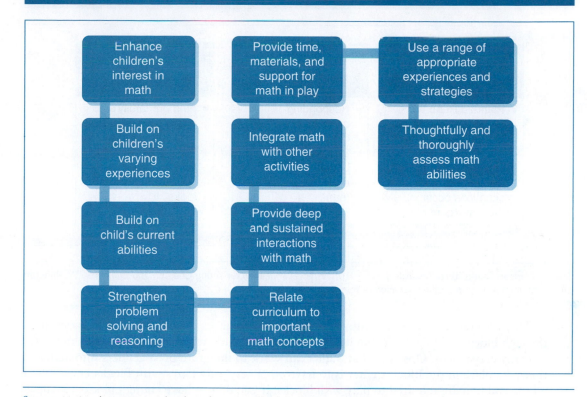

Source: National Association for the Education of Young Children (NAEYC) and the National Council of Teachers of Mathematics (NCTM). (2002/2010). *Early Childhood Mathematics: Promoting Good Beginnings.* Retrieved from http://www.naeyc.org/files/naeyc/file/positions/psmath.pdf.

experiences across math and literacy set a strong foundation for academic language. Students learn that thinking and language transfer across the curriculum when asked to think about content in similar ways.

Mathematics Challenge: Gender-Biased Issues

According to Derman-Sparks and Edwards (2010), children around the age of 2 years begin to notice physical differences and to describe themselves as being either a boy or girl. By about the age of 3, children begin to identify specific behaviors with specific genders. For example, children will state to a boy, "You're playing with a doll. You're a girl." By the age of 4, children will begin asserting gender role behaviors that are stereotypical, such as "Girls can't play here" or "Boys can't do this."

Similarly, many families tend to draw boys' attention to number concepts far more often than they do girls' (Chen, 2010). Research states that the use of cardinal numbers in speech to boys as young as 22 months of age can be three times more than their use to girls. For example, mothers tend to say to boys, "Look at these two cars" or "Here are three grapes" much more than they would say these phrases to girls.

Three ways of developing a healthy, non-biased gender approach in an early education classroom is to engage in the following activities: (1) have gender discussions about differences in anatomy, (2) be responsive to children's questions about anatomy differences, and (3) work with families on understanding ways to help their children form healthy gender identities (Derman-Sparks & Edwards, 2010). Figure 12.6 presents examples of these activities.

Figure 12.6   Strategies for Assisting Children in Understanding Gender Anatomy and Identity

Discussions on Gender Anatomy	Distinguishing Between Anatomy and Identity	Work Sensitively With Families
• Planned Read Alouds using books that address gender issues • Unplanned discussions when situations occur in the classroom	• Responding honestly to children's questions • Showing respect for bodies by using standard anatomical terms	• Find out family's views on gender and ways they address it • Have a clear idea of how a gender-equitable classroom looks

Source: Derman-Sparks, L., & Edwards, J. O. (2010). *Anti-bias Education for Young Children and Ourselves.* Washington, DC: National Association for the Education of Young Children.

This chapter later presents information on the value of developing mathematics skills through block building. Unfortunately, block play currently tends to be very male dominated in many classrooms. One way that adults can work to integrate both genders into activities that take place in the Block Center is to have an "Everybody Plays with Blocks Day," where all the children are required to play with blocks. If you do not have enough blocks to engage everyone, collaborate with another teacher to use the blocks from that classroom. If both of you schedule this type of day on different days, both will have access to double the amount of regularly available blocks.

If problems continue with having females comfortably participate in activities at the block center, the adults can declare one day a week as "Only Girls Play" during block time. This is also a good time to have open discussions with the class about all children needing to participate in block activities in the classroom. According to Derman-Sparks and Edwards (2010), "girls only" days are usually successful and can produce profound changes in a short period of time.

REFLECT AND APPLY EXERCISE 12.1

Non-Gender-Biased Field Trips

Reflect

You are working in an early education class where you have observed some actions and statements among the children reflecting gender bias. You have a plan to work with your staff on modeling acceptable behavior and language, and a plan for working with the children's families.

Apply

You also want to take your children on field trips to local places that do not demonstrate gender bias. Think of some places that you could take them and what would assist them in developing non-gender biases.

Mathematics and Play

Through the use of guided play (see Chapter 8) that includes carefully planned activities that are sensitive to children's learning needs, adults can prompt young children to successfully advance their mathematical thinking. Such interviews will provide children with the understanding of how mathematical activities relate to their everyday lives. For example, when children are playing in the playhouse, just suggesting the use of place settings for all children could expand the following mathematics skills: one-to-one correspondence, patterning, and counting.

Interestingly, the passage of No Child Left Behind in 2001 and the dominating focus on early literacy development have led to a decrease in both play and mathematics activities in early childhood programs. With very constricted daily schedules, some teachers are concerned that engaging in mathematics will decrease the amount of time that children devote to language and literacy activities. However, mathematics proponents respond that mathematics is similar to literacy development in a number of ways (Sarama, Lange, Clements, & Wolfe, 2012).

First, around the age of 2, children tend to naturally learn number words at the same time that they are learning other words—including colors, foods, toys, and family members. As children develop, they know which words are number words. They also use them appropriately in the correct contexts, similar to the way they use other new vocabulary words.

Second, literacy requires children first to learn a concept, then a word, then the syllables of the word, and finally the letters that make up the word. Similarly, children learn numbers by first learning about the concept of numbers and then learning about the different composites of numbers that can make up that number. By the age of 6, most children realize that words are created out of single letters and that numbers are composed of different combinations of other numbers.

Third, as discussed in Chapters 4 and 10, children create play narratives at a very young age. These narratives exhibit the ability to identify the main events of a story in an orderly fashion and then to predict specific outcomes. Similarly, mathematics involves putting pieces of information together in an orderly fashion and predicting further outcomes, such as identifying different types of patterns.

Finally, literacy skills involve distinguishing between letters of the alphabet and the sounds they produce. Interestingly, alphabet letters are made up of different geometric configurations. For example, a "b" is made up of a straight line and a circle on the bottom right side, whereas a "q" is made up of a circle with a straight line on the right side going downward. These shapes and directions are based on mathematical concepts of shape, placement, and direction (Andersen, Andersen, & Shapiro, 2005).

Figure 12.7 summarizes the similarities between literacy and mathematics skill development. Understandably, most children who have a delay in attaining literacy skills also have a delay in the development of mathematics.

Literacy and mathematics share many similar developmental characteristics, and literacy skills can be developed through play activities. Accordingly, it is readily understandable that play is also a developmentally appropriate practice for the acquisition of mathematics skills. Additionally, there is no evidence that focusing on the development of mathematics skills will negatively impact the learning of literacy skills (Sarama et al., 2012).

Socio-dramatic play areas are places where numerous mathematics concepts can be integrated and children can learn to use number, patterning, measurement, geometric, and data analysis collection skills in everyday activities. Figure 12.8 lists the 20 play themes that were stated in the previous chapter and mathematics skills that are naturally associated with these themes.

Figure 12.7   Similarities Between Literacy and Mathematics Skill Development

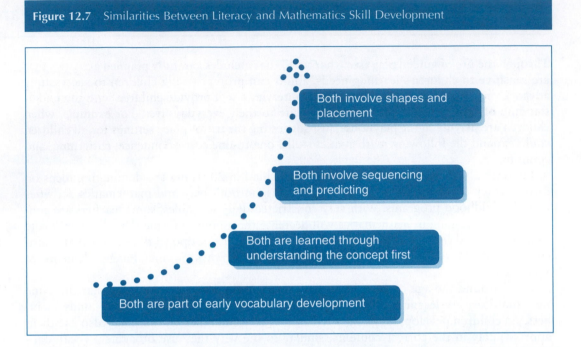

Both involve shapes and placement

Both involve sequencing and predicting

Both are learned through understanding the concept first

Both are part of early vocabulary development

Figure 12.8   Mathematics Activities for Different Play Themes

Play Theme	Realistic Objects
Bank	Money, safe combinations, check writing, deposits, loans, budget
Beach	Temperature, distance, tide, rentals, sand castles, waves
Beauty Salon	Appointments, money, tips, cash register, length, shampoo amounts
Camping	Distances, supplies, campfire, compass, map, directions, fire danger
Car Wash	Money, specials, receipts, cash register, gasoline, tips
Fire Station	Maps, helmet number, length of hose, alarms, gloves
Gas Station	Money, gallons, amount of air, oil quarts, receipts, mini-market
Hardware Store	Cash registers, number of items, categories, patterns, balancing
Medical Center	Appointments, x-rays, bills, number of pills, amount of ointment
Outer Space	Countdown, weight, time, orbits, controls
Paint Store	Paint numbers, measuring, patterns, gallons, quarts, specials
Photo Studio	Film numbers, picture sizes, specials, bills, computers
Pizza Parlor	Cash register, sizes, phone, pizza shapes, number of toppings
Post Office	Stamps, scale, number of items, sizes, prices, lengths, addresses
Rock Store	Cash register, order pads, scale, number, categories, flyers
Shoe Store	Sizes, pairing, sales receipts, sale signs, price tags, balancing
Theater	Tickets, money, times, candy/sodas sales, prices
Travel Agency	Tickets, times, maps, schedules, passports, time changes, trip lengths
Veterinarian Office	Prescriptions, cages per animal, x-rays, schedule, appointments
Zoo	Tickets, prices, feeding schedules, stands, sizes of enclosures

Guiding Mathematics Skills With Learning Standards

Head Start Mathematics Elements

Along with understanding traditional development of number concepts and operations, the Head Start Framework (Head Start, 2011) calls for children in early childhood programs to learn mathematical concepts such as geometry and spatial sense, patterns, and measurement. All of these concepts can be developed through young children's participation in play activities. The following are the specific Head Start Mathematical Elements that children need to learn during their preschool years.

Number Concepts and Quantities. Young children can understand that numbers reflect specific quantities and represent a certain order, a particular size, or a position on a list. According to Clements and Sarama (2009), children should be encouraged to enhance the following four characteristics of early number knowledge:

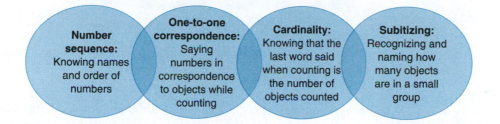

In the opening scenario, the children were asked to record the number of pieces that they used to create an object. This activity enhanced their ability to count in sequence and use one-to-one correspondence. Additionally, by recording the total number that they used to create a geometric figure, they were enhancing the characteristics of cardinality and subitizing.

Clements and Sarama (2007) have found that some young children can recognize quantities that are three or less without counting. Figure 12.9 illustrates what researchers have discovered when it comes to approximate ages and number-counting skills.

Number Relationships and Operations. The children in the opening scenario could have engaged in number-relationship activities by comparing the different objects and the number of pieces needed. Similarly, children could participate in similar discussions when designing block formations and creating wood structures.

The following are two skills that contribute to understanding number relationships:

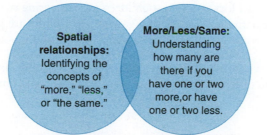

Typical activities that expand children's understanding of number relationships and operations are the following: bar graphs, board games with a spinner or dice, scales, stacking cups to make a pyramid, abacus, and small counters such as bears, fruits, animals, and insects.

Figure 12.9   Number and Counting Skills and Approximate Ages

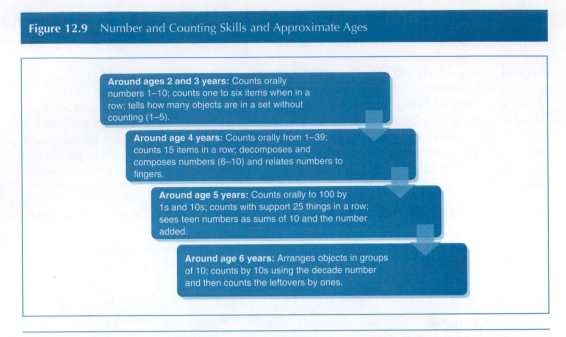

Around ages 2 and 3 years: Counts orally numbers 1–10; counts one to six items when in a row; tells how many objects are in a set without counting (1–5).

Around age 4 years: Counts orally from 1–39; counts 15 items in a row; decomposes and composes numbers (6–10) and relates numbers to fingers.

Around age 5 years: Counts orally to 100 by 1s and 10s; counts with support 25 things in a row; sees teen numbers as sums of 10 and the number added.

Around age 6 years: Arranges objects in groups of 10; counts by 10s using the decade number and then counts the leftovers by ones.

Source: National Research Council. (2009). *Mathematics Learning in Early Childhood: Paths Toward Excellence and Equality.* Washington, DC: The National Academies Press.

Geometry and Spatial Sense. Many play activities provide children multiple opportunities to explore shapes of objects and the properties of those shapes, as well as how these objects relate to one another. Van de Walle et al. (2013) suggest that geometry involves the following aspects:

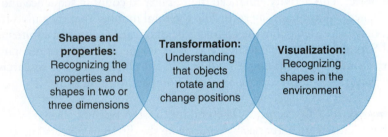

Shapes and properties: Recognizing the properties and shapes in two or three dimensions

Transformation: Understanding that objects rotate and change positions

Visualization: Recognizing shapes in the environment

Again, the children in the opening scenario were arranging different shapes into other shapes, experimenting with turning shapes in different directions to create a larger imagined object, and recording the various sizes and shapes needed to complete their object. Figure 12.10 includes examples of how blocks can assist children in discovering two- and three-dimensional shapes. Other popular activities that encourage geometric skills are geocards, geometry hopscotch, shape hunts, Legos, foam shapes, color/shape bingo, and wooden pattern blocks.

Patterns. When they work with patterns, children are learning different designs that are sequenced in a specific order, and they are predicting what will come next in the pattern.

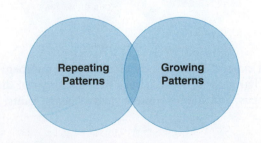

Repeating Patterns

Growing Patterns

Figure 12.10 Using Blocks to Create Geometric Shapes

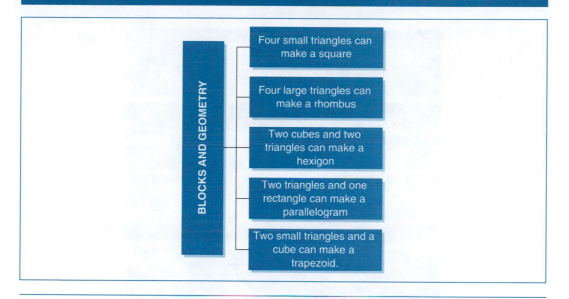

Source: Copley, J. V. (2010). *The Young Child and Mathematics*. Washington, DC: National Association for the Education of Young Children.

As young children become more aware of shapes in their environment, they begin to see specific patterns. These geometric patterns can either be *repeating patterns* or *growing patterns*. Repeating patterns are ones that repeat a core set of shapes. A growing pattern produces a progressive pattern from one step to another. Figure 12.11 has examples of these types of patterns. Figure 12.12 provides 10 examples of how to tie a play theme in with patterning. Finally, children enjoy enhancing their patterning skills by stringing beads, playing with pattern blocks, tic-tac-toe games, stacking items, with art projects, Unifix cubes, and movement sequences.

According to Geist, Geist, and Kuznik (2012), teaching patterns to young children is a key concept in emergent mathematics, which parallels the idea of emergent literacy. Emergent mathematics suggests that:

- Mathematical learning begins early in life.
- Mathematics is related to other developmental milestones.
- Mathematics develops from real-life situations.
- Children learn mathematics through actively engaging their minds in many different ways.
- Thinking about relationships plays a special role in children's mathematical development.
- Learning mathematics is a developmental process that is nurtured by stimulating mathematical environments.

Figure 12.11 Different Types of Patterns

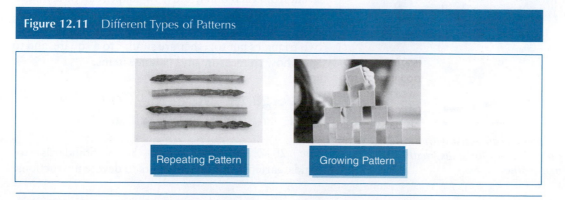

Sources: Blue Jeans Images/Photodisc/Thinkstock; Comstock Images/Stockbyte/Thinkstock.

Figure 12.12   Examples of Integrating Mathematics Activities Into Centers

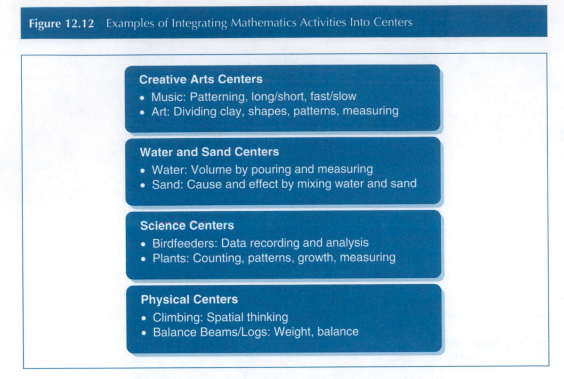

Creative Arts Centers
- Music: Patterning, long/short, fast/slow
- Art: Dividing clay, shapes, patterns, measuring

Water and Sand Centers
- Water: Volume by pouring and measuring
- Sand: Cause and effect by mixing water and sand

Science Centers
- Birdfeeders: Data recording and analysis
- Plants: Counting, patterns, growth, measuring

Physical Centers
- Climbing: Spatial thinking
- Balance Beams/Logs: Weight, balance

Many mathematical skills are expanded through playing simple board games that use manipulatives and allow children to recognize the numbers on the dice, relate those numbers to the number of spaces that they can move, and realize that each movement brings them closer to a desired goal. Finally, they learn how to use game-playing language such as turn-taking, being the "winner" or "loser," or even having a "tie" game.

As children explore and talk about patterns, they continue to build the academic language they will use across the curriculum when working with patterns. Understanding patterns will support students' thinking when reading and writing in other content areas. These rich conceptual experiences in mathematics prepare children for thinking about other content.

Mathematics activities can be integrated into all learning centers so that children will enhance their skills through self-motivated, playful, peer interactions. Figure 12.13 provides suggestions of some activities that can occur in typical early education learning centers.

The last half of this chapter will discuss how children can directly interact with manipulatives, blocks, wood pieces, and manipulative games to gain an understanding of mathematics concepts. For example, blocks can assist children in learning how shapes are similar and different from each other, and how shapes can be arranged in a certain order to accomplish a specific design task. Additionally, children can use blocks to understand that two triangles put together are similar to a square, and to learn how to measure and balance items.

Kindergarten Common Core State Mathematics Standards

©iStockphoto.com/diane39

Simple board games can assist with the development of fine motor skills, mathematics skills, and many other skills.

The 2012 Common Core State Standards for Kindergarten encourage teachers to devote instructional

Figure 12.13 Use of Manipulatives With Play Themes

Play Theme	Manipulatives
Astronauts	Rockets, stars/planets, moon boots
Car wash/auto shop	Miniature cars, traffic signs, money
Fishing	Fishes, bobbers, nets/poles, worms
Hair Stylist	Combs/brushes, colored clips
Housekeeping	Keys, cups, utensils, food items
Painter	Colors, brushes with paint on them
Pizza Parlor	Boxes, toppings, pizza sizes, money
Post Office	Stamps, packages, pieces of string
Wedding	Veils/bow ties, flowers, rings, cakes
Zoo Keeper	Animals, foods, tickets, workers

time to two critical areas of mathematics: (1) the representation, relation, and operation of whole numbers, initially with sets of objects; and (2) descriptions of shapes and how they can be used in spaces. These standards encourage dedicating more learning time during kindergarten to numbers than to other areas of skill development in mathematics. Through continual engagement with blocks, manipulatives, and woodcrafts, kindergarteners can participate in mathematics activities that enrich their understanding of counting, number operations, measurement, data collection, and geometry.

Participation in activities involving blocks, manipulatives, and wood allows children to practice counting and comparing numbers. Specifically, block structures require children to count the number of blocks and reproduce an equal number on the other side in order to have a balanced structure. Children can use measurement data, such as length or weight, to create structural foundations that will support further additions. By manipulating geometric wooden blocks and carefully placing them in positions in space, children build two- and three-dimensional creations.

©iStock.com/BrianAJackson

Children engage in complex mathematics activities while involved in playful activities.

Block Centers

Block building has been a part of children's play for well over a century. Wooden blocks have been commercially produced in the United States since shortly after the Civil War (Hewitt, 2001). The first blocks produced were similar to the ones used today. Block construction activities have always been intended to educate children. The first wooden blocks displayed symbols such as letters, words, or short narratives.

For over a hundred years, children have enjoyed playing with blocks.

Today, along with the traditional wooden building blocks, other blocks are available that are made out of various types of materials. Contemporary blocks include hollow wooden blocks, cardboard blocks, plastic blocks, foam blocks, and stacking/nesting blocks. There are also wooden people, vehicles, and storefronts that accompany the blocks, and the availability of these items encourages children to integrate socio-dramatic play activities into block constructions.

As Figure 12.14 illustrates, blocks can be used by people of all ages, starting at infancy and continuing through adulthood. With the introduction in 1949 of the Lego, which is a combination of a block and a manipulative, block building has become a hobby for people of all ages. Research has now confirmed that block building enhances skills in multiple developmental and learning areas. Clark (2009), in *The Integrative Education Model*, explains, "Making movement and physical encoding a part of the learning experience results in better retention of information and a deeper level of understanding" (p. 146).

Developmental Stages of Block Play

When children play with blocks, they typically progress through specific and recognizable stages of development. Early education professionals need to be familiar with this sequence so that they can (1) provide developmentally appropriate materials and (2) advance the children's skills by scaffolding their interactions with the blocks. The stages through which children progress are:

Stage 1: Gathering, Carrying, and Dumping Blocks. At about two years of age, children become interested in block play. This development occurs at the same time that children start intentionally moving items around in their immediate environment. During the first stage of block play, children are not interested in building structures. Instead, they engage in hands-on activities that allow them to gather sensory information about the blocks.

Stage 2: Functional Use by Creating Rows and Stacking. As children further investigate the qualities and usefulness of blocks, they begin to use them as a "tool" for accomplishing certain tasks. At this stage, children typically place blocks flat on the floor and then put one next to another to create a row of two or three blocks. After realizing that they can accomplish this task, they begin to extend their rows farther and farther out, sometimes expanding them across a room. Next, children discover that they can stack one block on top of another to make a short tower.

The first activity of building with blocks typically involves creating a row or stack of blocks.

Stage 3: Bridging. Once children have become successful with stacking blocks, they start to construct bridges. This activity is complex due to the various balancing and spatial relationship skills required. Children must mathematically problem-solve by estimating how far apart to place the two support blocks and what size of connecting block to use. Bridging is the first activity in which children actually build a structure with blocks. It is also the first time that children intentionally use blocks to replicate a specific image from their minds.

REFLECT AND APPLY EXERCISE 12.2

Beyond Stacking and Crashing

Reflect

Two children in your class have been going to the block center every day for over two weeks. The only activity that they appear to engage in is stacking blocks and knocking them so that they crash over.

Apply

You would like to see them advance their skills. What would be some of the next skills that you would expect to see them display? How could you encourage them to develop these skills?

Figure 12.14   Use of Blocks at Different Developmental Ages

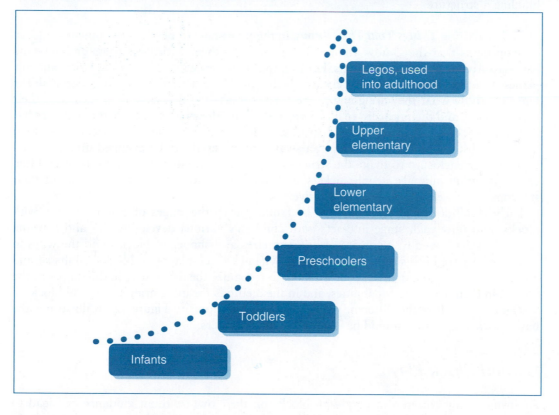

Stage 4: Enclosing. Once children begin to build regularly with blocks, they progress from constructing bridges to creating enclosures. Knowing how to make an enclosure provides children with a variety of options. Children quickly realize that they can increase the number of enclosures so they have multiple structures. Additionally, they learn that they can create enclosures in different sizes and different shapes—circular enclosures, rectangular enclosures, square enclosures, and triangular enclosures.

Children create complex stories to accompany their elaborate structures.

©iStockphoto.com/ johnbloor

Stage 5: Creating Complex Structures. At this stage, children truly enjoy creating intricate structures that usually include a variety of different types of arrangements. Children take great pride in the structures they build and in the structures' level of complexity. Plenty of space and time is needed for success at this stage; children cannot be cramped or rushed. Also, when some children have created a special structure that they are proud of, they enjoy having their structure remain intact the way they have created it for a longer period of time. They feel satisfied when they can return to the structure to make further modifications and additions. Therefore, allowing them to delay in the cleanup process is very appropriate.

Stage 6: Creating Socio-Dramatic Play Structures.
Once children have developed the skills necessary to build complex block structures—skills that most children become quite adept at—they then begin to label their structures with names. Children also start to integrate socio-dramatic play behaviors into their block play, a development that usually begins by children copying what construction workers do when building a structure.

Stage 7: Creating Things That They Know. In the final stage of block development, children develop items that they know about. They then share them with their peers and generate play narratives using their creations. For example, children will build houses, cities, and airplanes, and they will then become characters that use these structures. At this stage, children typically know what they are going to create, announce and negotiate their idea with their play partners, and then proceed to collaboratively build the structure. Once the structure has been created, children incorporate other objects and props into that structure, thus making it more realistic looking. For example, a swatch of material can be propped up and added to a circular enclosure to make the structure represent a circus tent. Additionally, children can then gather animals, people, tickets, and other items to enhance the meaning of their structure and to enrich their play narrative.

Early childhood professionals must be familiar with the stages of children's play with blocks, and how each stage interacts with children's various developmental and learning stages. Children need to be aware of different sizes and shapes of blocks, and the ways in which blocks are both similar and different. When children play with blocks, adults should continually talk to them and encourage them to recognize the differences in the shapes of the blocks, in their symbolic capabilities, and in the methods for integrating props and blocks.

Figure 12.15 lists the different stages of block development. Figure 12.16 illustrates the basic block shapes that should be included in block centers.

Guided Block Play

Allowing young children to play with blocks on their own without guidance can lead to unpleasant situations. Because of the skills needed to balance the blocks, reproduce a mental image, and communicate information about the structure, beginning block-builders left unassisted will often become frustrated with their unsuccessful attempts. In turn, their frustration will lead them to demolish their creation.

However, with guidance children can learn how to be successful in block building activities. The block center is an area where guidance can take place through questioning, scaffolding, and modeling (Park, Chae, & Boyd, 2008).

Figure 12.15   Stages of Block Play Development

Stage 1
- Gathering, Carrying, and Dumping

Stage 2
- Functional—Making Rows and Stacking

Stage 3
- Bridging

Stage 4
- Enclosing

Stage 5
- Creating Complex Structures

Stage 6
- Creating Dramatic Play Structures

Stage 7
- Creating Known Structures

Figure 12.16   Block Shapes and Storage

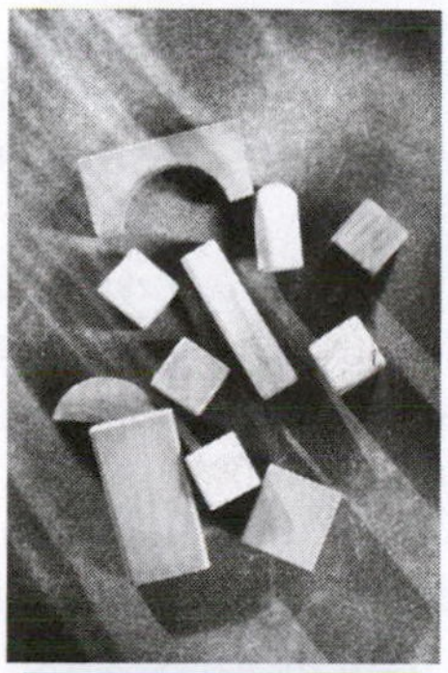

Basic Block Shapes

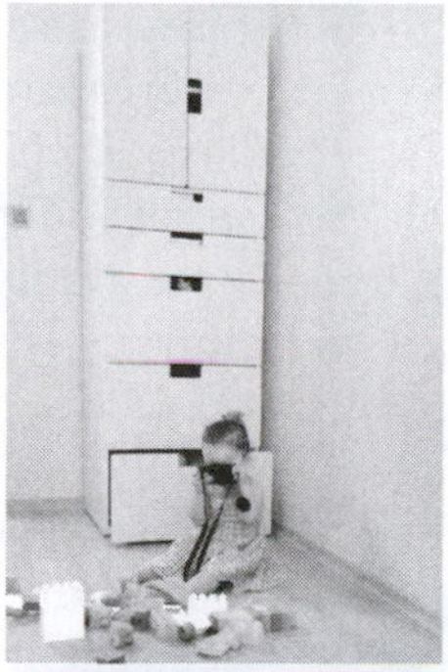

Appropriate Block Storage

Sources: Comstock Images/Stockbyte/Thinkstock; ©iStock.com/uchar.

The time and effort dedicated to supporting these various tasks with blocks—what the children can construct, where the construction activities will take place, what amount of time and space will be involved, and who will control the deconstruction of the structure—are part of guiding strategies that professionals can use. These strategies assist children

Children must have access to materials and enough space to create complex structures.

in producing high-quality block interactions and creations that enhance their social, motor, and academic abilities.

Creating a Mathematical Learning Environment With Blocks

As with all centers, special considerations must be evaluated and then implemented when designing the block center.

Location. Attention should be given to providing children with a definite space that is separated from the foot traffic of the classroom. Young children are typically unsteady on their feet. They can naturally stumble or trip when passing by and, in doing so, unintentionally knock over a structure that other children have created.

Similarly, the flooring that the students will use for block building needs to be secure and hard. Carpet makes it difficult to balance structures when building. If a classroom is carpeted, a piece of plywood, approximately 3 feet by 4 feet, should be provided to support the structures that each group of children is working on. These boards should be smoothly sanded on the sides and can be painted. If multiple boards are being concurrently used, ample space should be left between them so that children can freely move around to the different sides of their constructions.

Finally, block play can be a very noisy and exciting activity. Therefore, the center should be situated in a place near other noisy activities. Locating the block center near the book center would likely disturb those children who choose to relax and read a book. Placing the block center in the vicinity of the dramatic play center, which usually has a high level of activity and sounds, would be a better match. It can further lead to children's natural integration of their blocks into the dramatic play center.

Materials. Children should be provided with enough blocks to create the images that they might desire. They should have access to at least 200 blocks of varying sizes and shapes. The block center should have sufficient space to store the blocks in an orderly fashion, and that space must be accessible to all children, including those with disabilities. Low and sturdy bookshelves, such as the one shown in Figure 12.16, make ideal places to store blocks, and the bookshelves allow children to independently take the blocks and return them. Blocks should not be stored on the top, open shelf, as they could be knocked over and injure children sitting near the shelves.

The top, open shelf of the bookshelves can be a place to store plastic tubs with lids that contain the props for the wooden structures. The props include people, animals (especially those found in different places around the world), furniture, vehicles, space equipment, store items, and scraps of material. Diverse cultural representations of people, household items, and varying family groupings need to be included in the props. The use of such items encourages the development of socio-dramatic play activities within the block center and also decreases the use of aggressive behaviors by keeping children involved in

As children become more comfortable with blocks, they begin to imagine different uses for different block shapes.

creating a narrative around the structure (Hanline, Milton, & Phelps, 2009). The tubs should be labeled with the names or pictures of the objects they contain.

To enhance the learning activities that occur at the block center, books specializing in building, specific environments, fantasy, and structures should be neatly placed on the bookshelves. Special attention should be given to books on different cultures and the types of buildings that would be found in those environments. Posters can be attached to the walls of the center at the children's eye level to encourage ideas for various architectural or thematic structures (see Figure 12.17). Posters depicting architectural structures from familiar surrounding areas and different areas around the world assist children from diverse cultures in building structures that families might have pictures of at home. Also, compiling a Block Journal, a binder that stores photos of structures with captions, is an excellent resource for providing children with building ideas. Children enjoy taking the journal home and sharing these activity pictures with their families.

The following is a list of some suggested items that could be included in a block center to encourage social interactions and pretend play enactments.

Wooden ramps

Ropes/pulleys

Rulers/tape measures

Fabric

Vehicles

Brand X Pictures/Stockbyte/Thinkstock

All children should be encouraged to play in the block center.

Figure 12.17   Books With Suggestions for Block Centers

Houses	• Dorros, A. (1992). *This is my house.* New York, NY: Scholastic.
Ships	• Crowther, R. (2008). *Ships: A pop-up book.* Somerville, MA: Candlewick Press.
Bridges	• Prince, A. J. (2005). *Twenty-one elephants.* New York, NY: Houghton Mifflin.
Buildings	• Macaulay, D. (2004). *Building big.* New York, NY: Houghton Mifflin.
Castles	• Macaulay, D. (1982). *Castle.* New York, NY: Houghton Mifflin.
Trains	• Balkwill, R. (2008). *The best book of trains.* Boston, MA: Kingfisher.
Airplanes	• Bingham, C. (2001). *Big book of airplanes.* New York, NY: Dorling Kindersley.

Small trees/plants

Clipboards/paper

Boxes

Animals

Cardboard

Doll house furniture

Maps

LEARNING FOR ALL CHILDREN
Block Activities and Culture

Block play requires that children possess the verbal negotiation skills that will allow them to develop common representational narratives while creating block structures. A study by Cohen and Uhry (2009) suggests that bilingual preschoolers playing with blocks, who were performing at an average or above-average range on oral language assessments, produced a somewhat lower number of play episodes than children who were not bilingual when playing with blocks. The explanation for this outcome likely lies in that fact that block play differs from socio-dramatic play. Block play has fewer props and requires more sophisticated verbal descriptions and negotiations than socio-dramatic play. Therefore, because of the complex language demands of block play, bilingual students could benefit if they spent time in the block center where they engaged in useful strategies to successfully communicate with their peers.

©iStockphoto.com/AndreyPopov

Children engage in challenging language activities while participating in block and manipulative play activities.

Additionally, the study found that the integration of block accessories, writing and sign-making supplies, and recycled materials (e.g., foam cubes, fabric scraps, and film canisters) could enhance the participants' language and literacy skills. Therefore, teachers should observe bilingual children in block play and determine their following behaviors:

1. How are the children using the play materials?

2. Who plays regularly in the block center, and who does not?

3. Who is rejected from the block center?

4. Why do certain children have trouble in the block center?

5. Which children are skilled at constructing and decorating block structures?

These observations can help the teacher provide the necessary support for helping all students feel included and successful in the block center.

Adult Block Guidance

Similar to the socio-dramatic play center, the block center is an excellent environment in which to integrate literacy-based objects. Diagrams, maps, paper, pencils, rulers, clipboards, catalogues, advertisements, and sale flyers from hardware stores are natural objects to have available for construction work. Additionally, literacy items related to other activities can encourage the building of different structures and the enactment of related narratives around those themes. Examples of these types of items are scraps of paper or sticky notes for traffic tickets, shopping lists, medical prescription pads, and pay checks.

Before children actually begin to play with blocks, the educators might want to provide some adult-directed instruction on activities that could occur with the blocks. For example, the class could review a particular book that they have read and discuss how to create representations of pictures from the book. Alternatively, the adult could choose a couple of blocks and then discuss their shapes, how they compare to other blocks, and ways that the children might use them when constructing a structure.

Finally, the props for the block center should be rotated periodically. When new ones are placed in the center, the teacher may want to talk about them and encourage suggestions from children on how they might be used. Situations like this one provide opportunities for the children to enhance their vocabulary and representational concepts.

Once children have completed their block constructions, they should be given time to share their creations with the class, and the class should be allowed to ask them questions about how they designed their structure and why they did so. Examples of appropriate questions are: "What was the most important thing you did while you were building this?" and "What blocks did you use to build your structure? Why?" Questions like these have been found to promote conversations by children and also assist them in developing block-building strategies (Cohen & Uhry, 2009). Figure 12.18 lists specific mathematics skills and examples that can be developed through the use of block building.

Cleaning-Up Blocks: A Challenging Situation

Cleaning up the blocks can be a frustrating and challenging time, especially for young children. Blocks are big and take up a lot of space. Children often will become overwhelmed when they look at the blocks spread out all over the floor and contemplate having to clean

Figure 12.18   Specific Mathematics Skill Development With Blocks

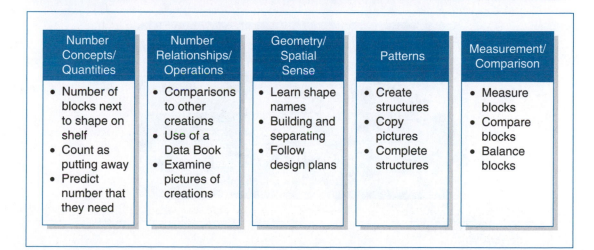

Number Concepts/ Quantities	Number Relationships/ Operations	Geometry/ Spatial Sense	Patterns	Measurement/ Comparison
• Number of blocks next to shape on shelf • Count as putting away • Predict number that they need	• Comparisons to other creations • Use of a Data Book • Examine pictures of creations	• Learn shape names • Building and separating • Follow design plans	• Create structures • Copy pictures • Complete structures	• Measure blocks • Compare blocks • Balance blocks

Working together to clean up the blocks can make the task more enjoyable and manageable.

all of them up. Therefore, the staff should think through the procedure that will work best with each particular group. Because putting all the blocks away may appear overwhelming to young children, they will often need the assistance of an adult to get them started with this task.

Cleanup time is not wasted. During that time children can develop motor skills, visual perceptual skills, language skills, cognitive skills, and social skills. Because of the learning opportunities that cleaning up the blocks offers for children, they should not be rushed through this task. Often, they should be granted extra time to complete the task if necessary.

To enhance children's visual-perceptual and organizational skills, adhesive silhouettes of the block shapes can be purchased and placed on the bookshelves where the blocks are to be placed. Block silhouettes can also be traced on black paper, cut out, and taped to the bookshelves. Children can then be expected to match the blocks to the silhouette images of the blocks and put the blocks away in an orderly manner. To enhance classification concepts, block placements should be arranged on the shelves according to shapes—for example, all squares together, all rectangles together. Additionally, they should be placed in ascending order of size from left to right, thus to encouraging left-to-right progression.

One way of enticing children to put the blocks away is to use an "assembly line," where children pass the blocks from one person to another. This type of activity encourages social and language skills among peers. Using an assembly line is an excellent method for involving some children with cognitive and attention disabilities; at the same time, however, it might be challenging for some children with physical disabilities. Children who find the process physically challenging can be assigned the job of "overseeing" the process and making sure that the items are returned to their correct locations. Figure 12.19 summarizes strategies that can be used for the orderly cleaning up of the block center.

Figure 12.19 Guiding Block Cleanup

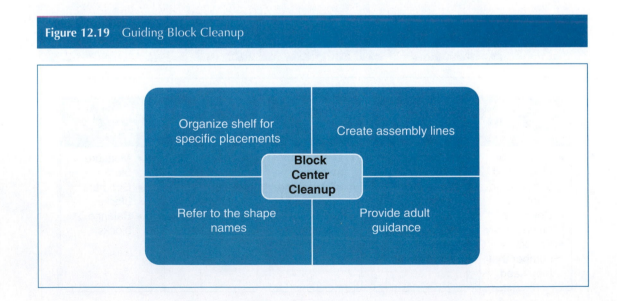

The different shapes of the blocks have specific names, and the adults should use those names when referencing the blocks. If the children have advanced to the point where the name can be printed on the shelf instead of the silhouette, or along with the silhouette, then that action should be taken. Using these organization strategies integrates the use of higher level language and literacy skills. Accordingly, they benefit young children, especially those learning English as their second language. It helps them learn the new label (the English vocabulary term) for a known or familiar concept.

Generally, an adult can observe the skills used by children who are involved in block play. Specifically, the adult should note the changes that occur in the following behaviors that contribute to development and learning: use and size and shape of blocks; time spent playing by self or with another; language used with self and with others; level of representational play used; and collaborative interactions with peers.

Kindergarten and Blocks

Today's Common Core State Standards require children not merely to understand rote mathematical concepts, but also to use representational abilities that involve problem-solving as well as social and linguistic skills (Bergen, 2007). These skills can be attained through carefully planned, day-to-day interactions with blocks, manipulatives, and woodcrafts. However, many parents, policy makers, and school administrators are uncomfortable with allowing primary grade children to create block structures during the school hours. Instead, they choose to implement policies that reduce the time spent in these social/cognitive experiences and then increase time performing more "officially" targeted early education activities involving the use of pencil and paper.

Educators today need to resist this trend. Play experiences involving the high-quality use of blocks, manipulatives, and woodcrafts impacts children's long-term capacities related to problem-solving, social cognition, and academic skill development. Teachers must provide children with opportunities not only to develop mathematical skills, but also to develop language and learning skills. All of these skills contribute to later school success and the enhancement of cognitive and academic abilities.

REFLECT AND APPLY EXERCISE 12.3

Everyone Needs to Clean Up

Reflect

Four children have been enjoying activities in the block center for the past week. Yesterday, two of the children complained to an adult that the other two children never help put the blocks away. You watch the center today and noticed that they are correct. When it was time to clean up, two of the children in the block center continued to play and then began wandering around the room.

Apply

What are some playful techniques that you could use that will engage all the children at the block center in the task of putting away the blocks? What skills will they develop while participating in these activities?

LEARNING FOR ALL CHILDREN
Block Activities and Disabilities

By using blocks children enhance their abilities to problem solve, think logically, and learn early mathematics skills—for example, counting, sorting, classifying, identifying shapes, and understanding whole-part relationships. Hanline et al. (2009) examined the relationship between block construction representations and the early mathematics abilities of typically and atypically developing preschoolers. The latter category included preschoolers with Down syndrome, prematurity, Autism Spectrum Disorder, physical impairments, and speech and language disorders. The authors found no predictive relationship between block construction and mathematics abilities. However, they did conclude that children who exhibited higher use of blocks as representational objects also had higher reading abilities and a faster rate of academic growth during the elementary grades. Additionally, although children with disabilities had similar block skills, they nonetheless had lower predicted reading scores and progressed at a slower rate in reading abilities, a pattern similar to other research findings associated with the learning and development of children with disabilities. Figure 12.20 suggests ways to support the use of blocks by children with disabilities (Phelps & Hanline, 1999).

Figure 12.20 Accommodations/Supports for Children With Disabilities During Block Play

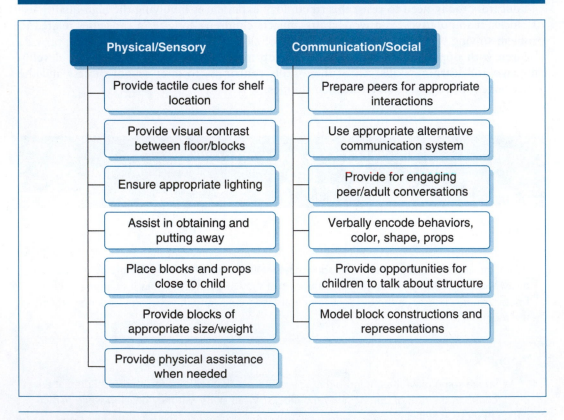

Source: Phelps, P., & Hanline, M. F. (1999). Let's Play Blocks! Creating Effective Learning Experiences for Young Children. *Teaching Exceptional Children, 32,* 62–67.

As children become more skilled at block building, they begin to rebuild structures and modify them by integrating different items into them. The following observation sheet contains information from Newburger and Vaughan (2006) and can be used for analyzing children's mathematics skills through the observation of block activities and relates those skills to the CCSS Kindergarten Standards of Mathematics on Measurement/Data and Geometry.

BLOCK SKILLS AND CCSS—KINDERGARTEN		
Block Skill	*CCSS Kindergarten Mathematics Standard*	*Observations*
Builds a block structure from a picture	*Geometry (5.b):* Analyze, compare, create, and compose shapes	
Talks about the basic features of the shapes	*Geometry (5.a):* Identify and describe shapes	
Uses measuring tools to accurately measure a structure to be copied	*Measurement and Data (4.b):* Classify objects and count the number of objects in categories	
Recognizes odd three-sided figures as triangles	*Measurement and Data (4.a):* Describe and compare measurable attributes	

Manipulatives Centers

Manipulative toys enhance children's fine motor skills as well as their understanding of mathematics, their development of perceptual skills, and their familiarity with language and use of symbols. Manipulatives are either produced commercially or made from common items found in children's environments.

All children benefit in different ways from block or manipulative activities.

©iStockphoto.com/CEFutcher

Commercial Manipulatives

Although there are numerous commercial manipulative products, certain special ones are long-time favorites in early childhood classrooms. For example, wooden puzzles are found in almost every early childhood room. The simplest forms of puzzles have only a few individual pieces, and children may pick up each piece by grabbing an attached wooden dowel. As children advance their motor and cognitive skills, they begin to use their fingers to lift and replace puzzle pieces that fit together.

One way to personalize puzzles is to trace a puzzle piece onto a picture of a child, cut out the picture in the shape of the puzzle piece, and stick the traced picture in the slot where the puzzle piece goes. Then, place the puzzle piece on top of the picture. This process makes puzzle activities more special and exciting, for when the child lifts the piece up, the child finds his or her picture or a picture of a peer child. Personalizing the puzzle in this way makes puzzle activities

©iStockphoto.com/Paha_L

Children enjoy exploring small items that are meaningful in their everyday activities.

focus not only on fine motor and problem-solving skills, but also encourages children to talk about pictures of themselves or their peers. Additionally, early childhood professionals can also make puzzles more personal by purchasing puzzles that reflect the people from diverse cultures and cultural items, foods, and homes that children in the classroom may recognize.

Another commercial manipulative toy that has been popular for a long time is Mr. and Mrs. Potato Head. Playing with the Potato Heads not only develops children's fine motor skills, but also their mathematical, perceptual, language, and self-identity skills. Additionally, using a variety of nesting dolls from different cultures encourages an appreciation of diversity while, at the same time, teaching fine motor, sequencing, and vocabulary skills.

A large number of other commercially produced, small block-like items greatly interest children and enhance their mathematical and manipulative skills. These include waffle blocks, Duplos, Legos, magnetic tiles, and tube or pipe builders. These types of manipulatives work on children's fine motor skills, visual-perceptual skills, and creativity. Similar to wooden blocks, playing with these items provides excellent opportunities for grouping children to work collaboratively, thereby enhancing their social skills and language skills.

Finally, a number of commercially made manipulative toys involve shoestrings and small block objects with a hole in the middle. These toys allow children to string the blocks on the shoestring. Like use of the items mentioned above, stringing blocks requires eye-hand coordination as well as holding the string and picking up the block. Children can be asked to reproduce specific color and/or shape patterns through their use of the blocks on the string.

Common Manipulatives

Many items that are commonly found in a household environment can be used as manipulative toys. These include the following:

Keys	Paper shapes
Nails	Plastic bottles
Bolts/screws	Jar lids
Golf tees	Rocks
Flowers	Balls
Coins	Cardboard tubes
Shells	Beans
Bottle caps	Sticks
Nuts	Pasta noodles
Pipes	Buttons

Everyday manipulatives must be safe for the children of specific age groups using them. They also should encourage the children's development of skills such as sorting, classifying, comparing, patterning, or graphing. Children need to be provided with an appropriate object that will allow them to organize the items in a way that is familiar to them. Small trays with dividers, cupcake tins, cookie box trays, dishes, cups, baby food jars, jar lids, and desk organizers are excellent sorting items. Using common items as manipulatives is an excellent teaching technique that allows children to learn various classifying concepts. Children with advanced fine motor and visual-perceptual skills will enjoy sorting everyday manipulatives by using ice tongs, tweezers, clothespins, and magnets as sorting devices.

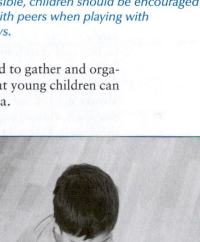

As much as possible, children should be encouraged to collaborate with peers when playing with manipulative toys.

Performing Statistics With Manipulatives: A Four-Step Process

As children engage in manipulative activities, they should be encouraged to gather and organize their data. Van de Walle et al. (2013) suggest a four-step process that young children can use when they are involved in projects that require them to analyze data.

Step 1: Formulate Questions. Before getting started on data collection, everyone must have a clear idea of what the goal is behind the activity. The questions can either be determined by the adults or the children in the class. For example, if the class has access to a variety of shells, children may be asked to manipulate the shells so that they are classified as either smooth/rough, strong/fragile, or having/not having points. If shoes are in the room, children might want to classify them as shoes for sports, shoes for dressy activities, and shoes for different types of weather. If the class is working on an optometrist theme and has a collection of eyeglasses, the children may want to classify the eyeglasses as fancy glasses/everyday glasses, or sports' glasses/reading glasses. Whatever the items are, an interesting and clear question is needed to analyze them.

Step 2: Collect Data. Children now think about the data that are going to be collected. If comparisons are going to be made, specific groupings need to be thought through and discussed. For example, with a collection of nuts and bolts, the children might want to determine how many have matching nuts and bolts and how many do not. Children can also collect numerical data. For example, they may want to determine how many of the bolts are short/medium/long or whether their weight is heavy/light. Consideration should be given to how the data are going to be collected. Will the objects be counted, measured, weighed, or felt?

Children enjoy playing with items found around their houses that families have donated to the school.

Step 3: Analyze Data. Next, the data will be analyzed. For this step, children must be taught to refer back to the question. Will the answer be graphed or counted? Are children going to determine which leaves are the widest by measuring them, or are they going to determine how many have more than one point?

Step 4: Interpret Results. Finally, a discussion needs to occur regarding the collected data. Children need to discuss what the numbers tell them. Who will they share these data with? What do the findings not tell us? What new questions do we have based on the data?

Children can use many different types of graphs to represent their findings. Figure 12.21 provides pictures of an object graph, picture graph, line plot, and bar graph.

Creating a Mathematics Learning Environment With Manipulatives

All of the manipulative items should be placed in a manipulatives center. This center should be organized in a very orderly manner so children can easily access the items. The items should be kept securely in containers with lids that will prevent them from spilling and that, at the same time, are easy to open and put back on. One efficient way of separately organizing many of these items is to use clear, plastic zippered pencil cases that may be inserted into binders.

The center should also be designed so that a variety of materials are available to children at different learning levels. Grouping items so that similar ones are placed together is always a good idea. For example, different types of block stringing activities could be on one shelf, classifying objects could be on another shelf, and commercial board games on a third shelf. Like all the centers, items should be rotated in and out of the center regularly so that students will not become bored with the available selection. If the program is a full-day program, children should have access to different arrays of materials in the morning and in the afternoon.

When teachers create manipulative games for children, they should evaluate strategies for making these activities more culturally diverse. Using pictures of children from other

Figure 12.21   Different Types of Graphs

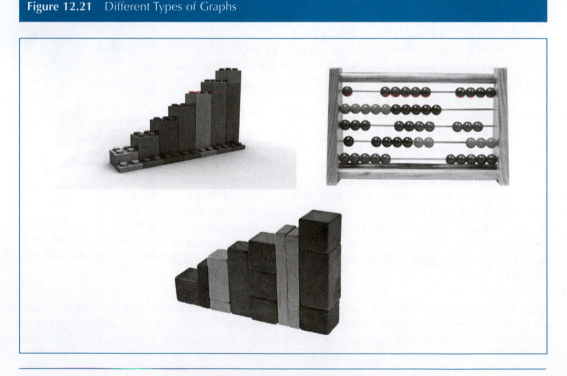

Sources: ©iStock.com/homeworks255; ©iStock.com/RogiervdE; Stockbyte/Stockbyte/Thinkstock.

cultures or with disabilities on game boards can help all children become more comfortable with diversity. Additionally, the use of stickers and bulletin board borders that depict multicultural children, art, celebrations, and architecture can encourage familiarity among all children. Figure 12.22 provides suggestions when using manipulatives.

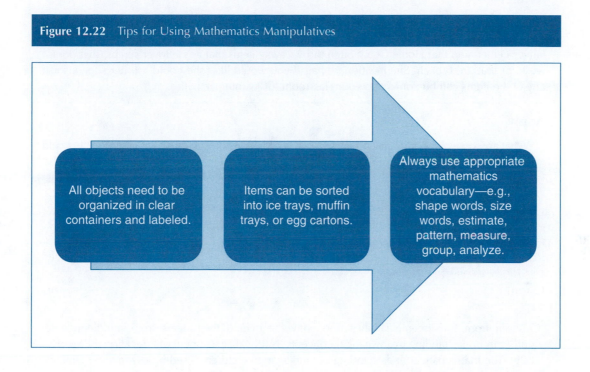

Figure 12.22 Tips for Using Mathematics Manipulatives

All objects need to be organized in clear containers and labeled.

Items can be sorted into ice trays, muffin trays, or egg cartons.

Always use appropriate mathematics vocabulary—e.g., shape words, size words, estimate, pattern, measure, group, analyze.

Kindergarteners and Manipulatives

Engaging in simple board games and manipulating play objects allows children to count and categorize commercially designed objects or everyday objects that are familiar to them. Additionally, the children begin to add and subtract objects as they move their place markers while playing games. They enhance their understanding of quantities above "9," and their understanding of "more than" and "less than" attributes. Through these self-motivating, everyday activities, children learn how to represent, relate, and use numbers in a meaningful manner.

The Kindergarten CCSS expect children to be capable of the following skills by the time that they are ready to transition into the first grade:

- Represent and compare whole numbers
- Describe shapes and spaces

Manipulatives are certainly objects that children can use, and the children can be required to write the numerals for the total number of items used. They can then be asked to examine different shapes and write down the numbers for the different shapes that add up to that total number. They can compare the different sets of numbers that they have by putting them in order from smallest to largest, or largest to smallest.

Finally, children can be asked to do similar activities with two-dimensional objects such as squares, triangles, circles, rectangles, and hexagons. They then need to learn how to identify these basic shapes in three-dimensional objects such as cubes, cones, cylinders, and spheres.

REFLECT AND APPLY EXERCISE 12.4
Creating a Wish List

Reflect

The mother of a child in your class informs you that she has a job working at Home Depot. She mentions to you that she has observed some of the common items that you have at your manipulatives center, and that Home Depot often throws away items that are leftover scraps, that do not work, or that are broken. She mentioned that, if you would like, she could ask her supervisor if any of the items can be donated to your classroom for learning activities.

Apply

What are some of the items mentioned that you could use in the manipulatives center? How could you use those items to assist your students with fine motor, mathematics, and other academic skills?

 # LEARNING FOR ALL CHILDREN
Manipulatives Activities and Poverty

Children from low-income families frequently lag behind their peers from middle-income families in understanding mathematical concepts (National Assessment of Educational Progress, 2009). The mathematical understanding of kindergarten children raised in low-income families strongly predicts their future math achievement at 8, 10, and 14 years of age (Jordan, Kaplan, Olah, & Locuniak, 2006). One area on which low-income children tend to score poorly in kindergarten evaluations is estimating the location where a number would appear on a number line. Siegler and Ramani (2008) found that 4-year-old children from impoverished backgrounds improved their skills at identifying number placements on a number line after playing an hour of simple manipulative board games, such as Chutes and Ladders or The Great Race. They noted that when the population played these games, the children improved their skills in counting, number identification, and comparisons of numerical magnitudes.

In a more recent study by the same authors (Ramani & Siegler, 2011), 4- and 5-year-olds were involved in the application of a simple game that used a spinner with numbers and a game board with 10 equal-sized, connected squares placed in a linear design. They found that preschool children from low-income backgrounds using this application were able to increase their learning rate so that it was greater than 3- and 4-year-old preschoolers from middle-income backgrounds. The finding suggests that children can enhance their mathematics skills when they are involved in informal, age-appropriate activities, such as manipulative board games.

Parents and teachers should encourage young children to participate frequently in linear numerical board games, which are easy and inexpensive to make. Such activities appear to benefit young children who are likely to start the school system behind their peers. Five things to consider when purchasing board games for children:

- Look for the age range on the game box. If it is too easy, children will not be interested in it. If it is too hard, they will become discouraged.
- Try to get a game that can be adapted in a number of ways so that you get more "bang for your buck."
- Make sure that it is a fun game that has a theme in which the children have shown interest.
- Review the directions and make sure that they are simple.
- Check online to see what others say about the game.

Woodcraft Centers

Creating objects out of wood can be an inspiring activity for many young children. A minimum age is required, however. Children younger than 4 years of age should not use wood. Instead, they should engage in activities using plastic hammers and other types of commercially made plastic construction materials similar to the Little Tykes workbench. Once children reach the age of 4, they should exhibit the eye-hand coordination and the hand and arm muscle strength needed to participate in activities that involve real, lightweight tools. "Child-size" tools can usually be purchased at large hardware stores for around $20. Suggested woodcraft skill development is listed in Figure 12.23.

Creating a Mathematics Learning Environment With Woodcraft

When designing a woodcraft center focusing on lumber, nails, and hammers, paramount attention must be give to safety. Therefore, the following considerations must be followed:

- The center should be highly visible, but away from foot traffic.
- An adult must always be present.
- Equipment should be stored away and brought out only for activities.
- Very specific rules must be posted and discussed with the children.
- Children should always wear goggles.
- Only two or three children should work at the center at one time. Having a limited number of goggles can solve this concern.
- Children must be taught to respect tools and handle them properly.

Children should understand that the woodcraft center is a place where they will start out slowly and gradually work up to creating more complex objects. They should understand

Figure 12.23 Stages of Development in Woodcrafting

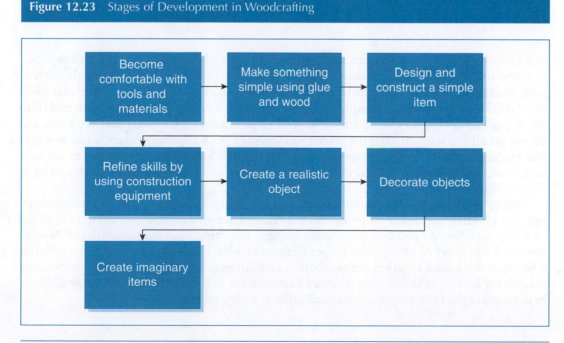

Source: Huber, L. K. (1999). Woodworking With Young Children: You Can Do It! *Young Children, 54*(6), 32–34.

that they have to develop strength in their hands and arms, similar to the way that runners develop strength in their legs and feet, before they move on to more challenging projects. Children can begin by arranging the wood scrap pieces so that they are together with common shapes, sanding them down, practicing hammering golf tees into Styrofoam blocks with rubber mallets, gluing pieces of wood together, and painting their creations. See Figure 12.24 for a list of further tools that can be used.

Figure 12.24   Tools for Woodcraft Center

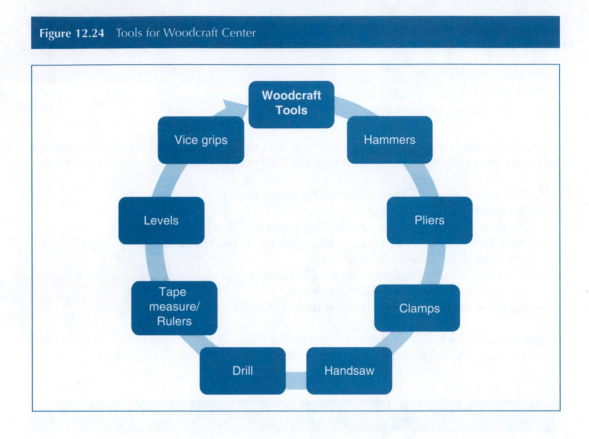

Children just beginning to learn woodworking skills can be permitted to use a screwdriver to screw items onto a piece of wood. The best types of wood to use are soft woods, such as pine, cedar, fir, or redwood. Hardware stores, lumber companies, and cabinetmakers will often donate scraps of wood to educational programs. When it is time to introduce nails into the woodcraft center, they should be ones with large heads (roofer nails) that are short and do not go all the way through the wood. Additionally, with beginning users, some teachers like placing a plastic comb between the head of the nail and the child's fingers to act as a barrier and prevent injuries. Figure 12.25 provides a list of other materials that should be in the woodcraft center.

As their eye-hand coordination improves and the strength in their hands and wrists develops, the children are ready to enjoy more advanced activities, such as nailing two pieces of wood together. As children participate in these activities, conversations should develop around the number of objects, the shapes of those objects, how the shapes of objects change when they are joined together, the similarities and differences between different shapes, and reasons for arranging things a certain way. Participation in these activities will assist children in developing the following mathematical skills in a very self-motivating way:

Figure 12.25　Other Materials in the Woodcraft Center

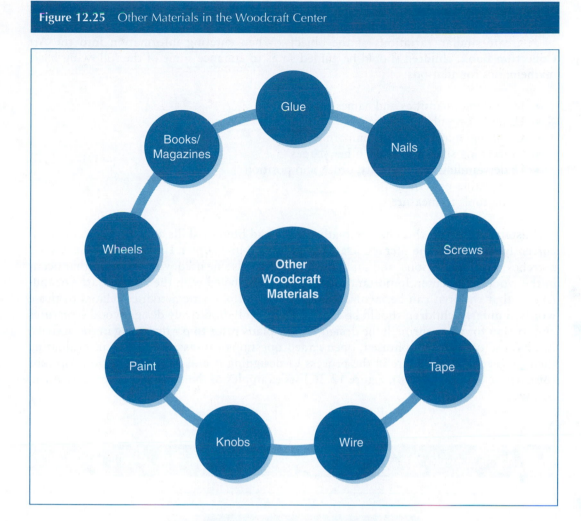

- Problem solving
- Matching and classifying
- Sorting
- Comparing and measuring
- Conceptualizing

Woodcraft and Materials

The woodcraft center also should have other materials available for children to integrate into their creations, such as tongue depressors, fabric scraps, yarn, dowels, paints, and markers. Many communities have nonprofit organizations that recycle art materials for a small donation. They are typically managed by artists who are members of the community and can be found by "googling" the following term: "recycled art supplies."

Once they have created their woodworking objects, children should be allowed to display them in the classroom, explain to the class the sequence they used in making them, and discuss the different shapes, measurements, balancing challenges, and modifications that they made. Additionally, if the children wish, their creations can be used in the block center or the socio-dramatic play center. Finally, a picture should be taken of each child's object and placed in the Art Collection Book with either dictated and/or written directions by the child on how to make such an item. Other children in the class can use the book to re-create similar variations of the objects. When entering information into the Art Collection Book, children should be guided so as to enhance some of the following basic mathematics foundations:

- Identifying quantities and names of numbers
- Using last number name to identify a quantity
- Counting, matching, and comparing
- Combining shapes to make other shapes
- Understanding directionality, order, and position
- Duplicating patterns
- Using tools to measure

As stated earlier in this chapter, mathematics and literacy skills appear to develop concurrently. Therefore, the literacy strategies presented in Chapter 10 (i.e., play plans, word searches, word dissections, and shared writings) can also be used with activities that occur in the woodcraft center. Important items should be labeled with the appropriate vocabulary so that children can be involved in alphabet and phonetic activities related to those words. Similarly, children should be encouraged to collaboratively design wood structures and to plan for them through the design of play plans prior to participating in the activity. Adults' use of carefully phrased, open-ended questions can assist children in evaluating their project while they are in the process of designing it and analyzing various options (Bisgaier & Samaras, 2008). Figure 12.26 lists examples of the types of questions that can be used.

Figure 12.26   Questions That Assist Children in Analyzing Their Options for Designing a Sculpture

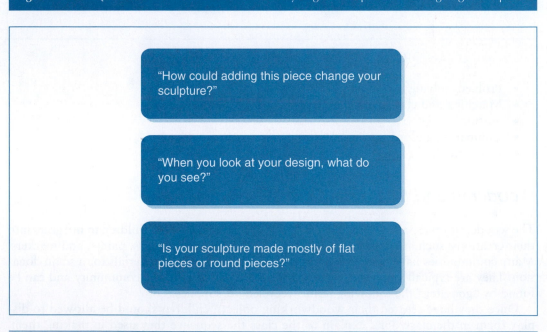

"How could adding this piece change your sculpture?"

"When you look at your design, what do you see?"

"Is your sculpture made mostly of flat pieces or round pieces?"

Source: Bisgaier, C. S., & Samaras, T. (2008). Using Wood, Glue, and Words to Enhance Learning, In D. Koralek (Ed.), *Spotlight on Young Children and the Creative Arts* (pp. 12–18). Washington, DC: National Association for the Education of Young Children.

Chapter Summary

Math activities occur everywhere in children's environments. Children see math when they weigh food at the market, when they look at numbers on the clock in their house, when they observe the shapes of indoor and outdoor objects, and when they analyze the patterns on the clothes they wear. They also see math when parents reason with them about items that cannot be purchased, or activities that cannot be undertaken, due to the household budget.

Engaging in block building, manipulative activities, and creating wooden objects enhances children's math, language, literacy, and logic skills. These developmentally appropriate activities, when guided by adults, allow children to become successful in high-quality learning activities. Only after children develop these skills in a comfortable, playful, and realistic context can they then use the skills in other situations requiring more abstract thinking.

HOME AND COMMUNITY CONNECTIONS

Implementing Play Activities in the Mathematics Center

Count everything! How many chairs at the table, How long it takes to put on your shoes, How many birds on the wire, How many trees on the block.

CHAPTER 12 FIRST-PERSON INTERVIEW

Children Taking Ownership of Their Learning

Gregory Uba

Early Education Teacher, Sacramento, CA

Although the number of males in early education is small, we have become increasingly well organized. There are a number of formal and informal associations that bring us together to discuss our careers and challenges. Social media has led to a number of Facebook groups dedicated to advocates for men in early education. A number of local organizations, professional association committees, and a national organization, MenTeach.org, serve to support, promote, and encourage the participation of men in the lives of young children.

The data on males teaching in early education programs are not encouraging. According to the U.S. Bureau of Labor, in 2002 only 2.3% of pre-K and kindergarten teachers were males. Ten years later, in 2011, that figure was still the same. However, from a low in 2004 of 1.9% to its peak in 2010 of 3%, the number of male teachers in early education has failed to achieve any significant traction.

What's the big deal? Why is the gender of early education teachers important? Don't we simply want good teachers for our young children? Stereotypes notwithstanding, I believe that there is, to some extent, a culture related to gender that men can and do bring to the early education classroom. It seems to me that males tend to have a higher threshold for risk-taking when children are involved in physical play. I know that I tend to be less cautious than many of my female colleagues with whom I work. For example, instead of saying to the children that they can jump from no higher than the third rung of a climbing structure, I tend to leave it up to the children to determine what they feel safe with. Of course, I am right there watching them, and usually nothing happens. Don't get me wrong—occasionally there will be a bloody nose or scraped knee, but that happens with other activities too.

(Continued)

(Continued)

My feeling is that we have to let children establish their own limits of competence with physical play just as we encourage them to establish their limits in other areas. For example, we don't discourage children from taking chances in reading and writing; we get excited when they do it. Well, the same is true about physical play.

I fondly remember one day—there was a girl in the class who was working really hard at building a tower with big plastic blocks. Although she was the shortest child in the classroom, she looked like she really wanted to make a tall tower. We sort of have a rule of "Build it no taller than you are," but I could see that she wasn't going to stop with that. After she got the block tower to her height, she went over and got a chair so she could climb up higher to make a taller tower. As I watched this, I, the human being self, not just the teacher self, really didn't want to stop it. I looked around and saw some boys playing with trucks close by her tower. So, I went over and told them to get the construction hats from the dramatic play area and wear them, just in case the tower came tumbling down. Then I hung some yarn from the ceiling and she anchored it between two of the bricks so the tower had some extra support. She was so determined to do this that I just couldn't put limits on her physical play. Children really know what they can do and what they cannot do, and we need to trust them.

I have learned other important lessons about trust from children. One day the children were out playing in the sandbox, and when it was time to clean up, I realized that I could work with them on classifying skills in a very natural and playful way. We have these milk bottle crates that we usually toss all the sand toys into at the end of the day. Quite impressed with my teaching strategy, I started putting all the shovels into one crate, the buckets into another, the sand molds into another, and so forth. Suddenly, I noticed that a child was behind me taking them out and putting other things into the crates. It surprised me and I said, "Dude, what are you doing?" He just looked at me and said "Blue," and continued putting all the blue objects into the crate. It was then that I realized that he got the concept and that he was categorizing the objects the way that he wanted to do it. He had taken ownership of the concept of classification that was meaningful to him. It hit me that I needed to stop being so much of a teacher—to become better at watching and listening—because the children really know how to teach themselves!

Student Study Site

Visit the Student Study Site at **www.sagepub.com/selmi** to access additional study tools including mobile-friendly eFlashcards and links to video and web resources.

Sample Learning Activities

Curricular Area: Math

Core Vocabulary: Alike, same, different, bigger, smaller, count, curved, straight, equal, greater, less, more, object, shape, size

Guide Questions:

How are . . . alike?

How are . . . different?

What is the shape of your object?

Which one is bigger?

Which one is smaller?

Let's count the . . .

How many are there?

Resources:

Christelow, Eileen. (2012). *Five Little Monkeys Jumping on the Bed.* HMH Books for Young Readers.

Coffelt, Nancy. (2009). *Big, Bigger, Biggest.* Henry Holt and Co.

Diehl, David. (2007). *A Circle Here, A Square There.* Lark Books.

Martin, Bill, & Sampson, Michael. (2004). *Chicka Chicka 1-2-3.* Simon and Schuster Books for Young Readers.

Miranda, Anne. (2002). *Monster Math.* HMH Books for Young Readers.

Rosenthal, Amy Krouse. (2011). *This Plus That: Life's Little Equations.* HarperCollins.

Core Text: *Fish Eyes,* by Lois Ehlert

- Skills: Counting, counting on, describing
- Levels of Questions: What do you see? How many fish do you see? Why does it help to count things we see? Would you want to swim with fish? Why or why not?
- Product: Paper plate aquarium, fish mosaic with tissue paper

Learning Centers:

- Explore through literacy: Fill your library with books that help students learn math content such as the titles recommended
- Create: Provide students with different materials to create a fish

  o Construction paper
  o Buttons
  o Tissue paper
  o Paper plates
  o Modeling clay

- Outdoor Play: Hop Scotch, Duck-Duck-Goose, Jump Rope (counting the number of jumps)
- Dramatic Play: Shopping at the store

  o What are you shopping for?
  o How many are you buying?
  o How much does it cost?

Key Term

manipulative toys

Some Children's Books About Mathematics and Blocks

The Doorbell Rang, by Pat Hutchins

Five Creatures, by Emily Jenkins

Houses and Homes, by Ann Morris

Let's Count, by Tana Hoban

One Duck Stuck, by Phyllis Root

Tools, by Taro Miura

What Do Wheels Do All Day? by April Jones Prince

Useful Websites

Figure This: http://www.figurethis.org

Math Perspectives: http:/www.mathperspectives.com

NAEYC Blocks: http://www.naeyc.org/files/tyc/file/TYC_V3N3_StrasserandKoeppel.pdf

NAEYC Position Paper on Math: http://www.naeyc.org/positionstatements/mathematics

National Council of Teachers of Mathematics: http://www.nctm.org

National Library of Virtual Manipulatives: http://nlvm.usu.edu

National Library of Virtual Manipulatives: http://nlvm.usu.edu/en/nav/vlibrary.html

Reflective Question

You are a teacher for a preschool class that is preparing to enter kindergarten in the fall. A few parents of your students have mentioned to you that they think their children are spending too much time playing with blocks. You discussed their concern with your director, and she suggested that you and your partner teacher design a presentation for parents on how block play enhances academic skills. What information would you provide to the parents?

13

Integrating Play Activities in the Social Studies and Book Centers

---

THE BUS TRIP

©iStock.com/matka_Wariatka

A preschooler who is hearing-impaired and learning to speak is playing in a room with other hearing-impaired preschoolers. She goes over to the kitchen play area in the classroom, opens a cupboard, and pulls out a black purse that she holds up over her head. Another preschooler who is also hearing-impaired is across the room. She looks up at the purse and quickly walks over to the girl with the purse. The girl with the purse points to the other girl and herself repeatedly. Both girls then begin to pull items out of a nearby closet and dress in adult hats, dresses, and purses, while interacting with each other through vocalizations and gestures. The girl with the purse gives the other girl a straw suitcase.

When dressed, both exit the kitchen play area and walk around the perimeter of the room, with the girl with the purse slightly ahead of the girl with the suitcase. They point to things as they gesture and vocalize to each other, and they look as they walk.

A preschool boy who is hearing-impaired stands to the right side of the kitchen area. He is intentionally pushing the keys on a cash register and occasionally looking up at the girls who are walking around the room. Another boy who is hearing-impaired and younger stands behind the stove watching what the boy is doing at the cash register. As the two walking girls approach the right side of room, the boy at the cash register leaves and gets two desk chairs, and places them

(Continued)

369

(Continued)

side by side, facing in the same direction. He then places a third chair in front of the chair on the left, also facing in the same direction. He steps over to the right side of the chair arrangement and stands with his hand out and his palm up.

As the girls are meandering around the classroom, they point at the boy standing by the chairs, vocalize, and walk quickly toward him. When they get to him, they each reach into their purses and place their hands into the boy's hand. The boy looks at his hand, nods his head, and pretends to give them something back. He then steps aside.

The girls walk past the boy to the side-by-side chairs and sit down next to each other. The boy then walks over to the single chair in front and sits down. He stretches out his right hand and then pulls his arm back in close to his side. He then starts moving both hands in an arched motion in front of him. The girls, who are sitting behind the boy, start pointing at things to the left side of them, vocalizing, and gesturing. The younger boy is still standing near the cash register but watching the three other children.

The older boy suddenly stops making the arched motions with his hands, stands up, and walks to the right. He then waves to the girls to get off, which the girls do. The girls walk back to the housekeeping area. As the older boy is standing there, the younger boy suddenly gets down on his hands and knees, and goes galloping up to the older boy. The older boy grabs the younger boy by his shirt neck and drags him to the house. While passing a bookcase, he takes a piece of paper off a shelf and sticks it in his pocket. He then pretends to knock and one of the girls comes over, facing him. He shakes his finger at the girl, as if to be scolding her, and gives her the piece of paper. The girl takes the young boy, who is still on his hands and knees, by the shirt neck and drags him into the house area, where he goes over and curls up in a dog bed in the house area.

T he scenario demonstrates children who are making sense of the community in which they live. They are learning about typical community activities through participation in enjoyable role-playing events such as taking a trip, driving a bus, and being a dogcatcher. These playful activities are expanding their understanding of social studies skills by providing the children with opportunities to organize settings and props, and to create narratives about familiar community activities.

This chapter discusses how to create developmentally appropriate social studies activities that expand children's understanding of themselves as members of a family, community, and diverse world. Because children learn about the world and faraway places by reading books and using technology, this chapter also includes information on using technology with young children and a section on designing book centers. Specifically, the chapter addresses the following questions:

- What are ways that play activities can enhance children's department of social studies concepts?

- How can social studies centers be organized as anti-bias learning environments?

- What are strategies for integrating technology into early childhood learning environments?

- How can book centers be designed to support learning activities?

Early Social Studies Skills

Social studies content is a combination of history, geography, sociology, and civics. It is designed to provide children with an understanding of their national heritage and the beginning skills that they will need to participate as active adult members of a democracy (Maxim, 2006). During the early education years, children start this learning process by engaging in activities that enhance their understanding of the concepts of self, family, and community. Programs frequently provide children with opportunities to discuss individual differences, examine diverse family celebrations, and learn about community workers.

Early education centers are designed to be caring communities, where each child's uniqueness and diversity are valued. When children begin early education programs, they learn how to participate in day-to-day, routine group schedules. Throughout the day, they learn how to collaborate with others, control their emotions, respect differences, and resolve conflicts. These activities encourage the development of appropriate social skills that ultimately should contribute to their becoming responsible workers and productive members of society. Activities such as block building, pretend playing, picture painting, and creative dancing offer opportunities for children to take pride in their products and their surroundings by working hard on projects and then tidying up before leaving their learning environments. Additionally, when children engage in conversations about their activities, a practice that is encouraged throughout this book, they enhance their understanding that people are responsible for their own actions and for contributing to the success of the larger, learning community.

Through play activities, early education centers typically assist children in learning about themselves and the community in which they live. Similar to the activities in the opening scenario of this chapter, children participate in activities centered on various types of local public and private facilities. These facilities include hospitals, religious places, parks, shops, offices, firehouses, police stations, entertainment places, transportation centers, restaurants, recreation centers, and senior centers. Books, field trips, and technology enrich children's learning about how their families and local communities are both similar to and different from those throughout the world, and how families and communities have changed over time. All of these civic-related play situations create practical opportunities for children to engage in meaningful learning activities about geography and history through the integration of maps, globes, books, and technology.

Additionally, social studies is further enhanced in a personal way by the variety of ethnic cultures, cultural events, and cultural traditions that each individual child brings to an early education center. Through peer sharing of books, songs, dances, poems, foods, and languages, young children learn to respect the everyday practices of their peers as well as to understand the various religious and ethnic holidays they are familiar with. Discussions and reflections about both distant and local civic and religious concepts create a foundation for understanding the diverse local, state, country, and world events that occur.

Playful activities enhance children's understanding of social studies concepts.

©iStock.com/McIninch

Young children love to participate in map activities.

Jupiterimages/BananaStock/Thinkstock

A major part of social studies curriculum is for children to study about themselves and their families. Having children bring in pictures of their families and make small posters of their families encourages discussions about similarities and differences in home life. If these posters are laminated, young children can keep them under their nap cots and pull them out should they feel lonely at naptime, which could ease that anxious feeling.

LEARNING FOR ALL CHILDREN
Books From Cultures Around the World

One of the benefits of having diverse populations attend early education programs is that the children can be provided with books from different countries that have been translated into English. Such books assist children in understanding each other. Additionally, many children's books that have been written in English have now been translated into other languages. In turn, this assists children from other countries in understanding the customs and habits of their North American peers. Full benefits from translated books can be observed when teachers invite children's family members to the classroom to read books to the class in the language in which they were written (Gillanders & Castro, 2011; National Center on Cultural and Linguistic Responsiveness, n.d.).

Lo and Cantrell (2002) supply a framework for choosing multicultural books that have been translated into English and that are appropriate for beginning readers. Through the use of international literature, both early childhood professionals and children can learn about customs, lifestyles, languages, and families from different countries.

Teachers should choose translated books for use in much the same manner that they would choose books to read to the class or for children to read independently (Lo & Cantrell, 2002). Figure 13.1 provides guidelines that can be used. Teachers should make sure that the quality of the story will engage the children. The opening lines, the plot, and the subject matter are obviously important considerations when analyzing books. Additionally, the illustrations should be reviewed to determine if they add to the children's understanding of the language, culture, environment, and customs.

For more advanced readers, the chapter headings in books that have been translated into English should provide support for the story. As with other books, teachers should consider the number and length of the chapters in translated books to ensure that they correspond to the children's reading abilities. Additionally, presenting books to a group using a Dialogic Read Aloud approach, which is addressed later in this chapter, can help guide young children's comprehension. Finally, Lo and Cantrell caution that a teacher must review translated books to make sure that the quality of the translation is linguistically correct and that they retain the books' cultural flavor and have not overly "Americanized" the text.

Translated books come in a variety of formats:

- Side-by-side translations in the same book
- Separately published translated book
- Scattering of words in another language throughout a book written in English

The HighScope Curriculum (see Chapter 2) supports the following six key development indicators for preschool social studies activities. These same concepts tend to be the core for many comprehensive early education social studies programs.

- **Diversity:** People have diverse characteristics, interests, and abilities.
- **Community roles:** People have different roles and functions in the community.
- **Decision making:** Communities are impacted by various decisions, similar to classrooms.
- **Geography:** Communities have different features and locations.
- **History:** Communities are impacted by their past, present, and future.
- **Ecology:** Communities must care for their environments.

Social Studies and Play

Playful activities with music, songs, art materials, and play props can be adapted so that children engage in exciting developmentally appropriate practices that enhance their understanding of their families, communities, and the world. When young children transition for

Figure 13.1 Criteria for Choosing International Books as Early Reader Selections

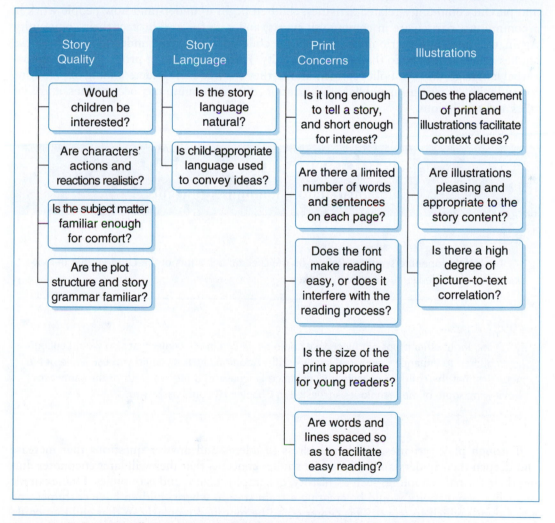

Source: Lo, D. E., & Cantrell, D. E. (2002). Global Perspectives for Young Readers: Easy Readers and Picture Book Read-Alouds From Around the World. *Childhood Education, 79*(1), 21–25.

©iStockphoto.com/Imgorthand

One way for children to understand about the passage of time is to have them dress and participate in activities that occurred in the past.

the first time from the home to the school environment, having a play center where they can participate in familiar home activities softens the impact of this change in daily routines. Engaging with familiar home objects and in customary activities provides children with the comfort and support that they need to adapt to the classroom environment. Therefore, the socio-dramatic play center should also include foods and meal utensils from different cultures. For example, the house could be adapted to have a low Japanese tea table, or a French cafe table, or to have Mexican, Indian, Brazilian, or Chinese food products.

As children become familiar with and successfully participate in school events, play center themes can be broadened to include familiar community institutions and activities in which the children engage with their families outside of the home—such as the post office, a fast-food restaurant, the library, and a supermarket. At a young age and by participating in these pretend and playful community-related activities, children begin to understand how people work in a community, participate in community events, and care for and protect their community. Again, the opening scenario illustrates that the children who played understood many social studies concepts related to their own community. Through the use of props, verbal and nonverbal language, and symbolic representations, they showed their understanding of preparing for and taking a trip, using public transportation, different community occupations, and civic rules and regulations.

REFLECT AND APPLY EXERCISE 13.1

Demonstrating Community Concepts

Reflect

Re-read the opening scenario. Reflect on the specific behaviors of the children that demonstrate their knowledge of community workers.

Apply

Think about other props or objects that could be placed in the center that also would encourage children to enhance their social studies skills. Additionally, how could you use some of the activities that the children engage in to enhance language and literacy skills at the same time? Reviewing some of the techniques suggested in Chapter 10 could assist you.

Through play activities, children address problems and answer questions that increase and deepen their understanding of social studies concepts that they will later encounter during their formal schooling, such as history, geography, civics, and economics. One example of such a play activity would be creating a train station where children have costumes and a train with which to travel. This center could be modified regularly so that children could engage in a number of different experiences and roles:

Younger children (approximately 2 to 5 years old):

- **Community roles:** Arranging the center with wall posters, books, artifacts, and clothing that represent current community roles; for example a school crossing guard, road repair workers, animal control officers.
- **Geographical experiences:** Arranging a center with wall posters, books, artifacts, and clothing that represent a different natural environment; for example, a forest or a desert.

Older children (approximately 5 to 7 years old):

- **Diversity experiences:** Arranging the center with wall posters, books, cultural artifacts, and clothing that represent life in another country, such as China, Nigeria, Mexico, or Saudi Arabia.
- **Historical experiences:** Arranging the center with wall posters, books, artifacts, and clothing that represent a different period of time, for example the Prehistoric Era or the Feudal Era.

Of course, children's understanding of social studies content is further enhanced through participation in language and literacy activities that relate to their play enactments. Activities such as making play plans, creating shared writings, and participating in dialogic readings (described later in this chapter) augment not only language and literacy abilities but also understanding of social studies concepts. Through collaborative activities at different learning centers (e.g., making music with instruments, proving scientific concepts, creating artifacts, preparing foods, and designing block structures) social studies concepts are even further enhanced. Careful planning of center activities allows children to continually discuss, problem-solve, and question social studies themes. Through careful observations, concerns and interests expressed by the children can become the cornerstone for small and large group activities or for designing further centers. Figure 13.2 suggests some ways in which socio-dramatic play centers can be modified to support the development of social studies concepts.

Figure 13.2 Integrating Play and Social Studies Themes

Colonial Housekeeping: History (different appliances, clothing, toys), community roles (diverse responsibilities), geography (rural settings)

Toy Store: Economics (selling), diversity (cultural toys), community roles (consumers), ecology (recycled materials)

Pet Store: Community roles (occupations), decision making (adopting a pet), geography (different climates and pet care)

Super Heroes: Geography (natural disasters), decision making (disaster prevention), community roles (community protection)

Social Studies Concepts

Neighborhood and Community Outings

Children should explore their neighborhoods and communities by having planned group outings during the school day. These situations provide children with firsthand experiences with social studies topics that cannot be duplicated in the classroom or at the school. They can then return to the school and use playful interactions to reenact what they have learned on the outing.

The first step in planning a group outing is for the adults to decide on the goal of the outing and determine if it can be attained in a different way. Asking questions similar to the following will assist with this process: Do we need to go to the train station? Would inviting an employee from the station to the class accomplish the same goal?

If the decision is made to go on an outing, the adults must then carefully think through experiences that the children need prior to, during, and after the outing. Adults should consider what Seefeldt (2004) labels the *integrative power* of a group outing. An example of reflecting on the integrative power of an outing would be asking the question, "How will the outing enhance the children's language arts, mathematics, art, and social skills?" As adults prepare the students for the outing, they will need to focus on the areas of development along with the development of social studies content skills. For example, children can draw pictures of what they expect to see on the outing and dictate stories about it. When they return, they can re-create what they learned through socio-dramatic play activities inside and outside the classroom.

Seefeldt and Galper (2006) provide safety tips for class outings, which are listed in Figure 13.3. Additionally, they offer the following guidelines for meaningful class outings:

- Keep the outing simple for young children, and increase the complexity as they develop.
- Consider the mode of transportation. Walking is best for most children.
- Consider the special needs of all children in the classroom.
- Introduce the outing experience through discussions, pictures, mapping, reading, and art experiences.
- Organize your classroom play activities around the place to be visited.
- Prepare the children for how to gather data on the outing.
- Allow children to reflect on the outing by having enough materials and time.
- Welcome parent participation during any phase of the outing—for example, planning, implementing, or following up.

Figure 13.3   Some Safety Tips for Class Outings

Obtain parental permission	Check the route and site ahead of time for hazards	Make sure at least one adult is trained in first aid and CPR	Take a first aid kit on the outing
Check children's medical forms for allergies	Always walk on the left, facing the traffic	Be sure children know to observe small animals, not handle them	Have children practice transportation rules
Consider adult/child ratios. 1:3 or 4 at the most	Take an updated list of children's emergency numbers	Small outings might be best for all learners	Be sure the site meets the needs for children with disabilities

Source: Seefeldt, C., & Galper, A. (2006). *Active Experiences for Active Children: Social Studies.* New York, NY: Pearson.

Social Studies Standards

Engaging in social studies activities advances children's understanding of themselves, their families, and the communities in which they live. Through these activities, children begin to examine how people interact with different social and physical environments.

Head Start Early Learning Social Studies Elements

Children begin to understand their roles as members of a family and community through the understanding of history, culture, and environment. Through hands-on experiences they begin to make sense of different types of cultures from either distant places or different times in history, and how those cultures interacted with the geographical environment around them.

The Head Start Framework (Head Start, 2011) focuses on how young children develop skills across the following three social studies themes:

- **Self, family, and community:** Children develop an understanding of their relationships to their family and community, and the various roles in their family and community, and a respect for diversity within families and communities (e.g., family structures, traditions, jobs, and rules).
- **People and the environment:** Children begin to understand the relationship between people and the environment in which they live (e.g., roads, buildings, water, animals, plants, and protection through recycling).
- **History and events:** Children compare events that happened in the past and how these events relate to their self, family, and community (e.g., past, present, future; personal and family histories; and people changing over time).

Specific examples of skills relating to these themes are listed on the following website: http://eclkc.ohs.acf.hhs.gov/hslc/tta-system/teaching/eecd/Assessment/Child%20Outcomes/HS_Revised_Child_Outcomes_Framework%28rev-Sept2011%29.pdf.

Vygotsky's (1978) theory of learning suggests that children need the assistance of another person to expand their knowledge to an independent level. Therefore, by knowing the child's existing level of understanding, adults can expand the child's understanding through the following activities (Seefeldt & Galper, 2006):

- Providing children with references—for example, story and informational books, poems, pictures, reference books, and a display table
- Showing a video, pictures, or photographs
- Demonstrating to children how to do something
- Sharing a new fact or piece of information
- Questioning children
- Asking children to observe and listen
- Asking children to use the computer as a resource
- Using new vocabulary that will expand children's language
- Providing experiences
- Providing peer-learning opportunities

As discussed in Chapter 5 of this book, today's classroom intersects with different types of families—including single parent, two parents, unmarried partners, gay and lesbian parents, and extended families. Through early education social studies activities that are both planned and unplanned, young children will enhance their understanding that families provide basic functions, rear children differently, have different values, and can form positive relationships with other families that are different. For example, you can read books on different families;

make bar graphs of the different types of families of the students; make collages of each child's family and discuss similarities; discuss families' different living environments; discuss the meaning of "home"; have children bring in recipes and foods from home; have clothing, objects, and music that might be in the homes of children from different cultures; and talk about different family celebrations and routines. Again, learning about these concepts, and how they are similar and different among families, can be done through formal and informal discussions, children's books, music and dance, art projects, display tables, teacher-directed lessons, and classroom outings.

National Council for the Social Studies (NCSS) Standards

The NCSS (2012) has also published a framework for prekindergarten through 12th grade learning that includes grade-level standards organized around 10 social studies themes. By participating in developmentally appropriate activities that integrate these standards, children develop a sense of civic responsibility and are introduced to concepts relating to the democratic process. Children can be guided to enhance their understanding of many social studies themes through their continual engagement in everyday activities like the following:

- **Play activities** that involve neighborhood activities and community services
- **Map activities** focusing on classroom, school, neighborhood, and community
- **Family timeline activities** that compare how families are made up of different members
- **Rule-making activities** that problem-solve class organization and behavior issues

©iStockphoto.com/mediaphotos

Involvement in everyday collaborative activities can provide the foundation for social studies concepts.

As children design opportunities for continual participation in classroom collaborative activities, they must consider others and their values and beliefs, collaborate and be team members, show interest in others, and negotiate and compromise (Mindes, 2006). Everyday participation in these natural early education activities contributes to children's understanding of their own social studies responsibilities of being capable of making informed and reasoned decisions as members of a culturally diverse and democratic society. Older children in the beginning primary grades can participate in activities to develop social studies skills such as the following: collecting their own data, making timelines, creating books, designing collections, and interviewing people.

Social Studies Centers

Social studies involves understanding how and why people live a certain way. Therefore, social studies learning activities for young children should not be segregated into individualized learning activities; rather, the activities should be presented through an integrated, cross-disciplinary learning approach. Similar to other learning activities, integrating multiple daily opportunities with themes that relate history, geography, and civics allows children to meaningfully interact with social studies concepts. Therefore, through reflective planning, activities involving early literacy, play, mathematics, science, and creative arts can engage children in enriching their understanding of social studies content.

Figure 13.4 provides a list of the 10 NCSS themes, questions that can assist in guiding young children to develop these skills (Hutton, 2011), and suggestions for activities in which these social studies themes can be encouraged. Again, as stated before, the use of language and literacy learning activities, such as the ones presented in Chapter 10, should regularly occur with these social studies activities.

Social Studies Centers: Concept of Time

A careful examination of Figure 13.4 reveals the recurring social studies theme of the **passage of time**, or the concept that with time, some things change and some do not. Not only is time one of the major NCSS themes, it is also a concept that is integrated into the other themes. For example, children learn how *people, places, and environments* change over time; how *their individual development and identity* changes with time; how *production, distribution, and consumption* change over time; and how *science, technology, and society* change over time.

Although young children have a vague understanding of time, they need assistance in furthering their understanding of this concept. Children's understanding of the passage of time can be fostered by talking to them about the personal experiences they have encountered throughout the day, and by using time as a reference for those experiences. Talking about what happened today, yesterday, last month, or next week provides children with a personal understanding of changes in time. One way to assist children's understanding of the passage of time is to take photos of them involved in activities and then to put those pictures in a photo album or on a bulletin board, or arrange them neatly on a table. Children enjoy looking at pictures of themselves and their peers, handling the pictures, and talking about them. As they engage in conversations with peers about their photos, they can be encouraged to reference different times at which these activities took place. Additionally, placing some of the photos in picture albums and allowing children to take them home will increase the opportunities for children to comfortably explore the concept of the passage of time.

Carefully planned questions can assist young children with the development of time concepts.

Sharing objects with children helps them understand the passage of time. For example, showing them a hand-operated mixer and comparing it to a state-of-the-art electronic mixer helps children understand how things change as time passes. Also, bringing in outdated clothing and talking about how it might be different and similar to today's clothing can also assist. Finally, looking at old postcards or photographs of their town or city and comparing those to how things look today also expands their understanding of how time passes and changes occur.

The following are social studies questions suggested by Seefeldt and Galper (2006) that can be asked of children to assist them in improving their understanding of the concept of time passing:

- How many days since we had the police officer's visit to our classroom?
- What did you like best about our field trip to the supermarket that we might be able to do when we go on our field trip to the library?
- Who can tell me something what we did last week?
- What did you like in our lunch yesterday that you would like to have today?
- What types of clothing are we wearing this month that we did not wear last month?

Figure 13.4   NCSS Themes, Questions, and Activities

NCSS Themes	Exploratory Questions	Play Center Activities to Develop Concepts
Culture: Children learn how people create, learn, share, and adapt to culture.	• What is culture? • How are groups of people alike and different? • In what ways are cultures similar and different (food, music, clothing, language)?	*Socio-Dramatic:* Taking shoes off inside, eating utensils, not eating certain foods *Creative Arts:* Dance, music, instruments, sports, birthday celebrations *Mathematics:* Number words
Time, Continuity, and Change: Children learn about everyday life in different times and places around the world.	• What happened in the past? • How do we know about the past? • How was life in the past different from and similar to today?	*Manipulatives:* Jacks, marbles, jackstraw (pick-up sticks with twigs or straw) *Motor Games:* Ring (rope) toss, jump rope, tag *Socio-Dramatic:* Rag dolls, mob caps, cocked hats, old-fashion kitchen
People, Places, and Environments: Children explore different spatial and geographic concepts and the interaction between people and places.	• Where am I? • What are some landforms and bodies of water? • Why do people move? • How do people impact the environment? • How does the environment impact people?	*Socio-Dramatic:* Travel agent (maps, globes, travel clothing); recycling center *Science:* Impact of weather on clothing, recreation, and food. *Blocks:* Different types of housing
Individual Development and Identity: Children learn that family, friends, culture and institutions shape their personal identity.	• How am I the same as and different from other people? • How can I learn to cooperate and collaborate with others? • How has my family and culture contributed to my identity?	*Socio-Dramatic:* Birthday/Holiday center (different ways people celebrate birthdays and holidays) *Manipulatives:* Picking things up with spoons, chopsticks, shells *Mathematics:* Child-made bulletin board demonstrating differences in classroom families and number of guardians, siblings, grandparents, others living in house, and pets
Individual, Groups, and Institutions: Learners examine families, schools, governments, and courts.	• How do I influence groups, and how do groups influence me?	*Science:* Create a scientific experiment as a group *Music:* Collaboratively create a musical instrument using paper plates, beans, yarn, and other items
Power, Authority, and Governance: Children examine rules, fairness, and responsibilities within their families, groups, and classrooms.	• Why do we need rules and laws? • What are my responsibilities as a student? As a citizen? • What happens when you do not agree about something?	*Socio-Dramatic:* Voting place, police station, forest ranger station *Science:* Environment, recycling *Classroom Responsibilities:* Class duties, rules

NCSS Themes	Exploratory Questions	Play Center Activities to Develop Concepts
Production, Distribution, and Consumption: Children relate their wants and needs to personal economic experiences.	• What are goods and services? • How are goods made, delivered, and used? • What is the difference between a need and a want?	*Socio-Dramatic:* Bank, market, farm *Mathematics:* Money *Science:* Growing plants, hatching chickens or butterflies, producing honey or milk
Science, Technology, and Society: Children study how their lives are impacted by technology.	• What are some science and technology examples in our daily lives? • How do the media influence us?	*Socio-Dramatic:* Computer repair shop, office, hospital, newspaper or media reporter *Manipulatives:* Making gadgets with Legos *Science:* Experiments
Global Connections: Children discover how things that happen around the world impact their lives.	• How are people, places, and environments connected around the world? • What are examples of global connections in communities?	*Socio-Dramatic:* Shoe or clothing store (What countries do items come from?), food *Manipulatives:* What countries did they come from?
Civic Ideals and Practices: Children participate in classroom communities by following rules, sharing, and collaborating.	• What are rights and responsibilities in communities? • What is fair? • What are democratic practices?	*Socio-Dramatic:* Polling place, court *Collaborative learning activities* *Child-developed classroom rules*

Social Studies Centers: Anti-Bias Activities

Teachers need to provide an anti-bias approach, which includes the fair treatment of people and materials through attitudes, beliefs, and feelings, to learning in order to promote an authentic multicultural understanding of social studies themes. Perhaps unthinkingly, some teachers tend to use what is currently being termed a tourist approach toward multiculturalism. This approach involves presenting themes in simplistic, isolated activities without much discussion. To be a more culturally responsive person requires teachers to reflect on their own personal cultural background and values, to learn about other cultures and how those cultures differ from their own culture, and to continually integrate diversity in literature and activities in their classrooms (Mindes, 2006). According to Derman-Sparks and Edwards (2010), effective anti-bias education happens when all four of the following goals are part of the curriculum (pp. 3–7):

- Each child is encouraged to demonstrate self-awareness, confidence, family pride, and positive social identities.
- Each child expresses comfort and joy with human diversity; accurate language for human differences; and deep, caring human connections.
- Each child recognizes unfairness, has language to describe unfairness, and understands that unfairness hurts.
- Each child demonstrates empowerment and the skills to act, with others or alone, against prejudice and/or discriminatory actions.

Figure 13.5 suggests ways to integrate anti-bias activities into the 10 social studies themes to enhance children's understanding that all people are made equitable, and that all children and adults together can provide a safe and supportive learning community. Once children have these understandings, they are able to develop to their fullest potential and begin to work toward being productive members of society in the future.

Creating a caring group of children should naturally result in providing an anti-bias education. However, children are influenced by what they hear and see at home and in the community. Therefore, children will ask questions about other children's differences that might be uncomfortable to answer. In these situations, adults should not attempt to silence children. Instead, Eric Hoffman (1999) suggests the following guidelines for addressing children's curiosity:

- Just listen—Stay calm and interested, but don't make judgments about the child
- Determine what the child really wants to know
- Listen for feelings behind the words
- Answer simply and matter-of-factly, using appropriate language
- Always respond—If you do not know the answer, tell the child that you will get back to him or her; remember to get back to the child
- Follow up—Decide if the particular child's question deserves follow-up activities for all children

Through daily interactions, adults can expand children's anti-bias skills. Derman-Sparks and Edwards (2010) suggest using the following strategies:

- Encourage discussions and activities about people's attributes
- Model respect for others' emotions and try to work out conflicts
- Never allow personal attributes to be a reason for a decision

Figure 13.5 Examples of Anti-Bias Activities

Self-Awareness	• Equal respect for each child by inviting families in to share cultural foods, dress, and/or customs
Human Diversity	• Guardians are different in number, sexes, ages, ethnicity, names, and relationship, but are similar in love, support, care, and guidance
Fairness	• Inclusive classroom members consider physical, developmental, behavior challenges, and hearing and vision impairments
Empowerment	• Continual discussions on feelings, family's approaches to problem solving, and identification of unfair practices

- Assist all children in all activities
- Teach children to recognize stereotypes
- Handle toileting and diapering routines without shame
- Use holiday traditions and celebrations
- Incorporate children's family traditions
- Customize December holidays—read books about all winter holidays

---

REFLECT AND APPLY EXERCISE 13.2

Demonstrating Community Concepts

Reflect

Many children in early education centers use biased language without even knowing what they are doing. For example, children may refer to community helpers as a fireman and a policeman.

Apply

Think about how you would respond to children in your class if they were using biased phrases and words. How would you work with children in your class to make sure that they did not continue to use such phrases and words?

Technology Use and Young Children

Technology dominates today's world. It is ever-present in homes, offices, schools, public facilities, purses, and pockets. There are many new and clever ways in which teachers can use technology with children to guide their understanding about history, geography, and civics in their local areas. Through technology use, children can then compare their communities with other communities around the world. The challenge for professionals working with young children is how to integrate hands-on, everyday developmentally appropriate activities with current technological media.

Similar to other learning material, like blocks, manipulatives, or woodcraft objects, the effectiveness of technology does not depend on the product. Rather, it depends on how that product is being integrated into a child's life. Technology products can be hands-on, interactive, and encouraging tools for children's learning if they are presented to the children in a thoughtful and playful manner. However, as with any learning material, early educators need to ensure that technology is integrated into a child's day with the appropriate guidance. Teachers need to reflectively plan what they want children to do with technology and how long each child should be permitted to engage in a technology activity. Technology experiences

Technology can be a hands-on, interactive, and engaging way for children to learn.

©iStockphoto.com/Dean Mitchell

should not take away from children's social interactions, creative play activities, physical activities, or outside explorations. Instead, such experiences should be used to support those activities.

In 2012, the NAEYC published the position statement *Technology and Interactive Media in Early Childhood Programs.* That statement encouraged the use of technology in programs to extend learning opportunities for those children who need assistive devices to learn, move, communicate, and create. Additionally, the statement emphasized how technology could enhance collaboration with families through the development of digital portfolios that document children's progress. However, when using technology to enhance home–school connections it is important to understand the diversity of technology available to families outside the classroom. Many families may not have access to technology in a way that provides them equal access to the classroom or their child's progress. Teachers should survey families at the beginning of the year to learn about the technology families have in their homes. Using this information, teachers can plan for the use of technology along with traditional forms of communication to ensure all families feel included. This can also provide an opportunity for schools to introduce families to varied forms of technology when helping in the classroom or during family-related events. Finally, the NAEYC stressed that technology could be used as a tool for creating new exploration opportunities for children by making books of the children's work.

NAEYC and the Fred Rogers Center for Early Learning and Children's Media at Saint Vincent College (2012) recommend that early childhood educators engage in the following activities:

- Select, use, integrate, and evaluate technology and interactive media tools by giving careful attention to the appropriateness and the quality of the content, the child's experience, and the opportunities for co-engagement
- Provide a balance of activities for children, recognizing that technology is one tool that can be used for learning
- Prohibit the passive use of television, videos, DVDs, and other non-interactive technology and media
- Limit any use of technology and interactive media (see Figure 13.6 and Figure 13.7)
- Carefully consider the screen time recommendations from public health organizations for children; screen time is the amount of time spent in front of a computer screen
- Provide leadership in ensuring equitable access to technology and interactive media experiences for the children in their care and for parents and families

Additionally, the NAEYC position statement recommends that adults who are working with young children need to model good digital use by using technology in safe, healthy, responsible, and socially positive ways. Although further research is needed to help guide the development of policies and practices for using technology with young children, intentional (see Chapter 7) and developmentally appropriate (see Chapter 1) use of technology and interactive media should be considered for all young children. Figure 13.8 summarizes some of the effective classroom practices that the NAEYC recommends for integrating technology tools and interactive media in early learning environments for infants, toddlers, preschoolers, and kindergarteners.

Book Centers

Because so much of children's learning about different cultures, histories, and geographies comes from reading books and because so much information on literacy development was presented in Chapter 10, the following section on designing a Book Center has been included

Figure 13.6 American Academy of Pediatrics (AAP) Recommendations on Media for Children (2013)

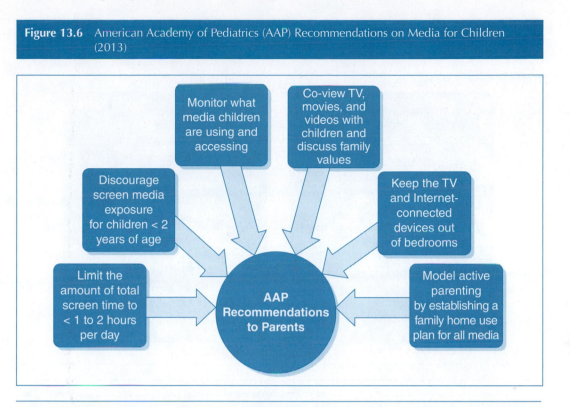

Source: American Academy of Pediatrics Council on Communications and Media. (2013, October). Children, Adolescents, and the Media. *Pediatrics*. Retrieved from http://pediatrics.aappublications.org/content/132/5/958.full .pdf+html

Figure 13.7 American Academy of Pediatrics (AAP) Recommendations on Media for Schools (2013)

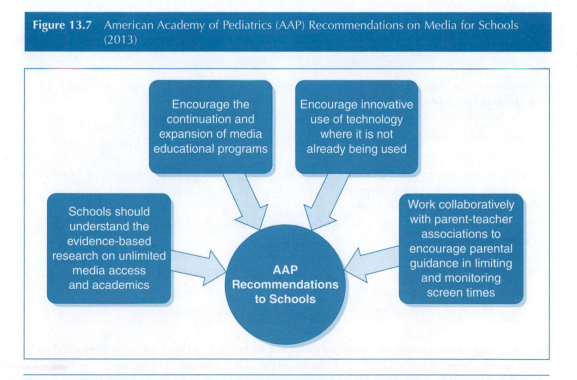

Source: American Academy of Pediatrics Council on Communications and Media. (2013, October). Children, Adolescents, and the Media. *Pediatrics*. Retrieved from http://pediatrics.aappublications.org/content/132/5/958.full .pdf+html

Figure 13.8 Effective Classroom Use of Technology

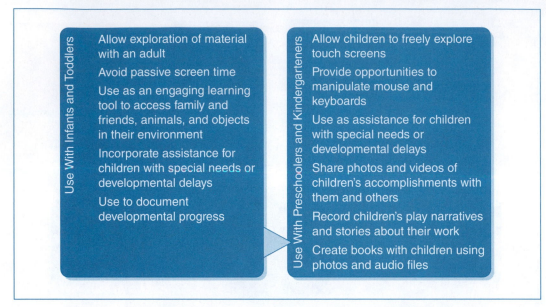

Use With Infants and Toddlers

Allow exploration of material with an adult

Avoid passive screen time

Use as an engaging learning tool to access family and friends, animals, and objects in their environment

Incorporate assistance for children with special needs or developmental delays

Use to document developmental progress

Use With Preschoolers and Kindergarteners

Allow children to freely explore touch screens

Provide opportunities to manipulate mouse and keyboards

Use as assistance for children with special needs or developmental delays

Share photos and videos of children's accomplishments with them and others

Record children's play narratives and stories about their work

Create books with children using photos and audio files

Source: National Association for the Education of Young Children and the Fred Rogers Center for Early Learning and Children's Media at Saint Vincent College. (2012, January). *Position Statement: Technology and Interactive Media as Tools in Early Childhood Programs Serving Children From Birth Through Age 8.* Retrieved from http://www.naeyc .org/files/naeyc/PS_technology_WEB.pdf

CHECKLIST FOR COMPUTER USAGE WITH YOUNG CHILDREN

Computers should supplement educational activities such as play, music, reading, movement, art, and social interactions.

Adults should always be present to guide children's computer work.

Adults should observe children's amount of use on the computer and types of activities. Children must participate in alternate activities.

Children should be guided to work with peers on the computer to enhance social skills, turn-taking, cooperation, and language skills.

Adults must monitor the software products that children are using for inappropriate language, violence, or lack of stimulation.

in this chapter. However, book centers should not be limited to these subjects; they need to be more comprehensive and include books from all the classroom areas of interests. Additionally, they should include both fictional and informational books and other varied forms of print (e.g., children's magazines, newspapers, catalogues, advertisements).

Interacting With Books

As early as 5 months in age, some babies will sit in an adult's lap and quietly look at a book. If other infants are placed in an adult's lap, however, they will quickly begin to wiggle around and attempt to get down on the floor where they are less confined. In short, infants differ widely and, because of these differences, their interest in books and book reading activities depends on multiple factors. Three factors are particularly important:

- **Infants' styles of interaction.** Some children enjoy being cuddled, while others do not. Many children feel uncomfortable spending much of their time in a constrained position; therefore, they do not favor the restricted feeling that they experience when looking at a picture book with an adult. Other infants enjoy every engaging moment provided by the infant-adult interaction in book reading.
- **Infants develop at various rates.** Some children will adapt to book reading activities earlier than others, in the same way that some children walk before others.
- **All children are different.** Books are more pleasing to some infants than they are to other infants. Rather than look at a book, some children might be more interested in watching a ball roll past them or a sibling involved in a play activity.

Because the attitudes of young children toward book activities are varied and unpredictable, adults must be sensitive to signals given by babies. Adults need to let the baby's feelings guide the length and physical context of a reading experience so that, at a young age, children will associate books with positive and enjoyable memories.

Around the age of 12 to 18 months, most children begin to sit on an adult's lap and enjoy having a book read to them. At this point, children will attempt to repeat actions illustrated in the book. If the book shows a picture of children clapping their hands, the child looking at the book will perform a similar activity. Figure 13.9 suggests simple types of books for reading with babies. Figure 13.10 illustrates how keeping books in baskets on the floor allows infants easy access to them.

As children enter into toddlerhood, they should be encouraged not only to enjoy the book but also to participate in the entire process of book reading. Specifically, toddlers should be

Figure 13.9 Types of Books for Infants

What Books to Read?	How to Read Books?	Which Types of Books?
Infants: Books with bright colors, contrasting patterns, and faces	Cuddle	Textures
	Repetition	Mirrors
4–6 Months: Vinyl or cloth, repetition	Use expression	Flaps with surprises
	Animal and vehicle sounds	Easy to turn pages
6–12 Months: Pictures of familiar objects	Stop and talk or ask questions	Rhyming words
		Waterproof
12 Months: Books that they can turn and feel the pages	Encourage touching — books need to be durable	Small photo albums
		Toy catalogs

allowed to choose the book that they want to read and to determine how much of the book that they are interested in reading. Then, when their interest wanes, they should be allowed to return the book back to the shelf or basket, and then to engage in a more desirable activity. Figure 13.11 demonstrates different book activities and suggests approximate ages when they should appear (Schickedanz, 1999).

Figure 13.10   Books in a Basket on the Floor Allow Infants Easy Access

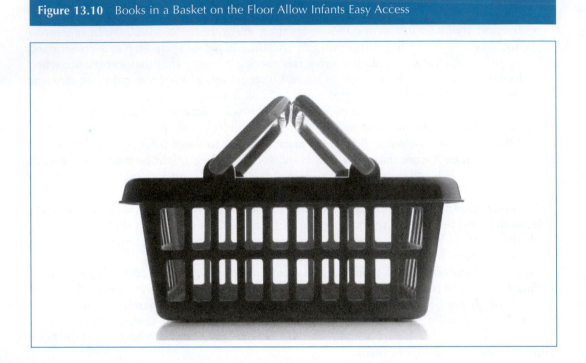

By the time children reach preschool, they should be familiar with how to use books and should enjoy interacting with them. Unfortunately, although benefits accrue from early book reading with young children, research has shown that most teachers read to children only an average of 8 minutes a day, with only 4% of teachers reading more than 20 minutes a day (Dickinson & Tabors, 2001). Furthermore, data from the National Institute of Child Health and Human Development (NICHD) Early Child Care Research Network (2000) concluded that preschool programs for low-income children tend to provide their children with even less reading time than that reported.

Teachers attempting to address the needs of diverse populations, including many children from low-income situations, must be aware of these findings. These teachers must strive to provide students in their programs with at least 20 minutes a day of reading time.

Designing Book Centers

Part I of this book demonstrated that literacy is an active process that requires children to think about print. The book center should

Nick White/Photodisc/Thinkstock

Book reading activities should be collaborative and fun for children of all ages.

Figure 13.11 Infants' and Toddlers' Behaviors Demonstrating Understanding of Pictures in Books

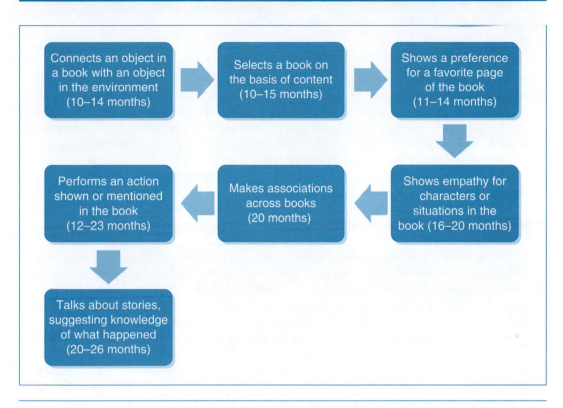

Source: Adapted from Schickedanz, J. A. (1999). *Much More Than the A B Cs: The Early Stages of Reading and Writing*. Washington, DC: The National Association for the Education of Young Children.

include both fiction and informational books. The center should not contain just books, but also have materials that will engage children in enjoyable and meaningful reading and writing activities. Because young children are skillful at learning through interactions with their peers, the book center should also maximize opportunities for peer collaborations. However, these interactions should focus around peaceful and relaxing activities, encouraging a tranquil environment for the book center.

Along with books, the book center should contain multiple types of paper, writing materials, tablets, journals, alphabet stamps, a CD player or other portable music players, a computer or electronic tablet, and alphabet and word games. Not all of these items should be displayed at once, and the ones that are exhibited should be organized in an orderly and user-friendly manner.

©iStockphoto.com/lostinbids

Throughout the day, teachers should pick up a book and read it to the children who are interested.

LEARNING FOR ALL CHILDREN
Book Centers and Disabilities

Dennis, Lynch, and Stockall (2012) suggest many ways to modify literacy environments to assist both disabled and nondisabled children. They recommend that the book center be a comfortable and quiet setting where children can relax and read books or listen to audio books. Some children will enjoy the opportunity to snuggle in a corner on a large pillow, while others will prefer a chair and table.

Children with posture and muscle challenges might require book holders to support the books that they choose to read. These holders are typically made of lightweight plastic, and some have adjustable clips to hold the book open.

Additionally, having books that focus on children and adults with disabilities is also important. The website section at the end of this chapter contains suggestions on where such books can be located.

Children with visual impairments, who are learning to read with Braille overlays, should be provided with overlays for all the books in which they are interested. Children with low vision who are learning to read print will likely benefit from books with high contrast print, bold fonts, adequate spacing between the lines, and plenty of white space on the page (Dennis, Lynch, & Stockall, 2012). A vision specialist should be consulted before such decisions are made.

Children with language problems will often understand language better than they can express it. Therefore, they will have difficulty verbally answering questions. However, if they receive minimal supports—such as being asked to fill in words, to select a picture or object, or to place items in the correct sequence in which they appeared in the story—such children can usually do better when required to verbally sequence events.

Story boxes, bags, or baskets that contain real objects talked about in the books can assist children with language delays in developing vocabulary. Additionally, allowing them to integrate some of these items into their socio-dramatic play centers or puppet centers encourages them to act out the stories in which all of the players have background knowledge. As a result, language-delayed children will depend less on the use of metacommunications for sharing their play intentions with their partners. Finally, it is always beneficial to supply visually impaired children with the real objects that are being discussed in the book so that they can feel and manipulate those objects.

Many children with special needs also have attention challenges. Teachers can call children's attention to specific print in the book, a practice referred to as *print referencing*. According to Justice and Ezell (2004), there are three specific strategies for print referencing: (1) asking children questions about print, (2) commenting about print, and (3) tracking the print with your finger. These three strategies, together with encouraging children to identify specific letters or words, enhance early literacy skills.

Using open-ended dialogic reading prompts particularly benefits children with language disorders. By using "wh" questions (e.g., when, where, what, why, which), adults encourage children to comprehend the questions and to respond with the language that they know. If children have difficulty responding to open-ended questions, teachers can assist them by showing them pictures that have been copied directly from the book or that have been cut out of a second book.

In short, through all of these experiences, children with and without disabilities enhance their understanding of the form and function of print in their lives and in books. As a result, they become more comfortable with decontextualized print, letters of the alphabet, and phonemes. Being comfortable with the function of print enhances young children's self-motivation to pursue reading and writing tasks.

Strategies that will assist children in becoming comfortable with print:

- Read stories aloud
- Let children handle books and pretend to read
- Allow children to scribble and draw for writing
- Ask children to predict what will come next in a story or poem
- Summarize the story
- Use writing to communicate with children
- Talk about words and letters
- Connect single letters with sounds they can make
- Point out simple and meaningful words
- Write words and simple sentences

Location and Structure. The location of the book center is a main contributor to engaging children in literacy activities. Choosing the appropriate location is challenging because a book center should be situated in a quiet part of the classroom, preferably away from the socio-dramatic and block centers. Books should not be stacked on the shelves for children to pursue aimlessly; rather, books should be grouped according to categories. For young children who cannot yet categorize books, the books could be placed in plastic containers that fit on the bookshelves. Containers can be labeled on the front of the container with print and with pictures that represent the category. For infants, books can be neatly arranged in baskets on the floor to make access easier for children who are still crawling.

All children benefit when special reading environments are created both inside the classroom and outside the classroom.

The center should be comfortably furnished so that children can sit to read or write, mostly with peers but sometimes by themselves. Children may prefer soft pillows or beanbag chairs that allow them to relax while enjoying reading or listening to a book. Additionally, the center should have an area where children can group together and share books. Some teachers are fortunate to have parents who will contribute their time to building a simple wooden structure that can be used for children to sit in when at the center—like a "book boat," a "literacy launch pad," or a "reading race car." These specially designed, nook-like structures are usually lined with pillows so that children can cuddle up together and enjoy reading a book or e-book, or listening to a book on tape.

For those teachers who lack the support of parent groups, a few trips to the Goodwill store or garage sales will usually result in locating a moderately priced children's swimming pool, blow-up canoe or boat, or small tent. Each of these items can easily be converted into a comfortable and relaxing nook area for reading. Additionally, placing a number of stuffed animals or cloth dolls in these special reading areas can encourage children to relax and enjoy the literacy activities. Finally, placing a lamp on one of the shelves will also make the center appear more tranquil, and for tent-reading activities having a flashlight in the tent will add excitement.

The center should also contain a study table and chairs for children who choose to participate in writing and game activities. Additionally, the book center is an excellent location for a computer station where two children can sit together at the computer and collaboratively engage in listening to stories and playing computer literacy games. Additionally, children enjoy having access to a simple audio recorder that they can use to record their own stories and then listen to those stories or to those of their peers. Children, however, must be first taught how to appropriately operate the audio recorder; many children may require adult assistance when using it.

Materials and Resources. Posters that encourage reading and writing can be hung on the walls of the book center. Frequently, local bookstores and libraries have posters that they will donate to teachers. Additionally, having a book checkout system with library cards, checkout cards, and date stamps allows children to learn library procedures while engaging in literacy pretend play enactments. Placing a calendar at the checkout counter of the book center assists children in determining due dates. As an art project, children can make bookmark that can be kept in the book center for children to use when they need to mark their place in a book.

The books available in the center should focus on diverse topics that interest the children. The center should contain a variety of types of books, including fiction, poems, and information books, and special books should be displayed using a book rack on a top shelf. Adults should pay attention to which books attract the most children and should routinely rotate out books that the children have lost interest in reading.

Having different types of paper and fun pens available will undoubtedly encourage children to engage in writing activities while in the book center. Using clipboards makes it possible for children to write while they are relaxing on pillows and beanbags. Also, having stationery, old cards that stores might be discarding, invitations, and postcards (including ones that the children can make) will engage students in literacy activities and assist as play props. Alphabet letters, such as magnetic ones that can be used with magnetic boards or cookie sheets, alphabet stamps and pictures, and alphabet games, such as bingo, can all be carefully situated in the book center. Figure 13.12 illustrates some of the items that can be included in a book center.

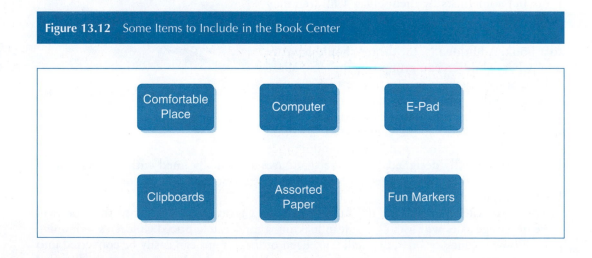

Figure 13.12   Some Items to Include in the Book Center

| Comfortable Place | Computer | E-Pad |
| Clipboards | Assorted Paper | Fun Markers |

Book Center Activities

Here are examples of simple and easy activities that children enjoy and that keep them engaged with books.

Game: Count the letter: _____.

Count the letter is a game that children can play on their own and that focuses them on finding a specific letter in a book.

How Do Children Play Count the Letter: An adult completes the phrase "Count the letter: _____" by putting a letter on the blank line.
  The game proceeds as follows:

1. The children will need the card with the letter on it, clipboards, paper, pencils, and either a flyswatter, a pointer, or a wand.

2. Two children play at a time. One child has the clipboard, pencil, and paper. The other child has the wand, pointer, or flyswatter.

3. The children choose a book. The child with the pointer then finds the designated letter and points to it or swats it with the flyswatter. The other child with the clipboard makes a mark every time the letter is found.

4. They tally up the marks and then switch positions.

5. When the second person completes their book, they tally up their numbers and then compare to see who found the most.

6. If children are just learning to count, they can be provided with a piece of paper with a row of 10 boxes on it. A mark can be put in a box every time they find the letter. Whoever has the most boxes with marks will be the winner.

7. Words or rhyming objects can be used in place of letters. Most children never appear to tire of this activity!

Guided Questions

Most preschool children will develop literacy skills if they are provided regular and consistent opportunities to interact with books. However, the children cannot just be left on their own with the books. Instead, adults must provide practices, like the following ones, that will guide children toward advancing their literacy skills at a young age:

*   Reading and discussing what is being read
*   Showing the print and pointing out the relationships between printed forms, including pictures, and spoken words
*   Providing opportunities for children to explain and to predict stories

Figure 13.13 presents three question-asking strategies that have been proven to assist young children in the development of literacy skills (Barclay, Benelli, & Gudt, 1998). Similarly, Wasik, Bond, and Hindman (2006) found that asking questions, building vocabulary, and making connections between events in the book and events in the children's lives greatly contribute to the literacy development of disadvantaged children.

Book Reading Guided Questions Strategy #1. Before exposing children to a book, adults should identify the vocabulary in the book that their students will find challenging. The adult can use real objects to introduce new words and can ask the children questions such as the following:

"What is this called?"

"What can we do with this?"

Figure 13.13   Simple Tips for Reading Stories to Young Children

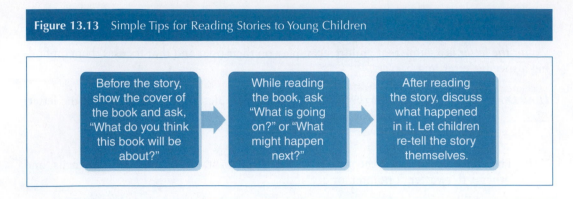

Source: Barclay, K., Benelli, C., & Gudt, P. T. (1998). It's Never Too Soon: Building a Firm Foundation for Reading and Writing. *The Magazine of the National Head Start Association, 17*(3), 38–44.

This type of interaction will provide the adult with information on what the students know and what they need to learn.

Book Reading Guided Questions Strategy #2. During the reading of a book, problem-solving discussions can be prompted by asking questions similar to the following:

"Who can tell me what is happening on this page?"

"What do you think will happen next? How do you know? What were the clues?"

Book Reading Guided Questions Strategy #3. After the story is read, children can reflect on their feelings about the book by the adult asking:

"What part of the book did you like best?"

"Tell me why you think that person did what he did? What made you think that?"

Guided questions like these allow children to actively participate in book reading activities. They also encourage children to elaborate on their ideas, feelings, and reactions to the stories that use decontextualized language. The Common Core State Standards emphasize students' ability to use text evidence to support their thinking. Asking students to explain their answers and show where in the text their answer came from sets a strong foundation for future reading and writing success in alignment with the CCSS. Research has found that if teachers employ these types of interactive reading activities, young children begin to develop critical reading skills and demonstrate considerable improvement in their language and literacy skills despite economic challenges (Wasik et al., 2006).

Dialogic Reading

Dialogic reading is another guided reading strategy that research has found to enhance the literacy skills of young children (Bowman et al., 2001). Dialogic reading experiences are conversations that the adult reader has with the children, as pictured in Figure 13.14. These conversations are geared toward enhancing the children's use of the language presented in the story. Through the adult's use of five different types of prompts, children become more involved in the reading of the story. The following is a list of these prompts accompanied by examples:

Completion Prompts	• Leave a blank at the end of a sentence
Recall Prompts	• Encourage children to remember what happened
Open-Ended Prompts	• Encourage children to re-tell the story by focusing on the pictures
What, Where, When, and Why Prompts	• Encourage children to use their own vocabulary to talk about pictures
Distancing Prompts	• Guide children to make connections between the book and their experiences

Figure 13.14 Adults and Children Participating in a Conversation About What They Are Thinking While Reading a Story

Dialogic Reading Activity

"Hum. I am wondering if maybe the....
Who would like to share what they are
wondering?"

Once again, the use of these prompts encourages children to use decontextualized language in telling about events that they were exposed to through written text.

In summary, books have a special place in the development of children's literacy skills. Additionally, shared book reading is considered one of the most important activities that occur between a child and caregiver. Huge disparities exist in the amount of time spent in

Through appropriate questioning, adults can guide children to higher levels of reading skills.

shared reading between a caregiver and child in a middle-income home, and the time for this activity spent in a low-income home. Adams (1990) reported that typical middle-class children enter first grade after they have been read to for approximately 1,000 hours; in contrast, low-income families average just about 25 hours for this activity.

To make up for the disparity between the two populations, children must be provided with a greater number of playful and stimulating experiences with books (Neuman, 1999). Just placing books in the physical proximity of children is not enough. Instead, along with the books, children must have adults who can read more often to the children and can offer them individual assistance and encouragement. Neuman's study found that supplying books and adult guidance over a year resulted in substantial improvements in children's concepts of print, writing, letter name knowledge, and concepts of narrative.

Chapter Summary

HOME AND COMMUNITY CONNECTIONS

Integrating Play Activities in the Social Studies and Book Center

Meet the neighborhood. Take a drive or walk around the neighborhood and label what you see; a grocery store, the post office, the park, the police station, the neighbors, apartments, houses, the mall, the street signs, the name of your street.

Early childhood curricula typically include lessons that explore themes of *me, my family, my neighborhood,* and *my community.* They also include topics on how diversity exists in the world around them and exists in comparison to the past and to the future. Children use books and technology to gather information on individuals who are both similar to and different from them so that they can understand others' cultures and traditions, and learn methods for caring about the world around them. Implementing these social studies skills requires children to develop a wide range of social behaviors, many of which are similar to those acquired through socio-dramatic play interactions. Therefore, integrating play and social studies skills is a natural and comfortable process for young children. Classrooms should have appropriate and well-planned book centers that support children's development of social studies skills.

CHAPTER 13 FIRST-PERSON INTERVIEW

Children Feeling Comfortable With Traditions

I have been working with the same special education partner-teacher, Vera, for 5 or 6 years. I really can't remember how long it has been. One year the principal split us up, but we were put back together the following year by the new principal, and we were both delighted! When we initially started working together, we spent lots of time planning, but now we don't need to spend that much time. Don't get me wrong; we plan! But the way we plan now is so different. It's more informal, and we don't need to focus so much on the details. We have learned to work with each other quite well.

Theresa Lawrence

Collaborative Early Education Teacher, Carson, CA

Every day, we each lead a large circle activity. I tend to run the early morning circle, and Vera does the later one. But that's not always the case. This year, some of the children we have are more challenging than before. So, if Vera needs to sit near one of them, I will take over the large group activity. However, often I will sit near the challenging child and that works out too. You know, none of the children know which teacher is with special education and which one is not, we do not separate ourselves in that way. They don't see any differences in us, and often I have trouble seeing any difference in the children, as children are generally at varying developmental levels. When they are playing together, you just don't see differences. You really cannot tell who is receiving Special Education services and who is not. They are just groups of children busy learning while having fun.

We use a social studies curriculum for a framework on what themes the children are going to explore. However, Vera and I really like to alter what we do so we can address the needs of all the children. We always bring in our own ideas and activities for the children to supplement the theme. Sometime we spend one week on a theme, and other times we will spend two weeks. It just depends on how interested the children are in the topic. Our days are very fast-paced, and we definitely know when the children are interested or not interested in the activities. We use the social studies themes to assist the children in developing their self-esteem. We want all of our children to recognize ways in which they are similar to their peers, and the ways in which they are different from each other. We truly cherish diversity in our class and focus on how differences are good in almost everything we do. We want the children to look at each other and see the uniqueness of each person in our class because we are all so different when it comes down to it.

We are always reading books about how people are different—some people have curly hair, some have no hair, and some have long hair. We are always talking about how everyone is different and, at the same time, we talk about how much we are alike—we all play, talk, eat, feel sad, happy, and have fun. We discuss the different types of families in our classroom. Some children live with grandmas or uncles. We have children who have two mommies or two daddies. We have children who have a parent incarcerated. We have children who have a parent who has died. Even with all these different types of families, we still talk about how similar parents and guardians are—they take care of you, they love you, they help you, and they want the best for you.

Our current theme is "celebrations." The other day we were discussing the different types of celebrations that we have. Because it was December, we had a word web with many different types of holiday words on it using the word "celebration" as the root. While we were talking about the words, one little boy said in a positive tone, "We don't have a tree at our house." I simply responded with, "It's fine not to celebrate certain holidays, but I know you have events you celebrate, like your birthday," and we moved on with our activity. I couldn't help thinking about how comfortable he appeared to feel when talking about something he did not do and what he does do that was different from many of the other children, and how accepting the children were about his comment.

Student Study Site

Visit the Student Study Site at **www.sagepub.com/selmi** to access additional study tools including mobile-friendly eFlashcards and links to video and web resources.

Sample Learning Activities

Curricular Area: Social Studies

Core Vocabulary: Community, family, fair, teamwork, roles, responsibility, neighborhood

Guide Questions:

What is a community?

What does it mean to be part of a community?

Why is it important for us to work together?

What is teamwork?

How can we help our families and communities?

Resources:

Andreae, Giles. (1999, 2012). *Giraffes Can't Dance.* Cartwheel Books; Brdbk edition.

Bullard, Lisa. (2002). *My Neighborhood Places and Faces.* Picture Window Books.

Finn, Carrie. (2007). *Manners at School.* Picture Window Books.

Martin, Bill, Sampson, Michael, & Raschka, Chris. (2004). *I Pledge Allegiance.* Candlewick Press.

Ritchie, Scot. (2009). *Follow That Map!* Kids Can Press.

Sweeney, Joan. (2000). *Me and My Family Tree.* Dragonfly Books.

Core Text: The Recess Queen, by Alexis O'Neill

- Skills: Acceptance, fair play, rhyming, verbs, text features (bold, font, large print, small print) for emphasis
- Levels of Questions: Who was the story about? What happened in the story? Was it right for Jean to treat the kids the way she did? What was special about Katie Sue? Do you think it is OK for someone to order you around on the playground? How can you be a good friend on the playground?
- Product: Map of the school, map of the playground, class rules

Learning Centers:

- Explore through literacy: Books on different types of communities
- Create: Make a map of the playground using various materials: construction paper, recycled boxes, toilet paper rolls, scissors, glue, crayons, modeling clay. Provide a wide array of materials for students to self-select how they will create their playground map.
- Outdoor play: Allow students to play freely with the materials and apparatuses already available. But use the guide questions to help them understand the concepts of teamwork and fair play as they interact with one another.
- Dramatic play: At home with the family, coaching their favorite professional team

Key Terms

anti-bias	screen time
culturally responsive	social studies
passage of time	tourist approach

Some Children's Books About Social Studies

Beautiful Blackbird, by Ashley Bryan

Castles, Caves, and Honeycombs, by Linda Ashman

Everybody Bakes Bread, by Norah Dooley

Lots of Grandparents, by Shelley Rotner & Sheila Kelly

My Best Friend, by Pat Hutchins

Send It! by Don Carter

Stars and Stripes: The Story of the American Flag, by Sarah L. Thomson

Supermarket, by Kathleen Krull

Sweet Music in Harlem, by Debbie A. Taylor

Trucks, by Donald Crews

Whistle for Willie, by Ezra Jack Keats

Useful Websites

American Academy of Pediatrics Report on Screen Time: http://pediatrics.aappublications
.org/content/132/5/958.full.pdf+html

National Council for the Social Studies: http://www.socialstudies.org

Reflective Question

Social studies skills need to be integrated into typical daily early education classrooms. How could the opening scenario be expanded to enhance language and literacy skills, mathematical skills, and further social studies skills?

14 Integrating Play Activities in the Creative Arts Centers

BUSY EXPRESSING THEIR IDEAS

George Doyle/Stockbyte/Thinkstock

At this preschool the days typically begin with children choosing to participate in activities that are set up in seven different centers: the manipulatives center, the dramatic play center, the block center, the snack center, and the three creative arts centers. On this particular day, the creative arts centers consist of a painting activity, a foil art activity, and a modeling clay activity. The following are samples of the types of interactions that occur during activities at two of these creative arts centers, the painting activity and the foil art activity.

At the painting center, two boys are sitting with an adult who controls an older looking record player. One boy is using a pencil to punch a hole in the middle of a white paper plate. He then positions the plate on the center of the record player so it is secure. Next he tells the other boy sitting at the table that he is going to use the colors yellow and red to make a "hot planet." The other boy responds that he wants to use blue and purple because his planet is cold.

The adult asks the boy who has just placed the plate on the record player what is going to happen on his hot planet. The boy starts telling her how only very hot things can live there like rocks and lava. He hopes that the rocket ship will not crash into it because the ship will melt. Next, the boy who is going to create a cold planet, starts talking to the other boy about how they have to get these planets made so that they can get back to the rocket ships before someone else gets their rockets.

The adult then shows the children how to hold two marking pens at once and how to apply enough pressure so that the pens will make marks while the plate still rotates around. The adult and the boys spend some time talking about what they know about the word "rotate" and how

(Continued)

(Continued)

that knowledge might apply to what they will do with the pens, plate, and record player. The adult asks the boy with the yellow and red markers to go first. The boy holds his hand in a somewhat steady position for a couple of minutes while the plate rotates around.

At the foil art table, four children are sitting with an adult and creating different objects out of foil, such as a necklace, hat, and letters of the alphabet. A girl who was at the dramatic play center comes over and asks the adult for a blanket for her doll. The adult asks if anyone at the table can make a blanket for the doll that is getting cold. One boy volunteers and firmly covers the doll with a piece of foil. The doll's legs and feet remain uncovered, so the boy gets another piece of foil and presses it against the original piece to further extend the blanket. The girl returns to the dramatic play center with her doll and blanket.

Next, the adult places a piece of foil on her head and says that she is going to make a hat. As she molds it to her head, the foil slips down over her eyes a bit. A boy who was watching the adult asks if he could make a space helmet. The adult takes the piece of foil off of her head, gives it to the boy, and assists him in molding it to his head. She then suggests that he could go over to the full-length mirror in the dramatic play center to work further on it. Another child is busy squishing foil and making it into a long, rope-shaped object. He then starts to swing the object around, and the adult suggests that perhaps it could be a leash for walking a dog. The boy starts to walk toward the dramatic house center with the foil strip behind him. He announces to the children playing there that he is walking his dog and needs some water fast "because it is so hot and smoggy here."

Back at the foil art table, the adult picks up another flat piece of foil and announces that she is reading her newspaper. Next, she rolls it up and says, "What happened to my newspaper? Did it become a magic wand?"

Art, music, movement, and drama have traditionally constituted the areas of creative arts that are recognized as integral to young children's development. Local communities and educational programs have long provided an array of activities that engage children and their parents in activities involving these areas. Unfortunately, in recent decades severe budget cuts and an increasing emphasis on the development of academically isolated discrete skills have limited these types of activities. However, research now demonstrates that carefully planned creative arts activities can expand some foundational academic skills.

This chapter examines different types of creative arts activities and illustrates how to implement pretend play interactions to expand these activities into a vital component of young children's curriculum. The chapter then suggests ways in which the activities can impact children's development and learning processes. Specifically, the following questions will be addressed:

> How can creative arts enhance children's development and learning?

> Why would it be important to create contexts for expressive play interactions?

> What are some of the important components for the following creative arts centers: art centers, music and movement centers, drama centers, and puppet centers?

Early Creative Arts Skills and Development

Although several creative arts activities differ in both appearance and routine, all of them focus on expanding similar abilities in children. Through hands-on activities, children receive opportunities to communicate their own thoughts using a range of representational symbols. A child who is excited about spending the afternoon with "Papa," can paint a picture of the ice cream cone that the child knows they will get, sing a happy song about grandparents, create a socio-dramatic play episode about spending the afternoon with Papa, or move to music to express the feeling of glee that will be felt when Papa appears at the classroom door.

Unlike the academic domains, the creative arts do not focus entirely on spoken and written language. Instead, expressions of thoughts and ideas are created using visual, kinesthetic, aural, and tactile means. Through these creative expressions, children enhance their cognitive, language, motor, social, and perceptual abilities.

The creative arts encourage many of the abilities that are critical to typical developmental patterns and vital lifelong skills. These include awareness of space, use of body parts, creation of stories, and the development of higher level thinking. Figure 14.1 provides descriptions of how some creative arts skills develop in children from birth through 8 years of age.

Figure 14.1   Examples of Arts Experiences That Develop in Young Children

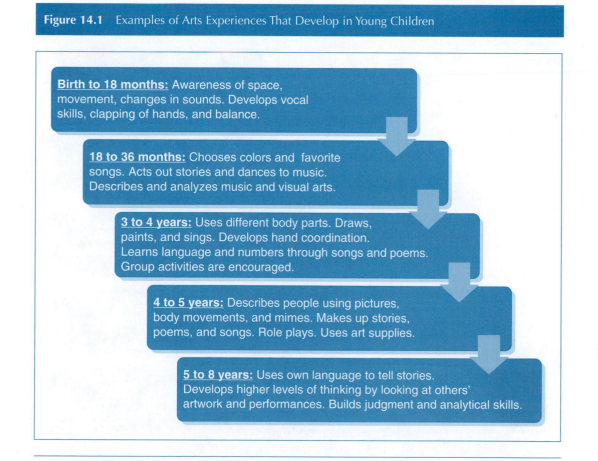

Birth to 18 months: Awareness of space, movement, changes in sounds. Develops vocal skills, clapping of hands, and balance.

18 to 36 months: Chooses colors and favorite songs. Acts out stories and dances to music. Describes and analyzes music and visual arts.

3 to 4 years: Uses different body parts. Draws, paints, and sings. Develops hand coordination. Learns language and numbers through songs and poems. Group activities are encouraged.

4 to 5 years: Describes people using pictures, body movements, and mimes. Makes up stories, poems, and songs. Role plays. Uses art supplies.

5 to 8 years: Uses own language to tell stories. Develops higher levels of thinking by looking at others' artwork and performances. Builds judgment and analytical skills.

Source: Adapted from Arts Education Partnership, http://www.aep-arts.org

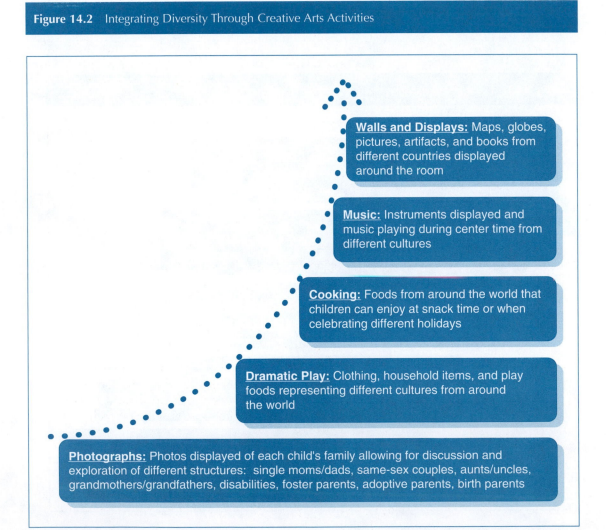

Creative arts activities allow children to express thoughts and ideas.

Creative arts also assist children in learning how to respect and understand distinct forms of art that are treasured by different families and cultures. Not only will all children develop a broader concept of the arts, they will also enhance their social-emotional skills as they learn to integrate the different cultural forms of art, music, dance, and drama valued by the families of their peers. Figure 14.2 suggests some techniques for illustrating culturally diverse creative arts around the classroom.

Music also assists children in developing English when songs are taught to them using direct instruction (Paquette & Rieg, 2008). They are exposed to new vocabulary, hear how the English language sounds, phonology, and the prosodic nature of the language. Through the combination of enjoyable interactions and implicit

Figure 14.2   Integrating Diversity Through Creative Arts Activities

Walls and Displays: Maps, globes, pictures, artifacts, and books from different countries displayed around the room

Music: Instruments displayed and music playing during center time from different cultures

Cooking: Foods from around the world that children can enjoy at snack time or when celebrating different holidays

Dramatic Play: Clothing, household items, and play foods representing different cultures from around the world

Photographs: Photos displayed of each child's family allowing for discussion and exploration of different structures: single moms/dads, same-sex couples, aunts/uncles, grandmothers/grandfathers, disabilities, foster parents, adoptive parents, birth parents

instructions, children are exposed to vocabulary from the language that they are learning. They learn how to use that language in a meaningful manner. Figure 14.3 provides steps that can be used when teaching language through songs (Isenberg & Jalongo, 2013).

Figure 14.3   Steps for Teaching Songs to English Language Learners

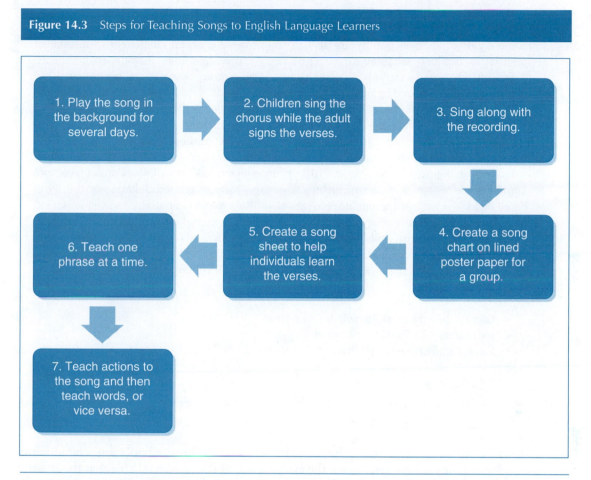

Source: Isenberg, J. P., & Jalongo, M. R. (2006). *Creative Thinking and Arts-Based Learning; Preschool Through Fourth Grade* (4th ed.). Upper Saddle River, NJ: Pearson.

Current Status of Creative Arts in the Schools

Since 1969, the U.S. government has published the *National Assessment of Educational Progress,* which includes periodic assessment of the academic achievement of elementary students in all educational areas. Disturbingly, in 2008, results showed that only 57% of the eighth-grade students in the United States attended schools where music instruction was provided three to four times a week, and only 47% attended schools where visual arts instruction was frequently provided. Moreover, when students were tested on their creative arts knowledge, children from lower economic families scored 28 points lower in music and 9 points lower in the visual arts than students who came from more economically advantaged families. Finally, students attending city schools had lower scores than students from suburban, town, and rural schools. These data demonstrate that the creative arts continue to be neglected in all areas of education, especially at schools that serve students who have diverse economic, social, and academic challenges.

LEARNING FOR ALL CHILDREN
Creative Arts and Poverty

Some children raised in poverty are at high risk of developmental challenges as a result of prenatal malnutrition, exposure to teratogens, and impoverished home learning environments. Noise, crowding, and instability, all of which can undermine the development of emotional and behavioral abilities, can dominate their home life.

Creative arts experiences can provide a variety of channels for learning cognitive skills that may assist children who have developmental difficulties associated with poverty (Gregoire & Lupinetti, 2005). These activities can impact the academic readiness skills of young children who have different levels of learning because they come from economically challenging situations (Brown, Benedett, & Armistead, 2010). Integrating the arts into all areas of the preschool curriculum recognizes that the arts can offer advantages to impoverished children who are at risk of failing to develop age-appropriate readiness skills. Participation in music, creative movement, and visual arts instruction that is integrated into daily activities allows children to expand the emotional and behavioral skills needed to assist with cognitive, language, literacy, mathematics, science, and other school readiness skills (Brown et al., 2010).

Through regular participation in creative arts activities, all children can expand the following developmental skills:

- Express their thoughts, knowledge, and ideas
- Investigate their feelings and emotions
- Explore and create with different types of materials
- Be creative
- Experiment with colors, forms, shapes, and textures

Today's early education professionals must be aware of how schools and communities are neglecting the creative arts. Given the evidence about the important role that the creative arts play in children's development, early education teachers must advocate for opportunities both inside and outside of the school environment that will assist in developing creative arts skills starting at a young age. Teachers must continually inform families of the various cultural activities in the creative arts that the community does provide and encourage them to participate in these activities. Similarly, teachers must invite local community arts representatives to the family and classroom activities at their schools, and then design classroom activities that stem from these community activities.

Creative Arts, Play, and Literacy

As demonstrated in the opening scenario, when arts activities are integrated into socio-dramatic play activities, they can provide valuable opportunities for children to enhance their academic abilities. With adult guidance, the children in the scenario were designing play props that would expand their play narrative stories, such as different planets, a blanket to keep a baby warm, a leash for walking a dog, and a helmet for outer space exploration.

Carefully planned art and play experiences afford opportunities for children to develop social skills by producing collaborative projects, mathematical skills by sequencing or patterning activities, and language and literacy skills by discussing their process, negotiating ideas, and explaining finished projects to class peers. Similarly, well-planned music activities can allow children to experiment with different types of sounds in ways that may excite some children more than words do and additionally, develop phonemic awareness. Movement activities not only strengthen children's bodies, they also help children learn about spatial relationships. Finally, dramatic enactments can contribute to children's development of attentiveness, recall, language, literacy, and social skills.

Creative arts activities need to provide opportunities for exchanging ideas and creating together.

Research has revealed the value of encouraging expressive interactions that allow young children to participate in playful and enjoyable creative arts activities and to share their ideas and activities with peers (Koralek, 2008). Centers should not be a place where children drift in and out, or where they merely replicate a displayed item. Instead the centers should be contexts in which children create items that express their own thoughts and ideas using the provided materials. Opportunities should encourage the collaborative production of playful creations through children's interacting and working with peers. For example:

- **Music center:** Classroom that encourages children to engage with musical instruments, songs, musical devices, and have enough space for children to move to the music they create.
- **Movement center:** An area in the classroom that is large enough to encourage children to engage with gross motor movements that accompany music.
- **Art center:** Children are provided opportunities to work side by side, expressing thoughts and observing different artistic techniques applied by peers.
- **Dramatic center:** Children collaboratively express developmental and learning abilities through co-production of familiar stories and events that involve pretense.

REFLECT AND APPLY EXERCISE 14.1

Learning Vocabulary Through Songs

Reflect

All of us learned songs when we were young children. Think about a song that you learned.

Apply

Choose three words from the song that you remember and think of how you would teach those words to children who did not know them. Would you teach them about those words before you introduced the song, during the song, or after they had been exposed to the song? Why?

Creative Arts and Motor Standards

Beginning at birth, infants quickly learn how to communicate their feelings, thoughts, and imaginations through actions, sounds, and words. As they become proficient communicators, they learn how to express their thoughts through drawings, paintings, movement, singing, and constructing three-dimensional creations. Young children do not restrict themselves to just one form of creative symbolic representation. Instead, they move in a natural way between all the different modes of creative expressions, picking and choosing the one that best fits the message they are attempting to create (Fawcett & Hay, 2004). These early experiences with diverse forms of representing their experiences and ideas set a strong foundation for future writing development. Students will learn to make decisions about how to best present their learning through a variety of genres, mediums, and discourse structures. Having children draw or paint to different types of music and then discuss how the music impacted their creation is a natural way to integrate creative activities.

Therefore, as demonstrated in the opening scenario for this chapter, the creative arts can become social acts in which children playfully express themselves through exploring, thinking, representing, and discussing their creations. The specific art objects were designed to be included in play activities through the use of play communications or metacommunications (see Chapter 4). Teachers need to respect the processes that children choose to create artistic products rather than focusing solely on the end artistic products that children create. When children are involved in creative arts events, their activities should be monitored for the primary purpose of enhancing the development of their communication abilities along with their creative abilities. Questions as well as responsive and sensitive comments provide ideal opportunities for children to increase their familiarity with the use of symbolic representations that express their thoughts and feelings through these enjoyable, social creative arts activities. The adults in the opening scenario demonstrate how to naturally integrate open-ended questions and comments into creative arts activities.

Through creative arts, music, movement, and drama, children learn how to imagine, express themselves, and interact with others. Using their bodies and minds, they listen, observe, discuss, move, problem-solve, and imagine options. When curriculum content is integrated into these activities, children link the activities that they are participating in to the knowledge that they are gaining, and meaningful learning occurs in all areas of development.

Early Creative Arts Standards

The National Association for Music Education has established standards for preschool children in the following areas: singing and playing instruments, creating music, responding to music, and understanding music. Kim and Robinson (2010) suggest that teachers follow four steps to effectively implement these standards, which are listed in Figure 14.4.

Children need to participate in activities that continually link moving physical muscles with mind muscles (Marigliano & Russo, 2011). For example, children can be asked how a certain activity makes their body feel? Makes their skin feel? Makes their hair feel? Then they can engage in another activity and be asked to compare how that activity makes them feel and to compare their responses to the feelings from the initial activity.

Through the adult scaffolding techniques of *engaging, expanding, and empowering*, rich learning environments are created for young children. The National Dance Education Organization has designed standards for dance in early childhood. These standards encourage adults to engage children in playful and meaningful problem-solving activities with their peers. During these activities, adults can use open-ended prompts to expand children's experiences. Children feel empowered when adults first acknowledge what a child has done and then ask if anyone can do that same activity in a different way.

Figure 14.4 Four-Step Process to Incorporate Music Standards

1. Read the music standards	• The standards provide guidelines in four content areas: singing and playing instruments, creating music, responding to music, and understanding music
2. Learn music terminology related to the standards	• Music instruments: Timbre or instrument's unique sound • Music elements/expressions: Beat/rhythm; tempo/dynamics; pitch/melody • Music awareness: Music symbols
3. Implement the music standards	• Implement music standards during choice time, during read alouds to accompany story sounds, or by helping children find connections between visual patterns and musical rhythm.
4. Check the music standards	• Make and use a checklist to determine if the activities satisfy the music standards. If they do not fully meet the standards, additional activities need to be planned.

Source: Kim, J., & Robinson, H. M. (2010). Four Steps for Becoming Familiar With Early Music Standards. *Young Children, 65*(2), 42–48.

The Head Start Child Development and Early Learning Framework (Head Start, 2010) has a complete list of the Creative Arts Expression Elements and Examples in the areas of art, music, movement, and drama for children 3 to 5 years old. These elements include the following areas:

- Using a range of media and materials to create art objects
- Using voice and instruments to create sounds
- Using body to move to music and express feelings
- Using acting, props, and language to portray events and stories

Head Start Motor Skills Elements

Creative arts activities encourage the development of motor activities in young children. During the early childhood years, adults tend to give particular attention to children's physical development, and they do so with justification. The coordination of body movement is a complex process that begins at infancy (Batshaw, Roizen, & Lotrecchiano, 2012). The bones, muscles, and joints in the human body are connected by ligaments and tendons. Nerves and neurons provide the connection between the body and the brain, and this connection allows for coordinated body movement to occur. As children's bodies move, continual signals to the brain provide information about the body's position in space, and that information assists in the development of both gross motor (i.e., large muscle) and fine motor (i.e., small muscle) skills.

©iStockphoto.com/ktaylorg

Manipulative toys assist children with the development of muscles that are needed for drawing and writing.

Gross Motor Skills Development. As children develop their **gross motor skills** (e.g., crawling, standing, and walking), they become more coordinated in their body movements, more sophisticated in the activities in which they engage, and more advanced in physical skills that provide a foundation for academics—for example, eye-hand coordination and balance. Many gross motor skills are enhanced through creative arts activities such as movement and drama. Specifically, the Head Start Framework identifies the following gross motor skills as ones that preschoolers should be encouraged to develop:

Movement: Coordination of body alone and when using objects
   Example: Children sitting on a chair with shoes and socks off, picking up small objects with toes and depositing them in a nearby bucket

Navigation: Movement of body through space and use of directionality
   Example: Placing a hard-cooked egg on a spoon and having children walk from Point A to Point B. Having them on their hands and knees and pushing an egg with their nose from Point A to Point B.

Balance: Control of body during physical movements
   Example: Arranging several hula hoops of different colors on the floor, and having children jump from one color to another, and then hop to the closest hula hoop

Fine Motor Skills Development. People typically tend to associate the development of gross motor skills with the milestones for learning during early years of life. By contrast, they do not pay as much attention when children develop **fine motor skills**, such as picking things up or transferring objects from one hand to another. Additionally, most people tend to associate the term fine motor skills with coloring, cutting, and writing, and, therefore, think that these skills develop during preschool. However, like all other motor skills, these skills begin to develop early in life.

Figure 14.5 provides a sequential summary of some of the fine motor skills that develop from birth to 6 years of age. These are, however, only a few examples, and not all children develop at the same rate. Therefore, if a child is unable to achieve some of these skills at the noted time, the child's inability to do so does not necessarily indicate a delay in development. These are average time estimates; thus, some typically developing children achieved a particular skill either before or after the average date stated in the table.

An examination of the Head Start Framework (Head Start, 2011) reveals that using writing and art tools are complex activities. They occur only after a child has developed strength and dexterity, eye-hand coordination, and the ability to manipulate objects in the environment. Children must be afforded the opportunity to develop the prerequisite skills before they use crayons, scissors, and other paper-related materials. Through the development of such motor skills, children are able to explore and function in different learning environments. The following are examples of the fine motor skills that children should be expected to develop during their preschool years, according to the *Head Start Child Development and Early Learning Framework* (Head Start, 2010).

- Control of small muscles when using utensils
- Control of small muscles when using self-care practices
- Control of small muscles when building and exploring

Figure 14.5 Summary of Development of Some Fine Motor Skills

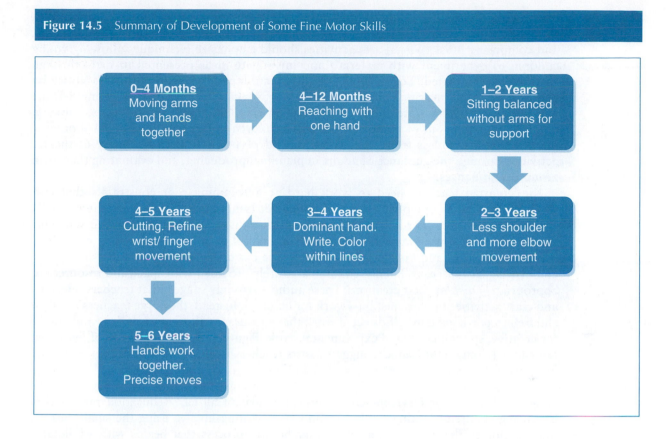

Kindergarten Standards

In 1994, the Consortium of National Arts Education Associations established K–12 content standards in the traditional subject areas of visual arts, music, movement, dance, and drama. These standards, which are available at www.ed.gov/pubs/ArtsStandards.html, focus on what the children will know and be able to do in the creative arts area throughout their education. Currently, the National Coalition for Core Arts Standards (NCCAS) is revising those standards and including standards that will also focus on creating media arts standards for pre-K–12 media, which should be available online after June 2014.

The current standards describe skills that students should possess at the end of their secondary education. Students should:

- Be able to communicate at a basic level in the four art disciplines—dance, music, theater, and visual arts.
- Be able to communicate proficiently in at least one art form using insight, reason, and technical proficiency.
- Be able to develop and present basic analyses of works of arts from structural, historical, and cultural perspectives.
- Have an informed acquaintance with exemplary works of art from a variety of cultures and historical periods.
- Be able to relate various types of arts knowledge and skills within and across the arts disciplines.

Children in Grades K through 4 need to learn to use the arts both as a natural means of communication for the expression of self and as a way to respond to the expressions of others. In kindergarten, children are expected to engage in body awareness and movement activities that recognize and appreciate both themselves and others. Additionally, they should learn ways to express their creativity through singing, playing instruments, and composing music. Visual arts activities should emphasize techniques allowing young children to experiment with materials and investigate ideas presented to them through works already created. For example, children can expand their visual arts abilities by painting, drawing, making collages, printmaking, making stained glass, creating 3-D art and structures, using watercolors and modeling clay, designing nature crafts, cooking, and making object out of home items. Finally, children in Grades Preschool–4 should be provided with seamless transitions from pretend play activities to the study of theater activities through the guidance of adults in planning, producing, and evaluating their own group performances.

Kindergarten teachers need to work hard at overcoming four constraints that currently dilute activities involving the arts (Jalongo & Isenberg, 2006). First, teachers usually choose art activities according to the amount of *time* they have available in their schedule. Second, they often use *inexpensive materials* instead of high-quality ones that contribute to specific textures and illusions. Third, adults are extremely concerned about being *neat* and making *cleanup* easy. Finally, children are rarely provided with space and resources to appropriately *display* their creations. These authors strongly suggest that teachers reject art and craft activities that are just busywork for children. Instead, they urge teachers to allow children to participate in self-directed work that encourages alternative designs and allows for creative, spontaneous, and experimental work. Figure 14.6 provides a list of five questions that Jalongo and Isenberg suggest assists teachers in encouraging children to engage in creative thought.

Stages of Fine Motor Development. A principal goal of all early education programs is enhancing children's writing skills. Not only does writing involve using the small muscles that develop in the hand, it is also a comprehensive process that begins with whole arm movements and ends up with small finger coordination. The development of fine motor skills is a complex process. It involves the ability to control muscles, be patient, make judgments, and coordinate information from the brain (Carvell, 2006). Specifically, four stages of fine motor development provide the foundation for the development of writing skills: whole arm, whole hand, pincer, and pincer coordination.

According to Carvell, the first stage of the writing development process begins with strengthening the muscles of the entire arm. Participation in activities that build large muscle strength, such as painting on an easel and arm-stretching exercises, is a precursor to the development of hand muscles. In the next stage, children begin to develop strength in

Figure 14.6   Questions That Assist Teachers in Encouraging Creative Thought in Children

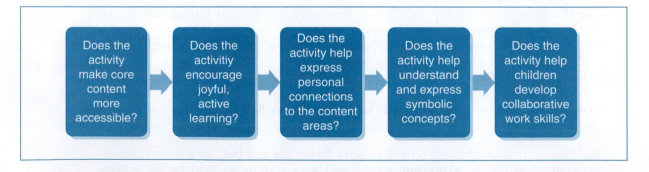

Source: Jalongo, M. R., & Isenberg, J. P. (2006). Creative Expression and Thought in Kindergarten. In D. F. Gullo (Ed.), *K Today: Teaching and Learning in the Kindergarten Year* (pp. 116–126). Washington, DC: National Association for the Education of Young Children.

their entire hand. Through activities such as pouring dried beans, dried rice, and water, and squeezing and painting with sponges, young children strengthen and coordinate the use of their hands and fingers in a natural and fun way.

The third stage involves building up the use of pinching by pressing the thumb and index finger together. Many types of manipulative activities can assist in developing a firm pinch. These include picking up puzzle pieces, placing keys in the correct categories, stringing wooden beads, and stacking blocks.

Finally, the child is ready for the last stage: pincer coordination. To successfully perform this type of activity, children must be capable of placing their thumb, index, and middle fingers together so that they act as a tripod supporting the writing utensil. Once children achieve this steady position, they can then begin working on using their hand to create small and highly coordinated finger movements with markers, crayons, pencils, and other writing utensils. Figure 14.7 offers suggestions on how activities previously mentioned in this book relate to the different stages of fine motor development.

Adults must observe how children use their arms, hands, and fingers during a variety of school activities throughout the day so they can be sensitive to when children are ready to progress to the next step in writing development. They also must be aware when children are becoming frustrated with a specific aspect of writing development. Children develop motor skills at very different rates, and teachers must encourage the development of such skills by providing developmentally appropriate practices for each child.

Therefore, adults need to bolster the development of fine motor skills by providing activities that support differentiated instruction for each stage of the child's physical development (Huffman & Fortenberry, 2011). Through the sequential development of children's whole-arm, whole-hand, pincer, and pincer coordination, young children can eagerly and enthusiastically learn to use writing as a symbolic tool for expressing their thoughts.

Art Centers

When designing art projects, teachers must recognize that the most valuable learning element of this activity is the process that children engage in, not the artistic product that they produce. Children delight in investigating objects and experimenting with the impact that their actions have upon those objects. They take great pride in products that they produce on their

Figure 14.7 Four Stages of Fine Motor Development and Activities From This Book

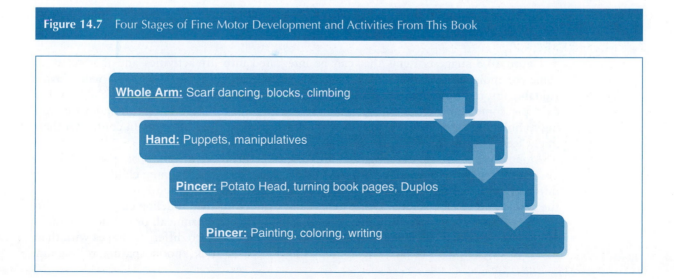

Whole Arm: Scarf dancing, blocks, climbing

Hand: Puppets, manipulatives

Pincer: Potato Head, turning book pages, Duplos

Pincer: Painting, coloring, writing

Children need the space and time to create objects reflecting their unique ideas.

own. In the opening scenario, the children appeared much more excited about what they were going to do with their colored paper plates then in the process of making them. Therefore, the art centers should be places where children can safely test their ideas, and share with and receive suggestions from peers that impact the procedure they use. They should not focus on merely having children replicate an adult-made creation.

Art centers should be large enough in area so that children can expand their projects without any concern about interfering with other activities. If children have designed a cardboard box creation and wish to extend it by attaching a variety of boxes, they should have the space to do so. Similarly, the art center should be located in a low-traffic area so that children are not worried about other children disturbing them when those children spread out their own projects. As in the block center, children in the art center should have the option of letting their projects remain in the center for a couple of days, allowing for them to return with fresh ideas about modifying their creations.

Art centers should always be arranged so that children can work together whenever possible. Large painting easels should be placed side by side, encouraging children to interact with peers, share ideas and comments, and observe different artistic styles and techniques.

Different types of materials should be rotated into the centers for children to experiment with and analyze how these various materials might be used with their projects. As in this chapter's opening scenario, a variety of types of paper and objects should be available—such as white paper, cardboard, foil, cellophane, boxes, egg cartons, and paper tubes. Over time, different types and textures of paint should be integrated into the center—for example, tempera paints, finger paints, watercolors, sand paint, vegetable oil, and colored glue. The materials used for painting can be systematically changed. Some items that children can paint with, and the activity that the item is associated with, are:

- Fruits and vegetables when they are learning about healthy foods
- Pine tree branches when studying plants
- Corks and jar lids when learning about floating and sinking
- Feather dusters and different types of brushes and rollers when learning about household items

Figure 14.8 suggests items that can be integrated into art activities and that relate to some common socio-dramatic play themes. Careful and continual observation will provide valuable information on what works and what does not work for individual children. For example, some young children, including those with physical disabilities, can find it frustrating to hold a large paintbrush and make marks on a large piece of paper. In contrast, others might feel very comfortable undertaking that activity.

Along with painting, drawing, and creating structures out of boxes or wood, children also enjoy exploring with modeling clay. An excellent activity for young children is placing different colors of modeling clay into zip-type plastic bags and then having children mix the colors and see the results. Other items can be added to the modeling clay to create different textures, such as seeds, glitter, sawdust, pine needles, cornmeal, or oatmeal. Aromas might also be added. Children enjoy molding modeling clay into different shapes with their hands or spreading it out on a flat surface using a Popsicle stick, spoon, spatula, rolling pin,

Figure 14.8 Items to Use in Art Centers According to Themes

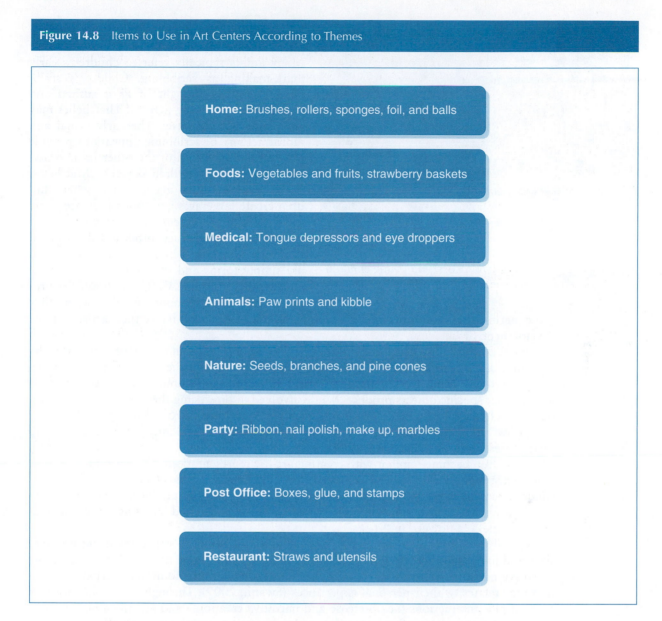

Home: Brushes, rollers, sponges, foil, and balls

Foods: Vegetables and fruits, strawberry baskets

Medical: Tongue depressors and eye droppers

Animals: Paw prints and kibble

Nature: Seeds, branches, and pine cones

Party: Ribbon, nail polish, make up, marbles

Post Office: Boxes, glue, and stamps

Restaurant: Straws and utensils

plastic or wooden hammer, or paint roller with wax paper from the kitchen on it. All of these activities not only enhance creative abilities, they also assist in strengthening the small hand muscles.

As with other centers, children should always be responsible for cleaning up after art activities. Small hand broom and dustpans make this job easy and fun for young children, and using them will also improve their eye-hand coordination skills. At the end of the day, the staff needs to make sure that the art center is clean for the next day, with paint containers free of drips and brushes washed and drying in a tall, washed-out milk carton. Plastic cookie trays can be used to organize crayons so that they are classified by colors. A clean, well-organized art play center where children are allowed to work as independently as possible will encourage the production of more creative and experimental products. Again, special attention must be given to the process that the children will be experimenting with (e.g., the sequence of activities, the problem solving, and cause and effect), while the actual product that they will produce should receive less attention.

Stages of Drawing

©iStockphoto.com/ConstanceMcGuire

Drawing is a developmental process, and young children should be allowed to experiment with it.

Many adults typically refer to children's early mark-making as scribbling. Children's scribbling is usually thought of as a rushed and careless early drawing activity. That belief may well be wrong, however. The early visual and motor activity of scribbling appears to provide the foundation for all of the other basic drawing patterns that children develop (Matthews, 1994). Specifically, at a young age, when children create large arcs and loops they are using them as a *pre-representational symbol,* which will be used to construct forms and shapes used in future drawing activities. These markings are simply forms and shapes that do not have an intended meaning. Children should be provided with ample amounts of space where they can experiment with and practice drawing arches and loops to enhance their artistic motor development.

Similar to how play develops, children begin demonstrating initial artistic creations by depicting *action representations.* As children pretend through their drawing or painting, they experiment using arcs, loops, and up and down lines to symbolize different aspects of motion that specific objects produce. While involved in producing these artistic representations, children typically make comments such as "It just went around the corner" or "It's gone now," indicating that a quality of movement through time and space is attached to their representations (Matthews, 1994).

As children become familiar with creating artistic representations, they begin to generate their first straight lines, followed by angled structures and then cross-structures. At this point, children become interested in producing *figurative representations* of objects. These representations are ones that are unidentifiable to others but that the child labels as objects such as "an airplane," "a flower," or "rocks."

Typically, children then advance to producing more complex structures using different sizes and lines, and increasing the amount of details. At the same time, children craft more extensive narratives about their artistic creations by integrating additional verbal information that relates to their personal experiences (Swann, 2009). Through the combination of pretend play interactions (i.e., pretense and narrative creations) and art, the ability to produce representational art (i.e., art creations that represent something in real life) emerges in young children, as demonstrated in Figure 14.9. As will be explained below, adults can assist children with this developmental process by guiding them with specific theme suggestions and drawing materials.

Guiding With Open-Ended Art Materials

Expressive interactions with peers are enhanced when children are given the freedom to create their own new expressions. Open-ended materials, which are everyday items that can be used in a variety of ways, can contribute to creative expressions. Using open-ended art materials—such as beads, feathers, yarn, milk cartons, paper rolls, wire, tubing, material scraps, dried foods, pebbles, and shells—challenges children to share their new creative thoughts and ideas. Additionally, creating music instruments and drama props out of open-ended materials provides opportunities for children to modify previously known knowledge through the creation of new expressions.

Figure 14.9 Stages of the Development of Representational Art

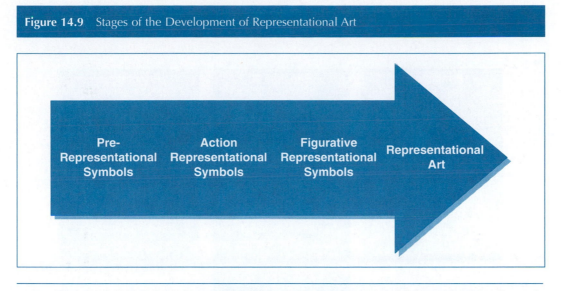

Source: Matthews, J. (1994). Deep Structures in Children's Art: Development and Culture. *Visual Arts Research, 20*(2), 29–50.

Similar to socio-dramatic play, when young children are involved in creative activities with peers, they will engage in higher levels of pretending and interacting. For example, the scenario at the beginning of this chapter demonstrates how children were self-motivated to use foil to collaboratively create objects that they imagined, such as a blanket, a dog leash, and a space helmet.

Specifically, the use of open-ended materials provides an effective artistic vehicle that children can use to collaboratively explore and problem-solve (Drew & Rankin, 2008). Open-ended materials afford children the freedom to express their feelings, thoughts, and communications through movements as well as through, visual, aural, and auditory representations. Just as skilled children have the ability to realize alternative possibilities by assigning meaning to their collaborative play interactions, they can use the creative arts to accomplish the same result. Through expressive play interactions, children can suspend familiar everyday rules and express themselves in a manner that they choose and enjoy.

In a time when concrete learning standards and skill-based outcomes dominate education, children must be afforded regular opportunities to playfully explore open-ended materials in ways that will assist them in meeting expected learning standards (Drew & Rankin, 2008). Teachers need to be well versed in the value of creative arts and in the use of creative arts activities to promote the skills articulated in the early standards.

Figure 14.10 lists seven principles justifying the use of open-ended materials that allow children to express themselves and to learn and develop. These principles support the idea that creativity develops in children a strong sense of their abilities and a way in which they can effectively approach learning (Principle 1). Creativity should not be relegated to a separate part of the curriculum; rather, it should be carefully integrated into content learning areas, thus allowing children to express their knowledge and feelings about the learning activities in which they are involved (Principle 2). As children grow in different areas of learning and development, they should be allowed to work in small groups to produce creative and unique projects (Principles 3 and 4). These collaborative learning activities allow children to move forward with their learning and understanding of the construction of knowledge, and they provide insights for adults on what children are interested in learning (Principles 5, 6, and 7).

Figure 14.10   Key Principles for Using Open-Ended Materials in Early Education Classrooms

Principle 1:
Spontaneous, creative self-expression increases competence and well-being now and into adulthood.

Principle 2:
Creativity extends and deepens children's understandings through multiple, hands-on experiences.

Principle 3:
Creative activities with peers support learning and a growing sense of competence.

Principle 4:
Literacy, science, and mathematics skills are learned through interactions with diverse, open-ended materials.

Principle 5:
Children learn best in open-ended explorations when teachers help them make connections.

Principle 6:
Teachers are nourished by observing children's joy and learning.

Principle 7:
Ongoing self-reflection among teachers in community is needed to support these practices.

Source: Drew, W. F., & Rankin, B. (2008). Promoting Creativity for Life Using Open-Ended Materials. In D. Koralek (Ed.), *Spotlight on Young Children and the Creative Arts* (pp. 32–39). Washington, DC: National Association for the Education of Young Children.

REFLECT AND APPLY EXERCISE 14.2

Encouraging Expressive Play Interactions

Reflect

In the opening scenario, three creative arts centers are described that focus on the development of expressive play interactions. Re-read the information presented on one of the centers and identify the practices in this center that encourages expressive play interactions.

Apply

Using the same center, think of some ways that you could continue to enhance expressive play interactions of the children while they are involved in the activity that is described.

Art projects should afford opportunities for young children to experiment with different procedures and techniques. Experimentation of this type will result in an enhanced understanding of the process of "cause and effect" and will lead the children to a higher level of cognitive development. While investigating and manipulating art materials, children should be encouraged to describe their findings and ideas to their peers. This activity will expand the children's language abilities and enhance their feelings of self-worth. With the guidance of an adult, children can explore various ways to use household materials to create with modeling clay, paints, crayons and chalk, stamps, and colored beads.

Typically, art center activities have difficulty competing in popularity with other more lively and interactive centers, such as the dramatic play center and the block center. However, the number of participants in the art center will increase if the center is designed to provide opportunities for children to combine social and representational activities similar to those occurring at the other, more popular centers.

Around 3 years of age, children become perceptually, cognitively, and physically capable of demonstrating symbolically represented information. As pretend verbal interactions increase, so do representational drawings (Escobedo, 1999; McCune, 1985). When art activities are combined with pretend play activities, and peers collaboratively create artistic representations, they also tend to create shared play narratives around these artistic creations. For example, Swann (2009) found that children's interest in a previously unpopular art center was ignited when a teacher taped a 6-foot-long piece of butcher paper to a table and demonstrated how simple roads could be drawn. The children were then shown how small toy cars could be maneuvered on the roads, and the center suddenly became one of the most popular areas in the class. Children maintained their interest in the activity as they enhanced their drawing skills by creating a complex road system and drawing houses, stores, and other community institutions (e.g., zoo, car wash) along the roadway at which the cars could stop.

Interestingly, when some girls started to engage in the activity of the small toy cars, they integrated dolls and stuffed animals into this event by having them stationed in places near the roads and developing car activities that involved them. The addition of these play items encouraged more complex play narratives, increased the use of new vocabulary, and enhanced the incorporation of more abstract symbols and images into the drawings. Integrating play activities with art thus appears to encourage both sustained interactions among children and more creative activity.

Swann suggests four steps for guiding children's artistic play activities to produce high-quality interactions. These steps are listed in Figure 14.11.

Figure 14.11 Suggestions for Guiding the Children to Experiment With Art and Play Combinations Using Small Props: Dolls, Animals, Furniture, Vehicles

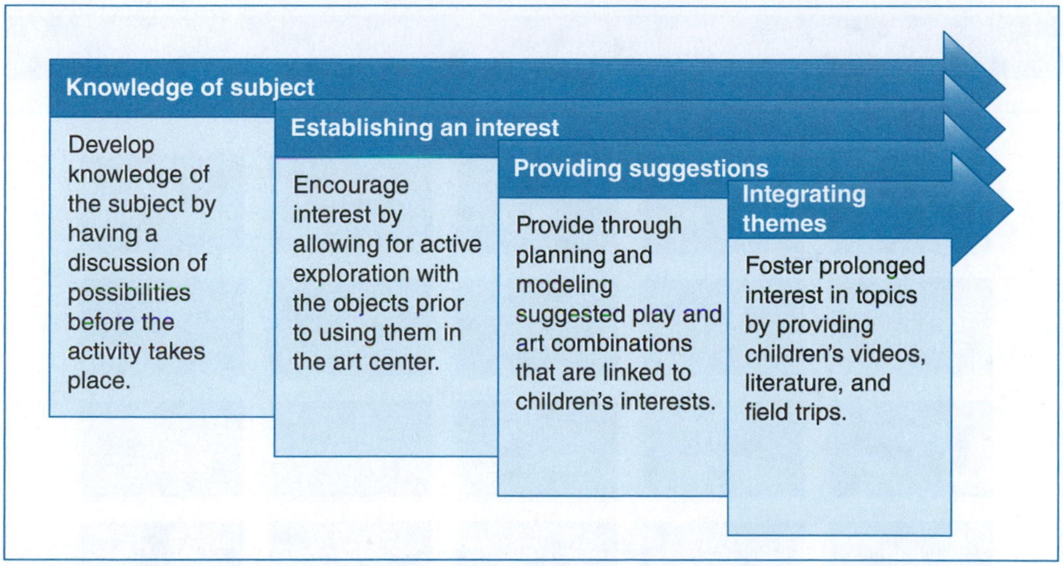

Knowledge of subject

Develop knowledge of the subject by having a discussion of possibilities before the activity takes place.

Establishing an interest

Encourage interest by allowing for active exploration with the objects prior to using them in the art center.

Providing suggestions

Provide through planning and modeling suggested play and art combinations that are linked to children's interests.

Integrating themes

Foster prolonged interest in topics by providing children's videos, literature, and field trips.

Source: Swann, A. C. (2009). An Intriguing Link Between Drawing and Play With Toys. *Childhood Education, 85,* 230–236.

REFLECT AND APPLY EXERCISE 14.3

Encouraging Drawing Activities

Reflect

A classroom has three children who only want to play "Robin Hood," where one boy is Robin, another is Little John, and a girl is Maid Marion. As the teacher, you feel that this activity has occurred too often and would like to engage these children in a drawing activity.

Apply

Think of ways that you and your staff could guide these children to engage in expressive play interactions involving drawing. How could you design these activities so that the children are motivated to engage with each other while, at the same time, they advance their drawing skills? You may want to use the suggestions in Figure 14.11 to assist you.

Figure 14.12 provides 20 suggestions for developmentally appropriate nature art ideas that children can create to their liking.

Music and Movement Centers

Young children find it almost impossible to separate music and movement. For them, music is not just an auditory process involving listening; it also consists of moving their body to the music. Since birth, children have moved around exploring their environment and have learned about the world from different sounds that they have heard. Therefore, when children

Figure 14.12 Twenty Nature Art Project Ideas

Sun Prints	Colored Acorn Art	Twig Frames	Leaf Crowns	Stick People
Mud Painting	Flower Painting	Rock Art	Leaves in Clay	Shell Art
Nature Mobiles	Bird Feeders	Salt Dough Leaf Prints	Key Chimes	Tree Rubbings
Wind Spinners	Leaf Prints	Dandelion Painting	Pine Cone Critters	Corn Cob Painting

listen to music, they naturally use body movements to explore the sounds and to express their feelings.

Movement is the main vehicle that young children use to learn how to coordinate their bodies. *Creative movement* is a form of creative arts in which the human body engages in various movements in space involving different timing and the use of energy.

Music and creative movement can assist in promoting a variety of developmental and learning skills. Unfortunately, many teachers only offer music opportunities during "circle time" when children are asked to join the teacher in singing a few songs. Instead, music and movement should be incorporated into a variety of the early childhood curriculum areas.

Dow (2010) outlines seven benefits of providing music and movement centers for young children. First, music and movement can provide equal access to activities for all children. Aside from the space required, the only other items needed might be some instruments to provide auditory cues and a CD player. Modifications to the activities can be made for those with disabilities by having children in a wheelchair shake their heads or hands, or move their arms instead of their legs in a specific manner. For children with hearing losses, most auditory devices today are capable of picking up some rhythmic information from music.

All children can participate in music and movement activities.

Second, curriculum content can be integrated into the music and movement activities. For example, if the class is studying different types of transportation, the children could be provided with music and movement activities that relate to vehicles and their equipment. If they are studying nature, the creative activities can focus on replicating leaves falling from a tree, boats bouncing up and down on the ocean, people climbing to the top of a mountain, and so forth.

Third, music and movement assist children with their physical development. Marching, galloping, stomping, hopping, jumping, and turning around will strengthen children's gross motor abilities. After children develop these skills, they can add more advanced skills to their repertoire, such as skipping and leaping.

Fourth, physical movement also addresses the current concern that American children and adolescents are too often either overweight or at risk of becoming obese. Without utilizing extra time in an already tight school-day schedule, music and movement instruct children on the positive impact that body activities can have on how they feel physically and ultimately on their feeling of self-worth.

Fifth, music and movement provide wonderful opportunities for the development of social and emotional skills. These activities encourage children to work as group members; they will observe and learn from each other, and often have to find solutions to problems posed by an adult. For children who have trouble expressing their feelings or who express their feelings inappropriately, creative movement can offer structured activities in which they can release their feelings and emotions in an acceptable manner.

Sixth, creative movement helps children learn to use their bodies to explore new questions and discover innovative solutions to problems. These skills are critical in a world where thinking skills and collaboration with others are needed to succeed. Through creative movement activities, children begin to develop some of the foundational skills that they will use later in life when they enter the workforce.

Finally, a strong connection exists between the mind and the body, and body movements impact the learning process. Research has found that exercise assists in the growth of new brain cells that facilitate learning. Creative movement is an excellent way to develop a mind-body connection in young children.

Like play, music and creative movement are exploratory, interactive, social, creative, academic, and joyful activities (Kemple, Batey, & Hartle, 2008). Play, music, and creative movement are also alike in that they all have a symbolic and rule-governed system, require active participation, and convey meaning (Morin, 2001). Children's involvement in music and movement should be as frequent as their involvement in play activities (Neelly, 2001).

According to Schwartz (2008), the following qualities of play should also be the hallmark of creating a musical environment for all young children (pp. 125–126).

Play	Being playful means
is spontaneous	responding in the moment
is child centered	playing at the child's developmental level
is child directed	focusing on the child and the child's needs
happens when it happens	not limiting experiences
does not require a product	valuing the experience
has meaning to the child	respecting the child's boundaries
can be solitary or with a group	making objects or thoughts available
can be with objects or with thoughts	

©iStockphoto.com/omgimages

Children find it natural to combine music and movement, along with enjoying friends.

Almost all very young children enjoy moving around when they hear music. They are intrinsically motivated to choose and create their own movements to accompany the music that they hear. Preschoolers also love to learn songs and then create their own words to songs that they know. However, adults often control music and movement activities by turning them into teacher-centered activities whose primary goal is for the children to follow what the teacher does. Such restrictions, however, are rarely placed on children involved in socio-dramatic play activities and, therefore, should also be implemented cautiously during the music and creative movement activities.

One of the most basic movements for young children to learn is balance. The following are 10 simple ways to integrate balance activities into children's everyday activities:

1. Walking on curbs
2. Riding scooters
3. Walking on uneven ground
4. Kicking balls
5. Playing Follow the Leader to different rates of walking
6. Pretending to walk on a tightrope
7. Putting pants on while standing
8. Walking on a balance beam
9. Walking on logs
10. Riding a bike

Motor Skills Development

Music and creative movement assist young children in the development of motor, movement, and body awareness skills. Children can enhance their gross motor skills by participating in activities that require them to listen to music and clap, move scarves in broad movements, and jump on bubble wrap. These activities strengthen and coordinate the muscles in children's arms, legs, and torso. Movement to music requires children to move their hands and fingers, skills that strengthen the muscles used for future writing and other advanced fine motor skills. When moving to music, children also develop the ability to balance and coordinate body movements that require them to cross all three midlines of their bodies: bending at the waist, crossing from the right side to the left and the left side to the right, and crossing from facing frontward to backward. All of these activities greatly contribute to the development of balance, control, body awareness, and strengthening of large and small muscles.

Familiar songs that get children moving and also expand their language abilities are the following:

- Heads, Shoulders, Knees, and Toes
- If You're Happy and You Know It, Clap Your Hands
- The Wheels on the Bus
- Five Little Speckled Frogs
- Five Little Monkeys
- Here We Go Round the Mulberry Bush
- Hokey Pokey
- Ring Around the Rosie

Social and Emotional Development

Music and creative movement can also enrich social and emotional development. Children tend to calm down when they hear quiet music and/or feel slow rhythmic movements. This calming using music and movement affords children the opportunity to practice and develop their own ability to self-regulate their emotions. Additionally, music and creative movement can be used to assist children in identifying emotions and in expressing themselves. For example, by 5 months of age, some children can discriminate between happy and sad music (Flom, Gentile, & Pick, 2008).

Involvement in music and movement activities also helps children learn how to be group members and assists them in learning how to share and wait for a turn. Through these activities, children participate in collaborative activities that provide opportunities for them to engage in group processes and to periodically take on the role of group leader. As a result, music and creative movement can enhance a child's emotional feeling of self-esteem. When children produce the appropriate music and movements, and then receive positive responses from those around them, they feel proud of themselves. Additionally, experiences using culturally diverse music and movements encourage children to feel pride in their culture while, at the same time, providing the types of positive home–school connections described earlier in this chapter.

Cognitive Development

Music and movement also assist in developing young children's cognitive skills. Songs and movements require children to count, pattern, and memorize specific beats and activities. For example, through music and movement, young children learn about differences and similarities in pitches, tones, volumes, speeds, and rhythms. Children around 2 years of age are capable of symbolically acting out familiar movements to music. They can trot like a slow horse and fly like a fast-moving airplane when they hear the corresponding sounds.

When children reach preschool, they use music and creative movements to express more sophisticated symbolic activities. They are able to act out sequenced movements to songs and take on imaginary roles. As their abilities increase to reproduce longer and more complex music and sounds, their attention span and vocabulary become more enhanced. Figure 14.13 suggests ways to create musical instruments with preschoolers.

Figure 14.13   Suggestions for Creating Music/Movement Play Centers for Preschoolers

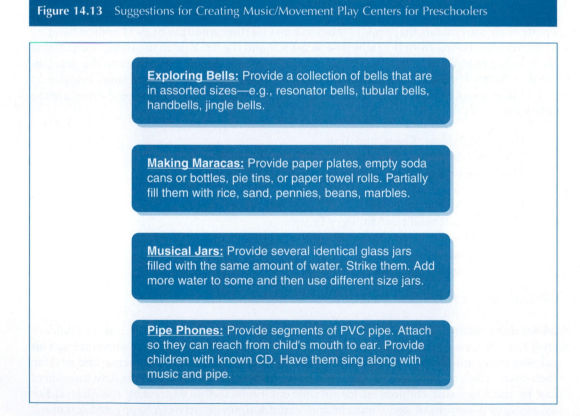

Exploring Bells: Provide a collection of bells that are in assorted sizes—e.g., resonator bells, tubular bells, handbells, jingle bells.

Making Maracas: Provide paper plates, empty soda cans or bottles, pie tins, or paper towel rolls. Partially fill them with rice, sand, pennies, beans, marbles.

Musical Jars: Provide several identical glass jars filled with the same amount of water. Strike them. Add more water to some and then use different size jars.

Pipe Phones: Provide segments of PVC pipe. Attach so they can reach from child's mouth to ear. Provide children with known CD. Have them sing along with music and pipe.

Source: Kemple, K. M., Batey, J. J., & Hartle, L. C. (2008). Music Play: Creating Centers for Musical Play and Exploration. In D. Koralek (Ed.), *Spotlight on Young Children and the Creative Arts* (pp. 24–31). Washington, DC: National Association for the Education of Young Children.

Language and Literacy Development

Music and movement can increase children's language and literacy abilities (Gromko, 2005). Children can learn new vocabulary and begin to use those words to express ideas. Children will experiment with using words or phrases from songs in their everyday spoken interactions with peers and adults. Music can also expand children's phonemic awareness by having them identify repetitive and rhyming sounds that they hear in songs. Figure 14.14 suggests developmentally appropriate ways that adults can support learning through music and creative movement activities (Parlakian & Lerner, 2010).

Figure 14.14	Supporting and Nurturing Young Children's Developmental Skills Through Music			
	Social-Emotional	*Physical*	*Cognitive*	*Language/Literacy*
Infants to 12 Months	Notice the songs they enjoy. Use their names in the songs you sing.	Assist in moving their bodies when listening to music.	Encourage making of homemade instruments using plastic containers and utensils.	Sing simple songs with corresponding finger movements. They begin to use fingers at about 9 months and sing at about 12 months.
12 to 24 Months	Encourage them to play together music parade and song-based games—e.g., Ring Around the Rosie.	Select songs that build on body awareness—e.g., If You're Happy and You Know It.	Associate songs with activities, and that will assist in learning the sequence.	Pause and let children fill in the blank "How much is that doggy in the ____ ."
24 to 36 Months	Encourage children to create music—e.g., happy music, mad music, silly music.	Introduce creative movement experiences when singing—e.g., Pop Goes the Weasel.	Provide a symbol for a song—e.g., ball for On top of Old Smokey.	Use songs as a way to tell stories. Hearing stories through music assists with understanding the sequence.

Source: Parlakian, R., & Lerner, C. (2010). Beyond Twinkle Twinkle: Using Music With Infants and Toddlers. *Young Children, 65*(2), 14–19.

Researchers have found that implementing an instructional music curriculum in pre-schools tends to produce children who have higher academic abilities and are more successful at separating words phonemically (Schellenberg, 2006). Teachers who value music and movement use them frequently to engage children's academic and social skills and to assist with classroom routines such as cleaning up before moving to the next activity (Gillespie & Glider, 2010). Unfortunately, although most teachers routinely include music and movement as part of their circle time, only a small number of teachers dedicate a specific time of the day to music and movement development. The following sections suggest how teachers can place music and movement in a more pronounced position in young children's curriculum.

Schwartz (2008) suggests that music and movement can assist children who have obstacles that might be preventing them from learning how to read. The following are some comparisons that she makes in her book (p. 142):

Music and Literacy
There is a developmental progression to learning literacy
Literacy involves both decoding and determining meanings for words
Songs can be paired with all steps of learning to read
Music can provide temporal structure to encourage book handling
Words of books can be set to music, making them easier to remember
Lullabies and music can be paired with book reading to make it enjoyable
Music reflecting the emotional content of written stories can assist with comprehension
Music can help with story sequencing

Pretense Development

Coupling movement with pretend activities can assist children's ability to pay attention, speed of learning, retention of information, and overall enjoyment of learning (Lorenzo-Lasa, Ideishi, & Ideishi, 2007; Sacha & Russ, 2006). Attaching an animal image to a movement assists children in learning how to physically act out the movement by providing a mental image of that animal. That process results in the enhancement of motor, cognitive, and language abilities. For example, assigning the label "butterfly" to the gross movement of extending arms and moving them up and down, or the label "seal" to hopping around while clapping hands and having heads up in the air, assists children with gross motor development. At the same time, these activities enhance self-awareness, social interactions, emotional responses, cognitive development, and attention skills (Lorenzo-Lasa et al., 2007).

Using music and movement activities as props can also engage children while assisting with the development of cognitive, academic, and language learning skills. The development of a mental image can be promoted by placing a blue piece of material or carpet square in the middle of the group and then telling the children that it represents a pond or a river. Similarly, by having a couple of children stand by that image with their hands stretched out and then labeling them as "the trees" or "the forest," teachers encourage children in developing abstract symbolic representation skills. Music also can be used as a prop. Using slow and soft music can create a backdrop for children who are pretending that they are the raindrops from a spring rain shower. In contrast, louder and faster music can assist in creating the environment for fishes swimming away from a large shark.

Pairing movement and language can support children who have delayed language skills or who are developing a second language. Parts of the body can be learned in a playful manner by having children pretend to "glue" a specific part of their body to the floor, a wall, or another object in the classroom. Further instructions can be presented on ways in which the teacher or selected children can move

Use of objects for symbolic representations can enhance children's movement activities and their cognitive skills.

©iStock.com/lanych

parts of the body. Activities like these require children to concurrently move and use their memory to hold information over a few seconds while directions are provided. Discussing the children's feelings after finishing these activities can assist them in understanding more about balance and frustration, and how these activities and feelings can be associated with other real-life activities.

Another movement activity involves asking a child to choose a partner and converse with that partner using a sound or sounds instead of words. Before beginning this activity, the adult must model it, demonstrating how to use body movements and facial expressions that will assist in conveying the meaning of the sounds. During the activity, one partner observes the other partner and determines what the partner "said." An adult can assist the children by showing the children a picture of something and then telling them that their "conversation" must relate to that picture in some way. To make the activity even more challenging, children can be required to communicate without any sounds, using only body movements and facial expressions. This sets the stage for understanding that communication involves more than just speaking. They will learn to speak with their eyes, their hands, their tone, and their posture.

LEARNING FOR ALL CHILDREN
Music, Movement, and Disabilities

Most early education programs are witnessing an increase in enrollments of children with disabilities. Research shows that young children with disabilities can develop skills more easily when these skills are embedded in natural play activities. However, modifications to these play activities must occur in an orderly and thoughtful manner.

The program titled Materials + Objectives + Space + Time (MOST) addresses four specific needs that most children with disabilities have and for which teachers need to plan (Mitchell, 2008). For some children, the materials will need to be modified to meet the specific needs of the child. For example, some children might need to have a bookrack to hold the book as they look at it. Others may require modifications to their crayons or pencils so that they can more easily manipulate them.

Children with disabilities typically have an Individualized Education Program (IEP) that includes individual learning objectives. Therefore, teachers need to be aware of those learning objectives and design ways to measure the child's progress to attaining those objectives. If a child has a patterning objective (i.e., identification of a repeating sequence), the teacher might choose to measure the attainment of that objective by the child's ability to clap out certain nursery rhymes that have been reviewed in class.

Some children who have physical and visual disabilities will need ample space for their equipment so they can participate in movement activities. Special attention must be given to this adjustment when planning the activities with the staff.

Finally, children with disabilities might require more time to complete an activity, or they might be successful only if they are provided with successive short periods of time to work on the activity. As a result, the school staff needs to remain flexible so that all children will have the amount of time that they need to complete a specific activity. Figure 14.15 provides some of the suggestions that Mitchell (2008) proposes when modifying materials, space, and time.

Additionally, teachers should always consider the following strategies when working with all young children on expanding their music skills:

(Continued)

(Continued)

- Have children be part of the decision-making process through discussions
- Have music be a time in which learning can be scaffolded
- Make sure to assess children's musical progress
- Engage children in learning about particular musical elements by using open-ended prompts

Figure 14.16 provides 20 suggestions for integrating music and movement activities into everyday activities for young children.

Classroom Transitions

Early education schedules include an abundance of transitions that occur throughout the day: arrival, snack, centers, circle, lunch, outdoor play, returning to the classroom, story time, and dismissal. Young children, however, can find it challenging to transition successfully from one activity to another. Transitions that are not planned ahead of time can easily become very disorderly, wasting valuable learning time. Transition can be linked to a unit or theme that the children are studying, and a movement from one of the unit's activities can be implemented as part of the transition. For example, if the class is studying pets, children

Figure 14.15   Planning Tips for Modifying Materials, Space, and Time

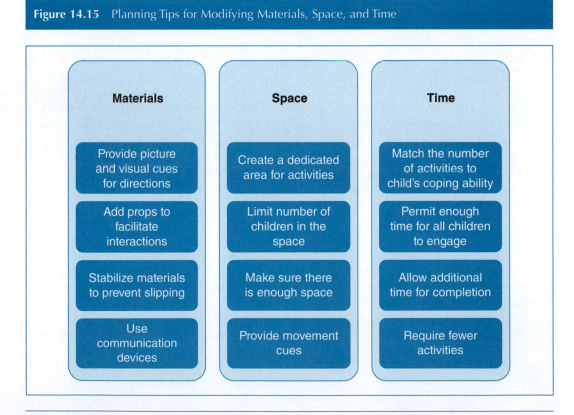

Materials	Space	Time
Provide picture and visual cues for directions	Create a dedicated area for activities	Match the number of activities to child's coping ability
Add props to facilitate interactions	Limit number of children in the space	Permit enough time for all children to engage
Stabilize materials to prevent slipping	Make sure there is enough space	Allow additional time for completion
Use communication devices	Provide movement cues	Require fewer activities

Source: Mitchell, L. C. (2008). Making the Most of Creativity in Activities for Young Children With Disabilities. In D. Koralek (Ed.), *Spotlight on Young Children and the Creative Arts* (pp. 40–43). Washington, DC: National Association for the Education of Young Children.

Figure 14.16 Twenty Suggestions for Integrating Music and Movement Into Everyday Activities

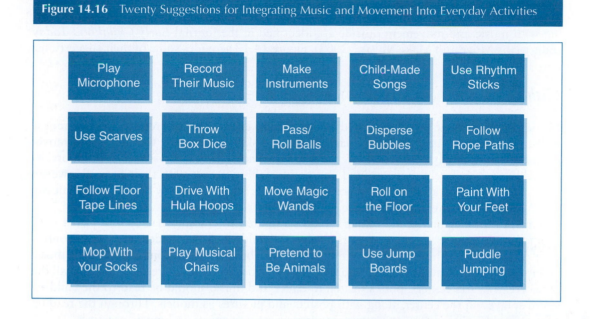

Play Microphone	Record Their Music	Make Instruments	Child-Made Songs	Use Rhythm Sticks
Use Scarves	Throw Box Dice	Pass/ Roll Balls	Disperse Bubbles	Follow Rope Paths
Follow Floor Tape Lines	Drive With Hula Hoops	Move Magic Wands	Roll on the Floor	Paint With Your Feet
Mop With Your Socks	Play Musical Chairs	Pretend to Be Animals	Use Jump Boards	Puddle Jumping

can be asked to move like a frog, a fish, or a bird to the next scheduled activity. Similarly, if the children are engaged in a unit on car washes, they can be asked to move like spinning brushes or people who polish cars while they transition from one activity to another. Making transitions fun, interesting, and reflective will encourage children to listen for the special notification that requires them to finish their work and move on to the next activity.

When choosing transition movements, adults should also consider the mood of the activity to which the children are going (Pica, 2009). For example, children who are transitioning to outdoor play activities might participate in more invigorating movements, such as spinning like carwash brushes or hopping like bunnies. In contrast, when children transition to naps, they should engage in slower movements, such as pretending that they are

Transitions from one activity to another provide an excellent opportunity for integrating movement activities that relate to a concept being studied.

newly born kittens or emulating the pace of a car going through a car wash.

In sum, transitions need to be planned, orderly, and enjoyable. They need to couple a physical movement with a mental image so that learning occurs.

Outdoor Activities

An excellent place for movement and music activities is the outside playground. This area typically provides children with ample space to move around creatively. Children who might feel shy or inhibited about singing inside, frequently feel more expressive on the playground. However, before starting an activity outdoors, the supervising adult needs to gather the children together to make sure that they understand both what they are going to do and what the rules are for the activity. If children are involved in the rule-making process, they are more likely to respect the rules.

Libraries, bookstores, and teaching supply stores have books that suggest outdoor music and movement activities. A number of activities that children can engage in when exploring with music and movement outside are identified in the journal *Early Childhood Today* (Editorial, "Move and Make Music," 2003). Figure 14.17 provides some of their suggestions.

Guiding Music and Movement Activities

Music and movement activities should be designed to encourage children to integrate motor skills, problem-solving skills, and social interaction skills. Therefore, the music and movement center ultimately will need a large amount of space, either indoors and/or outdoors, so that children can freely move around and comfortably interact with their peers. However, when presented with a large open-spaced area, young children typically run around aimlessly and frequently become uncontrollable.

Thus, in the beginning, the center should be limited to a somewhat confined area with room for only two or three participants, so that the children can be guided on ways to control their movements without disrupting others. As they become more comfortable with music and movement routines, the space and number of participants can increase. Similar to all the other creative arts centers, books related to dance and music should be read to the children and displayed in the center, along with posters and pictures as models. Through the reading of these books, discussions can occur on appropriate movement and music practices.

Teachers need to treat music and movement like the activities in other centers. Thus, children should be encouraged to participate as independently as possible in the activities. Additionally, adults need to adapt to multiple roles when guiding children's music activities. Those roles include planning, observing, participating, extending, modeling, and motivating children (Kemple et al., 2008). Figure 14.18 defines these roles and shows how adults can implement them in the music and movement center.

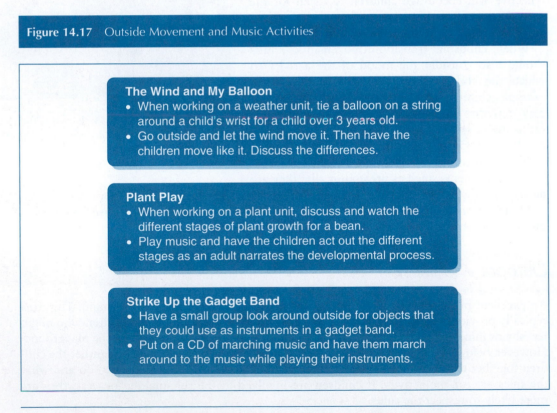

Figure 14.17   Outside Movement and Music Activities

The Wind and My Balloon
- When working on a weather unit, tie a balloon on a string around a child's wrist for a child over 3 years old.
- Go outside and let the wind move it. Then have the children move like it. Discuss the differences.

Plant Play
- When working on a plant unit, discuss and watch the different stages of plant growth for a bean.
- Play music and have the children act out the different stages as an adult narrates the developmental process.

Strike Up the Gadget Band
- Have a small group look around outside for objects that they could use as instruments in a gadget band.
- Put on a CD of marching music and have them march around to the music while playing their instruments.

Source: Editorial. (2003, June/July/August). Move and Make Music. *Early Childhood Today, 17*(8), 12–13.

Figure 14.18 Multiple Roles for Adults When Engaging Children in Play and Music

Planning	• Set the stage for introducing new materials in interesting ways.
Observing	• Observe children's reactions to new materials and each other. Determine if guidance is needed.
Practicing	• Share and enjoy the music, and play with children, rather than direct them.
Extending	• Enhance exploration by asking well-chosen, open-ended questions; adding a new material; or suggesting ideas.
Modeling	• Join in and demonstrate a new behavior or thought nonintrusively, via parallel play.
Motivating	• Encourage children to participate in the activities.

Source: Kemple, K. M., Batey, J. J., & Hartle, L. C. (2008). Music Play: Creating Centers for Musical Play and Exploration. In D. Koralek (Ed.), *Spotlight on Young Children and the Creative Arts* (pp. 24–31). Washington, DC: National Association for the Education of Young Children.

REFLECT AND APPLY EXERCISE 14.4

Justifying Music and Movement Activities

Reflect

You and your staff believe that you are implementing an excellent creative arts curriculum for your preschool children. You are particularly pleased with how you have integrated music and movement activities into the content areas that you are teaching. However, some of the children's parents have begun to question you gently about the amount of time being dedicated to such play activities. They worry that these activities are taking time away from the more structured activities that are supposed to prepare their children for kindergarten in the fall.

Apply

You and your staff decide to organize a meeting of the families to discuss several topics, one of which will be the impact of music and movement on development and learning. What information will you share with the families about the impact of music and movement on development and learning? How do these expressive play activities relate to the more academic activities that the children will be expected to perform next fall when they enter kindergarten?

Drama Centers

Creative drama, when children are directed by an adult to attain specific goals through storytelling, is an activity different from socio-dramatic play. However, early childhood educators who are not well versed in child-centered, socio-dramatic play often consider creative play and socio-dramatic play to be one and the same. This misunderstanding frequently occurs when adults do not recognize the value of allowing children to independently engage in the creation of pretend play enactments. As discussed in Part I of this book, child-driven pretend enactments provide multiple opportunities for development and learning to occur. Unfortunately, too frequently adults directly intervene in children's socio-dramatic play and alter the nature of that activity by changing the goal from pleasing the participants to attaining the adult's goals (Furman, 2000).

The use of a director in children's play often results in activities that are referred to as *creative drama*. Socio-dramatic play and creative drama are similar in that both respect children's words and ideas, share a feeling of joy and creativity centered on a story, enhance the feeling of community among children, and encourage storytelling and writing skills. However, in creative drama the director focuses the children's attention on attaining curricular goals that children, if left alone, often may view as unimportant.

Michael Blann/Photodisc/Thinkstock

Differences can be seen between socio-dramatic play productions and creative drama productions.

Guiding Children's Drama Productions

Children as young as 2 and 3 years of age are capable of participating in creative drama activities (Wanerman, 2010). However, the difference between these very young actors and 4-year-olds is that the younger children do not understand the need to "script" roles and actions so that the production evolves sequentially. In contrast, creative drama productions by older children can involve some children directing others while, at the same time, participating in activities that foster exploration of and participation in meaningful roles (Paley, 1990).

Instead of children making up stories, use of storybooks as working scripts has proven successful in assisting children in carrying out creative drama enactments. In "From Page to Stage: Story Drama in Five Basic Steps," Wanerman (2010) describes a process that has proven successful with young children. The steps in this process are described below and are listed in Figure 14.19.

Step 1: Read and Re-read Children's Favorite Books. One of the most important tasks is to observe the books that children are reading and then to choose one of those books for a creative drama activity. Opportunities to continually reread the story or parts of the story must be provided so that most of the children become very familiar with the text and are interested in turning the story into a creative drama.

Step 2: Use the Story as a Strong Scaffold. The story selected should have clearly described characters and activities that can be incorporated into a classroom setting. The book itself can be used as a visual scaffold when young children are creating the drama production. Holding the book up and allowing children say to the dialogue directly from the book is

Figure 14.19 From Page to Stage: Story Drama in Five Basic Steps

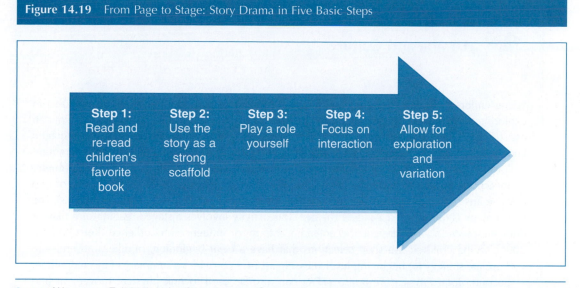

Step 1: Read and re-read children's favorite book

Step 2: Use the story as a strong scaffold

Step 3: Play a role yourself

Step 4: Focus on interaction

Step 5: Allow for exploration and variation

Source: Wanerman, T. (2010). Using Story Drama with Young Preschoolers. *Young Children, 65*(2), 20–28.

a way to keep the children engaged in the production while, at the same time, promoting language development.

Step 3: Play a Role Yourself. An adult can provide a model for young children to observe and imitate. Through adult involvement in the production, the story keeps moving with a minimum amount of interruptions and confusion. Additionally, the adult participant can always play the role of a frightening or unsympathetic character in the story, if the children are apprehensive about doing so.

Step 4: Focus on Interactions. A primary goal of creative drama productions is to enhance the language and social skills of young children. Therefore, special attention should be given to the collaborative dialogue and actions that occur throughout the drama. Whenever possible, children should be encouraged to interact with each other, talk about their activities, and comment to each other on what might happen next in the story.

Step 5: Allow for Exploration and Variation. This final step is very challenging, but it is the most important phase of producing a drama. Very young children are often too inexperienced to deviate from the story line. However, as they become comfortable with producing creative dramas as a form of expressive art, and as their language and problem-solving skills develop, they should be encouraged to create new endings to the stories that they enact. Affording children this opportunity will foster their storytelling and their cognitive ability to predict multiple possible outcomes. This leads to an understanding of their own creative abilities that will lead to other adaptations to the story. Drama centers are wonderful for rehearsing nursery rhymes.

As children become comfortable with and knowledgeable about creative drama enactments, support from adults and books can decrease, and children can be encouraged to take over more of the organization of the production. Around 4 years of age, children usually become capable of taking ownership of both the language and the story, and they should begin integrating their own ideas into the script (Paley, 1990). At this point, children begin to use their own language to create their own stories, and they begin to understand the impact that language use has on a creative production.

LEARNING FOR ALL CHILDREN
Drama and Culture

Young children's brains learn best and retain the most information when they are involved in exploring materials and questioning how the materials can be used. Drama and movement can assist English language learners in developing decoding skills, fluency, vocabulary, syntactic knowledge, discourse knowledge, and thinking skills (Sun, 2003). Drama and movement require children to listen and produce language in a meaningful, fun, and nonthreatening environment.

Incorporating drama and movement into classroom activities contributes to the use of two creative arts strategies that support literacy development in English language learners (ELLs). The first strategy is the use of a **Readers Theater**. This activity involves a staged reading of a play or dramatic piece of work designed to entertain, inform, or influence an audience (Kerry Moran, 2006). Young children use short selections that have a clear beginning, middle, and end—an appropriate strategy for beginning-level ELLs. Figure 14.20 provides a summary of this technique.

Second, *Total Physical Response (TPR)* can also be used to link physical movement and learning for children developing a second language. TPR involves the teacher beginning with simple action commands such as "stand up" and "sit down." As students become increasingly proficient, the teacher provides more complex commands such as "put the block on the table." The TPR process begins with explicit teacher models and scaffolds and gradually releases the responsibility to the students to independently demonstrate their knowledge and proficiency with the language. These types of directions by the teacher directly link actions with learning. Figure 14.21 provides information on songs that emphasize the TPR concept.

A third creative arts activity that has been found successful in teaching children learning English is the use of shared writings. This technique, which was discussed in Chapter 10, provides children with activity-based experiences that they later (1) share; (2) read, write, or talk about; or (3) listen to others talk about. By engaging in a common, hands-on experience, discussing it, and writing about it in a journal or as a group, children actively learn about math, science, social studies, and other curricular areas.

The use of drama, movement, and music offers young children—especially English language learners—opportunities to actively learn and retain information. When these creative arts activities are integrated into all classroom learning content areas, they support learning as an active, physical, and meaningful process.

Classroom drama activities for all children should enhance their development in the following areas:

- Intellectual—increase organizing and planning skills and skills for retelling familiar stories
- Physical—enhance gross and fine motor skills and coordination
- Social—expand turn-taking skills, cooperation and impulse control
- Emotional—develop self-esteem, positive sense of self and individual, and take pride in accomplishments

Puppet Centers

Puppets have been around for thousands of years, and cultures throughout the world have used them for storytelling (Salmon & Sainato, 2005). Puppets provide a safe environment where children can try out new words and linguistic structures, and not feel ashamed of making a mistake (Rule & Zhbanova, 2012). Because of the exaggerated gestures that can

Figure 14.20 Suggestions for Implementing Readers Theater

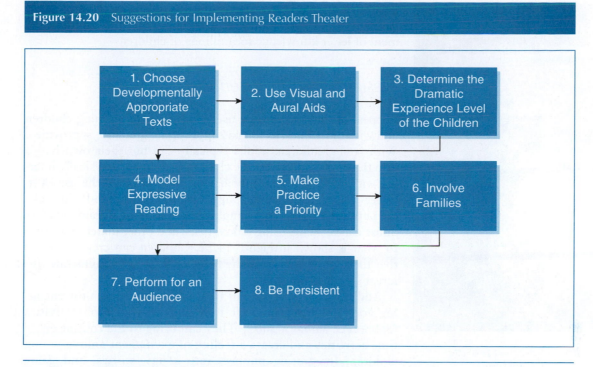

Source: Kerry Moran, K. J. (2006). Nurturing Emergent Readers Through Readers Theater. *Early Childhood Education Journal, 33,* 317–323.

Figure 14.21 Using TPR With Music to Teach Concepts

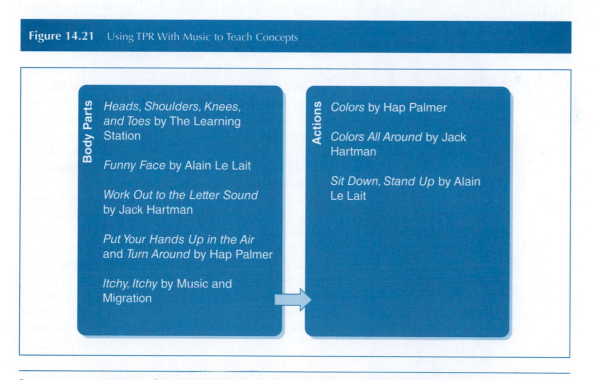

Source: Jensen, E. (2000). Moving With the Brain in Mind. *Educational Leadership, 58*(3), 34–37.

be made with puppets, they are ideal for use when singing songs or reciting nursery rhymes. An adult can use them to depict prepositions and also to note connections between rhyming words. Puppets can assist in enhancing children's phonological awareness skills while the

Playing with puppets can provide endless hours of enjoyment.

Figure 14.22 Dramatic Playhouse

children engage in a fun activity. Finally, for more than 40 years, *Sesame Street's* Bert and Ernie have contributed to the development of letter knowledge for millions of children.

Designing Puppet Centers

Puppets can be successfully used both with very young children and with older ones, as long as appropriate guidance is provided. With young children, adults typically can put their own hands into the puppet, allowing the child to verbally or physically interact with the puppet without having to coordinate the use of it. Older children can put the puppet on their own hand and make the puppet come to life. A simple puppet stage or a dramatic playhouse can be made using a box, pens, and other material, similar to what is shown in Figure 14.22. Children can create pictures that they can place across the front of the stage to illustrate different scenes.

Additionally, puppets can be used in classrooms for engaging young children in circle time and for transition activities (Salmon & Sainato, 2005). They can bring to life routine circle time activities and create a feeling of excitement among young children. Integrating puppets into songs, stories, and game activities can engage many of those young children who tend to lose interest during everyday activities. Puppets also can be employed to introduce new concepts and reinforce old ones, as well as to announce the day's activities at the beginning of class or to review them when the day concludes.

During transition times from one activity to the next, puppets can alert the children that it is time for them to clean up and move. A puppet going around the room ringing a hand bell is often more noticeable to young children than having an adult take that same action (Salmon & Sainato, 2005). Figure 14.23 provides specific suggestions for using puppets when transitioning from one activity to another.

As a method for linking school with home, Salmon and Sainato (2005) suggest having students take home a "traveling puppet" for a visit. Sending a puppet packed in a tote bag home with children, along with a journal and a pen, allows children to record the highlights of the evening that the puppet visited their home and family. Including a storybook or two that relate to the puppet in the tote bag also encourages families to spend some time with their child in literacy-related activities.

Guiding Children's Puppet Productions

Puppets provide a playful and comfortable support to engage children in motivating activities. Puppets are also useful for asking the children to share information, questions, and events related to stories. These requests

Figure 14.23	Suggestions for Using Puppets for Transitions

Transition Prompter	• Use a puppet to signal a transition between activities. The puppet can shake a bell indicating when it is time to move to another activity.
Attention Getter	• Use a puppet to quickly capture the attention of a busy group of children and lead them to the next activity.
Transition Helper	• Allow children to take turns using a puppet to ready the class for special activities such as library time, music, or art class.
Cleanup Time	• Use a puppet to model the expected behavior, such as placing blocks in a bin.
Line Leader	• Guide the class to the library, gym, or music class using a puppet to increase the attention of the group.

Source: Adapted from Salmon, M. D., & Sainato, D. M. (2005). Beyond Pinocchio: Puppets as Teaching Tools in Inclusive Early Childhood Classrooms. *Young Exceptional Children, 8*(3), 12–19.

of the children can occur either during or after the stories are read to them. Children who are reluctant to share their thoughts and ideas often tend to become more involved and willing to share when they can do so by using a puppet (Keogh & Naylor, 2009). Research has found that, when puppets are used, children have higher levels of engagement and motivation, use more reasoning, give more explanations, and provide more linked justifications for event happenings in stories (Belohlawek, Keogh, & Naylor, 2010). Having a puppet read a story to a group and then discuss the different forms of print that exist in the story will focus all of the children's attention on the print in the book.

Chapter Summary

Participation in creative arts activities, such as art, music and movement, and drama, encourages the development of children's gross and fine motor, sensory, creative, and perceptual skills. All of these skills are critical for academic success in the primary grades. Art activities that are typically presented in early education programs and that enhance young children's development and learning are: drawing, gluing, painting, and adapting three-dimensional materials. Playful art activities, where children are required to work with peers in creating works or objects, exploring new artistic techniques, and discussing completed products, also greatly contribute to learning and development.

Young children love to hear their own voice and to use their voice to chant. Similarly, they enjoy expressing themselves through the physical movements of their bodies. Music and movement programs provide opportunities for children to sing and move

HOME AND COMMUNITY CONNECTIONS

Implementing Play Activities in the Creative Arts Centers

Fill the house with music and songs. Sing a song as your child engages in everyday activities. *Brush, brush, brush your teeth, Brush, brush, brush your teeth, Brush, brush, brush your teeth till they're clean and shiny.*

throughout the day. When music and movement activities are integrated into the daily learning curriculum, they afford children opportunities to simultaneously participate in enjoyable and meaningful performing arts as well as in content-learning activities.

Children are also capable of producing guided creative dramatic and puppet enactments. These activities should be designed to assist children in learning language and developing social and emotional skills—skills needed to participate successfully as a group member. As children become older and more experienced with creating dramatic productions, responsibility for those productions can gradually be transferred to the children.

CHAPTER 14 FIRST-PERSON INTERVIEW

Children Are Natural Movers and Doers

Kaitlan Fisher

Dance and Movement Instructor, Newport Beach, CA

Teachers find it challenging to teach the creative arts because they usually do not have a background in those areas. When I was in school, students either enjoyed academics, athletics, or the arts. Just a few people were able to cross over and be good in more than one of these areas. People that go into teaching are usually those who enjoy the academics.

I went to very good schools, but the focus was on academics. Most of the education that I received in the arts was from after-school programs that my parents enrolled me in and paid for me to attend. Not a lot of people can afford to do that.

Even though I have a strong background in movement and dance, I still find it very difficult to integrate those activities into the academic learning areas for young children. There's nothing out there to guide you, so you need to spend long hours thinking about how to adapt what you really want the children to learn into meaningful and enjoyable creative activities. Sure, you can just teach them about the academics, but some young children struggle to learn that way. Most of them are "movers and doers," and I have found out that they learn more and faster if music, movement, or drama reinforces the academic information. I just love using songs and stories when I am teaching.

If I want children to learn about a concept, I often use objects or have children pretend they have objects. For example, when we were studying about triangles, the children certainly understood more about this type of shape when I related it to the shape of a piece of pizza. However, my students really got the idea when I had them sit on the floor and stretch their legs out with their feet apart. I then went around the circle with my pretend wand and turned their legs into pizza pieces. We spent time talking about math concepts such as comparing the length of the sides and the sizes of the angles. We also worked on motor skills such as flexing our toes. A child would circle around the group with a "pretend wand" and touch different children's feet with the "magic wand," and those children would have to flex their toes as hard as they could.

There are many areas to use music and movement for learning. I always use it with science. The other day we were learning about evaporation and the effect of heat on water. We then talked about the song "The Itsy, Bitsy Spider." Next, children and I made up our own verses to the song using different animal situations where water evaporated. For example, the big splashing whales went swimming through the ocean, and the rain did not wash them out. However, when the sun did come up and dried up a lot of the ocean, the whales did not have as much space to swim. I was amazed how the children began to apply the concept to other situations!

I am also amazed at how much older children enjoy these activities. Although I teach younger children, I often have fifth graders come in and help in the classroom. They really get into the activities, and that makes the younger children even more interested. We had the best time a few months ago when the presidential election was going on. I had just finished reading my students the book *Charlotte's Web*. With the election approaching, I decided to read them *Duck for President*. After reading the book, we then agreed to have a pretend campaign in the classroom, and the people running for the office of president would be characters from *Charlotte's Web*. Some children volunteered to be specific characters and others volunteered to make posters or work on a speech that would state how they would improve Charlotte's barn. We all had so much fun with this activity, including the fifth graders who came in to help that day. At the end of the day, the characters gave their speeches and we cast our votes. We counted the votes, talked about "having the most votes," and found out that Farmer Brown won. The children still play this game on their own.

Creative arts really help children with their social and emotional needs. I teach at a school where the children come from very challenging backgrounds. One day, when I was leaving school, I went through the office and noticed that a boy was there with a police officer. Evidently, the boy had become sick at school that morning and his mother was called. When she neglected to come and pick him up within a reasonable amount of time, the police were called in because of child neglect. The boy looked sick and was obviously very frightened. I felt he needed some extra attention, so I sat with him and we sang songs, read and discussed books, and did gentle relaxing movements. Within a short time, he appeared to feel a little more peaceful about his situation.

I work with a lot of children who are learning to speak English. Just last week, a 3-year-old child who only spoke Russian started in my class. This week his mother communicated to me that at home he is singing songs using English words.

I don't know how I could even control my class if I didn't use movement and music. When I want to get the children's attention, I simply say, "Okay, it's time for everyone to stop what they are doing and catch a bubble." The classroom suddenly becomes quiet, while everyone looks at and copies me as I extend my arms out, carefully pretend to catch a bubble, and gently pull it in close to my body. It always works! Sometimes I will say, "It's time for everyone to copy the three movements that Enrique is going to make." Everyone then looks at Enrique and follows his movements.

When we need to have the children go somewhere in a line, I have a line leader decide on an animal and pretend to be that animal for about ten seconds. Everyone in the line has to follow the leader's movements. Then we stop, and after the leader moves to the back of the line, the new leader gets to choose a movement for all of the children to do for the next ten seconds. Doing these movements keeps the children's interest, allows them to exercise different parts of their bodies, and makes them think of movement sequences and learn language. And it is fun. Why wouldn't you do it?

Student Study Site

Visit the Student Study Site at **www.sagepub.com/selmi** to access additional study tools including mobile-friendly eFlashcards and links to video and web resources.

Sample Learning Activities

Curricular Area: Creative Arts

Core Vocabulary: Music, performance, create, movement, dance, art, appreciation, stretch, twist, gallop, freeze, bold, light, strong, tempo, rhythm, sequences, instruments

Guide Questions:

How can we express ourselves through movement?

How can we express ourselves through pictures and paintings?

How can you make your body move?

What colors did you use in your painting? How does it make you feel?

When you watched _____, what did it make you think about? How did it make you feel?

What is a performance?

What sounds do you hear? What is creating those sounds?

Resources:

Daywalt, Drew. (2013). *The Day the Crayons Quit*. Philomel.

Potter, Debra. (2005). *I Am the Music Man*. Child's Play.

Lewison, Wendy. (1996). *I Wear My Tutu Everywhere*. Grosset & Dunlap.

McDonnell, Patrick. (2006). *Art*. Little, Brown Books for Young Readers; Library Binding Edition.

Reynolds, Peter. (2003). *The Dot*. Candlewick.

Core Text: Ish, by Peter Reynolds

- Skills: Perspective, creativity, appreciation, acceptance, confidence, drawing
- Levels of Questions: What is the story about? What does "-ish" mean? What do you like to draw? What does it mean to draw well? What can we learn from this story?
- Product: Create their own -ish drawings. Create a class art gallery.

Learning Centers:

- Explore through literacy: A variety of books on the arts and artists
- Create: Provide a wide range of drawing tools such as colored pencils, crayons, pastels, markers, water colors, and oil pastels for students to create pictures. While they are creating ask questions such as, "What are you working on? What are you using to make your picture? What colors have you selected?"
- Outdoor play: Have music playing outside for students to engage in expressive movement
- Dramatic play suggestions: Visiting the art gallery, tour guide

Key Terms

art center

fine motor skills

gross motor skills

movement center

music center

Readers Theater

Some Children's Books About Creative Arts

The Day the Crayons Quit, by Drew Daywalt

De Colores, by Jose-Luis Orozco

From Head to Toe, by Eric Carle

Get Up and Go, by Nancy Carlson

Hands: Growing Up to Be an Artist, by Lois Ehlert

I Ain't Gonna Paint No More! by Karen Beaumont

Little Yoga: A Toddler's First Book of Yoga, by Rebecca Whitford

Music Music for Everyone, by Vera B. Williams

This Jazz Man, by Karen Ehrhardt

We All Sing With the Same Voice, by J. Philip Miller and Sheppard Greene

We're Going on a Bear Hunt, by Michael Rosen

Useful Websites

Arts Education Partnership: http://aep-arts.org

National Art Education Association: http://www.naea-reston.org

National Association for Music Education: http://www.nafme.org

National Coalition for Core Arts Standards: http://nccas.wikispaces.com

National Dance Education Organization: http://www.ndeo.org

Wolf Trap Foundation for Performing Arts: http://www.wolftrap.org

Reflective Questions

1. Describe examples of socio-dramatic play and creative drama that have similar themes. Analyze the similarities and differences between these two activities.

2. Use the three creative arts centers described in the chapter's opening scenario to discuss how that preschool might have addressed modifying these three centers using different materials, space, and time, as suggested in Figure 14.15.

References

Adams, M. (1990). *Beginning to read.* Cambridge, MA: MIT Press.

Albert Shanker Institute. (2009). *Preschool curriculum: What's in it for children and teachers.* Washington, DC: Albert Shanker Institute.

American Academy of Pediatrics Council on Communications and Media. (2013, October). Children, Adolescents, and the Media. *Pediatrics.* Retrieved from http://pediatrics.aappublications.org/content/132/5/958.full.pdf+html

Andersen, A., Andersen, J., & Shapiro, J. (2005). Supporting multiple literacies: Parents' and children's talk within story reading. *Mathematics Education Research Journal, 16*(3), 5–26.

Apgar, V. (1953). A proposal for a new method of evaluation of the newborn infant. *Current Researches in Anesthesia and Analgesia, 32*(4), 260–267.

Ashbrook, P., & Chalufour, I. (2013). *Introduction to spotlight on young children: Exploring science.* In A. Shillady (Ed.), *Spotlight on young children: Exploring science* (pp. 2–4). Washington, DC: National Association for the Education of Young Children.

Bagdi, A., & Vacca, J. (2005). Supporting early childhood social-emotional well being: The building blocks for early learning and school success. *Early Childhood Education Journal, 33,* 145–150.

Barclay, K., Benelli, C., & Gudt, P. T. (1998). It's never too soon: Building a firm foundation for reading and writing. *The Magazine of the National Head Start Association, 17,* 38–44.

Barnett, W. S., Carolan, M. E., Fitzgerald, J., & Squires, J. H. (2012). *The state of preschool 2012: State preschool yearbook.* New Brunswick, NJ: National Institute for Early Education Research.

Barnett, W. S., & Yarosz, D. J. (2007). *Who goes to preschool and why does it matter?* (Preschool Policy Brief No. 15). Available at http://nieer.org

Barton, E. E., & Pavilanis, R. (2012). Teaching pretend play to children with autism. *Young Exceptional Children, 15,* 5–17.

Batshaw, M. L., Roizen, N. J., & Lotrecchiano, G. R. (2012). *Children with disabilities.* Baltimore, MD: Paul H. Brookes.

Baumeister, R. F., & Vohs, K. D. (2004). *Handbook of self-regulation: Research theory, and applications.* New York: Guilford Press.

Beckwith, L., Rodning, C., Norris, D., Phillipsen, L., Khandabi, P., & Howard, J. (1994). Spontaneous play in two-year-olds born to substance-abusing mothers. *Infant Mental Health Journal, 15,* 189–210.

Belohlawek, J., Keogh, B., & Naylor, S. (2010). The PUPPETS project hits WA. *Teaching Science, 56,* 36–38.

Bergen, D. (2007). The role of pretend play in children's cognitive development. *Early Childhood Research and Practice, 4*(1), 1–10.

Berk, L. E., Mann, T. D., & Ogan, A. T. (2006). Make-believe play: Wellspring for development of self-regulation. In D. G. Singer, R. M. Golinkoff, & K. Hirsh-Pasek (Eds.), *Play = learning: How play motivates and enhances children's cognitive and social-emotional growth* (pp. 74–100). New York, NY: Oxford University Press.

Bisgaier, C. S., & Samaras, T. (2008). Using wood, glue, and words to enhance learning. In D. Koralek (Ed.), *Spotlight on young children and the creative arts* (pp. 12–18). Washington, DC: National Association for the Education of Young Children.

Blair, C., Knipe, H., Cummings, E., Baker, D., Gamson, P., Eslinger, P., & Thorne, S. L. (2007). A developmental neuroscience approach to the study of school readiness. In R. C. Planta, M. J. Cox, & K. L. Snow (Eds.), *School readiness and the transition to kindergarten in the era of accountability* (pp. 121–148). Baltimore, MD: Paul H. Brookes.

Bodrova, E., & Leong, D. J. (2003). Chopsticks and counting chips: Do play and foundational skills need to compete for the teacher's attention in an early childhood classroom. *Young Children, 58*(Part 3), 10–17. Retrieved from https://www.naeyc.org/files/yc/file/200305/Chopsticks_Bodrova.pdf

Bodrova, E., & Leong, D. J. (2007). *Tools of the mind.* Upper Saddle River, NJ: Pearson Education.

Bodrova, E., Leong, D. J., Paynter, D. E., & Hensen, R. (2003). *Scaffolding literacy development in the preschool classroom.* Aurora, CO: Mid-continent Research for Education and Learning.

Bondioli, A. (2001). The adult as a tutor in fostering children's symbolic play. In A. Goncu & E. L. Klein (Eds.), *Children in play, story, and school* (pp. 107–131). New York, NY: Guilford Press.

Bornstein, M. H., Haynes, O. M., Pascual, L., Painter, K. M., & Galperin, C. (1999). Play in two societies: Pervasiveness of process, specificity of structure. *Child Development, 70,* 2910–2929.

Bornstein, M. H., & O'Reilly, A. W. (Eds.). (1993). *The role of play in the development of thought.* San Francisco, CA: Jossey-Bass.

Bornstein, M. H., Selmi, A. M., Haynes, O. M., Painter, K. M., & Marx, E. S. (1999). Representational abilities of the hearing status of child/mother dyads. *Child Development, 70,* 833–852.

Bornstein, M. H., & Tamis-LeMonda, C. S. (1997). Maternal responsiveness and infant mental abilities: Specific predictive relations. *Infant Behavior and Development, 20, (3),* 283–296.

Bosse, S., Jacobs, G., & Anderson, T. L. (2009). Science in the air. *Young Children, 64*(6), 10–15.

Bouley-Picard, T. M. (2005). Preservice teachers and preschools: The development of thematic literacy play centers. *Journal of Early Childhood Teacher Education, 25,* 211–222.

Bowman, B. T., Donovan, S., & Burns, M. S. (2001). *Eager to learn: Educating our preschoolers.* Washington, DC: National Academies Press.

Bowman, D. H. (2005, July/August). From literacy to learning: An interview with Catherine Snow on vocabulary, comprehension, and the achievement gap. *Harvard Education Letter, 21*(4). Retrieved from http://hepg.org/hel/article/290

Bradley, B. A., & Jones, J. (2010). Sharing alphabet books in early childhood classrooms. In D. S. Strickland (Ed.), *Essential readings on early literacy* (pp. 70–82). Newark, DE: International Reading Association.

Bredekamp, S. (2002). *Developmentally appropriate practice in early childhood programs serving children from birth through age 8* (2nd ed.). Washington, DC: National Association for the Education of Young Children.

Britto, P. R., Fuligni, A. S., & Brooks-Gunn, J. (2006). Reading ahead: Effective interventions for young children's early literacy development. In D. K. Dickinson & S. B. Neuman (Eds.), *Handbook of early literacy research* (pp. 311–332). New York, NY: Guilford Press.

Brown, E. D., Benedett, B., & Armistead, M. A. E. (2010). Arts enrichment and school readiness for children at risk. *Early Childhood Research Quarterly, 25,* 112–124.

Bruner, J. (1960). *The process of education.* Cambridge, MA: Harvard University Press.

Bruner, J. (1986). *Actual minds, possible worlds.* Cambridge, MA: Harvard University Press.

Bryk, A., Sebring, P. B., Allensworth, E., Luppescu, S., & Easton, J. (2009). *Organizing schools for improvement: Lessons from Chicago.* Chicago, IL: University of Chicago Press.

Bulotsky-Shearer, R. J., Bell, E. R., Romero, S. L., & Carter, T. M. (2012). Preschool interactive peer play mediates problem behavior and learning for low-income children. *Journal of Applied Developmental Psychology, 33,* 53–65.

Burghardt, G. M. (2011). Defining and recognizing play. In A. Pellegrini (Ed.), *The Oxford handbook of the development of play* (pp. 9–18). New York, NY: Oxford University Press.

Burt, T., Gelnaw, A., & Lesser, L. K. (2010). Do no harm: Creating welcoming and inclusive environments for lesbian, gay, bisexual, and transgender (LGBT) families in early childhood settings. *Young Children.* Retrieved from https://www.naeyc.org/files/yc/file/201001/LesserOnlineExtra2.pdf

Buysse, V., Goldman, B. D., & Skinner, M. L. (2002). Setting effects on friendship formation among young children with and without disabilities. *Exceptional Children, 68,* 503–517.

Cabell, S. A., Justice, L. M., Vukelich, C., Buell, M. J., & Han, M. (2008). Strategic and intentional shared storybook reading. In L. M. Justice & C. Vukelich (Eds.), *Achieving excellence in preschool literacy instruction* (pp. 161–181). New York, NY: Guilford Press.

Cabell, S. Q., Torterelli, L. S., & Gerde, H. K. (2013). How do I write. . . . ?: Scaffolding preschoolers' early writing skills. *Reading Teacher, 66,* 650–659.

Carey, S. (1978). The child as word learner. In M. Halle, J. Bresnan, & G. Miller (Eds.), *Linguistic theory and psychological reality.* Cambridge, MA: MIT Press.

Carlson, F. M. (2011a). *Big body play: Why boisterous, vigorous, and very physical play is essential for children's development and learning.* Washington, DC: The National Association for the Education of Young Children.

Carlson, F. M. (2011b). Rough play: One of the most challenging behaviors. *Young Children, 66,* 18–25.

Carson, M. S. (1989). *The scientific kid: Projects, experiments and adventures.* New York: Harper & Row.

Carvell, N. R. (2006). *Language enrichment activities program (LEAP)* (Vol. 1). Dallas, TX: Southern Methodist University.

Center for Research on Education, Diversity, & Excellence. (2002). *Study on effectiveness of school programs for language minority students posted online.* Retrieved from http://www.crede.ucsc.edu

Champion, T. B., Katz, L., Muldrow, R., & Rochelle, D. (1999). Storytelling and storymaking in an urban preschool classroom: Building bridges from home to school culture. *Topics in Language Disorders, 19*(3), 52–67.

Charman, T., Howlin, P., Berry, B., & Prince, E. (2004). Measuring developmental progress of children with autism spectrum disorder on school entry using parent report. *Autism, 8,* 89–100.

Chen, J. (2010). Gender issues in externalizing problems among preschool children: Implications for early childhood educators. *Early Child Development and Care, 108,* 463–474.

Chien, N. C., Howes, C., Burchinal, M., Pianta, R. C., Ritchie, S., Bryant, D. M., . . . & Barbarin, O. A. (2010). Children's classroom engagement and school readiness gains in prekindergarten. *Child Development, 81,* 1534–1549.

Child Trends Data Bank. (2012). *Early childhood program enrollment: Indicators on children and youth.* Bethesda, MD: Author. Retrieved from http://www.childtrends.org/?indicators=early-childhood-program-enrollment

Childress, D. C. (2011). Play behaviors of parents and their young children with disabilities. *Topics in Early Childhood Special Education, 31,* 112–120.

Chouinard, M., Harris P., & Maratsos, M. (2007). Children's questions: A mechanism for cognitive development. *Monographs of the Society for Research in Child Development, 72,* 1–129.

Christ, T., & Wang, X. C. (2010). Bridging the vocabulary gap: What the research tell us about vocabulary instruction in early education. *Young Children, 65*(4), 84–91.

Christensen, A., & Kelly, K. (2003). No time for play: Throwing the baby out with the bath water. *The Reading Teacher, 56,* 528–530.

Christie, J. F. (1991). *Play and early literacy development.* Albany: State University of New York Press.

Clark, B. (2009). The integrative education model. In *Systems and models for developing programs for the gifted & talented* (2nd ed., pp. 143–102). Mansfield, CT: Creative Learning Press.

Clay, M. (1979). *The early detection of reading difficulties: A diagnostic survey with recovery procedures.* Portsmouth, NH: Heinemann Educational Books.

Clay, M. M. (1998). *By different paths to common outcomes.* York, ME: Stenhouse Publishers.

Clements, D., & Sarama, J. A. (2007). Effects of a preschool mathematics curriculum: Summative research on the Building Blocks project. *Journal for Research in Mathematics Education, 38,* 136–163.

Clements, D., & Sarama, J. A. (2009). *Learning and teaching early math: The learning trajectories approach.* New York, NY: Taylor & Francis.

Cohen, L., & Uhry, J. (2009). Young children's discourse strategies during block play: A Bakhtinian approach. *Journal of Research in Childhood Education, 21,* 302–315.

Colvin, G., Flannery, K., Sugai, G., & Monegan, J. (2009). Using observational data to provide performance feedback to teachers: A high school case study. *Preventing School Failure, 53,* 95–104.

Conezio, K., & French, L. (200s2). Science in the preschool classroom: Capitalizing on children's fascination with the everyday world to foster language and literacy development. *Young Children, 57*(5), 12–18.

Cook, R. E., Klein, M. D., & Chen, D. (2012). *Adapting early childhood curricula for children with special needs.* New York, NY: Pearson.

Copley, J. V. (2010). *The young child and mathematics.* Washington, DC: National Association for the Education of Young Children.

Copple, C., & Bredekamp, S. (2009). *Developmentally appropriate practice in early childhood programs serving children from birth through age 8.* Washington, DC: National Association for the Education of Young Children.

Corsaro, W. A. (1987). *Friendship and peer culture in the early years.* Norwood, NJ: Ablex.

Cote, L. R., & Bornstein, M. H. (2005). Child and mother play in cultures of origin, acculturating cultures, and cultures of destination. *International Journal of Behavioral Development, 29,* 479–488.

Cress, C. J., Arens, K. B., & Zajicek, A. K. (2007). Comparisons of engagement pattern of young children with developmental disabilities between structured and free play. *Training in Developmental Disabilities, 42,* 152–164.

Cummins, J. (2000). *Language, power and pedagogy: Bilingual children in the crossfire.* Clevedon, UK: Multilingual Matters.

Curran, J. M. (1999). Constraints of pretend play: Explicit and implicit rules. *Journal of Research in Childhood, 14,* 47–55.

de Falco, S., Esposito, G., Venuti, P., & Bornstein, M. H. (2010). Mothers and fathers at play with their children with Down Syndrome: Influences on child exploratory and symbolic activity. *Journal of Applied Research in Intellectual Disabilities, 23,* 597–605.

DeBaryshe, B. D., Gorecki, D. M., & Mishima-Young, L. N. (2009). Differentiated instruction to support high-risk preschool learners. *NHSA Dialog, 12,* 227–244.

Dennis, L. R., Lynch, S. A., & Stockall, N. (2012). Planning literacy environments for diverse preschoolers. *Young Exceptional Children, 15,* 3–19.

Denton, P., & Kriete, R. (2000). *The first six weeks of school.* Greenfield, MA: National Foundation for Children.

Derman-Sparks, L., & Edwards, J. O. (2010). *Anti-bias education for young children and ourselves.* Washington, DC: National Association for the Education of Young Children.

DeStefano, L., & Rempert, T. (2007). *Year one evaluation of Chicago Early Reading First.* Champaign: University of Illinois at Urbana-Champaign.

DeStefano, L., Rempert, T., & O'Dell, L. (2008). *Year two evaluation of Chicago Early Reading First.* Champaign: University of Illinois at Urbana-Champaign.

DeTemple, J. M. (2001). Parents and children reading books together. In D. K. Dickinson & P. O. Tabors (Eds.), *Beginning literacy with language* (pp. 31–51). Baltimore, MD: Paul H. Brooks.

Dever, M. T., & Falconer, R. C. (2008). *Foundations and changes in early childhood education.* New York, NY: Wiley.

Dewey, J. (1910). *How we think.* Boston: D. C. Heath.

Dewey, J. (1966). *Democracy and education: An introduction to the philosophy of education.* New York, NY: Free Press. (Original work published 1916)

Dickinson, D. K., & Neuman, S. B. (Eds.). (2006). *Handbook of early literacy research: Volume 2.* New York, NY: Guilford Press.

Dickinson, D. K., & Tabors, P. O. (2001). *Beginning literacy with language.* Baltimore, MD: Paul H. Brookes.

Donaldson, M. (1978). *Children's minds.* New York, NY: W. W. Norton.

Douglas-Hall, A., & Chau, M. (2008). *Basic facts about low-income children, birth to age 6.* New York, NY: Columbia University, National Center on Children's Poverty. Retrieved from http://www.nccp.org/publications/pub_847.html

Doussard-Roosevelt, J. A., Joe, C. M., Bazhenova, O. V., & Porges, S. W. (2003). Mother-child interaction in autistic and nonautistic children: Characteristics of maternal approach behaviors and child social responses. *Development and Psychopathology, 15*(2), 277–295

Dow, C. B. (2010). Young children and movement: The power of creative dance. *Young Children, 65,* 30–35.

Drew, W. F., & Rankin, B. (2008). Promoting creativity for life using open-ended materials. In D. Koralek (Ed.), *Spotlight on young children and the creative arts* (pp. 32–39). Washington, DC: National Association for the Education of Young Children.

Dunn, J. (2006). *Children's friendships: The beginning of intimacy.* Malden, MA: Blackwell.

Early Childhood Education Assessment. (2007). *State early learning standards and early childhood program standards birth to third grade.* Retrieved from http://ccsso.org/projects/scass/projects/early_childhood_education_assessment_consortium/publications_and_products/3688.cfn

Eberly, J. L., Joshi, A., & Kozal, J. (2007). Communicating with families across cultures: An investigation of teacher perception and practices. *The School Community Journal, 17,* 7–26.

Editorial. (2003, June/July/August). Move and make music. *Early Childhood Today, 17*(8), 12–13.

Edmiaston, R. K., & Fitzgerald, L. M. (2000). How Reggio Emilia encourages inclusion. *Educational Leadership, 58*(1), 66–69.

Elias, C. L., & Berk, L. E. (2002). Self-regulation in young children: Is there a role for sociodramatic play? *Early Childhood Research Quarterly, 17,* 216–238.

Elkind, D. (2007). *The power of play: How spontaneous, imaginative activities lead to happier, healthier children.* Berkeley, CA: Da Capo Press.

Elkonin, D. (1977). Toward the problem of stages in the mental development of the child. In M. Cole (Ed.), *Soviet developmental psychology* (pp. 538–563). White Plains, NY: M. E. Sharpe.

Enz, B., & Christie, J. (1997). Teacher play interaction styles: Effects on play behavior and relationships with teacher training and experience. *International Journal of Early Childhood Education, 2,* 55–69.

Epstein, A. S. (2007). *The intentional teacher: Choosing the best strategies for young children's learning.* Washington, DC: National Association for the Education of Young Children.

Escobedo, T. (1999). The canvas of play: A study of children's play behaviors while drawing. In S. Reifel (Ed.), *Play and culture studies* (pp. 101–122). Stamford, CT: Ablex.

Farver, J. A. & Shin, Y. L. (1997). Social pretend play in Korean- and Anglo-American preschoolers. *Child Development, 68,* 544–456.

Farver, J. M., & Howes, C. (1993). Cultural differences in American and Mexican mother-child pretend play. *Merrill-Palmer Quarterly, 39,* 344–358.

Fawcett, M., & Hay, P. (2004). 5x5x5 = Creativity in the early years. *International Journal of Art & Design Education, 23,* 234–245.

Fisher, K., Hirsh-Pasek, K., Golinkoff, R. M., Singer, D., & Berk, L. (2011). Playing around in school: Implications for learning and educational policy. In A. D. Pellegrini (Ed.), *The Oxford handbook of the development of play* (pp. 341–360). New York, NY: Oxford University Press.

Flom, R., Gentile, D. A., & Pick, A. D. (2008). Infants' discrimination of happy and sad music. *Infant Behavior and Development, 31,* 716–728.

Freeman, R., Eber, L., Andersen, C., Irvin, L., Bounds, M., Dunlap, G., & Horner, R. (2006). Building inclusive school cultures using school-wide PBS: Designing effective individual support systems for students with significant disabilities. *Research and Practice for Persons With Severe Disabilities, 31,* 4–17.

Friend, M., & Bursuck, W. D. (2012). *Including students with special needs: A practical guide for classroom teachers* (6th ed.). Boston, MA: Pearson.

Friend, M., & Cook, L. (2007). *Interactions: Collaboration skills for school professionals* (5th ed.). Boston, MA: Pearson.

Friend, M., & Cook, L. (2013). *Interactions: Collaboration skills for school professionals* (7th ed.). Boston, MA: Pearson.

Furman, L. (2000). In support of drama in early childhood education, again. *Early Childhood Education Journal, 27,* 173–178.

Gadzikowski, A. (2013). Preschool and kindergarten classroom strategies for young scientists. In A. Shillady (Ed.), *Spotlight on young children: Exploring science* (pp. 36–40). Washington, DC: National Association for the Education of Young Children.

Gallagher, R. J., LaMontagne, M. J., & Johnson, L. J. (1994). Early collaboration: The collaborative challenge. In L. J. Johnson, R. J. Gallagher, M. J. LaMontagne, J. B. Jordan, J. J. Gallagher, P. L. Hutinger, & M. B. Karnes (Eds.), *Meeting early intervention challenges: Issues from birth to three* (2nd ed., pp. 235–250). Baltimore, MD: Paul H. Brookes.

Ganz, J. B., & Flores, M. M. (2010). Implementing visual cues for young children with autism spectrum disorders and their classmates. *Young Children, 65,* 78–83.

Geist, K., Geist, E. A., & Kuznik, K. (2012). The patterns of music: Young children learning mathematics through beat, rhythm, and melody. *Young children, 67*(1), 74–79.

Gelman, R., Brenneman, K., MacDonald, G., & Roman, M. (2010). *Preschool pathways to science: Facilitating scientific ways of thinking, talking, doing and understanding.* Baltimore, MD: Paul H. Brookes.

Gerde, H. K., & Bingham, G. E. (2012, July). Examining material and interaction supports for children's writing in preschool classrooms. In H. K. Gerde (Chair), *Writing in early childhood: Development, variation, and contextual supports.* Symposium conducted at the meeting of Scientific Study of Reading, Montreal, Quebec, Canada.

Gibbons, P. (2003). Mediating language learning: Teacher interactions with ESL students in a content-based classroom. *TESOL Quarterly, 37,* 247–273.

Gillanders, C., & Castro, D. C. (2011). Storybook reading for young dual language learners. *Young Children, 66,* 91–95.

Gillespie, C. W., & Glider, K. R. (2010). Preschool teachers' use of music to scaffold children's learning and behavior. *Early Child Development and Care, 180,* 799–808.

Ginsburg, K. R. (2007). The importance of play in promoting healthy child development and maintaining strong parent-child bonds. *Pediatrics, 119,* 182–191.

Goldenberg, C. (2008). Teaching English language learners: What the research does and does not say. *American Educator, 32*(2), 8–11.

Goncu, A., & Gaskins, S. (2011). Comparing and extending Piaget's and Vygotsky's understanding of play: Symbolic play as individual, sociocultural, and educational interpretation. In A. D. Pellegrini (Ed.), *The Oxford handbook of the development of play* (pp. 341–360). New York, NY: Oxford University Press.

Gopnik, A. (2009). *The philosophical baby: What children's minds tell us about the meaning of life.* New York, NY: Farrar, Straus & Giroux.

Gordon, A. (2013). *Kids with autism benefit from outdoor classroom.* Retrieved from: http://www.thestar.com/life/parent/2013/07/05/kids_with_autism_benefit_from_outdoor_classroom.html

Gormley, W. T. (2005, December). Is it time for universal pre-K? *The Education Digest, 71*(4), 47–53.

Gregoire, M. A., & Lupinetti, J. (2005). Supporting diversity through the arts. *Kappa Delta Pi Record, 41,* 159–162.

Grisham-Brown, J., Pretti-Frontczak, K., Hawkins, S. R., & Winchell, B. N. (2009). Addressing early learning standards for all children within blended preschool programs. *Topics in Early Childhood Special Education, 29,* 131–142.

Gromko, J. E. (2005). The effect of music instruction on phonemic awareness in beginning readers. *Journal of Research in Music Education, 53,* 199–209.

Guralnick, M. J. (2001). A framework for change in early education inclusion. In M. J. Guralnick (Ed.), *Early childhood inclusion: Focus on change* (pp. 3–35). Baltimore, MD: Brookes.

Haight, W. L., & Miller, P. J. (1992). The development of everyday pretend play: A longitudinal study of mothers' participation. *Merrill-Palmer Quarterly, 38,* 331–349.

Haight, W. L., & Miller, P. J. (1993). *Pretending at home: Early development in the sociocultural context.* Albany: State University of New York Press.

Halfon, N., Olson, L., Inkelas, M., & Lange, L. (2002). Summary statistics from the National Survey of Early Childhood Health, 2000. National Center for Health Statistics. *Vital Health Statistics, 15,* 1–34.

Hamlin, M., & Wisneski, D. B. (2012). Supporting the scientific thinking and inquiry of toddlers and preschoolers through play. *Young Children, 62*(3), 82–88.

Hanline, M. F., Milton, S., & Phelps, P. (2009). The relationship between preschool block play and reading and math abilities in early elementary school: A longitudinal study of children with and without disabilities. *Early Child Development and Care, 180,* 1005–1007.

Harger, J. (2008). The Montessori model in Puebla, Mexico: How one nonprofit is helping children. *Montessori Life, 1,* 20–25.

Harry, B., Klingner, J., & Cramer, E. (2007). *Case studies of minority student placement in special education.* New York, NY: Teachers College Press.

Hart, B., & Risley, T. (1995). *Meaningful differences in everyday experiences of young American children.* Baltimore, MD: Paul H. Brookes.

Hatcher, B., & Perry, K. (2004) Visible thought in dramatic play. *Young Children, 59,* 79–82.

Head Start. (2010). *The Head Start child development and early learning framework: Promoting positive outcomes in early childhood programs serving children 3–5 years old.* Arlington, VA: Head Start Resource Center.

Head Start. (2011). *The Head Start child development and early learning framework: Promoting positive outcomes in early childhood programs serving children 3–5 years old.* Arlington, VA: Head Start Resource Center.

Heath, S. B. (1986). Taking a cross-cultural look at narratives. *Topics in Language Disorders, 7*(1), 84–94.

Hebert, H., Swank, P., Smith, K., & Landry, S. (2004). Maternal support for play and language across early childhood. *Early Education & Development, 15,* 93–113.

Hedges, H., Cullen, J., & Jordan, B. (2011). Early years curriculum: Funds of knowledge as a conceptual framework for children's interests. *Journal of Curriculum Studies, 43,* 185–205.

Helm, J. H., & Katz, L. (2011). *Young investigators: The project approach in the early years.* New York, NY: Teachers College Press.

Henderson, S. D., Many, J. E., Wellborn, H. P., & Ward, J. (2002). How scaffolding nurtures the development of young children's literacy repertoire: Insiders' and outsiders' collaborative understandings. *Reading Research and Instruction, 41,* 309–330.

Hewitt, K. (2001). Blocks as a tool for learning: Historical and contemporary perspectives. *Young Children, 56,* 61–67.

Highland, J., McNally, P., & Peart, M. (1999). *Improving student behavior through the use of multiple intelligences.* (ERIC Document Reproduction Service No. ED434774)

Hirsh-Pasek, K., & Golinkoff, M. (2011). The great balancing act: Optimizing core curricula through playful pedagogy. In E. Zigler, W. S. Gilliam, & W. S. Barnett (Eds.), *The pre-K debates: Current controversies and issues* (pp. 110–116). Baltimore, MD: Paul H. Brookes.

Hirsh-Pasek, K., Golinkoff, R. M., Berk, L. E., & Singer, D. E. (2009). *A mandate for playful learning in preschool.* New York, NY: Oxford University Press.

Hoffman, E. (1999). *Best best colors/Los mejores colores.* St. Paul, MN: Red Leaf.

Honig, A. S. (2007). Play: Ten power boosts for children's early learning. *Young Children, 51,* 72–78.

Howes, C. (1992). *The collaborative construction of pretend: Social pretend play functions.* Albany: State University of New York Press.

Howes, C., Burchinal, M., Pianta, R., Bryant, D., Early, D., Clifford, R., & Barbarin, O. (2008). Ready to learn? Children's pre-academic achievement in pre-kindergarten programs. *Early Childhood Research Quarterly, 23,* 27–50.

Howes, C., & Wishard, A. G. (2004). Revisiting shared meaning: Looking through the lens of culture and linking shared pretend play through proto-narrative development to emergent literacy. In E. F. Zigler, D. G. Singer, & S. Bishop-Josef (Eds.), *Children's play: The roots of reading* (pp. 143–158). Washington, DC: Zero to Three Press.

Huber, L. K. (1999). Woodworking With Young Children: You Can Do It! *Young Children, 54*(6), 32–34.

Huffman, D. (2002). Evaluating science inquiry: A mixed-method approach. In J. W. Altschuld & D. D. Kumar (Eds.), *Evaluation of science and technology education at the dawn of a new millennium* (pp. 219–242). Newell, MA: Kluwer Academic/Plenum.

Huffman, J. M., & Fortenberry, C. (2011). Helping preschoolers prepare for writing: Developing fine motor skills. *Young Children, 66,* 100–103.

Hutton, L. A. (2011). *The dreamery: Educational underpinnings.* Unpublished manuscript, Department of Liberal Studies, College of Education, California State University, Carson, CA.

Ilgaz, H., & Aksu-Koc, A. (2005). Episodic development in preschool children's play-prompted and direct-elicited narratives. *Cognitive Development, 20,* 526–544.

Inan, H. Z., Trundle, K. C., & Kantor, R. (2010). Understanding natural sciences education in a Reggio Emilia-inspired preschool. *Journal of Research in Science Education, 47,* 1186–1208.

International Reading Association (IRA), Common Core State Standards (CCSS) Committee. (2012). *Literacy implementation guidance for the ELA Common Core State Standards.* Retrieved from http://www.reading.org/Libraries/association-documents/ira_ccss_guidelines.pdf

Isenberg, J. P., & Jalongo, M. R. (2013). *Creative thinking and arts-based learning: Preschool through fourth grade* (6th ed.). Upper Saddle River, NJ: Pearson.

Isquith, P. K., Gioia, G., & Espy, K. A. (2004). Executive function in preschool children: Examination through everyday behavior. *Developmental Neuropsychology, 26,* 403–422.

Jackson, J. J. (2011). Effective child development strategies. In E. Zigler, W. S. Gilliam, & W. S. Barnett (Eds.), *The pre-K debates: Current controversies and issues* (pp. 2–8). Baltimore, MD: Paul H. Brookes.

Jalongo, M. R., & Isenberg, J. P. (2006). Creative expression and thought in kindergarten. In D. F. Gullo (Ed.), *K today: Teaching and learning in the kindergarten year.* (pp. 116–126). Washington, DC: National Association for the Education of Young Children.

Jensen, E. (2000). Moving with the brain in mind. *Educational Leadership, 58*(3), 34–37.

Jordan, N. C., Kaplan, D., Olah, L. N., & Locuniak, M. N. (2006). Number sense growth in kindergarten: A longitudinal investigation of children at risk for mathematical difficulties. *Child Development, 77,* 153–175.

Justice, L. M. (2004). Creating language-rich preschool classroom environments. *Teaching Exceptional Children, 2,* 36–44.

Justice, L. M., & Ezell, H. L. (2004). Print referencing: An emergent literacy enhancement strategy and its clinical applications. *Language, Speech, and Hearing Services in Schools, 35,* 185–193.

Kaderavek, J. N., & Justice, L. (2000). Children with LD as emergent readers: Bridging the gap to conventional reading. *Intervention in School and Clinic, 36*(2), 82–93.

Kaplan, S. N. (2002). Differentiated curriculum: Multiple means and fixed ends. *Social Studies Review, 41*(2), 14.

Kaplan, S. N. (2008). Curriculum consequences: If you learn this, then . . . *Gifted Child Today, 31*(1), 41–42.

Kasari, C., Freeman, S., & Paparella, T. (2006). Joint attention and symbolic play in young children with autism: A randomized controlled intervention study. *Journal of Child Psychology and Psychiatry, 47,* 611–620.

Katz, J. R. (2001). Playing at home: The talk of pretend play. In D. K. Dickinson & P. O. Tabors (Eds.), *Beginning literacy with language* (pp. 53–73). Baltimore, MD: Paul H. Brookes.

Katz, J. R. (2004). Building peer relationships in talk: Toddlers' peer conversations in childcare. *Discourse Studies, 6*(3), 329–346.

Keilty, B., & Galvin, K. M. (2006). Physical and social adaptations of families to promote learning in everyday experiences. *Early Education & Development, 26,* 219–233.

Kemple, K. M., Batey, J. J., & Hartle, L. C. (2008). Music play: Creating centers for musical play and exploration. In D. Koralek (Ed.), *Spotlight on young children and the creative arts* (pp. 24–31). Washington, DC: National Association for the Education of Young Children.

Kendall, J. S. (2003). Setting standards in early childhood education. *Educational Leadership, 60,* 64–68.

Keogh, B., & Naylor, S. (2009). Puppets count. *Mathematics Teaching, 213,* 32–34.

Kepner, H. (2010, February). A missed opportunity: Mathematics in early childhood. *NCTM Summing Up.* Retrieved from http://www.nctm.org/about/content.aspx?id=25054

Kermani, H., & Brenner, M. E. (2000). Maternal scaffolding in the child's zone of proximal development across tasks: Cross-cultural perspectives. *Journal of Research in Childhood Education International, 15,* 30–52.

Kerry Moran, K. J. (2006). Nurturing emergent readers through Readers Theater. *Early Childhood Education Journal, 33,* 317–323.

Kim, J., & Robinson, H. M. (2010). Four steps for becoming familiar with early music standards. *Young Children, 65*(2), 42–48.

King, K. A. (2012). Writing workshops in preschool: Acknowledging children as writers. *The Reading Teacher, 65,* 392–401.

Klein, L. G., & Knitzer, J. (2006). *Effective preschool curricula and teaching strategies* (Pathways to Early School Success, Issue Brief No. 2). New York, NY: Columbia University, National Center for Children in Poverty.

Koralek, D. (2008). *Spotlight on young children and the creative arts.* Washington, DC: National Association for the Education of Young Children.

Krafft, K. C., & Berk, L. E. (1990). Private speech in two preschools: Significance of open-ended activities and make-believe play for verbal self-regulation. *Early Childhood Research Quarterly, 13,* 637–658.

Krashen, S. D., & Terrell, T. D. (1983). *The natural approach: Language acquisition in the classroom.* London, UK: Prentice Hall Europe.

Lai, W. F., Lee, Y. J., & Lee, J. (2010). Visiting doctors' offices: A comparison of Korean and Taiwanese preschool children's narrative development. *Early Education and Development, 21,* 445–467.

Laminack, L. (2013). *Flirting with literacy: Sparking a life-long love affair with literature.* Keynote speech at Early Literacy Institute, International Reading Association, San Antonio, TX.

Lawrence, J. F., & Snow, C. E. (2011). Oral discourse and reading. In M. L. Kamil, P. D. Pearson, E. B. Moje, & P. P. Afflerbach (Eds.), *Handbook of reading research* (Vol. 4, pp. 320–338). New York, NY: Routledge.

Lembke, E., McMaster, K., & Stecker, P. (2010). The prevention science of reading research within a response-to-intervention model. *Psychology in the Schools, 48*(1), 22–35.

Leyva, D., Reese, E., Grolnick, W., & Price, C. (2008). Elaboration and autonomy support in low-income mothers' reminiscing: Links to children's autobiographical narratives. *Journal of Cognition and Development, 9,* 363–389.

Lifter, K., & Bloom, L. (1998). Intentionality and the role of play in the transition to language. In A. M. Wetherby, S. F. Warren, & J. Reichle (Eds.), *Transitions in prelinguistic communication: Preintentional to intentional and presymbolic to symbolic* (pp. 161–198). Baltimore, MD: Paul H. Brookes.

Lifter, K., Mason, E. J., & Barton, E. E. (2011). Children's play: Where we have been and where we could go. *Journal of Early Intervention, 33,* 281–297.

Lillard, A. S., & Witherington, D. C. (2004). Mothers' behavior modifications during pretense snacks and their possible signal and value for toddlers. *Developmental Psychology, 40,* 95–113.

Lo, D. E., & Cantrell, D. E. (2002). Global perspectives for young readers: Easy readers and picture book Read-Alouds from around the world. *Childhood Education, 79,* 21–25.

Lonigan, C. J. (2006). Conceptualizing phonological processing skills in prereaders. In D. K. Dickinson

& S. B. Neuman (Eds.), *Handbook of early literacy research*. New York, NY: Guilford Press.

Lorenzo-Lasa, R., Ideishi, R. I., & Ideishi, S. K. (2007). Facilitating preschool learning and movement through dance. *Early Childhood Educational Journal, 35*(1), 25–31.

Lynch, E. W., & Hanson, M. J. (2004). *Developing cross-cultural competence: A framework for working with children and their families* (3rd ed.). Baltimore, MD: Paul H. Brookes.

Machado, J. M. (2007). *Early childhood experiences in language arts*. Belmont, CA: Wadsworth.

Marigliano, M. L., & Russo, M. J. (2011). Moving bodies, building minds: Fostering preschoolers' critical thinking and problem solving through movement. *Young Children, 66*(5), 44–49.

Marrow, M. L. (2005). *Literacy development in the early years*. New York, NY: Pearson.

Matthews, J. (1994). Deep structures in children's art: Development and culture. *Visual Arts Research, 20*(2), 29–50.

Maxim, G. W. (2006). *Dynamic social studies for constructivist classrooms: Inspiring tomorrow's social scientists*. Upper Saddle River, NJ: Merrill.

McAfee, O., & Leong, D. J. (2007). *Assessing and guiding young children's development and learning* (4th ed.). New York, NY: Allyn and Bacon.

McCabe, L. A., Cunnington, M., & Brooks-Gunn, J. (2004). The development of self-regulation in young children. In R. F. Baumeister & K. D. Vohs (Eds.), *Handbook of self-regulation: Research, theory, and applications* (pp. 340–356). New York, NY: Guilford Press.

McCune, L. (1985). Play-language relationships and symbolic development. In C. C. Brown & A. W. Gottfried (Eds.), *Play interactions* (pp. 28–45). Skillman, NJ: Johnson & Johnson Baby Products.

McCune-Nicolich, L. (1981). Toward symbolic functioning: Structures of early pretend games and potential parallels with language. *Child Development, 52,* 785–797.

McGee, L. M., & Richgels, D. J. (2012). *Literacy beginnings: Supporting young readers and writers*. Boston: Pearson Education.

McKeown, M. G., & Beck, I. L. (2006). Encouraging young children's language interactions with stories. In D. K. Dickinson & S. B. Neuman (Eds.), *Handbook of early literacy research: Volume 2* (pp. 181–194). New York, NY: Guilford Press.

Meece, D., & Soderman, A. K. (2010). Positive verbal environments: Setting the stage for young children's social development. *Young Children, 65*(5), 81–86.

Mezzacappa, E. (2003). Alerting, orienting, and executive attention: Developmental and socio-demographic properties in an epidemiological sample of young, urban children. *Child Development, 75,* 1375–1386.

Miller, E., & Almon, J. (2009). *Crisis in the kindergarten: Why children need to play in school*. College Park, MD: Alliance for Children.

Milteer, R. M., Ginsburg, K. R., Council on Communications and Media, Committee on Psychosocial Aspects of Child and Family Health, & Mulligan, D. A. (2012). The importance of play in promoting healthy child development and maintaining strong parent-child bond: Focus on children in poverty. *Pediatrics, 129,* 204–213.

Mindes, G. (2006). Social studies in kindergarten. In D. F. Gullo (Ed.), *K today: Teaching and learning in the kindergarten years* (pp. 107–115). Washington, DC: National Association for the Education of Young Children.

Mitchell, L. C. (2008). Making the most of creativity in activities for young children with disabilities. In D. Koralek (Ed.), *Spotlight on young children and the creative arts* (pp. 40–43). Washington, DC: National Association for the Education of Young Children.

Molfese, V. J., Modglin, A. A., Beswick, J. L., Neamon, J. D., Berg, D. A., Berg, C. J., & Molnar, A. (2006). Letter knowledge, phonological processing, and print language: Skill development in nonreading preschool children. *Journal of Learning Disabilities, 39*(4), 296–305.

Moll, L. C., Amanti, C., Neff, D., & Gonzalez, N. (1992). Funds of knowledge for teaching: Using a qualitative approach to connect homes and classrooms. *Theory Into Practice, 31*(2), 132–141.

Morin, L. B. (2001). Cultivating music play: The need for change in teaching practice. *General Music Today, 14*(2), 24–29.

Morrow, L. M. (2005). *Literacy development in the early years*. New York, NY: Pearson.

Morrow, L. M., & Schickedanz, J. A. (2006). The relationship between sociodramatic play and literacy development. In D. K. Dickinson & S. B. Neuman (Eds.), *Handbook of early literacy research* (pp. 269–280). New York, NY: Guilford Press.

National Assessment of Educational Progress. (2009). *The nation's report card: Mathematics*. Retrieved from http://nationsreportcard.gov/math_2011/summary.asp?tab_id=tab3&subtab_id=Tab_1#chart

National Association for the Education of Young Children (NAEYC). (2001). *Standards for early childhood professional preparation initial licensure programs.* Retrieved from http://www .naeyc.org

National Association for the Education of Young Children (NAEYC). (2005). *Code of ethical conduct and statement of commitment* (Position statement). Available from http://www.naeyc .org/store/node/450

National Association for the Education of Young Children (NAEYC). (2009a). *Developmentally appropriate practice in early childhood programs serving children from birth through age 8.* Retrieved from: www.naeyc.org.

National Association for the Education of Young Children (NAEYC) . (2009b). *Where we stand on early learning standards.* Retrieved from http://www.naeyc.org/positionstatements/ learning_standards

National Association for the Education of Young Children (NAEYC), Division of Early Childhood (DEC), & National Head Start Association (NHSA). (2012). *Frameworks for Response to Intervention in early childhood education: Description and implications.* Retrieved from http://www.naeyc.org

National Association for the Education of Young Children (NAEYC) & National Association of Early Childhood Specialists in State Departments of Education (NAECS/SDE). (2002). *Early learning standards: Creating the conditions for success* (Joint position statement). Retrieved from http://www.naeyc.org/positionstatements/ learning_standards

National Association for the Education of Young Children (NAEYC) & National Association of Early Childhood Specialists in State Departments of Education (NAECS/SDE). (2003). *Early childhood curriculum, assessment, and evaluation: Building an effective, accountable system in programs for children birth through age 8* (Joint position statement). Retrieved from http://www.naeyc.org/position statements/cape

National Association for the Education of Young Children (NAEYC) & National Association of Early Childhood Specialists in State Departments of Education (NAECS/SDE). (2009). *Early childhood curriculum, assessment, and program evaluation.* Retrieved from http:// www.naeyc.org

National Association for the Education of Young Children (NAEYC) & National Association for Early Childhood Specialists in State Departments of Education (NAECS/SDE). (2010). *Joint statement on the Common Core Standards initiative related to Grades Kindergarten through Third Grade.* Retrieved from http://www.naeyc.org/ files/naeyc/file/policy/NAEYC-NAECS-SDE-Core-Standards-Statement.pdf

National Association for the Education of Young Children (NAEYC) & the Fred Rogers Center for Early Learning and Children's Media at Saint Vincent College. (2012, January). *Technology and interactive media as tools in early childhood programs serving children from birth through age 8.* Retrieved from: http://www .naeyc.org/files/naeyc/PS_technology_WEB.pdf

National Association for the Education of Young Children (NAEYC) & the National Council of Teachers of Mathematics (NCTM). (2010), *Early childhood mathematics: Promoting good beginnings.* Retrieved from http://www.naeyc .org/files/naeyc/file/positions/psmath.pdf

National Autism Center. (2009). *Evidence-based practices in the schools.* Randolph, MA: National Autism Center.

National Center on Cultural and Linguistic Responsiveness. (n.d.). *How to use bilingual books.* U.S. Department of Health and Human Services. Retrieved from http://eclkc.ohs.acf .hhs.gov/hslc/tta-system/cultural-linguistic/docs/ ncclr-qguide-how-to-use-bilingual-books.pdf

National Council for the Social Studies (NCSS). (2012). *The national curriculum standards for social studies.* Silver Spring, MD: National Council for the Social Studies.

National Institute for Early Education Research (NIEER). (2008). *State-funded preschool enrollment passes one million mark, yet most 3- and 4-year olds are denied access to public preschool programs.* Retrieved from http://nieer .org/news-events/news-releases/state-funded-preschool-enrollment-passes-one-million-mark-yet-most-3-and-4

National Institute for Early Education Research (NIEER). (2010). *The state of preschool 2010.* Retrieved from http://nieer.org/publications/ state-preschool-2010

National Institute for Early Education Research (NIEER). (2012). *The state of preschool 2012.* Retrieved from http://nieer.org/yearbook

National Institute of Child Health and Human Development (NICHD), Early Child Care Research Network. (2000). The relation of child care to cognitive and language development. *Child Development, 71,* 960–980.

National Research Council (NRC). (2009). *Mathematics Learning in Early Childhood: Paths Toward Excellence and Equality.* Washington, DC: The National Academies Press.

National Research Council (NRC). (2011). *Successful K–12 education: Identifying effective approaches in science, technology, engineering, and mathematics.* Washington, DC: National Academies Press.

National Research Council (NRC). (2012). *A framework for K–12 science education: Practices, crosscutting themes, and core ideas.* Washington, DC: National Academies Press.

National Research Council (NRC). (2013). *Next Generation Science Standards: Appendix D—All standards, all students: Making Next Generation Science Standards accessible to all students.* Washington, DC: National Academies Press.

Nation's Report Card. (2008). *National assessment of educational progress at Grade 8: Arts 2008.* Retrieved from http://nces.ed.gov/nationsreportcard/twd/analysis/infer.asp

Neelly, L. P. (2001). Developmentally appropriate music practice: Children learn what they live. *Young Children, 56*(3), 32–37.

Nelson, E. (2012). *Cultivating outdoor classrooms: Designing and implementing child-centered learning environments.* St. Paul, MN: Redleaf Press.

Nelson, H. D., Nygren, P., Walker, M., & Panoscha, R. (2006). Screening for speech and language delays in preschool children: Systematic evidence review for the U.S. Preventive Services Task Force. *Pediatrics, 117*(2), 298–317.

Neuman, S. B. (1999). Books make a difference: A study of access to literacy. *Reading Research Quarterly, 34,* 286–311.

Neuman, S. B. (2004). The effect of print-rich classroom environments on early literacy growth. *The Reading Teacher, 58,* 89–91.

Neuman, S. B., & Dickinson, D. K. (2001). *Handbook of early literacy research: Volume 1.* New York, NY: Guilford Press.

Neuman, S. B., & Dickinson, D. K. (2011). *Handbook of early literacy research: Volume 3.* New York, NY: Guilford Press.

Neuman, S. B., & Roskos, K. (1997). Literacy knowledge in practice: Contexts of participation for young writers and readers. *Reading Research Quarterly, 32*(1), 10–32.

Newburger, A., & Vaughan, E. (2006). *Teaching numeracy, language, and literacy with blocks.* St. Paul, MN: Redleaf Press.

Ochs, E., & Schieffelin, B. B. (1984). Language acquisition and socialization: Three developmental stories and their implications. In R. Schweder & R. A. LeVine (Eds.), *Culture theory: Essays on mind, self, and emotion* (pp. XX). New York, NY: Cambridge University Press.

Odom, S. L., Buysse, V., & Soukakou, E. (2011). Inclusion for young children with disabilities: A quarter century of research perspectives. *Journal of Early Intervention, 33*(4), 344–356.

Odom, S. L., & Diamond, K. E. (1998). Inclusion of young children with special needs in early childhood education: The research base. *Early Childhood Research Quarterly, 13,* 3–25.

Odom, S. L., Li, S., Sandall, S., Zercher, C., Marquart, J. M., & Brown, W. H. (2006). Social acceptance and rejection of preschool children with disabilities: A mixed-method analysis. *Journal of Educational Psychology, 98,* 807–823.

Office of Planning, Research, and Evaluation (OPRE). (2012). *Head Start research: Third grade follow-up to the Head Start Impact Study.* Retrieved from http://www.acf.hhs.gov/programs/opre/resource/third-grade-follow-up-to-the-head-start-impact-study-final-report

Ogu, U., & Schmidt, S. R. (2013). Kindergarteners investigate rocks and sand: Addressing multiple learning styles through an inquiry-based approach. In A. Shillady (Ed.), *Spotlight on young children: Exploring science* (pp. 61–67). Washington, DC: National Association for the Education of Young Children.

Paley, V. G. (1990). *The boy who wanted to be a helicopter: The use of storytelling in the classroom.* Cambridge, MA: Harvard University Press.

Paquette, D., Carbonneau, R., Dubeau, D., & Tremblay, R. E. (2003). Prevalence of father-child rough-and-tumble play and physical aggression in preschool children. *European Journal of Psychology of Education, 18,* 171–189.

Paquette, K. R., & Rieg, S. A. (2008). Using music to support the literacy of young English language learners. *Early Childhood Education Journal, 36,* 227–232.

Park, B., Chae, J. L., & Boyd, B. F. (2008). Young children's block play and mathematical learning. *Journal of Research in Childhood Education, 23,* 157–162.

Parlakian, R., & Lerner, C. (2010). Beyond twinkle twinkle: Using music with infants and toddlers. *Young Children, 65*(2), 14–19.

Patrick, H., Mantzicoppulos, P., & Samarapungavan, A. (2013). Integrating science inquiry with reading and writing in kindergarten. In A. Shillady (Ed.), *Spotlight on young children:*

Exploring science (pp. 48–54). Washington, DC: National Association for the Education of Young Children.

Paul, R., & Elder, L. (2009). *Critical thinking: Concepts and tools* (6th ed.). Tomales, CA: Foundation for Critical Thinking.

Pavri, S. (2012). Response to intervention in the social-emotional-behavioral domain: Perspectives from urban schools. *Teaching Exceptional Children Plus, 6.* Retrieved from http://escholarshiop .bc.edu/education/tecplus

Pellegrini, A. D. (1985). The narrative organization of children's fantasy play. *Educational Psychology, 5*(1), 291–304.

Pellegrini, A. D. (2011). *The Oxford handbook of the development of play.* New York, NY: Oxford University Press.

Pellegrini, A. D., & Galda, L. (1993). Ten years later: A reexamination of symbolic play and literacy research. *Reading Quarterly, 28,* 162–175.

Peña, E. D., & Halle, T. G. (2011). Assessing preschool dual language learners: Traveling a multiforked road. *Child Development Perspectives, 5,* 28–32.

Perry, J. P. (2001). *Outdoor play: Teaching strategies with young children.* New York, NY: Teachers College Press.

Phelps, P., & Hanline, M. F. (1999). Let's play blocks! Creating effective learning experiences for young children. *Teaching Exceptional Children, 32,* 62–67.

Piaget, J. (1959). *The language and thought of the child.* London, UK: Routledge & Kegan Paul.

Piaget, J. (1962). *Play, dreams, and imitation in childhood.* New York, NY: W. W. Norton.

Pica, R. (2009). Learning by leaps and bounds: Make a little music. *Young Children, 64*(6), 74–75.

Pierangelo, R., & Guiliani, G. A. (2012). *Assessment in special education: A practical approach* (4th ed.). Boston, MA: Pearson.

Pizzolongo, P. J., & Hunter, A. (2011). I am safe and secure: Promoting resilience in young children. *Young Children, 66,* 67–69.

Planty, M., Husser, W., Snyder, T., Provasnik, S., Kena, G., Dinkes, R., . . . Kemp, J. (2008). *The conditions of education 2008* (NCES 2008-031). Washington, DC: National Center for Education Statistics, Institute of Education Sciences, U.S. Department of Education.

Powell, D., Fixsen, D., Dunlap, G., Smith, B., & Fox, L. (2007). A synthesis of knowledge relevant to pathways of service delivery for young children with or at risk of challenging behavior. *Journal of Early Intervention, 29,* 81–106.

Price, J. R., Roberts, J. E., & Jackson, S. C. (2006). Structural development of the fictional narratives of African American preschoolers. *Language, Speech, and Hearing Services in the Schools, 37*(3), 178–190.

Pugach, M. C., & Johnson, L. J. (1995). *Collaborative practitioners collaborative schools.* Denver, CO: Love Publishing.

Pugach, M. C., Johnson, L. J., Drame, E. R., & Williamson, P. (2012). *Collaborative practitioners collaborative schools* (3rd ed.). Denver, CO: Love Publishing.

Purcell, T., & Rosemary, C. A. (2007). Differentiated instruction in the preschool classroom: Bridging emergent literacy instruction and developmentally appropriate practice. In L. Justice & C. Vukelich (Eds.), *Achieving excellence in preschool literacy instruction* (pp. 221–241). New York, NY: Guilford Press.

Ramani, G. B., & Siegler, R. (2011). Reducing the gap in numerical knowledge between low- and middle-income preschoolers. *Journal of Applied Developmental Psychology, 32,* 146–159.

Raver, C. C., Farner, P. W., & Smith-Donald, R. (2007). The roles of emotion regulation and emotion knowledge for children's academic readiness: Are the links causal? In R. C. Planta, M. J. Cox, & K. L. Snow (Eds.), *School readiness and the transition to kindergarten in the era of accountability* (pp. 121–148). Baltimore, MD: Paul H. Brookes.

Reese, E., Leyva, D., Sparks, A., & Grolnick, W. (2010). Maternal elaborative reminiscing increases low-income children's narrative skills relative to dialogic reading. *Early Education and Development, 21*(3), 318–342.

Resnick, L. B., & Snow, C. E. (2009). *Speaking and listening for preschool through third grade.* Newark, DE: International Reading Association.

Rettig, M. (2005). Using the multiple intelligences to enhance instruction for young children and young children with disabilities. *Early Childhood Education Journal, 32,* 255–259.

Reynolds, A. J., & Temple, J. A. (2005). Priorities for a new century of early childhood programs. *Infants & Young Children, 18*(2), 104–118.

Robinson, W. Y. (2006). Culture, race, diversity: How Montessori spells success in public schools. *Montessori Life, 4,* 9.

Roehler, L. R., & Cantlon, D. J. (1997). Scaffolding: A powerful tool in social constructivist classrooms. In K. Hogan & M. Pressley (Eds.), *Scaffolding student learning: Instructional approaches and issues* (pp. 6–42). Cambridge, MA: Brookline.

Roopnarine, J. (2011). Cultural variation in beliefs about play, parent-child play, and children's play: Meaning for childhood development. In A. D. Pellegrini (Ed.)., *The Oxford handbook of the development of play*. New York: Oxford University Press.

Roskos, K. A., & Christie, J. F. (2000). *Play and literacy in early childhood: Research from multiple perspectives*. Mahwah, NJ: Erlbaum.

Roskos, K., & Neuman, S. B. (2003). Environment and its influences for early literacy teaching and learning. In S. B. Neuman & D. K. Dickinson (Eds.), *Handbook of early literacy research: Volume 1*. New York, NY: Guilford Press.

Rothman, H. (2012, July/August). Nine way the Common Core will change classroom practice. *Harvard Education Letter, 28*(4). Available online at http://hepg.org/hel/article/543

Ruddell, R. B., & Ruddell, M. R. (1995). *Teaching children to read and write: Becoming an influential teacher*. Needham Heights, MA: Allyn and Bacon.

Rule, A. C., & Zhbanova, K. S. (2012). Changing perceptions of unpopular animals through fact, poetry, crafts, and puppet plays. *Early Childhood Education Journal, 40*, 223–230.

Sacha, T. J., & Russ, S. W. (2006). Effects of pretend imagery on learning dance in preschool children. *Early Childhood Education Journal, 33*, 341–345.

Sachs, J. (1980). The role of adult-child play in language development. In K. H. Rubin (Ed.), *Children's play*. San Francisco, CA: Jossey-Bass.

Salmon, M. D., & Sainato, D. M. (2005). Beyond Pinocchio: Puppets as teaching tools in inclusive early childhood classrooms. *Young Exceptional Children, 8*(3), 12–19.

Salvia, J., Ysseldyke, J., & Bolt, S. (2007). *Assessment in special and inclusive education* (11th ed.). Boston, MA: Houghton Mifflin.

Sameroff, A. J. (2010). A unified theory of development: A dialectic integration of nature and nurture. *Child Development, 81*, 6–22.

Sameroff, A. J., & Chandler, M. (1975). Reproductive risk and the continuum of caretaking causality. In F. D. Horowitz (Ed.), *Review of Child Development Research (Vol. 4)*. Chicago: University of Chicago Press.

Sameroff, A. J., & Fiese, B. H. (2000). Transactional regulation: The developmental ecology of early intervention. In J. P. Shonkoff & S. J. Meisels (Eds.), *Early intervention: A handbook of theory, practice, and analysis* (2nd ed., pp. 135–159). Cambridge, UK: Cambridge University Press.

Sanders, K., & Downer, J. (2012). Predicting acceptance of diversity in pre-kindergarten class rooms. *Early Childhood Research Quarterly, 27*, 503–511.

Sarama, J. A., Lange, A., Clements, D. H., & Wolfe, C. B. (2012). The impacts of an early mathematics curriculum on oral language and literacy. *Early Childhood Research Quarterly, 27*, 489–502.

Saul, J. D., & Saul, B. (2002). Multicultural activities throughout the year. *Multicultural Education, 8*, 38–40.

Scales, B., Perry, J., & Tracy, R. (2012). Creating a classroom of inquiry at the University of California at Berkeley: The Harold E. Jones Child Study Center. *Early Education and Development, 23*, 165–180.

Schellenberg, E. G. (2006). Long-term positive associations between music lessons and IQ. *Journal of Educational Psychology, 98*, 457–468.

Schickedanz, J. A. (1999). *Much more than the A B Cs: The early stages of reading and writing*. Washington, DC: The National Association for the Education of Young Children.

Schwartz, E. (2008). *Music, therapy, and early childhood: A developmental approach*. Gilsum, NH: Barcelona Publishers.

Schwartz, S. L., & Copeland, S. M. (2010). *Connecting emergent curriculum and standards in the early childhood classroom*. New York, NY: Teachers College Press.

Seefeldt, C. (2004). *Social studies for the preschool/primary child*. New York, NY: Pearson.

Seefeldt, C., & Galper, A. (2006). *Active experiences for active children: Social studies*. New York, NY: Pearson.

Segal, M. (2004). The roots and fruits of pretending. In E. F. Zigler, D. G. Singer, & S. J. Bishop-Josef (Eds.), *Children's play: The roots of reading* (pp. 33–48). Washington, DC: Zero to Three Press.

Seligman, M., & Darling, R. B. (2007). *Ordinary families, special children: A systems approach to childhood disability* (3rd ed.). New York, NY: Guilford Press.

Sherratt, D., & Donald, G. (2004). Connectedness: Developing a shared construction of affect and cognition in children with autism. *British Journal of Special Education, 31*, 10–15.

Shim, S., Herwig, J. E., & Shelley, M. (2001). Preschoolers' play behaviors with peers in classroom and playground settings. *Journal of Research in Childhood Education, 15*(2), 149–158.

Shonkoff, J. P., & Phillips. D. A. (Eds.). (2001). *From neurons to neighborhoods: The science of early childhood development.* Washington, DC: National Academy Press.

Siegler, R., & Ramani, G. B. (2008). Playing linear numerical board games promotes low-income children's numerical development. *Developmental Science, 11,* 655–661.

Singer, D. G., Golinkoff, R. M., & Hirsh-Pasek, K. (2006). *Play = learning: How play motivates and enhances children's cognitive and social-emotional growth.* New York, NY: Oxford University Press.

Skibbe, L., Behnke, M., & Justice, L. M. (2004). Parental scaffolding of children's phonological awareness: Interactions between mothers and their preschoolers with language difficulties. *Communication Disorders Quarterly, 25,* 189–209.

Snell, M. E., Berlin, R. A., Voorhees, M. D., Stanton-Chapman, T. L., & Hadden, S. (2012). A survey of preschool staff concerning problem behavior and its prevention in Head Start classrooms. *Journal of Positive Behavior Interventions, 14,* 98–107.

Snow, C. E., Burns, M. S., & Griffin, P. (Eds.). (1998). *Preventing reading difficulties in young children.* Washington, DC: National Academy Press.

Soderman, A. K., Gregory, K. M., & McCarty, L. T. (2005). *Scaffolding emergent literacy: A child-centered approach for preschool through grade 5.* New York, NY: Pearson Education.

Sorace, A., & Ladd, B. (2005). *Raising bilingual children.* Washington, DC: Linguistic Society of America. Retrieved from http://www.linguisticsociety.org/resource/faq-raising-bilingual-children

Stanton-Chapman, T. L., Chapman, D. A., Kaiser, A. P., & Hancock, T. B. (2004). Cumulative risk and low-income children's language development. *Topics in Early Childhood Special Education, 24*(4), 227–237.

Stoll, J., Hamilton, A. A., Oxley, E., Eastman, A. M., & Brent, R. (2012). Young thinkers in motion: Problem solving and physics in preschool. *Young Children, 67*(2), 20–26.

Stott, F. (2003). Making standards meaningful. *Early Childhood Today, 18,* 19–22.

Sun, P.-Y. (2003). *Using drama and theater to promote literacy development: Some basic classroom applications.* Retrieved from ERIC database. (ED477613). Available at http://eric.ed.gov/?id=ED477613

Swann, A. C. (2009). An intriguing link between drawing and play with toys. *Childhood Education, 85,* 230–236.

Taba, H. (1962). *Curriculum development: Theory and practice.* New York, NY: Harcourt, Brace & World.

Tharp, R. G., & Gallimore, R. (1990). *Rousing minds to life.* New York: Cambridge University Press.

Tough, G. (2008). *Whatever it takes: Geoffrey Canada's quest to change Harlem and America.* New York, NY: Houghton Mifflin.

Trommsdorff, G., Friedlmeier, W., & Mayer, B. (2007). Sympathy, distress, and prosocial behavior of preschool children from four cultures. *International Journal of Behavioral Development, 31,* 284–293.

Turnbull, A., & Turnbull, H. R. (2001). *Families, professionals, and exceptionality: Collaboration for empowerment* (4th ed.). Upper Saddle River, NJ: Merrill/Prentice Hall.

Turnbull, A. P., Turnbull, H. R., Erwin, E., & Soodak, L. (2006). *Families, professionals, and exceptionality: Positive outcomes through partnerships and trust* (5th ed.). Upper Saddle River, NJ: Merrill/Prentice Hall.

Turnbull, A. P., Turnbull, H. R., Shank, M., & Leal, D. (1995). *Exceptional lives: Special education in today's schools.* Englewood Cliffs, NJ: Merrill/Prentice Hall.

United States Census Bureau. (n.d.). *Current population survey data collection.* Retrieved from http://www.census.gov/hhes/socdemo/children/data/cps.html

University of Texas Health Science Center at Houston. (2002). *National Head Start S.T.E.P. teacher's manual.* Washington, DC: United States Department of Health and Human Services, Office of Human Development Services, Administration for Children, Youth and Families, Head Start Bureau.

U.S. Department of Education. (2010). *The nation's report card: National assessment of educational progress in reading 2009.* Washington, DC: NCES 2010–458. Retrieved from http://nces.ed.gov/nationsreportcard/pdf/main2009/2010458.pdf

Van de Walle, J. A., Lovin, L. A. H., Karp, K. H., & Williams, J. M. B. (2013). *Teaching student-centered mathematics: Developmentally appropriate instruction for Grades pre-K–2* (Vol. 1). New York, NY: Pearson.

Vaughn, S., Linan-Thompson, S., Pollard-Durodola, S. D., Mathes, P. G., & Hagan, E. C. (2006). Effective interventions for English

Language Learners (Spanish-English) at risk for reading difficulties. In D. K. Dickinson & S. B. Neuman (Eds.), *Handbook of early literacy research* (pp. 185–197). New York, NY: Guilford Press.

Vukelich, C., & Christie, J. (2009). *Building a foundation for preschool literacy*. Newark, DE: International Reading Association.

Vygotsky, L. S. (1978). *Mind in society: The development of higher mental processes* (M. Cole, V. John-Steiner, S. Scribner, & E. Souberman, Eds. & Trans.). Cambridge, MA: Harvard University Press. (Original work published 1930–1935)

Wanerman, T. (2010). Using story drama with young preschoolers. *Young Children, 65*(2), 20–28.

Wasik, B. A., Bond, M. A., & Hindman, A. (2006). The effects of language and literacy intervention on Head Start children and teachers. *Journal of Educational Psychology, 98*, 63–74.

Wasik, B. A., & Hindman, A. H. (2013/2014). Realizing the promise of open-ended questions. *The Reading Teacher, 67*, 302–311.

West, S., & Cox, A. (2004). *Literacy play*. Lewisville, NC: Gryphon House.

WestEd. (2011). *California preschool curriculum framework* [Draft]. Retrieved from http://www.wested.org/online_pubs/ccfs/preschool-curriculum-framework.pdf

White, S. H. (1996). The child's entry into the "Age of Reason." In A. J. Sameroff & M. M. Haith (Eds.), *The five to seven year shift: The age of reason and responsibility* (pp. 17–30). Chicago, IL: University of Chicago Press.

Whitehurst, G. J., & Lonigan, C. J. (1998). Child development and emergent literacy. *Child Development, 68*, 848–872.

Williams, E. (2003). A comparative review of early forms of object-directed play and parent-infant play in typical infants and young children with autism. *Autism, 7*, 361–377.

Wilson, D. M. (2009). Developmentally appropriate practice in the age of testing. *Harvard Education Letter, 25*, 158–159.

Wood, D., Bruner, J. S., & Ross, G. (1976). The role of tutoring in problem solving. *Journal of Psychology and Psychiatry, 17*, 89–100.

Woodward, J. (2003). *Making things happen: A theory of causal exploration*. New York, NY: Oxford University Press.

Xu, F., & Garcia, V. (2008). Intuitive statistics by 8-month-old infants. *Proceedings of the National Academy of Science, 105*, 5012–5015.

Yamamoto, Y., & Li, J. (2012). What makes a high-quality preschool? Similarities and differences between Chinese immigrant and European American parents' views. *Early Childhood Research Quarterly, 27*, 306–315.

Yopp, H. K., & Yopp, R. H. (2009). Phonological awareness is child's play. *Young Children, 64*(1), 1–9.

Zigler, E., Gilliam, W. S., & Barnett, W. S. (2011). *The pre-k debates: Current controversies and issues*. Baltimore, MD: Paul Brookes Publishing.

Glossary

ability groups Groups that are formed when children are placed in groups with peers who have similar abilities.

accommodate The mental activity of modifying existing knowledge to incorporate new information.

achievement gap The gap on educational measures that exists among various economic groups, racial and ethnic groups, special education populations, and English language learner groups.

activity materials Items that will be used when participating in an activity.

activity space The amount of physical space needed for children to participate comfortably in a play activity.

activity time The amount of time it will take to have children complete an activity.

adult suggestions Verbal or nonverbal prompts designed to assist children in learning at a higher level.

adult-directed learning Activities in which adults lead children through specific steps of a learning activity.

alphabet recognition The ability to recognize the letters of the alphabet.

alternating teaching When different teachers teach different-sized groups with the larger group usually moving at a faster rate of learning than the smaller group.

anti-bias Attitudes, beliefs, and feelings that address the identity of people and materials through the use of fair treatments.

Apgar score An assessment administered to infants immediately following birth to estimate general health status of the infant by examining appearance, pulse, grimace, activity, and respiration.

art centers Places where children can safely test out their ability to create objects and pictures that express their own thoughts and feelings.

assessment Examination of learning and developmental abilities of individuals. For the purposes of this text, assessment is a planned process for systematically gathering, synthesizing, and interpreting information.

assimilation When children incorporate new information into their already accumulated body of knowledge.

authentic assessment Collecting of data on young children's abilities from realistic or natural learning settings to determine actual learning during instructional activities.

big ideas General themes that comprise the superstructure for planning and guiding project-based child-centered learning.

bullying Using force or intimidation with others that results in suffering and loss of self-confidence.

center teaching A teaching arrangement when both teachers are actively involved in instruction. Each assumes responsibility for planning and teaching related portions of a lesson in a particular center. This approach requires planning and coordination and requires transition time while children move from one center to another.

checklists Commercial or teacher-made lists that offer an efficient method for observing and gathering authentic data on language, cognitive, social, and emotional abilities.

child-centered activities Interactions focusing on meaningful learning activities that the child is self-motivated to accomplish.

collaboration Interaction when people who are committed to common goals share planning, teaching, and evaluation of those goals because their relationship is based on respect and shared responsibility.

Common Core State Standards (CCSS) K–12 learning standards for integrated language arts, math, and literacy across the curriculum that provide a consistent and clear understanding of what students are expected to learn.

common underlying proficiency (CUP) When people learn something, they have processed the concept and meaning; they have registered the experience and the knowledge.

concrete operational stage Stage of development during which children expand their use of abstract thought with concrete thinking processes.

conflict resolution A behavior modification process implemented when someone continually refuses to follow a group's accepted rules.

co-teaching, co-partnering Method in which more than one teacher determines roles each teacher assumes, how children will be grouped, what co-teaching models will be incorporated in the classroom, and how educational decisions will be made.

Council for Exceptional Children (CEC) A national organization that advocates for the rights for persons with disabilities and has a subgroup called the Division of Early Childhood (DEC) that promotes the rights of young children with disabilities between birth and 6 years of age and their families.

culturally responsive Reflecting on one's own personal cultural background and values with the intent of learning about other cultures and how those cultures differ from one's own culture.

decontextualized narratives Stories that are removed from the everyday and tangible experiences of an immediate context.

developmentally appropriate practices (DAP) Activities that are appropriate to age and developmental abilities, are attuned to a person's uniqueness, and are responsive to the social and cultural contexts in which the person lives.

differentiated instruction A philosophy of teaching that recognizes children's individual differences in three specific, related areas of learning readiness skills, interests, and learning styles.

dissecting words Activity where children take apart words, phrases, and sentences, and then recreate them.

early intervention Programs for families of very young children who need to develop the skills necessary for successful school participation.

early learning standards Desired outcomes and content for young children.

Early Start Program Federal program that promotes the school readiness of children ages birth to 2 years old from low-income families by enhancing their cognitive, social, and emotional development.

egocentric Self-centered thinking that uses both actions and language that focus on the self.

emergent literacy Development by very young children of skills, knowledge, and attitude toward reading and writing that are acquired through observing everyday literacy activities.

equilibrium The balancing of information that is already known with new information that is being learned.

expressive language Language used to share thoughts and comments through the use of voice, gestures, signs, or symbols (including written language).

fine motor skills Skills that require the use of small muscles, such as finger, toes, wrists, tongue, and lips.

flexible groupings Various group sizes and configurations (i.e., large, small, interest based, ability based, and centers groups) that engage children in learning different skills.

formal assessment Activities that have a single set of expectations and a prescribed method for scoring and interpreting the results.

formal operational stage A developmental stage in which language becomes the core of all abstract thought.

free play Spontaneous activities by children that rarely involve adult interactions.

friendships Voluntary relationships with others that typically involve the sharing of companionship, intimacy, and affection.

full-day program Programs that children attend for an entire day and that assume some responsibility for providing both education and childcare activities.

functional behavior assessment Observations and analysis of a child's behavior with the goal of modifying conditions that are causing the child to behave inappropriately.

funds of knowledge Understanding how and what children have learned through their active participation in household and community activities and applying that information to classroom learning activities.

gross motor skills Skills that require the movement of large muscles such as arms, legs, feet, and torso, for rolling, walking, running, throwing, and kicking, for example.

guided play A form of child-centered play where adults structure the environment around general curricular goals designed to stimulate children's natural curiosity, exploration, and play through interactions with objects and peers.

Half-Day Program Programs where children have the option of attending either a three- or four-hour morning or afternoon session.

Head Start Framework Learning elements that can be used for collecting data to determine developmental progress and to identify areas of focus for future learning activities.

Head Start Program Federal program that promotes the school readiness of children ages 3 to 5 years old from low-income families by enhancing their cognitive, social, and emotional development.

high-quality activities Activities that are age-appropriate, individually appropriate, and socially/cultural appropriate.

high-quality programs Activities that typically have low adult-child ratios, continually provide safe and intellectually stimulating environments, and encourage children to interact with peers to expand their understanding of the world.

HighScope Preschool program in Ypsilanti, Michigan, that focuses on enhancing educational experiences of at-risk children from poor neighborhoods.

home literacy Literacy that develops in the homes through experiences that demonstrate how language and literacy are used to communicate with and learn from their environment.

horizontal curriculum integration Integrating new activities with earlier learned activities with the goal of children developing and using their growing knowledge base as they move through child-centered learning activities.

inclusion Combining children with disabilities and children who do not have disabilities, and addressing all children's individual needs through activity participation, peer relationship development, and academic achievement.

Individual Family Service Plan (IFSP) A written plan of needed services for a family with a child who has a developmental disability who is under 3 years of age.

Individualized Education Program (IEP) A plan of educational goals and objectives written for students from 3 through 21 years old who are eligible for special education.

Individuals with Disabilities Education Act (IDEA) A federal law that allows children with disabilities to participate in a free and appropriate public education and the right to access and participate in natural environments that encourage inclusive practices not only in early education centers but also in society as a whole.

indoor play activities Carefully planned and designed activities that enhance children's pretend and social interactions in the home, school, or community center.

informal assessment Data obtained from natural learning activities in which the children are involved and that are used by teachers to design high-quality learning activities that enhance children's abilities.

inside play context The area in which the play activity is taking place.

inside-out process Skills that relate to the coded aspects of reading and that center on the ability to understand rules for translating print into meaningful sounds—for example, recognition of alphabet letters and awareness of their sounds.

intentional teaching Carefully crafted play environments and activities that reflect the individual needs of the children and the skills needed to contribute to academic success and a successful life.

interests What self-motivates and engages the child to interact with people, objects, and activities.

iterative process Revisiting an idea or process for continuous refinement or improvement; a cyclical process of discovery.

journals Commercial or teacher-made booklets in which children are encouraged to make regular entries by drawing and/or writing common pictures, letters, words, or stories.

language   The process that we use to communicate with other people and that is made up of socially shared rules such as word meanings, word order, and word combinations.

language acquisition process   An unconscious process for young children whose focus is getting their needs met through language.

large group activities   Lessons focusing on presenting general concepts or ideas that include either the entire class or about half of the class and that last for about 10 to 15 minutes, depending on the interests of the children.

learning center activities   Well-planned indoor or outdoor activities that focus on activities designed to meet the specific developmental needs of children.

learning style   The technique that a person chooses to use to learn, such as visual, verbal, logical, physical, aural, or a combination of any.

lesson plans   Well-organized, thorough, and detailed, written educational "road maps" that teachers develop and use to guide their teaching, thus ensuring that children learning will be held to the highest expectations.

literacy   The ability to access information about the world, process its meaning, and produce knowledge to be shared with others.

literacy play contexts   Play environments in which actual literacy skills are practiced, such as a bookstore, library, post office, or stationery store.

literacy-enriched play objects   Play items that encourage children to read and write, such as pens, paper, books, schedules, calendars, stationery, keyboards, and receipts.

manipulative toys   Toys that enhance children's fine motor skills.

metacommunications   Verbal or nonverbal communications that contribute to the construction of a play context and allow the plot to be coordinated, sustained, and negotiated.

Montessori   An approach to learning that respects children as innate learners with a natural capacity to learn.

morphology   The study of word structures that govern the meanings of word units (e.g., tense markers, suffixes, plural markers).

movement center   An area in the classroom that is large enough to encourage children to engage with gross motor movements that accompany music.

multidisciplinary team   A group typically comprised of educators, the child's parents, a psychologist, and support services personnel who determine whether a child is eligible for special education services.

multiple intelligences   A theory that suggests that intelligence is composed of multiple modalities rather than a single general cognitive ability.

music center   An area in the classroom that encourages children to engage with musical instruments, songs, musical devices, and has enough space for children to move to the music that they create.

National Association for the Education of Young children (NAEYC)   A national organization for early childhood professionals dedicated to establishing research-based standards for programs and professionals, providing resources to improve the quality of early education programs, assisting families in learning how to identify high-quality educational programs, and enhancing professionals' knowledge.

National Head Start Association (NHSA)   An organization that advocates on behalf of two federally funded programs, the Early Start Program, and Head Start Program

natural environments   The learning settings in which children can be found engaged in play, constructing, exploring, and interacting with other children and adults.

No Child Left Behind Act (NCLB)   A federal act mandating that, for states to receive federal funding for education, they must assess children, establish measurable academic performance standards, and demonstrate improved learning growth.

object permanency   Understanding by children that objects continue to exist even when they cannot be seen.

observational notes   Written or typed descriptions of activities compiled after watching children with minimal intrusion in a natural learning setting, and then writing informal and brief notes about the behaviors observed.

one teaching, one assisting   Instructional technique in which one teacher assumes the major responsibility for instruction while the other teacher provides support.

one teaching, one observing Instructional technique in which one teacher assumes primary responsibility for delivering the lesson while the second teacher observes individual students or small groups of students.

open-ended prompts Statements in which teachers respect children as active learners by inviting them to share their knowledge.

outdoor play activities Well-planned, outdoor learning environments that afford children opportunities to explore, investigate, experiment with, problem-solve and pursue outdoor interests.

outside-in process A way of understanding the context in which writing is produced—for example, knowledge of the world and how to use print.

parallel play Play activities in which children observe another child's play activities and attempt to replicate those play activities from afar.

parallel teaching Instructional technique in which each teacher teaches a group of children using similar lessons that have been jointly planned by all the teachers.

paraprofessional aide An adult who works in the classroom and assists the teacher and the students.

passage of time Understanding that over time some things change and some things remain the same.

philosophy statement A set of principles that defines the beliefs that the adults in a classroom put into practice every day.

phonemic awareness The understanding that individual sounds make up spoken words through, for example, the analysis, synthesis, and manipulation of phonemes.

phonological awareness Through engaging in oral communication, children develop the ability to hear, distinguish, and manipulate individual sounds of speech, such as syllables and rhymes.

phonology A component of language that addresses the smallest unit of speech sounds, such as /a/, /b/, /k/.

Piaget A Swiss-born developmental psychologist who was the first to introduce the concept that children think differently than adults.

PL 99-457 A federal law that mandates educational services for children with disabilities from 3 years of age and encourages the participation of young children with disabilities in early education programs for children without disabilities and provides families of children with disabilities with assistance in determining support services.

planned inquiry activities A method of instruction that places equal emphasis on the introduction of both content and learning experiences to inspire children to investigate occurrences that are happening and allow them to use observations from these investigations to build on their current knowledge. These activities build on children's natural curiosity and nurture development of conceptual knowledge and children's scientific processing skills.

play center space An area that is large enough to accommodate all the children wishing to play and that is set off to the side of the room so that the play activity is not interrupted.

play communications Literal statements or behaviors that relate to the roles, actions, or object symbolic representations in a play event.

play plans Proposals for what children want to do during a play activity that are created just before the children participate in the play activity.

portfolio A collection of a student's work from multiple sources and using multiple methods that shows growth over time.

positive behavior support Addresses specific challenging behaviors that appear to recur and interfere with a child's academic and social development.

pragmatics The component of language that focuses on the purpose or intention of the message in context.

preoperational stage Stage of development in which children use language of their world context to determine meanings, but they may not be ready to express their ideas orally.

props Realistic- and unrealistic-looking play materials that provide children with support for the content of their play activities.

prosocial behaviors Voluntary acts that assist young children in showing their peers concern for their well-being, such as caring, sharing, and helping peers.

Readers Theater A staged reading activity of a play or dramatic piece of work designed to entertain, inform, or influence an audience.

readiness skills   The specific skills that a child cannot produce alone but needs the support of a more experienced person to successfully generate them.

recasting   An adult repeats a child's incorrect language by naturally and correctly restating it in a nonthreatening way.

receptive language   The understanding of the language that is being spoken or read.

reciprocal relationships   Interactions in which stakeholders, including families, continually demonstrate awareness of others' abilities to interact with one another and with children in an appropriate manner.

Reggio Emilia   Supportive and enriched environments that provide child-centered, self-guided, activities focusing on a sense of respect, responsibility, and community.

Response to Intervention (RtI)   A systematic observation, assessment, and intervention process for ameliorating children's learning challenges in the general education classroom.

responsive classrooms   Classrooms using a collaborative approach where children and adults determine and enforce classroom rules.

scaffolding   A learning process where a more knowledgeable person guides a novice learner to think and/or complete tasks at a higher level than the novice learner could achieve unassisted.

scientific inquiry process   A procedure that allows children to question, explore, and problem-solve as they collect and compare data through carefully planned, hands-on, and adult-facilitated activity.

screen time   The amount of time that a person spends in front of a computer screen.

self-regulation   The ability of children to regulate their own social, emotional, and cognitive abilities, which contributes to classroom success.

semantics   The component of language focusing on the words that a person understands or uses to convey meaning (e.g., vocabulary).

sensorimotor stage   Learning that occurs through sensory explorations, such as what a child hears, sees, tastes, and feels.

shared writings   Reading texts that are composed from children's own oral language with the written support of an adult.

small group activities   Lessons that involve a staff member working with a limited number of children (3–6) on activities that will move the children's skills to an independent level of mastery.

social play   Play at around 2 years of age and along with the onset of language in which children begin to participate in overt activities by directly sharing their play creations with their peers.

social proximity   Standing close enough to communicate and to demonstrate interest of another person.

social studies   The combination study of content from history, geography, sociology, and civics that provides children with an understanding of their national heritage and the beginning skills that they will need to participate as active, adult members of a democracy.

socio-dramatic play   A type of social play in which children create pretend play narratives that are collaboratively sequenced and incorporate planning, coordinating, and negotiating in order to sustain the activity.

solitary play   A type of play in which very young children play independently but rarely interact with other children while playing.

speech   Verbal production of language that is used for communicating and consists of articulation (speech sounds), voice, and fluency (speech rhythm).

stages of block development   The developmental process in which children develop more complex block-building skills.

Student Assistance Team   Group of school professionals that support teachers who have concerns about a particular student's educational progress.

supporting from outside the play context   Situations in which an adult stays outside the play activity but provides verbal or nonverbal support for the children's play.

supporting inside play context   Situations in which an adult joins in the play activity and interacts with and supports the children's play.

symbolic play   Play activities where roles, actions, and objects become something that they do not typically represent by taking on a new function (e.g., a bucket becomes a hat).

syntax The component of language that focuses on how language is organized to convey messages, including the elements used to form phrases or sentences (grammar).

teaming Teachers plan and implement their teaching duties by sharing instruction, usually in a large group. The teachers, however, may divide up tasks.

theme The topic for play enactment that makes it a cohesive and integrated narrative interaction.

tourist approach When cultural information is presented using simplistic themes and isolated activities that do not focus on much discussion.

transactive model of assessment Assessment process that accounts for how children interact with objects, people, and the environment to determine how they learn, what they know, and how they develop new skills.

types of family structures Diverse family types such as single-parent families, blended and extended families, adoptive families, foster families, and conditionally separated families.

vertical curriculum integration Science curricula that present planned activities based on broad themes and include other subject matter development, such as mathematics, reading, social studies, and language arts.

visual schedules A column or row of pictures, objects, or words that represents major daily activities and assists children with processing the day's sequence of events.

Vygotsky Russian scientist who proposed that learning first occurs through the interaction between children and the environment where the learning activity will take place.

word knowledge Understanding that spoken words can be represented by print.

word searches A literacy activity that encourages children to focus on environmental print both in and outside the classroom.

zone of proximal development The zone where children gradually become more capable of producing and demonstrating skills with less support.

Index

AAP. *See* American Academy of Pediatrics
Ability groups, 155
Academic precursors, 6–7, 107, 139
   See also Literacy development
Accommodation of new information, 32, 33
   in block activities, 354
   in book centers, 390
   for creative arts activities, 427, 428
   for learning, 274
   technology use, 384
Achievement gap, 20
Adams, M., 396
Adoptive families, 117
Adult interactions
   avoiding taking control, 214–215
   in creative drama, 432, 433
   in high-quality classrooms, 170–171
   in learning centers, 192, 193
   in music and movement activities, 430–431
   in play centers, 260–261
   in Reggio Emilia programs, 45–46
   in science centers, 318–319
   support services staff, 126, 242
   See also Guided play; Parents; Scaffolding
Adult-child ratios, 170
Adult-directed learning, 7–8, 14, 17, 18–20, 107, 330–331
Adult-guided activities
   inappropriate increases in, 4, 14, 17
   integrating with child-centered activities, 173–175, 187
   negative effects, 7–8, 18–20
   pressures to increase, 18, 107, 353
   See also Guided play; Learning centers
Aides, 125, 126, 129, 130
Almon, J., 17
Alphabet
   awareness, 7
   learning, 107
   writing, 104–105
Alternating teaching, 128
Amanti, C., 187–188
American Academy of Pediatrics (AAP), 17, 162, 385
Anti-biased activities, 381–383
Apgar, Virginia, 226

Apgar scores, 226
Arithmetic. *See* Mathematics
Armstrong, Brian, 109–110
Art centers
   activities, 407, 413–420
   cleaning up, 415
   designing, 413–414
   locations, 414
   materials, 414–415, 416–419
   See also Creative arts
Art Collection Books, 363–364
Art materials
   cleaning and storing, 415
   modeling clay, 414–415
   open-ended, 416–419
   painting, 414
   play themes and, 414, 415
   recycled, 363
Assessment
   achievement gap, 20
   authentic, 231–236, 243
   of children with disabilities, 235
   child's involvement, 237, 239, 245–246
   collaboration with families, 235, 238
   cultural differences and, 230
   definition, 227
   formal, 227, 229–231
   informal, 227–229, 231–233
   instability, 230–231
   of language, 229–230
   language delay screening, 91, 92
   ongoing, 227–229, 237, 238, 243
   photographs, 234–235, 238–239
   reflective questions, 236, 245–246
   Response to Intervention, 239–242
   special education placements, 240, 242–243
   teams, 239, 240, 242
   tools, 233–235, 237, 238–239
   transactive model of, 243–246
   types, 227, 228
   uses, 227–229
   valid and reliable methods, 227, 228
   See also Head Start Framework
Assimilation of new information, 32, 33
Ateliers, 46

Authentic assessments, 231–236, 243
  See also Assessment
Autism spectrum disorders
  language delays, 93
  socio-dramatic play and, 77–79
  visual schedules, 150–152
  See also Disabilities, children with

Balance, 423
  See also Movement
Behaviors
  functional behavior assessment, 163
  positive behavior support, 162–164
  prosocial, 159, 160
  unacceptable, 20, 161–163
Behnke, M., 217
Bell, E. R., 161–162
Berk, L., 208
Berk, L. E., 206
Berry, B., 235
Biases
  anti-biased activities, 381–383
  gender, 335–336
  of teachers, 120
Big body play. *See* Rough-and-tumble play
Big ideas, 316, 321–323
Bilingual development, 89–90, 230, 280
  See also English language learners
Block activities
  children with disabilities and, 354
  cleaning up, 346, 351–353
  cultural differences and, 350
  developmental stages, 344–346, 347
  gender differences, 336
  geometric shapes, 340, 341
  guided play, 346–348, 351
  journals, 349
  in kindergarten, 353–355
  skills developed, 330, 331, 344,
    351, 354, 355
  stringing blocks, 356
Block centers
  locations, 348
  materials, 348–350, 351
  observing, 350
Blocks
  materials, 343–344
  shapes, 341, 347, 352, 353
  storage, 347, 348–349, 352, 353
Bloom, L., 36
Bodrova, E., 259, 285–286
Bond, M. A., 393
Book centers
  activities, 392–396
  children with disabilities and, 390–391
  designing, 384–386, 388–392
  locations, 391
  materials, 389, 392
  reading areas, 391

Books
  choosing, 372, 373
  creative drama scripts, 432–433
  cultural diversity in, 372, 373
  interacting with, 387–388
  "Picture Walks," 156
  pictures in, 389
  print referencing, 390
  reading to children, 388, 395–396
  in science centers, 323
  storage, 391
  translated, 372
Bradley, B. A., 292
Brady, Renee, 221–222
Bredekamp, S., 173
Brenner, M. E., 216
Brent, R., 307–308
Britto, P. R., 104
Bruner, Jerome, 203
Buddy Play Plans, 285, 286
Bullying, 80–81
Bulotsky-Schearer, R. J., 161–162
Burghardt, G. M., 37
Burt, T., 116, 117
Bush, George W., 18
Buysse, V., 14, 15

Cabell, S. A., 279
Cameras. *See* Photographs
Canada, Geoffrey, 12
Cantrell, D. E., 372
Carlson, F. M., 146–147
Carter, T. M., 161–162
Carvell, N. R., 412
CCSS. *See* Common Core State Standards
CEC. *See* Council for Exceptional Children
Center for American Progress, 12
Center for Research on Education, Diversity, and
    Excellence, 230
Center learning. *See* Learning centers
Center teaching, 127, 129
Centers. *See* Learning centers; Play centers
Change
  passage of time theme, 379
  as science theme, 301–302, 317–318, 319, 320–323
Charman, T., 235
Charsha, Beverly, 297–298
Checklists, 235
Chien, N. C., 171, 191
Child-centered activities
  benefits, 7
  guided play as, 219
  integrating with adult-guided activities, 173–175, 187
  interests of children, 179, 183, 204–205
  learning opportunities, 139–141, 202
  literacy development, 172, 202
  music, 422
  planning, 246, 259–260, 284–286
  in Reggio Emilia programs, 46

science, 322
at transitions, 196
See also Play
Childress, D. C., 208
Christ, T., 94
Christie, J., 219
Christie, J. F., 202
Circle Time, 149, 294, 421, 425, 436
Civics. *See* Social studies
Clark, B., 344
Class sizes, 170
Classroom management
conflict resolution, 161, 163
responsive classrooms, 159–160
unacceptable behaviors, 20, 161–163
Classroom organization
activities, 139–141
for effective learning, 138–141, 153
flexible groupings, 155–159
furniture, 141
home-like items, 141, 142
interactions, 139, 140
settings, 139–140
student involvement, 137–138
See also Learning centers; Play centers; Schedules
Classrooms
language-rich, 124–125
lighting, 141
links to outdoors, 141–142
Reggio Emilia programs, 46
See also Learning centers; Play centers
Clay, Marie, 30, 37, 103
Clay, modeling, 414–415
Clements, D., 339
Cognitive decentering, 138–139
Cognitive development stages
concrete operational, 32, 33
formal operational, 32, 33
preoperational, 32, 33, 34
sensorimotor, 32, 33
Cognitive skills
creative arts and, 406, 424
development, 40, 60, 76
multiple intelligences programs, 50–52
Piaget's theory, 32–34
use in play, 80, 95, 146, 188, 259–260
Vygotsky's theory, 34, 36
Cohen, L., 350
Collaboration
among children, 75, 115
benefits, 122–124, 126, 127
co-teaching, 125–129
culture of, 115
definition, 121
justification, 114–115
language-rich classrooms, 124–125
mutual roles, 125–126
with professionals, 115, 121–129
Reggio Emilia programs, 47

Response to Intervention activities, 240–241
successful, 121
See also Families, collaboration with; Teams
Collaborative play. *See* Socio-dramatic play
Common Core State Standards (CCSS)
accommodations, 274
English Language Arts, 273, 285, 319, 320
foundational skills, 198
implementation, 274
integrating, 319, 320
K-12, 272–274
limitations, 273–274
literacy skills, 8, 273
mathematics, 319, 320, 342–343, 353–355, 359
nonfiction texts, 8, 102
observation worksheet, 251–254, 255–256
play-based curricula and, 8
reasoning skills, 394
transitions from Head Start Framework, 273
Common underlying proficiency (CUP) model, 90
Communication
encouraging, 90
meta-, 97, 99–100, 217
nonverbal, 74
observation of, 261–262
oral, 7, 172–173
play, 97, 98–99, 261–262
in socio-dramatic play, 97–100
See also Language; Speech
Communities
field trips, 185–186, 376
learning about, 371
play center themes, 374–375
See also Social studies
Computers. *See* Technology
Concrete operational stage, 32, 33
Conflict resolution, 161, 163
Consortium of National Arts Education
Associations, 411
Content areas, 42–43
See also Learning centers; Mathematics; Science;
Social studies
Conversations
benefits, 371
dialogic reading, 390, 394–395
structured, 279–280
unstructured, 280
See also Social skills; Speech
Cook, L., 121, 126, 127
Cooperation. *See* Collaboration
Copeland, S. M., 175
Copley, J. V., 331
Copple, C., 173
Corsaro, W. A., 75, 214–215
Co-teaching, 125–129
Council for Exceptional Children (CEC), 14
Count the Letter game, 393
Counting, 339–340
See also Mathematics skills

Cox, A., 217
Craft, Diane, 25–26
Creative arts
 accommodations, 427, 428
 children with disabilities and, 406
 cultural differences and, 404
 dance, 408
 experimentation, 418–419
 integration in curriculum, 406, 417
 play activities and, 406–407, 408, 417, 419
 puppets, 434–437
 Reggio Emilia programs, 46
 in schools, 405–406, 412
 skill development and, 403–405, 406, 407, 408,
  412–413, 421, 423–427
 standards, 408–409, 411–412
 See also Art centers; Music
Creative drama
 adult roles, 432, 433
 books as scripts, 432–433
 definition, 432
 dramatic centers, 407
 Readers Theater, 434, 435
 skills developed, 433
Creative movement, 421–427
 See also Movement
Cultural diversity
 anti-biased activities, 381–383
 assessment and, 230
 awareness, 10
 block activities and, 350
 in classrooms, 160, 187–191, 371
 collaboration with families, 120, 141, 195–196
 creative arts and, 404
 guided play and, 216
 increase in, 13–14
 learning about, 371, 372–373, 375
 learning center materials, 194–196
 manipulative toys and, 356, 358–359
 in narratives, 102
 in parenting styles, 216
 play goals, 60–61, 70
 play objects, 141, 216, 374
 prosocial behaviors, 160
 symbolic play and, 70
 tourist approach, 381
 See also English language learners
Cultural responsiveness, 381
Cummins, J., 90
CUP model. *See* Common underlying proficiency model
Curriculum
 adult-directed, 7–8, 14, 17, 18–20, 107
 arts integration, 406, 417
 current challenges, 17–20
 HighScope programs, 47, 48, 372–373
 horizontal integration, 317
 music and movement integration, 421, 425, 428–429
 science, 312, 313–318, 321–323
 vertical integration, 317

Dance, 408
DAP. *See* Developmentally Appropriate Practices
Darling, R. B., 116
Data collection, with manipulatives, 357
 See also Assessment; Observation
DEC. *See* Division for Early Childhood
Decontextualized narratives, 276
Decontextualized objects, 63, 67
Demographics, 9–12
 See also Diversity
Dennis, L. R., 390
Derman-Sparks, L., 117, 335, 336,
  381, 382
Developmental diversity, 14–16, 406
 See also Accommodations; Disabilities,
  children with
Developmentally Appropriate
  Practices (DAP)
 benefits, 3–4, 7–8, 161, 175
 best practices, 5
 definition, 5
 differentiated instruction, 177–181
 inclusion and, 15
 for literacy development, 108, 172
 principles, 8–9, 20
 See also Play
Dever, M. T., 214
Dialogic reading, 269, 390, 394–395
Dickinson, D. K., 107–108
Differentiated instruction, 177–181
Disabilities, children with
 assessments, 235
 attention to play, 71
 block activities, 354
 book centers and, 390–391
 co-teaching, 125–127
 creative arts activities, 427–428
 developmental delays, 406
 educational rights, 14
 families, 118
 friendships, 16, 81–82
 guided play, 208, 211
 inclusion, 14–16, 47, 82, 125–127, 158–159
 Individualized Education Programs,
  118, 243, 427
 language delays, 91–93
 learning centers, 158–159
 movement activities, 421, 427
 multiple intelligences approach, 52
 outdoor learning benefits, 147–148
 Reggio Emilia programs, 47
 Response to Intervention activities, 239–241
 self-regulation, 77
 social interactions, 74
 speech disorders, 91
 symbolic play, 74
 visual schedules, 150–152
 See also Accommodations; Autism spectrum
  disorders; Developmental diversity

Dissecting words, 289–292
Diversity
    awareness, 10, 11–12
    economic, 10, 12–13, 18–20
    ethnic, 10, 13–14, 60–61
    of families, 116, 377–378
    gender, 10
    language, 10, 13–14
    of population, 9–12
    religious, 10
    respect for, 116, 117
    See also Cultural diversity; Developmental diversity
Division for Early Childhood (DEC), 240–241, 242
Donald, G., 78
Dow, C. B., 421
Dramatic centers, 407
    See also Creative drama
Dramatic play. See Socio-dramatic play
Drawing, 416, 419
Dropout rates, 20
Dunn, J., 80, 81

Early education
    adult-directed curriculum, 7–8, 14, 17,
        18–20, 107
    enrollments, 11
    evaluations, 49
    high-quality programs, 6, 12, 170, 171, 205
    learning theories and, 43–53
    state spending, 16
    See also Child-centered activities; Head Start
Early intervention, 6
Early learning standards
    creative arts, 408–409, 411–412
    NAEYC position statement, 4–5
    readiness skills, 178
    of states, 178, 181, 197–198, 271
    use of, 198
    See also Common Core State Standards;
        Head Start Framework
Early Start Program, 5, 6
Eastman, A. M., 307–308
Eberly, J. L., 120
Ecology. See Social studies
Economic diversity, 10, 12–13, 18–20
    See also Low-income families
Economics. See Social studies
Edwards, J. O., 117, 335, 336, 381, 382
Egocentrism, 32
Elkind, D., 17, 58, 60, 261, 305
Elliott, Elizabeth, 264–265
Emergent literacy, 101, 103–104
Emotional power, 80
Emotional skills
    development, 80
    omission from Common Core, 273
Emotions
    activities and, 188–189
    love, 58–60

English Language Arts, Common Core State Standards,
        273, 285, 319, 320
    See also Language
English language learners
    creative arts activities, 434
    reading skills, 283
    songs, 405
    spoken language activities, 280
    See also Bilingual development
Enz, B., 219
Epstein, A. S., 174
Equilibrium, 32, 33
Ethnic diversity, 10, 13–14, 60–61, 102
    See also Cultural diversity
Expressive language, 91, 92
Expulsions, 20
Ezell, H. L., 390

Falconer, R. C., 214
Families
    activities, 130
    guided play activities, 206–207
    Individual Family Service Plans, 243
    learning opportunities, 12–13
    literacy activities, 6–7, 18–20, 107–108, 294
    members, 116
    nuclear, 116
    pictures of, 372
    puppet visits, 436
    separations, 117
    storytelling, 103
    structures, 117, 377–378
    See also Cultural diversity; Low-income families;
        Parents
Families, collaboration with
    assessment, 235, 238
    benefits, 119, 120
    classroom involvement, 118–119
    communications, 115, 119, 129–130
    cultural differences and, 120, 141, 195–196
    encouraging, 120, 131
    family structures and, 116–118
    importance, 118–121
    learning center design, 188–189, 190
    Montessori programs, 44
    reciprocal relationships, 119, 120, 122, 129–131
    Reggio Emilia programs, 45–46
    respect, 116, 117
    technology use, 384
Fathers. See Families; Parents
Field trips, 185–186, 376
Fighting, distinction from big body play, 144–146
Fine motor skills, 281, 355–356,
        410–411, 412–413
    See also Manipulative toys
Fisher, K., 208
Fisher, Kaitlan, 438–439
Flexible groupings, 155–159
    See also Groups; Learning centers

Flores, M. M., 78, 79
Formal assessment, 227, 229–231
    See also Assessment
Formal operational stage, 32, 33
Foster families, 117
Free play, 17, 21, 171, 205
    See also Play
Freeman, S., 78
Friend, M., 121, 126, 127
Friendships
    boss relationships, 80
    of children with disabilities, 16, 81–82
    definition, 80
    developing, 80, 81
    give and take relationships, 80
    leader-follower relationships, 80
    play and, 80
Full-day programs, 148
    See also Schedules
Functional behavior assessment, 163
Functional play, 309–310
Funds of knowledge, 12–13, 187–188

Galper, A., 376, 379
Galvin, K. M., 208
Games
    board, 342, 359, 360
    with books, 393
    rules, 311
    See also Play
Ganz, J. B., 78, 79
Garcia, V., 30, 330
Gardner, Howard, 50
Geist, E. A., 341
Geist, K., 341
Gelman, R., 317
Gelnaw, A., 116, 117
Gender
    awareness, 335
    diversity, 10
    of early education teachers, 365–366
    physical differences, 335–336
    stereotypes, 281, 335
Gender bias, in mathematics, 335–336
Geography. *See* Social studies
Geometry, 340, 341
    See also Mathematics skills
Ginsburg, K. R., 11
Golinkoff, M., 38
Golinkoff, R. M., 208
Gonzalez, N., 187–188
Gordon, A., 147
Grammar. *See* Language; Syntax
Gross motor skills, 148, 281, 410
Groups
    Circle Time, 149, 294, 421, 425, 436
    large, 149, 155–156
    small, 155, 156–157, 283–284
    See also Learning centers

Guided play
    activities, 20–21
    adult roles, 204–208, 209–220
    block activities, 346–348, 351
    challenges, 207
    with children with disabilities, 208, 211
    cultural differences and, 216
    definition, 38, 204
    distinction from free play, 21
    in families, 206–207
    guidance from inside play setting, 214–220
    guidance from outside play context, 209–214
    language in, 217–219
    learning through, 21, 207
    literacy activities, 283–297
    literacy play contexts, 212–213
    literacy supports, 206
    mathematics activities, 333, 334, 337
    with more-experienced peers, 204, 210
    props, 210–213, 281–283
    research on, 21, 206, 207–208, 214–215
    skills, 206
    strategies, 208
    suggestions, 213
    themes, 210, 211, 281–282
    woodcraft activities, 364
    See also Play; Play centers
Guided questions, 393–394

Half-day programs, 148
    See also Schedules
Halle, T. G., 230
Hamilton, A. A., 307–308
Hamlin, M., 306
Hanline, M. F., 354
Harger, J., 44
Head Start Framework
    creative arts elements, 409
    learning standard outcomes, 271–272
    mathematics elements, 339–341
    motor skills elements, 409–411
    science elements, 311–312
    skills, 275–276
    social studies elements, 377–378
    transitions to Common Core Standards, 273
Head Start Program, 5, 6, 12, 13, 247–259
Head Start Research Third Grade Follow-Up Impact
        Study, 93–94
Health, benefits of play, 17
    See also Physical development
Heath, S. B., 102
Helm, J. H., 322
Highland, J., 52
High-quality activities, 170
High-quality programs
    adult-child ratios, 170
    benchmarks, 170, 171
    class sizes, 170
    impact on children from low-income families, 12

play activities, 205
value, 6
High-quality teaching strategies
assessment and, 227–229
differentiated instruction, 177–181
integrating child-centered and adult-guided
activities, 173–175, 187
intentional teaching, 172–176, 303
interactions with children, 170–171
lesson plans, 181
open-ended prompts, 175–177
See also Scaffolding
HighScope programs
conflict resolution, 161, 163
curriculum, 47, 48, 372–373
evaluations, 49, 94
learning theories and, 46–48
plan-do-review activities, 47–48
Hindman, A. H., 176, 393
Hirsh-Pasek, K., 38, 208
History. *See* Social studies
Hoffman, Eric, 382
Home literacy programs, 107–108
Homes. *See* Families
Honig, A. S., 53
Horizontal curriculum integration, 317
Howes, C., 17, 62, 95, 170
Howlin, P., 235
Hunter, A., 31

IDEA. *See* Individuals with Disabilities Education Act
IEPs. *See* Individualized Education Programs
IFSPs. *See* Individual Family Service Plans
Imagination, 58
See also Symbolic play
Inclusion
advantages, 16, 82
concerns about, 15
co-teaching, 125–127
definition, 14–15
developmentally appropriate practices, 15
full or partial, 15
learning center activities, 158–159
Reggio Emilia programs, 47
Individual Family Service Plans (IFSPs), 243
Individualized Education Programs (IEPs),
118, 243, 427
See also Disabilities, children with
Individuals with Disabilities Education
Act (IDEA), 14
Indoor learning settings. *See* Classrooms;
Learning centers
Infants
Apgar scores, 226
creative expression, 408
interacting with books, 387
language development, 86–87, 88
learning, 30–31
love, work, and play, 58

play activities, 280, 309
prematurity, 74
Informal assessment, 227–229, 231–233
See also Assessment
Inquiry process environments, 305
See also Planned inquiry activities
Inside-out process, 104–106
Instructional methods
adult-directed, 7–8, 14, 17, 18–20, 107
differentiated, 177–181
individualized, 283–284
See also Developmentally Appropriate Practices;
High-quality teaching strategies
Intelligences. *See* Multiple intelligences programs
Intentional teaching, 172–176, 303
Interactive media. *See* Technology
Interactive play. *See* Socio-dramatic play
Interests of children, 179, 183, 204–205
International Reading Association
(IRA), 273–274
Interventions. *See* Response to Intervention
IRA. *See* International Reading Association
Iterative process, 306–307

Jones, J., 292
Jones, Katrina, 132–133
Joshi, A., 120
Journals, 235, 323, 349
Justice, L. M., 124, 217, 390

Karp, K. H., 333
Kasari, C., 78
Katz, J. R., 99
Katz, L., 322
Keilty, B., 208
Kermani, H., 216
Kim, J., 408
Kindergarten
block activities, 353–355
creative arts standards, 411–412
manipulative toys, 359
science curriculum, 313–316
See also Common Core State Standards
Kozal, J., 120
Krashen, S. D., 87
Kuznik, K., 341

LaFoe, Danelle, 199–200
Laminack, Lester, 103
Language
as academic precursor, 6–7
alphabet, 7, 104–105, 107
assessment instruments, 229–230
content, 91
definition, 86, 92
expressive, 91, 92
form, 91
morphemes, 86–87
morphology, 92

oral, 7, 172–173
phonology, 7, 87, 92
pragmatics, 92
receptive, 91, 92
semantics, 92
in socio-dramatic play, 74–76, 78
symbolic object representations and, 64–65
syntax, 87, 92
terms and definitions, 92
use, 91
See also English language learners; Literacy;
    Reading; Speech
Language acquisition process, 87–88, 89
Language development
    bilingual, 89–90, 230, 280
    collaborative teaching, 124–125
    in creative drama, 433
    delays, 87–88, 91–93, 390
    in early childhood, 86–89
    importance, 88–89
    music and, 404–405, 407, 425, 426
    phonological awareness, 7, 87
    poverty and, 93–94
    questions, 176
    scaffolding, 217–219, 220
    skills, 64–65, 88, 172
    socio-dramatic play and, 62, 95–97
    vocabulary teaching, 94–95
Language diversity, 10, 13–14
    See also Cultural diversity
Language-rich classrooms, 124–125
Large group activities, 143, 149, 155–156
Lawrence, Theresa, 396–397
Leal, D., 118–119, 122–123
Learning
    active, 176
    cultural differences and, 216
    early, 30–31
    Head Start Framework, 271–272
    integrative, 140–141
    interactions with others and environment,
        30–31, 34–35, 46
    See also Early learning standards
Learning Center Observation Worksheets,
    243–244, 247–259
Learning centers
    accessibility, 208
    activities, 22, 183–184, 186–191, 192–193
    adult roles, 192, 193, 196
    areas and boundaries, 193
    children with disabilities in, 158–159
    definition, 157
    designing, 22, 183–191, 193, 196
    goals, 181–182
    Head Start Framework, 271–272
    high-quality, 181–191
    indoor, 183
    introducing, 191, 196

learning opportunities, 22, 157–158, 183–184,
    186–187, 280–281
literacy-enriched, 182, 183–184, 186,
    191–192, 194
managing, 191–193
materials, 184–186, 187, 193–196
mathematics activities, 341, 342
NAEYC principles, 22–23
number of children, 158, 192
outdoor, 143, 145, 183
play centers as, 22, 205
socio-dramatic play, 182, 184, 196
See also Play centers; Science centers;
    Social studies centers
Learning environments. *See* Classrooms; Natural
    environments; Outdoor play activities
Learning styles, 179–180
Learning theories
    early education programs and, 43–53
    multiple intelligences, 50–52
    of Piaget, 32–34, 38–39, 44–45, 47, 48
    See also Vygotsky, Lev
Lego blocks, 344, 356
Leong, D. J., 259, 285–286
Lesser, L. K., 116, 117
Lesson plans, 51, 52, 181, 182
Letters. *See* Alphabet; Writing
Libraries, 392
Lifter, K., 36
Literacy
    as academic precursor, 6–7, 107
    definition, 103
    home, 107–108
    See also Language; Reading; Writing
Literacy activities
    dissecting words, 289–292
    in families, 6–7, 18–20, 107–108, 294
    guided play, 283–297
    outdoor, 143–144
    play plans, 284–286
    in science centers, 317, 319
    shared writings, 292–296
    in social studies centers, 375, 379
    in socio-dramatic play, 213, 275–276, 283–286
    word searches, 286–289
    See also Books
Literacy development
    child-centered activities, 172, 202
    classroom activities, 106–107, 108, 393–394
    emergent, 101, 103–104
    guided play, 206
    individualized instruction, 283–284
    inside-out process, 104–106
    mathematics skills and, 334–335, 337–338, 364
    outside-in process, 104–106
    play and, 41–42, 275–280
    play center activities, 280–297
    research on, 103–104, 108

small-group activities, 283–284
writing skills, 104–105, 107
Literacy play contexts, 212–213
Literacy skills
checklist, 296
Common Core State Standards, 273
in content areas, 8
contextual clues, 8
real-world activities, 13
speech, 172–173, 279–280
symbolic object representations and, 64–65
teaching strategies, 103
writing, 104–105, 107, 278–279
Literacy-enriched learning centers,
182, 183–184, 186, 191–192, 194
Literacy-enriched play objects
in block centers, 351
in book centers, 389, 392
guided play, 212–213, 282–283
See also Props
Lo, D. E., 372
Lonigan, C. J., 103, 104
Love, 58–60
Lovin, L. A. H., 333
Low-income families
activities, 130
collaboration with, 44
disadvantages, 13
early education programs, 5, 6, 12
language development, 93–94
literacy activities, 18–20, 107, 294
mathematical skill development, 360
play activities, 162
reading to children, 395–396
See also Families; Poverty
Luckenbill, Julie, 263–264
Lynch, S. A., 390

Madsen, Tiffany, 165–166
Make-believe. See Pretend play;
Symbolic play
Malaguzzi, Loris, 45
Manipulative toys
commercial, 355–356
common objects, 356–357
cultural differences and, 356, 358–359
in kindergarten, 359
play themes, 343
puzzles, 205, 355–356
skills developed, 330, 331, 357, 359
statistical operations, 357–358
storage, 358
Manipulatives centers, 358
Mann, T. D., 206
Martinez, Vicki, 83
Materials. See Art materials; Props
Materials + Objectives + Space + Time
(MOST), 427

Mathematics
Common Core State Standards, 319, 320, 342–343,
353–355, 359
concepts, 331
emergent, 341
gender bias in, 335–336
processes, 331, 332
Mathematics skills
block activities, 351
content areas, 331, 333
data collection and analysis, 357–358
early development, 30, 330–331, 334, 337, 341
importance, 334
in learning centers, 341, 342
literacy development and, 334–335, 337–338, 364
manipulatives and, 330, 331, 343, 355–359
natural activities, 330, 331
play activities, 330, 332–333, 337–338, 342
poverty and, 360
recommended practices, 334, 335
rote learning, 330–331
in science centers, 318, 319
standards, 339–343
time spent on, 332–334, 337
in woodcraft activities, 362–363, 364
McGee, L. M., 217, 218
McNally, P., 52
MDTs. See Multidisciplinary teams
Meals
schedules, 149
transitions, 153
Meece, D., 90
Mental representations, 139
Metacommunications, 97, 99–100, 217
Miller, E., 17
Milteer, R. M., 11
Minority groups, 12, 13–14, 102
See also Cultural diversity; Ethnic diversity
Mitchell, L. C., 427
Moll, L. C., 13, 130, 187–188
Montessori, Maria, 43
Montessori programs, 43–45
Mora, Sandra, 325–326
Moral and ethical principles, 16
Moreno, Jaime, 26–27
Morphemes, 86–87
Morphology, 92
Morrow, M. L., 295
MOST. See Materials + Objectives + Space + Time
Mother-child symbolic play representations, 70
Mothers. See Families; Parents
Motivation, 138, 179
See also Interests of children
Motor skills
assessment, 237
development, 281, 423
fine, 281, 355–356, 410–411, 412–413
gross, 148, 281, 410

standards, 409–411
  See also Physical development
Movement
  balance, 423
  creative, 421–427
  dance, 408
  integration in curriculum, 428–429
  music and, 420–424
  outdoor activities, 429–430
  pretend play and, 426–427
  skill development, 423
  Total Physical Response, 434, 435
  during transitions, 154, 428–429
  See also Physical activity
Movement centers
  activities, 423–424, 426–427, 434
  adult roles, 430–431
  areas, 430
  definition, 407
  materials, 421
Multicultural books, 372
  See also Cultural diversity
Multidisciplinary teams (MDTs), 240, 242
Multiple intelligences programs, 50–52
Music
  child-centered activities, 422
  integration in curriculum, 421, 425, 429
  language development and, 404–405, 407, 425, 426
  movement and, 420–424
  play and, 422, 426, 429–430
  standards, 408, 409
  at transitions, 154
Music centers
  activities, 423–424
  adult roles, 430–431
  areas, 430
  definition, 407
  instruments, 424
  materials, 421, 424

NAECS/SDE. *See* National Association of Early Childhood Specialists in State Departments of Education
NAEYC. *See* National Association for the Education of Young Children
Narrative productions, 96
Narratives
  cultural differences, 102
  decontextualized, 276
  development, 78, 101–102, 209
  pretend play, 206
  shared play, 69
  shared writings, 292–296, 434
  themes, 210
National Academy of Sciences, 103–104
National Assessment of Educational Progress, 405
National Association for Music Education, 408

National Association for the Education of Young Children (NAEYC)
  assessment principles, 227
  Code of Ethical Conduct, 116
  on collaboration, 131
  on Common Core Standards, 273
  on developmentally appropriate practices, 5, 20, 172, 175, 177
  on early learning, 4–5, 197–198
  evidence-based findings, 6–7
  on mathematics skills, 334, 335
  principles, 22–23
  on Response to Intervention, 240–241, 242
  on technology use, 384
National Association of Early Childhood Specialists in State Departments of Education (NAECS/SDE), 197–198, 227, 273
National Coalition for Core Arts Standards (NCCAS), 411
National Council for Social Studies (NCSS), 378, 379, 380–381
National Council of Teachers of Mathematics (NCTM), 332, 334, 335
National Dance Education Organization, 408
National Dissemination Center for Young Children with Disabilities (NICHCY), 87, 91
National Head Start Association (NHSA), 5, 242
National Household Education Survey, 12, 13
National Institute for Early Education Research (NIEER), 170, 171, 198
National Research Council (NRC), 308, 313–316, 318
Natural environments
  assessment in, 231, 237, 238
  children with disabilities in, 14
  See also Inclusion
Nature, art projects, 420
  See also Outdoor play activities; Science
NCCAS. *See* National Coalition for Core Arts Standards
NCLB. *See* No Child Left Behind Act
NCSS. *See* National Council for Social Studies
NCTM. *See* National Council of Teachers of Mathematics
Neff, D., 187–188
Neighborhoods. *See* Communities
Nelson, E., 142
Neuman, S. B., 184, 294, 396
New York City, Harlem schools, 12
Newburger, A., 355
Next Generation Science Standards (NGSS), 313, 319, 320
NHSA. *See* National Head Start Association
NICHCY. *See* National Dissemination Center for Young Children with Disabilities
NICHD Early Child Care Research Network, 388
NIEER. *See* National Institute for Early Education Research

No Child Left Behind Act (NCLB), 18, 106, 179, 197, 337
Nonfiction texts, 8, 102
Notes, observational, 233–234
NRC. *See* National Research Council
Numbers, 339–340
   See also Mathematics

Obama, Barack, 49
Object permanency, 58–59, 60
Objects, decontextualized, 63, 67
   See also Manipulative toys; Props; Symbolic play
      representations
Observation
   analysis of data, 262
   authentic assessment, 231–236, 237, 238
   of block centers, 350
   of communication skills, 261–262
   notes, 233–234
   of participation, 260–261
   of planning activities, 246, 259–260
   of play activities, 262
   Response to Intervention, 239–242
   of social interactions, 260, 261
   transactive, 243–246
   worksheets, 247–259
   See also Assessment
Odom, S. L., 14, 15
Ogan, A. T., 206
One teaching, one assisting, 128–129
One teaching, one observing, 127
Open-ended art materials, 416–419
Open-ended prompts, 175–177
Oral communication, 7, 172–173
   See also Speech
Outdoor play activities
   for children with disabilities, 147–148
   decreased time available, 19
   definition, 147
   developmental impact, 142–143, 144, 146, 147–148
   information for families, 146–147
   learning centers, 183
   literacy activities, 143–144
   movement activities, 429–430
   music and, 429–430
   in Reggio Emilia programs, 46, 141
   rough-and-tumble play, 144–147
   rules, 429
   safety, 143, 147
   schedules, 149
   settings, 141–142, 143–144, 145, 148
   supervising, 147
Outings. *See* Field trips
Outside-in process, 104–106
Oxley, E., 307–308

Paparella, T., 78
Parallel play, 61–62, 148

Parallel teaching, 128
Paraprofessional aides, 125, 126, 129, 130
Parents
   assessment involvement, 235
   of children with disabilities, 208
   cultural differences, 216
   field trip participation, 376
   guided play activities, 206–207, 208
   interactions with children, 70, 79, 94
   roles in learning, 45–46
   rough-and-tumble play, 146
   single, 117
   See also Families
Passage of time, 379
Patterns, 340–342
   See also Mathematics skills
PBS. *See* Positive behavior support
Peabody Picture Vocabulary Test, 229
Peart, M., 52
Peña, E. D., 230
Perry, J. P., 144
Perry Preschool Research Study, 49, 94
   See also HighScope programs
Philosophy statements, 125
Phonological awareness, 7, 87
Phonology, 87, 92
Photographs
   assessment use, 234–235, 238–239
   of families, 372
   learning about passage of time, 379
   portfolios, 234–235
   of woodcraft objects, 363–364
Physical activity
   importance, 25–26, 142–143, 408, 421
   learning and, 421
   See also Movement; Outdoor play activities
Physical development
   of children, 146, 421
   of children with disabilities, 281
   See also Motor skills
Physical spaces, learning and, 244–245
   See also Classroom organization; Learning centers;
      Outdoor play activities; Play centers
Piaget, Jean, 32–34, 38–39, 44–45, 47, 48
"Picture Walks," 156
Pizzolongo, P. J., 31
PL 99-457, 14
Plan-do-review activities, 47–48
Planned inquiry activities, 303–305, 307
Planning, by children, 246, 259–260, 284–286
Plans, lesson. *See* Lesson plans
Play
   characteristics, 36–37, 59, 422
   cognitive levels, 61–62
   common characteristics with literacy, 276–277
   creative arts and, 406–407, 408, 417, 419
   decreased opportunities, 17
   definition, 36

as foundation for learning, 4, 138–139
free, 17, 21, 171, 205
friendships and, 80
functional, 309–310
health benefits, 17
importance, 20, 58
learning opportunities, 3–4, 38–43, 53, 172–173,
     202, 309
literacy development and, 41–42, 275–280
love, work, and, 58–60
parallel, 61–62, 148
with peers, 17
Piagetian perspective, 38–39
rough-and-tumble, 144–147
seen as non-essential, 17
skill development, 4–5, 37–38
social, 62, 63
solitary, 61, 64, 148
types, 61–63
Vygotsky on, 39, 40–42
See also Guided play; Outdoor play activities;
     Pretend play; Socio-dramatic play
Play center spaces, 209
Play centers
     accessibility, 208
     areas, 209
     art centers, 407, 413–420
     block centers, 348–350, 351
     boundaries, 209
     as learning centers, 22, 205
     literacy skill development, 280–297
     locations, 209
     manipulatives centers, 358
     materials, 210–213, 262, 281–283
     observing, 243–244, 246, 259–262
     organizing, 282–283
     supports, 260–261
     themes, 281–282, 374–375
     woodcraft, 361–364
     See also Guided play; Learning centers;
          Movement centers
Play communications, 97, 98–99
Play objects. *See* Literacy-enriched play objects;
     Manipulative toys; Props
Play plans, 246, 259–260, 284–286
Playground safety, 143, 147
     See also Outdoor play activities
Plays. *See* Creative drama
Portfolios, 234–235
Positive behavior support (PBS), 162–164
Potato Heads, 356
Poverty
     children in, 12, 13, 406
     language development and, 93–94
     Montessori programs and, 44
     stresses, 13
     See also Low-income families
Pragmatics, 92
Prenatally drug-exposed children, 71

Preoperational stage, 32, 33, 34
Preschool. *See* Early education; Head Start Program
Preschool Language Scale, 229–230
Pretend play
     by age, 72–73
     centers, 22
     decreased opportunities, 17
     learning through, 38–40, 63, 95–96
     movement and, 426–427
     See also Play; Socio-dramatic play; Symbolic play
Price, J. R., 102
Prince, E., 235
Print awareness, 7, 286–289, 294, 390
Print referencing, 390
Probability experiment, 30, 31
Problem-solving
     in mathematics, 331
     in science education, 307–308
Projects, 141
Props
     culturally diverse, 141, 216, 374
     for guided play, 210–212, 281–283
     household items, 141, 142, 211
     learning about, 262
     literacy-enriched, 212–213, 282–283,
          351, 389, 392
     number of, 211, 283
     organization and storage, 282–283
     realistic, 211, 276, 277–278, 281–282, 374
     for socio-dramatic play, 63, 184–186, 187,
          281–282, 374
     See also Manipulative toys
Prosocial behaviors, 159, 160
Puppet centers, 434–437
Puzzles, 205, 355–356

Questions
     guided, 393–394
     open-ended prompts, 175–177
     reflective, 236, 245–246

Ramani, G. B., 360
Readers Theater, 434, 435
Readiness skills, 177–178
Reading
     to children, 388, 395–396
     comprehension skills, 6, 104
     dialogic, 269, 390, 394–395
     skills, 103, 107
     See also Books; Literacy
Recasting, 207
Receptive language, 91, 92
Reciprocal relationships, with families, 119, 120, 122,
     129–131
Reflective questions, in assessment, 236, 245–246
Reggio Emilia programs
     children with special rights, 47
     collaboration, 45–46, 47
     learning theories and, 45–46

outdoor learning, 46, 141
principles, 45, 304, 308–309
Religious diversity, 10
See also Cultural diversity
Resilience, 31
Resnick, L. B., 89, 219
Response to Intervention (RtI), 239–242
Responsibility, encouraging, 49
Responsive classrooms, 159–160, 171–172, 173
Rettig, M., 51
Richgels, D. J., 217, 218
Robinson, H. M., 408
Romero, S. L., 161–162
Roskos, K., 184
Roskos, K. A., 202
Rough-and-tumble play, 144–147
Routines. See Schedules
RtI. See Response to Intervention

Safety
field trips, 376
outdoor play, 143, 147
woodcraft, 361
Sainato, D. M., 436
Salmon, M. D., 436
Sarama, J. A., 339
SATs. See Student Assistance Teams
Scaffolding
cultural differences and, 216
definition, 171
evidence-based strategies, 204
language development, 217–219, 220
by parents, 216
successful, 203, 205
See also Guided play
Schedules
arrivals and departures, 153–154
full-day programs, 148
large group activities, 156
posting, 149
sample, 149, 150, 151
visual, 150–152, 191–192
See also Transitions
Schickedanz, J. A., 105
Schwartz, E., 422, 426
Schwartz, S. L., 175
Science
concepts, 302
content, 302, 303, 305
distinguishing practices, 313–316, 318
Head Start Framework, 311–312
inquiry learning environment, 303–308, 313, 317–321
kindergarten curriculum, 313–316
Next Generation Science Standards, 313, 319, 320
play and, 309–311
practices, 313–316
preschool curriculum, 312, 316–318, 321–323

problem-solving format, 307–308
teaching methods, 305–306
Science centers
adult roles, 318–319
books, 323
developing, 316–324
literacy activities, 317, 319
mathematics skills, 318, 319
tools and materials, 323–324
See also Learning centers
Scientific inquiry process, 302–304, 311, 313
Screen time, 384
Screenings. See Assessment
Seefeldt, C., 376, 379
Segal, M., 36
Self-assessment, 237
See also Assessment
Self-guided speech, 76
Self-reflection, 245–246
Self-regulation
of children with disabilities, 77
definition, 76
development, 7, 76–77
in socio-dramatic play, 76–77, 261
work and, 60
Seligman, M., 116
Semantics, 92
Sensorimotor stage, 32, 33
Sesame Street, 436
Shank, M., 118–119, 122–123
Shared writings, 292–296, 435
Sherratt, D., 78
Siegler, R., 360
Sight words, 291
Sign language, 88
Singer, D., 208
Skibbe, L., 217
Small group activities, 155, 156–157, 283–284
See also Learning centers; Play centers
Snow, C. E., 12, 89, 219
Social play, 62, 63
Social proximity, 261
Social sharing, 97
Social skills
in creative drama, 433
development, 371, 421, 423–424
music and movement activities, 423–424
observing, 260, 261
omission from Common Core, 273
See also Conversations
Social studies
content, 371–373
field trips, 376
play activities, 373–375
standards, 377–378
Social studies centers
anti-biased activities, 381–383
integration in curriculum, 378

literacy activities, 375, 379
passage of time theme, 379
technology use, 383–384
themes, 379, 380–381
Sociocultural learning theory, 216–217
   See also Vygotsky, Lev
Socio-dramatic play
   autism and, 77–79
   block play and, 346
   communicating during, 97–100
   components, 95–97
   controlling, 75–76
   distinction from creative drama, 432
   encouraging, 184, 219
   excluding peers, 75, 139
   in families, 206
   importance, 71–72
   language, 74–76, 78
   language development and, 62, 95–97
   in learning centers, 182, 184, 196
   learning opportunities, 63, 95–96, 139
   literacy activities, 213, 275–276, 283–286
   mathematics activities, 337–338
   narratives, 101–102, 206
   objects (props), 63, 184–186, 187, 281–282, 374
   plans, 284–286
   rules, 74–75, 95, 97, 139, 311
   self-regulation and, 76–77, 261
   skill development, 261
   social studies themes, 375
   See also Guided play; Play; Pretend play;
      Symbolic play
Socio-dramatic play representations, 72–73, 95
   See also Symbolic play representations
Soderman, A. K., 90, 216–217
Solitary play, 61, 64, 148
Songs
   language development, 404–405
   movement to, 423, 434, 435
   new words, 422
   at transitions, 154
   See also Music
Soukakou, E., 14, 15
Sound awareness games, 290
Special education placement, 240, 242–243
   See also Developmental diversity; Disabilities,
      children with; Individualized Education
      Programs
Speech
   definition, 92
   development, 87
   development delays, 91–93
   encouraging, 88–89, 90
   links to writing, 286, 287, 294
   self-guided, 76
   skills, 172–173, 279–280
   structured conversations, 279–280
   unstructured conversations, 280
   See also Language

Spoken language. *See* Speech
Standards. *See* Common Core State
      Standards; Early learning standards;
      Head Start Framework
Statistics
   data collection and analysis, 357–358
   probability experiment, 30
Stereotypes, 10, 281, 335
Stockall, N., 390
Stoll, J., 307–308
Stories. *See* Books; Narratives
Student Assistance Teams (SATs), 239
Substance abuse, 71
Support services staff, 126, 242
Swann, A. C., 419
Syllable awareness games, 290
Symbolic play
   by age, 72–73
   of children with disabilities, 74
   cultural differences and, 70
   learning through, 59
   levels, 64, 65
   objects, 58, 62, 78
   science learning, 310
   See also Pretend play; Socio-dramatic play
Symbolic play representations
   actions, 72, 96–97
   appropriate combinational activity, 66
   creating, 59
   development, 64–65
   functional unitary activity, 65
   inappropriate combinational activity, 65–66
   levels, 65–69
   mother-child, 70
   objects, 72, 96–97
   other-directed pretense, 67–68
   roles, 72, 96–97
   rule making, 97
   self-directed pretense, 67
   sequential pretense, 68
   sharing, 97
   substitution pretense, 69
   transitional activities, 66–67
Syntax, 87, 92

Tabors, P. O., 107–108
Teachers
   academic activities, 7–8, 17, 18–20, 107
   cultural biases, 120
   male, 365–366
   See also Adult interactions; Collaboration
Teaching strategies. *See* High-quality teaching
      strategies; Instructional methods
Team play, 63
Teaming, 128
Teams
   assessment, 239, 240, 242
   classroom, 125
   multidisciplinary, 240, 242

student assistance, 239
See also Collaboration
Technology, 383–384, 385, 386, 391–392
Terrell, T. D., 87
Theater. *See* Creative drama
Themes
  from community, 374–375
  of guided play, 210, 211, 281–282
  manipulative toys, 343
  of narratives, 210
  of play centers, 281–282, 374–375
  in Reggio Emilia programs, 46
  social studies, 375, 379, 380–381
  use of, 141
Thrall, Joanna, 54
Time, passage of, 379
Total Physical Response (TPR),
    434, 435
Tourist approach, 381
Toys. *See* Manipulative toys; Props
TPR. *See* Total Physical Response
Transactive model of assessment, 243–246
Transitions
  child-centered, 196
  cleaning up, 137–138, 153, 346,
    351–353, 415
  between learning centers, 158
  for meals, 153
  movement during, 154, 428–429
  music, 154
  puppets, 436
  puppets in, 437
  reducing stress, 153–154, 160
Trust, 59, 114–115, 122
Turnbull, A. P., 118–119, 122–123
Turnbull, H. R., 118–119, 122–123

Uba, Gregory, 365–366
Uhry, J., 350
Units, 141
U.S. Department of Education, 11
  Office of Special Education Programs, 15

Van de Walle, J. A., 333, 340, 357
Vaughan, E., 355
Vertical curriculum integration, 317
Visual arts, 412, 414, 416
  See also Art centers; Creative arts;
    Drawing
Visual cues, 78–79
Visual impairments, 390
  See also Disabilities, children with
Visual schedules, 150–152, 191–192
Vocabulary, 94–95
  See also Literacy; Words

Vygotsky, Lev, learning theory of
  in HighScope Curriculum, 48
  independent learning, 34, 36, 216–217
  learning through assistance, 34, 35, 36, 203,
    216–217, 377
  play contexts, 39, 40–41, 42
  in Reggio Emilia programs, 46
  self-guided speech, 76
  zone of proximal development, 34–36, 39, 61, 177,
    179, 203, 217

Wanerman, T., 432
Wang, X. C., 94
Wasik, B. A., 176, 393
Weikart, David, 46
West, S., 217
White, E. G., *Charlotte's Web*, 276
Whitehurst, G. J., 103, 104
Williams, J. M. B., 333
Wishard, A. G., 17
Wisneski, D. B., 306
Wood, Audrey, *The Napping House*, 276
Woodcock Johnson Test of Achievement, 230
Woodcraft centers
  activities, 362
  ages, 361
  designing, 361
  development stages, 361–362
  displays, 363–364
  guided play, 364
  materials, 363
  mathematics skills, 362–363, 364
  safety, 361
  skills developed, 330, 331, 364
  tools, 361, 362
Word searches, 286–289
Word Walls, 289
Words
  dissecting, 289–292
  sight, 291
  vocabulary, 94–95
  See also Language; Literacy
Work, 58–60
Writing
  fine motor skills, 412–413
  journals, 235
  links to speech, 286, 287, 294
  skill development, 104–105, 107, 278–279
  skill levels, 278–279
  See also Literacy

Xu, F., 30, 330

Zone of proximal development, 34–36, 39, 61, 177,
    179, 203, 217

About the Authors

Ann M. Selmi has taught for over 40 years, and most of her career has been spent working with young children with or without disabilities and their teachers. For the past 8 years she has taught teachers at California State University, Dominguez Hills, where she prepares early childhood teachers to address some of the most challenging situations in the Los Angeles area. Her research focuses on the relationship between the development of language and play. She also worked for 5 years as a researcher on the cochlear implant program for young deaf children at the House Ear Institute in Los Angeles, and she spent one year as a visiting researcher at the National Institute of Child Health and Development in the Child and Family Research Section in Bethesda, Maryland.

Raymond J. Gallagher began his career as a general education teacher and as a teacher in special education. As a university educator, he has been involved in research concerning the development of young children who are at risk for and diagnosed with disabilities, and the ways they and their families are served. He continues to be involved in personnel development preparing individuals to teach in P–12 settings that serve the educational needs of all youngsters. Dr. Gallagher is a Professor of Clinical Education in the Rossier School of Education at the University of Southern California.

Eugenia R. Mora-Flores is an Associate Professor in the Rossier School of Education at the University of Southern California (USC). She teaches courses on first and second language acquisition, Latino culture, and in literacy development for elementary and secondary students. Her research interests include studies on effective practices in developing the language and literacy skills of English learners in Grades Pre-K–12. She has written more than four books in the area of literacy and academic language development (ALD) for English learners. She also works as a consultant for a variety of elementary, middle, and high schools in the areas of English language development, ALD, and writing.

SAGE researchmethods

The essential online tool for researchers from the world's leading methods publisher

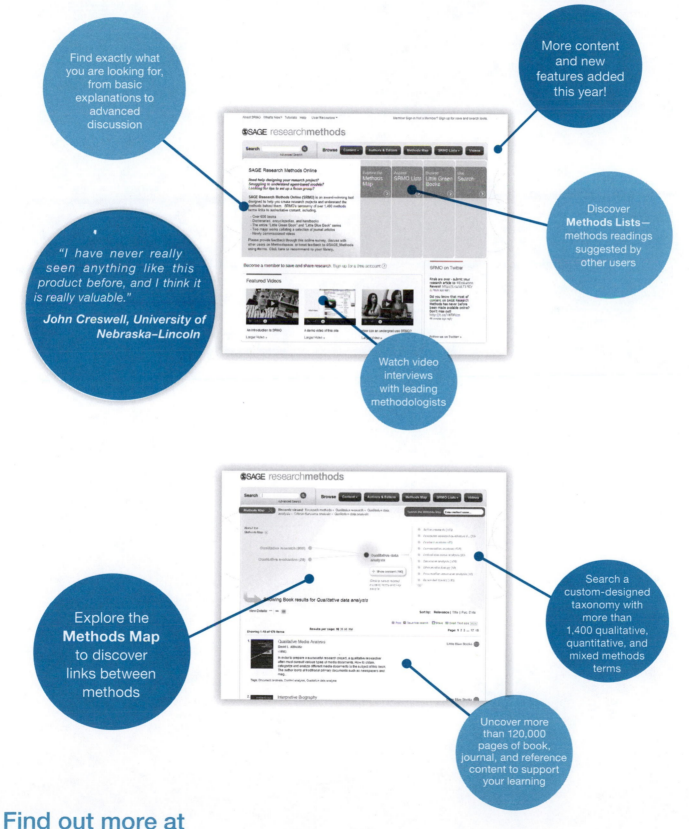

Find exactly what you are looking for, from basic explanations to advanced discussion

More content and new features added this year!

"I have never really seen anything like this product before, and I think it is really valuable."

John Creswell, University of Nebraska–Lincoln

Discover **Methods Lists**— methods readings suggested by other users

Watch video interviews with leading methodologists

Explore the **Methods Map** to discover links between methods

Search a custom-designed taxonomy with more than 1,400 qualitative, quantitative, and mixed methods terms

Uncover more than 120,000 pages of book, journal, and reference content to support your learning

Find out more at
www.sageresearchmethods.com